FIELDING'S
SPAIN
1996

Fielding Titles

Fielding's Alaska Cruises/Inside Passage
Fielding's Amazon
Fielding's Australia
Fielding's Bahamas
Fielding's Belgium
Fielding's Bermuda
Fielding's Borneo
Fielding's Brazil
Fielding's Britain
Fielding's Budget Europe
Fielding's Caribbean
Fielding's Caribbean Cruises
Fielding's Caribbean East
Fielding's Caribbean West
Fielding's Europe
Fielding's European Cruises
Fielding's Far East
Fielding's France
Fielding's Freewheelin' USA
Fielding's Guide to the World's Most Dangerous Places
Fielding's Guide to Kenya's Best Hotels, Lodges & Homestays
Fielding's Hawaii
Fielding's Holland
Fielding's Italy
Fielding's Las Vegas Agenda
Fielding's London Agenda
Fielding's Los Angeles Agenda
Fielding's Malaysia and Singapore
Fielding's Mexico
Fielding's New York Agenda
Fielding's New Zealand
Fielding's Paris Agenda
Fielding's Portugal
Fielding's Rome Agenda
Fielding's San Diego Agenda
Fielding's Scandinavia
Fielding's Southeast Asia
Fielding's Southern Vietnam on Two Wheels
Fielding's Spain
Fielding's Thailand Including Cambodia, Laos, Myanmar
Fielding's Vacation Places Rated
Fielding's Vietnam
Fielding's Worldwide Cruises
The Indiana Jones Survival Guide

FIELDING'S SPAIN 1996

The Most In-Depth Guide to the Spectacle and Romance of Spain

A. Hoyt Hobbs & Joy Adzigian

Fielding Worldwide, Inc.
308 South Catalina Avenue
Redondo Beach, California 90277 U.S.A.

Fielding's Spain 1996

Published by Fielding Worldwide, Inc.

Text Copyright ©1995 A. Hoyt Hobbs and Joy Adzigian

Icons & Illustrations Copyright ©1995 FWI

FIELDING WORLDWIDE INC.

PUBLISHER AND CEO	**Robert Young Pelton**
PUBLISHING DIRECTOR	**Paul T. Snapp**
ELECTRONIC PUBLISHING DIRECTOR	**Larry E. Hart**
PUBLIC RELATIONS DIRECTOR	**Beverly Riess**
ACCOUNT SERVICES MANAGER	**Christy Harp**
PROJECT MANAGER	**Chris Snyder**

EDITORS

Linda Charlton   **Kathy Knoles**

PRODUCTION

Gini Sardo-Martin   **Craig South**

Janice Whitby

COVER DESIGNED BY	**Digital Artists, Inc.**
COVER PHOTOGRAPHERS — Front Cover	**Robert Young Pelton/Westlight**
Background Photo, Front Cover	**Mark Stephenson/Westlight**
Back Cover	**Robert Young Pelton/Westlight**
INSIDE PHOTOS	**Robert Young Pelton/Westlight, National Tourist Office of Spain**

Inquiries should be addressed to: Fielding Worldwide, Inc., 308 South Catalina Ave., Redondo Beach, California 90277 U.S.A., ☎ *(310) 372-4474*, Facsimile *(310) 376-8064*, 8:30 a.m.–5:30 p.m. Pacific Standard Time.

ISBN 1-56952-094-1

Printed in the United States of America

Dedication

We gratefully dedicate this book to a spirit on high—Eunice Riedel, our mentor and guide.

Letter from the Publisher

In 1946, Temple Fielding began the first of what would be a remarkable new series of well-written, highly personalized guidebooks for independent travelers. Temple's opinionated, witty and oft-imitated books have now guided travelers for almost a half-century. More important to some was Fielding's humorous and direct method of steering travelers away from the dull and the insipid. Today, Fielding Travel Guides are still written by experienced travelers for experienced travelers. Our authors carry on Fielding's reputation for creating travel experiences that deliver insight with a sense of discovery and style.

Unforgettable. That's what you'll say after a vacation in Spain the Fielding way. Hoyt Hobbs and Joy Adzigian have been traveling through Europe for the past 20 years, searching for the dramatic, the little-known, the romantic attractions and the pristine beaches that make Spain one of the most entertaining countries in Europe. In Fielding's *Spain*, Hoyt and Joy have created the perfect balance of entertainment and education, all in a historical context. You won't forget Spain. Not with Fielding.

Today, the concept of independent travel has never been bigger. Our policy of *brutal honesty* and a highly personal point of view has never changed; it just seems the travel world has caught up with us.

Enjoy your Spanish adventure with Hoyt Hobbs, Joy Adzigian and Fielding.

Robert Young Pelton
Publisher and C.E.O.
Fielding Worldwide, Inc.

ABOUT THE AUTHORS

Hoyt Hobbs and Joy Adzigian

Hoyt Hobbs and Joy Adzigian have traveled extensively throughout Europe and North Africa since 1973. They first visited Spain in 1975 while living in the south of France, and felt an immediate affection for the peoples and cultures of the Iberian peninsula. Their passion for art and architecture, as well as for food and wine, had met its match, and Spain drew them back again and again.

The couple wrote their first guidebook in 1979—to Egypt—when, after numerous trips, they had been unable to find a guidebook to their liking.

Popular guides conveyed too little understanding of history and culture, while more scholarly books hid what was interesting within reams of detail. Reviewers applauded their balanced approach. *The Library Journal* said: "...with only this book [one can] enjoy a more comprehensive, efficient and informative tour...than is possible with any of the classical travel guides." According to *Traveler's Book Society* "...the level here is almost exactly right for the intelligent traveler....This is a book to travel with as well as to use in planning a tour...." "This book is a model of specific, useful, honest travel advice and concise, vivid historical exposition," noted the *Chattanooga Times*, adding that "you ought to buy this book at once." In 1981 their Egypt guide was selected for publication as the first of the Fielding's country guides. Now they have applied their successful and informative approach to Spain.

Dr. Hobbs, an associate professor of philosophy at Long Island University, is widely read in history, architecture and diverse cultures; Joy Adzigian, a stylist and producer, brings a background strong in literature, art and design. Both are highly experienced students of food and wine who enjoy the discovery of the new and superior. They report the findings of their Spanish explorations in this lively, comprehensive guide.

The authors are married and live in New York City.

ACKNOWLEDGMENTS

A project such as this could never have been completed without substantial assistance from a large number of people and organizations.

We owe a great debt to Jean Miserandino from the Spanish National Tourist Office in New York who performed miracles without complaint. Thanks to Pilar Vico from Travel Ahead who makes the impossible possible.

Carmen Casadella, our travel associate and a model Catalan, corrected so many mistakes and supplied such intelligent observations that she improved the book immeasurably.

In Spain, special thanks are due Diego Franco of Córdoba, Felisa Hernandez of Seville, Tomás Gómez Quesada of Granada, and José Ballesteros of Santiago de Compostella.

We are grateful to our good friends Pamela Dailey and Arthur Krystal for timely and astute editorial assistance. Donna Wayne transcribed hours of tape into readable notes, with unfailing good spirit. Dr. and Mrs. Albert H. Hobbs laid all the groundwork for this book with a lifetime of lessons. Lastly, we thank all our friends and family for their patience and we want them to know that, for better or worse, we are available again.

Fielding Rating Icons

The Fielding Rating Icons are highly personal and awarded to help the besieged traveler choose from among the dizzying array of activities, attractions, hotels, restaurants and sights. The awarding of an icon denotes unusual or exceptional qualities in the relevant category.

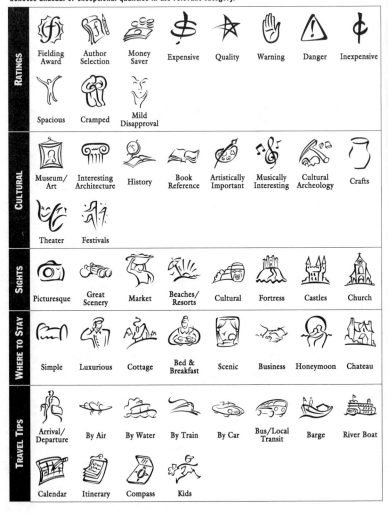

RATINGS

Fielding Award	Author Selection	Money Saver	Expensive	Quality	Warning	Danger	Inexpensive
Spacious	Cramped	Mild Disapproval					

CULTURAL

Museum/Art	Interesting Architecture	History	Book Reference	Artistically Important	Musically Interesting	Cultural Archeology	Crafts
Theater	Festivals						

SIGHTS

Picturesque	Great Scenery	Market	Beaches/ Resorts	Cultural	Fortress	Castles	Church

WHERE TO STAY

Simple	Luxurious	Cottage	Bed & Breakfast	Scenic	Business	Honeymoon	Chateau

TRAVEL TIPS

Arrival/ Departure	By Air	By Water	By Train	By Car	Bus/Local Transit	Barge	River Boat
Calendar	Itinerary	Compass	Kids				

ACTIVITIES

Downhill Skiing	X-country Skiing	Water Sports	Sailing
Scuba Diving	Snorkeling/ Diving	Deep-sea Fishing	Freshwater Fishing
Swimming	Hiking	Walking	Relaxing
Golf	Tennis	Horseback Riding	General Sports
Cycling	Workout		

SPECIAL INTEREST

Nightlife	Singles	Romantic	Nude Beaches
Lecture	Spectacular Cuisine	Wine Tasting	Shopping
Cafe Stops	Gardening	Pro Sports	Mystery

TABLE OF CONTENTS

LIST OF MAPS

SPAIN AND PORTUGAL

INTRODUCTION

Spain welcomes tourists and is in turn embraced by more visitors than any other country in Europe. The reasons for its popularity are abundantly clear. Spain pampers travelers in paradors, warms them on sandy beaches, dazzles them with scenery and art, delights them with flavorful cuisine, and—most of all—surprises. Spain is not a European Mexico with mariachi music and Indian civilizations, but a different culture entirely—venerable, yet lively and cosmopolitan, graced by striking art and awesome architecture.

Because Spain isolated itself from world politics through the 1960s, however, North Americans know less about it than many other European countries. While the names of the Costa del Sol, Madrid, Barcelona, Seville and Granada will generally be recognized, those of Salamanca, Segovia, Santiago de Compostela, Oviedo, Burgos, or even Córdoba—any one of which would captivate most visitors—are less well known. Spain's northern and western beaches—more scenic than the overpopulated Costa del Sol and long appreciated by Europeans—are virtually barren of Americans. One of our aims is to entice you to those areas we know you'll enjoy; another is to warn you about locales overblown by their descriptions in articles or travel brochures.

In addition to guiding you to enjoyable places, we want to enhance your appreciation of them. Because Spain's long seclusion has obscured its formative historical events and figures, visitors frequently miss the significance of what they see. For this reason we provide more historical and cultural background than most travel guides take time for and include specific commentaries on individual buildings and works of art.

1996

This year Spain offers visitors two special dividends. Although the American dollar has fallen sharply on international markets, travelers will find their budgets stretching further in Spain than in almost any other Western European country. Hotels have held the line, depending as they do on foreign visitors. Only restaurants pinch the pocketbook more than last year. Travelers will also find a country prepared for them as few places in the world have ever been. Spain accomplished wonders in producing both the 1992 Summer Olympics and the 1992 World's Fair, the first time one country ever staged two such mammoth events in a single year. To enhance those productions the Spanish government granted loans to remodel hotels throughout the country, with terms so attractive that most seized the opportunity. This was only one phase of an unprecedented effort to spruce up the country for the events of 1992. Every museum and historic monument that needed renovation received it. Major roads were repaired, and routes to important sights were repaved, straightened and widened. The hundred miles of winding road from Cáceres to Guadalupe that had formerly taken three hours to travel, for example, can now be negotiated in half that time. A high speed train line was constructed to whisk riders between Madrid and Seville in three, rather than the five hours it used to take. All these improvements mean that a tourist to Spain in 1996 will be greeted by a country in better, cleaner, and fresher condition than any other in the world.

Using This Guide

Following introductory chapters about trip preparation and background, we divide the sights of Spain into seven manageable geographic areas approximating seven of Spain's traditional kingdoms.

Our Rating System

Apart from giving you information about what is available to see and do in Spain and background about its history and culture, the most valuable help we can provide is to evaluate sights, monuments, hotels and restaurants. For easy reference, we codify our opinions within a star system:

★★★★★   Outstanding anywhere in the world

★★★★   Exceptional, among the best in the country

★★★   Superior for a particular area of the country

★★   Good, a clear step above the average

★   Above average

For hotels and restaurants we provide two additional types of information. We indicate the price category of each establishment (explained under "Prices") and, in the case of hotels, we also specify which services they offer. However, since value is an important consideration in selecting hotels and restaurants, it affects our assignment of stars. We award a hotel or restaurant an extra star (or even two) if the quality of its service, style and/or cuisine sufficiently surpasses that of its higher-priced competitors in the same class. Conversely, we award fewer stars to establishments charging higher prices than their accommodations or food merit. Read our descriptions of any hotel or restaurant to understand its rating

In addition, we selected our very favorite hotels and restaurants and awarded them a "Fielding's choice," the script *"f "* you will see in margins throughout the book.

Note, the stars we award are based on quite different criteria from those displayed outside every hotel entrance in Spain. Those government awarded stars rank a hotel by the number and kinds of services it provides, such as whether bedrooms contain telephones, televisions and minibars, or whether saunas, restaurants or conference rooms are available. Although many of these services are incidental to a tourist, the greater their number, the more official stars a hotel receives. No account of comfort, attractiveness or the quality of service is taken by these official stars.

In this guide we indicate the services available by assigning a class category. A **Deluxe** or a **First-class** hotel will provide every possible facility and service; a **2nd-class** hotel will offer a restaurant and room TV, but usually not saunas, conference rooms or other infrequently used extras; and a **3rd-class** accommodation, while often as pleasant as hotels receiving higher class designations, may begin and end with a comfortable room.

As in many European countries, the Spanish government also assigns from one to four stars to unofficial hotels, variously called *residencias, pensiónes, fondas* or *hostals,* which provide a smaller range of services than similarly rated official hotels. Such accommodations might lack an elevator, overnight desk staff or an on-premises restaurant. To many travelers the absence of such features may be of little concern, and the otherwise fine accommodations may be well worth your consideration. A relatively new sort of accommodation in Spain is the apartment-hotel which adds cooking facilities to the normal room, often in larger spaces. We include all these such lodgings in our hotel listings, but distinguish them with the letters "R," "Hs," "P," or "A" for *residencia, hostal, pensión or apartment-hotel.*

Since we don't believe that an endless Yellow Pages of hotels and restaurants is what most tourists to a foreign country want or need, we've selected and described a range of good hotels in all price ranges with locations convenient for a sightseer. Because Spain offers such an abundance of fine hotels, we tell you about bad ones only when a desirable location might tempt you to book them.

Prices

Because daily international currency fluctuations prevent us from telling you the exact dollar costs of the hotels and restaurants we review, we group their prices into more stable general categories: **Very Expensive**, **Expensive**, **Moderate** and **Inexpensive**. Note that cost is not relative for us; a moderate hotel is one that charges under $100, whether its price is higher than most of the other hotels in its area or not.

Price Category	HOTEL (per night, double occupancy)	RESTAURANT (full meal for 1, +house wine)
Very Expensive	$200+	$50+
Expensive	$100-$200	$30+
Moderate	$50-$99	$15-$30
Inexpensive	Less than $50	Less than $15

Changes

The prospect of introducing Spain to visitors carries the excitement of giving a present the receiver is sure to love. At the same time it's a humbling prospect. Our information is based on inspecting hundreds of hotels and restaurants over many visits, but we are aware that others may have improved, declined or closed too recently to be included in our reviews. If you locate some treasure we've missed, we'd love hearing about it so we can visit it for possible inclusion in future editions. Similarly, if you receive bad food or inadequate service in any of the establishments we list, please let us know so others can be warned about it. While no hotel or restaurant treats everyone the same, egregious service or behavior is never acceptable. Your comments and suggestions are welcome and helpful. Write us c/o Fielding Worldwide, *308 Catalina Avenue, Redondo Beach, CA 90277,* or FAX us at *(310) 376-8064,* 8:30 a.m.–5:30 p.m. Pacific Standard Time.

Most important, have a wonderful trip!

PRACTICAL MATTERS

For Information

The Tourist Office of Spain is a valuable resource for information and answering questions.

- **California**: San Vicente Plaza Bldg., 8383 Wilshire Boulevard, Suite 960, Beverly Hills, CA 90211 (☎ *213-658 7188; FAX 213-658 1061*)

- **Florida**: 1221 Brickell Avenue, Suite 1850, Miami, Fl 33131 (☎ *305-358 1992; FAX 305-358 8223*)

- **Illinois**: Water Tower Place, 845 N. Michigan Avenue, Suite 915E, Chicago, Il 60611 (☎ *312-642 1992; FAX 312-642 9817*)

- **New York City**: 665 Fifth Avenue, New York, NY 10022 (☎ *212-759 8822; FAX 212-980 1053*)

Travel to Spain

By Plane

Direct flights to Spain depart from New York City (Iberia, TWA, TAP), Newark (Continental), Dallas/Fort Worth (American), Atlanta (Delta), Miami (Iberia, Aeromexico), Washington, DC (United), Atlanta (Delta), Toronto and Montreal (Air Canada and Iberia). Flight time is roughly seven hours from New York City to Madrid. Only Iberia and TWA fly every day to Madrid, the others four to five times a week. Iberia and Delta also fly daily from New York to Barcelona through Madrid. British Airways arranges connecting flights through London to various Spanish cities; Air France provides the same service through Paris; and KLM stops over at Amsterdam. All these can fly directly from their stop-overs to Málaga, Barcelona or Madrid. In addition, charter flights abound.

Since airfares were deregulated, competition has led to complex, changing rates along with exotic giveaways and deals. Like specials at the supermarket, prices change continually so that only a travel agent will know what is available at a given time. However, some principles are constant.

Prices change with the seasons and are most expensive from June through August and during Christmas and Easter; least expensive both from November to the middle of December and from the second of January through the first half of March; and between the two extremes at other times. Whatever the season, about $50 on a round-trip ticket can be saved by flying on weekdays.

First-class fares will be the most expensive way to fly by a factor of three or four times the least expensive. For that price, a traveler is provided free stopovers, extra leg room and quiet. Meals are more elaborate, and drinks and headsets are free—though the high fare covers such generosity many times over. Most carriers also offer a class of fares between first class and economy, called "Business Class," "Preference Class" or some such designation, with about the same benefits as first class, except for a tad less room, and at about half the price.

Most of us cram into tourist, economy or coach class. The names vary but not the fact that this is the low end, both of comfort and cost. Here rates grow complex.

In addition to regular economy (tourist, coach or whatever-the-name) fares, there are also discount economy fares which reduce the number of free stopovers allowed. If a flier does not plan any stopovers, he travels exactly as do those paying the full economy fares, but for less. "Excursion" fares are even lower in cost—economy-class travel with required minimum and maximum stays that happily correspond to the duration of most vacations. APEX (Advanced Purchase Excursion) fares are special excursion fares that require full payment for tickets two weeks or so before departure. All excursion fares carry an expensive penalty for changing a reservation, and APEX fares involve a penalty for cancelling the trip. But savings, which can be half what a regular economy ticket would cost, mean that most tourists opt for such arrangements.

Stand-by fares, once the bargain-hunter's treasure, have been discontinued by most airlines (Virgin Atlantic to London is an exception), because of inconvenienced and sometimes irate travelers. A true bargain hunter might, however, call airlines to check the current status.

Charter flights were once great bargains. They were also risky—if the charter company failed, the price of the paid-in-advance ticket could be lost.

Since scheduled airlines have lowered their fares, the savings on charter flights today are less than they used to be, although still real. Generally there is little or no flexibility in dates of travel, and advance payment is always required. Planes tend to be overcrowded, accommodations cramped. If you cancel your trip, you forfeit the entire price of the ticket, but the charter company may cancel its flight, up to ten days before scheduled departure, as long as it refunds your money. So if your charter leaves as scheduled, you can be sure it will be full—the company would have cancelled otherwise. Also, departure delays are common. Still, we have seen one-way flights from New York to Madrid for a very tempting $200. For more information ask your travel agent, check the travel section of the newspaper or try **Council Charter**, *205 East 42nd Street, New York, NY 10017* (☎ *800-800-8222*).

Alternatively, ticket consolidators can provide tickets as cheaply as most charters with less risk. These firms sell at discounts the tickets that airlines were unable to at higher fares. Thus space will not be available for every flight, and never for popular times. But discounts range from 20 percent and more off standard fares. A sampling of consolidators is: **Access International,** *101 West 31st Street, New York, NY 10016* (☎ *212-465 0707; 800-825-3633*), **Travel Avenue,** *180 North Des Plaines, Chicago, IL 60661* (☎ *800-333-3335*), **UniTravel,** *Box 12485, Street Louis, MO* (☎ *800-325-2222*), **Council Charter,** *205 E. 42nd Street, New York, NY* (☎ *800-800-8222*) and **Sunline Express Holidays, Inc.,** *607 Market Street, San Francisco, CA 94105* (☎ *800-SUN-LINE*) and **Travac**, *989 Sixth Avenue, New York, NY 10018* (☎ *800-872-8800*).

Although requiring a nominal membership fee, joining a travel club is another way to save because such organizations buy tickets in volume. Try **Moment's Notice**, *425 Madison Avenue, New York, NY 10017* (☎ *212-486-0503*); **Discount Travel International**, *114 Forrest Avenue, Narberth, PA 19072* (☎ *800-334-9294*); or **Worldwide Discount Club**, *1674 Meridian Avenue, Miami Beach, FL 33139* (☎ *305-534-2028*) for more information.

More offbeat for the venturesome or desperate, is generic air travel. **Airhitch** is the best known (*2641 Broadway, New York, NY 10025*, ☎ *212-864-2000*). You register by paying a small fee and specify a range of departure dates and a preferred destination, along with alternatives. About a week before your first desired departure you are offered at least two flights meeting those specifications. If you do not accept any, your fee is forfeited; otherwise you pay the balance minus the fee. Savings can be great, as low as the lowest charters, with less money risked up front. Write or call for details and other variations on this theme.

Note: there is a book describing the ins and outs of bargain airfares, including flying as a courier. The *Worldwide Guide to Cheap Airfares*, by Michael Wm. McColl, is published by Insider Books and could save its cost many times over. With a credit card handy, you can order the book by calling: ☎ *1-800-78-BOOKS.*

After paying, the question remains what to take with you. Each economy passenger is allowed two pieces of luggage, neither of which can exceed 70 pounds, and whose combined dimension (length, width, plus height) measures no more than 62 inches for one piece and 55 for the other; one carry-on with dimensions totaling no more than 45 inches; and one shoulder bag. Higher classes of fares are allowed more. These limits apply to adults and to those children paying at least half of the adult fare; children paying less than half-price fares are permitted less. If you must take more than what the airline allows, come early to the check-in and expect to pay for overweight.

Seats in the rear of a plane rock and shake more than those farther forward. Tall travelers should request seats behind the door or the emergency exit, as these provide the most leg room. All told, the last row of seats is the worst, not even reclining fully. Note that foreign flights are not subject to the same non-smoking regulations as our domestic ones, so request whichever section is appropriate. One food tip is to ask for a special dietary meal both at reservation time and again when you confirm. The special diet can be kosher, low sodium, low cholesterol or any other, but such meals generally will be prepared with more care than your seatmate's.

By Car

Numerous border crossings link France with Spain. The most travelled are La Jonquera from Perpignan, on the extreme east coast, and Irún from Bayonne, on the extreme west coast. Both routes avoid mountain travel through the Pyrenees and remain open 24 hours a day, even through the winter. The most interesting Pyrenees route is through the tiny country of Andorra, enticing for its duty-free shopping. Portugal connects with Spain in 14 places, but the common crossings are from Élvas to Badajoz, in the center, from Valencia to Tui, in the north, and from the Algarve through Spain's Ayamonte in the far south.

A car ferry links Spain with Morocco. Boats leave either Ceuta, a Spanish enclave in Morocco, or Tangier, for Algeciras in Spain. The trip takes one and one-half hours from Ceuta, an hour longer from Tangier. Especially if bringing a car, reservations should be made in advance through a travel agent, or directly through **Compania Trasmediterranea** (*2 Calle Pedro Muñoz Seca, Madrid, España 28011,* ☎ *91-431-0700*).

By Train

Express trains leave Paris' Austerlitz station every evening, arriving at Madrid 13 hours later (or at Barcelona 11-1/2 hours later). The most modern train is the *Talgo* which currently departs from Paris at 8 p.m., and arrives at 8:30 a.m. in Chamartin station, Madrid. The Puerta del Sol is older, and leaves at 5:45 p.m. for a 9:55 a.m. arrival in Madrid. The Talgo also leaves for Barcelona from Paris at 9 p.m. for an 8:30 a.m. arrival. Sleeping accommodations must be reserved well in advance. Trains can also be picked up south of Paris, through Biarritz for Donostia (San Sebastian) and Madrid, and through Perpignan for Figueres and Barcelona on Spain's east coast. In most cases the train costs as much as flying and sometimes more.

From Lisbon, the *Lusitania Express* leaves at 9:45 p.m. for arrival at Madrid's Chamartin Station at 8:55 a.m. The *Luiz de Camões*, in the daytime, is faster by a couple of hours. In the other direction, trains leave Madrid at 1:50 and 11 p.m. for Lisbon. The reason the trip takes so long is that trains have to be changed at Entroncamento because of wider-gauged Spanish rails.

Package Tours

A package tour combines travel and hotel costs in a single price. Since the packager deals in volume, he books flights and rooms more cheaply than individuals can. Even after the packager's profit, the combination should cost less than the same arrangements made individually. On the minus side, the hotels provided are seldom the best choices in the price range and the itinerary may be rigid. Note that the prices cited for packages generally are *per person* in a double occupancy room. Figure the costs of the tour you would arrange for yourself and see if the savings of a package tour makes it worthwhile. On your own, you can find accommodations more interesting than what the package offers. Our book is filled with such suggestions, but you will have to work to select and reserve. Of course a travel agent can make the reservations you want for no fee to you.

Travel sections of newspapers often advertise package tours. Travel agents will know many more. In choosing a package tour ask whether there is a guarantee that the price at booking time will not be raised, and whether you'll receive a full refund if any part of the package promised should become unavailable.

Package tours come in three distinct kinds, with ascending levels of price. "Independent packages," called FITs in the industry, allow the most freedom since they involve only a combination of hotel and flight arrangements, sometimes with a car as well. More familiar are "escorted tours" where you join a group to travel together, often by bus, under the direction of a leader, which means activities are ensemble, but all problems are the leader's responsibility. Such tours are the most carefree way to travel, but throw you in with a group of strangers and restrict your freedom to do what you want when you wish. The third type, a variation on the first is a "special interest tour." The difference from other escorted tours is that the leader is an expert on Spanish art, wine, food or whatever the specialization of the company.

Such a tour provides an education impossible to gain on one's own. Since the expenses include a fee for the leader, this sort of tour will cost more than other package tours, probably raising the price to about what individual arrangements would cost.

Major airlines flying to Spain generally offer independent packages, as do some independent companies:

American Airlines Vacations
☎ 800-241-1700).

Continental Airlines' Grand Destinations
☎ 800-634-5555).

Delta's Dream Vacations
☎ 800-872-7786).

TWA Getaway Vacations
☎ 800-GETAWAY).

United Airlines' Vacation
☎ 800-328-6877).

Travel Bound
☎ 800-456-8656).

In addition, American Express Vacations, Gadabout, Petrabax and Odysseys Adventures offer FITs, as well as the escorted tours listed below.

The following is a list of companies that offer escorted tour programs and that will be pleased to send information about their offerings:

Abreu Tours, Inc.
317 East 34th Street, New York, NY 10016 (☎ 212-661-0555 or 800-223-1580).

American Express Vacations
Local American Express offices, or 300 Pinnacle Way, Norcross, GA 30071 (☎ 800-241-1700).

Cosmos Tours
95-25 Queens Boulevard, Rego Park, NY 11374 (☎ 800-221-0090).

Globus-Gateway Tours
Same address as Cosmo Tours, above.

Welcome Tours Hispanidad
99 Tulip Avenue, Suite 208, Floral Park, NY 11001 (☎ 800-274-4400; FAX 516-352-4943).

M.I. Travel, Inc.
450 Seventh Avenue, Suite 1805, New York, NY 10123 (☎ 212-967-6565 or 800-848-2314).

Odyssey Adventures
537 Chestnut Street, Cedarhurst, NY 11516 (☎ 516-569-2813 or 800-344-0013; FAX 516-569-2998).

Petrabax USA
97-45 Queens Boulevard, Suite 600, Rego Park, NY 11374 (☎ 718-897-7272 or 800-367-6611).

Spanish Heritage Tours
    116-47 Queens Boulevard, Forest Hills, NY 11375 (☎ 718-544-2752 or 800-221-2580).; FAX 718-793-4278

Sun Holidays
    26 Sixth Street, Suite 603, Stamford, CT 06905 (☎ 800-243-2057, FAX 203-323-3843).

Tour Directions International, Inc.
    70 West 36th Street, Suite 1004, New York, NY 10018 (☎ 212-564-3236 or 800-423-4460; FAX 212-629-5934).

Trafalgar Tours
    11 East 26th Street, Suite 1300, New York, NY 10010 (☎ 212-689-8977 or 800-626-6603).

Special interest tours include the following:

For Art:

Jacqueline Moss Museum Tours
    131 Davenport Ridge Lane, Stamford, CT 06903 (☎ 203-322-8709).

For wine:

Odysseys Adventures
    (see previous listing).

For Jewish heritage:

Odysseys Adventures
    (see previous listing).

For golf:

Petrabax
    (see previous listing).

Adventures in Golf
    29 Valencia Drive, Nashua, NH 03062 (☎ 603-882-8367; FAX 603-595-6514).

Golfing Holidays
    231 E. Millbrae Avenue, Millbrae, CA 94030 (☎ 800-652-7847).

ITC Golf Tours
    4134 Atlantic Avenue, Long Beach, CA 90807 (☎ 800-257-4981; FAX 310-424-6683).

Perry Golf
    8302 Bunwoodie Place, Atlanta, GA 30350 (☎ 800-344-5257; FAX 404-641-9798).

Wide World of Golf
    P.O. Box 5217, Carmel, CA 93921 (☎ 408-624-6667; FAX 408-625-9671).

For Horses:

FITS Equestrian
    685 Lateen Road, Solvang, CA 93463 (☎ 805-688-9494; FAX 805-688-2493).

For cycling:

Cycling Through the Centuries
    P.O. Box 877, San Antonio, FL 33576 (☎ 800-245-4226; FAX 916-541-0956).

Costs

Alas, the days of truly cheap travel in Spain are gone, at least for the near future. Twenty years ago a moderate hotel charged $10 for a double, and the same amount bought a pleasant dinner for two with a house wine. Of course $10 bought more at home then too, but the loosening of government price controls on Spanish hotels and restaurants and the fall of the dollar have changed that situation even more drastically than inflation has. This is not to say that Spain costs as much as France, England or Italy. It never has, and probably never will. Spain remains one of the least expensive European countries for travelers, but none can be considered cheap today.

Comfortable double rooms in moderately priced hotels in tourist areas and resorts cost about $80 ($100 in Madrid or Barcelona). The same room in a town less frequented by tourists will be 25 percent less. Count on $20 per person for an adequate dinner with wine. Museums can charge $3 or so, and gasoline in Spain is a significant expense as you will discover when you peal off almost $40 to fill up the tank. Thus, the current budget for a couple to travel modestly in Spain in the high season of July and August averages a daily minimum of $180. This does not include transportation—either getting to or around the country. It is, however, about half the figure needed for France or Italy.

However, hotels drop their prices by at least 20 percent at times other than high summer and during Christmas and Easter seasons. If a given city hosts a special festival, such as Seville with its April Fair or Pamplona with its San Fermin, top prices will also be charged at that time. At any other time of the year significant savings are possible. In general a hotel will charge 25 percent less than its high season prices in off-season. We list hotels by their high-season charges in this book; if traveling at other times, discount our listings by that much.

When to Go: Climate and Seasons

In latitude Spain sits opposite that part of the United States stretching from Boston to Baltimore, but because of proximity to the Mediterranean Sea its climate is substantially warmer.

Spain's geography covers several different climates. The center, sealed from the sea by mountains north, south and west, experiences weather similar to most western European countries: hot summers, cold winters (but rarely with snow), low rainfall and low humidity. January temperatures average in the 40s in Madrid—11 is the record low—and rise to an average of 90 on August days. The slight rainfall averages a misleading inch per month because most of it falls in spring and autumn. Significant precipitation falls on the Cordillera Mountains surrounding this center, however, where six feet of moisture produces deep winter snow and good skiing.

The north of Spain, especially the northwest—Galicia, Asturias and Cantabria—makes up for the aridity of the center. Santiago de Compostela averages five feet of rain annually, most of it falling in winter. With some precipitation every other day, the buildings actually grow moss. On the other hand, the northwest is warmer in winter and cooler in summer than the central plateau.

The most pleasant year-round temperatures in Spain are those of the eastern coast, from Catalonia to the Levant. Geographically a continuation of the French Riviera, it shares that climate, except for generally milder winters. Valencia averages 50 degrees in winter, Catalonia a few degrees less. August days reach 90, and swimming is comfortable in tepid 70-degree water through October. Almost all the rain falls in spring and autumn. Temperatures rise four to five degrees higher to the south in Murcia, but its most noteworthy climactic feature is an oppressive summer heat haze, called the *calina*, that turns sun and moon red and greys the sky on most days.

The southern coastline of Spain enjoys the warmest winters in mainland Europe, with temperatures averaging 55 degrees in January. Almost no rain falls on the eastern half of this coast in summer, and not much during the rest of the year. Málaga boasts of almost 200 days of utterly cloudless skies. Coastal temperatures in August rise to mid or even high 90s. Inland, winter days average 10 degrees lower and summer days a few degrees higher. Winter nights can be decidedly cool.

Snow never causes problems for places that most visitors go, but it can make the highest mountains impassable. The two major passes through the Pyrenees—Irún and La Jonquera—are never closed by snow, although smaller passes sometimes are. However, in winter, night fogs can slow mountain traffic to a crawl.

Average Daily Temperatures
Day (Night)

	Madrid	Barcelona	Seville	Santiago
January	48 (36)	55 (43)	59 (42)	50 (39)
February	52 (37)	57 (45)	63 (44)	55 (40)
March	59 (41)	60 (48)	68 (48)	59 (42)
April	64 (45)	65 (52)	74 (52)	62 (44)
May	70 (50)	72 (57)	80 (56)	66 (43)
June	81 (59)	79 (65)	90 (64)	70 (56)
July	88 (63)	82 (70)	91 (65)	75 (58)
August	86 (63)	83 (70)	96 (70)	76 (59)
September	77 (57)	77 (66)	91 (65)	70 (53)
October	66 (50)	70 (58)	78 (57)	60 (46)

Average Daily Temperatures
Day (Night)

	Madrid	Barcelona	Seville	Santiago
November	55 (41)	62 (51)	68 (51)	55 (44)
December	48 (36)	56 (46)	60 (45)	53 (42)

Whatever the season, ideal weather exists somewhere in Spain. Spring and fall are ideal in the center of Spain, although summers can be uncomfortably hot and winters require bundling up. The northeast of Spain is best visited in summer, for winters bring frequent rain, though spring and fall are also pleasant. Catalonia and the Levant are balmy all year. Their seas are even swimmable in early fall, at least for those used to Maine bathing. Because of heat haze, Murcia is best in seasons other than summer. Barcelona, too, is not at its most enjoyable on steamy summer days. Andalusia remains pleasant year-long, though cool on winter evenings. However, nowhere in Spain is the weather ever inhospitable enough to prevent a trip.

Crowds are a consideration, too, in deciding when to visit. Spain doubles its population each summer, filling beaches, resort hotels and restaurants. In particular, August is the time when the Spanish themselves vacation, adding their numbers to beach crowds and leaving behind restaurants closed for vacation. Prices rise to accommodate the crowds. Overall, spring would be the ideal season to cover Spain's terrain, and early summer months are preferable to crowded August.

Holidays and Special Events

The dates of holidays are important because businesses, certainly, and sights, possibly, will be closed. But holidays also offer the best opportunities to view and take part in the local color of the country.

National Holidays
All offices closed. When occurring near a weekend, the holiday becomes a four-day weekend.

January 1, Año Nuevo
(New Year) Everyone is in the streets on New Year's Eve, and crowds gather in Madrid's Puerto del Sol munching grapes in time to chiming of the clock at midnight.

January 6, Epifania del Señor
(Epiphany) Presents are given to children, rather than on Christmas day.

March 19, San Jaime
(Saint James' day).

April 11, Jueves Santo
(Maundy Thursday).

April 12, Viernes Santo
   (Good Friday).

April 14, Dia de Pascua
   (Easter Sunday) Processions of floats in many towns bear holy statues.

May 1, Fiesta del Trabajo
   (Labor Day).

August 15, Asunción de la Virgen
   (Assumption Day).

October 12, Día Nacional de España
   (Hispanic Day).

November 1, Todos los Santos
   (All Saints' Day).

December 6, Constitución Española
   (Constitution Day).

December 8, Inmaculada Concepción
   (Immaculate Conception).

December 25, Natividad del Señor
   (Christmas).

Various regions and towns celebrate their own festivals at appointed times during the year. Check with the National Tourist Office of Spain for exact dates, but they line up as follows.

February 18-21, Carnival
   Festive parades mark this festival before Lent.

March 24, Fallas
   Processions of huge papier-mâché figures in Valencia.

April 7-14, Semana Santa
   Processions of life-sized statues of the Holy Family, especially festive in Cádiz, Málaga, Seville, Toledo and Valladolid.

April 12, Viernes Santo
   (*Good Friday*). Processions of floats bearing holy statues in many towns (especially Seville, Málaga and Cádiz.

April 15-21, April Fair
   Seville's picturesque festival where everyone dresses as if for *Carmen*.

April 27-29, Battle of Moors and Christian
   Reenactment of the Reconquest in Alcoy. Similar celebrations in other Andalusian towns occur later in summer.

May 10-16, Jerez Horse Fair
   Horses, bullfighting and Flamenco.

May 18-25, San Isidro
   Madrid's patron saint is celebrated for a week, and includes the best bullfights.

June 25, Corpus Christi
   Processions, especially colorful in Toledo.

July 9-16, Running of the Bulls
> Pamplona's famed macho festival.

July 25, Santiago Apóstol
> (*Feast of Santiago*) Celebrated in odd numbered years only, i.e., not this year.

October 12, El Pilar
> Zaragoza's costumed festival.

January 2, Granada
> Commemoration of the end of the Reconquest.

January 17, most towns
> San António (*the blessing of animals*).

Passports

The single requirement for the average tourist entering Spain is a valid passport. No shots are needed. No visa is necessary except for stays longer than 90 days (though this is seldom enforced) or to work in the country. Visa applications and information are available at the nearest Spanish consulate. (**Spanish Embassy:** *2700 15th Street NW Washington, DC 20009,* ☎ *202-265-0190;* **Spanish Consulate**: *150 E. 58th Street, New York, NY 10155,* ☎ *212-555-4080*)

U. S. State Department passport agencies are located in Boston, Chicago, Honolulu, Houston, Los Angeles, Miami, New Orleans, New York, Philadelphia, San Francisco, Seattle, Stamford (CT) and Washington D.C. Federal or state courthouses also issue passports, as do many post offices.

Expired passports can be renewed by mail, providing that no more than 12 years have elapsed since the date of issue and the applicant was at least 16 years old at the time. Enclose the expired passport and two, two inches square, full-faced photographs taken against a light background. Sign them on the center back, include a completed application form (obtainable at one of the offices listed above), and a check or money order payable to the U.S. Passport Agency for $35. Processing can take up to a month during the busy summer season, after which you will receive your old passport, cancelled, and a new one valid for ten years.

First passports and replacements for those already expired must be applied for in person at one of the offices listed above. Usually the process involves two trips, one to submit the forms and a second to pick up the passport. Proof of citizenship must be presented, which can be a previous passport, a copy of a birth certificate or a Certificate of Naturalization or Citizenship. A proof of identity is also required that may be satisfied by a driver's license or other ID with your picture on it. Credit cards are not sufficient proof of identity, but a friend of two-years' standing is. You will also need two full-faced photographs, two inches square, taken against a light background. The fee is $42 for adults eighteen and over, or $27 for minors. A charge is added for a first passport, a rush order, or a passport issued by a post office or courthouse. It can take up to six weeks for a first-time passport to arrive.

Though not publicized or promised, renewals in person usually can be managed on an emergency basis in 24 hours at State Department offices. Frequent travelers may request double the normal 24 pages at no extra cost.

Car Rental

Although car rentals can be done on the spot, comparison shopping is easier from home and prices are lower. All major U.S. rental companies have Spanish subsidiaries. Your travel agent can make arrangements, or you can call directly for prices or reservations. Lesser known companies act as brokers to find the least expensive European rental for the type of car you specify. Generally, either Auto Europe or Europe by Car will have the lowest prices. Note that Spanish rentals will bill at 12 percent more than the price charged, because of its IVA tax.

Despite the fact that the legal driving age in Spain is 18, most Spanish rental agencies require a driver to be at least 21. Check in advance. Estimate about $365 per week for a compact car with automatic transmission, or about half that price for a smaller, manual-drive car without AC.

Avis
☎ *800-331-1084, or* ☎ *800-879-2847 in Canada.*

Auto Europe
☎ *800-223-5555, or* ☎ *800-458-9503 in Canada.*

Budget
☎ *800-527-0700.*

Dollar (EuroDollar in Europe)
☎ *800-800-6000.*

Europe by Car
☎ *800-223-1516 or* ☎ *212-581-3040.*

Foremost Euro-Car
☎ *800-272-3299, in California* ☎ *800-272-3299.*

Hertz
☎ *800-654-3001 or* ☎ *800-263-0600 in Canada*

Kemwel
☎ *800-678-0678.*

National
☎ *800-227-3876.*

Sometimes the least expensive rental will be through a Spanish company. Names can be provided by the National Tourist Office of Spain. Some have U.S. representatives.

ATESA

Spain's largest, is represented by **Reshotel Marketing**, *70 West 36th Street, New York, NY 10018* (☎ *212-564-2300 or 800-423-4460*).

M.I.

Brokers all major U.S. and Spanish companies, so can locate the best deal. **M.I. Travel, Inc.** *450 Seventh Avenue, Suite 1805, New York, NY 10123* (☎ *212-967-6565 or 800-327-1515*).

In addition, most rental companies and major airlines offer fly/drive packages that bundle airfare and car rental prices, frequently with very attractive savings.

Renting a car for foreign use raises the issue of insurance. Rentals generally include collision insurance in the price—though this should be checked when comparing costs—but often leave a deductible of $1000 or more for damage to the rented car. In such a case, a collision damage waiver should be considered even though it can add $10 per day or more to the rental fee. Note that insurance policies covering damage waivers on rental cars at home generally do not apply to overseas rentals, although rentals via credit card often do.

A major credit card is sufficient for renting any car, but the lack of such plastic makes difficulties, here or there. Some companies will not rent at all to cardless clients; others require substantial deposits.

An International Driving Permit is strongly recommended, for it is understood throughout Europe. Branches of the American Automobile Club can supply one. Bring along two passport-sized photos, a valid driver's license and a $5 fee. Incidentally, AAA has reciprocal arrangements with automobile clubs in Spain that provide similar services for AAA members from the U.S. **Real Automóvil Club de España** is located at *C. José Abascal, 10, Madrid 28003* (☎ *1-447 3200*).

A good map of Spain is a necessity when driving, such as Michelin's *Spain*. Old, haphazardly developed cities can be mazes of tiny, one-way streets. If aiming for the center, follow signs for "*Centro*."

Customs' Requirements

Spain allows visitors to bring any items intended for personal use with them. This includes one carton of cigarettes and one liter of alcohol per adult. Expensive equipment—cameras, computers, etc.—should be registered with U.S. Customs before leaving the U.S. to ensure that they are not charged a duty on return. A proof of U.S. purchase will also serve.

On the return home, U.S. customs does not charge duty on a resident's first $400 of purchases for personal use or on gifts that accompany the traveler, providing his last allotment was claimed one month or more before. A family is permitted to pool its individual allotments as they wish. One carton of cigarettes is also duty-free for each adult, as are 100 cigars (not Cuban, of course), one liter of alcohol, and one bottle of perfume (if sold in the U.S, more otherwise). The next $1000 of personal merchandise or gifts is taxed at 10 percent. Above that amount, rates vary. Save receipts in case of questions. Antiques with proof from the seller that they are over 100 years old are duty-free, as are one-of-a-kind artworks.

Packages mailed home, unless clearly marked "American Goods Returned" or "Unsolicited Gift under $50" will be assessed a duty when delivered. In either case, they do not count as part of your custom's allotment.

Clothes and Packing

Most travelers bring more clothes than they need or use, and since living out of a suitcase means having to carry it, the best advice about packing is that less is better.

Remember that, except at resorts, you'll be visiting cities and towns where most people are dressed for work. You might be on vacation, but everyone else is heading for the office. Although Spain is less formal than other European tourist destinations, jackets, shirts and—except in the hottest weather—ties are the norm for men, and skirts or dresses are customary for women.

Street clothes tend toward more somber hues than many Americans wear. Yet black, grey and navy—standard for Europeans because they withstand wear—also work well for tourists. Given the lack of one-hour cleaners, a spill on a brightly colored dress or jacket might retire it for the rest of your trip.

A pair—or two, for alternating—of comfortable leather walking shoes is preferable in town to sneakers, which are primarily seen on school children. Use insoles rather than your uncushioned feet to take the battering of medieval cobblestones .

For most of the year, raincoats with linings are ideal—single garments that fend off cool, cold or rain. Natural fiber clothing is best—it's lightweight, packs well, and both holds warmth in winter and permits circulation in summer.

Of course at resorts and on holiday or summer weekend trips, Spanish men and women can be spotted in that universal fashion statement—jeans, polo or tee-shirts and sneaks.

A final note: since churches are places of worship, shorts and sleeveless tops are inappropriate.

Do not be overly concerned about forgetting something. Spain is a civilized country where almost anything forgotten or lost can be replaced. Still, it's convenient to have things at hand rather than having to search for them in a store. The following can prove useful:

- Small sewing kit
- First aid kit
- Sunglasses
- Travel alarm
- Penknife
- Ziplock bags
- Safety pins
- String
- Sunscreen

Camera film is expensive in Spain, but bringing your own risks fogging from airport x-rays (despite the disclaimer to the contrary).

Hotels and Other Accommodations

Hotels in Spain are numerous and high in quality. Nowhere in the world will you find more truly grand accommodations, or more delightful inns at modest rates. Service is excellent and cleanliness exemplary, with very rare exceptions. In almost every case you will receive more for your hotel dollar than at home.

As an experience, a night spent at an extraordinary hotel is at least the equal of visiting a special museum or church. Indeed, many tourists orchestrate their visits to Spain as hotel tours. With a few exceptions, extraordinary accommodations are not so expensive as to frighten even moderate travelers, who, if they cannot pass every night at wondrous hotels, can do so from time to time.

Unless money is not a consideration, we suggest using hotels in three ways. Some provide such special service, views or atmosphere that spending the night is well worth their assault on the budget. Other hotels are simply comfortable places to sleep at affordable prices. Last come those hotels that offer the simplest rooms at very modest charges. Spending a few nights in these inexpensive places can gain the savings to cover a memorable stay at one of the extraordinary hotels.

These are Spain's most extraordinary hotels (all expensive unless otherwise indicated):

The Best
Hostal de los Reyes Católicos, Santiago de Compostela

Parador Castillo de Sigüenza, Sigüenza

Alfonso XIII, Seville (Very Exp.)

De la Reconquesta, Oviedo

Ritz, Madrid (Very Exp.)

Santo Mauro, Madrid (Very Exp.)

Ritz, Barcelona (Very Exp.)

Parador San Marcos, León

Special

Rector, Salamanca

Parador de Olite, Olite (near Pamplona)

Parador Duques de Cardona, Cardona (near Barcelona)

Hostal del Cardenal, Toledo

Landa Palace, Burgos

Alhambra Palace, Granada (but see the review for warnings)

Virtually every public accommodation in Spain is listed in the annual *Guía de Hoteles*, published by the Secretaria General de Turismo and available in the U.S. at the **National Tourist Office of Spain** (*665 Fifth Avenue, New York, NY 10022,* ☎ *(212) 759-8822, FAX (212) 980-1053*), as well as at some travel agencies. The Secretaria General de Turismo rates establishments with a system of stars based on measurable features such as the percentage of rooms with private baths, air conditioning, etc., though not for such immeasurable qualities as comfort, efficiency and friendly service. Such ratings obviously provide only a rough guide to price and quality, and should be read in conjunction with our descriptions and alternative star-system (see, *Introduction*, "Ratings.") A white and blue metal plaque outside the establishment will indicate its official rating and type—"H" a *hotel*, "HR" a *residencia*, and "Hs" a *hostale*.

Paradors are an extraordinary Spanish institution—hotels that can enrich any trip. In 1926 the first parador was built as a hunting lodge for the wealthy, but soon others began serving tourists who demanded better lodgings than Spanish hotels of the era could provide. Faced with an oversupply of historical buildings whose owners could not afford their upkeep, the government began buying and remodeling grand edifices into hotels. The program proved immensely successful; it preserved irreplaceable treasures while offering tourists a chance to eat and sleep in the palaces, castles and convents in which ordinarily they could only sightsee. Eighty-six paradors now dot the country, about half of which are historical monuments with many of the rest showcasing modern architects.

Because paradors are government-owned they are less costly than other hotels of similar ratings. A night's pampered stay in a 15th century castle about $100 strikes most people as a bargain indeed. Some paradors are truly magnificent, memorable places, such as Los Reyes Católicos in Santiago de Compostela, Olite near Pamplona, Cardona near Barcelona, San Marcos in León, Sigüenza an hour east of Segovia, and De la Reconquista in Oviedo, to mention just a few. Others offer more ordinary, but comfortable, accommodations in areas lacking sufficient hotels. A list and brochure are available from the National Tourist Office of Spain (see address earlier in this section) or from the booking agent for the U.S. and Canada, **Marketing Ahead, Inc**. at *433 Fifth Avenue, New York, NY 10016*(☎ *(212) 686-9213, FAX (212) 686-0271*). Note that popular paradors fill up quickly. Reservations should be made as early as possible, at least five months in advance for smaller ones in high seasons. Note also that parador meals are seldom adventurous or remarkable, but served in dining rooms whose style almost makes up for ordinary cuisine. Recently, paradors have begun serving regional dishes, providing visitors with a convenient way to sample local specialties.

Not all the wonderful hotels in Spain are paradors. The Alhambra Palace in Granada can (assuming you stay on the upper floors) provide as memorable an experience as the parador nearby, though the parador is the most heavily booked hotel in Spain. No hotel in the world can surpass the privately-owned Palace in Madrid or the Ritz in Barcelona. And both the Hostal del Cardenal in Toledo and the Rector in Salamanca far surpass the quality of their neighboring paradors. Even if the idea of a parador seems wonderful, it's a good idea to check the ratings and descriptions of an area's other hotels before automatically booking into the parador.

First-class and luxury hotels all include TVs in every room and those mini-bars that represent luxury to the Spanish. In addition, each hotel of this class provides a concierge, that is, a kind of ombudsman who can help with almost any problem. He (or she) can locate tickets for almost any event, confirm travel arrangements or make them, recommend restaurants and shops, and deal with emergencies. Their knowledge and expertise are always impressive and make otherwise difficult chores effortless. The concierge should be tipped according to the number of requests, usually 100 pesetas each. Second-class hotels include TVs, but not always mini-bars. TVs are rare in lesser classes.

In our reviews of individual hotels we will not remark on such things as TVs and mini-bars or other expected features unless it is a class of hotel where such things are not usual.

If you're looking for a hotel room in person, remember that Europeans frequently ask to see their room before they register so hotels expect inspections. Simple English will generally be understood. If not, a single room is *una habitación individual,* a double is *una habitación doble. Con baño* means with bath. Few double rooms contain a large bed for two (*cama de matrimo-*

nio), though one can ask. A single room should be no more than 80 percent of the price of a double. The quoted price for a room in Spain includes taxes and usually, though not always, a surcharge for service. In case of a dispute, asking for the *libro de reclamaciónes* (complaint book) often wins the day.

The least expensive accommodations will always be **Youth Hostels**. Like college dorms in the old days, you sleep in largish rooms with strangers and are locked in after curfew (usually at midnight). However, a few double rooms are available at about double the dorm rate. Note that the word "youth" refers to spirit rather than age, for tender years is not a requirement. Despite being communal, hostels are invariably clean since they are supervised by a large and powerful international organization. Costs average about 1000$00 per night in Madrid, less outside the capitol. To stay at official hostels an official HI (Hostels International) card is required, and easier to get in this country than abroad. Contact **American Youth Hostels,** *733 15th Street NW, Suite 840, Washington, DC 20005 (☎ 202 783 6161; FAX 202 783 6171).* New memberships currently cost $25, renewals $20, with discounts for those over 55 and for families.

The way to sleep most cheaply in Spain is to pay nothing for accommodations. That is sometimes possible through a system of international house exchanges. Although the location of your lodging is fixed, it can be used as a base for side trips, and sometimes cars are included in the deal. Of course, your own home should be located in or near an area of interest to foreign visitors, and the odds of an agreeable arrangement improve the longer in advance that inquiries are initiated. Several companies specialize in such arrangements for a fee of $35-$75:

International Home Exchange/Intervac U.S.
   41 Sutter Street, Suite 1090, San Francisco, CA 94119 (☎ 800-788-2489).

Vacation Exchange Club
   Box 650, Key West, FL 33041 (☎ 800-638-3841).

For those willing to base in the same spot, an option is renting an apartment or villa. The following firms will help you find one for a fee:

At Home Abroad
   405 East 56th Street, Suite 6H, New York City, NY 10022 (☎ 212-421-9165).

Europe-Let
   92 North Main Street, Ashland, OR 97520 (☎ 800-462-4486)

Interhome, Inc.
   124 Little Falls Road, Fairfield, NJ 07004 (☎ 201-882-6864).

Overseas Connection
   31 North Harbor Drive, Sag Harbor, NY 11963 (☎ 616-725-9308).

Rent a Home International
   7200 34th Avenue NW, Seattle, WA 98117 (☎ 212-421-9165).

Vacation Home Rentals Worldwide

   235 Kensington Avenue, Norwood, NJ 07648 (☎ 201-767-9393).

Villas International

   605 Market Street, Suite 510, San Francisco, CA 94105 (☎ 415-281-0910).

Money

Spanish money is called *pesetas*, abbreviated "ptas." Coins exist in denominations of 1, 2, 5, 10, 25, 50, 100, 200 and 500 pesetas, and bills of 1000, 2000, 5000 and 10,000 pesetas. While the bills are unequivocal, coins arrive in a bewildering variety of sizes, shapes and colors. What makes things difficult is that neither the size of a coin nor its color indicate its value. In particular, 100 and 500 pta. coins are easily confused. When it is not convenient to read the denomination, thickness is the best indicator of worth.

One hundred and forty pesetas are presently worth about $1, but this is certain to fluctuate. Incidentally, the "Travel" section of the Sunday *New York Times* quotes rates buying and selling pesetas in this country, not in Spain, so the figures are low by twenty percent compared with what you will find when you arrive.

Safety argues for carrying traveler's checks rather than cash because they can be replaced if lost or stolen. Of course, traveler's checks usually cost one percent to buy, but not always. Currently American Express Traveler's Cheques are free at American Automobile Association offices for their members, and Thomas Cook Traveler's Cheques are free when travel arrangements are made through that agency. Inquire about the latest offers. If possible, exchange money only at banks—hotels, restaurants and stores give less favorable rates. Fees are charged for each transaction which argues against numerous small exchanges, but try not to convert more money than you will use, since converting back to dollars involves another exchange premium.

For some reason exchange rates are terrible in the U.S., so do not buy much foreign money before your trip. At most, purchase a small amount for the first day. Pesetas are hard to find in the U.S., although **Thomas Cook Currency Service** in New York at *630 Fifth Avenue (☎ 212 757-6915)* is an exception. Yet, this should not be necessary, for unless you land at some abnormal hour, you will be able to exchange dollars for pesetas at the airport when you arrive.

Bank hours are constricted in Spain—from 9 a.m. until 2 p.m. on weekdays only. However, the large El Corte Inglés department store chain changes money at bank rates and remains open when the banks are closed.

Popular credit cards are widely accepted in Spain, although Visa and MasterCard (called Eurocard in Spain) are recognized more generally than Amex or Diners' Club. Most restaurants, except very inexpensive ones, accept them, as do all first class and luxury hotels. Incidentally, payment by credit card ensures the best possible exchange rate.

Cash machines are becoming popular in Spain. ATMs on the CIRRUS and PLUS systems will be found in large cities and they accept American bank-cards, as well as Visa and MasterCard for cash advances. However, it is necessary to have a PIN number no longer than four digits. If yours is longer, the issuer of the card can change it for you before you depart for Spain.

Travel in Spain

Getting from one city to another in Spain is no more difficult than getting around anywhere else. You have the same choices—car, plane, train or bus.

By Car

Spanish roads generally are good enough, but not what you left at home. The majority of Spanish highways are two-lane roads that would be considered fair country roads in the U.S.

The quality of a Spanish road and whether it is multi-laned is indicated by its letter designation. "A" followed by a number, as in A-1, means an *autopista*, a well-paved four-lane or six-lane highway charging tolls (*peajes*) over most of its route. These roads will also have an "E" designation, since the major arteries in Europe are being systematically numbered throughout the European Economic Community. Toll roads are privately owned in Spain and charge truly exorbitant rates, but they do not pass through low-speed-limit villages, so save both time and gas.

"N" means a national road (*carretera Nacional*), and is followed by either a Roman or Arabic numeral. These are usually one lane in each direction and pass through towns and villages where speeds must be cut in half or more. The problem with one lane in each direction becomes painfully obvious when your're stuck behind a slow-moving vehicle. To help with such problems roads become three-laned up steep hills, allowing an opportunity to pass.

"D" and "C" prefix lesser roads, acceptably paved but even slower going, generally with more curves.

All roads are well marked with self-explanatory international highway symbols. Except for *autopistas*, Spanish roads present astonishing hairpin curves, especially over the mountains, but sometimes on perfectly flat terrain. These curves are usually well marked, and preceded by signs indicating an appropriate speed, but stay alert.

Speed limits are 120 kilometers per hour (75 m.p.h.) on *autopistas*, 100 (62 m.p.h.) on national highways, 90 (55 m.p.h.) on other roads, unless otherwise marked, and 60 (38 m.p.h.) to 40 in towns. Note that distances and speed limits will be measured in kilometers, approximately five-eighths of a mile. When passing, leave the left blinker on throughout your time in the passing lane, then signal right to return. Slow truckers will let you know when it is safe to pass them by signaling with their right blinker. Except for being occasionally more daring in passing, Spanish drivers are reasonably considerate and able.

Gas is a major expense in Europe, costing three times what it does in the U.S. Posted gas prices are initially deceptive for Americans because they are quoted by the liter (slightly more than a quart), as opposed to per gallon. "Fill her up" is *Encha o dispósito, por favor*. Stations are plentiful and remain open late throughout the country.

A good map of the area you plan to cover is a necessity when driving. Michelin map #990, covering all of Spain and Portugal, is recommended. Old, haphazardly developed cities can be mazes. If aiming for the center, follow signs saying "*Centro.*" Spanish authorities are serious about punishing drunken drivers, so don't take chances. And seatbelts must be worn outside of towns.

An International Driving Permit is required for foreigners driving in Spain. Branches of the American Automobile Club can supply one. Bring along two passport-sized photos, a valid driver's license and a $5 fee. Incidentally, AAA has reciprocal arrangements with automobile clubs in Spain that provide similar services for AAA members from the U.S. In Spain the emergency assistance number for RACE, the AAA affiliate, is ☎ *(91) 593 33 33*.

By Plane

The cheapest way to fly from one city to another in Spain is to use free stopovers if they are included in your trans-Atlantic fare. Sufficient free stopovers may permit you to fly without additional charge within Spain. Check with your travel agent.

Until recently Spain had only one domestic airline—Avianco, affiliated with international Iberia Airlines. Today three others add competition to lower prices that were already reasonable. Spain is a large country so flying is often the most convenient transportation. From Madrid, the longest flight to anywhere in Spain is under one hour. Sample flight times are:

- Barcelona: 55 minutes.
- Palma, Mallorca: one hour.
- Seville: 50 minutes.
- Valencia: 30 minutes.

Iberia always offers some inter-country special for foreign visitors. Currently on sale is a $300 pass (less out of season) for four cities of your choice, if purchased in conjunction with a ticket to Spain on Iberia Airlines. Check for current availability, price and other specials. Barcelona is served by a shuttle plane (Puente Aereo) that leaves Madrid every half hour, and requires no reservation.

By Train

Trains beat planes when the distance is 200 miles or less, because train stations are located downtown while airports are not. Trains go almost everywhere in Spain, though not always directly. RENFE (Red Nacional de los Ferrocarriles Español) radiates from its hub in Madrid to the corners of the country. Travel is convenient along any continuous radius, but requires retracing tracks to reach cities on different lines. RENFE ticket offices are centrally located in large cities.

The best trains for speed and service are international trains (EC, IC, TER, Electrotren, Pendular and Talga). Intra-country *"expreso"* and *"rapido"* come next. Seville is served by the splendid new, high-speed AVE, complete with airplane-like earphones, that takes less than three hours. Smaller cities, however, are connected by Motorail, which corresponds to our commuter train systems. The price depends on the caliber of train and whether you choose to travel in first or second class. So many types of discounts are offered that anyone paying full fare has simply not asked—round-trips, senior citizens, families, youths and certain days of the week are all assigned one discount or another. Better than standing in line at the train station is to drop in to any travel agency in Spain that displays a yellow and blue RENFE sign. It cost no more.

If planning a substantial amount of train travel, the best buy is a pass allowing unlimited rides during a fixed period. Eurail and Interail passes are valid on Spanish trains, as well as for the rest of Europe, but for such passes to prove worthwhile you must consume a great deal of mileage. Eurail Flexipasses, issued for fewer train days at lower prices, generally prove more suitable. Even less expensive, but purely for travel within Spain, are Spanish Rail Passes, called *Tarjeta Turistica*. They are issued only to tourists for three, five or 10 days of unlimited travel for fares as low as $175 for a second-class eight-day pass. More convenient, since most of us don't ride the rails every day of a vacation, is a Flexipass that allows, e.g., four days travel during a fifteen day period. Such a ticket costs about $130 for second-class travel (depending on the season). Another attractive deal is a Rail and Drive Pass that provides days of train travel with a car rental when you deboard. Information and current prices are available from travel agents. All such unlimited tickets must be purchased before leaving the U.S. The U.S. representative of **RENFE—Rail Europe**—is located at *230 Westchester Avenue, White Plains, NY 10604* (☎ *800-438-7245; FAX 914-682-2821*).

For train buffs, RENFE also offers special train tours. The most famous is the *Al Andalus Expreso*, a train of beautifully reconditioned cars from the 1920s and 1930s, which include shower rooms, a game room and a piano bar. The route varies, as does the number of days—between one and four—and service is offered only during May, June and September. Tickets are expensive—from $1700 per person for the four days, to $140 for one day, meals included—but it is an unmatchable experience. Information on this and other unique train tours is available through **Marketing Ahead** *(433 Fifth Avenue, New York, NY 10016;* ☎ *212-686-9213.*

By Bus

A bus is usually the cheapest form of travel, beating the cost of trains by about a third. Each city, village and hamlet contains a bus station, Madrid and Barcelona three. Addresses are noted in the "Directory" section for each city. The ticketing procedure is the same as at home. Pay as you board for a short trip or purchase a ticket in the station for a longer jaunt. Estimate about $5 per 100 km of ride. Although there is no provision for reservations, arriving early accomplishes the same thing.

Because there is no national bus company in Spain, numerous small firms divide up the country, so timetables and routes would fill a book, and do. The monthly *Horario Guía* lists times and routes, not only for all bus service, but also for trains and planes, and is available at any newsstand.

Restaurants

Restaurants in Spain serve filling meals at about the price of restaurants at home. If the cost is slightly greater, the portions will be too. The problem is the times these meals are served. The Spanish take siestas, which means they eat their large meal of the day at noon, just before a nap. Restaurants do not reopen for dinner until 8 p.m., at the earliest, or until 9 p.m. in metropolises such as Madrid or Barcelona. Hotel dining rooms are exceptions, since many of their guests can't wait so long to eat. Otherwise, when in Rome....

Spain boasts some utterly splendid restaurants that rank with the best in the world. Zalacaín in Madrid and Arzak in Donostia (San Sebastian) both have Basque chefs, impeccable service and sublime food, at a price (about $65 dollars a person for Zalacaín, and $60 for Arzak). But because the quality of available ingredients is outstanding throughout Spain, even a modest restaurant can provide delicious tastes. Vegetables are grown for flavor, not for their capacity to survive early picking and travel, as in the U.S. Humble chicken retains the taste we have all but forgotten, and bread always tastes homemade.

The Spanish love to dine out which generates an astonishing number of restaurants. In cities and towns, crowds wander the streets every evening, pause to study menus, and stop where their fancy dictates. Fortunately, few "tourist traps," where bad food is served at high prices, exist. Our selection of the very best restaurants in Spain are:

Zalacaín in Madrid

Arzak in Donostia

Akelarre in Donostia

Zuberoa in Oiartzun (near Donostia)

Neichel in Barcelona

Can Gaig in Barcelona

Girasol in Moraira (on the Costa del Azahar)

La Fonda in Marbella

Egaña Oriza in Seville

Chez Victor in Salamanca

All are expensive—in the range of $100 for dinner for two—and worth it. To whet your appetite, see the discussions in the relevant city section.

Even though restaurant prices are generally not exorbitant, eating out consumes the major part of most tourists' budgets. Costs can be reduced by ordering from the *Menú Turístico*, which all Spanish restaurants are obliged to offer (at least at lunch-time). This provides a three-course meal, usually including wine, and makes up for limited choices with savings of about half of à la carte orders. Many places offer *platos combinados* (combination plates), a filling meal and salad all on one plate, for five to 10 dollars, usually including wine on the side. Or try a sandwich (*bocadillo*) in any bar, or *tapas* (appetizers), enough for a meal in omnipresent tapas bars. Cafeterias and *auto-servicios* can be half the price of restaurants. And, should all else fail, major cities offer McDonald's and Kentucky Fried Chicken, just like at home—and at similar prices.

Shopping

Ceramics, leather, woven rugs, fashion, pearls, antiques and flea markets all call to the tourist's wallet in Spain.

Spain has been famous for **ceramics** since the time of the Moors, and its leather work so noted that "cordovan" became an English proper noun. Spain still produces colorful ceramics sold in a hundred shops at very attractive prices. The factories are located in Talavera de la Reina (near Toledo) and in the outskirts of Seville. Spain continues its tradition of fine **leather**, especially in Andalusia and in the famed Loewe's stores, with shoes best in Madrid, Barcelona and Seville.

Madrid and Barcelona are also budding centers for haute couture. No longer is Balenciaga Spain's only internationally recognized **designer**; today one might add Adolfo Dominquez, Alfredo Caral and Sybilla from Madrid, or, for men, José Tómas and Groc from Barcelona. New on the scene is Vittorio and Lucchino in Seville for true Spanish designs influenced by a Gypsy spirit.

Famed Majorca **pearls** can cost as much as 30 percent less in Spain. Spanish **antiques** have not yet escalated as precipitously as French, Italian or English articles; bargains, even in quality pieces, still exist. Costume **jewelry** is excellent and inexpensive. When one realizes that **gold** must be a minimum of 18 karat, one will see bargains. Colorful **rugs** can be spectacular. Toledo sells every kind of **weapon** imaginable, from copies of ancient ones to modern ones, from models to the real things.

The most entertaining shopping is to be found in local flea markets, in Madrid and elsewhere. Discussions of each city include appropriate specific information.

One unfamiliar complication to shopping in Europe is the Value Added Tax, added to purchase prices to equalize disparities among the countries of the European Economic Community. In Spain the Value Added Tax, or IVA, is 12 percent on most purchases, but 33 percent on luxury items. Needless to say, such a supplement can turn a bargain into a bad buy. In theory any foreigner who carries the merchandise home is entitled to a refund of the tax, provided the article cost over 47,000 ptas. In practice, the process is complex. Refund forms will be supplied by most stores or obtained at airport refund offices. Receipts and forms must be stamped by a customs official, who will ask to view the article, then you wait a month or more receive the refund, or for it to be reflected on your charge card. Galerias Preciados, one of the two major Spanish department store chains, offer a simpler way to deal with the IVA. Any tourist who requests it receives a card offering an immediate 10 percent deduction on every non-sale item, in lieu of the IVA refund.

Tipping

Scan the menu in restaurants for the words *servicio incluido*, which means your bill already includes tips. If so, a small additional gratuity is sufficient, say, five percent or the equivalent of a dollar, whichever is greater. Otherwise, 15 percent is a normal tip for underpaid wait-people in Spanish restaurants. When staying at a hotel of the third-class or above, the custom is to return some bills from your change for the staff. It is gracious to leave the equivalent of 100 ptas. per night in the room for the maid, while the concierge, doorman and porter should be tipped for specific services, say the equivalent of 100 ptas per bag carried, or a like amount for hailing a cab. In elegant restaurants where a captain orchestrates the meal and a sommelier presents the wine, the captain should receive five percent, the sommelier the equivalent of $2 and the waiter 15 percent.

Cab drivers expect a 10 percent tip unless the fare was negotiated beforehand, in which case the price includes the gratuity. Ushers are not tipped, but washroom attendants should be given a small coin. Anyone who opens a church or lights it merits 100 ptas. A guide expects 100 ptas per person. Hairdressers generally receive a 10 percent tip.

Time Zone and Official Hours

Clocks in Spain run six hours ahead of Eastern Standard Time in the U.S. Daylight saving time is observed in Spain from the last week in March to the end of September, so that during October the difference from E.S.T. declines to five hours.

The afternoon closings of shops, businesses, museums and monuments can be an avid tourist's bane, leaving him with nothing to do except eat and rest throughout the afternoon. Banks are generally open from 8:30 a.m. until 2 p.m. on weekdays, but may close an hour earlier in summer. A few remain open until 5 p.m. on Thursday. Shops generally start business at nine or 10 Monday through Saturday, but close from one or two, to three or four in the afternoon before opening again until eight in the evening. Businesses generally have similar hours, except for being closed on Saturday. Department stores remain open throughout the day.

After closing for the afternoon hiatus, museums generally reopen until seven in the evening. However, in winter most museums and monuments close at six, rather than seven. Almost all museums close on Mondays and open only until one or two on Sundays.

Restaurants open from one until four for lunch, then from nine or so until 11:30 or midnight for dinner. Of course, there are always exceptions.

August, the vacation month for most Spaniards, can complicate a tourist's itinerary. Especially in large cities such as Madrid or Barcelona, some museums and many restaurants close altogether or curtail their hours. The only rule is to check before setting out.

Mail, Telephones, Electricity and Measurement

Post offices, usually located in the center of a town, open from eight to noon and again from five to 7:30 p.m. on weekdays, but do not reopen in the evenings on Saturdays. However, main offices in large cities stay open all day. The mail is generally reliable, taking about a week for delivery to the U.S. Airmail postage to the U.S. cost 83 ptas. and letters within Spain, 35 ptas. Postcards are the same. Letters addressed to you can be sent to any Spanish city along with the words *Lista de Correos*. Such mail will be held until you pick it up, though it may be filed under your first name, in the Spanish style, rather than your last. American Express will also hold mail free for a month for card-holders or for those who carry Amex Traveler's Cheques.

The telephone system in Spain is perfectly adequate. A local call costs 25 pesetas. To call Spain from the U.S. or Canada, dial 011 for international calls, 34 for Spain, and the Spanish telephone number, but drop the "9" in the Spanish area code. For example, the area code for Madrid is 91. To call from the U.S., dial 011-34-1 plus the local number. To call the U.S. or Canada from Spain, dial 07, for overseas, and 1 for the U.S. or Canada, plus the local area code and number. To call the U.S. using an **AT&T** calling card dial *900-99-11* for an American operator; using an **MCI** calling card dial *900-99-14.*

To call a number in the same city in Spain just dial the local number, but to call a different city first dial 9, then the two or three digit area code, then the local number.

Calls from Spain to the U.S. cost about twice what they do in the other direction. If you use any of the international calling cards offered by U.S. long-distance telephone companies, however, the cost will be about the same as calling from home. As they do in this country, hotels often add exorbitant amounts for calls made from your room, adding three or four times the actual price of the call, but the alternative of using public pay phones means dealing with Spanish-speaking operators. At telephone offices, however, an agent will place the call for you. We list local telephone office addresses with each town or city entry.

Electricity in Spain runs at 220 or 240 volts, compared with 110 in the U.S. Unless an appliance has a 220 volt switch, it is likely to burn out in an Iberian socket when run at twice its power. Inexpensive converters are readily available in the U.S. Make sure you also buy an adapter for European sockets, which accept thin tubes, rather than our wider prongs.

Spanish measures are metric, as in most of the world. Distance is measured in kilometers, volume in liters and weight in grams.

Metric	U.S. Standard
1 kilometer	5/8 mile
1 liter	1.02 quarts
100 grams	3.5 ounces
100 kilometers	62 miles
4 liters	1.1 gallons
1 kilogram	2.2 pounds

Sports

Skiing

The season in Spain runs from December through May. Snow generally is abundant and good, the weather mild and skies clear. Costs will be a good third below those in the Alps.

Val d'Aran, in the Pyrenees of Catalonia, is international and sophisticated, a magnificent glacier-ringed valley. Tuca-Betrèn is the older and smaller of the two valley resorts, offering 18 slopes and trails. Modern Baqueiria-Beret is huge, with 41 slopes and trails, 19 lifts and helicopter skiing available. The French love it, but King Juan Carlos does too. A total of 5000 rooms exist in the valley. For information: Oficina d'Informació Turistica de Baqueira-Beret (*Apartado 60, Viella, Val d'Aran, 25530 Lérida, España:* ☎ *73 64 5050).*

El Formigal, almost a mile high in the Pyrenees of Aragon, is new, growing and lively. Twenty-three runs and trails with 17 lifts and tows exist presently, and the open country offers miles of off-trail possibilities. For information: Oficina de Turismo, Estacion de Formigal (*Sallent de Gallego, El Formigal, 22000 Huesca, España;* ☎ *74-22 5778).*

Cerler, also in Aragon, is larger and closer to the French border than El Formigal and more popular. Twenty-two trails exist at present. For information: Oficina de Turismo de Huesca (*23 Calle Coso Alto, 22000 Huesca, España:* ☎ *974-22 57 78).*

Solynieve in the Sierra Nevada near Granada lies at an altitude of almost 10,000 feet, yet only 60 miles from the tepid Mediterranean. The slopes here are not as demanding as some others, but snow is dependable late in the season. There is a parador. For information: Federacion Andaluza de Esquí (*78 Paseo de Ronda, Veleta, 18000 Granada, España;* ☎ *58-25 07 06).*

Alto Campo, Pajares (with a parador) and **San Isidro** all are scenically located in the Catabrian Mountains near Santander. Snow is reliable and lasts through May. For information: Oficina de Turismo (1 *Plaza Porticada, 39000 Santander, España;* ☎ *42-31 07 08).*

Golf

Spaniards golfed before Sevi Ballesteros; after all he had to practice somewhere. Spain offers 160 courses, mainly in the sunny south, although not so numerous as in some countries so the links grow crowded as golf's popularity increases. Figure about $50 for green fees, unless the links are connected with your hotel and included in the charges, and about $10 to rent clubs. Choice courses would be:

Real Sociedad Hípica Española Club de Campo in Madrid hosted one World's Cup and three Spanish Opens. For information: Real Sociedad Hípica Española Club de Campo (*Calle Fernanflor 6, 28014 Madrid, España;* ☎ *91-429 8889*).

La Manga Campo de Golf at Los Belones, 20 km from Cartagena in Murcia, provides gorgeous views and is superbly maintained. For information: La Manga Campo de Golf (*Los Belones, Cartagena, 30385 Murcia, España;* ☎ *68-56 45 11*).

Golf Torrequebrada in Benalmádena Costa near Málaga offers a five-star hotel with tennis and a casino in addition to the beautiful and difficult golf course. The small town contains very comfortable hotels at cheaper rates than the Torrequebrada, although staying there is the experience. For information: Golf Torrequebrada (*Apartado 67, Benalmádena Costa, 29630 Málaga, España;* ☎ *52-56 11 02, Fax 952-44 57 02*).

Hotel Byblos Andalus near Mijas outside Fuengirola possesses two difficult Robert Trent Jones courses beautifully set. This new hotel offers every facility for sport and comfort while doubling as a spa. It does cost 30,000 plus pesetas a day to exercise as kings do and then relax. For information: Hotel Byblos Andalus (*Apartado 138, Fuengirola, 29650 Málaga, España;* ☎ *5-247 30 50, Fax 5-247 67 83*).

Club de Golf Costa Brava in Santa Cristina de Arco near Barcelona is long established and a tough 18 holes. For information: Club de Golf Costa Brava (*Santa Cristina de Arco, 17246 Gerona, España;* ☎ *72-83 71 50; FAX 72-83 71 52*).

Real Golf de Pedreña in Santander, on a peninsula in an Atlantic bay, is Ballesteros' local course. This one requires that guests be accompanied by a member, but the Spanish are very friendly. For information: Real Golf de Pedreña (*Apartado 233, 39000 Santander, España;* ☎ *42-50 02 66*).

Real Sociedad de Golf de Neguri in Getxo (Agorta) near Bilbao is Spain's oldest course and reminiscent of Scotland, which is not bad. For information: Real Sociedad de Golf de Neguri (*Apartado de Correos 9, Getxo, 48990 Vizcaya, España;* ☎ *44-69 02 00*).

Tennis

Tennis has become Spain's fastest growing sport since the Sanchez brothers and sister became international stars and the Catalan Bruguera won two straight French Opens. Spain provides some cement courts but more red clay surfaces, like those in France. On the latter, be prepared to stay out for a while. Courts rent for about $10 per hour. Some choices in the sunny south of Spain are:

Don Carlos Hotel outside Marbella on the road to Málaga splits hard and clay courts on which Martina and Chris once played. At a couple of hundred dollars a night you can sail, ride horses and play tennis for "free." For information: Don Carlos Hotel (*29600 Málaga, Marbella, España;* ☎ *5-283 11 40, FAX 5-283 34 29; in the U.S., 212-949 7145, in NYC, or 800-338 4510 elsewhere*).

Marbella is a center for elegant sport hotels including: Los Monteros Hotel (☎ *5-277 17 00, FAX 5-282 58 46; in the U.S., 212-725 4500, in NYC, or 800-888 1199 elsewhere*), Puente Romano (☎ *5-277 01 00, FAX 5-277 57 66; in the U.S. 800-448 8355*), and Marbella Club Hotel (☎ *5-277 13 00, FAX 5-282 98 84; in the U.S. 212-838 3110, in NYC, 800-223 6800 elsewhere*).

Campo de Tenis de Lew Hoad at Mijas near Málaga is a very serious tennis camp, founded by Lew Hoad, though he no longer teaches. The courts are cement and the instruction is based on Australian principles. For information: Campo de Tenis de Lew Hoad (*Apartado 111, Fuengirola, 29640 Málaga, España;* ☎ *5-247 48 58*).

Fishing

Salt water fishing is so-so, but trout fishing in Spain can be fun indeed, although not for trophy fish. A license costing about $12 is required and can be purchased at the **Instituto Nacional para la Conservación de la Naturaleza** at Puerta de Toledo in Madrid at *Gran Via, 4* (☎ *1-347 6000*), or in regional offices. The season runs from spring through summer in Andalusia where good trout streams surround Granada and Jaen. Ávila in New Castile and Burgos in Old Castile are centers for trout, though the season is restricted and complex. Near Gerona and Lérida, around Barcelona, clear streams and lakes run with trout and bass.

Hiking

Spain offers abundant mountain wilderness for wandering feet, plus two special national parks. **Doñana National Park**, splitting the Costa da Luz, is the vast estuary of the Guadalquivir River that crowds in winter with migrating birds, in summer with deer and bulls. It may be visited only by tours arranged in advance through **Cooperativa Marismas del Rocío** in El Rocío near Huelva (☎ *955-43 04 32*); admission 1000 ptas. The tours leave from Matalascañas, 15 km south of Playa de Castila, on the Costa del Luz in Andalusia. No tours are offered in July or August, however. **Ordesa National Park**, in northern Aragon, provides the scenery of massive canyons cut by burbling streams. Open only from May through September, it may be visited by anyone and is described in the chapter on Aragón and Navarre.

Student Travel

Any student or person of student age or inclination seeking information on student travel should contact the **Council on International Educational Exchange (CIEE)**. In addition to its headquarters at *205 East 42nd Street, New*

York, NY 10017 (☎ 212-661-1414) branches are located near many large universities. The organization stores reams of information on work, study, education and travel programs for students. In addition it issues Federation of International Youth Travel Organization cards (and International Student Identity Cards, only for matriculating students) which discount transportation costs and museum fees, provide entrance to Youth Hostels and offer many other benefits. To apply for a card, send two passport-type pictures, a proof of birth date and a ten dollar fee. You need to be under 26, but not necessarily a matriculating student.

If you think you might enjoy living with a Spanish family for a week to a month, contact **Experiment in International Living**, *Kipling Road, Box E 10, Brattleboro, VT 05301 (☎ 802-257-7751)*. If you'd like to investigate study abroad, the subject is covered extensively in two books—*Academic Year Abroad* and *Vacation Study Abroad*, both published by **The Institute of International Education** *(809 UN Plaza, New York, NY 10017; ☎ 212-883-8200)*. Then contact the **Education Office of Spain** *(150 Fifth Avenue, Suite 918, New York, NY 10011; ☎ 212-741 5144)* for the specifics. A small selection of language schools offering Spanish courses, is:

EF International Language Schools, *1 Memorial Drive, Cambridge, MA 02142 (☎ 617-252-6100)* offers a nine month course in Barcelona for beginner to advanced that includes transportation and accommodations.

Escuela de Idiomas "Nerjo," Almirante Ferandiz, ☎ *73-29780.* Nerja Málaga, España *(☎ 52-16-87 or FAX 52-21-19)* offers reasonably priced intensive courses for five days to four weeks that include living with a Spanish family.

The Hispalis Center of the Instituto de Lenguas y Cultura Española at *Amor de Dios 31-2, E-41002 Seville, España (☎ 5-490 09 72)* covers courses from beginner to advanced lasting from two to eight weeks.

Centro de Lenguas e Intercambio Cultural in Seville offers from two weeks to sixteen weeks of intensive Spanish for beginner to advanced with various accommodations. Contact Language Study Abroad at *1301 North Maryland Avenue, Glendale, CA 91207 (☎ 818-242-5263).*

Centro de Idiomas at Sagasta 27, 3° Izq. 28004 Madrid, España *(☎ 446-69-79 or FAX 447-22-23)* offers a large variety of courses from two weeks to twenty-four and accommodations with Spanish families if desired.

Young people, 26 or under, are eligible for an especially inexpensive version of the Eurail Pass called Eurail Youthpass. It must be purchased before landing in Europe. Contact **Council Travel** *(205 East 42nd Street, New York, NY 10017; ☎ 212-661 1450)* for details. Or, in Spain, a Youth Pass for anyone under 26 may be purchased at RENFE stations for half-price travel on designated "Blue," off-peak days.

Any young person arriving in Spain should go to **Red Española de Albergues Juveniles** *(Calle José Ortega y Gasset 17, 28006 Madrid; ☎ 1-347 7629)* for an

International Youth Hostel Federation guest card (which costs about $20), and lists of available student hostels.

Young people will find living in Spain cheaper than any other European country and much cheaper than being home on their own. The only pleasure they might miss is the convenience of hitchhiking. Europeans generally show little consideration for those attempting the joys of the road and it is illegal.

Female Travelers

The situation for women in Spain, both native and visitor, has changed dramatically since the repressive Franco days when bare arms and short skirts were deemed illegal. Today Spanish women dress as stylishly as their counterparts anywhere in the world, and topless sunbathers on Spanish beaches are a non-event. Nonetheless, Spanish men retain elements of their Latin "machismo." That means that women traveling alone can be subject to sexual harassment. But, except for large cities or resorts in Andalusia where foreign women are sometimes regarded as prey, a female tourist should encounter no more serious problems than she would at home.

Naturally, harassment is worse for women alone. The situation is complicated when ignorance of Spanish means not knowing how to respond; still, the cold shoulder is understood internationally. Rape is infinitely rarer in Spain than in the U.S., but harassment can be unpleasant and is avoided only by taking the same precautions, including avoidance of isolating situations. None of this is meant to suggest that all Spanish men are cads, only that Spain has its share and that their activity should be more censured by their society than it is at present.

Crime

When Spain was a dictatorship under Franco, its crime rates approached zero. Today true democracy brings its worldwide accompaniments—drugs and thievery. Now Iberia calls for the same precautions as at home.

Unfortunately, more often than not, criminals prey upon tourists. As travelers we carry expensive cameras and probably more money than local citizens on their way to work, making ourselves good marks for pickpockets and snatchers. Just as we can spot a foreign visitor by his attire and attitude, so do we become easily identifiable in a foreign land. The question is not how to stop robberies, for we cannot solve that one at home, but how to decrease the odds that we will be chosen.

Thieves congregate where tourists are, which means that Madrid, Andalusia and Barcelona suffer Spain's highest crime rates. Think of Seville and Barcelona as the New Yorks of Spain (though their statistics are not nearly as bad as this model suggests), and the rest of the country as comfortably safe, given normal precautions. In these two locales try to be a more difficult mark by carrying as little as possible, thus leaving your hands free, and by holding pocketbooks or cameras close to the body. Most important, stay alert, especially at night, and avoid deserted areas. Such precautions should be sufficient. The usual street robbery consists either of youths cornering a victim on a street, or of a quick pocketbook or camera snatch, or of one accomplice creating a disturbance, perhaps by bumping into his victim, apologizing and distracting, while a confederate grabs what he can.

Cars pose another problem. Windshield stickers indicate a rented car that may contain valuable luggage or cameras. Whenever practical, it is best to empty your car before parking; next best is to be scrupulous in hiding visible signs that luggage waits inside, or even that the vehicle has been used for a long trip. So remove scraps, cups and maps from sight. Your goal is to discourage a thief's interest in your car.

Thefts in hotels are extremely rare, and violent crimes are a tiny percentage of U.S. figures. Outside of their few high crime areas, statistics show that traveling in Spain is considerably safer than traveling in the U.S. Be alert, take reasonable precautions and no untoward event should interrupt your trip.

Note: The police emergency number is *091*, anywhere in Spain.

Books

Nothing enhances a trip more than understanding, so read all you can before you go and while in Spain. A very selected list follows of informative books that present the variety of the country:

James Michener's *Iberia* conveys a love of Spain as does no other book. Published in 1968 and widely available in paperback, it is dated now, but remains interesting.

Jan Morris turns her keen and quirky eye in *Spain* on a country she did not fall in love with. The book shows something of the darker side of Spain.

Voices of the Old Sea, by Norman Lewis is an account of the clash of the modern world with older Spanish culture told through the events in one isolated village. The book is utterly captivating, and describes attitudes that remain present in modern Spain, even if submerged.

The classic travel book on Spain is George Borrow's *The Bible in Spain* written in 1843. If a copy is available at your library, get it. This is an opinionated, engaging old travelogue by an English Bible salesman. A more recent and informative effort, especially on the history is *Cities of Spain* by David Gilmour

For an insight into the modern Spaniard, John Hooper's *The Spaniards* is stimulating.

For food and drink, the premier book is Pennelope Casas' *The Foods and Wines of Spain*.

For Moorish art and architecture, Titus Burckhardt's *Moorish Culture in Spain* is the classic.

Washington Irving's *Tales of the Alhambra* remains evocative of these exotic buildings and times.

The Poem of El Cid is still fresh enough to enjoy, and conveys the flavor of Reconquista times.

William H. Prescott's *History of the Reign of Ferdinand and Isabella* has been the most readable book on this fascinating pair since 1838. Though long out of print, most libraries own a copy.

The best book on Columbus is Samuel Eliot Morison's *Christopher Columbus, Mariner*, accurate, though instilling great admiration for the man.

Peter Pierson chronicles the seminal king *Phillip II of Spain*, while Roger B. Merriman covers a wider canvas in *The Rise of the Spanish Empire in the Old World and the New*. Best of all is the elegant prose of J. H. Elliot in his *Imperial Spain 1469-1714*.

Jonathan Brown's *Velazquez, Painter and Courtier* is not just the best book on this painter, it is one of the best on any artist.

Jose Guidol is best on *Goya*.

The Spanish civil war has been extensively covered, usually from partisan points of view. A relatively balanced and moving presentation is Antony Beevor's *The Spanish Civil War*.

Gaudí is well served by two who knew him well in James Joseph Sweeney and Josep Luis Sert, *Antoni Gaudí*.

The acknowledged standard of books on Picasso is John Richardson's *A Life of Picasso*. However, it will test your interest.

Henry Myhill's *The Spanish Pyrenees* stands out among nature books for its lovely pictures, but the information contained in Frederic Grunfeld and Teresa Farino's *Wild Spain*, can't be beat.

For recent Spain, James Hooper's *The Spaniards: A Portrait of the New Spain* is good, though growing dated. But most stimulating, if taken as intelligent opinion rather than gospel is Ian Gibson's *Fire in the Blood*.

Robert Hughes wrote a celebrated book on the culture and architecture of *Barcelona*, that could be better but is often engaging.

THE LAND AND THE PEOPLE

Olive groves are familiar sights near Toledo.

The first and second surprises about Spain's geography are its size and its altitude. The country spreads over a quarter of a million square miles making it the third largest nation in Europe (after Russia and France). Only Switzerland comprises a more elevated average altitude—one Spanish peak tops 11,000 feet. Spain's third surprise is her people. This is not a country where the sun beams idly on guitar players while tourists loll on the sand. Although there is abundant sand along 2400 miles of coast and guitars and sun in evidence throughout, most of Spain is populated by city folk in business clothes and farmers in berets.

In shape Spain forms a 550 miles wide by 400 miles long shield, wider at the top and pointed at the bottom (the part that juts into the sea to reach for Gibraltar). Accidents of geography alone prevent it from belonging to Africa. A mere seven miles of sea separates Spain from Morocco, while Spain is tied to Europe by a 300-mile tab of northern isthmus consisting of the towering Pyrenees. This mountain wall is the reason that, throughout its history, Spain dealt as much with the Moors to its south as with French to the north.

Spain separates into three horizontal climatic regions. The Pyrenees continue across to the northwest corner of Spain, there renamed the Cantabrian Mountains, completing a mountain barrier that seals off the north of Spain. Rain clouds are held by these mountains to make the north green and wet. As opposed to this "wet Spain," the central part is arid. It is an immense, dusty plateau half a mile in altitude. This *Meseta* comprises La Mancha, where locals describe the climate as nine months of winter followed by three of hell. South of La Mancha stands a line of Sierra mountains to seal the cold from Andalusia, preserving a warm Mediterranean climate.

Ancient provincial differences remain strong in Spain, although technically the country was unified 500 years ago and a recent political subdivision sliced the traditional provinces into smaller "departments." The old provinces mean more to the traveler, and to the Spanish, for they encompass cultural and artistic differences that the new alignment does not. Running across the north of Spain, west to east, are the old provinces of Galicia, Asturias, Cantabria, the Basque provinces, Navarre, Aragón and Catalonia.

Galicia, tucked into Spain's northwestern corner, is hilly, misty, green and cut by precipitous deep inlets from the sea like Norwegian fjords. Fishing is a major business. Inland, verdant topsoil barely covers a granite bed, making farming difficult. Farms therefore are small, raising corn, apples, lumber and some beef cattle. The name "Galicia" derives from the Celtic word that also gave us "Gaul" and "Wales," for originally this was the land of Celts and the countryside does bring Wales to mind. Here, in the eighth century, shepherds followed a bright light to a crypt of ancient bones, claimed to be those of Saint James. Christian Europe rejoiced. To house these relics, one of the greatest medieval monuments in the world was raised on the site—the Romanesque Cathedral of Santiago de Compostela.

East of Galicia, **Asturias**, **Cantabria** and the **Basque Provinces** present the same green and moist appearance and temperatures as Galicia, but here the terrain is sedimentary rock instead of granite. Farms are consequently more fertile and larger, though growing crops similar to Galicia's. Asturian coal mines feed Spain's heavy industry, while the coast offers magnificent scenery and Donostia (San Sebastian), an elegant resort. All three provinces are home to Basques (*Vascos* in Spanish, *Euskaldi*, in their own tongue) in omnipresent berets, a people of enigmatic origin, language and robust national identity. Spain acknowledges their culinary expertise. Hard cider is the local drink (*sidra* in Spanish, *sagardua* in Basque). *Pelota, jai alai*, is the national sport, with a court in every village.

Navarre, next in line, is mountainous in the northeast, hilly in the north-west, and descends into cereal plains in the south. Rough stone houses sit on the mountains, and houses dug underground nestle into the plains. Vine-yards cover the southeast near Ribera, next to the famous Riojas wine area. Navarre is dotted with medieval monasteries that once provided shelter for pilgrim hordes marching to holy Santiago de Compostela in Galicia. Pam-plona, famous for its running of the bulls, is Navarre's capital.

The Pyrenees run through the north of **Aragón**, then descend to the basin of the Ebro River. Shut off from the tempering influence of the sea, South-ern Aragón grows olives and grapes and boils in summer while freezing in winter. This was the homeland of Ferdinand the Catholic who married Queen Isabella of Castile. Aragón also lay on the pilgrims' path to Santiago de Compostela, and abounds in ancient monasteries, the original hotels. Its major city—rebuilt in the 19th century—is Zaragoza, a friendlier town than its substantial size would suggest.

Catalonia, on the east coast, is more than Barcelona. The scenic and rocky north coast, called the *Costa Brava*, turns to golden sand in the south, and received the title *Costa Dorada*. The interior is dry but fertile. Catalans are fiercely independent, speaking a language of their own related to the Provençal dialect in the proximate area of France. They are renowned for business acumen, while their art is idiosyncratic both in continuing to em-ploy the Romanesque style later than other parts of Spain and in their avant-garde modern artists and architects: Gaudí, Sert, Miró and Dalí.

Below this belt of northern provinces, and to the west, sits the combined traditional kingdom of Old Castile and León, the largest ancient province. Beneath it, New Castile lies east, with Extremadura to its west. Valencia hugs the coast, east of New Castile and above Murcia.

The *Meseta* begins in **Old Castile and León** where horizons stretch wide de-spite low hills. To its east lies La Rioja, the great wine region of Spain. Else-where, wheat grows, sheep and cattle graze and people, concentrated in cities, are seldom seen. This is the land of medieval castles and of the first capitals of Spain during the Reconquest—León, Burgos, then Valladolid.

New Castile's Madrid is located almost exactly at the geographic center of the country, not far from medieval Toledo, massive El Escorial, Renaissance Salamanca and Segovia with its Roman aqueduct and fairy-tale castle. New Castile's southern half is called La Mancha, possibly derived from an Arabic word meaning "parched." This is the Meseta's heart, an almost featureless half-mile-high plateau empty of humans except in widely separated cities. Infinite wheat fields can be seen today, but in the past the land was ruined by millions of migratory merino sheep who ate every growing thing. Even today, Don Quixote can almost be seen on the distant horizons, passing the castles of Spain.

Extremadura, meaning "beyond the River Duero," is strewn with boulders which suggest Celtic dolmans at every turn. It is home to more sheep than humans, but even the sheep head for the hills during fiery summers. The land of Extremadura nurtured most of the conquistadores who, in turn, seized any opportunity to leave its inhospitable terrain. It boasts houses of the explorers, Guadalupe's holy monastery, Mérida's Roman ruins and Cáceres, a preserved Renaissance town.

Valencia and **Murcia,** on the east coast, are Extremadura's opposites. Here balmy fertile plains border a Mediterranean framed by grey mountains. Thanks to the legacy of the Moors, Valencia grows citrus trees, rice and olives. Perpetual sun shines on the white sands of the Costa Azahar in the north, and the Costa Blanca in the south. Temperatures seldom reach 90 or descend to 40 in busy Valencia, the major city. So arid is Murcia that it is a virtual desert, complete with stands of palms as if oases. The *calina*, a summer heat haze, can make activity difficult.

Andalusia, the southernmost part of the country, is everyone's ideal of Spain—the home of flamenco music and dance. The Sierra Nevada ("Snow Mountain"), capped all year in white, holds weather along the Costa del Sol to moderate Mediterranean temperatures. West, the Guadalquivir River breaks the mountains to form a wide basin that steams in summer. Further west, behind the Costa de la Luz ("Coast of Light"), rice, sugar and cotton extend on flat plains where the fighting bulls are raised. This is the fabled land of the Moors. A clear Andalusian sky reflects perpetually on Seville, Córdoba, Granada and the sherry production of Jerez de la Frontera.

According to Spain's 1981 census, its population approached 40 million. Now it certainly numbers more. About 40 percent of its people live in the ten largest cities, following a worldwide demographic trend of migration from rural toil to urban dreams. Whether the migrants' ambitions are realized is dubious, but they spawn boring suburbs around urban centers. A happy effect of this migration, however, is that the older towns and cities have not been forced to absorb increased population, thus preserving much of their original character. Even the centers of most Spanish cities retain their medieval or Renaissance character of narrow, crooked streets and ancient buildings. In the context of the rest of Europe, Spain remains poor, despite enormous economic strides through the 1980s, although poverty is not evident in either the look of the cities or the stylish dress of the people. Cities and towns sparkle, with little sign of dilapidation. Throughout the vast countryside, verdant farms cover the landscape, although only one Spaniard in six is a farmer today.

The recent recession hit Spain especially hard. Unemployment has risen to an astronomical 20 percent of the eligible workforce, in part because the huge foreign investment that came into Spain during the 80s moved out once Spanish wages climbed to European standards, and in part because Spanish work laws protect employees to a degree that hampers business. Crime has increased, but prices have recently declined in efforts to increase sales. Bargains now exist both in commodities and hotel accommodations.

The Spanish work hard. In the hot parts of the country, however, they fight a debilitating climate. Avoiding the outdoors during the heat of the day is a sensible adaptation, so the Spanish break to eat and rest from noon to two, or from one to three. But they come to work early and leave late to make up for the period away. You will seldom see an idle Spaniard.

The physical appearance of the people ranges from small, dark-complexioned Basques in the north to slender Andalusians in the south, where one finds the startling combination of raven hair crowning fair skin and blue eyes. The modern Spaniard is a mix of more races than he generally wishes to acknowledge. Originally there was a stock of native Iberians and Celts, along with Basques of unknown origin; then Romans intermingled, followed by German Vandals and Visigoths, and finally Moors and Jews.

Most characteristically, you will see the Spanish on their evening strolls, the *paseos*, when families come together for a walk at dusk along an avenue in each town appointed long ago for the purpose. There is something touching about the familial closeness this ritual involves, and the affectionate attention the adults devote to their children. You will wonder how such gentle people can enjoy the blood of bullfights, or how they could have fought so violently against each other in the Spanish Civil War. You will find no easy answer, for the Spanish are not a simple people.

WHERE TO GO

The beach at Santa Fe on the Costa del Sol attracts sun-worshippers.

Topping any list of sights would be Andalusia's three great cities located close enough to each other to be covered in one trip. **Granada ★ ★ ★ ★ ★** must be seen for its Alhambra Palace. This palace, arguably the finest Muslim structure in the world, is unlike any collection of buildings anywhere—perfect, exquisite and provoking. Together with its associated castle, fortified walls and the Generalife (summer palace nearby), it can be seen in half a day. Add the Capilla Real (Royal Chapel) and tomb of Isabella and Ferdinand to the other sights in the city, and Granada can be explored in a day or two. An hour away lies **Córdoba ★ ★ ★ ★** with its Mesquita, a perfectly preserved mosque. Inside, a forest of variegated columns incongruously houses a cathedral. The Mesquita, the lovely patios of the ancient Jewish Quarter, and the other sights of Córdoba consume one day. Two hours farther on waits **Seville** ★★★★★, a beautiful city that produced Expo '92, and contains the second best art museum in Spain, along with two resplendent examples of medieval Moorish-Christian architecture—the Alcázar (Fortress) and the Casa de Pilatos. At the minimum, Seville needs a three-day stay.

Next in priority is Madrid and the cities around it—Toledo, El Escorial, Segovia and Salamanca. **Toledo** ★★★★★ is a virtual museum city overflowing with El Grecos. It also possesses an awesome cathedral, an exquisite ancient synagogue, a fine art museum and more. Since Toledo lies within an hour of Madrid, visitors frequently make it a frenzied day-trip from the capital. Two days would be better. **Madrid** ★★★★★ is new in Spanish terms, but cosmopolitan and fun, combining pleasing sights with great museums. Two days hardly does justice to such a large and diverse city. A half-hour away, for a half-day excursion, stands **El Escorial** ★★★★, an imposing complex of palace, church and monastery from the 16th century. An hour farther along is **Segovia** ★★★★★, with a genuine castle looking strikingly like the fantasy one at Disneyland, an imposing cathedral and a dozen Romanesque churches all set on an imposing site—a visit requiring at least one hurried day. **Salamanca** ★★★★, at least another full day, is surely the finest city in Spain that tourists ignore. It is a treasure-house of intricate Renaissance *plateresque* architecture, much of it preserved on the grounds of its university, along with a 16th-century classroom. Salamanca also boasts one of the great churches in Spain—the Romanesque Catedral Vieja (Old Cathedral).

Barcelona ★★★★★ is a beautiful, cosmopolitan city offering much to do, pleasant walks while doing it and fine food to enjoy afterward. Beyond such simple pleasures, Barcelona bursts with so much architecture and art that it bids to be the one city in Spain to see if you can only see one. There is a fine cathedral standing in a preserved medieval quarter (the Barri Gòtic); the best Medieval and Renaissance museum in Spain (the Museu de Arte de Catalunya); some of the finest examples of modern art in the Miró and Picasso museums; and the astounding Sagrada Familia cathedral by Gaudí, to mention just the highlights. An absolute minimum stay in Barcelona demands three days; excursions to the surrounding area, which abounds in beaches, Greek and Roman ruins and medieval monasteries, can easily fill whatever additional time is available.

Santiago de Compostela ★★★★★ presents a great Romanesque cathedral set in the most beautiful of squares. Because one travels to Santiago to see only the cathedral and squares, it would be possible to spend a half day there, then continuing on one's way. But no one wants to. Everyone sits, charmed and contemplative, regretting their time of departure.

Just as grand, in a less insistent way, is the huge and flamboyantly Gothic cathedral of **Burgos** ★★★★. Burgos is a lively, lovely town that should receive at least a full day of one's time. Outside the city wait a medieval convent and a Renaissance monastery, each a gem.

The "royal" cities, successive early capitals of Spain established during its centuries of reconquest, come next on the list. Traveling north from Madrid, the first of these cities (but the last capital chronologically) is **Valladolid** ★★★. Less attractive than many other Spanish cities, it nevertheless houses an excellent collection of polychromed wood sculpture in a splendidly ornate Renaissance building (San Gregorio). The city also preserves the house in which Columbus died. An hour away and a little farther north is the second capital of Spain, **León** ★★★. Tourists come to admire its Gothic cathedral, patterned on the French model with acres of brilliant stained glass. While there, they also discover the city's atmospheric old quarter, its impressive San Marcos monastery and its Romanesque treasure—St. Isadore's church and pantheon. **Oviedo** ★★★, the first capital of Spain, waits three hours farther north. Nothing in the city limits must be seen, but a certain elegance captivates all who visit. Among other sights, Oviedo has a lovely cathedral containing ninth-century relics and carvings. On the outskirts of town, however, stands a treasure. Santa María del Naranco is Spain's oldest existing civil building, the remains of an eighth-century Visigothic palace. Valladolid, León and Oviedo each merit a day's visit.

The state of Extremadura encompasses a variety of sights spread throughout pleasant scenery. **Mérida** ★★ preserves Roman buildings, **Cáceres** ★ is a town of Renaissance houses, **Trujillo** ★★ invites with moody castle ruins and homes of the conquistadores, while **Guadalupe** ★★★ monastery glitters mysteriously in the mountain's heights. Extremadura is small—a tour of the state requires only three days—and lies close to Madrid.

Pamplona ★, the university town with its famous bullring, is the capital of Navarre. It is also the center for a collection of medieval monasteries that make pleasant excursions, especially to La Oliva and Leyre. Both are simple Cistercian structures—the former even simpler than when new because occupying French stripped it of decoration, the latter with a massive gloomy crypt well worth seeing.

Beaches

So far we've said nothing about beaches, as if relaxing were not a legitimate vacation enterprise. Spain is almost surrounded by beach, close to 2400 miles of it, some on the Atlantic, but most on the Mediterranean. Europeans are well aware of both the quality and quantity of Spain's shore, arriving in sufficient droves every summer to double the population of the country.

The northern beaches—those on the Atlantic—comprise some looking like Scandinavian fjords, and others dotted with elegant resorts. A tour of these beaches can pleasantly fill a vacation. Start at Santiago and head east to the coastal **Rias** ★ ★, headlands cut by river estuaries to form dramatic fjords. Or follow the coast east, pausing for days at Santillana del Mar, Santander and Donostia (also called San Sebastian) to explore the **Costa Verde** ★ ★ ★, perhaps pausing too at Oviedo, a half-mile inland. Or trace the route the other way around.

On the east coast, the rugged **Costa Brava** ★ ★ ★ runs north from Barcelona for almost 100 miles, as cliffs and headlands are broken by tranquil coves. Though much development has taken place since the 1960s, pockets of scenic beach remain to remind us of rugged Maine, though thankfully warmer. South of Barcelona, along the 100 miles to Valencia, lies the **Costa del Azahar** ★ ★ ★, the Coast of Orange Blossoms. The land flattens, beaches widen and stretch, and the scent of orange blossoms indeed hangs in the spring air. Housing developments reach into that same air, but not to the degree that they do farther south on the Costas del Sol and Blanca. A few scattered towns manage to retain their charm; beaches are ample, with Peñiscola the best. Thus, sunning opportunities run for over 100 miles both north and south of Barcelona. Transportation is ample too—using either trains or buses it is perfectly feasible to visit both Barcelona and its adjacent beaches without a car.

The most popular beaches in Spain, in fact in all of Europe, form the southern coast of Spain. East to west spread the Costa Blanca, Costa del Sol and Costa de la Luz. The **Costa Blanca** ★ ★ ★ is named for its fine white beaches that stretch for miles. Benidorm boasts of the best beaches in Spain, but the town itself is no longer attractive and space on the sand is hard to find at the height of the season. Nonetheless, there are pockets on this coast where crowds do not collect and bathing remains scenic and tranquil. The weather is wonderful—seldom are there clouds, let alone rain. The **Costa del Sol** ★ ★, running from Gibraltar east to Almeria, is a different cup of tea. Beaches are gritty, pebbles in the shallows make wading difficult, and high-rise developments stretch as far as the eye can see. Why then do all the people come? Because all the people come. These are Spain's most popular beaches by far and the most cosmopolitan and exciting, with crowded clubs, restaurants and bars. It is fun, and the sun shines almost every day, but such amusements are not cheap. West of Gibraltar begins the Atlantic Ocean and the **Costa de la Luz** ★ ★. Beaches consist of sand rather than grit, the Atlantic sends true waves, fresh seafood is delicious and the crowds and prices dip below those on the Costa del Sol.

Castles

Do you want to see fortresses, the fabled castles of Spain? Here is a list of the best, all close to Madrid. **Coca ★★**, near Segovia, is the epitome of a fortress; the Alcázar in **Segovia ★★★★** looks like a fairy-tale castle; and **Ávila ★★★★**, not far from Segovia, is the most complete medieval fortified town in Europe (tied with Carcassone in France). Not enough? Northeast of Coca, 35 miles from Valladolid, is the still-imposing castle of **Peñafiel ★★**, with parts as old as the 10th century, the rest from the 15th. South of Madrid, on the way to Andalusia, is a massive 15th-century castle in **Belmonte ★★**, complete with perimeter wall. Farther afield, the Alcázar of the Alhambra in **Granada ★★★★★**, along with its perimeter walls, calls insistently to the fortress lover, as do the walls of **Trujillo ★** in Extremadura. Would you like to spend the night in a castle? Near Madrid there is a large castle turned parador at **Siqüenza ★★★★**, or, for more intimate fortress surroundings, the parador castle at **Alarcón ★★★**. Near Pamplona at **Olite ★★★**, an archtypical castle has been turned into a parador open to anyone with the foresight to reserve ahead.

Cathedrals

Anyone in pursuit of cathedral glories will find a profusion in Spain. In particular those in **Toledo ★★★**, **Burgos ★★★★★** and **Seville ★★★★** represent the best and most impressive examples of the sumptuous Spanish Gothic. **León ★★★★** presents the airier French model, and **Santiago de Compostela ★★★★★**, the acme of the Romanesque, while **Salamanca's** Catedral Vieja **★★★★** is a quietly moving church. Outside **Oviedo** stand two tiny eighth-century progenitors of the larger churches to come. The church at **El Escorial ★★** and the cathedral at **Valladolid ★★**, both by the architect Herrera, are imposing neo-classical structures.

Virtually every city and most towns will possess a church of interest. And monasteries range from **Poblet ★★★**, near Barcelona (entirely restored, but moving nonetheless), to **Miraflores ★★★** and **Las Huelgas Convent ★★★★**, older and more atmospheric (both in the suburbs of **Burgos**), to **El Escorial ★★★★** (for its classical lines), and **Guadalupe ★★★** (full of religious mystery). Then there are the holy sites **Guadalupe ★★★**, for the Black Virgin, **Santiago de Compostela ★★★★★**, for its relics of Saint James, **Ávila ★★★**, for Saint Theresa; and **San Ignacio de Loyola Monastery ★**, half an hour from Donostia, and **Javier Castle ★**, near Pamplona, for Saint Francis Xavier's and Saint Loyola's respective birthplaces.

Charming Villages

Santiago de Compostela and **Segovia**, being large, stretch the village characterization, but both have that feel along with charm to spare. **Trujillo ★★** is sleepy and picturesque. **Ronda ★★**, in Andalusia, provides breathtaking vistas across the landscape. **Arcos de la Frontera ★★**, also in Andalusia, offers views almost as stunning from either the parador or the tiny El Convento Hotel. **Peñiscola ★★**, on the Costa del Azahar, offers vistas, miles of white beach and a lively town. **Donostia ★★★** on the Costa Verde is also much too large for the category, but its elegance immediately makes visitors forget that discrepancy.

Itineraries

Since too much of even a good thing can tire, we recommend that days of sights be broken either by beach lolling or an extra day with nothing on the agenda in a town you enjoy. That same wisdom argues against overloading a trip with any single type of sight, whether castles, cathedrals or museums. Variety, as someone should have said, is the spice of vacations. Suggested itineraries follow, though we leave it up to you how to implement our advice to serve your own interests.

The following ten itineraries cover most of Spain in trips that vary in length from one week to 15 days. Any two itineraries may be combined to form trips of longer duration, and too-long itineraries may be shortened by omissions. As to the time estimates, we are aware that many travelers want to fill every minute with activity. These people will find our estimates generous, for we add a few hours every day for whims, cafe sitting and napping. On the other hand, our itineraries are predicated on visits to only the most outstanding sights so they omit interesting and enjoyable activities for those with more time or energy. Impatient travelers can cut a day or two off our itineraries, while the thorough can add as much. Each itinerary assumes a first day consumed by travel, settling in a hotel and gaining bearings, and a last day taken up by departure arrangements, which in some cases might involve flying into Madrid for international connections. So, a week's itinerary comprises five sight-seeing days. Add to our itineraries whatever beach or rest days you wish.

IMPORTANT NOTE: Most museums in Spain are closed on Monday. If we list a museum for a day that falls on a Monday during your trip, interchange it with another day.

Madrid, seven days
This trip presents the flavor of Madrid and the Prado, one of the great museums of the world, as well as El Escorial, an imposing complex.

Day 1:   Travel to Madrid and settle into a hotel.

Day 2:   The Museo Nacional del Prado; Jardin del Retiro.

Day 3:   La Ciudad Antigua; Plaza Mayor; Convento Descalzes Reales; Convento de la Encarnación.

Day 4:   Excursion to El Escorial.

Day 5:   Museo Arqueológico Nacional; shopping; Museo Lázare Galdiano.

Day 6:   Palacio Real.

Day 7:   Departure.

Madrid and Toledo, seven days

This trip adds remarkable Toledo to the best of Madrid.

Day 1: Travel to Madrid and settle into a hotel.

Day 2: The Museo Nacional del Prado; Convento Descalzes Reales.

Day 3: La Ciudad Antigua; Plaza Mayor; Palacio Real.

Day 4: Museo Arqueológico Nacional; shopping; Museo Lázaro Galdiano.

Day 5: Travel to Toledo; settle into a hotel; Cathedral; Santo Tomé.

Day 6: Alcázar; El Tránsito Synagogue; Iglesia María Blanca; Santa Cruz Museum.

Day 7: Return to Madrid and departure.

Note: If an extra day is available, the fairy tale castle of Segovia lies an hour north of Madrid, with El Escorial on the way.

Barcelona, seven days

This trip introduces the cosmopolitan city of Barcelona, its extraordinary collections of medieval and modern Spanish art, and the charm of Gaudí's architecture.

Day 1: Travel to Barcelona and settle into a hotel.

Day 2: Barri Gótic; Cathedral; Palau de la Generalitat.

Day 3: Museo de Arte de Catalunya; Fondacion Joan Miró; Museu Arqueológico, if time.

Day 4: Museu Maritím; Museu Picasso; and the Textile and Costume Museum.

Day 5: Gaudí's works, including Sagrada Familia; shopping.

Day 6: Ramblas and Palácio de la Virreina; Santa Maria del Mar.

Day 7: Departure.

Note: This itinerary assumes flying directly to Barcelona. If landing in Madrid, you may need an extra day for travel to Barcelona, depending on connections. To include Madrid, add days two and three from the Madrid itinerary, but substitute the Museo Arqueológico Nacional for the Jardin del Retiro on the second day.

Madrid and Extremadura, eight days

This driving trip combines Madrid with a taste of the land which bred the Conquistadores. As a bonus it offers Roman ruins, a preserved renaissance town and the holy monastery of Guadalupe.

Day 1: Travel to Madrid and settle into a hotel.

Day 2: The Museo Nacional del Prado; Museo Arqueológico Nacional.

Day 3: La Ciudad Antigua; Plaza Mayor; Palacio Real.

Day 4: Travel to Cáceres and settle into a hotel.

Day 5: Ciudad Vieja and excursion to the Roman remains at Mérida.

Day 6: Excursion to Trujillo.

Day 7:   Return to Madrid, visiting Guadalupe Monastery on the way.

Day 8:   Departure.

The Levante and Murcia, eight days (or more)

This area is visited mainly for beaches—the Costa del Azahar and Costa Blanca. Valencia adds interest. Days should be added for relaxing in the sun.

Day 1:   Travel to Madrid and settle into a hotel.

Day 2:   Travel to Valencia and settle into a hotel.

Day 3:   Ciudad Vieja; Palacio de la Generalidad (only open Saturday mornings); Lonja; Museo Porvincial de Bellas Artes.

Day 4:   Museo Nacional de Ceramica; Iglesia de los Santos Janes; Colegio del Patriaca; Torres Serranos.

Day 5:   Excursion to scenic Peñiscola along the Costa Azahar, visiting Roman ruins at Sagunto on the way.

Day 6:   Travel down the Costa Blanca to Murcia and settle into a hotel, passing through once lovely Benidorm and pausing at Gandia to see the palace of the Borgias (Borjas in Spanish).

Day 7:   Cathedral. Travel to Madrid.

Day 8:   Departure.

Note: A boat ride through underground grottoes of San José is available outside Sagunto on the way from Valencia to Peñiscola. To include Madrid, add days two and three from the Madrid itinerary, but substitute the Museo Arqueológico Nacional for the Jardin del Retiro.

Seville, Granada, Córdoba, 10 days

This trip by car or train will give you the flavor of Andalusia, the Moors and Spanish architecture of the 14th and 15th centuries.

Day 1:   Travel to Madrid and settle into a hotel.

Day 2:   Travel to Seville and settle into a hotel. Cathedral; Torre Giralda.

Day 3:   Alcázar and gardens; Barrio de Santa Cruz; Museo Arqueológico.

Day 4:   Museo de Bellas Artes; Casa de Pilatos.

Day 5:   Travel to Córdoba and settle into a hotel. Mesquita.

Day 6:   Juderia; Alcázar and gardens; excursion to Medina el Azehara.

Day 7:   Travel to Granada and settle into a hotel. Cathedral and Capilla Real.

Day 8:   Alhambra; Palacio Carlos V; Generalife.

Day 9:   Albaicin; Cartuja, San Juan de Dios.

Day 10:   Departure.

Note: Any number of beach days on the Costa del Sol or Costa de la Luz can easily be added to this itinerary. To include Madrid, add days two and three from the Madrid itinerary, but substitute the Museo Arqueológico Nacional for the Jardin del Retiro.

Old Castile, 10 days

This whirlwind trip, for which a car is necessary, includes the best castles, fine Renaissance architecture, two spectacular cathedrals and a Roman aqueduct.

Day 1: Travel to Madrid and settle into a hotel.

Day 2: Travel to Segovia and settle into a hotel, visiting El Escorial on the way.

Day 3: Roman aqueduct; Alcázar; Ciudad Vieja and Cathedral.

Day 4: Travel to Salamanca and settle into a hotel, visiting Ávila and Coca castle on the way.

Day 5: Plaza Mayor; Patio de las Escuelas; Catedral Vieja; travel to Valladolid and settle into a hotel.

Day 6: Collegio San Gregorio and the town. Travel to León and settle into a hotel.

Day 7: Cathedral; Saint Isadore; excursion to San Miguel de Escalada.

Day 8: Travel to Burgos and settle into a hotel, visiting Fromista on the way.

Day 9: Cathedral; the monastery of Miraflores; Las Huelgas convent; return to Madrid with optional stops at Santo Domingo de Silos and Pedraza de la Sierra.

Day 10: Departure.

Note: To include Madrid, add days two and three from the Madrid itinerary, but substitute the Museo Arqueológico Nacional for the Jardin del Retiro.

Navarre and Aragón, 10 days

This driving trip offers medieval monasteries, scenically placed churches and Pamplona.

Day 1: Travel to Madrid and settle into a hotel.

Day 2: Travel to Pamplona and settle into a hotel.

Day 3: Cathedral; Museo Navarra and Ciudad Vieja.

Day 4: Excursion to Estella and Irache Monastery, stopping at Cirauqui and Puente la Reina on the way.

Day 5: Excursion to Olite; La Oliva Monastery; scenic Ujué and the monastery of Leyre.

Day 6: Travel to Zaragoza and settle into a hotel, stopping at Tudela on the way.

Day 7: Cathedral; Lonja; Nuestra Señora del Pilar; Aljaferia.

Day 8: Excursion to Veruela Monastery; Huesca; San Juan de la Peña Monastery.

Day 9: Return to Madrid.

Day 10: Departure.

Note: The park and waterfalls of Piedra Monastery make a nice excursion from Zaragoza, stopping at picturesque Daroca on the way. Also, from spring though fall, scenic walks are possible in Ordesa National Park. To include Madrid, add days two and three from the Madrid itinerary, but substitute the Museo Arqueológico Nacional for the Jardin del Retiro. If time allows, add Burgos from the Old Castile itinerary.

Santiago de Compostela, Galicia, and the Basque Counties, 12 days (or more)

In addition to the spectacular pilgrimage church of Santiago de Compostela, this driving trip offers rugged seacoast scenery and elegant beach resorts. Add days at Santillana del Mar, Santander, Laredo or Donostia (San Sebastian) for the beach.

Day 1:   Travel to Madrid and settle into a hotel.

Day 2:   Travel to Santiago de Compostela and settle into a hotel.

Day 3:   Cathedral; Ciudad Antigua; Hostal do los Reyes Católicos.

Day 4:   Excursion to Pazo de Oca, to ocean inlets at Mirador de la Curota and to Cabo Finisterre, the westernmost part of Europe.

Day 5:   Travel via the coast to Oviedo and settle into a hotel, pausing at Mondoñedo.

Day 6:   Ciudad Antigua; Cathedral; excursion to Santa Maria del Naranco.

Day 7:   Travel along the coast to Santillana del Mar, Santander or Laredo.

Day 8:   Explore the town.

Day 9:   Travel along the coast to Donostia (San Sebastian), detouring for San Ignacio de Loyola Monastery.

Day 10:   Ciudad Vieja; Mount Igueldo.

Day 11:   Return to Madrid.

Day 12:   Departure.

Note: From Santiago de Compostela an excursion can be made to Osera monastery and to Orense for its Cathedral and Old Town. The Altamira Caves lie outside of Santillana del Mar, but require advance permission to enter. Other painted prehistoric caves in the area that do not require permission are: Cueva Santimamine near Guernica on the way to Donostia; Cueva de Buxu in the Picos de Europa mountains between Oviedo and Santillana del Mar; Cueva el Castillo outside Puente Viesgo near Santillana del Mar; Cuevas Covalanas outside Ramales de la Victoria near Laredo; and Cueva Tito Bustillo outside Ribadesella on the way from Oviedo to Santillana del Mar. The road to Madrid goes through Burgos, with a magnificent Cathedral. To include Madrid, add days 2 and 3 from the Madrid itinerary, but substitute the Museo Arqueológico Nacional for the Jardin del Retiro.

Three Star Spain, 15 days

This trip covers the greatest sights in Spain, though it is light on local flavor and rest.

Day 1:   Travel to Madrid and settle into a hotel.

Day 2: The Museo Nacional del Prado; the Museo Arqueológico Nacional.

Day 3: Plaza Mayor; Palacio Real; excursion to El Escorial.

Day 4: Travel to Toledo and settle into a hotel. Cathedral; Santo Tomé.

Day 5: El Transito Synagogue; Iglesia María Blanca; Iglesia San Roman; Santa Cruz Museum.

Day 6: Travel to Seville and settle into a hotel. Cathedral; Torre Giralda.

Day 7: Alcázar and gardens; Barrio de Santa Cruz; Casa de Pilatos.

Day 8: Travel to Córdoba and settle into a hotel. Mesquita; Juderia; Alcázar and gardens.

Day 9: Travel to Granada and settle into a hotel. Cathedral and Capilla Real.

Day 10: Alhambra; Palacio Carlos V; Generalife.

Day 11: Travel to Santiago de Compostela and settle into a hotel.

Day 12: Cathedral; Hostal do los Reyes Católicos.

Day 13: Travel to Barcelona and settle into a hotel. Barri Gòtic; Cathedral.

Day 14: Museo de Arte de Catalunya; Museus Miró and Picasso; Gaudí's works, including Sagrada Familia.

Day 15: Departure.

Note: This itinerary assumes a departure from Barcelona. If leaving from Madrid one extra day may be needed for returning, depending on connections.

HISTORY

The regal tomb of Columbus is housed in Seville's Cathedral.

Spain's history is both long and unfamiliar which makes it difficult to digest. Yet nothing enriches a traveler's experience more than understanding the background of what he sees. We will provide that background in two ways. Below, historical chronology and overview presents the scope of Spain's history to serve as a ready point of reference. Historical profiles preceding each chapter on the sights will add the necessary details.

Prehistory to the Visigoths (to A.D. 711)

13,000 B.C.   Prehistoric people create cave paintings at Altamira.

1300 B.C.   Iberians inhabit Spain, perhaps migrating from North Africa.

1000 B.C.   Phoenicians colonize Cádiz and Málaga.

900 B.C.	Celts inhabit Spain, perhaps migrating from France.
650 B.C.	Greeks colonize the eastern coast of Spain.
250 B.C.	Carthaginians take over the south coast.
206 B.C.	The Roman general Scipio Africanus defeats the Carthaginians, beginning six centuries of Roman presence.
19 B.C.	Caesar Augustus completes the Roman conquest of Spain.
A.D. 74	Rome bestows citizenship on the Spanish.
A.D. 380	Emperor Theodotius declares Christianity the state religion of the Roman Empire.
A.D. 400	Germanic tribes invade Spain.
A.D. 500	Visigoths conquer Spain.
A.D. 711	Muslims from Morocco conquer the Visigoths.

Civilization existed in the Iberian Peninsula for at least 13,000 years before the Romans arrived to impose their way of life on its inhabitants. Not only do the megalithic Celtic dolmans preserved at Antequera prove the existence of a culture that spread from Brittany and Britain at the beginning of the last millennium B.C., but the haunting cave paintings in Altamira, dating from 13,000 years ago, force us to rethink our image of "primitive" cave dwellers. Before the Celts, two different peoples inhabited the land—Iberians, perhaps originally from North Africa, and Basques, who show little affinity to any other other people anywhere.

So Spain had lived in splendid isolation from the rest of the world until Phoenicians landed in 1000 B.C. to mine tin for the manufacture of bronze. They established permanent trading posts at Gades (Cádiz) and Malaca (Málaga), avoiding the inland territory belonging to those they referred to as "Celtiberians," mistakenly classifying two peoples as one. Greeks followed, but kept their distance by colonizing only the east coast of Spain, where major Greek ruins still remain north of Barcelona at Empúries.

As the fortunes of Phoenicia waned in the third century B.C., its former colony of Carthage took over control of the Spanish coast. This was too close to Italy for rival Roma's comfort and soon the two trading empires declared war. Just before the beginning of the second century B.C. the Romans first set foot on Spanish soil when they came to attack the supply lines of the Carthaginian general Hannibal during the Second Punic War. After winning, the Romans stayed in Spain and set out to do what no visitor had yet accomplished—the conquest of the interior.

Unlike most of Rome's opponents who fell quickly to her armies, Spain resisted for two centuries before its final defeat in 19 B.C. by Caesar Augustus. The peninsula, became a province of the Roman empire, growing over time more Roman than Rome, with senators, Latin writers and even emperors springing from its soil. In A.D. 74 the people of the peninsula were awarded Roman citizenship to acknowledge their importance in the Empire. Rome embarked on major construction projects throughout Iberia, building splendid bridges (at Alcantára), constructing huge aqueducts (still intact at Segovia) and running hundreds of miles of roads throughout the peninsula. In Mérida an elegant theater still stands beside a coliseum for gladiatorial and naval battles. The common tongue throughout the peninsula became Latin, which later separately evolved into Spanish and Portuguese.

As the years passed, Rome's power declined, allowing "barbarians" to break through the Empire's border defenses. In the fourth century A.D., Franks from Germany seized present-day France. With the eastern border of the Empire now vulnerable, other German tribes were free to invade and claim what they could. By the fifth century Alans and Swabians established settlements in eastern and western Iberia, respectively. Then the Vandals came, seized the south of Spain, and gave it their name, "Andalusia" (Vandal's Land). A century later, fleeing fierce Huns to their east, the mighty German tribe of the Visigoths poured into Spain. They chased the Vandals across the Gibraltar straits into Africa and conquered the other Germanic tribes and indigenous people to take command of all of Spain. With Toledo as their capital, they established an elected kingship, a caste of nobles, and a state religion (Christianity), all of which became Spanish institutions.

Moors and the Reconquest (711–1248)

711–716	Morocco conquers Spain in the name of Islam.
722	Pelayo achieves the first Christian military victory over the Moors, initiating the reconquest.
756	Moorish Spain, led by Abd er Rahman, secedes from the caliphate of Baghdad.
800	Santiago de Compostela, alleged burial site of St. James, achieves fame throughout Europe as a pilgrimage center.
912–961	Abd er Rahman III reigns as Spain's greatest caliph.
1072–1109	Alfonso VI reconquers most of Spain for the Christians, aided by El Cid.
1090	The Almoravids reconquer Spain for the Moors.
1147	The Almohades from Morocco conquer the Spanish Moors.
1212	Christian forces break the Moors' hold on Spain in the decisive battle of Las Navas de Tolosa.
1236–1248	Fernando III captures two of Spain's three Moorish strongholds, Córdoba and Seville, leaving only Granada under Moorish control.

A small Moroccan army crossed the Straits of Gibraltar in 711, first routed, then chased the Visigoths to small enclaves in the Pyrenees and northern Asturias. "Historical Profile: Moors and the Reconquest" on page 267

The Moors' domination of Spain would extend for 800 years—a span longer than the time that has elapsed since their final defeat in 1492. While the Dark Ages enveloped the rest of Europe, Spanish Muslims kept knowledge alive by maintaining disciplines rejected by the Christians—education, philosophy, poetry and cleanliness. Their architecture, especially in the Alhambra of **Granada** and the Mezquita of **Córdoba**, displayed a sensitivity never surpassed. The Moors appropriated the Visigoths' horseshoe arch as their most characteristic architectural element, and, because of religious proscriptions against depicting human and animal forms, adorned their buildings with intricate geometric and floral designs.

The Moors' capital of Córdoba soon became the largest city in Western Europe. But Moorish Spain remained a mere province within the Islamic empire until a dynastic change in Baghdad, the ruling center of Islam. The sole survivor of the previous dynasty, Abd er Rahman, fled to Spain where he claimed the allegiance of the Moors and forged Spain's independence. By the 10th century, under Abd er Rahman III, Moorish Spain had reached its apex, surpassing every other part of Europe in splendor, modernity and richness. This apex, however, was short-lived. The death of his grandson created problems of succession that split the Moors apart into separate weaker states.

In the meantime, Christians were attempting a reconquest of Spain from their northern confines. Tradition dates the beginning of the reconquest to 722 when Pelayo, a Visigoth noble, won the first Christian engagement against Moors. But no territory was regained in this skirmish. In fact, the Reconquest owed more to the discovery by shepherds of bones attributed to Saint James the Apostle, than to such raids. By the eighth century a church and a city—both called Santiago de Compostela—had grown around the sacred site. (Saint James in medieval Spanish was *Sant' Iago*.) It became a pilgrimage center, second only to the Holy Land and Rome, and drew Europeans by the hundreds of thousands to Christian Spain. With the pilgrims came the idea for a crusade to spread Christianity throughout the peninsula. Spain's epic reconquest, begun in this era, was followed by five centuries of struggle, both heroic and base.

Over time the northern state of Asturias conquered neighboring León. By the 11th century these combined states annexed the land to their south, called "Castile" after all the defensive castles there. Castile grew dominant in the coalition and powerful in the peninsula. Meantime, a separate Christian kingdom grew in Aragón and conducted its own reconquest down the eastern side of Spain. But Castile and Aragón grew into bitter rivals who fought against each other as often as they battled separately against the Moors.

By the end of the 11th century, however, a Castilian king, Alfonso VI, was strong enough to raid as far south as the Mediterranean coast and capture Toledo, the ancient Visigoth capital. Frightened Moors called for help from their Moroccan homeland. A fanatical sect called the Almoravids heeded the call and, with the exception of Valencia which was defended by the Spanish hero El Cid, reconquered all that their brethren had lost. When the religious fervor of the Almoravids abated, another fierce fundamentalist sect, the Almohades, took over and regained Valencia.

This revitalization of the Moors forced the Christian rivals, Castile and Aragón, to join forces in one campaign. In 1212, they summoned crusaders from the corners of Europe, formed an army that engaged the Islamic forces south of Toledo at Las Navas de Tolosa, and inflicted a defeat from which the Moors never recovered. After this great victory, Castile and Aragón once again parted ways.

Twenty-four years later, aided by civil wars that had sapped the Moors' strength, Castile's Fernando III was able to take the Moor's capital, Córdoba. Four years after that he seized Seville, while Aragón recaptured Valencia. The Reconquest was almost complete. Granada alone held out, though more than two centuries would pass before it fell.

Ferdinand, Isabella and Columbus (1369–1516)

1369–1379	Enrique Trastámara fathers a Castilian dynasty.
1451	Columbus is born.
1454–1474	The questionable legitimacy of Enrique the Impotent's designated heir places Isabella on Castile's throne.
1469	Isabella of Castile weds Ferdinand of Aragón.
1474	Isabella ascends the throne of Castile.
1479	Ferdinand ascends the throne of Aragón.
1481	The Inquisition begins.
1492	Granada surrenders, completing the Reconquest. Spain's Jews are expelled. Columbus sails for the Indies.
1502	Spain's Moors are expelled.
1504	Isabella dies.
1506	Columbus dies.
1512	Ferdinand conquers Navarre.
1516	Ferdinand dies.

The wedding of Isabella of Castile to Ferdinand of Aragón gave Christian Spain the unity it needed to complete the Reconquest. But before that Castile suffered two centuries of internecine violence and weak rulers. Foremost in this gallery of rogues was Pedro the Cruel. After Pedro killed one of his illegitimate half brothers, the other, Enrique of Trastámara, in turn murdered Pedro in 1369 and seized the throne, beginning the dynasty from which both Isabella and Ferdinand descended.

By the time Isabella's half-brother Enrique IV came to power a century later, so much authority had been transferred to the nobles of Spain by successive kings that Castile had dissolved into virtual anarchy. "Historical Profile: Ferdinand and Isabella" on page 185 Enrique IV claimed that his second wife's child was his heir, despite evidence to the contrary and his nickname of "the Impotent." To clear the succession for this "daughter" Enrique tried to marry his half-sister Isabella off to one prince after another, but Isabella defied him and, in 1469, secretly wed Ferdinand of Aragón. Enrique died in 1474, still protesting gossip about his daughter's paternity, but leaving Isabella's claim to the throne of Castile preeminent. Five years later, upon Ferdinand's ascension to his father's throne, the kingdoms of Castile and Aragón were finally united under Ferdinand and Isabella.

One of Isabella's first royal acts was to import Aragón's Inquisition to Castile. With its announced purpose of eliminating Christian heretics, the Inquisition persisted until the 19th century. What it actually accomplished, besides great personal and social disruption, was perhaps more pervasive: the esteem of "pure" bloodlines—those untainted by Jewish or Moorish ancestors.

Despite Ferdinand's generalship and Isabella's efficient organization, it required ten years of sustained warfare to subdue Granada. On January 2, 1492, Isabella and Ferdinand walked through the gates of Granada to conclude eight centuries of reconquest.

During that same year Isabella sent Christopher Columbus on his way to the New World "Historical Profile: Columbus and the Conquistadores" on page 369 and signed an order expelling all of Spain's Jews. Although Isabella lived only 12 years longer, before she died in 1504 she was to see one of her daughters marry the son of the Holy Roman Emperor—a union that would elevate Spain to the greatest power in Europe. Ferdinand survived his wife by another 12 years, during which he added Navarre to his kingdom, the territory that completes the map of modern Spain.

Habsburg Kings (1519–1700)

1519–1556	Carlos V becomes the first Habsburg king of Spain.
1519–1522	Cortéz conquers Mexico.
1532–1534	Pizarro conquers Peru.
1541–1614	The life of the painter El Greco.
1547–1616	The life of Miguel de Cervantes.
1556–1598	The reign of Felipe II.

1560	Felipe II makes Madrid the capital of Spain.
1567	Revolt against Spain begins in Holland.
1571	Spain defeats the Turkish fleet at Lepanto.
1580	Felipe II gains the throne of Portugal.
1588	The Great Armada is destroyed.
1598–1621	Felipe III succeeds his father.
1599–1660	The life of the master painter Velázquez.
1609	The Moroscos (converted Moors) are expelled from Spain.
1621–1665	The reign of Felipe IV. Velázquez appointed court painter.
1648	The treaty of Westphalia wins Holland's independence from Spain.
1640	Portugal regains its independence.
1665–1700	The reign of Carlos II ends the Spanish Habsburg dynasty.

The Habsburg dynasty in Spain began and ended with a Carlos, sandwiching three kings all named Felipe. Isabella and Ferdinand's daughter Juana, despite her obvious insanity, remained Spain's nominal ruler until her son Carlos V reached his majority. Carlos, a Habsburg on his father's side, also inherited control over Holland, Belgium, Austria and Germany along with his title of Holy Roman Emperor. Born and raised in Holland, Carlos introduced Spain to the culture and art of mainstream Europe. This opening of borders was a decidedly mixed blessing. By the time his son Felipe II succeeded him, the Low Countries, as Holland and Belgium were known, had begun a revolt that would last a hundred years and drain Spain of all its wealth from the New World. "Historical Profile: World Power and the Great Armada—Felipe II" on page 99

Felipe II established a new capital at Madrid, undertook massive building projects in the capital and constructed an imposing monastery at nearby El Escorial. Although he had vowed to keep his territory intact and defend the Catholic faith, his resolve was sorely tested by Protestant revolts in the Low Countries. He did defeat the Turks in a great sea engagement at Lepanto in 1571, and when, in 1580, the king of Portugal died heirless, Felipe II for a time united Portugal's throne with Spain's. In 1588, after discovering a secret alliance between England and the rebels in the Low Countries, Felipe assembled Spain's Great Armada and sent it to invade England. Only half of his ships returned. Ten years and two armadas later, Felipe died.

In 1609 his son, Felipe III, expelled all remaining Moors from Spain. In 1605 Miguel de Cervantes published *Don Quixote*, the first true novel. Felipe IV succeeded his father and lost Portugal in 1640 by violating an agreement that the Portuguese administer their own country. Although a low point in Spanish political history, the reign of Felipe IV witnessed the rise of most of Spain's greatest painters—Ribalta, Ribera, Murillo, Zurbarán, and, greatest of all, the court painter Velázquez.

Upon the death of Felipe IV in 1665, his son, a veritable idiot, ascended the throne. Somehow Carlos II managed to occupy his office for 35 years, but he never produced an heir and thus sealed the end of the Habsburg dynasty in Spain.

Bourbon Kings (1700–1930)

1700–1746	Felipe V becomes the first Bourbon king of Spain.
1702–1711	Attempting to regain the throne, Habsburgs precipitate the War of Spanish Succession.
1746–1759	Fernando VI promotes Spanish neutrality.
1759–1788	Carlos III brings prosperity to Spain.
1788–1808	Carlos IV rules. The weak king and his family are immortalized by Goya.
1789	The French Revolution produces Napoléon.
1809–1813	Britain and Portugal join Spanish guerrillas against France in the Peninsular War.
1814–1833	The absolutist Fernando VII defies the first constitution.
1833–1839	The First Carlist War brings civil war to Spain.
1843–1874	The reign and exile of Isabella II.
1874–1875	The First Republic.
1875–1885	Alfonso XII regains the throne.
1898	Spain loses Cuba, Puerto Rico and the Philippines in the Spanish-American War.
1902–1930	Alfonso XIII rules as Spain's last monarch before abdicating in favor of republican government.

In 1700, the childless last Habsburg, Carlos II, named Philip of Anjou as his successor. See "Historical Profile: From Habsburgs to Bourbons" on page 439. Under the title of Felipe V, he became the first Spanish monarch from the French Bourbon line (called Borbón in Spanish). His ascension precipitated a war, appropriately called the War of Spanish Succession, with the Austrian Habsburgs. Though Felipe eventually won, the war initiated two centuries of intermittent battles that would reduce Spain from a major world power to a pawn of newer European leaders.

After Felipe V, Fernando VI negotiated a series of neutrality treaties to help Spain recover from the devastations of civil war. His policies were continued by his half-brother Carlos III, whose astute economic planning moved Spain forward into the 18th century. He was succeeded by his son Carlos IV, an amiable dolt controlled by his wife, who, in turn, was under the spell of a favorite courtier. After the French Revolution, the unrealistic Carlos went so far as to send Spanish troops into France to restore its monarchy. His army was crushed, enabling France to demand that Carlos join her in war against Portugal and England. As the 19th century dawned, Spain entered the arena of European politics as a reluctant ally of Napoléon.

In 1808 Napoléon forced Carlos IV to resign in favor of his own brother Joseph. Outraged, the Spanish people rose in rebellion on the second of May, and fought a guerilla campaign until, four years later, aided by the British under the Duke of Wellington, they expelled the French. The great artist Goya immortalized the era with unforgettable etchings of the horrors of war and with royal portraits of the fat Carlos IV, his determined wife and plump children.

After the expulsion of the French, Spain found itself without a king for the first time since before the Visigoths. A constitution was drafted, and Carlos' son was invited to return from exile to reign as Spain's first constitutional monarch. Fernando VII had other ideas, however. He repudiated the constitution and seized control as an absolute monarch. In the meantime, most of Spain's American colonies had seized their independence while Spain was occupied by the French.

More trouble lay ahead. Fernando left only an underage daughter when he died, prompting his brother Don Carlos to wage five years of the First Carlist War to press his own royal claims. In the end, the carnage and destruction gained nothing, and the daughter, Isabella II, ascended her father's throne. She proved to be nothing like her namesake, preferring sexual dalliances to governing. A putsch of the army and navy ended her reign in 1868.

Since Isabella's son was too young to rule, Spain briefly enlisted two foreign relatives as king, before opting for a kingless republic for a year. By 1875 Isabella's son was judged old enough to become Spain's constitutional king, but his untimely death, ten years later, resulted in another regency. A rebellion in Cuba at the end of the century embroiled Spain in the Spanish-American War and cost her the last two of her American possessions—Cuba and Puerto Rico—along with the Philippines. In 1902 Alfonso XIII attained his majority and came to the throne, but the government had been so discredited in the eyes of both her citizens and her army, that only dictatorships and army revolts lay ahead.

The Spanish Civil War and After (1931–Present)

1931–1939	The Second Republic.
1936	The Spanish Civil War begins. Madrid resists.
1937	Destruction of the town of Guernica.
1939	Barcelona and Madrid fall. End of the Spanish Civil War.

1975	Franco dies. Juan Carlos I is crowned.
1978	A new constitution is approved.
1989	Felipe Gonzalez is reelected prime minister.

By 1931 world depression had pushed Spain, a poor country at best, into even deeper economic decline. "Historical Profile: The Spanish Civil War" on page 469 When Alfonso XIII called for elections, most of the large cities voted for socialists whose platform called for a republican government without a king. Lacking support, Alfonso abdicated. For the second time in Spain's history, counting the one-year experiment of 1874, Spain found herself a republic.

The 1930s were times of radical politics throughout the world. On the left, socialists, anarchists and communists in Spain gained ground in direct proportion to the deterioration of the economy, offering their new theories in place of traditional ideas that seemed no longer effective. On the right, the fascist Spanish Falange committed political murders that caused its leader José Antonio to be jailed and martyred. One socialist government in 1931 was replaced by a different one in the election of 1933, but proved equally unable to satisfy the conflicting desires of even its own supporters. Without political direction, violence and anarchy prevailed.

In 1936 the army revolted, attempting to seize the major cities of Spain. The revolt failed in its objectives, but evolved into a civil war of army, church, royalists and fascists fighting against the government and most of the people. In the first campaign Generalissimo Francisco Franco led the army toward Madrid. There the citizens staunchly resisted, surprising the world and their own elected officials, who had previously fled for safety.

With Madrid firm against them, the Nationalists (as the army called itself) then adopted a strategy of conquering the rest of the country so Madrid would fall from lack of support. First they waged a successful campaign in Spain's northern Basque country, although the destruction of the town of Guernica by Franco's German allies cost the Nationalists much in propaganda. The next year, 1938, the Nationalists turned west and surrounded Barcelona. The Republicans tried a valiant counterattack that exhausted their remaining supplies. Ironically, although the Nationalists were abundantly provisioned by fascist Germany and Italy, the democracies of America and Europe refused to aid the Republicans. Lacking rifles for its civilian troops, Barcelona fell in 1939. Madrid tumbled three months later.

Franco ruled Spain for almost three decades thereafter. He ruthlessly imprisoned Spanish liberals, but gained a great economic advantage for Spain over the war-torn countries of Europe by maintaining the country's neutrality during World War II.

With memories of the Civil War still fresh, many feared what might follow in the wake of Franco's death in 1975, but what transpired was a peaceful transition to democracy. Juan Carlos I, the son of Alfonso XIII, returned from exile, as Franco had wished, to become the constitutional monarch. He continues to reign today with his queen, Sofia, in much the manner that Elizabeth II rules Britain. In 1979 a constitution delineating this arrangement was approved by the electorate. But in 1981 a gang of Civil Guards, a group roughly corresponding to our state troopers, attacked a session of Parliament with automatic weapons and held its members hostage. All Spain waited to hear where Juan Carlos would stand—with the rightist forces, or with the Republic. When he announced his continued support of the constitution, the Civil Guards surrendered. The next year the Socialist Party won national elections by a narrow margin, and Felipe Gonzalez was named prime minister. By Spain's next election in 1989, Gonzalez had shown himself to be less a socialist than a pragmatist and won overwhelmingly.

Today, still under the leadership of Prime Minister Gonzalez, Spain stands at the center of the European political spectrum and holds a charter membership in the European Economic Community.

ART AND ARCHITECTURE

The College of San Gregorio in Valladolid features an intricate cloister.

The Spanish love dramatic light in their paintings, delighting in its contrasts, but dark in their cathedrals for its mystery. Spain's architecture came to be characterized by an emphasis on solidity over openness, longitude over height and surface decoration over architectural form. Over the centuries Spanish painting, on the other hand, evolved from conveying crude emotion through contorted bodies and copious blood to the most subtle depictions of face and form. At their height, Spanish artists achieved true miracles of the painter's craft.

Early Art and Architecture

Prehistoric, Celtiberian, Roman and Visigoth

Spain's oldest art does not suffer at all from comparison with the best the country would ever produced. The finest paleolithic paintings in the world, challenging those at Lascaux across the French border, adorn the ceilings of the cave of **Altamira**. The drawn animals seem to contort and breathe. The cave can hold only 15 people at a time, and admission is difficult to obtain, but *El Castillo* cave outside Puenta Viesgo near **Santillana del Mar** provides examples almost as striking without the need for prior arrangements. And no advance permission, only an admission charge to the Museo Arqueológico Nacional in **Madrid**, is required to view the artworks of the little-known Celt-iberians, a people whose unique art developed in isolation from classical influences. The Celtiberian masterpiece, the lovely sculpture *Dama de Elche* with its hauntingly foreign look, captivates all who view her.

Rome's domination of the Iberian Peninsula from the second century B.C. through the third century A.D. is evidenced by its architectural legacy throughout Spain. It bequeathed the *aqueduct* at **Segovia**, which is surpassed in size only by the Pont du Gard in France. The Roman *bridge* at **Alcantara**, though much repaired, preserves its original lines. Remains of a Roman city sprawl near **Empúries**, north of Barcelona; and at **Mérida**, in Extremadura, stands an intact *theater* beside the substantial remains of an *arena*; while the *Museo Arqueológico Nacional* in **Madrid** displays classical sculpture, mosaics and sarcophagi collected from all over Spain.

The Museum also houses jewels of the Visigoths, especially the rare solid gold *Crown of Reccesvinthus Rex*, with its embedded emeralds and sapphires and dangling pearls. The Visigoths began as farmers, turned migratory, then settled in Spain. Little of their art or architecture remains in their Germanic homeland, and little survives in Spain, for the Visigoths enjoyed only two centuries of dominance during which to refine their art. Their permanent buildings were almost all destroyed either by conquering Moors or by reconquering Christians, but, miraculously, a church of the Visigoths does survive intact outside Zamora, near **Valladolid**. *San Pedro de la Nave*, harmonious in its proportions and decorated with charming carvings, dates from the seventh century.

The Moors

No traveler to Spain should miss the 14th century *Alhambra* in **Granada**. Familiarity with western architecture does not prepare a visitor for transport to such a quiet, calm way of life. Rooms follow no prescribed plan, yet each attains an individual perfection while managing to compliment those it adjoins. But, above all, the Alhambra presents a unique solution to the problem of merging the constructions of men with nature. At the Alhambra, nature is brought inside with stalactite ceilings that convey the sense of a starry sky, while nature herself waits just outside in the form of gardens and pools. The intricate decoration of tile walls surmounted by fantastic carved ceilings should seem busy and gaudy, yet serve instead as restful study pieces. And everywhere the sound of running water tranquilizes, for no part of the Alhambra is more than a few feet from a patio or garden: the Moors knew secrets of peaceful architecture.

The *Mesquita* (mosque) in **Córdoba**, completed in the 10th century, shows how the Moors used their knowledge of architecture to serve religion. A striped forest of pillars and double tiered horseshoe arches creates an atmosphere of mystery and awe: this mosque has no parallel in the world. The exalted aesthetic of the Moors is evident as well in the collection of the Museo Arqueologico Nacional in **Madrid**. Consider the delicate ivory jar called the *Bote de Marfil*, with its sublimely harmonious decoration.

As the Reconquest advanced, some Moors found themselves behind the lines in Christian territory. Prizing their skills, the Christians engaged them, originating a style known as *Mudéjar*—Islamic art serving Christian ends. For examples of this fortunate collaboration, see the *Casa de Pilotes* and the *Alcázar* in **Seville**, parts of which bear comparison to the Alhambra, and the *El Tránsito* synagogue in **Toledo**. Less pleasing is *Mozarabic* work, done by Christians raised in Islamic territory but liberated by their kin. The ninth century Mozarabic church of *San Miquel de Escalada* near **León** is clean and airy, but the strong straight lines of the roof clash with the curves of horseshoe arches.

Architecture

The Reconquest: Romanesque

While it is not surprising that castles built to withstand assault might endure from the time of the reconquest, the wonder is that a civilian work, a palace, remains from the ninth century. Built by Ramiro I in the ninth century near **Oviedo**, and later used as a church—hence its name *Santa María de Naranco*—the palace suggests both the Romanesque style it prefigures, and its Byzantine source. The rough rocks of which it is composed should lend a rustic crudity, but instead convey refinement and harmony. Although the barrel vaulting of the ceiling, which would become a hallmark of the Romanesque, is supported by columns, the columns are carved in patterns which never materialized in that later style. It is a seminal and fascinating structure.

So many castles were built by both Christians and Moors to defend the border between them that the region was given the name "Castile." Castles, in all sizes and styles, still survive in profusion today. Those with round towers were generally designed by Christians while square towers usually indicate Moorish or Mudéjar architects. The walls of **Ávila**, punctuated by round towers, form one of the most extensive medieval fortresses extant. By the 15th century the rule about round and square towers no longer held, defied by the powerful structure erected at **Coca**, the most typical of all the world's castles, and by the fairy-like *Alcázar* (castle) at **Segovia**.

Throughout the time of the Reconquest, religious feeling was intense in the Christian parts of Spain. When, in the eighth century, bones believed to belong to Saint James were found at **Santiago de Compostela** the area blossomed into not just another pilgrimage center, but the holiest Catholic site outside of the Holy Land and Rome. By the 11th century one of the world's great churches had been erected there. Today the cathedral's splendid 18th century baroque front belies the majesty of its Romanesque interior—a towering barrel ceiling with massive ribs supported by colossal columns—whose sheer size inspires awe. The Romanesque style commands religious feeling through the power of its architecture—no filigree for these worshippers, no brightness let in by expanses of glass, no flying buttresses to permit slender columns, just awesome size. Introducing the cathedral is the *Door of Glory*, a masterpiece of Romanesque sculpture by Master Mateo, as he signed himself. At a time when other sculptors were fashioning staid statues, this genius created living beings from stone. Equally wondrous, on a smaller scale, is the *Catedral Vieja* (Old Cathedral) in **Salamanca**. A proper complement to the power of these cathedrals is *San Vicent*, a Romanesque church in **Cardona**, near **Barcelona**. Built at the same time as Santiago de Compostela, the purity and simplicity of the interior of this church evokes a different kind of respect. The dozen Romanesque churches sprinkled around **Segovia** inspire similar feelings.

Gothic

Influenced by Abbé Suger, the French lightened their churches in the 11th century with outside, "flying," buttresses that permitted less massive interior supporting columns, walls of glass to let in light, narrow ribs supporting arched ceilings, and, in place of the rounder Romanesque, pointed arches designed to raise the eye upward. Called Gothic, the new aesthetic style spread through Europe. The Spanish built one breathtaking church, complete with glorious stained glass windows, exactly on this model—the *Cathedral* at **León**. But by the 13th century the Spanish had modified the original style to create a new version—wider in plan and lightened more by ornate decoration than by the light of windows. The cathedrals at **Burgos** and **Toledo** are masterpieces of this Spanish Gothic style, ranking among the world's outstanding church architecture.

Renaissance: Isabeline and Plateresque

After their modification of the Gothic, Spanish architects continued to create new styles diverging from mainstream European architecture. Fifteenth century *Isabelline* buildings add a tracery of lacy decoration to otherwise bare walls, the prime example of which is the sumptuous entrance to the *Collegio San Gregorio* in **Valladolid**. The exuberance of the style, however, is most evident in **Granada** in the *Capilla Real* where Ferdinand and Isabella are buried. The architect Juan Guas let his fantasies run free. There also, carved in perfection by the master sculptor Bartolome Ordoñez, is the moving mausoleum of Isabella's son-in-law and daughter, Phillip the Handsome and Juana the Mad.

In the 16th century, the Isabelline effect evolved into the famed *plateresque*. The word "plateresque" means "like silverwork"—intricate, chiseled, curving and precious. As a style, the plateresque mainly refers to decoration that serves no structural function and obeys no laws of symmetry. It is an applique attracting the eye to an otherwise undistinguished wall, window or door. **Salamanca** is virtually a museum city of the plateresque—and its masterpiece is the entrance to its *university.*

Secondarily, plateresque refers to a retreat from Gothic design. Ceiling arches replace ribs and interior pillars substitute for outer buttresses. The plan and decoration of the interior of the *Cathedral* at **Granada** offers a particularly interesting example. (Its exterior belongs to the following century.) The plan is a rotunda with a circular ambulatory. If more were needed to distance these curves from their pointed Gothic counterparts, the decoration—recessed portals, where frames dominate what they enclose—proclaims the plateresque even more defiantly.

Classical and Baroque

However original and striking the plateresque may have been, it survived for only a century, ending when it lost favor among its royal patrons. As early as 1526, while the plateresque was still at its height, Carlos V had ordered a pupil of Michelangelo to design a classical *Palace* in **Granada**'s Alhambra precinct. Though the formality of the structure compares badly to the ethereal quality of the adjacent Alhambra, its plan of a circular courtyard within a square exterior is simple, dignified and impressive in its way—if only it were located elsewhere.

Throughout the remainder of the 16th century, Carlos' son, Felipe II, reacted against the decorative excesses of the plateresque by originating a new style, rather than adopting an older one as his father had done. *El Escorial*, outside Madrid, was the beginning. Designed by Juan Bautista de Toledo, another pupil of Michelangelo, the monastery of El Escorial is sometimes described as a fortress. In fact it is majestic, and appears stark only when viewed from a plateresque or Gothic perspective. When Bautista died four years into the project, he was replaced by the genius of Spanish architecture—Juan de Herrera. Untrained in architecture, Herrera followed no known style, only his feeling of what was right. The *church* in El Escorial is all his, unique and wonderful.

Herrera's originality died with him, to be replaced by a return to the ornate. The baroque excess of the 17th century holds its own fascination, as the Spanish version, called *Churrigueresque* (after the Churreguera family who originated it), exuberantly demonstrates. The original business of the Churrigueras was designing altars—the altarpiece in the *Convento de San Esteban* in **Salamanca** shows their extravagant work. When they turned to the larger scale of architecture, they expanded the ornate, entwined curves of their altars into buildings in which the eye finds no focus or rest, only stimulation. One acknowledged masterpiece resulted, the *Plaza Mayor* in **Salamanca**. Uncharacteristically for plazas of the period, the buildings around this square are agreeably combined to form one of the finest ensembles in Spain.

Neoclassic to Art Nouveau

In the 18th century, when Bourbon rule began in Spain, Felipe V built a "little" Versailles near **Segovia** to remind him of home. The palace at *La Granja* is sumptuous, the gardens grand. Succeeding sovereigns built extensively in Madrid, favoring architects of classical, Italian bent. One of the best was Juan de Villanueva who designed the *Museo del Prado*. So successful was his design that it spawned descendents around the world, including the Metropolitan Museum in New York.

Although there was little to distinguish Spanish architecture through most of the 1800s, as the century was closing Antoni Gaudí arrived to make up for lost time. It was the era of *art nouveau*—dripping, draping, decorative appendages, and buildings abhorring sharp corners. To these expressions of art nouveau, Spain contributed its own heritage of the Gothic and plateresque to nourish its genius Gaudí. In **Barcelona** stand his fantasies, from blocks of houses—*Casa Battló* and *Casa Mila*—to the amusement park *Güell*, to the unfinished masterpiece of *Sagrada Família*, like no church in this world.

Sculpture

Romanesque sculpture in Spain followed the path of sculpture elsewhere in Europe. Figures held rigid postures, faces were caricatures, and drapery fell stiffly. In such a context, the genius of Master Mateo (previously noted) leapt out at the viewer. By the 13th century, the time of the Gothic, figures became elongated to parallel the upward thrust of Gothic cathedrals. Sculpture also began to bend and move. Drapery, though still not natural, was consciously used to add rhythm to compositions, and faces began to reflect the individuality, if not the accuracy, of portraiture.

In 15th-century Spain, during the time of the Isabelline style, genius erupted again in the person of Gil de Siloé who decorated the monastery of *Cartuja de Miraflores* in **Burgos**. His altarpiece overwhelmed the more intricate altars of his contemporaries. In the same monastery he carved a tomb that conveys for all time the sadness of the death of the *Infante* (Prince) Don Alfonso, and, finest of all, a set of tombs for Juan II and his queen Isabel of Portugal. In his effigies, Siloé conveys the strongest emotions with the subtlest of lines.

In the 16th and 17th centuries Siloé's lead was followed by a number of great Spanish sculptors. Berruguete, influenced by the complex movements of the Greek statue of *Laocöon*, rediscovered during his time, carved tormented figures for the cathedral in **Toledo**. Although the choir stalls of that cathedral are entirely splendid, beginning with the lower parts depicting the conquest of Granada, it is the upper stalls on the left that are by this master. No one who takes the time to look can miss his genius. At first, compared to the higher relief of the other stalls, Berruguete's carvings seem reserved, for they are infinitely more subtle. With study, they come alive. Over the center, in high alabaster relief, flies his magnificent *Transfiguration*, subtly tense and moving.

Most characteristic of Spanish sculpture is its polychromed wood. Gregorio Fernández was a master of the genre. His haunting, living faces, better executed than his mannered bodies, are exhibited in the Museum of Polychrome Sculpture at **Valladolid**. The acknowledged giant of polychrome sculpture, however, is Juan Martinez Montañés who brought the art of painted wood to its summit during the 17th century. He was called *dios de la Madera*, the god of wood. His work is displayed in the Valladolid museum, but more can be seen in the churches of **Seville**, especially in the cathedral. See his *Christ of Clemency*, the *Virgin Primisima* and the *Christ Child Lifting his Arms*, all in the cathedral, and all conveying a stark and realistic dignity. Indeed, some find them too realistic to be considered art.

To all but lovers of romantic effect, sculpture had reached its pinnacle. The master of the 18th century was Nariciso Tomé, and his masterpiece, the *Transparente*, is displayed behind the altar of the **Toledo** Cathedral. When it was finished it was considered the eighth wonder of the world, although later generations damned it for maudlin extravagance. It is a work that people either love or hate, but nonetheless came to represent the sculptural ideal in Spain.

Painting

Romanesque and Gothic painting in Spain can best be appreciated in the superb collection of the Museo de Arte de Catalunya in **Barcelona**. Often captivating and always deeply expressive of the artist's religious feeling, early Spanish painting is remarkable for the quantity of blood it portrayed—a thinly veiled brutality. Perhaps the wars of the Reconquest that brought real blood into peoples' lives spilled into their art; perhaps Spain's Roman Catholicism, a particularly primitive, strict version, affected its artists; or perhaps that facet of the Spanish character that found excitement in the elaborate and bloody ritual of the bullfight migrated to its art.

By the time of the Renaissance, Spanish painting had advanced from concentrating on gore to enter the mainstream of European art. In fact, the greatest Spanish painters of that era all trained in Italy. Pedro Gonzalez Berruguete suggests Giotto in his *St. Dominic Before the Inquisition.* Fernando Yanez studied with Leonardo Da Vinci, but shows his own sensitivity in *Saint Catherine*, a painting remarkable for its appreciation of negative spaces. Pedro Machuca studied with Michelangelo, was greatly influenced by Caravaggio, and developed a style, especially evident in his *Madona del Suffragio*, of stark light and shadows. These paintings are included in the extraordinary Renaissance collection of the Museo del Prado in **Madrid**, a collection equally strong in both Italian and Spanish masters. Though not quite in the first rank, Spanish Renaissance painters are moving at their best and pleasing at their worst.

With the dawning of the 16th century, the quality of Spanish art underwent a dramatic change. Finally victorious in its long struggle against the Moors, Spain was free for the first time in centuries to turn its attentions outward to the rest of Europe. Spain's first sane monarch after Ferdinand and Isabella, Carlos V, pursued the twin goals of seeking out art from all the corners of Europe and of introducing his countrymen to an array of artistic styles. Carlos V became the patron of the Venetian Titian, whose genius epitomized European art at that time. Carlos was but the first of three generations of kings, from Felipe II to Felipe IV, who together acquired one of the finest art collections ever amassed—now housed in the Museo del Prado in **Madrid**. Dürer, Botticelli, Raphael, Caravaggio, Bosch, Titian and Rubens are only the best-known artists whose paintings are included in the superb royal collection that raised the standards of both art and its appreciation in Spain. More important, it stimulated her own artists to rise to unequalled heights.

At this time the first genius of Spanish painting emerged, although he was not born Spanish. Domenico Theotocopoulos, El Greco (the Greek), after studying with Titian in Italy, came to Spain from Crete hoping to find commissions as Titian had. In 1575, at age 35, he settled in Toledo, never to leave again. El Greco had studied Byzantine icon painting in which strong outlines make thin, elongated figures emerge from their background. He introduced the device to western art, along with a palette of luminous blues and reds acquired from his Italian teachers. El Greco was a man of devotion, searching for ways to express deep religious sentiment, and succeeded as no one had before. An ego of enormous proportions allowed him to resist pressures to make his art conform: he once told a pope that if the Sistine frescoes were removed, he could paint better ones.

El Greco first tried to sell paintings to Felipe II, who bought two. *The Martyrdom of St. Maurice* and *Adoration of the Holy Name of Jesus* still hang in Felipe's **Escorial**. In the latter work the great distance up and into the picture initially seems crude and childish, but, with study, the canvas opens up into eternity. El Greco drew from plastic models, not from life, producing angled figures and constant movement, but not realism. The Impressionists—especially Cézanne who copied El Greco's paintings repeatedly—learned much from him. But Felipe II found El Greco's paintings too radical and bought no others.

Thereafter, El Greco worked for wealthy private citizens and churches in **Toledo**. In the Hospital of Tavera, outside the city walls, two great works still hang. *The Baptism of Christ* is magnificent and the portrait of *Cardinal Tavera* haunting. The Museo Santa Cruz holds more than twenty El Grecos, including the famous *Altarpiece of the Assumption.* But the work most people call his best hangs alone inside the vestibule of the tiny church of Santo Tomé. *The Burial of Count Orgaz* is a late work (1586) and El Greco's largest. It incorporates all the original elements that this artist developed: elongated figures, drawn as if the painter were lying down looking up at his subjects; angry, living skies and raw emotion expressed as much in the mannered painting of fabric as in the faces of his subjects. If you can see only one El Greco, make it this one.

El Greco did not represent a culmination of European art; he followed his own muse. In the more realistic mainstream, Spain rose to dominance in the 17th century—the Golden Age of Spanish art. It began with Francisco Ribalta (1565–1628), a Catalan, who discovered his metier late in life. His finest works are the *Vision of Saint Francis* and *Bernard Embracing Christ* in the Museo del Prado in **Madrid**. Then Jusepe de Ribera (1591–1652) burst upon the art world. Ribera is the only painter who can be compared with Velázquez in electing to paint ordinary people instead of idealized images. Ribera painted seedy characters, and used them as models to portray saints and philosophers. His figures are real like no others. It has been argued that Ribera's paintings are stronger than Velázquez', and that he was more original in his themes. According to most, his masterpiece is *The Martyrdom of Saint Bartholomew* hanging in the Museo del Prado. But equally engaging are *Joseph with the Christ Child*, *Saint Alexis* and, most striking, *Trinity*. Study the strong diagonals created by the two inverted triangles of the design, the look on the face of God as he holds his dead Son, and the drapery. Ribera is a consummate master.

Genius seemed to inspire genius as Francisco de Zurbarán (1598–1661) followed Ribera. Zurbarán's paintings were the most spiritual of all, not with the fire of El Greco's work, but possessed, instead, of a quiet, bare, intensely reflective, almost mystical quality. Zurbarán's solitary figures in white robes against dark, featureless backgrounds display his extraordinary ability to combine spirituality with utter realism. *The Crucifixion* in the Museo de Bellas Artes in **Seville** is a superior example.

When the French invaded Spain early in the 19th century, they so admired Zurbarán's work that they pried his paintings from the walls of monasteries and churches, taking almost 100 works with them back to France, now all disbursed among the museums of the world. Spain retains some fine Zurbaráns, but, alas, not the best. Also in the Museo de Bellas Artes in **Seville** is *Blessed Henry Suso* in which the German mystic Suso, stands, uncharacteristically for Zurbarán, against a landscape setting. The figure of Henry Suso is prime Zurbarán, and sublime. The Museo del Prado in **Madrid** displays the best collection left in Spain. Outstanding are *Saint Luke before the Crucified*, *Saint Elizabeth of Portugal*, of the luminous clothes, the striking *Virgin of the Immaculate Conception*, and the unforgettable *Saint Peter Nolasco's Vision of the Crucified Saint Peter* with Saint Peter upside down.

Contemporary with Zurbarán, though worlds apart in his career and choice of subjects, was Diego Velázquez de Silva (1599–1660), whose work represents the culmination of Spanish painting. Recognized for his genius while still a youth, Velázquez studied in Seville, and was appointed a court painter by his twenties. Two early works before his appointment—*The Adoration of the Magi* and *Mother Jerónima de la Fuente*, with her piercing, determined gaze—show him already a master. These hang with all the other paintings we discuss in the premier Velázquez collection, that of the Museo del Prado in **Madrid**.

At court in Madrid, Velázquez became a royal portrait painter, entering a lifelong friendship with his patron and contemporary, the lonely Felipe IV. Velázquez' portraits of the king show his human side—a homely man with thinning hair and jutting Hapsburg jaw. The portrait of Felipe's brother *The Infante Don Carlos,* demonstrates Velázquez' mastery of the portrait genre. In 1628 Peter Paul Rubens, the most famous painter of the day visited Madrid. He had no use for any Spanish painter but Velázquez and undertook to teach him what he knew. These lessons are contained in Velázquez' disturbing *Feast of Bacchus,* in which the effete, half-naked, fair-skinned god of wine stares at us, surrounded by leathery peasants.

Beginning in 1629, Velázquez spent two years studying in Italy, funded by his patron Felipe. By the time he returned home, no project was beyond him. During this period he painted the epic *Surrender of Breda,* sometimes known as *Las Lanzas* for its most striking element. Velázquez drew everyone in the royal family and most of the jesters and dwarfs kept as pets. Most telling is his perceptive portrait of Queen Marianna showing her unpleasant character, lightened only by touches of vermilion ribbon.

Velázquez was ambitious, rising in position with the years. Added responsibilities for collecting art for the king, decorating rooms in the palaces at Madrid and El Escorial, and supervising other royal painters consumed time, constricting his own artistic output. In his last phase, Velázquez determinedly painted only works that were important to him, exercised to stretch his medium. Two acknowledged masterpieces resulted. *The Fable of Arachne,* by any measure a masterpiece of complexity, depicts a weaving contest between the mortal Arachne and the goddess Minerva.

Although it would be fruitless to try to decide what painting should be called the best in the world, Velázquez' last work, *Las Meninas* (Ladies in Waiting), tempts one against reason. The picture is complex and perfect, summarizing all the painting lessons learned through the ages. Velázquez died soon after finishing *Las Meninas,* but posthumously earned the Order of Santiago he had so assiduously sought in life. A thoughtful friend—some say it was the king himself—later painted a crimson cross, the sign of the order, on Velázquez' chest in the painting.

If Velázquez poses a problem it is that he is too accomplished. Everything seems so right and undramatic that it is possible to run quickly through a gallery of his work. His mastery requires study. Fortunately his paintings all invite contemplation, for such was his genius.

Bartolomé Esteban Murillo (1617–1682) followed Velázquez and was, in his own time, considered great. Later judgments deemed him mawkish and sentimental for choosing cute urchins as his subjects, although his star is ascending again. There is no question that he had every talent needed by a painter. Anyone who looks at his works displayed in the Museo del Prado can decide where to place Murillo, but no one will rank him with his predecessor. Velázquez could not be bettered.

Francisco de Goya (1746–1828) changed the direction of European painting. He first developed designs for tapestries, called "cartoons," at the royal tapestry works, before turning to portraits. By 1799 he was celebrated enough to be named painter to the king. The king happened to be a genial incompetent, dominated by his wife Maria Luisa and her lover, Godoy. Whether Goya's portraits of the royal family are the greatest art can be argued, but if art means showing the truth, these works make a case. Goya pushed his portraits toward caricature to reveal his subjects' inner character. Paintings such as *The Family of Carlos IV* in the Museo del Prado so ruthlessly display the emptiness of the king and the ambition of the queen, who takes center stage in the group, that one wonders why they allowed such a portrait to be displayed. Perhaps they could not see what was before their eyes, or perhaps Goya's bright but washed colors seduced his clients with their elegance. Conversely, when Goya's subject was a person of quality, as in the case of his friend and father-in-law Bayeu, the portrait exudes character. Goya could also be sensual, as in *Maja Clothed*—more erotic than the same subject and pose in *Maja Nude.*

Still, Goya's high position in the pantheon of art depends more on his fevered imagination than on his skill at portraiture. In 1808, when the French seized Spain, Goya painted two masterworks—*The Second of May* and *The Third of May*—depicting the uprising of Spanish citizens against their invaders. The first shows a battle, fierce with violence; the second, by artificially shortening the distance from the executioners' guns to the defenseless victims, shrieks of the horrors of death. Afterwards, Goya put anguish on canvas in his *Black Paintings* (named for their dominant color)—the unforgettable *Saturn Devouring One of His Sons, Dog Half-Submerged,* and *Witches' Sabbath.* Equally dramatic were his series of etchings on the *Horrors of War,* and *Caprichos,* caricatures of the great and of those who believed themselves to be. All are displayed with justifiable pride by the Prado.

Where was art to go after such geniuses? In the 20th century it became surreal or abstract, inspired by three founding fathers from Spain. The most prolific, versatile and influential modern artist surely was Pablo Ruiz Picasso (1881–1973). To those who claim modern art avoids realism because its practitioners lack talent, Picasso answered while a child by painting exceptional realistic works, but fought throughout his career to create new means of expression. Picasso, who lived in French exile most of his life, belongs to the world as much as to Spain; still, in the Museu Picasso in **Barcelona**, Spain displays a good collection of his works, stronger in early paintings than in later works. It is interesting to see the first realistic works of the teenaged Picasso and some favorite pieces from his rose and blue periods.

Picasso's most dramatic, and, many would say his finest work, the tormented *Guernica*, has finally been returned to Spain and is now displayed in Spain's new museum of modern art, the Centro de Arte Reina Sofia, in **Madrid**.

Spain does better in collecting the works of another native son, the Catalan Joan Miró (1893–1983). The Fondacio Miró in **Barcelona** presents the breadth of his work, from painting to sculpture to prints and fabrics, in a most appropriate building designed by Joseph Sert. Salvador Dalí (1904–1989), the great surrealist, has a worthy surreal gallery in the Museo-Teatro of his home town of **Figures**, northeast of Barcelona.

FOOD AND DRINK

Food markets, like this one, are typical throughout Spain.

The Spanish are robust in their tastes, adoring hearty food and animated conversation. Restaurants seem more like convivial meeting rooms than hallowed cathedrals of cuisine, and food portions are ample. As a result, dining customs and hours in Spain differ from our own.

Because the Spanish enjoy their leisurely main meal at two in the afternoon and follow it with an equally lengthy rest, restaurants do not reopen for dinner until eight or nine—or in Madrid, Barcelona and Andalusia at least ten at night—occasionally with restricted menus. Thus, an important consideration for visitors is not simply what to eat but when. For the most part, Americans in Spain stick to their habit of eating the main meal in the evening, causing them to search midday menus for light luncheon meals but discovering few choices among the full dinners. At night, after biding their time until the restaurants reopen, they find themselves the first arrivals, uncomfortably alone in the dining room.

Spain is relaxed about most things, including food and its availability, so it is perfectly possible to eat in Spain as you would at home. Below we explain how to find sandwiches and other light noon meals. On the other hand, it might prove interesting to try dining as the Spanish do. Take your main meal at midday, then snack on *tapas* at night. That way you'll be eating during the time many shops and sights are closed for their midday break, and you'll emerge fortified for serious sight-seeing. You will also sleep better for it.

The Spanish begin the day lightly with a *cafe completo*, a continental breakfast of delicious strong coffee and a roll or bread. Coffee is either *solo* (black), *con leche* (with milk) or *café américano*, a weaker version. Tea made from bags is available. Most hotels charge extra for breakfast, but any bar or cafe can provide it too. Those who wish more—some eggs, for example—are talking about *desayuno* (breakfast), which is generally available at hotels, often in the form of somewhat costly buffets that include cold cuts and fruit, along with ham, eggs and croissants.

At midday in any bar one can find *bocadillos* (sandwiches), consisting of rolls filled with delicious *tapas* selections, including tasty *jamón serrano* (like prosciutto). For more familiar lunch choices, stop at a cafeteria or an *autoservicio*. Alternatively, wait until one or two o'clock to eat a full meal in a restaurant.

By early evening (seven o'clock or so) groups begin gathering in the tapas bars. The name *tapas*, which means tops or lids, derives from a time when bartenders covered a glass of wine with a small plate—to ward off flies—on which they set free appetizers. Those free days are gone; today such appetizers cost a dollar or more. In a good tapas bar, always distinguished by a large crowd, choices will be varied—slices of omelette, *chorizo* (spicy dried sausage), marinated beef, squid, clams, oysters, mussels, octopus, shrimp, *jamón York* (boiled ham), *jamón serrano* (air-cured mountain ham—like prosciutto but stronger), rice and potatoes. Most of the food will be cold, but not all, and *raciones*, larger plates, may be ordered. Pointing is an acceptable way to select. When it is time to settle up, the waiter will count the empty plates to figure your bill. These delicacies may be sampled either standing at the bar or, for higher prices, sitting at a table. The food is washed down with wine, beer or sherry—usually a dry *fino*.

Dinner, *la cena*, is served beginning at nine or ten at night, depending on the area of Spain. However, some hotels open their restaurants earlier to accommodate our foreign habits.

Food

Spanish food is seldom spicy hot—in no way to be confused with Mexican cuisine and its generous use of chilies. What distinguishes Spanish food from northern European cooking is its use of olive oil for sautéing rather than butter. In general, Spanish cooking is based on the quality of the ingredients rather than on sauces as in French cuisine. The goal is to liberate the fresh tastes, instead of masking them with other flavors. At its best, Spanish food can be as subtle as the finest French; at its worst it can be heavy or greasy; but, in general, it provides tasty and satisfying sustenance.

Of course the quality of cooking varies, and restaurants are rated by the government through an assignment of from one through four forks, in addition to a *Lujo* (deluxe) rating. Each restaurant will have its rating posted on a plaque outside. This government assessment takes account of ambience, the variety of offerings and the elegance of service, but does not consider the quality of the cooking or the degree of graciousness with which it is placed before you. These ratings can be used as a rough measure of costs, but not of how enjoyable the dining experience will be. Our star ratings attempt to redress that lack.

Menus comprise à la carte choices, but all restaurants also offer either a *menú del día* or a *menú turistico* which provide complete meals at lower, all-encompassing prices, with a limited range of choices.

Note: the custom of serving a portion of vegetables with the main dish is not Spanish. At best you can hope for a small salad, unless you specifically order a vegetable side dish.

Spanish food comprises several regional cuisines, although a famous dish from a given region will be available in most cosmopolitan centers. Common to every region is a love of seafood, rushed fresh to cities as far from the coast as Madrid. A Spaniard, on average, eats 68 pounds of fish per year. And the Spanish love garlic. If you do not sympathize, avoid dishes with names containing the words *ajillo* or *ajo*.

Andalusia is famous for its cold soup, *gazpacho*—raw vegetables, especially onion and tomatoes, blended with olive oil, vinegar and garlic. From Málaga comes the interesting white *ajo blanco*, a cold blend of garlic, ground almonds, and floating grapes. *Sopa sevillana* is a rich fish stew flavored with mayonnaise and garnished with egg. *Fritura mixta de pescados* is a mixed fry of fresh seafood. Fresh sardines (*sardinas*) can be sublime, as can trout (*trucha*), fresh from nearby streams. A hearty casserole of lima beans and ham is called *habas con jamón*.

Valencia invented *paella*, now served all over Spain but nowhere done better than its home state. It is named for the special large skillet in which short-grained saffron rice is stewed with seafood, sausage, chicken and snails, all garnished with pimento. When seafood replaces all the meat, the name changes to *paella marinera*. Although a description of *paella's* ingredients seem to call for white wine, few whites can stand up to its rich flavors.

The center of Spain, **Old** and **New Castile**, is famed for its roast meat (*asados*). In crisp skin, *cochinillo* (suckling pig) falls off the bone, *cordero* (lamb) is memorable when roasted over wood fires called *hornos*, and *lechazo* (milk fed lamb) is a treat. A broth in which ham chunks, vegetables and eggs swim temptingly is called *sopa castellana*, while *cocido castellana* is a rich stew based on chick peas. The center for game, when it's in season, is Toledo.

Aragón and **Navarre** feature chicken and trout. *Pollo chilindron* is chicken in a peppery sauce, *trucha a la Navarra* is fried trout stuffed with *jamón serrano*.

The rest of Spain acknowledges that the **Basque Country**, where men form cooking societies, produces the finest chefs. *Pil pil*, a sort of chili sauce, is used for prawns (*gambas*) and codfish (*bacalao*). *Bacalao a la viscaina* is stewed cod in fresh tomatoes. A specialty is *merluza a la vasca*, baked hake in a casserole of clams. Basque *nuevo cochino* (Spanish nouvelle cuisine) is today the internationally "in" cuisine.

Galicia also merits a high reputation, not surprising given the availability of superb shellfish. *Centollos* consist of a huge local crab stuffed with its own minced meat. *Caldeirada gallega* is a heartier form of *bouillabaisse*, while *conchas de peregrino* will impress the scallop lover. *Empanada gallega* is a meat pie filled with either fish or meat.

Many dishes thought of as "Provençal," such as *bouillabaisse* and *cassoulet*, actually derive from **Catalonia**, where the cooking is similar to that of nearby French Provence. Mayonnaise was invented in Catalonia and brought to France in the 16th century. Pasta and snails (not in the same dish) are staples in Catalonia, though absent from menus in the rest of Spain. Fish stews are specialties—from *zarzuela de mariscos*, tomato based, to *romesco de peix*, with almonds and bread crumbs. Catalans make a delicious spicy sausage called *butifarras*. For dessert, *crema catalana* is a delectable *creme caramel*.

Drink

Wines in Spain are as various and as frequently drunk as those in France. They can be as good as all but the very highest level of French wines, which is very good indeed, and are available at more affordable prices. In any price category below the astronomical, a Spanish wine will beat its comparably priced French counterpart.

There are so many varieties of Spanish wine, however, that most names are unfamiliar except to specialists—a problem for the traveler who simply wants a wine to enjoy with his meal. Because its high alcohol and tannin content makes Spanish wine mature slowly, a good rule of thumb is to ignore the name and choose the oldest bottle in the price range you're considering.

Certain regions produce outstanding wines which are available all over Spain. Others make wines dispensed locally by the glass or carafe as *vino de la casa* or *del pais*, though even these generally prove enjoyable. Wine can be red (*tinto*), white (*blanco*) or rosé (*rosado*). Bottled wines are controlled to ensure quality by a *Denominación de Origen*, like the French "Appellation Controllée." *Reservas* are wines of good vintage, *Gran Reservas* are the best wines given bodega (winery) bottles.

The best known of Spain's wine regions is **Rioja** in the northwest corner of Old Castile. Here red wines are aged in oak casks for a minimum of two years (for as long as ten years in the case of *gran reservas*) before bottling—as opposed to the few months in a cask employed in French wine production. Long contact with oak gives Riojas a characteristic "vanilla" taste, and the high tannin content that is leeched makes for long wine life. Rioja white wine resembles white burgundies, although years in oak masks some delicacy of the grape. Wines from the northern Rioja Alta attain more subtlety and finesse than the higher (15 percent) alcohol wines of the southern Rioja Baja. With weather more consistent than that in France, even an average year's production is of such good quality that fewer vintage years are declared. If interested in a tour of this wine region, see the information under Haro in the León and Old Castile chapter.

For the best of the red Riojas, try any bottle of Marqués de Riscal or Marqués de Murrieta. Good, and less expensive, are Palacio's "Glorioso," Enrique Bilbao's "Vina Zaco," Gomez Cruzado's "Vina Dorana," La Rioja Alta, and CUNE, which costs even less, as does Marqués de Cáceres and Paternina's "Banda Azul". For whites, Marqués de Murrieta again rates high, along with CUNE's "Monople Blanco Seco" and Bilbainas' "Viña Pacta."

Connoisseurs single out Vega Sicilia, from the area of **Valladolid**, as Spain's finest red wine. It is richly expensive (up to five figures in pesetas) and difficult to find. The same company bottles a lesser wine—the equal of all but the finest Riojas—as "Valbuena," at one-third the price. And a vineyard near Vega Sicilia, Alejandro Fernandez, bottles the superb, if little known, "Pesquera Tinto" at a fifth of Sicilia's price.

La Mancha in New Castile produces wine in great quantity but, for the most part, of little distinction. One area's wine, that of **Valdepeñas**, near the border of Andalusia, rises above the rest, however. The supply is large and no bodega stands out, but a Valdepeñas is always a safe and satisfying choice in its modest price category.

An interesting choice in white wine for seafood is a "green" wine from **Galicia**. It is not named for its color, but for the fact that a shortened growing season in this cool region leads to early harvests. The wines are light, very dry and generally *petillant*—hinting at a sparkle on the tip of the tongue. The best come from Albarino.

Catalonia produces most of the sparkling wine in Spain along with enjoyable still wine. The area of **Penedés**, running from the coast south of Barcelona to the Monserat Mountains, bottles surprisingly good, moderately priced reds and whites. Villafranca de Penedés, 20 miles south of Barcelona, is the center of the wine region and has installed a fascinating museum of wine in a 14th-century palace of the kings of Aragón. Here too is the huge bodega (winery) of Torres. Its heavy "Sangre de Toro" is an undistinguished blend, but "Coronas" are vintage wines of strong bouquet and body. Torres' "Viña Sol" is a nice dry white. A lighter red is "Pleno" from Bodegas Cenalsa Murchante, or Jean León's "Cabernet Sauvignon," made from the famous Bordeaux grape allowed in Penedés, though not in Rioja, by the *Denominación de Origen.*

Most of the world's champagne comes from Penedés, though only that grown in the Champagne region of France may legally bear the name. Codorniú and Freixenet are both huge bottlers, though Conde de Caralt, Castellblanch, Rigol and de la Serra are all worthy. In the true champagne process, bubbles develop in the bottle over years of storage, recorking and decanting sediment. Wines made by this process are designated *cavas* in Spain because the bottles are stored in cool caves. Sparkling wines that lack this word on the bottle are more cheaply produced in bulk vats. Spanish sparkling wine is best compared to the French *blanc de blancs,* for it does not contain the Chardonnay or Pinot Noir grapes used in French champagne. It is softer, with less bite than the French, but neither does it carry as high a price. A Spanish *seco* (dry) can be enjoyed at a cost that permits it to be an everyday pleasure.

Sherry is Spain's great contribution to the world of wines. Americans seldom drink it, except in its sweeter versions, yet dry sherry is a splendid aperitif, stimulating to the palate, and even serves well accompanying a meal. Sherry is manufactured by allowing the juice of grapes to ferment in contact with air, a process that normally would turn the grape juice to vinegar. But at the western tip of Spain in **Jerez de la Frontera**, the juice develops a coating of yeast, a *flor* (flower), which protects against such oxidation. A richly complex wine, high in alcohol, results. The final product is aged in a system called *solera*, in which huge casks, each containing one year's vintage, are stacked by year with the oldest on the bottom. As a bottle is filled from the lowest (thus oldest) cask, wine from the cask above replenishes what was removed, the next cask above replenishes that one, and so on. In this way, younger vintages acquire character from older ones. Sherry does not age in the bottle, only in the solera, and since the oldest vintage is continually replaced, a vintage year can be stretched infinitely. Visiting the bodegas in Jerez is fascinating and modestly priced, or even free.

Sherries should not be judged by cream sherry, an uncharacteristic product that develops no flor. Cream sherry is produced by sweetening *oloroso*, a dark sherry so high in alcohol that it needs no flor to protect it. Try *fino*, which is light and dry, if slightly bitter. *Amontillado*, a more mature *fino*, is amber in color and nutty in flavor. An old one will be an expensive treat. Though less familiar, sherry-type wines are produced in quantity in the adjoining area of **Montilla**. The grape here is the Pedro Ximenez variety rather than the Palomino grape of Jerez, and their sugar content is not raised by sun drying. A montilla will generally be drier and possess greater finesse than a sherry, at least in the opinion of many.

The Spanish actually drink more brandy than sherry, though Spanish brandy pales beside the French, and most popular brands are raw indeed. Torres, however, puts out an acceptable medium-priced brandy called "Gran Reserva," and Gonzalez Byass' "Lepanto" is worth its extra cost. Spanish beer (*cerveza*) is good, if rather light, and is ordered by the bottle (*botellín*) or draft (*caña*). Hard, sparkling cider (*sidra*) is the drink of choice in the northwest of Spain. As to Spanish whiskey, it is best to remain silent, but liqueurs are a different matter. Many of the famous ones—such as Cointreau, Benedictine, Chartreuse and the fruit liqueurs of Marie Brizard, are produced under license in Spain at the cheapest prices anywhere.

When you are not in the mood for alcohol, bottled water (*agua con gas* or *sin gas*, water with or without carbonation) is always available, as is Coca-Cola.

BULLFIGHTING

Running of the bulls in Pamplona ends at the bullring.

Bullfighting is in decline. For the first time less than half of the Spanish admit to any affection for these events. Today, in part due to the excitement generated by nationwide betting, soccer captures the largest share of the sports audience, and golf and tennis, following recent international successes, grow increasingly popular. Yet, to 40 percent of the Spanish, the bulls still remain a passion. Madrid's Las Ventas arena fills to its 50,000-seat capacity most days during the season, and tickets are always scarce at Spain's score of regional rings.

The bullfight season extends from April through October in Madrid, with fights every day during the May **Fiesta de San Isidro**, and during special weeks in other cities. In the first week in July, Pamplona holds its **Fiesta de San Fer-**

min, more interesting for the running of the bulls than for the calibre of the fights. In conjunction with its April Fair, Seville opens the splendid *Maestranza* bullring for two weeks at the end of the month, and presents lesser events throughout the summer. One of two different categories of fight will be offered on a given day, corresponding to professional and semipro. *Novilladas*, which involve young bulls and apprentice matadors, appeal primarily to those interested in spotting future talent.

But do not attend a bullfight unless you are prepared to see blood, often great quantities of it. In Spanish culture, a bull is viewed as a symbol, although this may be difficult to remember when a team of horses drags away a bloody carcass that moments before was a proud animal. Still, a *corrida* is a vibrantly visual and auditory pageant, worth trying at least once.

The events of a *corrida* (bullfight) are easily described, but not so easily understood. What a corrida is *not* is a contest between a man and a bull: the bull always loses and is expected to. Of course the possibility exists that a bull may gore the matador, but such danger does not draw the crowds any more than the chance of serious injury to players brings fans to football games. The crowd cheers the matador's mastery of the bull more than the riskiness of his cape passes.

A bullfight is a drama whose every act has been rigidly choreographed since the 18th century, a kind of ballet whose steps are as well known to the audience as they would be to anyone seeing *Swan Lake* for the hundredth time. As in dance, grace and form count for everything. A bullfight is a ritual recounting man's mastery of nature as embodied by the most powerful animal of medieval Europe.

The drama is directed by the governor of the corrida, who presides in the first row of seats opposite the bull enclosure. When he flutters his white handkerchief, trumpets blare and the procession begins. Riders in 18th-century costume, mounted on padded horses, lead the parade, followed by marching banderilleros, then strutting matadors in their "suits of mirrors," who wave their hats at the cheering crowd. The governor tosses the key for the bull enclosure to the lead mounted *alguazil* (protector), who opens the gate to let in the first bull. The bull is huge—at least half a ton, in its prime at four to six years old and wearing ribbons on his withers to designate the ranch that bred him. Confused by the roar of the crowd and the unfamiliar terrain, the bull races about the circular arena in halts and charges. While the matadors observe him, a group of toreros play the bull with capes to run him through his paces, but rush for safety when his charges grow dangerous.

Next a *picador* on a padded horse stabs the bull's front withers with a lance, damaging his neck muscles so his head will droop by the time the matador engages him. A trio of *banderilleros* then run in turn at the bull, each leaping to plant a pair of ribboned darts in that neck wound until a total of six flop there. Now the matador walks magisterially alone into the ring, a long cape in hand, which he shakes to encourage charges from the color-blind bull. Deftly—and if he is any good—with aplomb and grace, the matador makes the bull rush close enough to graze his leg, then swirls the cape away. The crowd roars "olé" in one voice in time with the charges, participating in the rhythm of the fight. As the matador conducts pass (*faena*) after pass, "olés" can grow deafening, breaking into sustained applause for the rare virtuoso at the top of his form. The long cape is then exchanged for a shorter *muleta*, stiffened by an enclosed sword. By now the matador knows the moves of his bull, and the bull has grown confused by continually missing his quarry. The matador makes the animal rush in shorter and shorter charges until the bull stands with heaving sides. Disdainfully the matador walks away, showing his back to the beast.

The governor signals again, and trumpets announce that the matador has a fixed time to end the drama. He unsheathes his sword and moves slowly toward the victim, then quickens his pace, jumps and stabs the blade deep between the bull's shoulders into his heart. This finale is supposed to be clean and swiftly done: a single thrust that brings the bull immediately to his knees. If it is not, the crowd may demonstrate its disapproval vocally. As the bull is dying, the matador doffs his hat and bows to both the governor and the audience. An exceptional performance, as decided by the governor, can earn the matador a cheering parade around the ring and an ear from the bull or, more exceptionally, two ears and a tail.

While the sand is swept in preparation for the next bull, a team of horses drags out the carcass, already forgotten by the crowd engrossed in discussions of the performance. Usually a corrida consists of six fights, each lasting twenty minutes or so, the whole taking two and a half hours. It does not take that long to discern the difference between exceptional matadors and ordinary ones. The event is undeniably a splendid spectacle, often exciting and beautiful, but there is the blood and the death of a magnificent animal for our sensitivities to deal with.

THE SIGHTS

Isabeline entrance to the Museo de San Gregorio in Valladolid.

Spain's sights swell into the hundreds and include ancient ruins, historic and modern buildings, paintings, sculpture, scenery and relaxing beaches. Although no arrangement can anticipate everyone's interests, a geographical organization seems the best. After tiring of the beach or a succession of museums, you can look through the chapter describing the sights of the surrounding area to discover fresh alternatives nearby.

We divide our descriptions into seven geographical regions. First comes Madrid and the area around it, New Castile. Next is Old Castile and León, a convenient day's drive from Madrid. Then we describe the sights of Andalusia, a longer day's drive from Madrid, followed by those of Extremadura, which lies west of Madrid and can be included on the way to or from Andalusia. The area comprising Galicia, Asturias and Cantabria is a long day's drive north of Madrid, though more convenient to Old Castile and León. The Aragón and Navarre region with its famous city of Pamplona is described next because it lies on the way to Catalonia, which, with its jewel Barcelona, constitutes the final section.

MADRID AND
NEW CASTILE

Madrid's Plaza Neptuno is a pleasant stop on a walking tour.

Historical Profile:
World Power and the Great Armada—Felipe II

Felipe II (1556–1598) established Madrid as the capital of Spain and built New Castile's most imposing monument, so an account of his life provides a fitting background to this area. He was also the king who sent the Great Armada to England and waged Spain's longest, most complicated war. Although Felipe was the most powerful European of his time, he was a lonely man, so shy that his voice fell to a whisper in public.

This strange individual was the creature of his father, for whom he felt respect approaching veneration. After all, most of us do not have a father as mighty or busy as the Emperor Carlos V.

Carlos, the child of mad Queen Juana—a daughter of Ferdinand and Isabella—had been raised in the Netherlands, never setting foot in Spain until, at the age of 17, he arrived to be crowned its king. "Historical Profile: Ferdinand and Isabella" on page 185 Carlos had been cursed with a gawky frame, a sallow complexion and a huge, jutting jaw, an inheritance unfortunately passed on to his descendants.

Carlos thirsted for empire. Soon after he ascended the Spanish throne, his Hapsburg grandfather, the Holy Roman Emperor Maximilian, died. As one of his first acts of state, Carlos spent huge sums from the Spanish treasury to insure his election as Maximilian's successor. Already reigning as Duke of Burgundy and the Low Countries, King of Castile and León, King of Arágon, and King of Naples, by age 19 he had maneuvered his way to the additional title of Carlos V, Emperor of the Holy Roman Empire. Counting Mexico and Central and South America, Carlos thereby assumed rule over the largest kingdom since the Empire of the Mongols; his acquisitions changed Spain from an autonomous state into one of the pieces of an encompassing empire.

It was not long before the Spanish demonstrated their disapproval of their reduced state. When Carlos left for Germany in 1520 to receive his emperor's crown, protests broke out behind him in Spain. Unrest percolated for two years before erupting into a full-scale revolution. Led by the aptly named Juan Bravo from Segovia, the rebels called themselves *comuneros*, and fought resolutely for a ruler who would hold Spanish interests more deeply in his heart. With no possibility of quelling such a general uprising, Carlos acceded to the rebel's demands, agreeing to learn Spanish and take on Spanish advisors, marry a Portuguese princess, and raise any resulting children in Spain. Carlos began learning Spanish when peace was restored, but not until he had executed the ringleaders of the revolt.

After replacing his Flemish advisors with Spanish ministers, Carlos journeyed to Seville in 1526 to wed his cousin, Princess Isabella of Portugal. The two spent the summer—a far longer term than formality required—honeymooning in rooms Carlos reconstructed in the Alhambra Palace at Granada. There Felipe was conceived, to be born in the capital of Valladolid on May 21, 1527. Tenderly, Carlos sat beside Isabella through an agonizing 13-hour labor, during which she asked only that her face be veiled to hide her pain.

Felipe's dire need for fatherly approval can be traced to the abandonment he suffered as a child. Because Carlos was a prince of many countries rather than the ruler of a unified empire, he spent his life traveling from one realm to another. Of the 39 years that Carlos V ruled, he resided in Spain for less than 16. Felipe came to know his father primarily through frequent letters filled with stern advice and moral lectures.

Felipe's upbringing fell mainly to his mother until her death when he was 12; then, through his teenage years, he was raised by a succession of governors. His child household consisted of 51 pages, eight chaplains, a kitchen staff and assorted cleaners, totaling 191 people, none of whom were connected to Felipe by blood or friendship. Not surprisingly, as an adult he prized solitude and felt acutely uncomfortable in company other than his family. The young prince channeled his energies into physical activity, especially dancing, fishing, hunting with his crossbow, jousting and the new game of quoits, yet he was equally passionate about music and needlework. He read encyclopedically in Latin, Greek, Spanish and Italian, and owned books by Erasmus, Dürer and Copernicus, as well as many cabalistic works. Although his greatest love was history, of the 41 books beside his bed when he died, 40 were religious.

Felipe resembled his father physically, with the same blond hair, pale complexion and short stature. He had thick lips, piercing grey eyes reddened from the strain of constant reading, and a protruding chin that he hid behind a beard as soon as he could grow one. Yet, he was considered handsome, and when St. Ignatius Loyola, founder of the Jesuit Order, met him, he caught a "breath of goodness and sanctity" from the young prince. [Quoted by Geoffrey Parker, *Philip II*, p. 54.]

Carlos allowed his son no more time for childhood than he had enjoyed himself. After Felipe's 16th birthday, Carlos appointed him Regent of Spain and arranged a marriage to his cousin, the Portuguese princess María Manuela. Then Carlos left Felipe in charge of Spain for the next 14 years so he could deal with problems abroad. The companionship of Felipe's new wife proved temporary, for María died two years later after the birth of Prince Don Carlos. On Felipe's 19th birthday, Carlos decided that his son should become acquainted with his future domains and sent him on a two-year sojourn through Italy, Germany and The Netherlands. Felipe's aloof manner, attributable more to shyness than arrogance, made an unfavorable impression on his future subjects.

Nor were his father's political affairs going well. In 1551 France invaded Italy; Germany rose in rebellion, inflicting a severe defeat on Carlos; and Turkey invaded Spanish North Africa. Although Carlos mobilized 150,000 troops for these assorted wars, he realized that he needed an ally against France who could also help with smoldering problems in The Netherlands.

He chose England and, to cement the alliance, betrothed the young widower Felipe to Mary Tudor, England's queen.

Felipe sailed to England in July of 1554 to meet his bride. Mary adored him, but, at 26, he was not equally taken with the 37-year-old queen. Soon after, Carlos, exhausted from his wars, abdicated in favor of his son and retired to a monastery at Yuste in Extremadura. Two years later he died. At this news, Felipe left Mary after 15 months of marriage, and crossed the channel to The Netherlands never to see her again.

Felipe was again alone, at age 28, this time at the apex of a political empire. In his first year as monarch, Felipe won a major victory over the French at Saint Quentin on the border of The Netherlands, and won back Italy. His reign had begun auspiciously.

Before he could return to Spain, Felipe labored in The Netherlands for three years to untangle problems abandoned by Carlos. Once home, Felipe never left the peninsula again, in marked contrast to the peripatetic style of his father. By expanding an existing system of councils to deal with ongoing problems, and *juntas* to deal with temporary ones, he created a complex centralized government with which to control his disparate empire. He trusted no one. His ministers were informed about their areas of responsibility, nothing more, so that Felipe alone controlled global policy. He was a slow thinker and deliberate speaker who preferred reading and writing to speaking and listening. Only in isolation, without the pressure of others waiting for his words, could he reach decisions. Since most people of the time could neither read nor write, Felipe's methods seemed incomprehensible: he read every official document, at least in precis, and wrote every official policy, at least in outline.

A victim of his own mistrusting and solitary nature, Felipe assumed the burden of administering all details of the empire, agonizing as long over the pension-claim of a single soldier as over an issue of state. The pace of government naturally slowed, and the mass of his work came, in time, to consume Felipe's every waking hour.

There were family matters to deal with as well. When Mary Tudor died in 1558, Felipe married Elizabeth of Valois, the daughter of the king of France. She was 13, exactly half Felipe's age. The marriage took place with a proxy standing in for Felipe. Elizabeth came to Spain two years later, although two more years passed before she was deemed old enough for the marriage to be consummated. She conceived for the second time in 1566, after a miscarriage. Her concerned husband visited five times a day throughout the pregnancy and remained at her side during the labor and birth of their first daughter, Isabel. The following year Catalina was born. The next year, pregnant again, Elizabeth succumbed to fainting fits, but bloodletting so weakened her that she miscarried and died. Felipe sat with her as she expired. Now a widower three times over, Felipe sought refuge in a religious retreat.

That year, 1568, was a tragic time, for Felipe's only son and heir, by his first wife Maria Manuela, died as well. Don Carlos, the son of cousins and grandson of cousins, was the product of a severely constricted gene pool. He had an abnormally large head, a stammer, and a vicious personality that delighted in abusing animals and women. While at the University of Salamanca he had fallen down a flight of stairs in pursuit of a porter's daughter, incurring serious head injuries and blindness. Trepanning by the great Flemish physician Vesalius saved his life and restored his sight, but did not improve his mental condition. Once, when a shoemaker delivered boots that fit too snugly, Don Carlos forced him to eat his wares. As he grew older, he began to scheme for power, collecting money from courtiers to travel to The Netherlands to seize control for himself. No matter how reduced his mental faculties, Don Carlos' royal blood made him dangerous, forcing Felipe to imprison his son. Don Carlos tried a variety of suicidal means to gain his release, refusing food, then eating gluttonously, and undressing in cold seasons. Eventually he succeeded—in his own death, if not his freedom.

Felipe married for the last time in 1570. Although he was 20 years older than the bride, his niece Ana of Austria, she nonetheless bore him four sons. Three died in childhood, but the last, a male named after his father, survived to become Felipe's heir. In 1580 both Felipe and his wife caught the flu; Ana, his fourth and last wife, died.

There was more to Felipe's life than work and suffering. He loved art, amassing the nucleus of the present Prado collection. His tastes were greatly influenced by his father's Dutch origins, but his favorites ran to extremes. He collected the fantastic paintings of Bosch, 33 in all, as well as Titian's courtly art. Although he commissioned several works by El Greco, the *Adoration of the Name of Jesus* being the most important, Felipe eventually came to dislike the artist's work.

Felipe also enjoyed building. In 1561 he settled on Madrid as his capital, moving from Valladolid, and set about refurbishing the Alcázar for his palace. Two years later he began his most ambitious project, constructing a palace that would also serve as a mausoleum for his father, himself and his family, and contain a monastery to provide perpetual prayers for their assorted souls. So that he could personally oversee the work, the complex was constructed at San Lorenzo de Escorial, close to his new capital. Whether the plan of the building represents the cross on which Saint Lawrence died, as some say, or the Temple of Solomon, as others claim, the most intriguing part of the palace is Felipe's bedroom. The chamber where he lived and worked is tiny and austere, more a large closet than a bedroom, but contains one door that leads directly into the adjoining church so Felipe could watch and listen even when not in formal attendance. The edifice of el Escorial covers four football fields and was completed in just 21 years. Felipe wept from disappointment when it was finished.

Above all he enjoyed his family, the only company with whom he could relax. Felipe loved his wives, except for Mary Tudor, and his children, particularly his daughters and especially Isabel. She often sat with him while he pursued his solitary tasks, silently handing him the next document that required attention. He loved her so much that he kept her with him until shortly before his death, not arranging a marriage until she had reached the exceptionally old age of 33.

The majority of Felipe's life, however, was spent on the affairs of his manifold territories. His statecraft is revealed in four major events: war against Turkey, the acquisition of Portugal, war in The Netherlands and the failed attempt to conquer England.

Along with the office of Holy Roman Emperor came the responsibility of leading Europe's ongoing struggle with the infidel, the Ottoman Empire. After his father's death, Europe looked to Felipe to lead the crusade. Felipe began his campaign with two defeats, losing almost all his Mediterranean galleys each time, and placing the countries around the Mediterranean in imminent danger. In 1570 the Turks demanded that Venice surrender Cyprus. Venice, by the narrowest of votes, decided to fight and called on the Pope to summon Christian aid. When Felipe agreed to supply half of the money and ships in exchange for the authority to appoint a commander, other countries fell in line. Felipe named Don Juan of Austria as his admiral.

Don Juan was the illegitimate son of Felipe's father and a Flemish girl, a young man Felipe had taken into his court hoping to find some enterprise worthy of his half-royal blood. In 1571, 100 Christian galleys under Don Juan bottled up a fleet of 230 Turkish ships at Lepanto in the straits of Greece. Don Juan won a resounding victory, capturing 100 enemy ships and sinking as many more. Among the Spanish sailors wounded in the fray was Miguel de Cervantes, later to write *Don Quixote*. In time the Turks were able to replenish their fleet, but the battle of Lepanto signaled the end of their Mediterranean dominance.

Seven years after the great victory at Lepanto, the king of Portugal died. His family suffered from an astonishing mortality rate, and he left only one grandson, Don Sebastiõ, to rule after him. Don Sebastiõ had no interest in women, caring only for hunting, war and devotions. After his coronation he set off with pomp to conquer Morocco. It was a debacle; surrounded, the entire Portuguese army surrendered when Don Sebastiõ was killed, leaving the flower of the Portuguese nobility captive. The remaining direct heir to the throne was a 66-year-old cardinal who died four years later and left no descendant.

Now the strongest claim to the Portuguese throne was Felipe's through his mother Isabella, the daughter of Portugal's king three reigns earlier. Felipe campaigned methodically to acquire the crown. He paid the ransom of the Portuguese nobles captive in Morocco, then lobbied extensively in the Portuguese Cortes to show merchants how they would benefit from a union with Spain's American empire. But Felipe's claim was challenged by an illegitimate grandson of a former king who found support in the common people and clergy. Just as the Portuguese Cortes was about to decide the succession, this pretender seized Lisbon, forcing the assembled delegates to flee.

Felipe then played his trump card. Prior to his death, the last Portuguese king had stipulated that a committee settle the succession, and, of the five members designated, three had fled to Spain. All three voted for Felipe, who, armed with this legitimacy, invaded Portugal and conquered it in five weeks. For the first time since Roman days, the peninsula was unified. Felipe aptly remarked of his new realm, "I inherited it; I bought it; I conquered it." [Quoted in John Lynch, *Spain under the Hapsburgs,* Vol. I, p. 327.]

By this time Felipe had been at war in The Netherlands for over a decade, a conflict that would break both his health and the Spanish economy. Although The Low Countries were predominantly Catholic, significant pockets of Lutherans, Calvinists and Anabaptists dotted the territory. Mixing politics with religion, Felipe's father had instituted an inquisition against Protestants in The Netherlands because he believed that "heretics should not only be persecuted for their beliefs, but also as creators of sedition, upheaval, riots and commotions in the state....Guilty of rebellion, they can expect no mercy." [Peter Pierson, *Philip II of Spain,* p. 44.]

Strife between Felipe and his Dutch subjects was inevitable. The Dutch were as forceful in defending religious freedom as the Spanish were in opposing it. Three years of consecutive bad harvests through 1566 frayed nerves on both sides. Then, Felipe's decision to increase the number of Low Country bishops from four to eighteen angered the Dutch, who viewed the policy both as an expansion of the Inquisition and a strengthening of the Spanish hold on their country. A Calvinist rampage that desecrated Catholic churches enraged Felipe.

The next year Felipe sent one of the grandees of Spain, the Duke of Alba, with 10,000 crack Spanish infantry to impose order on The Netherlands. Alba quickly ended the Calvinist rampage by arresting suspects by the hundreds. Felipe believed that The Netherlanders should foot the expenses of the campaign, and Alba imposed a new tax to that end, but the tolerance of most Netherlanders did not extend to taxes earmarked for their own persecution. War broke out again, and this time Spain could not end it.

When Alba's army attempted to win back a captured town in the southern Netherlands, they left the north undefended. Dutch privateers, known derisively as "Beggars," rushed from their haven in England to seize the undefended north, causing Alba to wheel back in an about-face. So it went for nine years. Alba could win any engagement against an army in the field, but he could not conquer the north while holding the south, or vice versa. The Dutch were everywhere that he was not.

These years of war in The Netherlands exhausted the Spanish treasury, including the millions shipped from silver mines and sugar and tobacco plantations in the New World. In 1575 Felipe declared his country bankrupt. His soldiers, part Spanish, part mercenary, were not paid for as long as a year at a time, leading to 46 mutinies over the course of the war.

Anxious for improvement, Felipe replaced Alba with his own half-brother Don Juan. But there was little Don Juan could do except sign a treaty acknowledging the status quo: the south, modern Belgium, remained Spanish; and the north, modern Holland, was granted independence.

Felipe refused to acknowledge the treaty, however, for he could not accept the loss of even a part of his domain. His father's advice had become Felipe's credo: "If you are forced to take a stand as champion or defender of our sacred religion, even should you lose all your kingdoms, God will receive you in glory, which is truly one goal worth striving for." [Quoted by Geoffrey Parker, *Philip II*, p. 44.]

So Felipe replaced Don Juan with the capable Alexander Farnese, Duke of Parma. Over the course of seven years, from 1578 to 1585, Parma employed an astute policy of dividing-and-conquering to gain back the south including Brussels, Antwerp and Flanders. Holland still held out, but prospects looked brighter for Spain than they had for decades. Then, in 1585, the Dutch rebels signed a treaty in Nonesuch Castle with Elizabeth of England, who promised money and troops for their cause.

Relations with England became intolerably strained thereafter. Previously, Felipe had wooed England as a balance against his main rival France, despite the fact that elsewhere he gloried in the defense of Catholicism. In fact, he had supported the Protestant Queen Elizabeth against the Pope, who twice had threatened to excommunicate her. True, Felipe had also encouraged at least three plots against Elizabeth, but such intrigues counted as statecraft in those days. Elizabeth had played a different game. She allowed Francis Drake to privateer Spanish fleets and towns in the Americas, and shifted alliances so cunningly that no one could fathom her intentions. The English Treaty of Nonesuch with the Dutch rebels could not be endured, however, not with its threat of halting Spain's dearly won momentum in The Netherlands. Felipe felt he had no choice but to invade England.

He drew up plans calling for a huge Spanish fleet carrying 60,000 troops to link with Parma's army and ferry it across the Dover Straits. Once the combined Spanish forces landed on English soil he believed that English Catholics, still a majority at the time, would add their support to deliver an easy conquest. In truth, the English army was small, but the planned 60,000 Spanish troops soon fell to a more realistic 30,000, then to 20,000, and the huge fleet proved difficult to assemble.

Only England and Venice had national navies at the time; other countries hired ships from private citizens as needed. While trying to maintain secrecy, Spain scoured the Mediterranean for tonnage from Genoa, Venice and her own citizen-sailors. Spain already possessed a powerful Atlantic fleet to guard treasure ships from the New World, and had access to the ships of Felipe's new Portuguese kingdom. Altogether, Spain collected 130 ships of all sorts and sizes, of which 20 were capital ships of the line, the battleships of the day. This motley collection was the Great Armada. The Spanish referred to it during preparations as "Invincible."

Many school-day impressions of the Spanish Armada are more romantic than accurate, especially the idea that a huge Spanish flotilla was defeated by a rag-tag collection of English ships. In fact, under John Hawkins, the English designed and built the best ships of the day, narrower and longer—to add speed and allow more broadside guns—and bare of raised "castles" (for boarding an enemy)—to lend greater maneuverability and reduce rolling. These were the ships of the future. The English could easily match the Spanish in numbers of ships, and surpassed them in seaworthiness. England also possessed an edge in firepower with more modern, longer cannons of smaller bores that could fire 18- or nine-pound shot 1000 yards.

Chaos attended preparations for the Armada, for collecting the thousands of men, the 100-odd ships, and the tons of stores for a campaign in enemy waters was a bureaucratic nightmare. The weight of preparation fell on Admiral Santa Cruz, the hero of a sea war in the Azores. Already in his 60s, these pressures caused him to suffer a stroke as arrangements neared completion. Desperate for a new commander, Felipe called on the Duke of Medina Sidonia, the highest grandee of Spain. Medina Sidonia had gained some fame by rescuing the port of Cádiz when a fleet under Francis Drake had invested the town the previous year. This raid caused little damage to the city but left major problems for the Armada, since Drake captured transport ships bringing wood to hold the fleet's water and food. Hastily improvised containers would prove inadequate, later leading to virtual starvation for the sailors of the Armada.

Medina Sidonia's main qualification was his nobility. The admiral had to be someone proud officers would consider their equal or better. However, at first Medina Sidonia refused the command on the reasonable basis that not only was he prone to terrible seasickness but also that he had never commanded forces either on land or sea. Medina Sidonia recommended someone else for the job, but succumbed to Felipe's persistence.

On May 9, 1588, one year later than scheduled, the Invincible Armada sailed from Lisbon proudly flying a banner that said "Arise, O Lord, and vindicate Thy cause." [cited in Garrett Mattingly, *The Armada*, p.215.] For three weeks freak storms held the ships just off the coast. After two weeks more, they had only reached Finisterre, the northernmost tip of Spain, where they put into port to repair the damage. Medina Sidonia wrote Felipe that the fleet was in terrible condition; he had better make peace with England. But Felipe would not be swayed. He had written about the invasion: "I am so attached to it in my heart, and I am so convinced that God our Savior must embrace it as his own cause, that I cannot be dissuaded from putting it into operation." [Quoted by Geoffrey Parker, *Philip II*, p. 57.] On July 21 the Armada steered for England.

The Spanish fleet first met the English off the coast of Plymouth, under Lord Admiral Charles Howard and Vice-Admiral Francis Drake. The Spanish immediately formed a crescent with the largest ships on the wings to embrace the enemy, impressing the English sailors by the facility with which they performed their maneuver. The English stood away and pounded the Spanish beyond the reach of the Spanish guns, while the Spanish tried to lure the English close enough to grapple and board where their manpower advantage could be decisive. But never in history had such large fleets engaged, and neither side knew quite what to do. The English strategy proved ineffectual because their guns and gunners lacked sufficient accuracy, and the gunpowder at their disposal was not powerful enough. When the rare shot hit a Spanish ship, it was usually so spent that it bounced harmlessly off the wooden hull. Nor could the Spanish board an enemy who refused to come near.

The Spanish fleet soon disengaged, unhurt, for its mission was to meet with Parma in The Netherlands and ferry troops to England, not fight naval engagements. It anchored off Calais, as close to shore as the ships' 20 feet of draft would allow, to await the Spanish army. The mystery of the campaign is why Parma was not at Calais, and why he had not collected the boats to ferry his troops to the Armada offshore. Perhaps he had little faith in the enterprise and did not want to waste his troops, or perhaps he feared for what would happen in The Netherlands if his army were removed. In any case, the Armada waited at anchor, and Parma didn't come.

On the night of August 7, the English floated eight blazing ships with primed cannons waiting for the heat to set them off toward the anchored

Spanish. These fire ships caused havoc. The Spanish upped anchor and scattered, crashing into one another in the darkness. Then came a devastating squall. When the Spanish regrouped and took inventory, they found that the 50 rounds of ammunition provisioned for each cannon had been spent, seven ships of the line had been lost, one fifth of the men were disabled or dead, and their food had spoiled. There was nothing to do but go home.

Rather than return through the Channel, blocked by the English fleet, Medina Sidonia steered around the British Isles, through the North Sea, past Scotland and Ireland. Plans for the invasion had carefully considered the weather and chosen the summer for its dependable calm. Yet never in recorded history had so many severe storms occurred as in the summer of 1588. The last and most vicious gale awaited the Armada off the Irish coast. The fleet scattered with the winds, tens of ships sank, and tens more put into Ireland, too damaged to sail. Thousands of Spanish drowned or were summarily killed by the English commander in Ireland, who feared an uprising if Spanish Catholics remained in his territory.

Only half of the Invincible Armada returned to Spain, routed more by freak weather and a general's refusal to follow orders than by the enemy, but Felipe searched his soul for some act of his that had caused God to desert him. Refusing to admit defeat, in 1596 he sent off another armada, and in 1597 one more. Each time storms dispersed his fleets.

There was nothing more that Felipe could do. He began to relax his hold on the government in 1595, transferring responsibilities to his son and heir, Felipe III. He ceded The Netherlands to his daughter Isabel, finally removing that problem while saving some face. On September 13, 1598, racked with fevers and arthritis, toothless, his bedridden body a mass of gaping sores, Felipe smiled and died. He left his heir a debt of 85 million ducats, six times the yearly income of the Spanish government. Prices had quadrupled over the course of his reign. The Low Countries were gone, the Americas decimated by avarice and disease—80 percent of the indigenous population of Mexico had died. The crown of the Holy Roman Empire would never again grace a Spanish head.

According to contemporaries, Felipe's aim had been "not to wage war so that he could add to his kingdoms, but to wage peace so he could keep the lands he had." [Quoted by Peter Pierson, *Philip II of Spain*, p. 131.] Perhaps no one could have kept such a diverse empire intact; at least it can be said of Felipe that he tried as hard as anyone could. He himself had written "I know very well that I should be in some other station in life, one not as exalted as the one God has given me, which for me alone is terrible." [Quoted by Geoffrey Parker, *Philip II*, p. 94.]

Affairs in Spain worsened after Felipe died. Felipe III undermined Spain's control of Portugal; his successor caused a revolution in Spain; then came a mental incompetent who ended the line. In 1605, seven years after the death of Felipe II, Cervantes published his great *Don Quixote,* the tale of a romantic who tilted at windmills. It could well have been a parable for Felipe and his Spain.

Felipe's most visible legacies in New Castile are the imposing monastery at **El Escorial**, a building that still reflects his character, lovely gardens at **Aranjuez**, and, of course, Spain's capital city itself—Real **Madrid**, which he founded.

New Castile

The geographic, political and spiritual heart of Spain is a windswept plateau called La Mancha that comprises New Castile. Divided by mountains both from Old Castile in the north and Andalusia in the south, the terrain between is covered with low crops reaching to distant rolling hills. This is the fabled land over which Cervantes, in his parable about the end of chivalry, sent Don Quixote to tilt at windmills. Here Toledo, the original capital of Spain during the time of the Visigoths, endured through conquest by the Moors, and reconquest by the early Spanish. In turn, Toledo preserves precious memorials of Christian, Moor and Jew.

New Castile received its name during the Reconquest from the abundance of castles guarding this battleground between Christians and Moors. Belmonte and Calatrava castles still survive from those days, and, later, through the 15th century, more castles were built to protect Castile from Aragón's challenge from the east. But it was not until the 16th century that New Castile regained the primacy it had enjoyed during the time of the Visigoths when Toledo served as the country's capital. As Spain reached the apex of its international power, King Felipe II chose an undistinguished provincial town named Madrid as his permanent capital. He built palaces and government offices, trebling the population into that of a city. Madrid has remained Spain's capital ever since.

Madrid sits almost exactly in the center of Spain. A marker at the Puerta del Sol in Madrid reads "0 kilometers," and from it are calculated distances to every village and hamlet in the country. As Castile continued to lead Spain's effort to regain the country from the Moors, Castilian Spanish—the victor's language—spread from this center to become the tongue of modern Spain. Savants in the capital still rule magisterially on every attempt to alter its vocabulary.

Today **Madrid ★★★★★** overwhelms all other cities in New Castile in size, and its attractions can easily hold a tourist's interest for two days or a week. **Toledo ★★★★★** outdoes this giant in both the quality and the quantity of its monuments, although its natural compactness allows exploration in just a day or two. The other fine sights of New Castile can either be arranged as day trips from Madrid, or visited during overnight stays. **El Escorial ★★★★** is an imposing Renaissance monastery-palace only 44 km north of Madrid. Franco's huge monument to the Spanish Civil War, the **Valle de los Caídos ★** (Valley of the Fallen), stands nearby. The Bourbon palace of **El Pardo ★★** lies even closer, only 13 km from Madrid, while the gardens of the palace at **Aranjuez ★★** display their beauties 46 km to the south. Somewhat farther afield are **Belmonte ★★**, a 15th-century castle, looking exactly as one imagines a castle should; and **Sigüenza** ★★★, displaying a wonderful 15th-century cathedral on an imposing site.

Aranjuez ★★

Population 35,936
Area code: 91; zip code: 28300

46 km south of Madrid on N-IV.

Entering Aranjuez is like coming into an oasis. Verdant with shrubs and leafy avenues, it is a favorite day excursion for Madrileños, especially in mid-summer when its celebrated strawberries with cream *(fresones con nata)* are sold by roadsides throughout town.

Before Felipe II settled on Madrid as the permanent royal capital, sovereigns would move with the seasons among several cities and palaces. Aranjuez was one such royal town and a favorite stop of Ferdinand and Isabella. Despite his preference for Madrid, Felipe II built a large palace here and surrounded it with the extensive gardens. Twice devastated by fire, the palace was rebuilt in the 18th century to the French tastes of the ruling Bourbon kings, who added pleasant walks and a gridded town plan.

Aranjuez' most historic moment came after Carlos IV foolishly invaded France and, when defeated, signed a treaty that allowed French troops to quarter in Spain. In March of 1808, when the French intention to seize Spain became apparent even to Carlos, he fled to Aranjuez palace on his way to escape in the Americas. He was accompanied by his Prime Minister, Godoy, a man hated by the Spanish for conceiving this foolish French treaty. On the 17th of March, the citizens of Aranjuez stormed the palace and forced Carlos to discharge his minister and abdicate.

In the middle of the 19th century, Isabella II began the tradition of traveling by train to the verdure and strawberries of Aranjuez. Ever since, the *Trena de la Fresa* (Strawberry Train) has been a favorite Madrid summer outing. (It still runs, now as a carefully restored steam train; see "Directory.") Yet the foliage and gardens are best in the spring, and it is the gardens that are Aranjuez' attraction. Half a day will permit ample enjoyment of all the sights and gardens.

On the road from Madrid, immediately after crossing the Tejo (Tagus), the Parterre gardens lie right with the rear of the palace behind them. Farther right and behind you is the Jardin de la Isla of Felipe II, behind you to the left spreads the Jardin del Pripice.

Palácio Real

Pl. Palacio, ☎ *891 13 44.*

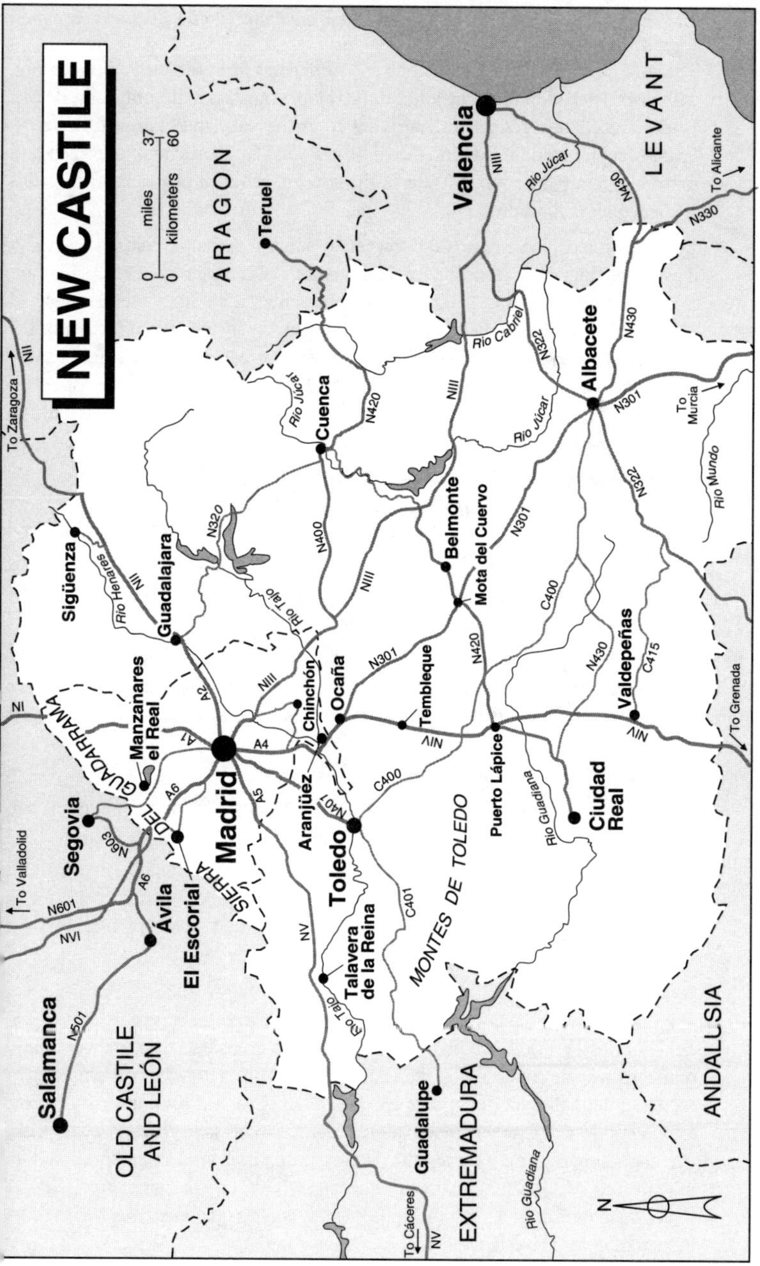
NEW CASTILE
0 miles 37
0 kilometers 60
ARAGON
Teruel
Valencia
LEVANT
To Alicante
N330
N430
NIII
Río Júcar
Río Cabriel
N322
Albacete
N301
To Murcia
Río Mundo
To Zaragoza
NII
Cuenca
N420
Belmonte
Mota del Cuervo
C400
Valdepeñas
C415
To Grenada
NIV
Sigüenza
Río Henares
Guadalajara
N320
N400
Río Tajo
Chinchón
Ocaña
Tembleque
NI
Manzanares el Real
A2
A1
A4
Madrid
A6
A5
Aranjüez
N401
Toledo
Puerto Lápice
Ciudad Real
Río Guadiana
Segovia
N603
To Valladolid
SIERRA DEL GUADARRAMA
El Escorial
Ávila
N601
NVI
Salamanca
N501
OLD CASTILE AND LEÓN
NV
Talavera de la Reina
C401
MONTES DE TOLEDO
Guadalupe
EXTREMADURA
To Cáceres
ANDALUSIA
N

Hours open: Tues.–Sun. 10 a.m.–1 p.m. and 3–5:30 p.m. (until 6:30 p.m. in summer). Closed Mon. and holidays.

The palace's classical brick-and-stone structure dates from the early 18th century, with many later additions. The interior today looks much as it did originally, despite Franco's occasional residence. Tapestries cover the walls and "Persian" carpets—Spanish copies made in Madrid—cover the floors. Opulent china, porcelain and mirrors decorate the rooms. It was in the crimson velvet throne room that Carlos IV signed his abdication.

The most interesting room is the **Porcelain Salon**, covered in colored relief tiles illustrating Chinese scenes. The royal pottery factory in Madrid's Buen Retiro Park manufactured these tiles with more pleasing effect than later ones installed in Madrid's Palácio Real. The king's **Arabian Salon**, a generous reproduction of the Sala Dos Hermanos in the Alhambra, shows that even a king's smoking was restricted to a special chamber. Only about 30 of the 300 rooms in the palace are open to view, but they are sufficient to convey the idea. *Admission: 600 ptas., to both the palace and museum, by tour only.*

Museum of Royal Robes

Same hours and ticket as for the palace.

The museum shows modern copies of regal dress before the reign of Ferdinand VII, and clothing actually worn by monarchs from 1812 on. Examples of the uniforms of various Spanish military orders are also displayed. Curious furniture is on view, along with a most interesting collection of fans, some dating from the 17th century.

Gardens

The gardens are free and open from 8 a.m. until sunset. The casas in the gardens open at 10 a.m., but are closed Tues. and holidays. A ticket to all the houses costs 400 ptas.

Parterre

A "small" formal garden in the French style stretches away from the back of the palace.

Jardin de la Isla

Across the canal along the palace's north side on an artificial island in the Tagus River is this large informal garden—still serene—planted in the 16th century for Felipe II.

Jardin del Principe

These fantastic gardens run for a mile. Within the park—for it is more than a garden—Carlos IV (Goya's patron), like his relative Louis XVIII in France, built a model farm so he could play at the rustic life. Signs direct you for one kilometer to the **Casa del Labrador** (Laborer's House), a classic case of royal understatement. Laborer, indeed! These accommodations are as luxurious as any sybarite could wish. The statues are classical antiques; the mosaics mostly Roman excavated from Mérida in Extremadura; Queen Maria Luisa's dressing-room is a jewel. Signs also direct you to the **Casa de Marinos** (Sailor's House) which contains the luxurious barges of six monarchs. Note the ceiling painted to resemble tapestry.

Where to Stay

Although both Toledo and Madrid are close enough to return to for the night, one nice hotel in Aranjuez provides a quiet place to lay your head.

Inexpensive (-$50)

Hostal Castilla   2nd-Class ★ ★

Carretera Andalucia, 98, Aranjuez (the main street through town), ☎ *891 26 27.*

Lodged in a lovely 18th century mansion, this hotel offers much more than its low prices suggest. Most rooms overlook a fountained courtyard and are decorated with some style. At these prices, don't expect luxury, but the owner is as sweet as the local strawberries. *17 rooms.*

Where to Eat

Expensive ($30+)

Casa José   ★★★

Abastos, 32 (near the town market), ☎ *891 14 88.*

Closed Sunday night, Monday, and from the last week in July to the last week in August.

Food of such quality in a provincial town is a find indeed. The decor is inviting, but does not suggest the elevated dining treat that lies in store. All the dishes are elegantly crafted, each with some innovative touch. The seabass is extraordinary, and the lamb with mushrooms is a treat. Reservations are recommended. Credit Cards: A, D, M, V.

Moderate ($15–30)

Rana Verde   ★

C. Reina, 1 (just east of the palace) ☎ *891 13 25.*

"The Green Frog," appropriately decked out in those colors, overlooks the river and provides more ambience than quality food. There is local asparagus in season, fish and, of course, strawberries in various guises, but no frogs, despite the name. Credit Cards: M, V.

Directory

Information

Located in the Pl. Santiago Rusiñol at the end of the Parterre garden. ☎ *891 04 27*

Trains and Buses

The station (☎ *891 02 02*) sits less than a mile west of town along C. Toledo. Trains connect with Madrid's Atocha station every twenty minutes. Toledo is a 40 minute ride. A special treat is the replica of the steam "Strawberry Train" that leaves Atocha station in Madrid at 10 a.m. on weekends and holidays during the summer, and returns at 8 p.m. A ticket costs about 2000 ptas, but includes all admission fees.

The bus station (☎ *891 01 83*) is located east of the main Pl. Rusiñolon at C. Infantas, 8. 17 buses per weekday connect with Madrid, half as many on Sun.

Belmonte ★ ★

Population 2811
Area code: 967; zip code: 16640

Take N-IV south from **Madrid** *for 57 km, exiting at Ocuña (11 km past Aranjuez). 76 km on N-301 (toward Albacete) brings you to Mota del Cuervo, then 16 K on N-420 (toward La Almarcha) brings Belmonte, for a trip of 149 km. You can return to N-IV, if continuing south to* **Granada**, *by taking N-420 through Mota for a connection at Puerto Lapice in 76 km. From* **Toledo** *take C-400 south to connect with N-IV at Madridejos in 87 km. Take N-IV south for 17 km to Puerto Lapice, where N-420 goes east to Belmonte in 76 km.*

Windmills can be seen from the highway surrounding **Mota del Cuervo**, a town also containing a ruined castle (formerly run by the Order of Santiago) that is worth wandering through. But the object of the trip is Belmonte, one of the most typical castles of Spain. It, along with the entire town, has been declared a national monument.

The **castle of Belmonte** was a fort, constructed in 1456 by Juan Pacheco, Marques of Villena, to defend his territory. It was a time of little central authority, for successive monarchs in vain attempts to curry favor, had dissipated their power to the realm's nobles. In this era, each grandee had to assume responsibility for his own defense. Christian lords built castles as much to defend themselves against other nobles, as for protection from the Moors.

 Some of the perimeter walls connecting the castle to the town remain, but it is the perfectly situated castle that most impresses. Hexagonally shaped, with circular towers to provide defenders with good angles from which to shoot attackers, the exterior of the 15th-century castle looks today almost exactly as it did five hundred years ago.

Castle of Belmonte

Hours open: 10 a.m.–2 p.m. and 4–8 p.m. (until 6:30 p.m. in winter). Closed the last week in August.

The castle was abandoned in the 17th century, not restored until the 19th and still needs work. Of course during the 200 years of its abandonment all the original furnishings disappeared. The red brickwork of the central courtyard was added for 19th-century tastes, but the empty rooms inside still exude a 15th century atmosphere. Some retain lovely wood ceilings in Moorish style—*Mudejar*, carved by Moors for Christian patrons. The one in the audience chamber is especially fine. The town **church** in Belmonte is also worth seeing for its polychrome altars and choirstalls. *Admission: 200 ptas.*

Caídos, Valle de Los (Valley of the Fallen) ★

Hours open: daily from 10 a.m.–7 p.m. (until 6 p.m. in winter). Closed all holidays.

See the directions to El Escorial. From **El Escorial** *take N-601 north for 8 km to turn at the sign for Valle de los Caídos.*

See the directions to El Escorial for **bus** *connections.*

This is Franco's memorial to the dead of the Spanish Civil War, though skeptics view it as a monument to himself. Regardless of the reason for the structure, its mountain setting is ruggedly beautiful amid granite outcrops and weathered pines. Inside a hill surmounted by a towering cross—400 feet high (with an elevator inside)—a huge underground basilica was excavated through the 1950s. Claims that this expensive basilica would exculpate the carnage and horrors of the civil war, clearing the consciences of both sides, are belied by the fact that Franco used Republican prisoners as forced labor to build the monument.

Franco wanted to awe. The nave of the underground basilica is larger than St. Peter's in Rome by a third. The cupola is huge and resplendent with bright mosaics of Spain's heroes and martyrs approaching Christ and Mary. Tapestries along the nave are 16th-century Belgian depictions of the Apocalypse, appropriately, while side chapels contain copies of famous Spanish statues of the Virgin. In a crypt behind the altar repose coffins of 40,000 unknown soldiers who died in the war, but the places of honor belong to Franco and José Antonio.

José Antonio Primo de Rivera, the son of a deposed dictatorial prime minister, led the small, quasi-fascist, Falange party during the political unrest leading up to the Spanish Civil War. "Historical Profile: The Spanish Civil War" on page 469 Convicted of political murder, Antonio was incarcerated as the war broke out and died in prison at age 33, to be promoted to martyr status by Franco and his Nationalist sympathizers. Antonio's remains are buried at the foot of the altar. Nearby, under a white slab, the Generalissimo himself sleeps forever. *Admission: 400 ptas. per car.*

El Escorial ★ ★ ★ ★

Population 6192
Area code: 91; zip code: 28280

From **Madrid** *take N-VI north for 16 km, then C-505 at the Las Rozas exit for 28 km. Well marked by signs. The total distance is 44 km.*

*Frequent **trains** leave Madrid's Atocha and Chamartín stations which deposit you a mile from the monument. Buses meet the trains to cover that distance.*

*A dozen Autocar Harranz **buses** (☎ 543 36 45) leave the Moncloa Metro stop in Madrid for El Escorial. The same line provides afternoon service from the El Escorial stop to The Valley of the Fallen and back.*

Felipe II was a complex and private monarch, deeply religious and greatly admiring of his father, Carlos V. He wanted to build a monument to God and to his father, and chose an insignificant village called San Lorenzo del Escorial for the site. This village was selected because it was near enough to Madrid that Felipe could travel to watch the work progress, as he often did, and for the name of the town. In his limited personal military career, Felipe had enjoyed one major success—over the French at St. Quentin in Flanders—in a battle won on August 10, the name-day of Saint Lawrence (San Lorenzo). The fact that the area contained abundant granite for building material clinched the choice.

At the time he constructed El Escorial, Felipe was the most powerful monarch in the world and put the resources of his empire to work on this, his favored project. It occupied 1000 workmen for 21 years, and when finished contained over 1000 doors, almost 3000 windows and corridors that ran for ten miles. Felipe wept when it was finished.

Felipe's structure was a mausoleum for his father and a pantheon for himself and his descendants. A monastery was included so monks could pray perpetually for all their souls. It also contained a palace so that Felipe could work near his father's remains, and a church, of course, for services. He commissioned Juan de Toledo, who had assisted Michelangelo and Bramante on St. Peter's in Rome, to design the building, and Felipe took an active interest in its design.

The structure stands as a reaction against the ornate Gothic, Isabelline and Plateresque styles of previous monarchs. It is monumentally simple and elegant in proportion, a brilliant solution to the problem of combining monastic austerity with the grandeur that a royal residence should express. Four years into the project the architect Juan de Toledo died, succeeded by his assistant Juan de Herrera, who carried out most of the design. To Herrera's genius is due the elegance of the details and, most significantly, the awesome church inside.

The exterior of the building is worth inspection from the courtyard. The facade stretches for two football fields, and runs one and a half more in depth, yet the expanse is neither boring nor busy with detail. Corner towers reward the left and right views, broken by roofcombs half way along. Windows are arranged in asymmetrical rows to avoid monotony, and the center entrance, with its carving and columns, gives a sense of more detail than it actually presents. The effect is somber, but stimulating and quietly elegant.

Plan on spending at least half a day to see everything that waits inside.

Monastery of San Lorenzo del Escorial ★★★★

C. San Lorenzo de El Escorial, ☎ *890 59 02.*
Hours open: Tues.–Sun. from 10 a.m.–1 p.m., and from 3:30–6:30p.m. (until 6 p.m. in winter). Closed Mon. and all holidays.
Entrance is through the King's courtyard, named for the six grotesque statues of kings of Judea high above the church facade. Ahead is the church, to the left a former college and to the right the monastery. Back along the right side of the church stands a cloister and chapterhouse, and, on the church's left, the royal apartments, where visits begin.

Stairs lead up to the **Battle Gallery**, a long hall of charming frescos. The ceiling is elegant with Roman-style decorative tracery, a common Renaissance theme. Wall murals display various battles painted to resemble tapestry—see the top and the surrounds of the "doorways." The long wall opposite the windows shows a battle against Moors that took place in Granada in the middle of the 15th century. It is curious to find this battle depicted because the Spanish, contrary to the message of the fresco, lost. The costumes are copied from an earlier work painted during the era of the actual battle, hence providing interesting documents. Both end walls show sea battles, with accurate depictions of Spanish galleons. The window wall presents the battle of Saint Quentin, Felipe's only personal victory.

Descending to the palace proper, the first rooms are those of Felipe's favorite daughter Isabel, and rather bare except for a portable organ. In Felipe's audience hall hang two fine Brussels tapestries and drawings of various royal residences. The next room is fronted by splendid German marquetry doors, followed by a room with a large sundial on the floor. Next comes Felipe's bedchamber, the size of a monk's cell, where he often worked and finally died. The poor man ended his days bedridden by pain and the sores of horrendous gout. Note the door opposite which leads into the church so Felipe could attend services without moving. The throne room—with a mere stool for a throne—seems plain, especially compared to that of Felipe's successors in the Palácio Real in Madrid. Indeed, despite beautiful objects, decorations and paintings, Felipe's palace conveys the sense of a simple life. The walls, for example, are whitewashed, rather than covered in velvet as in later palaces. In an alcove rests the litter that carried the invalid king during his final years.

Stairs lead to the new **museums** where some fine paintings are displayed. There is a Bosch *Ecce Homo*, and numerous Titians and Veroneses. A recess holds charming Dürer parchment paintings of birds, animals and flowers. Five Riberas, especially *Aesop*, are symphonies of light and dark. Other rooms display *Zurbaráns*, interesting for incorporating true background scenes, instead of the monotonic fields of most of his work. The two El Grecos that Felipe purchased are also here. One in particular, the *Martyrdom of St. Maurice and the Theban Legion*, was too innovative and acerbic in color for Felipe who never ordered another from the artist, although the painting is acknowledged today as a masterpiece. Do not miss Rogier van der Weyden's monotonic *Calvary*.

The later apartments built for Bourbon Kings are sumptuously out of character with Felipe's austerity. They hold some fine tapestries and lovely furniture.

Passing behind the church, a narrow stair-tunnel, luxuriously marbled, descends to the **Panteon de los Reyes**. This pantheon was built by Felipe's successor but not finished until the reign of the following king. It has none of the feel of the rest of El Escorial, although it is moving in a different way. At the bottom of the stairs comes the double shock of the intimacy of a small round marble room combined with a seemingly infinite ceiling. All around in stacked niches are simple yet monumental porphyry sarcophagi, each identical, of the great Hapsburg and Bourbon kings of Spain—Carlos V, Felipe II, and Felipe IV, Velázquez' friend and patron. Kings lie on the left, and include Isabella II who ruled, while consorts lie opposite, including Isabella's husband, Francisco Asis. Back up the stairs stretch gallery after gallery of deceased princes and princesses, including memorials to those stillborn—a reminder of the high rate of infant mortality then. One confection contains sixty little princes and princesses. Here, too, is the tomb of Don Juan, the victor of Lepanto. At the end of the galleries stands the *Pudridero* (Rotting Place), where corpses dried for ten years before internment in sarcophagi.

Next is the **church**, the masterpiece of Juan de Herrera. It exactly suits El Escorial without duplicating the style of the rest. Monumental, simple and perfect in proportion, this church by itself constitutes an architectural movement. Looking down the nave, the pillars at first seem intrusively massive before the effect of their fluting slenderizes them. Instead of the barrel vaulting characteristic of earlier churches, these pillars support a flat vault of daring span. The effect is awe-inspiring, as intended.

Subsidiary altars line both sides of the nave. In the altar to the right is a marble *Crucifixion* carved by Benvenuto Cellini. From one huge pillar hangs a painting of St. Maurice by an Italian named Cincinnato. This was the painting of St. Maurice that Felipe preferred to the masterpiece he commissioned from El Greco. The retable behind the altar consists of 100 feet of jasper, red marble and bronze designed by Herrera. It contains paintings of the Evangelists and Fathers of the Church. On both sides of the altar kneel bronze statues—on the left, of Carlos V and his wife, daughter and sisters; on the right, of Felipe and his fourth wife Ana, along with his third wife Isabel and his first wife María, presenting Don Carlos, the son who died. Felipe's second wife, Mary Tudor of England, is conspicuous by her absence.

If time permits, the **sacristy** to the right of the church is worth touring for its paintings, frescoed grand stairway and lovely cloister. Also interesting is the **library**, located to the right of the main entrance at the front of El Escorial, for its rich woodwork and rare books (including St. Teresa's diary and missals belonging to Ferdinand and Isabella, Carlos V and Felipe II).

In the same area as El Escorial, left and uphill, is the **Casita del Principe ★**, designed by Villanueva, the architect of Madrid's Prado Museum, for the prince who would become Carlos IV. It is situated in the new town, El Escorial de Abajo, southeast of the monastery on the road to the train station. This "Little House" is a model country cottage, resembling the Trianon at Versailles with its sumptuous interior and rich furnishings. One room is Pompeian; another is completely covered in tile. *Admission: 800 ptas.*

Madrid ★ ★ ★ ★ ★

Population 3,188,297
Area code: 91; zip code: 28000

Most travellers to Spain visit Madrid, if for no other reason than that their plane lands there. A better reason is to spend time in the **Museo del Prado**. The Prado cannot be called the best museum in the world, for it lacks broad coverage of the spectrum of world art exhibited by the Louvre and others. What it *is*, however, is the most exhilarating of museums. The paintings it displays achieve a consistently higher average than those in most other museums, and what it omits is not a detraction. The Prado chose to delight instead of edify, to take one's breath away rather than teach a course in art history. By itself the Prado repays a trip to Spain. And Madrid, the capital of the country for the last 400 years and the seat of the kings of Spain, houses national museums in buildings that only a monarch could produce, along with grand fountains and vistas.

Originally called *Majerit* by the Moors, a name that twisted off Spanish tongues as "Madrid," the city was founded as a Moorish fort to guard the northern approach to Toledo. The Spanish captured the fort in 1083, discovering a statue of the Virgin Mary in a granary (*al mudin* in Arabic) during the process. Since that time the patron saint of the city has been the Virgin of Almudina.

Although by no means a major town, Madrid's statue of the Virgin gave kings reason to visit from time to time. In the 14th century, Pedro the Cruel constructed Madrid's first castle on the site of the original Moorish fort. In the 15th century, Ferdinand and Isabella built a monastery, San Jerónimo el Real, and the following century Carlos V, their grandson, reconstructed Pedro's castle palatially.

In 1561, Carlos' son, Felipe II, decreed Madrid the permanent capital of Spain—*Real Madrid* (Royal Madrid). The reason is a subject of controversy, with most accounts attributing his decision to Madrid's central location. But Madrid is not exactly centered, and the centrality of a capital in Spain could not have been essential to a monarch whose territories extended far beyond the borders of this one domain. More likely the reason had to do with Madrid's proximity to the former capital, Valladolid. As the number of hearths in Valladolid increased, the supply of nearby trees became exhausted,

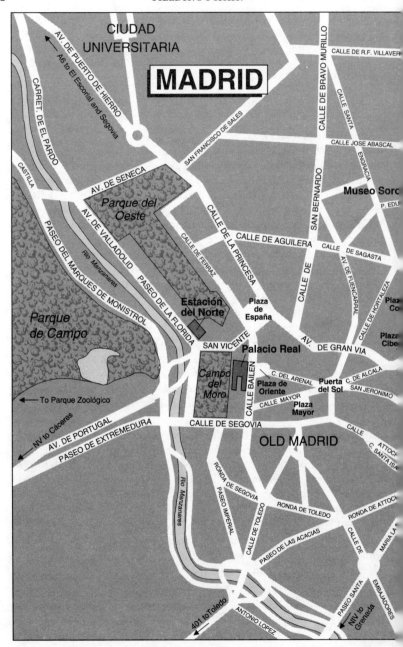

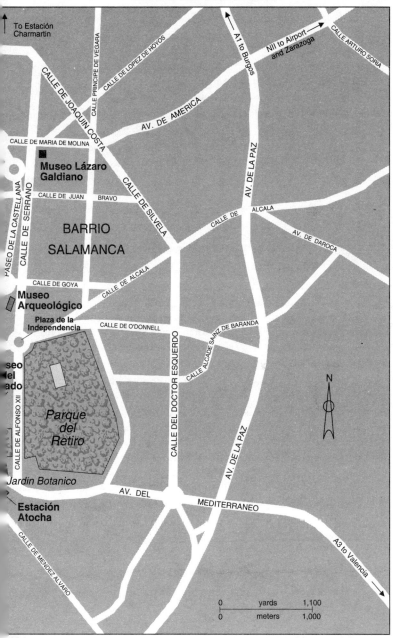

making firewood scarce. But Madrid still had stands of fresh timber, pure water and few hearths. It was time to move, and Madrid was conveniently close.

With the arrival of a king and his government came tens of thousands of functionaries requiring massive public buildings to house them. Most of those original government structures, however, including the palace, burned in cataclysmic fires during the 17th century. The present palace sits on the ashes of the original and dates from the middle of the 18th century.

After its initial influx, Madrid grew sporadically. Its population exploded from 20,000 to 175,000 in its first 100 years as Spain's capital, raising it to the fifth largest city in Europe. But Madrileños exhibited a talent for choosing the losing side in almost every national controversy, which periodically caused monarchs and their courts to avoid the city and growth to stagnate. Madrileños, for example, sided with Pedro the Cruel against his half-brother Enrique of Trastámara, the founder of the dynasty from which Isabella descended; they sided with "La Beltraneja," considered illegitimate, against her aunt, later Queen, Isabella; and they sided with the Republicans against Franco.

Most of Madrid's grand structures, including the Prado, were erected in a late 18th-century building spurt during the peaceful reign of King Carlos III, a monarch who earned the title "King-Mayor" for his sustained effort to raise Madrid to the standards of other European capitals. Historically and architecturally, Madrid is Europe's newest capital.

Napoléon's French troops seized Madrid in 1808. One month later, on the second of May, Madrileños revolted against their foreign occupiers. Goya immortalized the uprising in his famous *El Dos de Mayo*, and condemned the French atrocities that followed in his haunting *El Tres de Mayo*. Both hang in the Prado. During the Spanish Civil War, Madrid was a symbol to both Republicans, who strove to hold it, and to Franco's Nationalists, who attacked it in force when the war began. After a campaign of bloody battles around University City in the northwest, the determination of Madrid's citizens won the day.

Today four million people spread over miles of concrete suburbs. Happily, the original core of the city—the focus of virtually all a tourist's interest—remains relatively untouched by this growth. Most sights are an easy walk from this center, but since Madrid's original civil engineers never envisioned a city of such numbers, traffic can make traveling longer distances a problem. Streets clog, cars proceed slowly and parking in centercity is a challenge best avoided. An efficient subway system and inexpensive taxis, however, make driving unecessary.

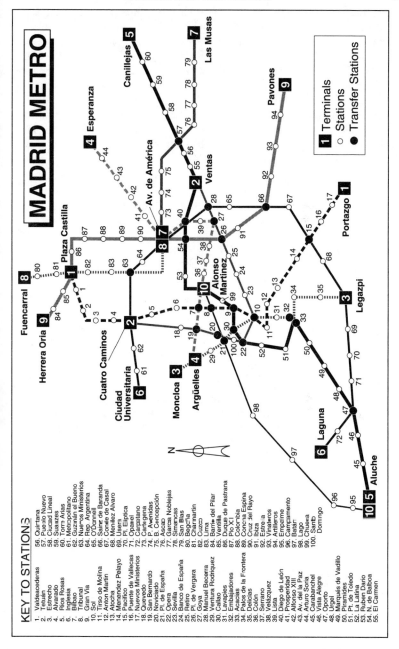

MADRID METRO

KEY TO STATIONS

1. Valdeacederas
2. Tetuán
3. Estrecho
4. Alvarado
5. Ríos Rosas
6. Iglesia
7. Bilbao
8. Tribunal
9. Gran Vía
10. Sol
11. Tirso de Molina
12. Antón Martín
13. Atocha
14. Menéndez Pelayo
15. Pacífico
16. Puente de Vallecas
17. Nuevos Ministerios
18. Quevedo
19. San Bernardo
20. Noviciado
21. Pl. de España
22. Opera
23. Sevilla
24. Banco de España
25. Retiro
26. Pl. de Vergara
27. Goya
28. Manuel Becerra
29. Ventura Rodríguez
30. Ventura
31. Lavapiés
32. Embajadores
33. Acacias
34. Palos de la Frontera
35. Delicias
36. Colón
37. Serrano
38. Velázquez
39. Lista
40. Diego de León
41. Prosperidad
42. Alfonso XIII
43. Av. del la Paz
44. Arturo Soria
45. Carabanchel
46. Vista Alegre
47. Oporto
48. Urgel
49. Marqués de Vadillo
50. Pirámides
51. Pl. de Toledo
52. La Latina
53. Rubén Darío
54. N. de Balboa
55. El Carmen

56. Quintana
57. Pueblo Nuevo
58. Ciudad Lineal
59. Suanzes
60. Torre Arias
61. Metropolitano
62. Guzmán el Bueno
63. Nuevos Ministerios
64. Rep. Argentina
65. O'Donnell
66. Sáinz de Baranda
67. Conde de Casal
68. Menéndez Alvaro
69. Usera
70. Pl. Elíptica
71. Opañel
72. Carpetana
73. Cartagena
74. P. Avenidas
75. B. Concepción
76. Ascao
77. Pl. de España
78. Simancas
79. García Noblejas
80. San Blas
81. Charnartín
82. Cuzco
83. Lima
84. Barrio del Pilar
85. Ventilla
86. Duque de Pastrana
87. Pío X
88. Colombia
89. Concha Espina
90. Cruz del Rayo
91. Ibiza
92. Estrella
93. Vinateros
94. Artilleros
95. Empalme
96. Campamento
97. Batán
98. Lago
99. Chueca
100. Santo Domingo

Terminals ■ 1
Stations ○
Transfer Stations ●

The Puerta del Sol is the midpoint of a line at whose eastern end stands the **Museo del Prado** with its **El Retiro Park** and at whose western end stands the **Palácio Real**. A mile and a quarter separates these monuments from each other, and between them lie most of the city's important sights. Along this axis is the Plaza Mayor, Madrid's Ciudad Antique, and the convents of Descalzas Real and Encarnación. Even the Sunday-morning flea market, **El Rastro**, is located only a few blocks south. Less than a mile due north of the Prado, the **Museo Arqueológico Nacional** displays the treasures of Spain's early history amid the Barrio Salamanca's elegant shops. Including the Archaeological Museum and its surrounding shops, the sights between the Prado and Palace can abundantly fill most visitors' schedules.

Madrid has always been the most lively of capitals, exuding energy and animation. One wonders when Madrileños sleep, for drawn by 3000 restaurants and tapas bars, they fill the sidewalks until the small hours of the night. Madrid is the culinary capital of Spain, with more restaurants offering more varieties of food than anywhere else in the country. Whatever the regional specialty—Basque, Galician, Valencian or Andalusian—Madrid serves its cuisine as well or better than its home territory. A visitor can perform a complete culinary tour of Spain without ever leaving Madrid.

What to See and Do

The **Museo del Prado** ★★★★★ is a high point, not simply of Madrid, but of Spain. The **Museo Arqueológico Nacional** ★★★ should not be missed. To experience the atmosphere of the city, take one or more **walking tours** ★ described below, preferably #1 and #2. The **Palácio Real** ★★★ is impressive for its excesses, if not tastefulness, and almost everyone should find the associated armory and carriage museums interesting. **El Retiro** ★ park, behind the Prado, offers an array of activities throughout the summer. Museums abound. The brand-new **Villahermosa Museum** ★★★ now fills the gaps in the Prado collection. The convents of the **Encarnación** ★ and **Descalzas Real** ★★ house impressive paintings. **Museo Lázaro Galdiano** ★★ displays exquisite ivories, enamelware and a few exceptional paintings. The **Museo Sorolla** ★ offers a different experience—turn-of-the-century paintings of light and life. The **Centro de Arte Reina Sofia** ★★ is rapidly becoming a premier museum of modern art. And then there is shopping—elegant in the **Barrio Salamanca** ★★, and, on Sunday mornings, fun in **El Rastro** ★, Madrid's flea market.

Museums

Museo del Prado

> *Paseo del Prado,* ☎ *420 28 36. Subway: Banco de España or Atocha. Buses: 10, 14, 27, 37, 45, M-6.*
> *Hours open: Tues.–Sat. 9 a.m.–6:30 p.m., (until 7 p.m. from May 15 to Oct. 15). Open Wed. night until 9 p.m. Open Sun. 9 a.m.–2 p.m.*

In 1785, as a major component of his plan to gentrify the capital, Carlos III commissioned the building of the stately Prado on the site of the Prado de San Jerónimo, or Saint Jerome's Meadow, formerly the gardens of a monastery built by

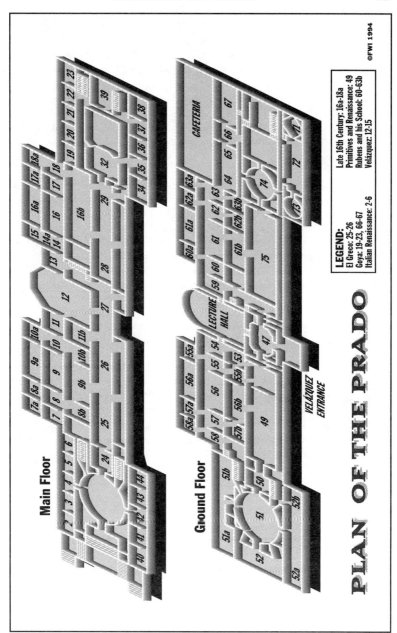

Main Floor

Ground Floor

CAFETERIA

VELÁZQUEZ
ENTRANCE

LECTURE
HALL

PLAN OF THE PRADO

©FWI 1994

LEGEND:
El Greco: 25-26
Goya: 19-23, 66-67
Italian Renaissance: 2-6

Late 16th Century: 16a-18a
Primitives and Renaissance: 49
Rubens and his School: 60-63b
Velázquez: 12-15

Isabella and Ferdinand. The meadow had long served as a favorite promenade for the beautiful people of Madrid, and the king hoped to edify his strolling subjects by housing natural science exhibits in their path. He gave the assignment to Juan de Villanueva, of neoclassical Italian bent, who designed a columned brick-and-stone structure with protruding end pavilions that generated countless similar museums around the world.

Before any exhibits could be installed, however, the French invaded Spain and lodged a troop of cavalry inside, greatly damaging the interior. When the French left, Carlos' grandson, Ferdinand VII, decided to use the abandoned building to house previously separate royal art collections under one roof. On November 19, 1817, shortly after the opening of the Louvre in Paris, the Museo del Prado first received the public.

A special aspect of the Prado collection is that, because it consists primarily of works chosen by a few Spanish kings for their own collections, it lends insight into royal tastes. Early in the 16th century, Carlos V, raised in The Netherlands before becoming Spain's king, assembled the beginning of the collection. His domains were extensive and he travelled throughout Europe, bringing a European sensibility to a Spain focused inward by its centuries of reconquest. Carlos purchased many Flemish works and, above all, paintings by the great Italian Titian, the master he admired above all others. Carlos' son, Felipe II, the enigmatic hermit-like king, greatly expanded the royal collection, adding fantastic works of Hieronymus Bosch, among others. In the 17th century, his grandson, Felipe IV, became an avid collector and also patron to the great Velázquez, who he sent to Italy to select works for royal purchase. Felipe IV bought Rubens' by the score and twice offered that artist the position of court painter, though Rubens declined each time. After Cromwell ousted Charles I from England's throne and offered the royal art collection for sale, agents of Felipe IV were the main bidders, sending home Dürer's *Self Portrait* among many others. Thus was the mass of the Prado's collection assembled.

Throughout the time of Carlos V and the collecting Felipes who succeeded him, Spain governed all of Italy south of Rome, which accounts for the Prado's superb collection of Italian masterworks, especially those from the 16th and 17th centuries. Thanks to Carlos V and Felipe II, Dutch and Flemish works are well represented, including a major Rembrandt purchased later. Still, the focus of the collection is on the incomparable Spanish masters, assiduously gathered in homage—unparalleled in any other country—to its native artists. Because Spain was a political rival of both England and France, the Prado is weak in English painting and spotty in French. And, despite three great works by Albrecht Dürer, the collection must also be considered weak in German painting, for its artists were generally ignored by the royal collectors.

No one should miss the three Dürers, Raphael's *Portrait of a Cardinal*, Bosch's paintings, all the Zurbaráns, all of Velázquez' works and Goya's portraits and "black paintings." In addition, the works of Berruguette, Ribera, El Greco, Pieter Bruegel the Elder, van der Weyden, Botticelli, Fra Angelico and Titian are outstanding, although other treasures will certainly call out to you as you pass. The Prado owns more than 6000 paintings. Since it chooses to display only about 500, every one will be special. Fortunately, the museum is not huge. How much time a visit requires will depend entirely on whether you wish to cover only its highlights, which can be seen in half a day, or to view its full hanging collection, which can be seen in a full day, or better still, enjoyed over a lifetime. Locations of paintings change frequently during the ongoing project of installing air conditioning, so directions and the location of the works we describe may need adjusting when you arrive.

Ground Floor

Left, as you enter the central "Velázquez Entrance," are paintings from the Renaissance, prefaced by medieval works. To the right hang works by members of the school of Rubens. Head left. You are on the way to Dürer and Bosch.

Off the long corridor of medieval paintings, three rows of rooms extend right. Work your way through the first row consisting of rooms 53, 55B, 56C, 56B and 57B.

By rooms 56B and 56C, the paintings begin to come alive. **Correa de Vivar** stands out. A sudden light comes in room 57B from *Virgin con Cabellero de Montessa*, attributed to the Italian **Pablo de San Leocadio**. Then back to room 57 in the next row. Here hang the paintings of Pedro Berruguette, the first genius of Spanish art.

Born in 1450, **Berruguete** worked in Italy before returning to Spain in 1483. He may have acquired technical mastery from his time abroad, but there is nothing Italian about his utter realism and fondness for decoration. Probably his finest work is the *Auto da Fé Presided over by St. Dominic de Guzmán*. It depicts the heretic Raymond talking to a priest who stands at the bottom of a stairway. With extended hand, the seated Saint Dominic pardons Raymond in front of a crowd that seems not to notice the event. This is the most Italian of Berruguette's works, but the colors surprise, as does the movement of the composition. Two other Berruguette paintings of Saint Dominic also deserve a look— *St. Dominic and the Albigenses* and *St. Dominic Restoring a Young Man to Life. San Pedro Martir* is a shattering work, heightened by the disquieting sight of an ax in the saint's head.

Left, in room 58, is an early innovator, the Fleming **Rogier van der Weyden** who died in 1464. His *Disposition* is a masterpiece of unforgettable faces. So too is *Pietà*, with a striking cross soaring heavenward. This is the first religious painting to include a portrait of an artist's patron—the solemn man with clasped hands.

Pass through room 56 and into room 55 to find works of **Machuca**, a contemporary of Berruguette, which display a liveliness not seen in the previous rooms. Notice *Disposición de la Cruz*, with its strong mood. And what a frame surrounds it—a rare preserved original frame for such an early work.

Proceed to room 54 where three extraordinary **Albrecht Dürers** wait on the far wall. *Adam and Eve*, so often reproduced, stand as tall as life—which is a surprise—on either side of the artist's *Self Portrait*. Dürer learned his trade in Italy, but his mathematical exactitude was natural, and he brought a Gothic palette of colors from his native land. This steely self-portrait must rank with the greatest of that genre, still earning admiration for the precision and profundity of its psychological self-study.

Move quickly through room 55A into 56A for a fantastic **Pieter Breugel**, the "Elder," the famous *El Triunfo de la Muerte* (Triumph of Death), from 1562. Nothing signals as strongly how removed this work is from the Italian aesthetic as the subjects Breugel chose: he depicts common folk in everyday scenes. Despite the religious theme of the inevitability of death, there are no religious references. Impossible juxtapositions make the whole truly surreal, revealing Breugel's debt to countryman Bosch. Encounters with death in all its varieties cover the canvas: humans flee from armies of skeletons who attempt to force them into a box, while two lovers in the right foreground, oblivious to all around them, adore each other. Bruegel's talent and accuracy are evident; it is no wonder that he inspired the work of his two sons and that of most Flemish artists for a century to come. But his paintings pale beside those of Bosch in the next room, 57A.

No matter how often seen in reproduction, the original *Garden of Delights* still seizes the attention and amazes. **Bosch** ("El Bosco," in Spanish) was a true original. The son of a modest painter in a small Dutch village, Bosch never felt the influences of cosmopolitan life. He joined an ascetic movement called the "Brethren of the Common Life," founded on the credo that pleasure is a sure road to hell. He painted this theory with a realism that makes one wonder how he could depict pleasures so convincingly. Rather than theorizing about his sanity or contemplating how his paintings prefigure surrealism, it is best to let the eye wander, discovering details. This much is clear: the left-hand triptych shows Paradise, the center depicts earthly delight, and the right, Hell.

The Adoration of the Magi calls for admiration of Bosch's mastery of technique and detail. Yet, there is that strange city in the background looking like a modern skyscraper metropolis. *The Haycart* is easier to understand. It illustrates a Dutch proverb referring to the world as a hay-cart from which each takes whatever he can. The poor scramble and fight to seize scraps from the central hay-cart. Christ watches from the extreme lower left, as above him nobles and high clergy approach. Monks and nuns in the foreground enjoy what they have already taken. The left panel tells the story of the expulsion from Eden, while the right displays the tortures awaiting us in Hell.

Entirely out of order, because of the impermanence of the current hangings, Ribera's works are hung in room 51B, in the pavilion extending from the right end of the long medieval corridor. **José Ribera** (1591–1652) is the only Spanish painter who can be compared with Velázquez in electing to paint ordinary people instead of idealized images. Study his masterpiece *The Trinity*: the strong diagonals—two inverted triangles, the look on God's face as he holds his dead Son, and the drapery. See also the powerful lines of *The Martyrdom of Saint Bartholomew*, and the smiling *Archimedes, Joseph with the Christ Child*, and *Saint Alexis*.

Retrace your path all the way back past the center entrance, to the rooms on its right. Again three rows stretch off the long hall. The first row, rooms 61B-63B, have **Rubens** and **Van Dycks**; the second row, rooms 59-63, more Rubens; and the last, rooms 60A-63A, display various landscapes and still-lives. Go farther right, off room 63, past rooms 64 and 65, for a temporary installation of the great **Goya** "Black Paintings" in room 67 and 68.

These paintings, dating between 1819 and 1823, are the works of Goya's old age and reflect a time of personal crisis. Goya had placed great faith in the enlightened ideas and secular government of the French, but his hopes for rationality among men had been dashed by France's invasion of Spain in 1808. Goya suffered a renewed attack of an illness that had earlier destroyed his hearing, and secluded himself in a house on the banks of the Manzanare, covering its walls with paintings called "Black" for their dominant tone. After Goya's death, the works were lifted off the walls and transferred to canvas as you see them.

See the famed *Saturn Devouring One of his Sons* and *Witches Sabbath*, but also the haunting *Dog Half Submerged*. *St. Isidore's Day* is a nightmarish self-satire of one of Goya's own exuberant, sun-filled early paintings under the same name displayed upstairs.

Upper Floor

To view the rest of the collection in order requires first retracing steps through the ground floor medieval hall to the pavilion on the far right, and then climbing to the upper floor. Around the rotunda toward the back hang early Italian masterworks. You enter into room four in the middle to see the splendid **Fra Angelico** *Annunciation*. The contrast between the detailed, almost Flemish, reminder of the Adam and Eve story outside, with the simple architectural shapes of the building where the Annunciation takes place, focuses all attention on the main event. The colors take one's breathe away.

Left, in room three, hang three parts of a four-painting series by **Sandro Botticelli**, *The Story of Nastagio Degli Onesti*. It depicts a tale from the Decameron in which Onesti, while wandering through a forest after rejection by his beloved, sees a knight murder a maiden and throwing her heart to a pack of dogs. The knight explains that he is condemned to repeat this act eternally because he killed himself after the maiden spurned his suit. Onesti invites his own beloved and her family to a picnic in the same forest so they might witness this result of rejected love. The happy aftermath is shown in the missing fourth painting. In the same room is a splendid **Mantegna**, *Death of the Virgin*.

Raphaels hang in room two, the next room to the left. Although he might be the most talented painter who ever lived, Raphael's fame seduced him into excesses that killed him by his early thirties. To meet the demand for his work, he organized a factory employing numerous assistants which produced art of such uneven quality that questions arise about whether the master's own hand had ever touched a given painting. The Prado, however, contains several of Raphael's acknowledged masterworks. *The Holy Family with Lamb* is reminiscent of Leonardo Di Vinci but with stronger colors and more expressive faces. Felipe IV bought *Christ Falls on the Way to Calvary*, and called it the "costliest gem in the world." Again the faces, especially those of the women, are miracles of expression—from concern, to love, to anguish. Most haunting is the *Portrait of a Cardinal*. The identity of the sitter remains in question but not the depth of Raphael's psychological study or the subtle richness of his subject's red silk robes.

Turning back to view the rooms following Fra Angelico's room four, we come to room five and **Andrea del Sarto**, an artist from the era of Raphael. *Lucrezia di Baccio del Fede* pictures del Sarto's wife. Stories describe her as cruel and unfaithful, but this portrait clearly shows why he kept her around. Work your way through room six, and through the three rows of rooms seven and eight, A and B for more Italian painting, including one by the genius **Caravaggio**, *David Victorious over Goliath*, of flawed composition but unearthly light.

Move into the long gallery, rooms 25 and 26, for **El Greco**. Domenicos Theotocopoulos, as he was baptized, came to Spain in 1576 after studying with Titian in Venice, and never left. El Greco had studied Byzantine icon painting in which strong outlines make thin, elongated figures stand out from their background. He introduced the device to western art, along with a palette of luminous blues and reds acquired from his Italian teachers. The Impressionists—especially Cezanne, who copied his paintings repeatedly—learned much from him.

El Greco's best work remains in Toledo, the city he made his home. The Prado, however, displays his finest portrait. *The Nobleman with his Hand on his Chest* was painted soon after El Greco landed in Spain, before the extreme elongation of figures and the fiery, yet paradoxically cool, colors of his later work. Still, there are hints of what was to come in the unknown sitter's long fingers and piercing gaze. Some of El Greco's mature work is also on view at the Prado, paintings which incorporate elongated figures, drawn as if the painter were lying down looking up at the subject; angry, living skies; and raw emotion expressed as much in the mannered painting of fabric as in the faces of his subjects. *Pentecost, The Trinity*, and especially, *The Adoration of the Shepherds* could only have been painted by this genius.

Moving down the long gallery, enter the large room 12 on the right, from which rooms 13-15 continue for the Spain's greatest painter, Velázquez.

The work of Diego **Velázquez** de Silva (1599–1660) represents the culmination of Spanish painting. Velázquez studied in Seville, and was appointed a court painter in his twenties. Two early paintings before this appointment show him already a master—*The Adoration of the Magi* and *Mother Jerónima de la Fuente*, with her piercing, determined gaze. At court in Madrid, Velázquez became a royal portrait painter, beginning a lifelong friendship with his patron and contemporary, the lonely Felipe IV. Velázquez' portraits of the king show his human side—a homely man with thinning hair and jutting Hapsburg jaw.

In 1628, Peter Paul Rubens, the most famous painter of the day, visited Madrid. He had no use for any Spanish painter but Velázquez, and undertook to teach him what he knew. These lessons are contained in Velázquez' disturbing *Feast of Bacchus*, in which the effete, half-naked, fair-skinned god of wine, surrounded by leathery peasants, stares at us. It is a flawed painting that foreshadows Manet's *Déjuner sur l'herbe* in its shock of contrasts.

Starting in 1629, Velázquez spent two years studying in Italy. The result was two large Italianate narrative works, *The Forge of Vulcan* and *Joseph's Bloodied Coat Presented to Jacob*. The former painting is a tour de force of surfaces, from gritty floor to burnished iron to gleaming armor. Figures of the cyclops show surprisingly lean, unidealized bodies. The latter is an annoying painting that does not seem to work until one steps twenty feet away and sees it come to life.

Back in Spain, Velázquez entered a mature phase when no project was beyond him. During this period he painted the epic *Surrender of Breda*, sometimes known as *Las Lanzas* for its most striking element. The work commemorates one of the few Spanish victories in the long war with The Netherlands, and the grace with which General Spinola accepted the Dutch surrender. *Count-Duke Olivares on Horseback* is a monumental homage to Velázquez' friend at court, a fellow Sevillano. The huge Count-Duke surveys his only military success. His depiction of *Diego de Corral y Arellano* is more subtle, the essence of portraiture.

Velázquez painted everyone in the royal family and most of the jesters and dwarfs kept as pets. Most charming is his perceptive portrait of *Queen Marianna* showing her determined, unpleasant character, lightened only by touches of vermilion ribbon.

Velázquez was ambitious, rising in position with the years. Added responsibilities for collecting art for the king, decorating rooms in the palaces at Madrid and El Escorial, and supervising other royal painters consumed time, constricting his own artistic output. In his last phase, Velázquez determinedly painted only works that were important to him, exercises to stretch the medium. Two acknowledged masterpieces resulted. *The Fable of Arachne* depicts a weaving contest between the mortal Arachne and the goddess Minerva. In the myth, the contest results in a tie, demonstrating Arachne's ability to weave divinely, and ends with the jealous Minerva transforming Arachne into a spider. In Velázquez' painting, Arachne stands in the sunlit background in front of her weaving. The weaving copies a known painting, *The Rape of Europa* by Titian. Velázquez' message is that Titian's painting is divine, which shows that artists transcend mere craftsmen. Velázquez was hoping at the time for a royal award never before given to a mere painter—the *Order of Santiago*; this painting was part of his campaign. Not incidentally, the painting is complex and fascinating.

Like no other painting, *Las Meninas*, Velázquez last work, makes the viewer a participant, for he stands exactly at the focus of all the activity. The princess Margaretta, her ladies-in-waiting, dog and dwarfs are all watching the subjects that the artist behind them, Velázquez himself, is painting. The models, the king and queen, are shown reflected in a mirror at the back, emphasized by the brilliant device of a courtier ascending sunlit stairs nearby. The picture is complex and perfect, summarizing all the lessons painting had discovered through the ages. Velázquez died soon after finishing *Las Meninas*, but posthumously earned the Order of Santiago he had so assiduously sought in life. A thoughtful friend—some say it was the king himself—later painted a crimson cross, the sign of the order, on Velázquez' chest in the painting.

If Velázquez poses a problem, it is that he is too accomplished. Everything seems so right and undramatic that it is possible to run quickly through a gallery of his work. His mastery requires study. Fortunately his paintings all invite contemplation, for such was his genius.

Finishing the three rows of rooms, pass through 16A-18A, all filled with Spanish works. There you can see an earlier Spanish luminary, **Ribalta**, especially the brilliantly-lit *Christ Embracing St. Bernard*, as well as **Murillo**, who followed Velázquez. Obvious comparisons with the master do not allow Murillo's works much of a chance.

Francisco de Zurbarán (1598–1661) followed Ribera, with paintings that are the most spiritual of all, not with the fire of El Greco's work, but possessed, instead, of a quiet, bare, intensely reflective, almost mystical quality. Zurbarán's solitary figures in white robes against dark, featureless backgrounds display his extraordinary ability to combine spirituality with utter realism. Outstanding are *Saint Luke before the Crucified*, *Saint Elizabeth of Portugal*, of the luminous clothes, the striking *Virgin of the Immaculate Conception*, and the unforgettable *Saint Peter Nolasco's Vision of the Crucified Saint Peter*, with Saint Peter upside down.

When the French invaded Spain in the 19th century, they so admired Zurbarán's work that they took almost 100 works back to France, now disbursed among the museums of the world. Spain retains some fine Zurbaráns, but, alas, not the best.

Returning to the front row, room 16B, we find **Titian**, so admired by Carlos V and by critics through the ages. Many of his works seem overly romantic today, but the collection is impressive and probably the best in the world. Especially memorable are *The Emperor Charles V at Muhlberg*, a portrait of his patron on horseback, and the artist's own *Self-Portrait*.

Continue through to the left pavilion, to room 19 and beyond, for someone who challenges even Velázquez, although in a radically different style. Here are the **Francisco de Goya** (1746-1828) rooms, his early and middle work prior to his last "Black Paintings."

Goya first painted designs for tapestries, called "cartoons," at the royal tapestry-works, before turning to portraits in which greys and watery colors dominate. By 1799 he was celebrated enough to be named painter to the king. The king happened to be a genial incompetent dominated by his wife, Maria Luisa, and her lover, Godoy. Whether Goya's portraits of the royal family are the greatest art can be argued, but if art means showing the truth, these works make a case. Goya pushed his portraits toward caricature to reveal his subject's inner character. Paintings such as *The Family of Carlos IV* so ruthlessly display the emptiness of the king and ambition of the queen, who takes centerstage in the group, that one wonders why they allowed such a portrait to be displayed. Perhaps these people could not see what was before their eyes, or perhaps Goya's bright but washed colors seduced his clients with their elegance. The portraits of Ferdinand VII are particularly unflattering. Goya disagreed with Ferdinand's policies so strongly that he fled Spain for voluntary exile in France. Ferdinand, for his part, wanted little to do with Goya. Goya's portraits of Ferdinand all incorporate the same face because the king refused to sit for the artist.

When Goya's subject was a person of quality, however, as in the case of his friend and father-in-law *The Painter Francisco Bayeu*, the paintings exude character and dignity. Goya could also be sensual, as in *Maja Clothed*, more erotic than the same subject and pose in *Maja Nude*. The sitter is not the Duchess of Alba, as some claim, but an unknown model. It is likely that these paintings were originally framed back to back, so the clothed version could be displayed for general viewing and the naked version turned forward for private contemplation.

Goya's high position in the pantheon of art depends more on his fevered imagination than on his skill at portraiture. In 1808, when the French seized Spain, Goya painted two masterworks, *The Second of May* and *The Third of May*, depicting the uprising of citizens against the invaders, shown in room 39. The first depicts a battle, fierce with violence; the second, by artificially shortening the distance from the executioners' guns to the defenseless victims, shrieks of the horror of death. *Admission: 450 ptas., which includes Casón del Buen Retiro.*

Museo Arqueológico Nacional ★★★

C. Serrano, 13, ☎ 577 79 12. Entrance in the rear on Paseo de Recoletas. Subway: Colón or Serrano. Buses: 1, 5, 9, 14, 19, 51, 74, M-2. See "Walking Tour #3."
Hours open: Tues.–Sat. 9:30 a.m.–8:30 p.m. Open Sun. 9:30 a.m.–2:30 p.m. Closed Mon. and holidays.

The National Archaeological Museum occupies the rear half of the large **Biblioteca Nacional**, with an entrance on C. Serrano. The building was opened in 1892 to celebrate the 400th anniversary of Columbus' discovery of America. While museums of archaeology abound throughout Spain, for the country is rich in artifacts of earlier civilizations, the very best examples have been assembled for display in this national collection.

The tour begins in room one with remains from Greek, Phoenician and Carthaginian civilizations, then leads into a display in room two of artifacts from the native ancient Iberian culture. Carthaginian influence is evident in the fourth-century B.C. *Dama de Elche*, the greatest known Iberian sculpture and the centerpiece of the room. She looks somehow foreign, of a culture outside the classical tradition, for the character of an alien aesthetic seems carved in her face. Other *damas* repose around her, almost as lovely as she. Following rooms contain Roman sculpture and mosaics of some interest.

The second floor begins with Visigothic jewelry. Three crowns turned into votive hangings are the star attractions, and that of Reccesvinthus Rex from circa 670 B.C. is particularly striking. Dangling gold letters spell his name, while the crown is embedded with uncut semiprecious stones. It is the world's loss that the most splendid crown in the collection was stolen in 1921 and never recovered.

Next comes incomparable Moorish art. The small objects, including the precious ivory box called the *Bote de Marfil*, repay study. Stucco work is also displayed, as are intricately coffered ceilings, all of which provide just a sample of the Moorish architecture that waits in Andalusia. Gothic sculpture comes next, and Renaissance objects and furniture follow. Higher floors display small collections of Egyptian and prehistoric art.

On the grounds by the entrance is an underground replica of Altamira cave. Although it is only a pale copy, with some quiet study the animals do begin to wriggle over your head. *Admission: 450 ptas.*

Palácio Real   ★★★

C. Bailén, ☎ *248 74 04. Subway: Opera. Buses: 3, 25, 33, 39, M-4. See "Walking Tour #2."*

Hours open: Tues.–Sat. 9 a.m.–6:15 p.m. (until 5:15 p.m. in winter.) Open Sun. and holidays 9 a.m.–2 p.m. Closed Mon.

In 1764, 26 years after the former Hapsburg palace was leveled by fire, this new palace was raised on the ashes of the old one. It was a new palace for a new dynasty. The final king of the Hapsburg line had been born mentally retarded and died childless, but, on his deathbed, willed the throne to a distant French relative, a cousin of the French Bourbon king. Thus did Felipe V initiate the present Bourbon line of Spanish monarchs. He ordered a palace to suit his French tastes designed by the Italian architect Sachetti.

But the building took decades to complete and Felipe died before it was finished. His son Carlos III, who did so much to make Madrid a worthy European capital, was the first king to inhabit the palace. Carlos took a personal interest in its decoration, even to founding a school for tile-painting in the Buen Retiro Palace, and did up his new residence in Baroque decor. While a palace is not a museum, of course, this one is filled with enough objects to serve both roles.

Entrance to the palace is through its south end where tickets are purchased, and a huge porticoed forecourt that leads to the palace proper. In addition to the palace proper there is the Library with its numismatic and music museum, the Real Farmacia (Royal Pharmacy), the Armería (Armory) and the Museo de Carruajes Reales (Royal Carriage Museum). At least the last two museums are worth a look. Including those, it will take several hours to see the palace.

Statues of Spanish monarchs intended for the roof were placed around the grounds when it was discovered that they were too heavy for the building. The exterior is a solemn white. Rows of pilasters and Corinthian columns run for over a block upon an entablature, surmounted by a hint of "icing" on the roof, all producing a stately facade. But the interior is another matter.

The apartments of the palace's first occupant, Carlos III, begin at the top of a grand stairway. The ceilings of two small rooms were painted by Mengs. Rooms lined with velvet, gilt and candelabras follow, and lead to a double throne room (one seat for the present King Juan Carlos, the other for his queen, Sofia) that tries hard to impress, but would be more appropriate as a Hollywood movie set—though there is that Tiepolo frescoed ceiling. The dining room sits 88 comfortably. Such rooms must be seen to be believed. Two thousand rooms fill the structure, though most are off-limits to tourists. The museum of painting, porcelain and crystal displays a Bosch, four Goyas and a Velázquez amid dinner services for scores.

Outside, in the west wing of the forecourt, is the **Real Armería** (Royal Armory), containing collections of the actual armor worn by 16th- and 17th-century kings. There is a fine tent captured from the French saint-king Francis I at the battle of Pavia, and armor for men, royalty, children, horses and dogs. The long length of the jousting lances are a surprise. The finest armor are the many suits worn by Carlos V, who needed them for a reign filled with wars. All the armor is functional and at the same time artistic, a happy blend of craft and aesthetics. Of course there are amusing excesses too, such as the plating that covers half a horse and culminates in ram's horns crowning the head-piece.

South of the palace is one of the largest churches in the world, **Nuestra Señora de la Almudena**. Construction began over 100 years ago and has not yet finished. It is possible that disappointment with the results to date has quenched the builders' incentive.

Outside in the Campo del Moro, the former royal park, is a modern building which houses the **Museo de Carruajes Reales** (Royal Carriage Museum). It contains elaborately decorated carriages, primarily from the late 18th century. The one in black ebony is the only carriage to have survived the fire that destroyed the former palace in the 18th century, and dates from a century earlier. Napoleon donated the one with the crown on top. The present coronation coach still bears the marks of an assassination attempt made on a former king and his bride in 1906. *By tour only, in Spanish or English. Admission: 500 ptas.*

Villahermosa Museum ★★★

Passeo del Prado, 8, ☎ 420 39 44. Across from the Prado. Subway: Banco de España or Atocha. Buses: 10, 14, 27, 43, 37, 45, M-6.
Hours open: Tues.–Sun. 10 a.m. to 7 p.m., (until 6:30 p.m. in winter). Closed Mon.
This museum completes the Prado collection by filling its gaps. Both Baron Thyssen-Bornemisza and his son spent a fortune from Dutch mining and shipping profits to acquire possibly the finest, and certainly the most extensive collection of art remaining in private hands, Queen Elizabeth excepted, and decided to sell the mass of it—nearly 800 paintings, sundry furniture, jewelry and statues—to Spain thanks in no small measure to the urgings of the Baron's Spanish wife. Here these treasures will reside for our enjoyment, displayed in a tasteful palace.

The installation was not complete at our last visit and was arranged in reverse order. Modern art inhabited the first floor, fine Impressionists the second, and masterpieces from the Renaissance through the 18th-century the third. Here the familiar, powerful *Portrait of Henry VIII* by Holbein the Younger was displayed, along with the captivating *Portrait of Giovanna Tornabuoni* by Ghirlandaio, and Caravaggio's unforgetable *St.Catherine of Alexandria*.

The next floor presents a surprising collection of great American canvases, then fine Impressionists followed by some dramatic expressionists, such as Munch. The modern art on the first floor falls below the standards of the rest, save for a fine Edward Hopper and a haunting painting of the Baron's father by Lucien Freud. *Admission: 650 ptas.*

Convento Descales Reales

Pl. de las Descalzas Reales, 3, ☎ *248 74 04. Subway: Puerta del Sol (directions in "Walking Tour #2"). buses: 1, 2, 5, 20, 46, 52, 53, 74.*
Hours open: Tues.–Thurs. and Sat. from 10:30 a.m.–12:30 p.m. and 4–5:15 p.m. Open Fri. 10:30 a.m.–12:30 p.m., Sun. to 1:30 p.m. Closed Mon. and all holidays.

Juana of Austria, the daughter of Carlos V, established this convent of Poor Clares in 1559 in a former Renaissance palace. The order had been founded a century before by St. Francis of Assisi, for his disciple St. Clare. After its founding, the order petitioned the pope for the "privilege of poverty," that is, for the right of its members to subsist on nothing but what they could beg.

However, there was no begging at this particular convent. It was restricted to "Poor" Clares of the highest nobility who used it as a periodic retreat from the pressures of high society. In return for their stays, they donated the sumptuous gifts now on display in buildings around the cloister.

Despite its austere exterior, the convent is a riot of decoration within. The tour passes through rooms containing fine paintings by Titian, Breugel the Elder, a splendid Zurbarán *St. Francis* and portraits of the Hapsburg royal family. Up a staircase for which "grandiose" is the only description, one enters the former dormitory hung with lovely 17th-century tapestries. The reliquary gallery displays impressive boxes and chests. This is a special museum, small but select.

The only sense of having visited a cloistered convent is by comparison—when you step outside and around the corner to the contemporary bustle of the el Corte Inglés department store. *By tour in Spanish only. Admission: 600 ptas.; free on Wed. The ticket serves also for the Convento de la Encarnación.*

Convento de la Encarnación

Pl. de la Encarnación, 1, ☎ *247 05 10. Subway: Opera (directions in "Walking Tour #2"), buses: 3, 25, 33, 39.*
Hours open: Tues.–Thurs. 10:30 a.m.–12:30 p.m. and 4–5:15 p.m. Open Fri., Sat. and 10:30 a.m.–12:30 p.m., Sun. to 1:30 p.m. Closed Mon. and all holidays.

See "Walking Tour #2." In 1611, Margarete of Austria, wife of Felipe III, commissioned Gómez de Mora, the architect who built Madrid's Plaza Mayor, to design this convent. She and succeeding monarchs donated generously to her pet project. The art in the galleries is not up to the standards of Descalzas Reales, but there is a Ribera, a fine polychrome sculpture by Gregorio Fernandez and pleasing 17th-century Madrid paintings. The 18th-century church is severe in design and Baroque in decoration. A sumptuously frescoed ceiling canopies equally dazzling reliquaries—over 1000 of them—in the gallery. The contrast with the private rooms of the convent is marked, for they offer a taste of simple cloistered life in the 17th century. *By tour in Spanish only. Admission: 600 ptas.; free on Wed. The ticket also serves as admission to Convento Descales Reales.*

Museo Lázaro Galdino

C. Serrano, 122, ☎ *561 60 84. Subway: Av. América. Buses: 9, 16, 19, 51, 89. This museum is situated in a "hole" in the subway system. The closest stop is Av. de América, six blocks due east along C. Maria de Molina.*
Hours open: Tues.–Sun. 10 a.m.–2 p.m. Closed Mon., all holidays and Aug.

This private collection gathered by José Lázaro demonstrates what good taste and piles of money can buy. The ground floor presents a veritable history of enameling up to the 17th century, charming ivories, fine medieval gold and silver, Renaissance jewelry and a crucifix said to be by Leonardo da Vinci. The next floor displays later statues and silver and gold work, although, with the exception of its Flemish primitives, it is more interesting for its furnishings than its paintings. Some very fine oils hang on the third floor: a moving Rembrandt portrait of his wife, two Bosches, Quentin Metsys, El Greco, Ribera, Zurbarán, Velázquez, Goya black period paintings and Tiepolo, along with some of the best English paintings in Spain, by Gainsborough, Turner, Reynolds and Constable. *Admission: 450 ptas; half price on Sun.*

Centro de Arte Reina Sofia ★★

C. Santa Isabel, 52, ☎ 467 50 62. Subway: Atocha, buses: 18, 59, 85, 86, C.
Hours open: Wed.–Mon. 10 a.m.–9 p.m. Closed Tues. and holidays.
Located one block northwest of the Atocha train and subway station, the building began as an 18th-century hospital. Now it has been spiffed up to house the best of Spain's modern art, including Picasso's *Guernica*.

Head straight to the second floor. There in Room 7 in the center is *Guernica*, to most experts the masterpiece of 20th-century art. Painted entirely in shades of black and white, it expresses the horrors of war in its depiction of the devastation of the Basque capital of Guernica. The town, in no way a military target, was carpet-bombed by wave upon wave of German planes during the Spanish Civil War. Scenes of civilians and animals contorted in agony fill the canvas. Because of Franco's involvement in the attack, Picasso would not permit this painting to be exhibited in Spain until after the dictator's regime ended. Picasso's studies for the work lend insight into its composition. If you allow it to, the painting will move you to a deep sadness.

The collection of Spanish modern art is unrivaled. There are major works by Miró, Dalí and Juan Gris, in addition to many Picassos. In particular, Picasso's series of drawings of Velázquez' *Las Meninas* will blow you away. As a collection it presents a tour-de-force of modern art, reminding us how great was the contribution of Spaniards.

The museum shop is worth a stop for its prints and posters. *Admission: 450 ptas.*

Museo Sorolla ★

Paseo del General Martinez Campos, 37, ☎ 410 15 84. Subway: Ruben Dario or Iglesia, buses: 5, 7, 16, 40, 61, M-3. By subway walk due north for two blocks from the Ruben Dario station on Miguel Angel to Paseo del General Martinez Campos, or walk due east on Paseo del General Martinez Campos from the Iglesia station.
Hours open: Tues.–Sun. 10 a.m.–2:30 p.m. Closed Mon. and all holidays.
This house was built in 1912 as the home and studio of an Impressionist of international renown, before art history passed him by and forgot him. It is a pity. Joaquin Sorolla's paintings possess a special light, inspired by that of his native Valencia, that gives his canvases life and spirit. Displaying the works in the turn-of-the-century surroundings where the artist lived adds intimacy. Those who take the time to visit are glad they did. *Admission: 450 ptas.*

Museo Panteon de Goya (Ermita de San Antonio)   ★

Glorieta de San Antonio de la Florida, ☎ *542 07 22. Subway: Norte, buses: 41, 46, 75, C.*
Hours open: Tues.–Fri. 10 a.m.–1 p.m., and 4–8 p.m., (until 7p.m. in winter). Open Sat. and Sun. for the morning hours only. Closed Mon. and all holidays.

Located three blocks north of the Estación del Norte, northwest of the Palácio Real, this chapel is a bit out of the way, but a mecca for fans of Goya. The church was built in 1798 by an Italian under orders from Carlos IV, and the king commissioned Goya, as his court painter, to decorate the cupola and vaults. The paintings are early Goya and romantic, but the cupola fresco of St. Antony of Padua surrounds the viewer and draws him in. As always, Goya's crowds, especially as they lean against and upon the painted railing, seem composed of real people, rather than, as with most artists, actors hired for the drama.

Appropriately, Goya's remains—except for his head which had disappeared—were disinterred about a century after his burial in France and entombed in this church in 1908. *Admission: 225 ptas.*

Real Academia de Bellas Artes de San Fernando   ★

C. de Alcalá, 13, ☎ *522 14 91. Subway: Sol, buses: 3, 5, 15, 20, 51, 52. See "Walking Tour #4."*
Hours open: daily 9 a.m.–7 p.m., except Mon. and Sat., when it closes at 3 p.m. Closed all holidays.

The building was designed by Villanueva who also constructed the Prado. The collection inside is a hodgepodge of over 1000 works, both good and bad, but includes Goyas and four fine Zurbaráns, along with fans and furniture. Nice prints from original plates by masters, such as Goya, are on sale in the gift shop. *Admission: 200 ptas.*

Walking Tours

The best way to experience any city is on foot. In Madrid, subways are convenient and taxis abundant and reasonable, so walking is seldom necessary but is certainly preferred. Each of the following walks includes a variety of sights that can be visited manageably in the time indicated.

1. Old Town (La Ciudad Antigua) ★ ★

This walk, a tour of 17th-century Madrid, will consume two hours or more, and should be taken early in the morning or late in the afternoon when the churches are open.

Plaza Mayor

Subway: Puerta del Sol. Buses: 3, 25, 33, 39, M-4. From the Puerta del Sol, head west on C. Mayor for two blocks, taking the third right into the Pl. Mayor.

This huge—football field-sized—square plaza is famed for being one of the largest and most architecturally integrated plazas in Spain. Although Felipe II had commissioned his favorite architect Juan de Herrera—responsible for such neoclassical work as *El Escorial*—to design a grand square in the capital, it was not until the reign of his son that construction began, and then under the supervision of the architect Juan Gómez de Mora. Completed over the course of just two years, the plaza officially opened in 1620 with ceremonies to celebrate the canonization of five Spanish saints: Sta. Theresa of Ávila, St.

Ignatius of Loyola, St. Francis Zavier, St. Isidro, the male patron saint of Madrid, and St. Felipe Neri.

Throughout the 17th century and into the 19th, the plaza served as an arena for so many spectacles—plays, *autos-da-fé*, fireworks, royal marriage celebrations and bull-fights—that the owners of the houses on the plaza's perimeter were required to lend their balconies to royalty during festivities. In the 1970s vehicles were barred from the plaza and diverted underground or around it. Thanks to the absence of traffic, today the plaza is a lively place in summer filled with crowds attending concerts and festivals, or simply milling about. In winter it is a quiet, open space useful for strolls or shortcuts. Tables spring up on Sunday mornings for a stamp fair.

On the plaza's north side is the **Casa de Panaderia**, once the home of the bakers' guild, but rebuilt in 1672 after a fire. The king often sat on its second floor to observe spectacles in the plaza. Today, **Felipe III ★** sculpted by the Italian Giovanni de Bologna, sits on horseback in the center of the plaza. With his beatific grin and baton of office held so insouciantly, his starched collar looks quite out of place, but is of no matter to the perching sparrows who love him dearly.

In the southwest corner of the plaza an archway leads to steps down to the **C. de Cuchilleros ★**, a strip of old *mesones* and *tabernas*, including the famous *Botín*. If you were to turn north, the street would become Cava de San Miguel, with more such dining places. (*Cava* was the name given to moats outside the original walls of medieval Madrid.) Instead turn right to the Pl. del Conde de Barajas, then left along its near edge down C. Lanzas to the **Plaza Puerta Cerrada**, an old city gate with a stone cross in the center, and surrounded by buildings with vegetable murals.

Turn right again (not the acute right) from the near side of the plaza up C. San Justo. Pass the convex statue-filled front of **Iglesia San Miguel**, an 18th-century church of Ital-ian Baroque style. The interior is elegant with bountiful stuccowork and a lovely oval cu-pola. On the corner of the other side of the street is the **Casa de Juan de Vargas**, where Isidro, the male patron saint of Madrid, worked as a servant. Follow C. del Codo along the north side of the church. When it bends around the end of a large building, you reach the atmospheric **Plaza de la Villa ★ ★**.

The large street bordering the plaza is C. Mayor, which leads leftward in two blocks to the Palácio Real. The building just passed is the **Torre de Los Lujanes**, the former resi-dence of an ancient family of Madrid grandees, in which Francis I of France was held pris-oner in 1325. Of the original Gothic building one side-door remains, the first door facing the plaza. Down into the plaza, beside Los Lujanes, is the smaller **Hemerotooa**, Periodi-cals Library, an annex of the City Library, with a Gothic entrance and two Renaissance tombs inside the vestibule. In the center of the plaza a 19th century statue honors **Alvaro de Bazan**, one of the heroes of the naval victory over the Turks at Lepanto. The noble building across the way is the present **Ayuntamiento ★** (City Hall) designed in 1640 by de Mora, the architect of the Plaza Mayor, to serve as both the meeting place for the town council and a prison—certainly an interesting combination. The Museo Municipal inside is open Tues.–Fri. 9:30 a.m.–3 p.m.; weekends 10 a.m.–2 p.m.; admission: 450 ptas. for tours of tapestries, furniture and paintings of Madrid (☎ *522 57 32*).

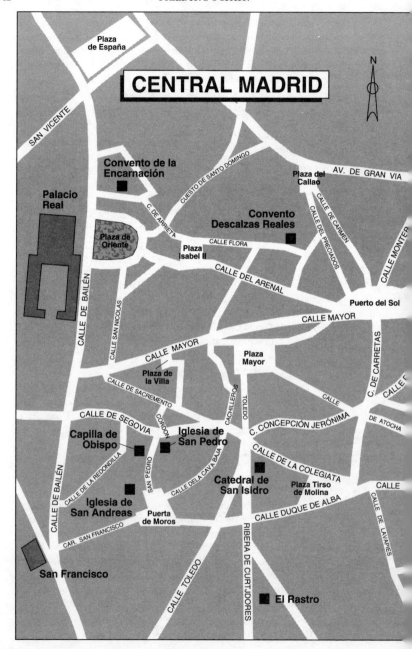

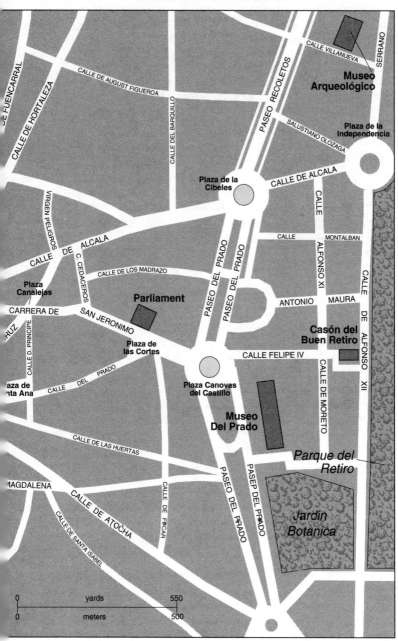

Calle Villanueva
Serrano
Calle de August Figueroa
Calle de Hortaleza
Calle de Fuencarral
Paseo Recoletos
Calle del Barquillo
Museo Arqueológico
Salustiano Olozaga
Plaza de la Independencia
Plaza de la Cibeles
Calle de Alcala
Calle de Alcala
Calle
Montalban
Alfonso XI
Calle
Virgen Peligros
C. Cedaceros
Calle de los Madrazo
Antonio
Maura
Plaza Canalejas
Parliament
Carrera de
San Jeronimo
Paseo del Prado
Paseo del Prado
Calle de Alfonso
Casón del Buen Retiro
Cruz
Calle D. Principe
Plaza de las Cortes
Calle Felipe IV
Calle de Moreto
aza de nta Ana
Calle del Prado
Plaza Canovas del Castillo
XII
Calle de las Huertas
Museo Del Prado
Parque del Retiro
Magdalena
Calle de Atocha
Calle de Ficar
Paseo del Prado
Pasep del Prado
Jardin Botanica
Calle de Santa Isabel

0	yards	550
0	meters	500

Walk down the plaza to the building at the end, connected by an archway to the Ayuntamiento, but pass along its side opposite the archway. This building, called the **Casa de Cisneros ★**, was erected in 1537 for the nephew of Jimenes de Cisneros, Isabella's chief minister who became the regent of Spain after her death. Now much restored, it retains one fine 16th-century window at the back overlooking the lovely Pl. del Cordón. Inside is an interesting collection of furniture and tapestries, although it is open only on Monday evenings from 5–7 p.m. Across the Pl. del Cordón carved cording surrounding the door of the large **Casa de los Alfaro** signifies that it once served as a bishopric.

Continue in the same direction through the plaza for a few feet along C. Cordón. Turn down the steps on the right just after the plaza. This lets you into the **Plazuela de San Javier ★**, an atmospheric corner of old Madrid.

Return to the C. Cordón and continue as it bends left to cross the C. de Segovia. On the other side stands the **Iglesia San Pedro el Vieja ★** with a soaring 14th-century Mudejar (i.e., built by Moors) tower. Inside is an exuberant retable by José Churriguera.

Off the right side of the church, as you face it, runs the C. del Principe Anglona. Follow it one block to the Pl. de la Paja, turn left down the side of the plaza to the 16th-century **Capilla del Obispo ★** (Chapel of the Bishop) at the end. Inside, illustrating the life of Christ, is a fine polychromed wood altarpiece by a talented pupil of Berruguette. In the south wall lies an elegant Plateresque tomb for the Archbishop of Plasencia. Carved by the same hand, the tombs of the archbishop's parents, who paid for the chapel, flank the altar.

Behind the chapel building is another religious structure. The 15th-century **Capilla de San Andrés** was reconstructed in the 18th century to house the remains of Saint Isidro, the male patron saint of Madrid. St. Isidro's remains, however, have been moved to Cathedral San Isidro discussed below.

Return past the Capilla Obispo up the west side of the charming Pl. de la Paja by the elegant restaurants, then turn left down C. Redondilla. At its end in two blocks you come into a large street named C. de Bailén. Head slightly leftward (not a hard left onto C. Don Pedro) to the huge neoclassical 18th-century church of **San Francisco el Grand ★★**, a project of Carlos III.

Inside, behind a facade by the architect Sabatini, designer of the Palácio Real, under one of the largest domes in the world (over 100 feet in diameter), are 15th-century choirstalls at the east end taken from El Paular monastery north of Madrid. In the first chapel on the left is a masterwork by the young Goya, *Sermon of San Bernardino to the King of Arágon*. Request that it be lit for you. The dome and chapel ceilings were frescoed by Bayeu, Goya's father-in-law, and others.

After viewing the inside, head up the Carrera San Francisco which leads away from the front of the church. Pass through Pl. Puerta de Moros directly across to Cava Alta, observing the front of Capilla San André along the way. When Cava Alta forks, go right, then take the first left which leads into C. Toledo. Across the street you see the **Catedral San Isidro** with massive 17th-century facade and twin towers. The inside is not special (it was gutted in 1936), except for containing the remains of St. Isidro in a silver shrine. This is only a temporary Cathedral, serving until the Cathedral de la Almundena beside the Palácio Real (see "Walking Tour #2") is completed.

(If you turn right onto C. Estudios, instead of left onto C. Toledo, it will lead, in two blocks, to the site of **el Rastro**, the famed Sunday- and holiday-morning flea market (open from dawn until 2 p.m.)

Walk north on bustling C. Toledo past San Isidro to take the second left onto C. Concepción Jerónima, then the first right onto C. Conde de Romanones. In one block you enter the Pl. de la Provincia dominated by the red **Ministerio de Asuntos Exteriores ★** (Ministry of Foreign Affairs). Originally built in 1629 by de Moro, the architect who constructed the Pl. Mayor, it is a dignified edifice with an elegant 17th-century cloister inside. The guard may let you peek in. Here newly-arrived foreign diplomats pull up in 17th-century carriages drawn by plumed horses to present their papers. The leftward street out of the plaza returns you to the Pl. Mayor.

2. Puerta del Sol, Descalzas Convent, Convento de la Encarnación and Pl. de Oriente ★ ★

This walk should consume less than two hours, including tours of the two convents and their art. It is best done in the morning when the convents remain open longer than they do in the afternoon. Check hours and days above. The walk leaves you in front of the Palácio Real which, if you want to include it in the tour, would add two or three hours more (and run into the midafternoon closings), although it could also easily be included after a pause for lunch. See the description of the Palácio above to decide.

Puerto del Sol ★

Subway: Puerta del Sol. Buses: 3, 25, 33, 39, M-4.

In every sense this plaza is the hub of Madrid, even of the country. Crowds bustle at any hour of the day or night.

North across the oval plaza is a small bronze statue of a bear and a strawberry plant, the emblem of the city of Madrid. East, at the entrance of C. Alcalá, is the imposing Treasury Building, the former royal Customs House. The tower with the clock, Madrid's Big Ben, was added to the former 17th-century post office, now reconstructed as the Gobernación (Ministry of the Interior). In front, on the sidewalk, a bronze plaque marks kilometer zero from which all distances in Spain are measured.

Shops of a lower caliber do their best to attract. But at the east end of the plaza, at #6, a called **La Pajareta** must be seen. It has been selling caramels here for over 150 years. A few doors east at #12, a store called **Casa de Diego** displays an astonishing number of umbrellas along with some fans. The window display is for tourists, but antique versions are stored away inside.

Head to the west end of the plaza and take the left of the forking streets there onto C. Arenal. Take the next left, C. Victoria, walking toward the el Corte Inglés department store. But just before you reach it, take the first right onto C. de San Martin. In a short block you enter the small Pl. de las Descalzas, for you just walked the width of the convent on your right.

See the description and hours of the Convento de las Descalzas ★★ *under "Museums" above.*

Return to C. Arenal and continue west (right) for two short blocks to enter the Pl. Isabela II. Across the plaza is the back of the Teatro Real, Madrid's opera house. Walking toward the plaza and right along the theater's back, you come to C. Arrieta which leads in one short block to the Convento de la Encarnación on the left.

See the description and hours of the Convento de la Encarnación ★ *under "Museums" above.*

The street that fronts the Pl. de la Encarnación leading northeast is C. de la Bola, on which a bistro called **La Bola** *at number 5 offers moderately-priced meals, if you are feeling hungry.*

Head north along the side of the convent to C. Toria. At the end of the street you face an 18th-century mansion once owned by Godoy, the Prime Minister of Carlos IV and lover of his queen Maria Louisa. Today, as the **Museo del Pueblo Español** ★, it houses an interesting collection of traditional costumes from all regions of Spain. Looking right up the street you see the **Palácio del Senado** (Senate Building). Formerly an Augustinian convent, it was converted to its present use at the beginning of this century. The Palácio seems small until one recalls that the Senate is a smaller group than the Parliament, which indeed meets in a larger building.

From here, if you have the energy for a walk of about a mile, you can head left to C. Bailén, then right as it leads over a pedestrian overpass, to view the monumental vista of the **Pl. de España**. *Today it is rather seedy, but statues commemorate Cervantes and his famous characters Don Quixote and Sancho Panza. Continue to your left into Parque del Oeste for greenery and a look at the complete Egyptian* **Temple of Debod** ★, *from Roman times. It was brought in pieces from Egypt when threatened by the rising waters of the Aswan Dam.*

From the Senate head due south through the **Pl. de Oriente** to pass the front of the **Teatro Real**, inaugurated in 1850. It is appropriately luxurious inside. This plaza owes a debt to Joseph Buonaparte, Napoleon's brother, who ordered the buildings crowding the palace to be razed. In the center of the plaza is a fine statue by the sculptor Montañés of the art collector Felipe IV, copied from a Velázquez portrait. The statue seems more heroic than what the truer eye of Velázquez permitted in his version, but the king never looked finer.

Across the street is the huge **Palácio Real** ★★★. *For a description see "Museums" above.*

3. Museo Arqueológico Nacional and Shopping: Barrio Salamanca ★★

This walk takes you to the Archaeological Museum to view superb Iberian, Visigoth and Moorish works, then through the Barrio Salamanca, Madrid's most fashionable shopping area. Expect to spend half a day—or more, if a true shopper.

The **Archaeological Museum** ★★★ *is the rear half of the large Biblioteca Nacional. The entrance is on C. Serrano. By subway, from the Colón station*

*head east across the Pl. Colón and you will see the front of the Biblioteca to
your right. From the Serrano station head south along C. Serrano for one
block to reach the museum.*

*See the description and hours of the Museo Arqueológico under "Muse-
ums," above.*

Barrio Salamanca ★ ★ North of the museum C. Serrano transforms into one of the
main shopping streets in Madrid. One block north (left when exiting the museum), C.
Goya crosses Serrano. The two streets form one corner of an area called the Barrio Salamanca, bordered by Serrano on the west, Goya on the south, Conde de Pañalver 10 short
blocks east, and José Ortega four blocks north. The Barrio Salamanca contains most of
the fine department, clothing, couture, antique, art and furniture shops of Madrid, with
the western half, where you're standing, the most interesting.

This area, one of the first urban developments, is named for the Marqués de Salamanca
who, in 1865, laid out this grid of streets which, at the time, extended beyond the walls
of Madrid.

Here is the layout of the Barrio. C. Serrano runs north-south. A short block east and
parallel to Serrano is C. Claudio Coello. Smaller streets run between. The first two after
Goya, Calles Hermosille and Ayala, are the most interesting. Wander as you will. Personal
favorites follow:

Plaza de Colon and the Biblioteca Nacional are worth a visit.

*Beginning a few blocks south of Goya on C. Serrano and walking north on
C. Serrano, you come to:*

#7: Farrutx. Fine designer shoes, its own brand and others.

#26: Loewe. The very finest in leather clothing, luggage and accessories, with prices to
match. Many branches throughout Spain and the U.S.

#27: Carrera Y Carrera. Fine jewelry and watches.

#28: Orlan. Leather bags, wallets and accessories, moderately priced.

#34: Afredo Caral. Designer fashion, superbly tailored.

> *C. de Jorge Juan is the street that crosses Serrano south of C. Goya. A couple of shops stand out on this street.*

#10: Sybilla. Off an unmarked courtyard is this impressive Spanish designer's boutique with prices that are fair for the quality.

#13: Gaitan. Handmade shoes and boots.

> *On C. Goya, a couple of blocks east, are two leather places worth a look.*

#68: Idee. Inexpensive shoes.

#75: Sara Navarro. A high fashion designer of leather clothes, shoes and bags.

> *Crossing C. Goya and continuing north on Serrano:*

#44: Rossy. Good costume jewelry.

#45: La Casa de las Maletas. Well crafted luggage at reasonable prices.

#47: Galarias Preciados. The Barrio Salamanca branch of this Spanish department store chain.

#48: Del Pino. Expensive costume jewelry.

#56: Talleries de Arte Granada. Fine art and furniture.

#56: Santa. Superb chocolate in a beautiful store.

#57: Cartier.

#59: Nesofsky. Fine furniture.

#63: Gonzapur Peleteria. Leather clothing at moderate prices.

#66: Gutierrez. Good shoes at reasonable prices.

#66: Breton. Elegant men's clothing.

#68: Los Pequeno Suizos. Good values in shoes and leathergoods.

#76: Manuel Herrero. Stylish leather.

#78: Cacherel.

#84: Fendi.

#92: Don Carlos. Boutique for the latest young styles.

#96-8: Adolfo Dominquez. Men's clothing by the designer who gave Don Johnson his look on *Miami Vice*.

Serrano crosses C. de José Ortega Y Gasset where, by going east, you can find **Vuitton** and **Courreges**, both at number 17.

4. Puerta del Sol, Pl. Santa Ana, The Cortes, and Pl. de Cibeles ★

This walk is light on historical buildings, but ambles through quaint streets and by shops lost in time, then lets into a charming square. Past the Senate building grand vistas open to the Paseo del Prado and the Pl. Cibeles. This is area the Madrid we think of when we are away. Unless you choose to view the art in the Real Academia de Bellas Artes, the walk can be made at a time when museums are closed.

Start in the Puerta del Sol ★. For directions and a description, see "Walking Tour #2."

At the east end of the plaza two major streets fork and head further east. Take the right one, Carrera de San Jerónimo. At San Jerónimo 2, note the shop called **Gil, Successor to Antolin Quevero**. The window is a classic—cheap fans mixed with the cheapest furs and Sevillano costumes. Better material is inside, but not by much.

At number eight you pass **Lhardy**, all mahogany wood and polished brass, here for over 150 years. If you can pass the delectable window display of food without entering, you have more will power than most. Incidentally, sandwiches and tapas will not break your budget, but the dinning room in the back is expensive.

At number nine elegance continues with **Villanueva Y Laisca**, outside all marble and brass, inside refinement. They sell small silver replicas, fine jewelry, china and war medals. The shop is on the corner of Pl. de Canalejas. Turn right around the plaza to look in an amazing shop called **La Violeta**. Yes, that is all that is sold from this exquisite stall—candied violets.

Continue across the plaza on C. de San Jerónimo. At number 11 is **Gutierrez** for designer shoes. At number 30, a block later, is **Casa Miró**, another candy store over a century and a half old, this one specializing in hard candy. At 34 is **Deogracias** for cabinets decorated to Spanish tastes, which is not everyone's.

As the street gradually widens, its name changes to Pl. de las Cortes. The **Cortes**, Spain's Parliament, is housed on the north side of the plaza in a gray building with steps leading up to Corinthian columns. The building was constructed in 1859, and its bronze lions were cast from cannons captured in Morocco in 1850.

Diagonally across from the Córtez is the **Palace Hotel**, one of Madrid's finest. On the street floor of the hotel, a spacious interior courtyard is surrounded by shops and contains an airy cafe at its center for relaxing.

Continue east to the end of C. de San Jerónimo and cross to the other side. At 48, opposite the Palace Hotel, you reach **Abelardo Linares**, a mansion filled with some of the best antiques in Spain. In a few more feet enter the Pl. Canovas del Castillo, with its Neptune fountain and views up and down the wide Paseo del Prado. Looking south is the **Museo del Prado**; to the north, the distant, lovely fountain of the Pl. de Cibeles, completed at the end of the 18th century and festive when lit at night.

Retrace your steps back to the small park opposite the Cortes building in which is located a once-influential private club, the **Ateneo de Madrid**. Here a small street called C. del Prado forks around the park. Numerous small and interesting antique shops line this street, a slice of old Madrid. So continue to follow it west. In five blocks the narrow street opens onto the green Pl. de Santa Ana, bounded on one side by the old Hotel Victoria. At the near end and left is the **Teatro Español**, whose productions are considered the best in Madrid.

Head north past the east side of the plaza along C. Principe. In one block you return to the Pl. Canalejas, where a left turn on C de San Jerónimo brings you back to the Puerta del Sol. To continue the tour, cross the plaza and head north on the large street called Sevilla, which, one block later, brings you to C. Alcalá, divided by a center strip.

At number 13, back west towards the Plaza del Sol, is the **Real Academia de Bellas Artes de San Fernando** ★ in a late 19th-century building designed by Villanueva, who planned the Museo del Prado. For a description of the museum and hours, see "Museums" above. Turning around to go east on C. Alcalá we pass number 15, the **Casino de Madrid**, which is not a casino at all but a private club. The late 17th-century church on the corner of C. Sevilla, **Las Calatravas**, contains an interesting retable.

Farther along, the street widens as Gran Via joins it from the northwest. Gran Via was once a fine shopping street, but now tourists visit mainly for the huge McDonald's restaurant and for the telephone office opposite that stays open day and night.

Continue past the imposing Banco de España building on the south side of Alcalá, to arrive, two blocks later, at the **Ministry of Defense**, set back in its park. The ministry occupies a former palace of Godoy, prime minister under Carlos IV and great and good friend of Carlos's queen, Maria Louisa. The fountain in the **Pl. de Cibeles** ★ ★, which you reach next, dates from 1780.

The fountain is as lovely as the splendid vistas stretching from it down Paseo del Prado to the Museum, and up Paseo de Recoletos, its continuation. Across the plaza and south is the pretentious Main Post Office, the Palácio de Comunicaciónes, built at the beginning of this century.

5. Parque del Retiro ★

This walk is just a stroll in the park, though summertime adds mimes, clowns, jugglers and assorted other entertainments.

The huge park, encompassing more than 300 acres, was originally a royal hunting preserve that contained a palace for royal vacations. Today, dotted with exposition buildings, it is part careful landscaping and part wild bushes and trees. In all, it is a restful place to amble. Note: the park closes at dusk, for it is not safe after dark.

If flora appeal, the **Jardín Botánico** waits at the south end of the Prado. In season, the roses are spectacular. *(Open daily 10 a.m. to 8 p.m.; admission: 80 ptas.)*

Start at the **Museo del Prado** (directions in the "Museums" section above). Walk due east from its northern end, past the Casón Del Buen Retiro annex, and into the park. A map at this entrance shows where sights are located, but directions hardly matter if your intent is to wander.

Straight ahead in a quarter mile is the **Palácio Velázquez**, an exhibition center. To its right is the **Palácio de Cristal**, named for its glass ceiling. To its north a lake for rowing fronts a monument to Alfonso XII, in pre-World War II monumental style. The statues of monarchs you pass were those made for the Palácio Real, but considered too heavy for its roof.

Where to Stay

Madrid is an expensive place to sleep whose few inexpensive rooms go quickly. Visitors generally have to increase their budget in this city. While many factors go into choosing a hotel, proximity to the center is an asset because it permits walking to most sights and restaurants. With literally hundreds of hotels to choose from, there is little reason to stay anywhere but in the old town, near it, or in the Barrio Salamanca where Madrid's elegant shops gather. A select list covering each price range follows.

Very Expensive ($200+)

Ritz   **Deluxe ★ ★ ★ ★ ★**

Pl. de la Lealtad, 5 (1 block north of the Prado), ☎ *521 28 57, FAX 532 87 76, Telex 43986, in the U.S., 800-223-6800.*

King Alfonso XIII personally oversaw the construction of the Ritz in 1910 because he considered no existing hotel suitable for his wedding guests. César Ritz himself, the hotelier whose name connotes luxury, received the commission. Here you actually feel like a guest of royalty, with the stiffness that implies (ties must be worn in the bar and eating areas), but with service that is noble. No two pastel-colored rooms are the same, but all are carpeted with rugs handmade in the Royal Tapestry Factory and decked out in embroidered linen, fresh flowers and dangling chandeliers. Everything is lux in a *Belle Époque* style harkening to a time when the rich certainly knew how to live. Naturally the Ritz' location is special—on its own park across from the Pl. Canovas del Castillo, the Palace Hotel and the Córtez building. From it you can hit the Museo del Prado with a stone, if so inclined. Such elegance costs a king's ransom, so estimate almost $400 a night for two. But even these prices aren't enough to keep the "squares" away, as this is one of the most heavily booked hotels in Madrid. Reserve far ahead and start saving, if you want a room. *127 rooms, plus 29 suites.*

Palace   **Deluxe ★ ★ ★ ★**

Pl. de las Cortes, 7 (1 block north of the Prado), ☎ *429 75 51, FAX 429 82 66, Telex 23903.*

Anywhere else this would be the most elegant hotel in town, but Madrid has the Ritz too. The lobby's all-glass cupola sets the stage for its *Belle Époque* decor and trompe l'oeil paintings. However, while the Palace's public rooms are sumptuous, its bedrooms are ordinary and so numerous that, despite superb management, the special attention for each guest these prices call for is sometimes labored. Still, it has that entrance, the location is as good as the Ritz and its charges are about a quarter less—though the Palace is about that much less grand. *436 rooms, plus 20 suites.*

Villa Real   **1st-class ★ ★ ★ ★**

Pl. de las Cortes, 10 (1 block north of the Prado), ☎ *420 37 67, FAX 420 25 47, Telex 44 600.*

Although designed to look 19th-century, these lovely accommodations actually opened in 1989. Unlike so many fancy hotels that emphasize their lobby, this one concentrates on its rooms. Everything about this hotel speaks of class and good taste. The bedrooms are more comfortable and attractive than those at the Palace, and they cost a few pesetas less, at a location that is exactly as convenient. Although it certainly isn't cheap, the Villa Real gives super value for your money. *96 rooms, plus 19 suites.*

Santo Mauro   **Deluxe ★ ★ ★ ★**

C. Zurbano, 36 (a block north of Pl. de Becerra, 1 mile west of the Pl. Cibeles), ☎ *319 69 00, FAX 308 54 77.*

This is as distinguished a hotel as anyone is likely to find anywhere. For starters, it is lodged around a garden in a small former palace that was restored lovingly, then decorated by the finest designers. Bedrooms contain every convenience, and the restaurant is world-class. Furthermore, it is small enough for intimacy and exquisite individual service. There are two drawbacks, however. It is located in the elegant Almagro quarter which is a mile and a half from the old town, and it charges almost as much as the Ritz. Of course the first problem is easily solved by a taxi, and the second by money. *33 rooms, plus four suites.*

Villa Magna   Deluxe ★ ★ ★

Paseo Castellana, 22, ☎ *578 20 00, FAX 575 31 58, Telex 229 14.*
Managed by the Hyatt chain, everything a modern hotel can provide is offered by the Villa Magna, but the elegance and atmosphere of an earlier era cannot be manufactured. For this reason it takes fourth place to the Villa Real and to the Ritz and Santo Mauro, although it has the nerve to outcharge them all. What it does offer is a good location for shopping in the Barrio Salamanca and ultra-modern comfort tempered with tasteful decor. However, the Hotel Wellington, described next, offers a similar location for a third less and four nights in the Serrano, can be had for the cost of one at the Villa Magna. *182 rooms.*

Wellington   Deluxe ★ ★

Velázquez, , 258 rooms. ☎ *575 44 00, FAX 576 41 64, Telex 22700.*
This aristocrat is well located for Barrio Salamanca shopping, yet close to the Prado and the old town. The owner is a bullfight aficionado so matadors crowd here during the season. The establishment has just been renovated, but retains an old-world feel *182 rooms..*

Expensive ($100–$199)

G. H. Reina Victoria   1st-class ★ ★ ★

Pl. Santa Ana, 14 (just north of C. de San Jerónimo, two blocks west of P. del Prado), ☎ *531 45 00, FAX 522 03 07, Telex 475 47.*

The eccentric facade of this Madrid institution has been declared a historic monument. Even better, it sits beside the quiet Plaza Ana park, yet is smack in the center of town. Manolete regularly stayed here as did Hemmingway and you can too at prices that are fair for Madrid. Recently it was taken over by the Tryp chain which improved the service and modernized it throughout. Comfortable, rather than fancy, rooms are bright and some include balconies overlooking the park. Now this is the place to stay in the old town (along with the Hotel Suecia, below). *195 rooms, plus six suites.*

Suecia   1st-class ★ ★

Marqués de Casa Ribera, 4 (Take the street going north along the west side of the Palácio Cortes on Carrera San Jerónimo. At the back, jag west, then north again, into the little square), ☎ *531 69 00, FAX 521 71 41, Telex 22313.*
The location is almost as good as that of the Victoria—in the old town, yet on a tiny quiet square. But the Suecia is new and glistening, compared to the Victoria's seasoned personality, so the choice is clear. In this category the Suecia's cleanliness and service can not be bettered in Madrid. Our only complaint is a certain coldness about the place. *119 rooms, plus six suites.*

Tryp Ambassador 1st-class ★ ★ ★

Cuesta de Santo Domingo, 5 (near the Palácio Real, 1 block north of the Opera), ☎ *541 67 00, FAX 559 10 40, Telex 49538.*

This is a most pleasant addition to Madrid's hotel inventory. As its grand stairway attests, the Ambassador is a renovated former palace from the 19th century. Graciously sized bedrooms all include separate sitting areas and are pleasantly accessorized. Businesspeople love it. The location is quiet and convenient to sights, somewhat less so for tapas-hopping. *163 rooms, plus 18 suites.*

Tryp Fenix 1st-class ★ ★ ★

Hermosilla, 2 (one block north of the Pl. Colón), ☎ *431 67 00, FAX 576 06 61.*

The location is convenient for shopping in the Barrio Salamanca, for the Archaeological Museum and a pleasant mile walk to the Prado and old town. This modern hotel gleams of marble and glass; rooms are large and decorated in muted tones. *213 rooms.*

Alcalá 1st-class ★ ★

Alcalá, 66, ☎ *435 10 60, FAX 435 11 05, Telex 48094.*

This is a modern, softly lit, executive-type hotel, located near the northeast corner of El Retiro Park. It is convenient to shopping in the Barrio Salamanca, but a bit of a walk to the Prado and old town. While walking, you can think about the prices that barely crest the expensive line. *153 rooms.*

Arosa 1st-class ★ ★

De la Salud, 21, ☎ *532 16 00, FAX 531 31 27, Telex 43618.*

Located just south of noisy Gran Via and two blocks west of the large C. Montera, this hotel offers a quiet atmosphere, nicely decorated rooms and an attentive staff for prices that barely enter the expensive range. *139 rooms.*

El Prado 2nd-class ★ ★

Prado, 11 (3 blocks along this quaint street that runs out of the Pl. Cortez), ☎ *369 02 34, FAX 429 28 29.*

Sitting on a little antique-shop street in the old town, the location of this hotel is superb for sights, tapas-hopping and restaurants. Doubly glazed windows keep the ample rooms quiet, and prices just rise into the moderate range. *47 rooms.*

Moderate ($50–$99)

Serrano 2nd-class ★ ★ ★

Marqués de Villamejor, 8 (around the corner from Serrano, the main shopping street of the Barrio Salamanca, and half way between Pl. Colón and the park), ☎ *435 52 00, FAX 435 48 49.*

We consider the intimate Serrano about the best moderately priced hotel in expensive Madrid. It is tastefully decorated, all the rooms include TVs and are nicely appointed, and the walk to the Prado passes some of Madrid's nicest stores. *30 rooms, plus 4 suites*

Regina 2nd-class ★ ★

Alcalá, 19 (one long block along this main street running west from the Pl. del Sol), ☎ *521 47 25, FAX 521 47 25, Telex 27500.*

Costing only a little more than the Inglés and Paris described in this section, the Regina's location is closer to the Puerta del Sol than theirs, while its rooms stand a clear level above them. *142 rooms.*

Don Diego
HR2nd-class ★

Velázquez, 45 (on one of the nice shopping streets of the Barrio Salamanca, four blocks north of the Parque del Buen Retiro), ☎ *435 07 60, FAX 431 42 63.*

The location is more convenient for shopping than the very expensive choices above, yet closer to the Prado and old town. This is an attractive place that provides pleasant balconies with some of the rooms. At such prices in this ritzy location, don't expect a TV in your room, however. *58 rooms.*

Carlos V
2nd-class ★

Maestro Vitoria, 5 (three short blocks north of the Pl. del Sol), ☎ *531 41 00, FAX 531 37 61.*

Located conveniently near the El Corte Inglés department store and the Convento de las Descalzas Reales, this venerable hotel counts as a bargain in expensive Madrid. Rooms are sufficiently comfortable and include satellite-TV, but noise can be a problem. Managed by Best-Western. *67 rooms.*

Inglés
3rd-class ★

Echegaray, 8, ☎ *429 65 51, FAX 420 24 23.*

Although its location is wonderful, (just off C. Prado east of Puerta del Sol, near the Prado and the Pl. Santa Ana in the old town), and despite its offering parking (which is unusual for the area), service at the Inglés is lackadaisical, uninterested and even rude. Its rooms, most of which are not air-conditioned, are strangely shaped and gloomy. Still, for the location and price, they may be worth putting up with. *58 rooms.*

París
2nd-class ★

Alcalá, 2, ☎ *521 64 96, Telex 43448.*

Although conveniently located at the east edge of the Puerta del Sol, this is a dowager of a hotel. As with the Inglés, its rooms are eccentric in shape and decor. The idea that a hotel room should be bright and cheery, yet restful, seems to have faded along with this hotel's freshness. *120 rooms.*

Inexpensive (Less than $50)

Francisco I
Hs2nd-class ★ ★ ★

Arenal, 15 (just west of the Pl. del Sol), ☎ *548 43 14, FAX 531 01 88.*

As far as we can tell this is the only genuine hotel in Madrid that charges such low prices. It is modern, clean, recently redecorated, has air conditioning in most rooms and provides hotel services, all in a fine location. Sound too good to be true? Only slightly. In truth the prices climb into the $60 range in high summer, only sinking into the truly inexpensive the rest of the year. *58 rooms.*

Hotel Residencia Lisboa
Hs2nd-class ★ ★

C. Ventura de la Vega, 17 (just off C. del Prado, near the Victoria in Pl. Santa Ana), ☎ *429 98 94.*

No frills, just a room to sleep in, but the rooms are larger than the low price would indicate and boast new private bathrooms. The location is superb. True, the hallways and public areas are low-wattage and the rooms sparsely and unfashionably furnished but, for the price, it is hard to do better in Madrid—and they accept credit cards. *23 rooms.*

Residencia Santander   **R2nd-class ★**

Echegaray, 1 (around the corner from C. San Jerónimo, four short blocks east of the Pl. del Sol), ☎ *429 95 51.*

The location is prime, except for street noise, but don't expect anything fancy at this price. All rooms have private baths but are sparsely furnished, although, surprisingly, some have TVs. No credit cards are accepted. *38 rooms.*

Mónaco   **R3rd-class ★**

Barbieri, 5 (Go west on Gran Via, after its start at the intersection with C. Alcalá, then take a right onto C. Hugo in one block. After two very short blocks on Hugo, jag left on C. Infantas, and take the immediate right onto Barbieri), ☎ *522 46 30, FAX 521 16 01.*

This one is a bit out of the way, located slightly north of Gran Via. The hotel is decorated in bright red, giving it an Egyptian look (or worse). Rooms are small, but include private baths. This neighborhood is replete with disco clubs and its strollers seem less amicable than those on the other side of Gran Via. *32 rooms.*

Youth Hostels

Albergue Juvenil Santa Cruz de Marcenado

C. Santa Cruz de Marcenado, 28, Madrid 28003 (from the Arguelles metro stop walk north on C. Princesa to take a left down C. Serrano Jover, then a right onto Marcenado), ☎ *547 45 32.*

Near the university, only a twenty minute walk from the Palácio Real, the location is good for a youth hostel in a large city. And the accommodations are bright and clean. Reception closes at 10:30 p.m. but the curfew is 1:30 a.m. Prices are a reasonable 650 ptas. However, a minimum stay of three days is required and reservations should be made a month in advance.

Albergue Juvenil Richard Shirrman

Casa de Campo, Madrid 28003 (in the park behind the Palácio Real. From the Lado metro stop go downhill and left, then look for signs directing a half mile walk, or, better, call and they will pick you up.), ☎ *463 56 99.*

The good news is that this one is in a park near a lake; the bad news is that the park is not safe to walk in at night. Clean and 650 ptas. is not a bad combo, though.

For a tight budget, numerous pensiones for $40 and under collect on the upper floors of **C. del Prado** and the small streets that lead away from it. A number of short streets in the area house as many as 10 separate pensiones. For example, at C. Echegaray, 5 (across from the hotel Iglés, noted above), there are four pensiones on various floors, each of which is very inexpensive and may suit.

Your range of choices can be expanded greatly if the requirement of sleeping within walking-distance of the sights is dropped. Near the southern Legazpi subway station, the **Hostal Auto ★** at *Paseo de la Chopera, 69* (☎ *539 66 00; FAX 530 67 03*) is a good moderate-inexpensive choice with parking. Near the northwestern Arguelles station, the **Hotel Tirol ★ ★** on *Marqués de Urquijo, 4* (☎ *548 19 00*) is a fine moderately-priced pick.

In a pinch the centrally-located and moderately-priced **Moderno** on *Arenal, 2* (☎ *531 09 00; FAX 531 35 50*), just past the west end of the Puerta del sol, will serve. Also centrally located but low-priced is the basic **Hostal Cervantes** with 12 rooms on the second floor at *C. Cervantes, 34* (☎ *429 27 45*). *Gran Via, 44* incorporates a number of small pensions, such as **Continental** with 29 rooms on the third and fourth floors (☎ *521 46 40*). Similar is the **Filo** at *Pl. del Angel, 15*, the same square as the Hotel Victoria, on the second floor (☎ *522 40 56*).

Where to Eat

You can eat in Madrid for whatever you care to spend. Of course the food generally improves as the prices rise. Specialties of Madrid are seafood and roast pig and lamb. Below we list our favorites in various price categories, but you can also do as the Madrileños do—stroll C. del Prado (which heads west from the Pl. de las Cortes) and amble up and down its adjacent side streets until a place strikes your fancy for tapas at the bar. Later, if you like what you nibbled, you can move back into the dining room for a meal.

Very Expensive ($50+)

Zalacaín

> *Álvarez de Baena, 4 (north, near the Museo de Cientas Naturales),* ☎ *561 48 40, FAX 561 47 32.*
> *Closed Saturday lunch, Sunday, Holy Week and August.*
> By all standards Zalacaín is the finest restaurant in Madrid, if not all of Spain. Even the Francophilic Michelin *Red Guide* awards this restaurant its highest rating. The decor is muted, elegant and comfortable, like a Velázquez painting, to focus all attention on what is arranged on your porcelain plate. And what lays on it will both look and taste sublime. Try the ravioli with setas, truffles and fois gras, or *bacalao tellagom*, or duck. Or for a sampling of the best, try the *Menu Degustacion*. This is a restaurant for serious connoisseurs who don't mind spending $100 each to enjoy an exquisite dining experience. Reservations weeks in advance are essential. Credit Cards: A, V, D.

El Amparo

> *Puigcerdá, 8 (one block east of Serrano, four blocks north of the park),* ☎ *431 64 58, FAX 575 54 91.*
> *Closed Sunday and August.*
> Catch Madrid's rising star, and look out Zalacaín! While Amparo can't match that venerable leader yet in style, it substitutes an attractive combination of rough wood amid high-tech. What is truly exceptional about Amparo, however, is the inventiveness of its Basque chef, who, breaking tradition, is a woman. Consider cold salmon with tomato sorbet, or rolled lobsters with soybean sauce. Of course, novelty without good taste is no asset, but there is discriminating sensibility to spare at this "refuge." Reservations are a must. Credit Cards: A, V, M.

Expensive ($30+)

La Trainera

> *Lagasca, 60 (two blocks east of Serrano, six short blocks north of the park),* ☎ *576 05 75, FAX 575 47 17.*
> *Closed Sunday and August.*
> Forget elegance and gentile service and think about the freshest possible fish. Here it is, served in a nest of little rooms decorated with utensils of the sea. Most of the shellfish is sold by weight and eaten as appetizers by the Spanish. You can make

them do for dinner or order selections from the menu, such as a delicious hake *gallega* style or salmonete (mullet) any old way. But do yourself a favor and start with the heavenly cream soup. This restaurant is very popular; reserve. Credit Cards: A, V, M.

El Pescador ★★★
José Ortega y Gasset, 75 (the northern limit of the Barrio Salamanca), ☎ *402 19 90.*
Closed Sunday, and August.
Seafood is expensive and this, or La Trainera above, is the best seafood restaurant in town, so its prices must be considered fair. The decor is seafaring, with checkered tablecloths, and the food incredibly fresh. The owner is from Galicia where they know how to cook a fish. Try the *crema tres eles* (if you have never tried eels) or the *salpicon*. Lobster, though delicious, will lift you into the very expensive category. Reservations are advised. Credit Cards: V, M.

El Cenador del Prado ★★★
C. del Prado, 4 (just off Pl. del las Cortes), ☎ *429 15 61.*
Closed Saturday lunch, Sunday, and the second half of August.
This restaurant continually improves, and is now as elegant as any in the country. Appropriately light and airy as a garden patio, this is the home of Spanish *cocina nueva*, with a menu that changes as frequently as the chef receives inspiration. If *patatas a la importancia con almajas* (potatoes with clams) is on the menu, by all means give it strong consideration. The banana ice cream is equally outstanding. Reservations are a must. Credit Cards: A, V, D, M.

Gure-Etxea ★★★
Pl. de la Paja, 12 (this pleasant plaza lies two blocks east of C. Bailén, running beside the Palace, and three blocks south of the Palace), ☎ *365 61 49.*
Closed Sunday, Holy Week and August.
The Spanish agree that Basque cooking is the best in Spain, and Gure-Etxea is our favorite Basque restaurant in Madrid, after Zalacaín of course. Here the cooking is unmodified by nouvelle flair. Two styles of dining are available in this former convent—elegance on the first floor, or exposed brick downstairs. The service is impeccable and the food first rate. Don't miss *porrusalda*, leek and potato soup with cod. Monkfish (rape) in green sauce and codfish (bacalao) with pil pil sauce are delectable. Lunchtime always includes some money-saving option that permits giving the restaurant a try without committing the entire dining budget. Reservations are advised. Credit Cards: A, D, M, V.

Café de Oriente ★★
Pl. de Oriente, 2 (facing the Palácio Real), ☎ *241 39 74.*
Closed Saturday for lunch, Sunday, and August.
The decor is glittering *Belle Époque*, the building and brick ovens date to the 18th century and views of the palace from a terrace chair (aperitif in hand) is spectacular at night. Two dining rooms wait in the back, one for Castilian food, exceptionally prepared, the other for more elegant and, to our tastes, too expensive Basque cooking. Credit Cards: A, D, M, V.

Saint James ★★
C. Juan Bravo, 26 (two blocks north of Ortega y Gasset at the north end of the Barrio Salamanca), ☎ *575 00 69.*

Closed Sunday.

If you crave paella, it is available at many Madrid restaurants, but this is where they do it best, along with many other Valencian rice dishes. The garden in summer is inviting, though the dining room is olive drab. Prices touch the low end of expensive. Reservations are required. Credit Cards: A.

El Mentidero de la Villa   ★ ★

Santo Tomé, 6 (two blocks north and three west of the Pl. de Cibeles), ☎ *308 12 85, FAX 318 87 92.*
Closed Saturday lunch, Sunday, holidays and the second week of August.

This is the trendy restaurant of the moment. The chef is Japanese and inventive with cold dishes and salads. Despite its effort to be au currant, the staff is friendly and the airy postmodern decor is restful. In our opinion, inventiveness has gotten a bit out of hand here, although traditional chocolate mousse is divine. Reservations are advised at this much touted place. Credit Cards: A, D, M, V.

Principe de Viana

Manuel de Falla, 5 (one block north of the Estadio Bernabeu, which is a mile and a half north of the park), ☎ *457 15 49, FAX 457 52 83.*
Closed Saturday lunch, Sunday, Holy Week and August.

Here you can watch a son try to follow in his father's large footsteps, for this restaurant is the creation of the son of Zalacaín's Sr. Oyarbide. Anyone must admit that his son inherited good taste in decor. We fear you will also be able to watch the son sink slowly into the sunset, for service fails to be truly gracious, the butter can be rancid and empty chairs lend a look of desolation. Credit Cards: A, V, D, M.

Moderate ($15–$30)

Brasserie de Lista   ★ ★

José Ortega y Gasset, 6 (on this fashionable street in Barrio Salamanca around the corner from Serrano, about eight short blocks north of the park), ☎ *435 28 18, FAX 576 28 17.*
Closed Sat. lunch and Sundays in August.

Tasteful nouvelle Spanish dishes are served in a relaxed, turn of the century bistro atmosphere. Waiters wear appropriate long white aprons. The menu also includes continental dishes and represents a bargain for such quality in Madrid. The only problem with de Lista is that it crowds at lunch when reservations are advised. Credit Cards: A, M, V.

Botín   ★ ★

C. Cuchilleros, 17 (out the southwest corner of the Pl. Mayor and down stairs), ☎ *366 42 17.*

According to *The Guinness Book of World Records* Botín, in continuous operation since 1725, is the oldest restaurant in the world. Its specialties are roast suckling pig (*cochinillo asado*) and roast baby lamb (*cordero asado*), cooked in ancient wood ovens (*hornos*). One or the other is always on the Menu del Día, and a price-saving when ordered that way. This is fortunate because Botín's prices are otherwise inflating it into the expensive category where it does not belong. The decor is rough-hewn wood beams and floors. Be warned: although the roasts are first-rate, this is a tourist favorite—we could do without the crowds and the roving musicians. Reserve, or be prepared to wait in line for up to an hour. Credit Cards: A, D, M, V.

La Bola

C. de la Bola, 5 (off the Pl. de Oriente, near the Palácio Real, as explained in "Walking Tour #1"), ☎ *547 69 30.*
Closed Sunday, and Saturday night in high summer.

Well over 100 years old, Bola is quiet and cozy with small dining areas for munching good Madrileño food. The specialty is *cocida Madrileño,* a stew of meat and chickpeas, served in two courses—as soup, then as meat. This dish appears only at lunch, when reservations are advised. But grills are good as well any time. Credit Cards: none.

Hylogui

Ventura de la Vega, 3 (off C. de San Jerónimo, four blocks east of Puerta del Sol), ☎ *429 73 57.*
Closed Sunday evening, and August.

This Madrid institution contains a series of dining rooms that extend on and on. The food is authentic Castilian and well prepared—the crowds would not come if the food were not first rate. This is the place to sample earthy Castilian cuisine. Credit Cards: A, M, V.

El Ingenio

Leganitos, 10 (follow C. Bailén north from the Palace for one block to Torija going right. In four blocks it runs into Leganitos; turn left), ☎ *541 91 33, FAX 547 35 34*
Closed Sun. and holidays in summer.

Sure, the Don Quixote decor is campy, but the simple food is first-rate and hugs the bottom of the moderate price range for a super value. Reservations should not be necessary. Credit Cards: A, D, M, V.

Casa Paco

Puerta Cerrada, 11 (this plaza is two blocks south of the Pl. Mayor), ☎ *366 31 66.*
Closed Sunday and August.

Hearty steaks are served in a festively tiled dining room past the bar. The beef is ordered by weight (1 pound is *medio kilo*). If you ache for a bloody steak, the meat here is first rate and done to a turn. Reservations are strongly advised, for Madrid offers few choices for really good steaks. Credit Cards: D , V.

Ciao Madrid

Argensola, 7 (from the southern end of the Archaeological Museum take C. Villanueva west for three blocks to turn right on Argensola), ☎ *308 25 19.*
Closed Saturday for lunch, Sunday and August.

There are times when nothing sounds as good as an Italian meal. This is Madrid's best Italian restaurant, a convivial place where the pasta is homemade, and keeping to the pasta produces a very reasonably priced dinner. But more expensive special ties, such as osso buco, will not break the budget either. Since it's guaranteed that you will not be the only person thinking Italian, reservations are advised. Credit Cards: A, D, V.

Armstrong's

Jovellanos, 5 (opposite the Teatro de la Zarzuela, one block north of C. San Jerónimo, and three blocks east of the Pl. Cortez), ☎ *522 42 30.*

There is nothing wrong with hankering for familiar food while in a foreign land. A London solicitor named Armstrong opened this attractively pink and white restaurant to answer such needs. The ambience is most pleasant and the food is good, as well as familiar. Credit Cards: A, D, M, V.

Inexpensive (Less than $15)

Luarqués ★

C. Ventura de la Vega, 16 (off C. de San Jerónimo, four blocks east of the Puerta del Sol), ☎ *429 61 74.*
Closed Sunday, Monday and August.
This is the place for hearty, "peasant" fare. The owners are Asturians who decorate their crowded dining room with rustic farm implements from home. Good value for the money makes this a popular place, sometimes with long waits, but C. Ventura de la Vega bids to be the most interesting restaurant street in Madrid, so if the wait is too long at Luarqués, you can move to Hylogui, described above, or to Asado or Puebla, described below. No reservations accepted. Credit Cards: none.

Paellería Valenciana ★★

Caballero de Gracia, 12 (this little street is just west of the fork where C. de Alcalá meets A. de Gran Via), ☎ *531 17 85.*
Open weekdays for lunch only.
You have to order ahead for paella and the portion is for two persons, but it is delicious and an excellent value. If you can live without the paella, you don't have to phone ahead. Walk in and down some hearty soup, followed by a lunch special. There is a three-course menu for less than $10 that includes a carafe of wine. Credit Cards: A, M, V.

Puebla ★

Ventura de la Vega, 12 (off C. de San Jerónimo, four blocks east of Puerta del Sol), ☎ *429 67 13.*
Closed Sunday.
Inexpensive, well prepared food makes up for the horrendous "decor." Madrid offers no greater food bargains. No reservations accepted. Credit Cards: none.

Foster's Hollywood

Velázquez, 80 (in Salamanca), ☎ *435 61 28.*
The name adequately suggests the decor which is bright and spare. Foster's forte is good old American hamburgers, large and in great variety. Of course, there are fries, tasty indeed, ribs and Tex-Mex, but don't neglect an order of superb onion rings. Credit Cards: A, D, M, V.

Los Gabrieles

C. Echegaray, 17 (the next street east of Ventura de la Vega).
Magnificent tiles make this bar-restaurant a feast for the eyes. The food isn't bad either.

McDonald's

Outlets are at Puerta del Sol and on Gran Via at C. Montera.

Shopping

The best buys in Madrid are leather goods, including shoes, along with antiques, and men's and women's high fashion clothing. See "Walking Tour 3" for specifics. Mammoth sales are held during the second week of January and from late July through the middle of August. Look for a sign saying *Rebajas*.

Leather

The best quality leather clothes and accessories are undoubtedly sold by the famous Spanish firm of **Loewe**. Prices are extravagant, but the quality is superb. Note that Barcelona offers similar quality for lower prices, but you do not save much at either location over the Loewe branch in New York. The firm maintains outlets in the best hotels but their most complete shops are at *C. Serrano 26* and, for men, *Serrano 34*, in the Barrio Salamanca. Less expensive and with a huge selection is **Lepanto** at *Pl. de Oriente*, 3 across from the Palácio Real. For high fashion shoes, **Farrutx** is a good bet on C. Serrano, 7, just south of the Museo Arqueológico. **Gutierrez** on C. Serrano, 66 has moderate prices, at a step down in quality. For good luggage try **La Casa de las Maletas** on *Claudio Coello, 45* in the Barrio Salamanca.

Antiques

Two of Madrid's finest antique establishments are located on either side of the Cortes building in the Pl. de la Cortes. **Galarias San Agustin** is at *San Agustin, 3* which branches off from the plaza, and **Abelardo Linares** stands at *San Jerónimo 48,* just west. Prices are high, but looking is free. **C. del Prado** leading off from the Pl. de las Cortes is a street filled with antique stores, some with reasonable prices. And around the El Rastro flea market numerous stores sell old things. At *12 Ribera de Curtidores*, in the heart of the market, are **Gonzalves** for brass and **José Maria del Rey** for fine antiques. *At 15 is* **Galería de Antiguedades**, an antique center, and at 27 is **Regalos Molina**, for ceramics (closed, for some reason on Sunday, the day that the market is held).

Jewelry

For fine *jewelry*, try **Carrera y Carrera** at *Serrano, 27*, for costume pieces try **Del Pino** at Serrano. *Silver* is luscious at **Lopez**, *C. del Prado, 3*, and **Villanueva y Laiseca** nearby at *Carrera de San Jerónimo, 9*.

Crafts

The best *crafts* are at **El Arco de Los Cuchilleros Artesania de Hoy** in the Plaza Mayor at 9. Next best is the elegant state-owned **ArtEspaña**, which has a fine outlet at *Pl. de las Cortes, 3*. Prices are not low, but the work from all over Spain is collected under one roof. For fans and umbrellas the place is **Casa de Diego** *in the Puerta del Sol at 12*.

The two best shops for *ceramics* are **Antiqua Casa Talavera** (☎ *247 34 17*) at *Isabel la Católica, 2*, just north of the Pl. Santo Domingo, a subway stop two blocks northeast of the Pl. del Oriente, and **Regalos Molina** *in el Rastro at Ribera de Curtidores 27*. (Ceramics prices, however, are better in Seville and Talavera de la Reina.)

Fine *engravings* from original plates by Goya and other great artists are sold at the **Instituto de Calcografía** in the Academia de Bellas Artes de San Fernando *at Alcalá 13*.

Department Stores

Spain has two large *department store chains*, both well represented by their Madrid branches. **El Corte Inglés** is the higher in quality of the two. Its largest store is off the Puerta del Sol on C. Preciados, another branch is in the Barrio Salamanca, at the corner of

Calles Goya and Alcalá. **Galarias Preciados** can cost less and has a branch near the El Corte Inglés on C. Gran Via near the Puerta del Sol. Both chains offer English interpreters. Preciados gives a 10 percent discount for tourists on every purchase made, in lieu of waiting for refunds of the IVA tax.

No Madrid shopping experience would be complete without a trip to the flea market, **El Rastro**, which takes place every Sunday. The stalls set up at about 9:30 a.m., the surrounding shops open at 11 a.m. and the whole area closes at 2 p.m. It is located along the wide street Ribera de Curtidores which runs south four blocks below the Pl. Mayor. You can take the subway to La Latina, walk a short block east, then south. The stalls in the streets mainly offer junk, but the fun is in the looking and the possibility of discovering a personal treasure. Stores lining both sides of the street carry generally better merchandise. Bargaining is expected, both at the stalls and in the stores, so do not assume the price quoted is the one you must pay. Watch your wallet or purse. On days of the week other than Sunday the true stores, as opposed to the street stalls, are open for more relaxed shopping.

Nightlife

For such a large and late-night city, Madrid offers less than you would expect in the way of nightclubs and their ilk. The best flamenco in Madrid is: **Café de Chinitas**, *at Torija, 7* (☎ *559 51 53*), and **Corral de la Pacheca** *at Juan Ramon Jimenez, 26* (☎ *458 26 72*). But Madrid's flamenco is not as good, and overpriced, in comparison to that in Seville. **La Scala Melia**, in the Melia Castilla Hotel, presents a Moulin-Rouge type review including topless "statues" *at Rosario Piño, 7* (☎ *571 44 11*). Of course there are discos. If you want to sample them, follow your ear through the maze of streets north of Gran Via. Archy's *at Marqués de Riscal, 11* (☎ *308 27 36*) and Pachá *at Barceló, 11* (☎ *446 01 37*) are the current "in" spots. Casino Gran Madrid (☎ *856 11 00*), the largest casino in Europe, lies twenty minutes from downtown. Free buses leave Pl. de España.

The true night life of Madrid, as in most Spanish cities, consists of the evening *paseo*, and tapas bar hopping. Crowds gather at dusk to wander through the old town until after midnight, popping into whatever place a convivial-looking group has assembled. The object is not to get drunk, but to socialize and mingle. To join in, walk down C. del Prado or any adjacent side street. A hipper crowd strolls along Paseo de la Castellana, north of the Archaeological Museum.

Sports

Bullfighting

Aficionados argue about which cities in Spain present the best spectacles, but most would settle on Madrid or Seville. The Madrid season runs from April through the beginning of November on every Sunday afternoon, but every day during the three-week festival of Saint Isidro in May. Tickets can be purchased at the **Las Ventas** ring at *C. Alcalá, 231* (Subway: Las Ventas), or through an agency at C. Victoria, 3, off the Puerta del Sol, or through the concierge at most hotels. Tickets are always hard to find and scalped for huge premiums during the three-week Saint Isidro festival when the best matadors come to town.

Soccer

The Spanish appreciate bullfighting, but they are crazy about soccer (*fútbol*). Madrid fields two rival teams, but the best is usually Real Madrid whose games are played in the huge (130,000 seats) **Santiago Bernabeu Stadium** at Paseo de Castellana, 140 (Subway: Lima). Agencies in major department stores sell tickets.

Directory

Addresses

American Express: *Pl. de las Cortes, 2* (☎ *332 50 50*)

Books in English:

Turner's English Bookstore, *Genova, 3* (which runs west of the Pl. Colón, near the Archaeology Museum; ☎ 319 28 67)

Washington Irving Center, *Marqués de Villamagna, 8* (☎ *435 69 22*), is an American library open Mon.–Fri. 2–6 p.m.

Car Rental Companies:

ATESA: *Gran Via, 59* (☎ *247 02 02*)

Avis: *Gran Via, 60* (☎ *247 20 48*) and Paseo de la Castellana, *57* (☎ *441 05 79*)

Europcar: *C. Orense, 29* (☎ *445 99 30*)

Hertz: *Gran Via, 88* (☎ *248 58 03*)

Embassies:

United States: *Serrano, 75* (☎ *576 34 00*)

Canada: *Núñez de Balboa, 35* (☎ *431 43 00*)

United Kingdom: *Fernando el Santo, 6* (☎ *308 04 59*)

Airport

Barajas Airport (☎ *305 4372*) is 12 km east of Madrid's center, not far removed for such a large city. A taxi into town costs about 2500 ptas. Alternatively, an airport bus, for 350 ptas., leaves every 15 minutes or so to the centrally located Pl. Colón, where taxis wait to carry you to your hotel. The bus stops under the plaza. Iberia branches dot the city, but the most convenient is in the Palace Hotel (☎ *563 99 66*, for international flights, ☎ *411 10 11*, for domestic).

Buses

The bus situation is complex, since eight separate stations house several times that number of independent bus companies. Try the Office of Tourism for information, or the largest of the eight stations, **Estación del Sur de Autobuses** on *Av. de Canarias, 17* (☎ *468 45 11*; Metro: Palos de Frontera). Generally bus fares are incredibly low by U.S. standards—for example, a round trip between Madrid and Barcelona costs in the neighborhood of $40—and only a tireless professional driver could better the eight-hour time.

City Tours

The following companies provide bus tours of the sights of Madrid: **Julia Tours,** *Gran Via, 68* (☎ *541 91 25*); **Pullmantur**, *Pl. de Oriente, 8* (☎ *541 18 07*); **Trapsatur**, *C. San Bernardo, 23* (☎ *541 63 20*). Brochures are available at most hotel desks. Pullmantur also offers excursions to nearby cities, such as Toledo, El Escorial and Segovia.

Driving Into Madrid

Unless your hotel is in the area between the Palácio Real and the Prado, where streets are narrow, driving should not be too difficult.

From the south by **A-4 (E-5)**, the highway turns into Av. de Andalucia inside Madrid. Choose between continuing on M-30 (*Av. de la Paz*), which you should take if going to the east or north of the center of town, or exiting on to Av. de Córdoba for the center. If aiming for the center, it is best to turn right to Pl. Arganzuela, continue straight across the plaza, and up the one-way Paseo de las Delicias which brings you into the large Pl. de Emperador Carlos V. The Atocha train station is located here. Take a true left up C. Atocha, for the area of the old town, or a less extreme left on the Paseo del Prado for beyond.

From the southwest on **A-5 (E-90)** it is straight sailing along the Av. de Portugal until signs for "Estación del Norte." Continue past the station to reach the signs to Puerta Florida, then turn right on Cuesta de San Vincente to Gran Via, for a left toward the center of town.

It is straight as an arrow from the northwest on **A-6,** except that street names change as you go deeper into Madrid. A-6 is called Av. Puerta de Hierro, which changes its name to C. Princesa, then becomes Gran Via.

From the north **A-1 (E-5)** is called Av. de la Paz (also known as M-30) as it enters Madrid. Turn right on C. Alcalá just past the Plaza de Toros (bullring)—signs might say "Puente de las Ventas." Stay on Alcalá as it passes alongside el Retiro Park to end at the Pl. Puerta de Alcalá. Continue straight across on Alcalá for the center of town, or take the first left, which is C. Serrano, for the Barrio Salamanca.

From the east and the airport **N-II (E-90)** becomes **A-2,** and is called Av. de América in Madrid. Where Costa Francisco Silvela crosses, Av. de América ends. Continue on the same street, now called C. Maria de Molina. It enters a large circle, the Pl. del Dr. Manañón. Turn left here on Paseo de la Castellaña, a huge multi-laned street, for both the Barrio Salamanca and the center of town.

N-III, from the southeast, changes its name to Av. del Mediterraneo in Madrid. It changes its name again on the other side of Pl. Manero de Cavia to Paseo de la Reina Cristina, then changes its name to Paseo de la Infanta Isabel as it bends right to enter the large Pl. del Emperador Carlos V. Take the second left up Paseo del Prado, the multi-laned street, for the Barrio Salamanca, or take the street straight across, C. Atocha, for the center of town.

Emergencies

Police • in the Puerta del Sol (☎ *221 65 16*; emergency: *091*)

Ambulance • ☎ *734 25 45*

English speaking doctors • (☎ *431 22 29*)

Information

Not centrally located, the Office of Tourism is north of the Pl. de España in the Torre Madrid Building at C. Princesa, 1 (see "Walking Tour #3"). Open weekdays 9 a.m. to 7 p.m., Saturday from 9:30 a.m. to 1:30 p.m. (☎ *541 23 25*). Another office is located in Barajas Airport, where, if needed, attendants will provide help in finding a hotel. An office of the City of Madrid is located at Pl. Mayor, 3, but stocks little information.

Post Office and Telephones

Madrid's main post office is located in the Pl. Cibeles and open weekdays from 9 a.m. to 10 p.m.; Sundays from 10 a.m. to 1 p.m.; and Saturdays until 8 p.m. The Telefonica on Gran Via 28 (opposite McDonald's) is open 24 hours every day. Long-distance calls are up to 50 percent cheaper here than those made from hotel phones.

Trains

RENFE's main ticket office is at *C. Alcalá, 44;* (☎ *563 02 02*); Metro: Banco de España. Madrid has three major train stations whose service overlaps. The largest is **Chamartín** Station, located in northern Madrid (Metro: Chamartín). It serves the north and east, including France, but not Galicia (☎ *323 21 21*). **Atocha** Station is located three long blocks south of the Prado (Metro: Atocha). It primarily serves the south, but also Extremadura, Portugal, and nearby northern cities, such as Ávila and Segovia ☎ *527 31 60*). **Norte** Station (Metro: Norte) serves Galicia and Salamanca, but also some nearby cities to the north (☎ *247 00 00*). RENFE can be called at ☎ *563 02 02* for information on all trains, in Spanish.

Travel in Madrid

Taxis are reasonable. The meter starts at 155 pesetas, then adds 70 pesetas each kilometer, although there is a surcharge of 150 pesetas at night and on holidays. Most trips from one sight to another will cost $4 or less. Taxis are white (though some are black) with a red stripe on the side. They can be flagged on the street or found waiting at taxi stands near sights or large hotels.

Buses, though numerous and inexpensive, are slow and require exact change. The fare currently is 125 pesetas. A sign at each stop lists the numbers of those buses that pick up there.

The subway (*Metro*) is frequent, clean and quick. It does close at 1:30 a.m., however. The fare is 125 pesetas, though a 10 ride *bonos* sells for only 600 ptas. The various lines are designated by the end station on their route, and maps are available at all stations.

Excursions from Madrid
El Escorial ★★★★ and Valle de Los Caídos ★

El Escorial stands among the great monuments in Spain. For descriptions and hours, see the "El Escorial" and "Valle de los Caídos" headings. Both lie about 50 km from Madrid; travel and sight-seeing will consume more than half a day.

Drive along C. Grand Via heading west. As it bends north it becomes first C. Princesa, then Av. Puerta de Hierro. Signs direct you to N-VI, going northwest. At 16 km exit left onto C-505 to El Escorial in 28 km, as the signs direct.

Trains leave every hour both from Atocha and Chamartin stations in Madrid. A bus meets the train in El Escorial. Incidentally, the train is on the Ávila and Segovia line, so either city can be included in the excursion.

Buses leave the Empresa Herranz station on C. Reina Victoria (near the Moncloa Metro stop) a dozen times per day. The same company runs a bus from the El Escorial stop to Valle de los Caídos at 3:15, returning at 6:15.

For directions to Valle de los Caídos, see the description of "El Escorial" in this chapter.

El Pardo ★★

This country palace only 13 km outside of Madrid is a more tasteful version of Madrid's Palácio Real, but not as memorable. For a description and hours see the "El Pardo" heading below in this chapter. Travel and sights will take up almost half a day.

Take C. Grand Via heading west. As it bends north it becomes C. Princesa, then Av. Puerta de Hierro. Bear to the right on C-601 for 13 km as it parallels the Manzanares River through scrub woods into the village of El Pardo.

Buses from C. Martin de los Heros (near the Moncloa Metro stop) leave every quarter hour during the day.

Toledo ★★★★★

For a description and hours of the sights see "Toledo" in this chapter. Travel and sights will consume a very full day.

Head down Paseo del Prado to the Pl. de Emperador Carlos V, where the Atocha train station is located. Drive through the plaza, past the train station, where four roads branch ahead. Take the second one from the right, which is the one directly ahead, called Paseo de Sta. Maria de la Cabeza. Signs will lead you to N 401 for Toledo, 70 km away.

Frequent trains leave Madrid's Atocha station for the 90 minute ride. Buses are a little faster and deposit you in the central Pl. de Zocodover. Continental Galiano buses (☎ 22 29 61) leave half hourly from the Estación Sur de Autobuses on C. Canarias, 17.

Segovia ★★★★★, Ávila ★★★, Coca Castle ★★ and Salamanca ★★★★

All can be reached in two or three hours by car. See the "Old Castile and Leon" chapter.

To leave Madrid, follow the directions to El Escorial, above, but continue north instead of exiting on C-505.

A dozen trains leave Madrid's Atocha station for the 2-1/2 hour trip to Segovia. Ávila trains go through El Escorial for a trip of under two hours; see the El Escorial information above. Few trains go directly from Madrid to

Salamanca. The better bet is to pick up one of the eight trains per day from Ávila to Salamanca.

Buses from La Sepulveda on P. de la Florida (Norte Metro stop) are faster to Segovia, but do only five trips per day. They match the train to Ávila.

El Pardo ★ ★

From **Madrid** *Gran Via heads west, bends northwest and changes its name to Calle Princesa, then changes its name again to Avenida Puerta de Hierro. Follow signs to A-6. Just past the University, a right fork onto C-601 to "El Monte de El Pardo" leads in 13 km to the palace.*

This is an older, more attractive palace than those in Madrid or Aranjuez. Half a day is plenty of time to see it and the other sights of interest as well.

For centuries the woods around El Pardo formed a royal hunting preserve for sylvan outings by Spanish kings "working" in Madrid. In fact, the original building on the site was a hunting lodge built in 1405 for Enrique III before Madrid even became the capital. After designating Madrid as his capital, Felipe II replaced that lodge with a palace and furnished it with fine art, which rather changed the hunt atmosphere. Fire, the scourge of so many palaces, later burned down half of it. Since the cataclysm occurred in 1604, however, much earlier than similar conflagrations in Madrid and Aranjuez, its latest—present—rebuilding dates to the time of Felipe III. Thus this is a Hapsburg structure, with Bourbon additions, as compared to the Bourbon palaces of Madrid and Aranjuez, although, its furnishings are to Bourbon tastes. It was Franco's favorite residence, and still filled with his mementos and uniforms. Today, the palace is sometimes used to entertain visiting dignitaries. The residence of the present king, Juan Carlos, is nearby.

Palácio del Pardo ★ ★

Hours open: Mon.–Sat. 10 a.m.–1 p.m., and 4–7 p.m. (opening and closing an hour earlier winter afternoons). Closed Sun.

The "Chinese" room and those with neoclassical furniture are the most interesting. Fine Sèvres porcelain and clocks are scattered throughout. Some of the ceiling frescoes and stuccowork are notable, and a huge collection of tapestries hangs on the walls, many, including designs by Goya, from the Spanish Royal Tapestry Factory. *Admission: 400 ptas., by guided tour only.*

Casita del Principe ★ ★

Same hours and ticket as the palace.

This is a twin to a similar building in El Escorial. It too was designed by Villanueva, the architect of the Museo del Prado, for the same prince who would become King Carlos IV. The rooms are tiny, which only intensifies the impact of their rich decoration and furniture. The dining room is a particular favorite. Some pleasing pastels by Tiepolo and some paintings by Mengs adorn the walls.

Note: The Convento de Capuchinos, on a hill to the west, contains a masterpiece of polychrome wood carving by Fernandez and two Ribera paintings.

Sigüenza ★ ★ ★

Population 6656
Area code: 911; zip code: 19250

104 km from Madrid. Head west from Madrid toward Barajas Airport on A2 (E90), which becomes N-II (E90) in the direction of Zaragoza. In 56 km comes Guadalajara. 48 km further, a turn left onto C-204 (there is a sign), reaches Sigüenza after 26 km of winding road.

This lovely hilltop town of Renaissance houses includes a fascinating Cathedral, containing a masterpiece of sculpture, and an imposing medieval fortress (now a parador) built for its bishops.

Calle de Medina leads uphill to the Cathedral. Construction began on this Gothic church in 1150, although by the following century it required repairs which were not completed—in the form seen today—until the end of the 15th century. Inside, the original Romanesque shape is rather simple, while the fortress-like exterior is a mixture of all the forms that Gothic architecture passed through—but with a French feel, for the early archbishops came from France.

Cathedral   ★ ★ ★

Hours open: by the sacristan from 11 a.m.–2 p.m. and 4–8 p.m. (6 p.m. in winter). Apply at the Sacristy at the rear of the Cathedral.

The sense of strength conveyed by the Cathedral's exterior is continued inside by high vaulting on massive pillars. Down the left side is a lovely doorway surrounded by painted Renaissance pilasters and Mudejar designs. The adjoining chapel contains a 15th-century triptych. A jasper doorway leads to a marbled late Gothic cloister with intricate Plateresque doors and a collection of Flemish tapestries located in a room off the north corner. Back in the church proper, after the door to the cloister, is a side altar designed by Covarrubias for Saint Librada and her eight sisters, all born on the same day, according to legend, and all martyred together. Next comes the sepulchre of Dom Fadrique of Portugal, one of the earliest examples of the Plateresque style. As the ambulatory begins, a door on the left leads into the sacristy, also designed by Covarrubias, with an astonishing painted and sculpted ceiling of thousands of staring cherubim.

Around the south side of the ambulatory, in the Doncel Chapel, waits the star of the Cathedral. Don Martin de Arca was a page (*doncel*) to Isabella and died in the Granada wars. His queen commissioned this sepulcher in early Isabelline style of a youth relaxed and reading. It is unlike any similar work in Spain in seeming so alive. Don Martin's parents lie in a mausoleum in the center of the chapel. *Admission: 125 ptas.*

Diocesan Museum ★

Hours open: Tues.–Sun. 11:30 a.m.–2 p.m., and 5–7 p.m. (During Jan. and Feb. open only Sun. and holidays).

The museum is located in a building across from the west side of the Cathedral. It contains prehistoric pieces, a collection of crucifixes, an El Greco and a superb Zurbarán of Mary floating above Seville—alone worth the price of admission. *Admission: 200 ptas.*

The Plaza Mayor ★ in front of the Cathedral is surrounded by late 15th- and early 16th-century porticos and balconies. The Ayuntamiento (city hall), from 1512, is located on the south side. Calle Mayor heads steeply up to the castle from the plaza.

Looking just as a fortress should (if you ignore the windows peering through what should be solid walls), the **castle** ★, which was erected in the 12th century to protect the archbishop of Sigüenza, was renovated in the 14th. For a time it served as a prison for the wife of Pedro the Cruel because he had already fallen in love with another woman while his wife-to-be was enroute to their wedding. It was too late to call off the ceremony, so Pedro went through with it, then imprisoned his new wife here. Now it is a parador, which explains its incongruous windows.

Where to Stay

Parador Castillo de Sigüenza   1st-class ★ ★ ★ ★

Plaza del Castillo, Sigüenza, . ☎ 39 01 00, FAX 39 13 64.

There is not a more authentically remodeled parador in Spain. Barely expensive, the price must be considered fair given how seldom one can stay in a castle in which a queen was imprisoned. The bedrooms are lovely, and some include canopied beds. *78 rooms, plus two suites*

Toledo ★ ★ ★ ★ ★

Population 57,769
Area code: 925; zip code: 45000

From **Madrid**, take Paseo del Prado to its southern end at the Plaza del Emperador Carlos V. Across the plaza take Paseo de Sta. Maria de la Cabeza, the middle of three branching streets. It becomes N-401 which reaches Toledo in 71 km.

From **Seville**, take N-IV (E5) east toward Córdoba. Continue through Córdoba, Bailén and Valdepeñas to Madridejos (in 286 km) where you exit for C-400 to Toledo for 70 km, a total trip of 346 km.

*For **trains** and **buses**, see Madrid "Excursions." The Toledo train
station lies outside of town, but any city bus will run you in.*

Toledo rises like Gibraltar from the plains of La Mancha, its peak formed
by cathedral spires and the turrets of the Alcázar. The sight is unforgettable.
Over millennia the river Tagus dug a ravine around three sides of Toledo,
leaving the hard bluff on which the city is situated rising high above. This geography prevented the city from expanding, concentrating all its treasures
atop one steep hill.

The Romans were not the first to appreciate the importance of Toledo's
site. They fought Iberians to capture it in 192 B.C. then fortified the hill and
founded a town called *Toletum*, from which the present name derives. In
turn, the Visigoths made Toledo the capital from which they ruled Spain.
When the Moors invaded in 711, they aimed straight for the capital, and
captured it in 712. It remained in Moorish hands for the next 300 years,
though reduced in political importance by incorporation into the Emirate
(later the Caliphate) of their own capital Córdoba. Eventually, disintegration
of the Caliphate into independent fiefdoms by 1012, left Toledo as the capital of its own Moorish state.

As a result of the Moor's toleration of other religions, at the time Toledo
contained one of the largest Jewish communities in Spain, numbering about
12,000, as well as a large Christian population. But when, after centuries of
harmony, the Moors attempted to extort a large sum for the defense budget
primarily from the Jewish community, Jews cried for help to the Spanish
Christian king. In 1085, Alfonso VI, aided by his general El Cid, attacked
Toledo and captured the city.

Under subsequent Christian kings the Jewish community thrived, making
important contributions to the wealth and learning of the town. Alfonso X
the Learned established a school of translators to disseminate the lore of Arabic culture throughout Europe which he staffed with Jews because only
they could understand both Arabic and Spanish. This happy condition
ended abruptly in pogroms in 1391 during which hundreds of Toledo Jews
were murdered by Christians. Finally, in 1492, all of Spain's Jews, the
sephardim, were expelled by Ferdinand and Isabella. Ironically, the grandfather of the future Saint Theresa had moved to Ávila and converted to Christianity just before the expulsion occurred.

The eviction of the Jews marked the beginning of Toledo's decline, hastened a century later by the banishment of those Moors who had evaded
exile by converting to Christianity. Toledo had been stripped of many of its
most accomplished citizens. What the city retained was their legacy—its
buildings.

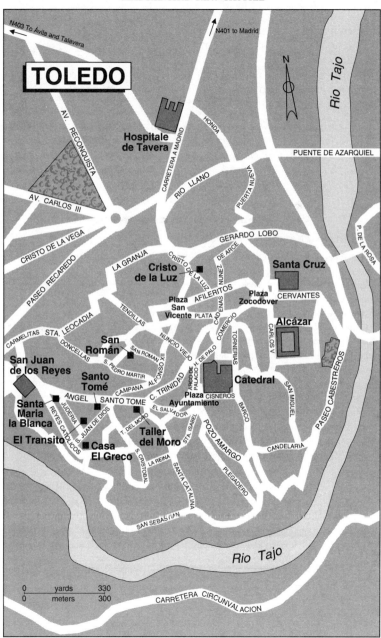

Toledo is special enough that UNESCO designates it part of mankind's cultural heritage. No city in Spain has more to see—one frantic day barely does it justice. But Toledo is also the only city in Spain where shopkeepers and their touts urge you to enter their establishments, conveying the impression that you've fallen into a tourist trap. In truth these stores sell decent wares and, because such insistence is not a natural Spanish trait, the effect is more a slight nuisance than a serious problem.

> *The Alcázar is the place to begin. If driving from Madrid, go left on the Carretera de Circunvalación, crossing the Tagus where N-401 intersects, then going left at the circle on the opposite side. Turn right up the winding road leading to the Alcázar. Here is the largest parking place in the city, though in summer parking can be difficult even here.*

What to See and Do

The following is a list of what should not be missed.

The **Alcázar** ★ is worth a visit to see the building, some of the military museums, and the room of General Moscardo, reconstructed exactly as it had been during the Civil War siege. The **Cathedral** ★ ★ ★ is the most sumptuous in Spain. **Santa Tomé** ★ ★ ★ houses what most people consider El Greco's greatest painting. **El Greco's House and Museum** ★ ★ displays more El Grecos than anywhere else, and is interesting as a period building. **El Tránsito Synagogue** ★ ★ ★ is a feast of Moorish decoration, and so is **Santa María la Blanca Synagogue** ★ ★. The **Santa Cruz Museum** ★ ★ ★ is spectacular as a building and for the art it contains. **San Juan de los Reyes** ★ ★ was built by Isabella and Ferdinand. **San Román** ★ ★ is a former 13th-century Church, now a museum of Visigothic artifacts, and **Ermita del Cristo de la Luz** ★ is a small, beautifully preserved mosque from the 11th century. All are within the old town walls. The atmospheric and memorable **Hospital de Tavera** ★ ★ stands just outside.

Note: Toledo is an old and concentrated town comprised of a maze of alleys, rather than a grid of streets. We present the best directions we can, but when confused you should feel free to ask passersby who are accustomed to such inquiries.

Alcázar   ★

Calle Capuchinos, ☎ 22 30 38. Entrance on the north side, farthest from the parking lot. Hours open: Tues.–Sun. 9:30 a.m.–1:30 p.m., and 4–6:30 p.m. (to 5:30 p.m. in winter). Closed Mon.

A fortress occupied this location at least since Moorish times, for the site so dominates both the town and surrounding plain that military engineers love it at first sight. Alfonso VI, who conquered Moorish Toledo, replaced the Alcázar of the Moors with his own fort, which El Cid commanded until the two quarreled. Later monarchs remade the building into more palace than fortress. Carlos V rebuilt it entirely in its present shape, using Covarrubias for his architect, but it was finished under Felipe II, Carlos's son, by Felipe's favorite architect Herrera (who designed the church at El Escorial). The north facade is Herrera's. What you see today, however, is entirely a reconstruction: the historic Alcázar was completely destroyed during the Spanish Civil War.

At the outbreak of war, the Alcázar served as an army headquarters. Most of the troops were home on leave, but soon the professional soldiers and cadets who remained were joined in the Alcázar by citizens of Nationalist sympathies. Since most of Toledo supported the opposition Republicans, its citizens surrounded the Alcázar and lay siege. For two months those in the building resisted artillery, mining and starvation before relief arrived at the last moment in the form of Generalissimo Franco with his army. Their stand became a symbol of determination to the Nationalists and, not surprisingly, Franco rebuilt the Alcázar after the war.

Architecturally the most interesting part of the Alcázar is its huge courtyard, which leads to entrances for various military museums. More such museums line the second floor, where the Alcázar's most moving display is also located. The office of General Moscardo, the defending Nationalist general, has been perfectly reconstructed as it was during the Civil War siege. You can see the dirt and bullet holes, the torn and hanging wallpaper, and the Spartan furnishings. Signs in all languages tell the story of how the Republicans surrounded the building and telephoned the general to inform him that his son was in their hands and would be killed if he did not surrender. General Moscardo asked to speak to his son and told him to prepare for death. It's a good story, but the son in question was discovered later enjoying life in Madrid. *Admission: 150 ptas.*

After touring the Alcázar, the time of day determines what to see next. To the right is the **Hospital of Santa Cruz***, a museum that should be seen, but which is open throughout the day so it can be saved for midday when the other sights close for lunch. Toward the left (south) is the* **Cathedral***.*

To reach the Cathedral, turn left on Calle Carlos V past the Alcázar to Pascuales San Miguel which cuts across it. Turn right. The name changes to Calle Coliseo as it bends right again, then turns left as it enters the Plaza Mayor. At the end of the plaza the Cathedral can be seen. A left would take you to the modern entrance, but it is worth viewing the facade first by going right instead, then left and left again into the Plaza del Ayuntamiento. The Cathedral facade is on the left; and on the right, angling away, is the **Episcopal Palace***. Further on, beside the palace, is the* **Ayuntamiento** *(city hall), with a classical front designed by Herrera, finished by El Greco's son. Straight ahead are* **law courts** *from the 14th century.*

Cathedral ★★★★

Plaza Mayor; ☎ *22 22 41. Entrance on the north facade.*
Hours open: daily 10:30 a.m.–1 p.m., and 3:30–7 p.m. (until 6 p.m. in winter, and on Sun.).
This is Spain's most important cathedral, and, after Burgos, its grandest. After razing the city mosque in 1227, building began on a typical French Gothic cathedral, but during its two centuries of construction the plan gradually changed to a squatter and broader version known as Spanish Gothic. The front, with its triangular top and asymmetrical towers, shows substantial Italian influence.

The present situation of the Cathedral suggests the effect of most cathedrals in the Middle Ages when they were new—all hemmed in by buildings so that no vantage permits a good view of the whole. Whether this was a calculated effect, or due to the difficulty or expense of removing neighboring buildings, is argued, but the clear result was to dramatize the openness of the interior.

Before entering, a look at the outside is in order. The tall and regular left tower is 15th century, showing Moorish influence, but spoiled at the top by a later lantern and overly-intricate spire. What should have been a tower on the right became instead a dome to cover the splendid Mozarabic chapel inside, designed by El Greco's son in the 17th century. The center portal, the Pardon Door, displays the best carving of the three main portals. In the center Mary offers her robe to Ildefonso, a Visigothic saint and patron of Toledo. The bronze door-covers are 14th century. Around the corner to the south side is the Puerta de los Leones, named for the lions on the railing columns, fronting a richly decorated portal.

Enter on the north side, through the cloisters. The interior conveys a sense of volume and strength, rather than the lightness of the soaring French Gothic. Gradually the sumptuousness of the decoration takes effect. The stained glass is of the period, multicolored and lovely; wrought iron and marble run rampant. Such richness threatens to dull the senses.

The **coro** (choir) in the center of the Cathedral nave contains some of the finest wood carving in Spain. The lower row of choirstalls, carved within a decade of the event, graphically depict the Christian conquest of Granada and constitute one of the best records of the battles. The upper tier of stalls on the right, are by the sculptor Alonso Berruguete. They are masterpieces of bas-relief, subtly conveying life and movement with figures that seem to push through the wood. At the back of the choir an alabaster Transfiguration, also by Berruguette, seems to rise and hover. Wait for a tour group to come by so that you can see the *coro* lit, or find the sacristan and offer a small gratuity.

Opposite the *coro* is the **sanctuary** and altar with its huge, flamboyantly-carved polychrome retable depicting the life of Christ. The silver statue of the Virgin in front seems lost in all the commotion. Royal tombs flank the altar: Alfonso VII on the left, Sancho II on the right. Behind the sanctuary, in the middle of the ambulatory, hangs a swirling Baroque *Transparante* slab by Tomé that seems out of place for all its prominence. Holes were cut in the Cathedral walls to allow the sun to illuminate it.

To the left (with your back to the Transparante) is a richly carved Gothic chapel to Santiago (usually locked). Lovely Gothic effigies of the chapel founder and his wife are inside. To the right, after the Chapel of San Ildefonso, a painted Mudejar portal leads to the **Capitular** room with its intricate 16th-century ceiling of surpassing elegance. Paintings of bishops of Toledo line the room, from the first century through the 19th. Although the artistic quality of the portraits is not high, they add a pleasant decorative touch, and include two painted by Goya. See if you can pick them out.

Returning back around the ambulatory, the tomb of Henrique of Trastámara, ancestor of both Isabella and Ferdinand, lies adjacent to the Santiago Chapel. Next in line is the **sacristy,** which presents a gallery of art under an imposing frescoed ceiling. The first gallery contains an awesome display of El Grecos, followed by rooms with Titian's great portrait of *Pope Paul IV*, some fine Van Dykes, an uninspired Goya, and a hauntingly "pretty" *Saint John the Baptist* by Caravaggio.

You cannot miss the huge fresco of Saint Christopher, almost 30 feet high, on the west transept. Its size lends it power beyond its artistic merit, but, for visitors, the chance of a blessing from this saint of travelers cannot hurt.

On the north side of the Cathedral front is the **tesoro** (treasury), entered through a Plateresque doorway. The Mudejar ceiling is lovely. Here you can see the 16th-century silver and gilt monstrance, weighing just under 400 pounds, which is carried through the streets during the Corpus Christi festival. A sword is displayed that belonged to Alfonso VI who conquered Toledo in 1085. Nearby is the library with richly illustrated medieval song books.

After all this splendor, the cloister disappoints. But not the **Mozarabic Chapel** that forms the front of the Cathedral on the south side. The chapel was constructed in 1504 so that those who still followed the Christian service as practiced by the Visigoths would have a place to worship. Most of those adherents had been isolated from their brethren because they lived in Moorish territory, and were thus called Mozarabs, "almost Arabs," by the other Christians. The decor of their chapel is elegantly frescoed, but the chapel is open only for their special services (at 9:30 a.m.). *Admission: 350 ptas.*

Afterwards, head left through the Plaza Arco de Palácio in front of the Cathedral, bearing right along the Archbishopric. Take the second right which is Calle San Salvador. At the corner, Santa Tomé with its wondrous El Greco lies straight ahead in one block. If time permits, first turn left, then quickly right to reach the **Taller del Moro**, *on the street of the same name.*

Taller del Moro ★

Calle Taller del Moro; ☎ *22 71 15.*
Hours open: Tues.–Sat. 10 a.m.–2 p.m., and 4–7 p.m. (until 6 p.m. in winter). Open Sun. from 10 a.m.–2 p.m. Closed Mon.
This is a museum displaying crafts and tools of the Moors, but it is most interesting as a building. The 14th-century structure was used by Moorish craftsmen as a workshop (*taller*), while they worked on the Cathedral. It retains lovely examples of stuccowork and inlaid ceilings from the period. *Admission: 200 Ptas., good also for San Román below.*

From the Taller continue to the corner and turn left along Plaza del Conde. At the end turn right, then left at the cross street, for Santa Tomé.

Santa Tomé ★★★

Plaza Conde, 1, ☎ *21 02 09.*
Hours open: daily 10:30 a.m.–1:45 p.m., and 3:30–7 p.m. (until 6 p.m. in winter).

Gonzalo Ruiz, Count of Orgaz, was a local lord of the Toledo area who donated much of the money to build this church and was buried inside when he died in 1323. Two centuries later, in 1586, urged on by his descendants the church commissioned El Greco to portray that burial. Naturally the appearance of the Count and those who attended were by then unknown, so El Greco used the faces of Toledoans of his day. A Mudejar tower stands beside the church as its annex, and in it hangs this masterpiece, so admired that there generally is a wait before admission to the small vestibule.

Recently restored to its former brightness, it now has the appearance of paint still wet. Tradition claimed that Sts. Stephen and Augustin attended the Count's burial to honor his charity, and El Greco shows them in rich capes supporting the deceased. El Greco's son stands in front pointing to the scene. (Inconspicuously inscribed on his handkerchief is the artist's signature.) All around in various attitudes stand citizens of Toledo, including El Greco himself, the sixth figure from the left. *Admission: 200 Ptas.*

Return to the corner where the church begins, turning right down the hill leading to the Plaza del Conde again. But go right on San Juan de Dios, instead of entering the plaza. Two alleyways later a sign directs you left to the House of El Greco.

Casa y Museo del Greco   ★★

Paseo del Tránsito; ☎ *22 40 46.*

Hours open: Tues.–Sat. 10 a.m.–2 p.m., and 4–7 p.m. (until 6 p.m. in winter). Open Sun. from 10 a.m.–2 p.m. Closed Mon.

Although the actual house in which El Greco lived has long since disappeared, this one was altered 100 years ago to suggest his style of living. The structure is an interesting reconstruction of a 16th-century private dwelling and displays a most amazing collection of El Greco's paintings, so brightly restored that they do not seem authentic. It is fun to inspect his large Views of Toledo (not the famous one, now in New York) now that you've seen the town yourself. *Admission: 225 ptas.; ticket good for Tránsito Synagogue.*

Return to Calle San Juan de Dios, continuing to the bottom of the street, where the Synagogue of the Tránsito stands.

Sinagoga del Tránsito   ★★★

Calle Samuel Ha-Levi, ☎ *22 36 55.*

Hours open: Tues.–Sat. 10 a.m.–2 p.m., and 4–7 p.m. (until 6 p.m. in winter). Open Sun. from 10 a.m.–2 p.m. Closed Mon.

Of eight known Toledo synagogues, only this and Santa María la Blanca Synagogue remain. It was begun in 1364 with a grant from Samuel Ha-Levi, the Treasurer of Spain during the reign of King Pedro the Cruel. Unfortunately, but characteristically, Pedro later turned on his treasurer, seized what remained of his wealth and put him to death. After the Jews were expelled from Spain, the synagogue was transformed into a church, from which comes its present name. It fell into neglect during the 18th century, until Francisco Perez Bayer, a Hebrew scholar, undertook the work of removing Christian overlays to restore it to its former splendor as a 13th-century synagogue. Inside you see the loving work of centuries of restoration.

The interior is basically one large two-story room. The balcony upstairs was for the women of the congregation. All around the upper walls, and covering the east end, run the most astonishing patterns of stuccowork inspired by the Moors. Hebrew inscriptions praise Pedro the Cruel, Samuel Ha-Levi, and God. Above the arches in the middle of the east end is a panel of delicate roses, surrounded by lovely designs. Fifty-four lacy windows are formed of stone tracery. Above the upstairs hall hangs an intricate cedarwood ceiling, with an effect that is altogether sublime. *Admission: 200 ptas.; ticket good for Casa del Greco.*

The large street perpendicular to C. San Juan de Dios is Reyes Católicos. Go right (north), arriving in two or three blocks at the Synagogue of Santa María la Blanca on the right.

Sinagoga Santa María la Blanca ★★

Calle Reyes Católicos, ☎ *22 84 29.*
Hours open: daily 10 a.m.–2 p.m., and 3:30–7 p.m. (until 6 p.m. in winter).
This was the principle synagogue of Toledo, rebuilt after a fire in 1250 on the site of its predecessor. Christians appropriated it after the programs in 1405, and transformed it into a church of the present name. In later years it was abandoned, then used successively as a barracks, a store and a workshop. Somehow much of the interior of the original synagogue remained intact, allowing accurate restoration.

Octagonal pillars with horseshoe arches form a main aisle with two more aisles on either side. Capitals are carved with intricate designs, relieving the whitewashed columns and walls. Above the arches sophisticated stucco designs reach to the ceiling, making the whole seem more like a mosque than a synagogue, but with a sophistication that few places of worship of any religion can claim. The incongruous sanctuary and retable were added in the middle of the 16th century. *Admission: 125 ptas.*

Continue past Santa María la Blanca on C. Reyes Católicos for one block to the monastery of San Juan de los Reyes.

San Juan de los Reyes ★★

Calle Reyes Católicos, ☎ *22 38 02.*
Hours open: daily 10 a.m.–2 p.m., and 3:30–7 p.m. (until 6 p.m. in winter).
The monastery was commissioned by Ferdinand and Isabella in gratitude for their triumph over "la Beltraneja," the pretender to Isabella's throne, and her Portuguese allies. "Historical Profile: Ferdinand and Isabella" on page 185 The monarchs' first architect, Juan Guas, finished the main structure in 1492 (although the whole was not completed until 1610). Ferdinand and Isabella so admired it that they planned to be buried here—before they conquered and were captivated by Granada. The facade is hung with over 100 fetters taken from Christian slaves freed during the liberation of Granada.

The restored cloister is elaborate yet graceful and its second story is especially to be appreciated, for its gallery retains a fine Mudejar ceiling. The church interior is composed of one impressively open aisle. Here and there characteristic Isabelline appliqué adds decorative interest. Where the transept crosses, openwork galleries display the entwined initials of Ferdinand and Isabella, along with a yoke and an arrow (in medieval Spanish these objects started with the first letter of the two monarchs' names), and the shields of Castile and Arágon. In no uncertain terms, the Catholic monarchs left their mark on this church. Supported by an eagle, amid statues of saints, powerful friezes of royal escutcheons line the transept walls. The heads carved beneath the arches are startling. *Admission: 125 ptas.*

Return through the C. Reyes Católicos to the first street on the left, Calle de Angel. Follow this for two blocks passing Santa Tomé. Take the narrow Calle Campaña across the intersection and left. Continue in the same direction across the next intersection where the street changes its name to Calle de Alfonso XII, which leads to the small Plaza Padre Mariana. Take the street leading from the left side of the plaza, Calle San Román, which quickly leads to the church of San Román around the corner.

Iglesia San Román   ★ ★

Calle San Clemente.
Hours open: Tues.–Sat. 10 a.m.–2 p.m., and 4–7 p.m. (until 6 p.m. in winter). Closed Sun. afternoon and all day Mon.
This 13th-century church demonstrates the extent to which the Moorish aesthetic dominated architecture in Toledo during its first century after passing into Christian hands. Both the outside and interior are Mudejar through and through, from the decorative brickwork to the horseshoe arches and their elaborate capitals. Today the church is a museum for Visigothic art, which is appropriate in the former capital of their domain. Note the jewelry especially. The lovely wall frescoes of the resurrection of the dead have been retained from the original church. *Admission: 200 ptas. (Good also for Taller del Moro, above.)*

If you have time for an act of homage, continue along C. San Román for one block to take the right fork. On the left is **Santa Domingo el Antiquo**. *Inside is an early view of Toledo by El Greco as well as the genius' last remains.*

Return along C. San Román, which becomes Calle Jesus y María after it crosses the intersection, then turn left at the next intersection onto Calle Trinidad. After a bend it enters the Plaza Arco de Palácio in front of the Cathedral. Continue across in the same direction, perpendicular to the Cathedral, into the large Calle Hombre de Palo. It narrows into Calle Comercio lined with shops, and in two blocks leaves you in the main square of Toledo, the Plaza Zocodover, which is lively and attractive. Here a right turn will take you to the **Museo de Santa Cruz**, *or a left will lead you to* **Santa Cristo del Luz** *(see descriptions in this section).*

Museo Santa Cruz   ★ ★ ★ ★

Calle Cervantes, ☎ *22 14 02.*
Hours open: Tues.–Sat. 10:30 a.m.–7 p.m. (until 6 p.m. in winter). Mon. 10 a.m. to 2 p.m. and 4:30–6:30 p.m. Closed Sun. afternoon at 2 p.m. and all day Mon.

Few museums in the world are housed in a more dramatic or beautiful building. It was built by Cardinal Mendoza, private confessor to Queen Isabella, as a hospital, a very sumptuous one, for the sick and orphaned of Toledo. Although the cardinal died before its completion, Isabella saw that his plans were carried through. Two fine architects of the day worked on it—Enrique Egas, on the interior, and Covarrubias, on the exterior. In truth the outside is not special, though the statue over the main portal of Cardinal Mendoza kneeling before the cross is worth a look, but the inside is magnificent.

It is a huge barn in the shape of a cross of equal sides, and seems to extend limitlessly in all four directions. Overhead runs an extraordinary wood ceiling. It would be hard to believe that paintings as spectacular as the collection in Santa Cruz would have to vie for attention against an architectural background, but architecture is seldom so dramatic.

The long entry hall is lined with fine 16th century tapestries and early furniture. The Zodiac tapestries have retained their rich blues and reds, and the figures are superb. At the end of the hall hangs the huge magnificent pennant from Don Juan's admiral's galley, flown during his victory over the Moors in 1571 at Lepanto. Then comes a corridor devoted to El Greco, in which over 20 canvases hang. The most famous is the *Altarpiece of the Assumption*, painted a few months before he died. Here the figures are more elongated than usual and the colors more acid. The virgin in the painting holds a book containing a record of El Greco's death, a detail added by his son. With its view of Toledo, *Saint Joseph and Child* is striking. Note the upside-down tumbling angels. On the second floor are two fine Riberas, mixed with less interesting paintings. The large *Holy Family* is reminiscent of Raphael. Tapestries depicting the history of Alexander the Great are striking, if more faded than the embroideries on the lower floor. An elegant Renaissance stair by Covarrubias leads down to a Plateresque patio, which in turn leads to small rooms housing archaeological finds. *Admission: 225 ptas.*

Ermita del Cristo de la Luz ★★

Cuesta del Cristo de la Luz. From the northwest side of the Plaza del Zocodover take Calle Silleria, which bends due west in one block. After the bend, take the third right onto Cuesta del Cristo de la Luz.

Hours open: any reasonable hour by applying to the gatekeeper.

This is a tiny, perfectly square mosque, built of brick in 922 on the site of a Visigothic church. It may well be the oldest surviving in Spain. Inside, it can be seen that pillars of the Visigothic church remain, remodeled by the Moors into superimposed arches like those in the Córdoba Mosque. Nine individual domes cover as many bays, resulting in a surprisingly harmonious composition. The apse is a Christian addition.

The name, "Christ of the Light" comes from a story that Alfonso VI's horse stopped here, when the king conquered Toledo, and knelt. (According to some versions, it was the horse of El Cid that bowed.) Investigation uncovered a Visigothic lamp still burning inside one wall, lighting a crucifix. This indeed would have been a miracle of candle-power, for the last Visigoths had departed 300 years before. *Admission: a tip to the gatekeeper.*

At least one monument outside the walls of Toledo is well worth seeing, the Hospital de Tavera. The building is remarkable, as is some of the art inside.

The Hospital is due north, at the end of a large square called Paseo de Merchan. It can be walked from the Ermita del Cristo de la Luz, although it is a hike of about half a mile. To walk, head north along Cuesta del Cristo de la Luz which leads into Calle Real de Arrabal. Continuing north, pass through the Puerta Nueva de Bisagra by Covarrubias, one of the gates of Toledo. Walk along Carretera a Madrid, by the east side of the square, to the Hospital at the garden's end. Alternatively, one can drive along the perimeter road and take a right on Carretaria a Madrid.

Hospital de Tavera   ★★

Passeo de Madrid, ☎ *22 04 51.*
Hours open: daily 10 a.m.–1:30 p.m. and 3:30–6 p.m.
Something sad emanates from this building, perhaps because, although it was never finished, it represents the final work of three great men.

This was the last building designed by Covarrubias; its stately form is a fitting memorial. He built it for Cardinal Tavera, descended from the combined great families of Medinaceli and Lerma. A double patio inside leads to a large chapel in which lay tombs of the Medinacelis—the most elegant being the tomb of Cardinal Tavera, the last work of the great sculptor Alonso Berruguete. Off the left side of the patio is a small museum of art and furniture belonging to the Dukes of Lerma. The huge dining hall displays Titian's *Portrait of Carlos V*, and a lovely Coello. In the library hangs a fine El Greco of *The Holy Family*, and a *Virgin*, unusual for actually being pretty. Ribera's *Philosophy* is nice, but the most striking Ribera—his strange painting of a bearded lady—is stashed in a small room. On the second floor is an utterly unforgettable painting by Zurbarán of the young Duke of Medinaceli, all in orange tones. On the same floor are a Tintoretto and a number of El Grecos, including his last canvas. *The Baptism of Christ by Saint John* is huge and includes all the characteristics that make El Greco the most recognizable of artists. *Admission: 600 ptas.*

Where to Stay

While hotels in Toledo are not numerous, they span all price ranges. Their number usually proves adequate since most visitors shortchange themselves by making Toledo only a day trip. July and August weekends are another matter, when reservations should be made in advance. The best news is that the three finest hotels are moderately priced, leaving the pleasant difficulty of choosing one over the other two.

Expensive ($100–$200)

Parador Conde de Orgaz   1st-class ★★★

Cerro del Emperador, Toledo (due south of the city, just off the circling road, Carretera de Circunvalación). ☎ *22 18 50, FAX. 22 51 66.*

This is one of Spain's modern paradors, and not our favorite by any means. True, it provides fine views of Toledo, but not spectacular enough to repay the inconvenience of being situated a long walk from town. Nor does the staff seem overly concerned with their clients' welfare. Avoid rooms 33 and 34, in which other guests' comings and goings and the elevator's rumble are clearly audible. *74 rooms, plus two suites.*

Moderate ($50–$99)

Hostal del Cardenal   R2nd-class ★ ★ ★ ★

Paseo Recaredo, 24, Toledo (In the northern wall of the city. The best route is to take the circular road past Paseo de Merchan, the large square that fronts the Hospital de Tavera, where a sign will point you left to parking for the hotel), ☎ *22 49 00, FAX 22 29 91.*

A better hotel would be hard to imagine: small, for intimacy; in a remodeled 18th-century cardinal's mansion, for history and elegance; and with a luscious garden, for peace, quiet and beauty. And, for an additional charge, you can have a suite with a terrace and still pay a moderate rate. Not that it matters, but the hotel is owned by the people who run the old taverna Botín in Madrid. What does matter is that there are so few rooms here, that reservations are advised. *25 rooms, plus two suites.*

María Cristina   2nd-class ★ ★ ★

Calle Marqués de Mendigorria, 1, Toled (opposite the Hospital de Tavera, north of the walls), ☎ *21 32 02, FAX 21 26 50, Telex 42827.*

This hotel should be the parador—a historic building located in the precinct of a historic sight. It is beautiful, run like a Swiss watch, and clean as can be. The rooms are about as attractive as those of the Hotel Cardinal, although the location is less convenient. *60 rooms, plus three suites.*

Carlos V   2nd-class ★ ★

Calle Horno de Magdalena, 1, Toledo (between the Alcázar and the Cathedral), ☎ *22 21 00, FAX 22 21 05.*

The location is in the heart of the city, so close to most sights it cannot be bettered. The hotel is modern, of no great architectural distinction, but half of the rooms have priceless views of the Cathedral. The rooms are merely hotel rooms, however. And being in the heart of town puts you in the center of city noise, not so loud in Toledo as in some other places, but not the quiet of the more highly recommended choices, either. *69 rooms.*

Inexpensive (Less than $50)

Los Cigarrales   3rd-class ★ ★

Carretera de Circunvalación, 32, Toledo (half a mile west of the parador), ☎ *22 00 53, FAX 21 55 46.*

Here you are presented with views as nice as those from the parador at much lower cost and amid friendly service. In addition, this hotel, a remodeled country house with wood beams in the rooms and tiles on the walls, is more attractive. To top it off, the dining room offers decent meals for less than $15. The hotel is, however, outside of town. *36 rooms.*

Imperio   R3rd-class ★ ★

Calle Cadenas, 5, Toledo (one block west of the Plaza del Zocodover), ☎ *22 76 50, FAX 25 31 83.*

The location is smack in the heart of medieval Toledo and the price is low enough to ease the most strained budget. The hotel is recently renovated, modern and clean, though the rooms are small. *21 rooms.*

Youth Hostel

Residencia Juvenil "San Servando

Castillo San Servando, Toledo (above the far bank of the Tajo, opposite the Alcázar. Cross the Alcántara Bridge), ☎ *22 45 54.*

For 775 ptas. you can stay in a castle and swim in the pool. That's the good news. Bring your own toilet paper; hot water stops at 9:30 a.m.; and reservations are imperative. That's the bad.

Where to Eat

Toledo is no gourmet paradise, nor does it tempt you with expensive restaurants since most are moderately priced. However, it is Spain's center for game, if such is your pleasure.

Expensive ($30+)

Asador Adolfo   ★★★

La Granada, 6 (head north along the facade of the Cathedral to reach the restaurant in twenty paces or so, at the corner of Hombre do Palo), ☎ *22 73 21.*
Closed Sunday evening, except before holidays.

Both the appropriate agedness of the surroundings and the quality of the food make this the best restaurant in Toledo. Parts of the restaurant date to the 15th century. The food is typical of the area, but cooked with extra refinement and care. It may be the best restaurant for game in all of Spain. Which is not to disparage the stuffed peppers or the special hake in saffron sauce. Even if you don't ordinarily like marzipan, try it here. Reservations are recommended. Credit Cards: A, D, M, V.

Moderate ($15–$30)

Cardenal   ★

Paseo Recaredo, 24 (see directions above to the hotel), ☎ *22 08 62.*

The garden outside is a delight, but accommodations are a bit cramped in the restaurant connected with this special hotel. You can watch the chef work in his kitchen, which is not our favorite dining view. At one time the food stood well above ordinary, though it has declined of late. Still you can get a decent suckling pig and the "Quarter of an Hour" fish soup is delicious. If asparagus is in season, there is none better. Credit Cards: A, D, M, V.

La Botica   ★

Plaza de Zocodover, 13, ☎ *22 55 57.*
Closed Sunday nights.

Eat in style in the dining room upstairs, or watch the passing throng from tables outside. The food is a clear cut above its competitors in the plaza, and the menu includes some original dishes, such as eggplant with cheese and shrimp. Finish with a refreshing fruit sherbet. Credit Cards: V.

Hierbabuena   ★

Calle Cristo de la Luz, 9 (just past the Ermita del Cristo de la Luz; see the directions to this sight.), ☎ *22 34 63.*

Closed Sun.

The Moorish ambience and candlelight make this a pleasant dining experience. The food, however, is ordinary. Credit Cards: A, D, M, V.

Casa Aurelio and Mesón Aurelio ★

C. Sinagoga, 6 and 1 (a tiny street a few steps north of the Cathedral), ☎ *22 20 97, and 22 13 92.*

The first restaurant is closed Wednesday and July; the second is closed Monday and August.

These neighbors are owned by the same family and serve comparable food. The food at either one should not disappoint, especially since prices are modest. The decor is informal, though the patio of the Casa is just a bit nicer than the setting of the Mesón. Credit Cards: A, M, V.

Inexpensive (Less than $15)

El Emperador ★

Carretera del Valle, 1 (follow the Carretera de Circunvalación around Toledo to the southwest of town where this restaurant is passed), ☎ *22 46 91*

Closed Monday and the first two weeks of September.

You can walk across the lovely 14th-century Puente de San Martin west of San Juan de los Reyes, then uphill to the left for a quarter of a mile. Views along the way are gorgeous, but a car or taxi is quicker. The best thing about "The Emperor" is terraced dining with views of Toledo. Decoration is dark wood, wrought iron and leather chairs—that is to say, Castilian. The food is simple and very reasonable. Credit Cards: M, V.

El Nido

Plaza de la Magdalena, 5 (a short block due south of the Plaza del Zocodover).

The prices of its special menus are the lowest in town. The food is hearty, if undistinguished.

Directory

Information

Located in the north end of the city at the Puerta Nueva de Bisagra, by the corner of the Plaza de Merchan. ☎ *22 08 43*. A convenient booth is set up in the Pl. Zocodover in summer.

Trains and Buses

The mudejar decorated train station (☎ *22 12 72*) is west of the city on Paseo de la Rosa. Direct trains to Madrid (one and one-half hour trip) leave 10 times per day through Aranjuez and cost less than $7. Service elsewhere involves changes. The local RENFE office is located at *Calle Silleria, 7*, just west of the Plaza del Zocodover.

Buses (☎ *22 58 50*), on Av. de Castilla la Mancha in the Zona Safón, are faster and cheaper than the train and deposit you a few blocks from the Pl. de Zocodover.

Post Office and Telephones

The post office (☎ *22 36 11*) is located at *C. de la Plata 1*, which is two blocks due north of the Cathedral, but hard to find, nonetheless. Telephones are available on the same street, west of the post office.

Police

Located in the Plaza del Zocodover at number 1 (☎ *21 34 00*; emergency: *091*).

Shopping

For centuries Toledo has been famed for inlaid steel (*damascene*), learned from the Moors. A great deal of **damascene** is offered in Toledo, but most is cheaply made by machine. Casa Bermejo, at *C. Airosas, 5* (☎ *22 03 46*) sells the good stuff. **Arms and knives** of all sorts are sold in shops lining the way to the Cathedral. **Marzipan** is a local specialty, made best at Casa Telesforo *in the Pl. Zocodover, 17* (☎ *22 33 79*).

A huge regional crafts fair for all of La Mancha is held the first two weeks of October in the north section of Toledo.

Taxis

There's a stand near the Alcázar, or call ☎ *22 16 98*.

Excursions

Aranjuez ★ ★ ★ is only 43 km east of Toledo, and its gardens provide lovely walks in season. N-400 leaves east from the circular road, Carretera Circunvalación, to take you there. A description of the town will be found under its own heading. The monastery of **Guadalupe** ★ ★ ★ lies in the mountains to the west, 178 scenic km away. See its separate description in the chapter on Extremadura. Take C-401 west from the circular road.

For the greatest variety and lowest prices in Spain on ceramics take an excursion to **Talavera de la Reina** ★ , 75 km west of Toledo. See below.

Talavera de la Reina ★

Population: 64,136
Area code: 925; zip code: 45600

> *From the circular road take N-403 heading northwest toward Torrijos. In 42k, just before Maqueda, this reaches N-V. Heading west along N-V, signs direct to Talavera in 33 km.*

Since the 15th century the name Talavera has meant ceramics. Famous for its designs in blue and yellow, today it is a center for ceramics factories that produce wares in most of the traditional colors of Spain, not only traditional blues and yellows. Factory showrooms are located on the west side of town. On N-V coming from the west you arrive exactly where the ceramic stores line the road—stores heaped with dishes and planters, vases and tiles, and objects you had never imagined could be fabricated in that material. The prices will astonish you in the most pleasant way.

Farther west for 24 km on N-V brings **Orpesa** with a fine 15th-century castle, now a parador. Another 7k brings the village of **Lagartera** where embroidered tablecloths and such have been sewn by local women for centuries (not the same women, of course). Almost every cottage displays the wares for sale.

OLD CASTILE AND LEÓN

As in a fairy-tale the Alcázar rises above Segovia.

Historical Profile:
Ferdinand and Isabella

Rank historical figures according to who imposed the greatest mark on modern Spain and Ferdinand and Isabella spring to the top. Before they came along, Spain had consisted of four fiercely independent territories ruled by four different kings. Spain was not a country until their marriage united the territory's two largest kingdoms and they conquered the rest. Ferdinand

and Isabella initiated the exploration of the New World, completed the re-conquest of Spain, and expanded the power of their kingship from a feudal office to a true monarchy. Equally consequential were their more blamewor-thy acts: they unleashed the pro-Catholic Inquisition, then banished both Jews and Moors from the soil of Spain.

Yet if a number of wildly improbably circumstances had not all come to-gether, neither Ferdinand nor Isabella would have been able to do anything for Spain. Each stood behind two more likely heirs until chance lifted them onto their thrones.

When Isabella's father, the King of Castile, died, he was succeeded by his eldest son Enrique IV. But her father had married twice and his second wife produced children as well: the first, on April 22, 1451, a daughter named Is-abella after her mother; the second, a son. The laws of succession dictated that the crown would pass next to King Enrique's children, so the second family could become eligible—first through its male—only if Enrique were to die childless. Whether Enrique did or did not leave a surviving child re-mains a mystery. What is certain is that Isabella's ascension to the throne hinged on the question of whether Enrique's designated heir was actually his child.

Enrique's reign began in kingly fashion with raids on the Moors at Grana-da. But the pleasures of monarchy—wine, women and courtly delights—soon started to appeal more strongly than royal duties. Enrique ceased rul-ing, entrusting his kingdom to ministers. Then, when his staid wife, Blanche of Aragón, paled as well in his eyes, Enrique moved to end his childless 12-year union. He applied to the pope for a dissolution of the marriage, claim-ing as his grounds the impotency of both parties. Thereby he won not only the annulment he desired but a nickname as well—"Enrique the Impotent."

Although Enrique next married the more lively Princess Juana of Portugal, it was not long before he tired of her as well, taking up with mistresses while his new wife cut a swathe through the ranks of the palace courtiers. One of these nobles, Beltran de la Cueva, emerged as Queen Juana's favorite. He challenged the other court knights to a joust to determine whose lady was fairest, and won the contest in Juana's name. For some reason this delighted the cuckolded Enrique, who celebrated the victory by endowing a new mon-astery. And so court life proceeded, until, eight years after marrying Enrique, Juana gave birth to a daughter.

Although named Juana after her mother, the daughter was maliciously re-ferred to as *la Beltraneja*, "the little Beltran girl," for few were persuaded of her royal paternity. Skeptics noted that Enrique had produced no children during 12 years of marriage to his first wife, and that their divorce had been based on his impotency. Further, this child had not been born until eight years of marriage to a second wife, notorious for her dalliances, while Enrique himself had produced no children at all by his many mistresses. It appeared to many that Enrique the Impotent was aptly named. So, when Enrique assembled the nobles of Castile to recognize the child as his heir, they refused.

Further, the Castilian nobles, their patience exhausted with this king who would not rule, demanded that Enrique acknowledge Alphonso, Isabella's brother, as his heir instead. Enrique initially agreed, but repudiated the arrangement as soon as the nobles disbursed. By now, so little respect remained for Enrique that his effigy was burned outside his own bedroom window, and supporters of Alphonso established a separate court, saddling Castile with two kings and a civil war. Three years later, Alphonso suddenly died and the rebels offered the crown to Isabella, who refused because Enrique, the rightful king, still reigned.

In the meantime, Enrique had been trying to marry off this potential contender for the throne. An early proposal from Ferdinand to Isabella had been rejected because his prospects for inheriting Aragón's throne were too slight. A match was made with Ferdinand's elder brother, however, although he died before the marriage could take place. Enrique next proposed the King of Portugal, but Isabella refused because he was too old. Finally, Enrique betrothed Isabella, without her consent, to one of Castile's main rebels in an attempt to isolate him from the other opposition leaders. Isabella's fiancé was not very appealing. He was much older, and had acquired a wide reputation for vice, despite presiding over a religious order. But he was eager, and applied to Rome for a release from his vow of celibacy. Fortunately for Isabella, while speeding towards the capital to complete their wedding arrangements, he died.

Other suitors, including Richard, soon to be Richard III of England, pursued her, as did both the brother of the king of France and a young man named Ferdinand from neighboring Aragón.

Ferdinand's course to Aragón's throne was as complex as the route Isabella had encountered in Castile. He was born on March 10, 1452, to the brother of Aragón's king. The king, however, having conquered southern Italy and finding it congenial, had taken up residence there, leaving the governance of Aragón to Ferdinand's father Juan (coincidently of the same name as Isabella's father). Like Isabella, Ferdinand was the offspring of a second marriage, the first of which had produced an older half-brother. By rights, if Ferdinand's father managed somehow to become king, Carlos, the elder half-brother, would succeed him. But Juan preferred Ferdinand over his other son so strongly that he waged war to deprive Carlos of the small kingdom of Navarre, inherited from his mother. Forced to leave Spain, Carlos wandered through Italy for ten years.

Why his father so favored Ferdinand remains a puzzle. Carlos possessed a superior intellect—he translated Aristotle's *Ethics* from the Greek—and had demonstrated a capacity for governing in Navarre. Although it is possible that Ferdinand's mother might have contrived to make her natural son favored, this is doubtful given that Juan was not the sort to be persuaded of anything he did not want. What is clear is that Ferdinand's father—after inheriting the throne of Aragón upon the death of his childless brother—refused to recognize Carlos as his heir. The nobles of Aragón then rose in arms to force Juan to acknowledge Carlos as heir-presumptive in conformity to law. But, at just that moment, Carlos died suddenly of mysterious, and some would claim suspicious, causes. Even after Carlos' death, half of Aragón still refused to recognize Ferdinand and seceded.

Juan, by now incapacitated by failing sight, left the conduct of the resulting war to his wife and the 16-year-old Ferdinand. Victory in that campaign finally secured the throne for Ferdinand, so he could begin the quest for a royal mate.

When Ferdinand sent an embassy to propose marriage directly to Isabella, she promptly accepted—the alternative being another of Enrique's unsuitable candidates. Here finally was a suitor close to herself in age and station, of proven accomplishments, and comely appearance. Her acceptance of Ferdinand's proposal, however, was given without Enrique's approval. When spies informed Enrique of the prospective match, he swore it would never take place, and dispatched a company of soldiers to kidnap Isabella, and stationing troops at the border to intercept Ferdinand. Fortunately, a group of Isabella's partisans prevented her capture, while Ferdinand evaded the border guards by disguising his attendants as traveling merchants and himself as their servant.

Isabella and Ferdinand wed on October 19, 1469, in a mansion in Dueñas, near the city of Valladolid. At 18, the bride was an acknowledged beauty, above middle height, blue-eyed and auburn-haired. Ferdinand, who stood shorter than his wife, possessed a full, square face, chestnut hair, a well proportioned body, and was younger by a year. Isabella had to borrow money from friends to pay their wedding expenses, and Ferdinand engaged in a piece of deception to ensure the ceremony's completion. Because the nuptial pair were cousins, papal dispensation was necessary to set aside consanguinity restrictions. When approval did not arrive in time, Ferdinand produced a forgery.

Despite Isabella's genuine desire for the marriage, she took care that her husband not exploit her position: the nuptial contract dictated that Ferdinand could not travel beyond the borders of Castile without Isabella's authorization, fill no positions in Castile's government without her consent, and authorize no royal ordinances without her countersignature.

News of the wedding enraged Enrique, who proclaimed that Isabella had forfeited the throne of Castile by marrying without his consent. Twice more he called on the nobles to ratify "la Beltraneja" as his legitimate heir, swearing sacred oaths that she was truly his daughter. Each time they declined his request. Four years later, the king, still protesting, died.

In 1474, Isabella was crowned ruler of Castile, and Ferdinand, in Aragón at the time, was coronated by proxy. "La Beltraneja", with her new husband, the King of Portugal, mustered forces to attack Castile. Five years of warfare ensued before Isabella routed the adherents of "La Beltraneja" in a decisive battle near Toro. That same year, 1479, Ferdinand's father died.

Against enormous odds, both Ferdinand and Isabella had attained the thrones of their separate states, forging, with their marriage, a union of mighty Castile and Aragón. At the time Castile consisted of Old Castile, plus land called New Castile that had been reclaimed from the Moors, and most of Andalusia. This kingdom covered the center, and encompassed more than half, of modern Spain. Aragón, originally a small territory, had expanded by conquest to include Catalonia and the rest of the eastern seacoast—altogether about a third of Spain's present territory. Except for the small northern kingdom of Navarre, and the ten percent of Moorish land around Granada, their marriage gave Isabella and Ferdinand control over the Spain we know today. However, the territory did not comprise a nation, for it lacked both common laws and common government; nor was it ruled by a unified monarchy: Isabella was Queen of Castile, while Ferdinand alone ruled Aragón. What their marriage did create was a means for future unification: their heir would govern all of Spain.

By the time Ferdinand and Isabella began their rule, the conquest of Granada had been a dream of Spanish monarchs for two centuries. It was Isabella who finally achieved the goal. She mustered and supplied troops for the campaign—in effect acting as commander-in-chief—while Ferdinand served as her general in the field. In a war that lasted a decade, she managed the financing, collecting and delivering of arms, horses, mules and food and drink for her troops—all accomplished during several pregnancies and births. In addition to this, she was inspired to establish the first field hospitals in history, and, despite the discouragement of authorities, she valued Columbus' project sufficiently to finance his explorations (See "Historical Profile: Columbus and the Conquistadores" on page 369.), bringing unheard-of fortunes to Spain in later years. But along with Isabella's accomplishments, her record includes one terrible stain.

In 1481 Spain instituted the Inquisition, although circumstances suggest that Ferdinand, more than Isabella, should be blamed for that institution of terror. (See "Historical Profile: Religion and the Inquisition" on page 395.) But, later, the notorious Inquisitor General and Isabella's childhood confessor, Tomás de Torquemada, used his considerable influence to persuade her to expel Spain's Jews. Spain's Jewish population, which counted for no more than a few percent, had never been a problem for the country. But Torquemada recited old wives' tales about Jews eating Christian babies, and argued relentlessly that because Christians were being seduced to convert to Judaism, his job of prosecuting heresy had grown impossible. Ignoring the fact that the Jewish religion had never proselytized, Torquemada further demanded that all Jews—not just convicted proselytizers—be punished because "a corporation convicted of a great crime should be disenfranchised, the innocent suffering with the guilty." [W. H. Prescott, *A History of the Reign of Ferdinand and Isabella*, Vol. II, p. 139] His persistence won out. Isabella, who had demonstrated genuine compassion both for her troops and for her subjects in need, signed the Edict of Expulsion in March, 1492.

Jews throughout Spain were given three months to either sell or forfeit all their property before leaving. Simultaneously, they were forbidden to carry gold or silver with them—that is to say money, for paper currency had yet to be invented. Perhaps 100,000 Jews departed under these harsh terms, most to neighboring Portugal. A minority chose to convert rather than suffer such a fate, but lying in wait for these "conversos" was the Inquisition. As Christians, they now fell within its purview. The damage Spain suffered from this expulsion is incalculable: departing Jews comprised both a sizable number of Spain's best-educated people and a large percentage of its merchants.

Despite their accomplishments, both good and evil, Ferdinand and Isabella were less powerful than we might expect. The power of their feudal thrones depended on the consent of the nobles, two or three of whom could raise more money and larger armies than could the king and queen. The Church, with its extensive land and riches, dominated by a foreign pope in Italy, constituted another powerful element beyond their control.

Undermining the strength of Spain's feudal lords required all the statecraft that Ferdinand and Isabella could summon. First they razed many of the kingdom's fortified buildings, thereby eliminating sanctuaries for potentially dissident nobles. Then they revoked awards of land and privileges that had been liberally distributed by King Enrique in a vain attempt to win the nobles over. Ferdinand and Isabella were less than consistent about this, however, for they heaped their own ample rewards upon those who had helped them conquer Granada. Last, and most importantly, they made ability, rather than nobility, the standard by which official appointments were made, often assigning government positions to men of common birth. This innovation deprived grandees of the added power of government offices, and allowed the government to separate itself from the nobility.

While the task of curbing the nobles was not completed until later reigns, Isabella was able to realize one goal during her tenure: she wrested the Span-

ish Church from the pope. In 1482, Isab██
over candidates for a vacant bishopric. For c██
appointments to high Church offices, often filling██
not infrequently, were their relatives, as the can██
objected. After the pope haughtily dismissed the ambass██
complain, she ordered all Spanish citizens to leave Rome,██
her intention to convene a council of Christian princes t██
Church. The vigor of her reaction so disturbed the pope that he se██
to mollify the Queen. When she refused him audience, the pope capit██
agreeing that future appointments would be made from a list proposed██
the Spanish monarch. Thus, the Roman Catholic church in Spain became
more nationalized than that in any other Catholic country.

Using her new ecclesiastical powers, Isabella appointed Francisco Jimenez de Cisneros as Archbishop of Toledo, the supreme prelate of Spain. Cisneros had practiced extreme asceticism as a young man, enduring the greatest privations to purify his soul. He lacked personal goals, but possessed a surfeit of ambition for his God. It was his purity that first brought him to Isabella's attention when he served as her confessor, but refused to live amid the luxuries of her palace.

Cisneros' first commission was to cleanse the Spanish church whose high offices were filled with nobles' sons and daughters, eager for the fortunes in revenue that accompanied these positions. Since religious belief had little to do with their appointments, prelates commonly lived as luxuriously as any noble, enjoying mistresses and siring children. Cisneros applied an ascetic broom that swept much of the luxury and sexual activity away.

His next goal was to convert as many Moors as possible to the true religion, as he saw it. Here his asceticism proved an impediment, for, despite the fact that the Granada Treaty of Surrender promised religious freedom to all, he resorted to imprisonment and torture to reconvert the few Muslims who had returned to Islam after a time as Christians. When Islamic leaders protested, they were imprisoned, causing the Muslim community to rise in rebellion, which Ferdinand put down only with difficulty. But rather than chastise the instigator Cisneros, Ferdinand punished those who rebelled. In 1502, Isabella and Ferdinand expelled all Moors from Spanish lands in the same callous way they had exiled Spain's Jews. In one stroke, Andalusia and Valencia lost almost all their farm workers, devastating Spain economically. Yet the misplaced goal of most of the country's Christians had now been accomplished—Spain was homogeneously Catholic.

The marriages that Ferdinand's and Isabella arranged for their children were equally consequential. The couple produced one son and four daughters. The eldest, a daughter named after her mother, wed the heir to the throne of Portugal, who died six months later after falling from his horse.

ir depression. The youngest, Cat-
, and then King Henry VIII of En-
Catherine of Aragón."

daughter of Maximilian, the Holy
a coalition of two mighty thrones.
the wedding. His wife, already preg-
l she delivered a stillborn child. But
aughter, named Juana, and they ar-
, Maximilian's son and heir.

ghter, Isabella, to try another marriage
e was betrothed to her first husband's
of Portugal. True to her mother's spir-
her fiancé promised to expel Portugal's

With the death of ___ Princess Isabella, as the eldest surviving child, added the title of heir to the throne of Spain to that of queen of Portugal. In her person lay the hope for a united peninsula. The poor woman, however, died in childbirth, and her sickly son survived for only two years.

Princess Isabella's death meant that inheritance of the throne of Castile evolved to Juana and her husband Philip. Philip was attractive enough to be called "the Handsome," and he brought a tidy inheritance to his marriage. From his mother's side, he had been bequeathed the Low Countries, modern-day Holland and Belgium. The pair produced a son, Carlos in February of 1500, who was to become the next king of Spain and the Low Countries, of the Holy Roman Empire and the Americas.

Isabella did not live to see her grandson rule the largest empire since the time of the Mongols. Her health had deteriorated with the passing of each beloved child, and her final burden was an inescapable awareness that something was wrong with Juana, now heir to the throne. In 1504 Isabella was attacked by a fever, lost her taste for food and suffered from an unquenchable thirst. In this condition she wrote her last will and testament. She named Juana "queen proprietor," along with her husband Philip. The laws of succession and his own children had eclipsed Ferdinand. Only if Juana were deemed incompetent, would Ferdinand continue to rule. To provide for her husband, whom she genuinely loved, she offered her best jewelry and one half of the royal revenues from the New World, which, if Ferdinand had actually received it, would have been a kingly sum indeed.

Shortly before noon on November 26, 1504, in the city of Medina del Campo, Isabella died. No family attended her. Ferdinand was away in Toledo on business; her few surviving children were living in foreign lands. She was 53 years old and in the 30th year of her reign. She was buried in Santa

Isabella church beside the Alhambra, without any memorial, having stipulated that the money thus saved should be given to the poor. In her will she added that

> *Should the king, my lord, prefer a sepulchre in some other place, then my will is that my body be there transported, and laid by his side; that the union we have enjoyed in this world, and, through the mercy of God, may hope again for our souls in heaven, may be represented by our bodies in the earth.*

W. H. Prescott, *Ferdinand and Isabella*, Vol. II, p.175.

On the evening of Isabella's death, Ferdinand resigned the throne of Castile, to which he no longer had title, then assembled the Cortes to declare Juana incompetent so he could assume the regency. The Cortes summarily affirmed Isabella's will, including Ferdinand's position as regent, but Ferdinand faced problems nonetheless. A strong minority of Castilian nobles, who regarded the unknown ways of Philip and Juana more optimistically than the known severity of Ferdinand, incited unrest in the kingdom and urged Philip to come to Spain. At the same time, both the King of France and Maximilian menaced Spain's borders.

Ferdinand responded by trying to produce an heir of his own. Within one year of Isabella's death, he wooed and married—in the same town of Dueñas in which a much younger Ferdinand had married Isabella 38 years before— an 18-year-old bride. The marriage, however, changed his situation—no longer was he the widower of the queen of Castile, now he was simply Ferdinand, the king of Aragón. Voices insisted more strongly that he resign the regency of Castile.

When Philip offered to come to Spain to co-rule, Ferdinand seized the offer as his only hope of retaining his hold on Castile. But Philip landed with hardened German troops, and announced that he had changed his mind about sharing the regency, refusing even to allow Ferdinand to see his own daughter. His options exhausted, Ferdinand ceded Castile to Juana and Philip. The Cortes then recognized Juana as monarch, with Carlos, her son, as heir. Philip gathered the reins of Castile, and Ferdinand left the peninsula to sojourn in Italy.

What had caused all this maneuvering for the regency was the fact that Juana, the rightful ruler, was insane. When, for example, she heard rumors that her husband had taken a lover, Juana attacked the woman in question and shaved her bald. It seems that Philip never cared for Juana, although she was thoroughly, and insanely, smitten with him. The shaving incident was Philip's final straw; he determined to have nothing more to do with Juana. But the less he cared for her, the more intensely jealous she became. Philip filled government offices with friends from abroad and lived off the fat of Castile for two months, then caught a chill while playing ball and died. Juana sat immobile for three months in the room where he died, seldom talking, signing no official documents and shedding no tears. Finally, she consented to bury her husband in Granada, provided that she accompany the funeral procession.

Thus began a mad cortege. The procession moved only by night because Juana insisted that "a widow, who had lost the sun of her own soul, should never expose herself to the light of day." [W.H. Prescott, *Ferdinand and Isabella*, Vol. I, P. 268]. The daylight hours were passed observing funeral services in some monastery or church enroute. One day they stopped mistakenly at a convent for nuns, believing it to be a male monastery. Juana ran out screaming that everyone must leave. She spent the rest of the day guarding Philip's coffin in fields nearby, terrified lest some nun lure her dead husband away.

Almost a year to the day after he left Spain, Ferdinand returned for good. From this time until his death he ruled Castile severely in Juana's name. In 1512, preparing for one of the recurring border wars with France, Ferdinand asked permission of the King of Navarre to send troops through that small territory in the shadow of the Pyrenees. When permission was refused, Ferdinand invaded and won the final piece of land that comprises modern Spain.

As if his job were now finished, Ferdinand's health began to decline. He experienced difficulty in breathing and complained about his heart. Returning from a hunt in January of 1516, Ferdinand died in a small house in Madrigalejo, near Trujillo. He was 63 years old and had ruled Spain for 41 years. His remains were buried beside Isabella's in Granada.

According to Machiavelli, Ferdinand had been the very model of a modern prince. His ambition was pure, undeterred by religion or other conceits. While devout Isabella toiled and bore his children, Ferdinand spawned illegitimate offspring wherever he went. He cared only for his own future: had his second marriage produced a male heir, Ferdinand would have preserved his personal power but undermined the future union of Castile and Aragón. He was acknowledged as the most astute politician in Europe of his time, possessing a cleverness that enabled him consistently to best France, though she was stronger in every military way. If Isabella was loved by her subjects and fondly remembered, Ferdinand was respected and feared.

During their long, eventful reigns, Ferdinand and Isabella commissioned an astonishing number of buildings. Many survive. Of course their tomb in **Granada** is a requirement for anyone interested in the pair, but there is also a fine church, San Juan de los Reyes, and an elegant hospital, Santa Cruz, that they commissioned in **Toledo**.

Old Castile and León, however, was the stage for most of the events of their lives and remains the repository for more Isabelline structures than any other area. Isabella's father, Juan II, is buried in Cartuja de Miraflores on the outskirts of **Burgos**. The nobles of Christian Spain first proclaimed Isabella as their monarch in the Alcázar of **Segovia**. She married Ferdinand in Dueñas, once a separate village, but now incorporated within the city of Valladolid. Unfortunately, the mansion in which the wedding took place no longer exists. Still surviving in **Valladolid**, however, are two of the greatest works of the architectural style that developed during their reign—Isabelline—in the portals of the San Gregorio and San Pedro churches. As young monarchs, Ferdinand and Isabella loved the monastery of San Tomás in **Ávila**, which they had built and where they planned to be buried. Here they stayed whenever duties permitted, often entertaining Torquemada, the Grand Inquisitor. After the tragic death of their only son Don Juan and his burial at San Tomás, however, it became a sad place for them thereafter. Ferdinand and Isabella also did much to encourage the University of **Salamanca** and are appropriately commemorated in the magnificent decorations in the School Square.

Old Castile and León

Madrid presents Spain's present, but Old Castile and León commemorates its past. Here, in the 10th century, Christian Spain came into being and grew to dominate the peninsula. As the center of the Reconquest, Old Castile and León defended against counterattacks from the Moors by erecting castles and fortresses over its terrain, in the process earning the first half of its name. But after the Reconquest, Old Castile and León faded, letting the new capital of Madrid lead Spain into modern times. History passed by Old Castile and León, but no area of Spain preserves a greater number of monuments from the era of the Reconquest.

When the Moors swept through the peninsula at the dawn of the eighth century, they pushed the Visigoths to footholds in Asturias, just north of León. Few and powerless, these Christians struggled for two centuries to regain a mere hundred miles of land to their south. Even so, that conquest involved a victory that seems astonishing in retrospect. Abd er Rahman III, the strongest Caliph who ever ruled Andalusia, determined in 939 to finish off the remaining northern Christians. He collected an army of 100,000 men for what he called his "Omnipotent Campaign." Outnumbered by at least ten to one, Christian forces somehow managed to rout his army at Simancas, near the present city of Valladolid in Old Castile. This victory allowed Christians from Asturias to flow 100 miles south into the territory they called León, after its major city. By 910, one noble was elected king.

Now the battleground between Christians and Moors shifted farther south to a 150-mile band stretching from León to just above Madrid—the territory of Old Castile. Neither the Christian King of León nor the Moorish Caliph could hold much of it for long, so local strongmen consolidated what power each could. When unification was finally effected, however, it was not by a leader from León, but by a Christian ruler from Navarre to the east. Sancho the Great of Navarre first conquered Aragón, then mastered Castile in 1029. Ironically, this unification caused the disharmony among the Christians that lasted for 500 years. For, when Sancho died one year after his conquest, he willed his new territory of Castile to one son, and the eastern territory of Aragón to another. Fernando I, the son who received Castile, quickly added León to his kingdom by marrying its heir, with the result that one king now ruled Castile and León, while another governed Aragón. And so the situation would remain for half a millennium.

Castile and León took the lead in the struggle to reconquer the Moorish lands in the south. (See "Historical Profile: Moors and the Reconquest" on page 267.) During this era, it functioned as a country with all the trappings of nationhood: a capital—first at León, then Burgos, then Toledo, then Valladolid; universities—at Palencia, Salamanca and Valladolid; and numerous

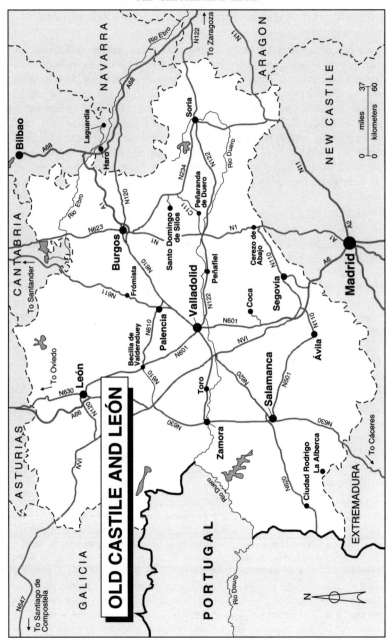

OLD CASTILE AND LEÓN

bishoprics, for the Christians were fervent, and their struggle with the Moors was a holy war.

Because of its leadership in the Reconquest, every Christian military success strengthened Castile and León. Before long it could count six million inhabitants which made it dominant in any Christian alliance. Leadership lasted for five centuries, until Isabella married Ferdinand from Aragón and together they defeated the last Moors in Granada. (See "Historical Profile: Ferdinand and Isabella" on page 185.) Castile and León remained the most powerful and populous region in Spain, until Felipe II moved the capital south to Madrid in 1561 to deprive Old Castile and León of its political importance. Stagnation set in, people migrated elsewhere, until the population declined to the two and a half million of today in a Spain grown four times as populous.

Old Castile and León make up one fifth of Spain. Except for mountains on its edges, it is a mesa that extends the landscape of La Mancha from New Castile. Similar crops of wheat and other grains grow on similar rust-clay soil in fields turned bright red in spring by a billion wild poppies. Today it is agriculturally rich, but it was not always so. From the 13th century until the modern era, monarchs favored sheep production over agriculture. Flocks of northern sheep would be gathered for migrations south in the winter, then home again in the spring. These flocks numbered many millions, and royal decrees gave sheep the right to cross any land in their way. Moving multitudes stripped vegetation like locusts as they passed, leaving the soil naked to the depredations of wind and rain, and destroying what had once been fertile land. Only in this century has prudent farming restored fertility, allowing agriculture to flourish again.

Despite the great expanse of land, dense communities developed. Most were founded during the Reconquest when the times required an architectural compactness that defensive walls could encircle. Population declines since the 16th century have allowed these towns to retain their character in a way that cities with expanding populations never could. These old towns make for unrivaled sight-seeing.

The area of Old Castile and León contains some of Spain's best sights. **Burgos** ★★★★ in the northeast boasts of the finest Medieval architecture in the country, including the finest Gothic cathedral and is itself a most pleasant city. In the same area are an elegant Romanesque monastery at **Santo Domingo de Silos** ★★★, a Renaissance palace at **Peñaranda de Duero** ★★ and the lovely town of **Soria** ★★.

Salamanca ★★★★, in the southwest, retains its ancient university, an architectural jewel of the Plateresque, and its Old Cathedral, a preserved marvel. **Zamora** ★★ and **Toro** ★★, nearby, display more Romanesque churches, while the entire town of **La Alberca** ★★ seems preserved from the Middle Ages. **Segovia** ★★★★★, in the south center, is spectacularly situated to display a castle like that at Disneyland. It also retains a perfect Roman aqueduct, an imposing cathedral, and a host of delicate Romanesque churches. In the 100 odd miles between Salamanca and Segovia lie **Ávila ★★★**, still surrounded by imposing medieval walls, and **Coca Castle ★★**, the paradigm of a Renaissance fortress. **León ★★★**, to the north, offers a Gothic cathedral to rival those in France, and its Old Quarter feels like the oldest in Spain. **Valladolid ★★**, in the center, is history personified. It was the capital for Ferdinand and Isabella, the city where Cervantes lived and Columbus died (both houses are preserved). Valladolid also offers a superb museum of wood sculpture. A splendid Romanesque church at **Frómista ★★** is in the same area (and equally close to Burgos). Lastly, the Rioja wine-growing region on the northeastern border, offers **Haro ★★** as a center for touring and sipping. The region of Old Castile and León can easily keep sightseers busy for two weeks.

Ávila ★★★

Population 41,735
Zip code: 05000; area code: 918

> *From* **Madrid** *take A-6 north, exiting at Villacastin (exit 4) for N-110 west, a trip of 132 km. From* **Salamanca** *take N-501 east for 98 km. From* **Segovia** *take N-110 west for 66 km.*

The most striking feature of Ávila is its walls. No other city in Spain and few in the world can rival its imposing picture of strength and age.

A town existed on these heights long before the walls went up. But in the 11th century, when Alfonso VI drove south to take Toledo, the center of his power shifted. He moved his fortifications southward, below Ávila, ordering the city to be fortified. Count Raymond of Burgundy, his son-in-law, completed the project in three years, by 1091. Two thousand citizens did the work of enclosing a rectangle almost 3000 by 1500 yards with walls 10 feet thick, over 40 feet high, punctuated by 88 round towers.

The huge fort required people to defend it, so Alfonso encouraged subjects from northern Asturias to migrate, along with knights who won renown as the Knights of Ávila. The strategy evidently succeeded, for no one ever breached these walls. During the late stages of the Reconquest, the Knights of Ávila assisted in winning Zaragoza, Córdoba and Seville, and their spoils fueled the desire for a commemorating cathedral. Work in the earliest Gothic style began in 1157 in the form of a fortress-church stuck into the town walls. By the 15th century, Ávila attained its greatest wealth, but began to decline with the end of the Reconquest. Decline accelerated when its gentry followed the Spanish court to Madrid. The expulsion of the Moors from Spain, in 1609, sealed Ávila's fate by depriving it of most of its craftsmen.

In 1515, Teresa Sanchez de Cepeda y Ahumanda was born and, as Saint Theresa, brought fame again to Ávila. At the age of seven, she attempted to run to the Moors, hoping to be martyred by them. She must have been an unusual little girl. Theresa's background was nobility tainted, from the Spanish point of view, by the blood of a Jewish grandfather. At puberty she began to experience mystical visions and religious dreams, all of which she wrote about exquisitely in diaries. At 19, she took the veil as a Carmelite nun. Led by visions to reform the Church, which had relaxed its views as it grew rich, she founded her own stricter version of the order, the Descalced (Barefoot) Carmelites. By the time she died in 1582, she had been interviewed by kings and earned a reputation as holy. This was confirmed by sainthood conferred only 40 years after her death. In 1975 she was named a Doctor of the Church, which put her in the company of Sts. Augustine and Thomas Aquinas.

Ávila's **walls** ★★★★ should be viewed and preferably walked. The **Cathedral** ★★ is an imposing monument; and the Romanesque basilica of San Vicente ★★ is huge and lovely. The **Monastery of Santo Tomás** ★★★ was founded by Ferdinand and Isabella and served as their palace, the mausoleum of their son, Don Juan, and the frequent residence of the Grand Inquisitor. For the Ávila of Sta. Teresa, see the **Convent of Sta. Teresa** ★, built on the site where she was born; the **Convent de La Encarnación** ★, where she lived as a nun for 20 years and experienced her visions; and the **Convent de San José** ★, the first for her new order. A half day is sufficient.

> *If arriving from* **Madrid** *or* **Segovia**, *turn left off of N-501, called Av. de Madrid, after passing the Basilica of San Vincente. At the park turn left and make the first right onto C. San Segundo which takes you past the town walls and Cathedral into the Pl. Sta. Teresa, for parking. If arriving from* **Salamanca** *turn left at the city walls onto Av. de Madrid. Circle the walls until the large basilica of San Vincente. Turn right. At the park turn left and take the first right onto C. San Segundo which follows the town walls, past the Cathedral, and into the Pl. Sta. Teresa for parking.*

Walls   ★★★★

These imposing barricades are almost 1000 years old, yet complete. Of course, some reconstruction has been necessary, but overall their character remains original. The walls should be scanned from a distance to gather their extent, viewed from the base to appreciate their height, and walked along (entrance beside the parador, see later in this section) to appreciate their massiveness and sense what it would be like to defend a medieval city.

> *Pass from Pl. Sta. Teresa through the gate into the old city. Once through, turn onto the second right, following the street as it bends left and right again until it reaches the Pl. de la Catedral. Ahead, on the right, is the front of the Cathedral; on the left is the 14th-century palace of a nobleman named Valderrabános, now a hotel.*

Cathedral

Pl. Catedral, ☎ *21 16 41.*

Hours open: daily 9 a.m.–1 p.m. and 3–7 p.m. (Opens at 10 a.m. in winter.)

The outside of massive grey granite is a curious architectural mishmash, punctuated by rows of balls. The 14th-century left door, carved of sandstone that weathered poorly, was moved from the west side of the church to its present protected location. The center portal, more animatedly carved than the others, was added in the 18th century. Most dramatic is the back of the church, so fortresslike that it is incorporated into the town walls.

The interior is a surprise after the dull fortress exterior. The nave soars and looks up to stones surprisingly patterned in red and yellow. Best of all, the clerestory stretches high, letting enough light inside to see the art clearly, a pleasant change from most Spanish churches. The altar is by the great Berruguete and others. At the center of the ambulatory resides a lovely alabaster tomb of Cardinal Madrigal, a 15th-century bishop of Ávila depicted sitting and reading. In the south (left-hand) aisle, the sacristy still wears enough original paint to suggest what a church of the period would look like when new—all colorful and bright. Its rear serves as a museum, containing an El Greco portrait and a huge monstrans (portable reliquary). A Romanesque doorway farther on leads to a delicate cloister. *Admission: 200 ptas., to the Sanctuary.*

C. Reyes Católicos runs behind the Palácio Valderrábanos hotel (opposite the Cathedral) west into the Pl. de la Victoria. The street going left across the plaza runs to the Pl. General Mola and the **Palace of Onates***, sporting a tower complete with battlements. A gentle right along the palace leads into the Pl. la Santa where the church of the* **Convent of Sta. Teresa** *is located.*

Convento de Sta. Teresa

Pl. de al Santa, ☎ *21 10 30.*

Hours open: daily 9 a.m.–1 p.m. and from 4–7 p.m.

The present Baroque edifice, dating from the late 17th century, is built on land once owned by Saint Theresa's father, where she was born and raised. Off the north transept an ornate chapel marks the place of her birth. Pieces of the saint are beside the gift shop. *Admission: free.*

West of the church front is the Renaissance **Palace de Nuñez Vela** ★ *with lovely windows and an elegant patio. Back at the Cathedral, a street along its north side leads through the main gate of the walls. Outside, straight ahead, a left from the Pl. de Italia leads to the* **Casa de los Deanes***.*

Casa de los Deanes

Pl de Navillos.

Hours open: Tues.–Sun. 10 a.m.–2 p.m. and 4–7 p.m. Open Sun. 11 a.m. to 1:30 p.m. Closed Mon.

This 16th-century palace, once the deanery of the Cathedral, is now the local museum. It contains a fine triptych attributed to Memling along with early furniture and some attractive ceramics. *Admission: 200 ptas.*

Past the Deanery, the first left runs to a park. A left turn along its far end, brings a first right which leads to the **Basilica of San Vicente**.

San Vicente   ★★

Pl. de San Vicente, ☎ *25 5230. Access is from the south side.*
Hours open: Tues.–Sun. 10 a.m.–1 p.m. and 4–7 p.m. (until 6 p.m. in winter and Sun.) Closed Mon.

The church commemorates the martyrdom in 303 of the child-saint Vincent and his sisters. The basilica was begun in the 12th century, but took 200 years to complete, so it mainly is Romanesque but incorporates early Gothic elements, such as ceiling ribs. The front displays unusually lively Romanesque carving around a double door-way. Inside, beneath a fine lantern tower, rests the 12th-century tomb of the Saint. The canopy is a later addition, but the carving on the tomb is of the period and depicts the martyrdom in an evocative and accomplished manner. A slab in the crypt below marks the supposed spot where the Romans killed these children. The ensemble and its display make a deeply felt memorial. *Admission: 100 ptas.*

The walls lead south to the parking in the Pl. Sta. Teresa, which at its east end presents the church of **San Pedro** ★ , *a fine Romanesque edifice, with an impressive lantern and rose windows. Pass along the north (left) side of the church to take the C. Duque de Alba, which heads left, for three blocks to the* **Convento of San José**.

Convento San José   ★

Pl. de Las Madres, ☎ *22 21 27.*
Hours open: daily 10 a.m.–1 p.m. and 4–7 p.m.

Saint Theresa began her reform of the Church with this convent in 1562 by offering the inhabitants a simple life of worship. Inside are tombs of the early adherents, including that of Lorenzo de Cepeda, the Saint's brother. A small museum displays mementos of the Saint and musical instruments the first nuns played. It seems that Theresa handled percussion. *Admission: 30 ptas.*

From the Pl. Sta. Teresa parking lot, past the front of San Pedro Church, then along its south face, the Av. de Alverez Provisional is entered. In a few blocks it passes the **Monesterio San Tomás**.

Monesterio San Tomás   ★★★

Pl. Granada, ☎ *22 21 27.*
Hours open: daily 10:30 a.m.–1 p.m. and 4–7 p.m.

For a time this monastery was the favorite residence of Ferdinand and Isabella. They commissioned it, funded it lavishly, and spent their summers here. Isabella's former confessor, Tomás de Torquemada, the first and most infamous Inquisitor General of the Inquisition, often joined them. He liked the place so much that he regularly convened tribunals of the Inquisitions here, and chose to be buried at this spot. Then tragedy struck when Ferdinand and Isabella's son, Don Juan, suddenly died. They buried him in this beloved monastery, but they could not bear to pass their summers here thereafter.

The facade displays the emblems of Ferdinand and Isabella—entwined arrows and yokes—the Spanish names for which (*flechas* and *yugo*) begin with their initials ("y" in the Middle Ages stood for the later "i" as the first letter of "Isabella"). Architectural details are highlighted throughout by rows of balls, the peculiar Ávila style.

Inside, at the crossing of the transept, is the mausoleum of the only son of Ferdinand and Isabella, who died at 19. The delicate tomb is a Renaissance marvel by the Florentine Domenico Fancelli, who years later carved another in Granada for the parents of the boy. The altar retable depicting the life of Saint Thomas in high relief is a masterpiece by Berruguete. In the third chapel on the north side are effigies of Juan D'Ávila and his wife, who were Prince Juan's tutors. A plain slab in the sacristy marks the final resting place (until he goes elsewhere) of Torquemada, the infamous Inquisitor General.

Three cloisters gird the church. The first is relatively unadorned, the second is the "Silent Cloister," intimate and richly decorated on the upper gallery. Stairs go up to a choral gallery furnished with finely carved 15th-century Gothic choir stalls. Then a second flight leads to a gallery overlooking the altar, and allows appreciation of its detail. Beyond the Silent Cloister is the third, larger, solemn "Cloister of the Catholic Monarchs." It displays a collection of oriental objects gathered by missionary brothers. Stairs lead up to a gallery in which Isabella and Ferdinand sat in virtual thrones. Notice their coats of arms on the balustrade. *Admission: 100 ptas., to the cloisters.*

Where to Stay

Ávila provides few hotels, but, except for July and August, since few people spend the night their number usually proves sufficient. Two special hotels are included.

Expensive ($100–$200)

Palacio de Valderrábanos   1st-class ★ ★ ★
Pl. de la Catedral, 9, Ávila, ☎ *21 10 23, FAX 25 16 91, Telex 22481.*
The building was a 14th-century palace for an early Bishop of Ávila. Despite the proximity of the equally historic parador, this hotel is the clear choice for spending an atmospheric night. The colors of the Palacio are rather loud and the interiors dark, with a feel of the '30s about the decoration. Once exceptionally grand, the hotel is showing signs of age and dust, but it remains a special place, especially for rooms overlook the Cathedral. *70 rooms, plus three suites.*

Parador Raimundo de Borgoña   1st-class ★ ★
Marqués de Canales y Chozas, 16, Ávila (by the middle of the north wall), ☎ *21 13 40, FAX 22 61 66.*
Although named after the man who oversaw the construction of the city walls, this parador is lodged in the former 15th-century Benavides Palace. Twelve of the rooms are in the palace, the rest in a modern addition of no special charm. Most of the furniture in the public areas is antique. The garden is lovely and leads to a stairway up to the city walls that non-guests may also traverse. *62 rooms, plus one suite.*

Moderate ($50–$99)

Hostería de Bracamonte   2nd-class ★ ★
Bracamonte, 6, Ávila (one block north of Pl. de Victoria, the main plaza within the walls), ☎ *25 12 80.*

The hotel is restful and quiet, not least because of a lovely patio. The decoration is attractive in a dark wood Castilian way. Prices for comfortable rooms are also appealing. *17 rooms, plus one suite.*

Inexpensive (Less than $50)

Hostale Continental   ★★

Pl. de la Cathedral, 6, Ávila, ☎ *21 15 02.*

This was a hotel, now degraded to hostale. The building remains from a bygone era with rooms as clean as any hotel but with lower prices. All in all, this is a comfortable place to lay your head. *54 rooms.*

El Rastro   ★

Pl. del Rastro, 1, Ávila (Halfway along the inside of the south wall of Ávila), ☎ *21 12 18, FAX 25 16 26.*

Known better as a restaurant, 14 comfortable, if small, rooms are offered for the night in a Renaissance building, and are rock-bottom in price. *14 rooms.*

Youth Hostel

Resudebcua Juvenal Duperier

Av. Juventud, Ávila (15 minutes southeast of Pl. Sta. Teresa along Av. Alférez Provisional), ☎ *21 35 48.*

Open only from the second week of July through the end of August, this is a small hostel (only 20 beds) so reservations are necessary. The curfew is 11 p.m., but a bed costs only 800 ptas.

Where to Eat

Specialties of the area are roasts, especially lamb (*cordero*) and veal (*tenera*). The special dish of the city is a dessert of clotted egg yolks called *yemas.*

Moderate ($15–$30)

El Molina de La Losa   ★★★

Bajada de La Losa, ☎ *21 11 01.*
Closed Monday in winter.

The setting could hardly be more pleasant. Head out of Ávila, following signs to Salamanca. Just past the west end of the walls, as the road crosses a bridge spanning the gentle Adaja River, look right to see this restaurant, looking like a French country inn on an isthmus in the river. In fact it is an ancient mill. Turn right across the bridge at the sign for the restaurant. Do not be put off by the rustic bar as you enter, the restaurant upstairs is pinewood bright with country furniture and gingham table cloths. Enjoy fine views of the river and Ávila's walls. The lamb is delicious here, but the specialty is fish fresh from the river. Credit Cards: M, V.

El Rastro   ★

Pl. del Rastro, 1, ☎ *21 31 43.*

Halfway along the inside of the south wall of Ávila is this noted restaurant, housed in a former palace, though the decor is more rustic than elegant. Roasts are the specialties. When the restaurant is crowded, as it is frequently, the service can be slow. Credit Cards: A, D, M, V.

Inexpensive (Less than $15)

A number of inexpensive restaurants surround the large Pl. de la Victoria, three short blocks west of the Cathedral. All serve reasonably prepared food.

Directory

Information

Located at Pl. de la Catedral, 4, opposite the Cathedral entrance, the Tourismo is open weekdays from 9 a.m. to 3 p.m. and from 5–7 p.m. Open until 2 p.m. on Saturdays.

Post Office and Telephones

The post office is located at *Pl. de la Catedral, 2*, with telephones next door.

Trains and Buses

The train station is at *Av. de Portugal, 17* (☎ *22 01 88*; information: ☎ *22 65 79*) at the end of Av. José Antonio, northeast of the walls. Service between Madrid (two hours, under 1000 ptas.) is frequent, as are connections to most cities in Old Castile.

The bus station is located at the intersection of *Av. Madrid and Av. Portugal*, two blocks due east of San Vicente basilica (☎ *22 01 54*). Because train service is so good, buses rather neglect Ávila.

Police

Av. José Antonio, 3 (☎ *21 11 88*).

Burgos ★ ★ ★ ★

Population: 156,449
Zip code: 09000; area code: 947

*From **Madrid** A-1 (E-5) becomes N-1, reaching Burgos in 235 km. From **Valladolid** take N-620 (E-80) for 125 km. From **Segovia** take N-110 for 57 km to Cerezo de Abajo where N-1 is picked up going north for a total of 194 km. From **León** take N-601 south towards Valladolid for 67 km to Becilla de Valderaduey where you change to N-610 to Palencia for 61 km. There pick up N-620 (E-80) for a total of 216 km. From **Valladolid** N-620 north reaches Burgos in 117 km, but be careful not to turn off into Palencia. From **Santander** N-623 goes south to Burgos in 93 km. From **Bilbao** A-68 heads south toward Logrono. Just before Miranda in 67 km, turn west onto either A-1 or N-1 for a continuation of 90 km. From **Pamplona** N-III heads west to Logrono in 92 km. There you take N-120 for 113 km further west.*

Burgos began as a military outpost to fend off Moors, but gained prominence when Count Fernán González briefly united the county of Castile in 950 and made Burgos his seat. The city's importance was enhanced by Fernando I, the first king of a united Castile and León, who appointed it his capital in 1037. Fifty years later, however, Alfonso VI captured Toledo and moved the capital there. Over the next 400 years, these two cities vied with one another for the honor of being Christian Spain's primary city. In 1221 Burgos commenced a great cathedral, in part to meet the "cathedral challenge" from Toledo. The rivalry became moot, however, after the conquest of Granada in 1492, when Ferdinand and Isabella chose still another city, Valladolid, as their capital. Burgos did not really need the status of a capital to be important, however, because it was situated at the crossroads of the main routes both to Santiago de Compostela and to southern Spain. It was and remains a commercial and military center, even to serving as the seat of Franco's government throughout Spain's Civil War.

Burgos claims El Cid as its most famous son, though, as Rodrigo Diaz, he was actually born in Vivar, six miles away. When Alfonso VI came to the throne after the suspicious death of his brother, the nobles appointed Diaz to extract a public oath from Alfonso that he bore no complicity in the death. Alfonso never forgave his vassal for this and soon found an excuse to expel him. Homeless, Rodrigo became a mercenary soldier who enjoyed outstanding success, campaigning both against and also for the Moors. Soon he was known by the Arabic title of El Sidi, "The Commander," which the Christians mispronounced as El Cid. El Cid's greatest feat was the conquest of a huge area around Valencia, which he held until he was defeated and killed by the Moors five years later. His wife, Doña Jimena, brought his body home, and today it lies in the Burgos Cathedral.

The Cathedral and old town lie along the Arlanzón River, which is lined on the north side with trees and flowered promenades. The old town, hemmed on its other side by a forested hill and ruined castle, is relatively small. The newer city spreads east and west and across the river, but offers little of historic or scenic interest. Unlike the typical medieval hill town with a maze of cobblestoned alleys, old Burgos seems green and light, a place to relax as well as to enjoy the sights.

Arriving from **Valladolid** *you enter the western part of Burgos and follow the Arlanzón River on Paseo del Empecinado as far as a pedestrian bridge opposite the Cathedral. Turn right here, away from the bridge, into the Pl. de Vega for parking. More parking is available at the next bridge after a right at the Pl. de Conde de Castro, where a large lot stands at the next left. From* **Madrid** *and* **Segovia** *on N-1, follow the opposite bank of the river and pass the lovely Pl. Miguel Primo de Riveira and bridge. Turn left and cross the river, then take the second left into a large parking lot. From the* **north** *you enter eastern Burgos. Cross, if necessary, to the southern side of the Arlanzón River and follow it until opposite the Cathedral. Turn left into the Pl. de Vega for parking.*

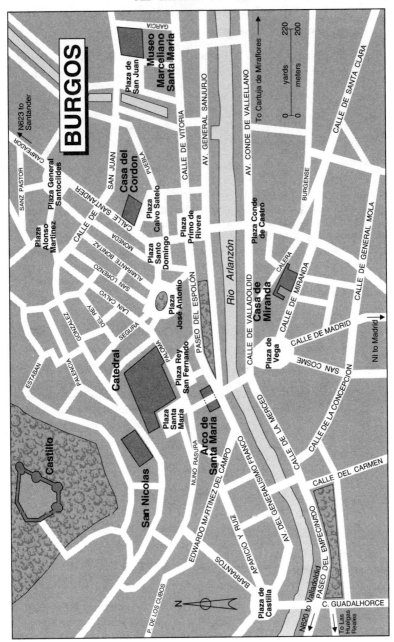

BURGOS

N623 to Santander

CAMPEADOR

SANZ PASTOR

Plaza Alonso Martinez

Plaza General Santocildes

Casa del Cordon

Museo Marceliano Santa Maria

GARCIA

Plaza de San Juan

SAN JUAN

CALLE SANTANDER

PUEBLA

Plaza Calvo Satelo

CALLE DE VITORIA

Plaza Santo Domingo

MONEDA

ALMIRANTE BONIFAZ

SAN LORENZO

LAIN CALVO

DEL REY

GONZALEZ

PALENCIA

ESTABAN

Plaza José Antonio

SEGURA

Plaza Primo de Rivera

AV. GENERAL SANJURJO

AV. CONDE DE VALLELLANO

To Cartuja de Miraflores

yards 0 220
meters 0 200

CALLE DE SANTA CLARA

BURGENSE

Plaza Conde de Castro

CALLE DE GENERAL MOLA

Río Arlanzón

PALOMA

PASEO DEL ESPOLÓN

Catedral

Plaza Santa Maria

Plaza Rey San Fernando

Arco de Santa Maria

NUNO RASURA

CALLE DE VALLADOLID

Casa de Miranda

CALERA

CALLE DE MIRANDA

Plaza de Vega

CALLE DE MADRID

SAN COSME

NI to Madrid

San Nicolas

Castilla

P. DE LOS CUBOS

EDWARDO MARTINEZ DEL CAMPO

APARICIO Y RUIZ

BARRANTOS

AV. DEL GENERALISIMO FRANCO

CALLE DE LA MERCED

CALLE DE LA CONCEPCIÓN

CALLE DEL CARMEN

PASEO DEL EMPECINADO

Plaza de Castilla

N620 to Valladolid

C. GUADALHORCE

To Las Huelgas Reales

N

What to See and Do

For most visitors, the paramount attraction of Burgos is her imposing **Cathedral ★ ★ ★ ★ ★**, the finest Gothic cathedral in Spain, especially when considering its setting. The **Casa de Miranda ★ ★** museum is also worth a look, as is the elegant facade of the **Casa del Cordón ★**, in which Ferdinand and Isabella met Columbus on his return from his second trip to the New World. But not to be missed are two exceptional early buildings in suburbs on either side of the city. **Las Huelgas Reales ★ ★ ★ ★** is a magnificent convent from the 12th century, displaying actual clothing of the period, and **Miraflores ★ ★ ★** is an elegant monastery from the 15th century, with exceptional sculpture. The number of sights in Burgos is not great, but their quality is.

Cathedral   ★ ★ ★ ★ ★

Pl. de Santa María, ☎ *20 4712.*

Hours open: daily 10 a.m.–1 p.m. and 4–7 p.m.

This is Spain's third largest cathedral, after Toledo and Seville, but its most imposing. It is variegated yet uniform, solidly standing as if for eternity—the finest example of the Spanish Gothic. The foundation was laid in 1221 by Fernando II, under the supervision of Bishop Mauricio. The mass of the Cathedral was completed by the end of that century. In the 15th century a second stage of construction took place. Tall spires were added to the front, the huge Condestable Chapel was appended to the rear, a cloister built on the side, and the interior chapels decorated anew. All this was effected by some of the great artists of the time who gathered in Burgos for the purpose. Thus, the interior decor and some exterior work are Plateresque. Slightly later, grand ramped stairways were added around the Cathedral so that a walk to the Cathedral would also involve a tour of its exterior.

Appreciation of the Cathedral starts outside with its front in the **Pl. Santa María**. Intricate openwork spires soar 300 feet into the sky, reminiscent of the Cathedral of Cologne. In fact, their architect was from Cologne and surely imported the design. Above the **rose window** in the center is a row of **statues** of kings of Castile and bishops of Burgos. Over the door an incongruous classical pediment separates a bishop leading a king on the right side and a queen on the left, each holding real spears.

Go left up the staired ramp that climbs to the **Coronería Portal**, located in the center of the northern side. Graceful draped statues line both sides of the door. Under Christ enthroned above the door is a traditional carving of heaven and hell, with hell, as usual, the more striking. Around the corner in a recess is the **Pellejería Portal**, which originally was the most convenient entrance for tanners whose factories were located on this side of the Cathedral. This portal is obviously Plateresque, though more balanced than usual and imposing. Around the back of the Cathedral is the famed **Chapel of the Condestable**, whose octagonal order contrasts with the busy Gothic spires above. From the rear, flying buttresses can be viewed in a lovely line. Farther around an elegant sweep of stairs leads down and past the splendid **Sacramental Portal**. Angels play while the four Evangelists write at their desks. Note the vigorous scene of hell, and the man praying, rather belatedly, in a boiling caldron.

Inside, the nave rises to vaulting made elegant with 15th-century ribs, though the view down the Cathedral is unfortunately obstructed by the choir. Atop a clock high on the left is the 16th-century *Papamosca*, "Flycatcher," a bird who opens his mouth each time the clock chimes. Proceed left.

The first chapel presents a riotously overblown 18th-century retablo dedicated to Saint Tecla. It is the work of a member of the Churriguera family who helped create the baroque churrigueresque style of architecture. Next is a chapel for Saint Ana, built a century and a half earlier. It contains a lovely retable by Gil de Siloé. The two chapels demonstrate, respectively, ornateness as opposed to art. At the transept, look left to a glorious diamond flight of **renaissance stairs**, all gilded and lovely, that merely lead to the outside.

Enter the nave to view the altar and choir, but look up first to see a Plateresque elegant lantern where the transept crosses the nave. Under the lantern, a plain copper slab marks the place where El Cid rests beside his wife Jimena. The 16th-century reredos behind the high altar effectively place Biblical figures in classical niches. Though ornate, the choirstalls in the coro are well done and are unusual for having inlays. In the center of the coro is the 13th-century coffin of the founding Archbishop, named Mauricio. His wood effigy is covered with embossed copper and Limoge enameling.

Continue around the left side of the apse to come to the chapel of Saint Nicolas, which contains a portable organ from the 16th century. Next is a 16th-century chapel with an **elliptical dome**, followed by two 13th-century chapels.

In the left rear is the outstanding **Chapel of the Condestable**. This addition to the Cathedral, a medley of the Isabelline, was fashioned in 1482 for the Constable of Castile and worked on by all the great artists in Burgos. Elegant vaulting meets in a star unexpectedly filled by glass. The pillars are carved with figures of the Apostles, rendered by the Renaissance master, Gil de Siloé. Compared with the usual busy altar retablo, this one is bold and dramatic, carved by Gil de Siloé's son Diego. The peaceful Constable and his wife, carved by an unknown artist, face the altar. Done in lovely Carrara marble, the artist obviously took delight in fabric folds. It was this couple who owned the Casa del Cordón (see below) where Columbus was received by Ferdinand and Isabella on his second return from the New World. Shields on the rear wall and the balustrade record the families of the Constable and his wife. To the right rear, a door leads to a sacristy in which hangs a Da Vinci-like painting of Mary Magdaline.

The Santiago Chapel next along in the apse carries a ceiling of delicate ribs. Continuing around to the right transept, a magnificent Gothic paneled door on the left leads into 14th-century cloisters, with statues everywhere and more chapels along the left side. The first of these chapels stores clerical vestments, plates and manuscripts, including the marriage contract of El Cid. The next room, the Chapterhouse, has a lovely Mudejar ceiling and displays a graceful Memling *Virgin and Child*, along with a Van Eyke. The *"Coffer of El Cid"* is bolted to the wall. This chest, purportedly El Cid's security for a loan worth far less than the gold that filled it, was found to hold sand when it was opened after repayment of the loan. In the adjoining Sacristy is a masterpiece of sculpture by Diego de Siloé of *Christ at the Column.*

Back in the Cathedral proper, return to the front along the right side of the nave. The large chapel of the Visitation contains a carved tomb of the Bishop of Lerma, a Renaissance masterpiece of a dour faced personage. Also in that chapel hangs a delicate painting of the Madonna and Child. Notice the beautiful vaulting above. In the front chapel on the far right is a gruesome crucifixion constructed with a figure made of buffalo hide that looks for all the world like human skin. *Admission: 350 ptas., for the treasury and cloister.*

Outside, take a look at the curious figures that make up the fountain in the plaza. Mary and her son wear real gilt crowns, while grotesques below ride fish with ears. Go up the ramped stair again, this time for a view of the **Church of San Nicolás***, directly ahead. Look opposite the church front at the engaging Renaissance* **Palace of Castrofuerte** *with a lovely patio.*

Iglesia de San Nicolás   ★

C. Fernán González.

Hours open: daily 9 a.m.–1:30 p.m. and from 4:30–6:30 p.m.

Although the architecture of this late Gothic church is not special, some of the art inside is. The retablo by Francisco de Colonia is huge and ornate, containing more than 400 of stone figures depicting the life of Saint Nicholas. At the base of the altar are two fine pairs of tombs of the church's patrons, Alfonso and Gonzalo Polanco, and their wives.

Walking directly along past the face of the Cathedral brings the Arch of Santa María.

Arco de Santa María   ★

Pl. Rey San Fernando.

At this spot once stood a gate through 11th-century walls that girded the town. Today only a few stones on either side of the arch remain, inscribed here and there with Arabic writing. Past the gate looking back in the direction of the Cathedral is the facade of the arch that, despite a more modern appearance, dates to 1550. Just before its construction citizens throughout Spain had risen against their new king, Carlos V, to protest his preference for foreign advisors and foreign affairs. This was the Comuneros Revolt which forced the king to accept many of the rebel's demands. After the king agreed to the will of the people, loyal citizens of Burgos raised this monument to atone for their participation in the uprising.

The center figure on the top register is Count Fernán González, the first man to unite Castile. On his left is Carlos V; on his right, El Cid. Below, two legendary early judges flank Diego Porcelos, the alleged founder of the city of Burgos. He was called Porcelos (Pig) because he was one of seven siblings, which is the size of a normal pig litter. With its tiny turrets evoking a castle, the arch seems a bit of fantasy.

Stretching west is the lovely Paseo del Espolan, lined with sycamores, flowers and topiary, where the citizens of Burgos stroll. The second left leads to

the **Plaza Mayor** ★ , a.k.a. **Plaza José Antonio**. *Unusual in its oval shape, the arcaded plaza presents an attractive appearance; it houses stores and numerous cafes. On the south side stands the Ayuntamiento (City Hall), opened in 1791. Leave the east side of the Plaza, opposite the Cathedral, to pass through the Pl. Santo Domingo. Take the next left onto the wide pedestrian walk, C. Santander. Turn right into the attractive Pl. de Calvo Sotelo for the Casa del Cordón, with the arresting carving of a rope forming a triangle over the door.*

Casa del Cordón   ★

Pl. de Calvo Sotelo.

Although it is now a bank, this handsome structure was once the palace of the Constables of Castile, at which the sovereigns of the time often stopped for extended visits. Here Ferdinand and Isabella met Columbus to learn about his second voyage. Here, too, Philip the Handsome, the young husband of their daughter Juana the Mad and father of Carlos V, died from a chill caught while playing ball with a retainer. (See "Historical Profile: Ferdinand and Isabella" on page 185.) Its popular name "House of the Rope," obviously comes from the carved Franciscan cord serving as a kind of tympanum to frame the coats-of-arms of the Constables of Castile. The "dogs (?)" in the top door corners are a whimsical touch.

The narrow C. de Puebla exiting the northeast corner of the plaza leads, after two long blocks, to the Pl. de San Juan and a museum displaying the work of a noted Spanish painter from the early part of the century. The statue in the plaza center is of Diego Rodriquez Porcelos, legendary founder of the city. Opposite are romantic ruins of the **Monastery of San Juan** ★ , *and, occupying the former cloisters, the* **Casa Cultural** ★ *with a fine Plateresque front.*

Museo Marceliano Santa María   ★

Pl. de San Juan. *20 56 87.*
Hours open: Tues.–Sat. 10 a.m.–2 p.m. and 4–7 p.m. (until 6 p.m. in winter.) Open Sun. morning. Closed Mon.

The first floor is for temporary shows, the second displays the works of a painter from Burgos named Marceliano Santa María, who painted in a "'30s" style. His work is clearly a cut above the ordinary, with unusual choices of subjects, nice coloring (purples and limes), and skillful use of light. *Admission: 100 ptas.*

Across the river, three streets back and midway between the pedestrian bridge which leads to the Arco Santa María and the vehicular bridge upstream, stands the **Casa de Miranda** *on C. Miranda.*

Casa de Miranda (Museo Arqueológico)   ★★

C. Miranda, 13, *26 58 75.*
Hours open: Tues.–Fri. 10 a.m.–2 p.m. and 4–7 p.m. Open Sat. and Sun. 11 a.m. to 1 p.m. Closed Mon.

The building, a 16th-century palace, is elegant with an unusual Plateresque patio containing columns that evoke the classical. Its grand staircase is imposing. The art collection is small but unusual too. The tomb of Juan de Padilla, a page of Isabella's killed during the siege of Granada, is a masterwork by Gil de Siloé. On the first floor is a collection of Visigothic sarcophagi, and also Gothic and Renaissance tombs. On the second floor are some extraordinary Moorish pieces, including a 10th-century ivory case for balls (perhaps for some sort of bowling), and an ivory casket from the 11th century with Limoges plaques for Christian use later affixed to the ends. There is also an interesting altar of beaten and enamelled copper images of saints from the 12th century. The paintings vary in quality, but a weeping, Flemish-style Christ is riveting. *Admission: 200 ptas.*

A convent and a monastery in opposite suburbs should not be missed. **Las Huelgas Reales Convent** *is 1.5 km west of the center. Take the river road on the bank opposite the Cathedral (signs point to N-630) until you see signs directing you to the convent.* **Cartuja de Miraflores Monastery** *is 4 km east of the city. Follow the river road east on the side opposite the Cathedral until signs direct you to the monastery.*

Buses leave Pl. de Calvo Sotelo (where the Casa del Cordón is) several times per day for each monastery, marked "Barrio de Pilar" and "Fuentes Blancas," respectively.

Convento Las Huelgas Reales

C. Compás de Adentro, ☎ 20 16 30. 1.5k. west of Burgos.
Hours open: Tues.–Sat. 10:30 a.m.–2 p.m. and 4–6:30 p.m. Open Sun. and holidays 11 a.m. to 3 p.m. Closed Mon.

The convent originally was a summer residence (*huelgas* means "repose") for the first kings of Castile. In 1187 this masculine lodge was converted to a convent by the queen of Alfonso VIII. She was Eleanor of Aquitaine, Richard the Lionheart's sister. The convent eventually controlled 50 manors and towns whose revenues supported the nunnery nicely enough that often queens would arrive to spend periods of retreat.

The convent grew in size over the centuries, accruing various architectural styles, and served as a royal pantheon for the first kings and queens of Castile. Napoléon's soldiers desecrated most of those tombs during their occupation in the 19th century, but fortunately missed a few early coffers that contained clothing miraculously preserved from the 12th and 13th centuries, now on display in the convent's **Museo de Talas**.

Past a Gothic arch and along the cloister, the church tower, with model castles on its top, beckons. The church is entered from a porch on which four early ornate sarcophagi still rest. The church is early 13th-century and its simple Cistercian style allows artworks clear display. Kneeling statues of the founders, Eleanor (Leonor in Spanish) of Aquitaine and Alfonso VIII, flank the altar. Royal tombs line the aisles, while the simple and moving tombs of the founders and their children are housed in the separate nun's choir. Here magnificent tapestries line the walls, and the wood floors seem too old to walk on.

The "Gothic" cloister retains enough intricate Mudejar stucco-work and wood ceiling to convey a sense of its original delicate appearance. Exquisite doors lead to the sacristy. The large chapterhouse with nine bays displays what is said to be the standard of the Moorish commander from the battle of Las Navas de Tolosa. If only one battle turned the tide for the Christians it was this victory in 1212 when they defeated a large army of fierce Almohad Moors. Although the "standard" is more likely a flap from a tent, it is still lovely and rich with history. This hall has seen its own history as well. It was here that Franco assembled his first government during the Spanish Civil War.

In the **Museo de Ricas Telas** (Clothing Museum), the former sewing room of the convent, clothing, jewelry and swords from the 12th and 13th century are simply displayed. Most remarkable is the equipment found with Infante Don Fernando de la Cerda, displayed in cases eight-11. But all of the clothing is striking for its intricacy and beauty. Don't miss the dress of María Almenar from 1196.

The Romanesque Cloister from the 12th century, the earlier of two, is simple with rounded arches. Rooms off this cloister constitute the royal apartments of the convent, with fine Mudejar decoration still intact in places. Across the garden stands the Chapel of Santiago, looking entirely Moorish, with fine wood paneling inside. A life-size statue of Saint James sits on a throne. His articulated right arm holds a sword that can be lowered through a series of counterbalances. It was used to dub new knights, usually princes, in the early 13th century. Tradition has it that it was built so the later Fernando III would not suffer the indignity of being knighted by an inferior. *Admission: 400 ptas., for guided tour in Spanish. Free Wed.*

Cartuja de Miraflores   ★★★

C. de Valladolid. Four km west of Burgos.
Hours open: Mon.–Sat. 10:30 a.m–3 p.m. and 4–6 p.m. Open Sun. and holidays 11:20 a.m.–12:30 and 1–3 p.m, then 4–7 p.m.

In 1442 King Juan II decided to erect a monastery on the site of one of his father's palaces to hold his family tomb. When the king died in 1454, the unfinished project was completed by his loving daughter Isabella the Catholic. She called on Juan de Colonia who worked on the second stage of the Burgos Cathedral to help her finish the memorial to her parents. He designed a plain exterior with only a florid Gothic doorway surmounted by the founder's lion-held shields to break the monotony, making the rich interior all the more impressive.

The superb altar and marble tombs are perhaps the finest works of Gil de Siloé, a rare instance of plan and execution by the same artist. Instead of the standard rectangular design, the gilt retable presents a great circle enclosing a crucifixion At its bottom, left and right, figures of the king and queen kneel beneath their coats of arms. But in front of the altar is the reason for the entire edifice—the paired tomb of Juan II and his wife, Doña Isabel of Portugal. Its base forms a star on which countless tiny figures, mostly characters from the New Testament, adore and watch over the recumbent king and queen above. The openwork carving is so intricate it is difficult to believe it could be fashioned from marble. The inscription reads: "It does not have an equal in the world and constitutes the principle adornment and glory of this church."

In a niche to the left is a tomb that almost rivals this one. It was made for the Infante Don Alfonso—Isabella's brother who would have been king instead of Isabella had he lived. But at age 14, he fell to his death from the walls of the Alcázar in Segovia, thereby allowing Isabella to ascend the throne. His tomb is masterful, if somewhat ornate, but the artistry of Gil de Siloé saves it from prettiness. The spectacled figure in the left bottom register is said to be the artist himself. In the chapel, to the left of the altar, usually hangs a splendid *Annunciation* by Pedro Berruguete, though it was not there on our last visit. *Admission: free.*

Where to Stay

Burgos offers one great hotel and a number of comfortable ones. Even the undistinguished hotels, however, charge in the expensive range. The reason is that Burgos is a prosperous city that caters to businesspeople.

Expensive ($100–$200)

Palacio Landa   Deluxe ★ ★ ★ ★

Carretera Madrid-Irun, at kilometer 236, ☎ *20 63 43, FAX 26 46 76.*

This is one of the most dramatic hotels in Spain, with an over-the-top elegance surpassed by few others, and its prices are improbably reasonable. Located 3.5 km south of Burgos on N-1, it can be reached by going south on Calle Madrid, which leads away from the Santa María pedestrian bridge. The hotel is built around a 14th-century castle which was carted here stone by stone. You see, the hotel is a fantasy of the owner's imagination. The Palacio Landa provides whatever the heart desires, including swimming. It is affiliated with the top-notch French Relais & Chateux chain (U.S. ☎ *800-677-3524*). *39 rooms, plus three suites.*

Condestable   1st-class ★ ★

C. Vitoria, 8, Burgos, ☎ *26 71 25, FAX 20 46 45, Telex 395 72.*

The location is good—one block north of the river on a nice shopping street, and four short blocks from the Cathedral. This is a modern hotel, efficiently run, with small, sleekly designed rooms and baths. *85 rooms.*

Almirante Bonifaz   1st-class ★ ★

C. Vitoria, 22, Burgos, ☎ *20 69 43, FAX 20 29 19, Telex 39430.*

This is the same type of hotel as the Condestable and equally efficient. Located on the same street, it is two short blocks farther east from the Cathedral. *79 rooms.*

Moderate ($50–$99)

Del Cid   2nd-class ★ ★ ★

Pl. Santa María, 8, Burgos ☎ *20 87 15, FAX 26 94 60.*

This hotel has lowered its prices just enough to fit in the moderate category. It also provides the best location possible—in the Cathedral square, off to the west side. In addition, part of the building is a 15th-century house, rambling and full of curiosities. Recently it became affiliated with the Best Western hotel chain, and we will have to see what that does to the service. So far only the public areas have been air-conditioned. Associated with the hotel is a good restaurant discussed in this section. *25 rooms, plus three suites.*

Fernán González   2nd-class ★ ★ ★

C. Calera, 17, Burgos (across the river from the old town, left from the Santa María pedestrian bridge), ☎ *20 94 41, FAX 27 47 21, Telex 39602.*

This is a perfectly acceptable hotel with more atmosphere than many in town, fair prices and views of the river, Espolón and Cathedral from the front rooms. Because it is an older hotel, it offers interesting architecture and antiques. Located just across the pedestrian Santa María bridge and left onto C. Calera. The restaurant is quite elegant. *84 rooms.*

Cordón   2nd-class ★ ★

La Puebla, 6, Burgos, ☎ *26 50 00, FAX 20 02 69.*

Still another modern hotel is this one, similar to the Condestable and located one block north of it. Its small size allows greater attention to each guest, though few of the staff speak English. *35 rooms.*

Inexpensive (Less than $50)

España   4th-class ★

Paseo de Espolón, Burgos ☎ *20 63 40, FAX 20 13 30.*

The hotel is situated beside the lovely Espolón and overlooks the river. It is modern and the staff is friendly, although its prices make the inexpensive category only out of season. *69 rooms.*

Inexpensive *hostales* concentrate around the Pl. de Vega, just across the river from the Santa María pedestrian bridge. None stands out enough to earn recommendation, but most serve their purpose.

Where to Eat

As in most of Old Castile, roast lamb and suckling pig are specialties, along with a local soup of lamb and shrimp.

Expensive ($30+)

Fernán Gonzáles   ★ ★ ★

C. Calera, 19. (across the river from the old town, left from the Santa María pedestrian bridge), ☎ *20 94 42.*

Located beside the hotel of the same name, this restaurant is elegant, yet more adventuresome than most in town. In addition to the usual roasts, there are *nueva cocina* specialties such as sole with shrimp sauce and green beans with foie gras and truffles. The owner knows wines—in fact he owns several vineyards—so his selection is exemplary. Credit Cards: A, D, V.

Moderate ($15–$30)

Mesón del Cid   ★ ★ ★

Pl. Santa María, 8 (to the west of the Cathedral square), ☎ *20 87 15.*
Closed Sunday evening.

Two ancient dining rooms on the second and third floors framed by hand-hewn wood present views of the Cathedral. Or try the pleasant terrace for fresh-air dining. The *sopa de Doña Jimena*, its version of garlic soup, is yummy, as is the baby lamb with mushrooms. Credit Cards: A, D, M, V.

Casa Ojeda   ★ ★ ★

C. Vitoria, 5 (opposite the Casa Cordón), ☎ *20 90 52.*

Closed Sunday night.

This well-known Burgos institution, with an elegant gourmet store adjacent and a fine upstairs dining room decorated in typical Castilian style, serves classical regional cooking. The cheeses are special. Credit Cards: A, D, M, V.

Rincón de España

C. Nuño Rasura, 11 (at the end of Pl. del Rey San Fernando, down the stairs from the Cathedral plaza), ☎ *20 59 55.*
Closed Tues. in winter.

A large light room inside or a terrace with awning outside are your choices. The food is decent, if limited in variety, and can be inexpensive if ordered from a special menu. Credit Cards: A, D, M, V.

Inexpensive (Less than $15)

Autoservicio Bonfin

C. Cadena (at the beginning of the Pl. del Rey San Fernando, down the stairs from the Cathedral plaza), ☎ *20 61 93.*
Open for lunch only.

Cafeteria-style service presents a choice of sandwiches and salads, as well as fuller meals. Convenient to the Cathedral for a rest, or a lunch.

Directory

Tourist Information

Located opposite the Cathedral front in the Pl. Alonzo Martínez. Open Mon.–Fri. from 10 a.m. to 2 p.m. and from 4–7 p.m., Sat. from 10 a.m. to 2 p.m. It provides a map and brochures in English.

Trains and Buses

Burgos is well served by trains because it lies on a main route between Madrid and the resort of Irun. The train station (☎ *20 35 60*) lies at the end of Av. Conde Guadalhorce, a 10-minute walk northeast of the Cathedral. Trains connect with León, Valladolid and Pamplona. The downtown RENFE office (☎ *20 91 31*) is at C. Moneda, 21, which leads off the eastern end of Pl. José Antonio, heading northeast.

Daily bus service connects Burgos with Madrid, León, Santander, Soria and San Sebastian. The main station (☎ *20 55 65*) is located at C. Miranda, 4, at the rear of the Casa Miranda, above.

Post Office and Telephones

Pl. Conde de Castro, 1 (☎ *26 27 50*), located across the river from the east end of the Espolón. Telephones are available at *C. de San Lesmes, 18.* Follow the narrow C. de Puebla exiting the northeast corner of the Pl. de Calvo Sotelo for two long blocks.

Police

General Vigon. ☎ *28 88 34* (*091*, for emergencies).

Excursions

On the route southeast to **Santo Domingo de Silos** ★ ★ ★, (which has a treasured cloister) famous today for its top-10 hit of Gregorian chant, a stop can be made at charming **Covarrubias** ★, and another at the interesting town of **Soria** ★★. **Peñaranda de Duero** ★★ due south, contains an elegant Renaissance palace in a pretty square. **Frómista** ★★★ church is a preserved Romanesque marvel, described under its own heading in this chapter.

Covarrubias ★

Population: 663

Leave Burgos on Av. Madrid heading due south from the Santa María pedestrian bridge, following signs to N-1. At 9.5 km fork left onto N-234 toward Soria. In 33.5 km at Hortiguela turn right onto C110 toward Covarrubias and Lerma. In 13 km you arrive.

Still partly girded by medieval ramparts, the town is guarded by the **Doña Urraca Tower** (a.k.a. **Fernán González Tower**). It rises with an extreme batter, in the shape of a truncated pyramid. A Renaissance palace leads to a picturesque old quarter with many restored, half-timbered house facades. The **Colegiata** church is crammed with attractive tombs, including that of Fernán González, who first united Castile, and his wife, Doña Sancha. The associated museum (open 10 a.m. to 2 p.m. and 4–7 p.m.; closed Tues.) contains some nice works, including a Berruguete, a Van Eyke and several fine primitives.

Santo Domingo de Silos ★★★

From Covarrubias take BU-903 south for 11.5 km, turning left past Santibañez del Val to Silos in seven km more.

All that remains of a monastery built in the 12th century is this Romanesque cloister. But what a cloister! Called the most beautiful in the world, its elegant shape and the animation of its carvings make it undeniably special. Apply at the porter's lodge; enter through the 18th-century church and descend to the lower cloister level. Take time to study the wondrous Romanesque carving on the columns, especially at the cloister corners, bases and capitals. The 14th-century painted Mudejar ceiling, though restored in large part, is still exquisite. On the north side, a sarcophagus lid in high relief supported by three lions, stands over Saint Dominic, who reconstructed the convent early in the 12th century and added the upper story. The small museum at the northwest corner holds an 11th-century chalice, a 10th-century manuscript, a gilt and enamel copper chest, and lovely ivories.

The associated church presents little of architectural interest but at 7 p.m. vespers one can hear the very best of Gregorian Chant by the monks, who improbably had a hit album a few years ago.

Soria ★★

Population: 32,039

From Santo Domingo de Silos continue on BU-903 for 18 km to N-234 south to Soria in 93 km. From Burgos, take N-234 south for 145 km. Once in Soria, drive along Paseo General Yague until the postmodern Museo Numantia appears on the left.

Though its charm lauded by poets has been obscured by modern buildings, Soria retains a pretty center with interesting sights.

The **Numantia Museum** ★★ *(open 10 a.m. to 2 p.m. and 4:30–9 p.m.; closed Sun. afternoon and Mon.; admission: 200 ptas.)* spaciously houses a good collection of Roman and Iberian pieces, especially those on the second floor from excavations at nearby Numantia.

Cross C. Ferial to enter the Pl. Ramon Benito Acona. A right and quick left brings you past the Diputacion into the Pl. San Esteban with a Romanesque church of harmonious lines. **San Juan de Rabanera** ★ has Byzantine-style vaulting, and a stunning Romanesque crucifix over the altar. Outside, turn left at the back of the church to enter the Pl. San Blas y el Rosel.

Directly ahead, across the plaza, is the long facade of the **Palace of the Counts of Gomara** ★. The two-story patio inside is elegant. On the west end of the palace, the street heading north leads in one block to **Santo Domingo** ★, which has one of the finest Romanesque facades in Spain. The central portal is covered with carving that well repays study. The interior, however, was redone in the 16th century.

Cross to the side of the plaza opposite Santo Domingo and go left down C. de la Aduana Vieja, passing the 18th-century **Casa de los Castejones** ★, with Baroque doorway, after which a right onto C. Ferial returns again to the Pl. Ramon y Cajal.

Peñaranda de Duero ★★

Population: 821

> *Leave Burgos on Av. Madrid leading due south from the Santa María pedestrian bridge, and follow signs to N-1. From N-1 exit at Aranda de Duero in 79 km to take C-111 east for 21 km to Peñaranda de Duero, a total trip of 100 km.*

This walled village is dominated by a square medieval keep. But it is the **Plaza Mayor** ★★★ and the palace fronting it that merits the trip. The plaza is a harmonious composition of half-timbered houses on massive stone pillars. In the center stands a stone pillory from the 15th century, unusual to see in Spain today. On the west side of the plaza stands the large **Palacio de los Condes de Miranda** ★★ with a noble facade (open 10 a.m.–1:30 p.m. and 4–7 p.m., until 6 p.m. in winter; closed Sun.). This is one of the great Renaissance palaces of Spain, and it combines architectural styles from Gothic to Mudejar to Plateresque. Inside is a lovely patio with surrounding gallery, a grand staircase and rooms with intricate wood ceilings.

Coca Fortress ★★

Population: 2127.

> *From **Segovia** take N-110 west toward Ávila, leaving west from the Pl. Azoguejo. At Villacastin in 37 km take N-VI north toward Valladolid. In about 40 km, at San Cristobal de la Vega, go right on C-603 following signs to Coca for 16 km, a total trip of 93 km. The final seven km on D-209 is bumpy. From **Ávila** take N-110 east toward Segovia to Villacastin in 29 km. Then follow the directions*

from Segovia above. From **Madrid** *take A-6 north, changing to N-VI at Villacastin in 83 km. Then follow the directions from Segovia above. Once reaching* **Valladolid** *take N-601 south toward Madrid for about 50 km, taking a left following signs for Coca in 19 km.*

This fortress is a singular example of Mudejar military architecture and one of the most famous sights in Spain. It is so often photographed because it looks just as we imagine a fortress should, if perhaps a little more massive and complex than we thought. To reach the fortress turn left just before the gate through what little remains of the town wall, or pass through the gate and turn left immediately after. In either case you end at the fortress in less than one kilometer.

Since the castle inside has been appropriated for a forestry school, only the walls can be toured, but for free. The fort dates to the 15th century and is still owned by the Duke of Alba. The surprise is that the fortress is made of fired brick. Mudejar architects made an art of laying bricks by varying the courses and colors to create patterns, and the whole feels entirely solid. The dry moat is deep and wide, the walls thick and the merloned turrets stand defiant. Despite such appearances, however, the building was never intended for defense. It was built for a funloving Archbishop as a stage for his parties.

Covarrubias

See Burgos excursions.

Frómista ★ ★ ★

Population: 1284

From **Burgos** *follow the directions for Valladolid, but in five km take N-120 west toward Osorno. In 60 km, at Osorno, take N-611 south toward Palencia for 18 km to Frómista, a trip of 78 km. From* **León** *take N-601 as if for Valladolid, but in 67 km at Becilla de Valderaduey take N-610 east to Palencia. At Palencia in 61 km take N-611 north for 32 km to Frómista, for a trip of 160 km. From* **Valladolid** *take N-620 (E-80) north to Palencia in 48 km, then follow the directions from León, for a trip of 80 km. From* **Madrid** *and* **Salamanca** *follow the directions from Valladolid. From Santander take N-611 south for 149 km.*

Today the town of Frómista seems sad and decayed, but once thousands of pilgrims stopped here on their way to the holy site of Santiago de Compostela. Still standing in the center of the village square is the pilgrim's interim destination. This church of San Martin once formed part of a large abbey with accommodations for all who asked. Only the extraordinary church remains. It was completed in 1066, before William the Conqueror landed in England. Because the village quickly declined, the abbey was abandoned by the time of the Catholic Monarchs. Thus, it has never been modified or added to and remains the purest Romanesque.

Iglesia San Martin   ★ ★ ★

Hours open: Wed.–Sun. 10 a.m.–2 p.m. and 4–7pm. Open Tues. 10 a.m. to 2 p.m. Closed Mon.

The church was built by the widow of Sancho the Great of Navarre, the man who conquered Castile before bequeathing it to his son Fernando I, the first king of a united Castile and León. This edifice embodied the first great success of the Romanesque style in Spain after earlier essays in the form, and served thereafter as the model for Romanesque churches. The purity of its Romanesque aesthetic is unsurpassed. Built of mammoth rough stones, every component of the church harmonizes with the rest.

Inside, pure lines sweep to the cradle vaulting and carry the eye as far as a squinch-supported dome. The ribbed arches are lovely, their capitals tastefully decorated. Unfortunately, overzealous restoration in the early part of this century imparts an uncharacteristic sense of newness. *Admission: 200 ptas.*

Haro and La Rioja ★ ★

Population: 8,581
Zip code: 26250; area code: 941

*From **Burgos** take either the toll road A-1 (E-5), or the parallel free N-1 east toward Vitoria-Gasteiz. From the toll road, just past Miranda de Ebro in 86 km, turn south toward Logrono, taking exit 9 for Haro, for a trip of 112 km. From N-1, just past Miranda de Ebro in 93 km, turn south on N-232, exiting for Horo in 15 km. From **Pamplona** take A-15 northwest for 23 km, turning onto N-240 at Iruzun going east toward Vitoria-Gasteiz. The road becomes N-1 (E5) in 29 km at Alsasua. 26 km past Vitoria-Gasteiz turn onto N-232 toward Logrono, exiting at Haro in 15 km, for a trip of 146 km. From **Bilbao** take the toll road A-68 (E-804) south toward Logrono, exiting at exit 9 for Haro for a trip of 89 km. From **south of Haro**, follow the directions from Burgos.*

NOTE ... *Most bodegas close from Aug. through the first half of Sept., and most allow tours only in the morning.*

Haro is a prosperous, attractive town that serves as the capital of Rioja Alta, the finest wine region in Spain. It is a pleasant place to rest while exploring the great bodegas (wineries). Old Haro covers a hill rising from the Plaza de la Paz, circled by an arcade of glass-balconied houses surrounding an old bandstand. Dating from 1769, the stately Ayuntamiento (city hall) across the plaza is a source of information about the area. **Santo Tomás ★**, a pretty 16th-century church, sits atop the hill. The south portal is a sumptuous with Plateresque carving; the interior is nicely Gothic.

But it is the wine that brings most people to Haro. Bodegas proliferate down the hill to the north, near the railway station from which they ship their wares. There the stream called Rio Oja, which gave its name to this region, enters the larger River Ebro. Bodega tours are given on an ad hoc basis, waiting for four or more tourists to assemble. Check with the tourist office for what is open and to make reservations. The best bodegas are **Lopez de Heredia, CVNE** (☎ *31 02 76*), **La Rioja Alta** (☎ *31 03 46*), **Muga** (☎ *31 04 98*), and Bilbaiñas.

Other good bodegas require a drive, but a pleasant one. Leave Haro east from the area of the bodegas, following signs to Labastida, four km northeast. From there follow signs to Logrono and N-232 (confusingly with the same designation as the different N-232 that passes south by Haro). On the right in 10 km pass by the picturesque hilltop village of **San Vicente de la Sonsierra ★**, surrounded by vineyards. Past Samaniego in seven km a sign points to the road for Puerto de Herrera, which in three km leads into the mountains for the **Balcon de la Rioja ★** and its panoramic views over the Rioja area. seven km farther, back on N-232, brings beautiful **Laguardia ★** (Biasteri, in Basque).

Laguardia retains its medieval village walls, gates, towers and grace. The town has ruins of a 10th-century castle, a Romanesque and a Gothic church, along with old mansions and the Bodegas Palacio, one of Spain's best. (**Marixa ★ ★**, just outside the walls, is a nice restaurant with moderate prices, and has 10 clean rooms for inexpensive rates. ☎ *10 01 65.*)

From Laguardia head south toward Elciego and Cenicero. **Elciego ★**, in four km, is another picturesque village that hosts the bodega of Marqués de Riscal, one of Spain's premier crus—and its oldest. Across the Ebro is Cenicero, the location of Bodegas Marqués de Cáceres, producer of a modest-quality wine. From here the better highway N-232 leads northwest back to Haro.

Where to Stay

In Haro or nearby are one excellent hotel and another of moderate price. Or, 16 km south in Calzada, one of those wonderful paradors beckons.

Moderate ($50–$99)

Los Augustinos   1st-class ★ ★ ★

San Agustin, 2, Haro, ☎ 31 13 08, FAX 30 31 48, Telex 37161.
This looks like a parador—it is housed in a reconstructed convent from the 14th century—though it is owned by a private chain. The hotel was renovated in 1990

and is top-grade throughout. Public spaces are nicely decorated with real and reproduction antiques, and the bedrooms are spotlessly modern. The sitting room is so
grand as to be slightly uncomfortable, bedrooms are less memorable. What we
don't understand is why it charges so little. *60 rooms.*

In Santo Domingo de la Calzada (16 km southwest of Haro on LO-750):

Parador Santo Domingo de la Calzada   1st-class ★ ★ ★

Pl. del Santa, 3, Haro, ☎ *34 03 00, FAX 34 03 25.*

This parador, once a palace of the kings of Navarre, was converted into a hospice for
pilgrims before reincarnation as a hotel. The public spaces retain the old stone that
oozes history. *61 rooms.*

Iturrimurri   2nd-class ★ ★

On N-232 1 km south of Haro, ☎ *31 12 13, FAX 31 17 21, Telex 37021.*
Closed the last week of December and the first week of January.

The hotel is functional and clean, with tennis court. a pool in a garden, and a moderately-priced restaurant. The staff is helpful. *36 rooms.*

Inexpensive (Less than $50)

In Laguardia (24 km from Haro):

Marixa   4th-class ★

Sancho Abarca, 8, Laguardia (just outside the walls), ☎ *10 01 65.*
Closed from the last week in December until the middle of January.

Pleasant rooms above this fine restaurant ★ ★ are small, but clean and attractive,
and some present panoramic views. *10 rooms.*

Where to Eat

Local restaurants serve mainly roasts and regional dishes, but naturally offer superb
wine selections.

Moderate ($15–$30)

Terete   ★ ★ ★

Lucrecia Arana, 17 (west of the plaza), ☎ *31 00 23.*
Closed Sunday night, Monday and October.

This is the outstanding Haro restaurant, over 100 years old. Nothing fancy—white
picnic tables upstairs—but roasts are perfectly seasoned and cooked in an ancient
horno. Naturally the selection of wines is exemplary. Credit Cards: V.

Directory

Information

The **Centro de Iniciativas Turisticas** in the Ayuntamiento at the end of C. Conde
de Haro serves as the information office *(*☎ *31 27 26).* Open Tues.–Sat. from
10:30 a.m. to 2 p.m. and from 5:30–8pm. Open Sun. from noon to 1 p.m.

Post Office and Telephone

The post office is located on C. de la Rioja *(*☎ *31 08 69),* along with telephones.

Trains and Buses

Service *(*☎ *31 15 97)* is possible to and from Bilbao and Donostia, three or four
times per day. From elsewhere, travel to Logroño for a leg to Haro.

León ★★★

Population: 131,134
Zip code: 24001; area code: 987

*From **Madrid** take A-6 northwest, changing to N-VI at exit 1 in 57 km. Stay on N-VI for 197 km to pass Benavente where you change to N-630 for 72 km. The total trip is 326 km. From **Ávila** take N-110 east for 29 km past Villacastin, joining N-VI north, then follow the directions from Madrid. The total trip is 294 km. From **Segovia** take N-110 west to Villacastin to join N-VI, then follow the directions from Madrid. The total trip is 302 km. From **Valladolid** take N-601 north for 139 km. From **Burgos** take N-620 (E-80) west for 77 km, turning on to N-610 at Magaz. N-610 enters Palencia in 11 km. Continue for 61 km past Palencia to Bacilla de Valderaduey where you go north on N-601 for 67 km to León. The total trip is 216 km. From **Salamanca** take N-630 north toward Zamora, continuing for 128 km to Caserio del Puente where you switch to N-VI going north for six km before rejoining N-630 for the final 72 km to León. The total trip is 206 km. From **Oviedo** take N-630 south through 115 km of slow going up and down mountains, or take the toll road A-66 after 36 km at **Campomanes** for a much faster trip.*

Despite a Leonese fixation with lions, the name of their city derives from the Latin *Legio Septima*, because the site was first settled by the Seventh Legion as a Roman bastion under Caesar Augustus. After conquest by first Visigoths, then Moors, Christians from Asturias in the north recaptured León in 850. But the Moors took it back in 996 and burned the town. In 1002 it was retaken by the Christians—this time for good—and made the capital of a province of the same name. With such status, the city became a haven for Christian refugees from Moorish territory and thus the Mozarabic center of Spain during the 11th and 12th centuries. The wonder is that there is not more fine Mozarabic architecture and art surviving. The present walls date to 1324, replacing an earlier construction that in turn replaced Roman walls. Parts remain standing in the old town along with a collection of houses from the 12th and 13th centuries. Still in use, the houses' exterior plaster sometimes flakes off to reveal their original half-timbered brick.

As the Reconquest gained territory, the capital of Christian Spain followed its armies further south and León languished. For centuries the town lay under the dust of decay. Then the citizens undertook a great cathedral, perhaps in memory of other times, incredibly raising a rival to those across the Pyrenees in France. In the 20th century rich deposits of iron and coal were discovered in the mountains north of León so today the city thrives again.

León is a city of modern buildings, wide avenues and fountains, yet maintains an old quarter from a different age.

Arriving from **Salamanca** *and* **Zamora** *on* **N-630** *travel on Av. Dr. Fleming past the northern train station. After the station turn acutely right onto C. Astorga. Astorga ends forcing a left onto Av. de Palencia which crosses the Bernesga River and empties into a large traffic circle (Guzman el Bueno). Continue through the circle to Ordoño II opposite, which leads in a few blocks to another circle, Pl. de Santo Domingo, with underground parking to the right. From* **N-601** **(Madrid**, **Valladolid** *and* **Burgos**) *drive down Alcalde Miguel Castana which soon ends at a confluence of large streets. Continue for a few blocks on the right street, Av. Independencia, until it lets into the circle of the Pl. de Santo Domingo with underground parking to the right. From the north on* **N-630** **(Oviedo**) *enter an intersection from which a right turn leads along Av. Asturia. In about two blocks, take the first left onto Av. del Padre Isla which in several blocks goes into the circle of the Pl. de Santo Domingo, with parking across the plaza.*

What to See and Do

The loveliest sight in León is the elegant French Gothic **Cathedral** ★ ★ ★ ★ with its thousand yards of stained glass windows. Noteworthy, too is the Romanesque basilica of **San Isadoro** ★ ★ ★ whose magnificent frescoes from the 12th century decorate a pantheon of the earliest kings of Spain. The **old town** ★ well repays a stroll. Massive and insistently elegant, the **Monastery of San Marcos** ★ ★ ★, now one of the great hotels in the world, should be seen. It contains an archaeological museum with a few nice pieces. Near the main plaza sits a 19th-century **palace designed by Gaudí** ★. In the environs of León waits a jewel of a ninth-century Mozarabic church at **San Miguel de Escalada** ★ ★. A full day would allow all these sights to be seen.

León's grand avenues all funnel into the large Plaza de Santo Domingo, a center from which the sights radiate. Walking east on Generalissimo Franco brings you to the Pl. de Regla and, three blocks later, the **Cathedral**. Walking north on C. Ramon y Caja brings **San Isidoro** in two blocks. Northwest along Av. de General Sanjurjo lies the **Monastery of San Marcos** nine blocks away.

Plaza de Santo Domingo   ★

San Marcelo church ★, rebuilt in the 16th century, stands at the east end of the plaza. It contains a moving wood sculpture by Gregorio Fernandez. Facing the church's south side is the **Ayuntamiento** ★ (city hall) from 1585 with the arms of León emblazoned on its facade. Across the plaza, opposite the Ayuntamiento, is the former **Casa de los Guzmanes**, now the Diputación, with a fine 16th-century patio and grillwork. Next to it, west, is the **Casa de Botines** ★ set back on its own lot. Now a bank, it was designed at the end of the 19th century by Antoni Gaudí as a small palace. Built to look Gothic, it shows Gaudí's mastery of that aesthetic, for it

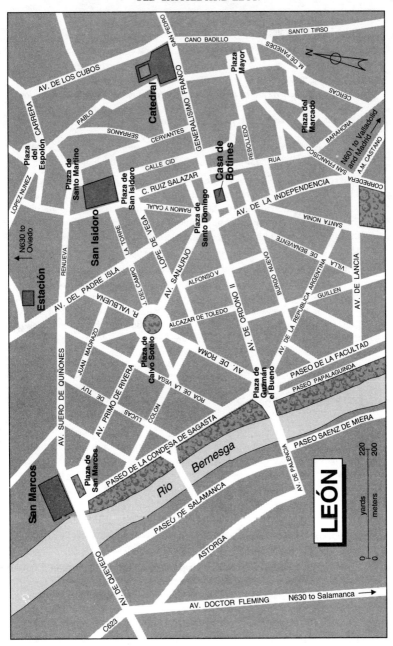

LEÓN

almost seems period though not exactly like any structure of that time. A walk east along Calle Generalissimo Franco past the Casa de los Guzmanes brings you to the Cathedral three blocks later.

Cathedral   ★★★★

Pl. de Regla, ☎ *23 00 60.*

Hours open: weekdays 9:30 a.m.–1:30 p.m. and 4–7 p.m. Sat. 9:30–1:30 p.m. Closed Sun.

Begun in the middle of the 13th century and finished 150 years later, it is surprising that this church reflects so little of the Spanish interpretation of Gothic that turned most of her churches into wider, less lofty, darker structures than those north of the Pyrenees. This Cathedral would suit any French town and bring glory to most.

Two equal but dissimilar towers frame the facade containing three portals beneath a great rose window. The central **portal** houses a vivid depiction of the fate of the damned; the left portal holds two fine depictions of prophets. A triple portal along the southern face is surmounted by a statue of Saint Froilan, the Bishop of León in the 10th century, and has lovely carvings decorating the door jambs. Continue around to the rear for a view of **buttresses** flying as they support the high nave.

Inside one is struck first by soaring height, then by all the glass. Even by Gothic standards the nave is narrow, which serves to emphasize its loftiness. Graceful piers carved to resemble bundled columns rise to an elegant ceiling traced with ribs. All around and behind in the rainbow's colors are a literal third of an acre of stained glass, the glory of the Cathedral. The front rose window and that in the chapels of the apse are the oldest; those in the nave are Renaissance and later, depicting flora and minerals beneath historic personages and their crests, surmounted by the blessed. The sun transforms the interior with heavenly colors.

Carved with painted alabaster reliefs, the trascoro in the center of the nave frames a central arch which gives the best view of the length of the Cathedral. The altar is later, 15th century, containing a nice depiction of the Entombment on the left side. Farther left is a *Pieta* by Rodger van der Weyden.

Both windows in the transepts are early. The one in the south wing is especially striking. Chapels in the apse behind the altar hold tombs of early bishops. The east chapel contains the tomb of **Condesa Sancha**, depicting horses tearing her nephew and heir to pieces in punishment for having killed her.

From the north end of the Cathedral (left) a fine Plateresque doorway lets into the **cloisters** adorned with fine frescoes. Museums are installed off the left and far sides, and display a 10th-century Visigothic Bible and a crucifix by Juan de Juni, among other miscellanies. *Admission: 300 ptas. for the museum and cloisters.*

Return to Pl. de Santo Domingo for the simplest route to San Isidoro. Take C. Ramon y Cajal north for two blocks to the basilica, still attached to the city walls.

San Isidoro el Real   ★★★

Pl. San Isidoro, 4, ☎ *22 96 08.*

Hours open: Tues.–Sat. 10 a.m.–2 p.m. and 4–8 p.m. (until 6 p.m. in winter). Open Sun. 10 a.m.–1:30 p.m. Closed Mon.

Fernando I, the first king of a united Castile and León, built a church here in the 11th century dedicated to St. Isidoro. This saint from Seville, not to be confused with Madrid's St. Isidro Labrador, was a seventh-century archbishop whose organization of church councils did much to define Catholic orthodoxy. Fernando I transferred the saint's bones here, before dying himself the next week. Building continued under the supervision of, at first, Fernando's daughter, then his son and in turn his grandson. By then the structure had been rededicated to serve as a pantheon for the kings of Asturias, León and those of the united Castile and León.

Of Fernando's church, only the narthex survives, housing its royal pantheon. The mass of the basilica was built about a century later by his successors. The look of the front was much altered by Gothic and Plateresque additions in the 16th century, including an equestrian statue of St. Isidoro. The **portals**, however, are original and the depiction of the sacrifice of Abraham in the **tympanum** is vivid. To the east a lovely early portal depicts Christ's descent from the cross.

The uncharacteristic height of the clerestory makes the small and almost square Romanesque interior unusually light. Yet it seems claustrophobic, almost subterranean, after the light of the soaring Cathedral. Huge pillars are surmounted by richly-sculpted capitals, while arches at the beginning of the nave and in the transepts show Mudejar influence. The retablo is late, early 16th-century, and overlooks a reliquary containing the bones of St. Isidoro. The north transept contains a 12th-century chapel retaining faded, but lively, **frescos**.

A doorway at the front of the basilica, left, leads to the **Pantheon of the Kings**. Carvings on the interior side of the portal and on the capitals of the columns are some of the earliest depictions of figures in all Spain. Two cryptlike rooms comprise the 11th-century structure raised by Fernando I, probably the first Spanish building in the Romanesque style. Here rested the remains of Alfonso V of León, Fernando I, Urrica, his daughter, and almost 20 other Infantes and Infantas until the French desecrated the building in the 19th century.

But they did not destroy the 12th-century frescos—still vibrant today thanks to the dry, airtight construction of the building. The vault ceilings depict New Testament episodes involving Christ, evangelists (with animal heads), saints and angels, and the **first Spanish nativity scene**. A charming calendar covers one archway, showing which farming tasks should be performed each month.

The adjoining Treasury contains 10th- and 11th-century pieces, including an enamel casket, another with ivory plaques and a chalice of two Roman agate cups mounted together in gold. *Admission: 300 ptas., for a guided tour of the Royal Pantheon.*

Old Town   ★

The basilica of **St. Isidoro** is in the area of the old walls which enclose a warren of streets, ending southeast at the Cathedral. Modern houses abut ancient buildings from the 13th century, which show their age by the half timbered brick exposed where plaster coatings have flaked off. Another concentration of ancient houses lies in the area between the arcaded Pl. Mayor, directly south of the Cathedral, and the Pl. del Mercado, to its southwest.

For a visit to the Monastery of San Marcos take the broad Av. General San-jurjo that leads northwest out of the Pl. de Santo Domingo for 10 blocks. The walk provides lovely views of the facade as you proceed.

Antiquo Monasterio de San Marcos   ★ ★ ★

Pl. San Marcos, 7, ☎ 23 73 00.
Hours open: (museum) Tues.–Sat. 10 a.m.–1 p.m. and 4–6pm. Open Sun. 10 a.m.–1 p.m. Closed Mon.

In the 12th century this was the mother house of the Order of Santiago, established to protect pilgrims on their way to Santiago de Compostela. Three centuries later Ferdinand the Catholic, as the order's Master, drew plans to embellish the monastery to proclaim the order's Reconquest accomplishments. The plan was finally carried out between 1513 and 1549 under the supervision of Ferdinand's successor Carlos V, in a style that was not his favorite.

The present imposing facade is the result—a sumptuous Plateresque monument stretching for over a football field. A baroque pediment added in the 18th century does not unduly disturb the original two-story design of regular windows, friezes, engaged columns and pilasters. Santiago (St. James) on horseback strides over the elaborate main door to the left, which includes scenes from his life. The right-hand door to the church is incomplete but covered with scallop shells, Santiago's symbol. All along, a row of medallions depicts assorted Biblical, Roman and Spanish personages, including Isabella the Catholic supported by Lucretia and Judith, and Carlos V supported by Trajan and Augustus.

Today most of the former monastery is given over to one of Spain's most deluxe paradors, though the church inside with its beautiful choir stalls remains open to all. Anyone can enter the hotel to look at the magnificent stone staircase leading from the lobby. The Chapterhouse, which now contains an archaeological museum under a splendid carved wood roof, and the sumptuously decorated sacristy, to the right, may be toured for a fee. Roman statuary and mosaics in the museum hold some interest, but the main treasures are the medieval works. Included are textiles and clothing, arms and religious articles, with one outstanding 11th-century Romanesque ivory, the Carrizo Crucifix, tiny, elongated and haunting. *Admission: 200 ptas.*

Where to Stay

For some reason few hotels inhabit this substantial city, but there is the elegant parador. It is expensive, about 18,000 pesetas a night for a couple, but large enough to almost always have available rooms. However, acceptable hotels exist in every price category so the situation should prove adequate, whatever your budget.

Expensive ($100–$200)

Parador San Marcos   Deluxe ★ ★ ★ ★ ★
Pl. San Marcos 7, León, ☎ 23 73 00, FAX 23 34 58, Telex 89809.

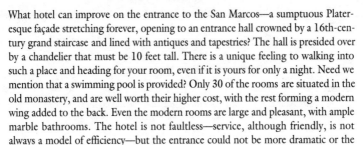

What hotel can improve on the entrance to the San Marcos—a sumptuous Plateresque façade stretching forever, opening to an entrance hall crowned by a 16th-century grand staircase and lined with antiques and tapestries? The hall is presided over by a chandelier that must be 10 feet tall. There is a unique feeling to walking into such a place and heading for your room, even if it is yours for only a night. Need we mention that a swimming pool is provided? Only 30 of the rooms are situated in the old monastery, and are well worth their higher cost, with the rest forming a modern wing added to the back. Even the modern rooms are large and pleasant, with ample marble bathrooms. The hotel is not faultless—service, although friendly, is not always a model of efficiency—but the entrance could not be more dramatic or the public areas more grand. *198 rooms, plus two suites.*

Moderate ($50–$99)

Quindós   **1st-class ★ ★ ★**

Av. José Antonio, 24, León, ☎ *23 62 00, FAX 24 22 01.*
This modern hotel provides what a hotel should—clean comfort with willing service. What makes it special is that it does all this for much less than what others charge, almost inexpensive prices. It is located in a quiet neighborhood one block north of Av. Gen. Sanjurjo and a block south of the Parador San Marcos. *96 rooms.*

Riosol   **R2nd-class ★**

Av. de Palencia, 3, León, ☎ *21 66 50, FAX 21 69 97, Telex 89693.*
Although the modern Riosol is actually closer to the center of town than the San Marcos, it feels out of things, across the river on an unattractive street near the train station. The rooms are comfortable enough, but the service is not as professional as it should be. The hotel is located five blocks due west of the Pl. Santo Domingo along Av. Ordoño II, which changes it name to Av. de Palencia after it crosses the river. *141 rooms.*

Inexpensive (Less than $50)

Don Suero   **HS2rd-class ★ ★**

Av. Suero de Quiñones, 15, León, ☎ *23 06 00.*
When you see this hotel you'll think we made a mistake. This hotel looks and acts much more expensive than it is. Actually, its rates are comfortably under the inexpensive limit. Altogether this modern professional place is a find indeed. **Note**: no credit cards are. *106 rooms.*

Where to Eat

Roast lamb and suckling pig are specialties, as with most of Old Castile, but León adds its own fresh trout. The three moderately priced restaurants below all serve good food in pleasant surroundings, though none stands much above the others.

Moderate ($15–$30)

Nuevo Racimo de Oro   **★ ★**

Pl. San Martin, 8, ☎ *21 47 67.*
Closed Sunday in summer and Wednesday the rest of the year.
The restaurant looks as a mesón should. It is installed on the second floor of an ancient tavern, and serves roasts from a wood fire oven, following a mandatory bowl

of steaming garlic soup (served in a wooden bowl with a wooden spoon). The place
is a mite touristy, but the food is good nonetheless, and a few dollars cheaper than
the restaurants that follow. Located at the north end of the Pl. Mercado, it can be
reached by walking east from Pl. de Santo Domingo to C. Rua going south, which
takes you to the Pl. Mercado in three blocks. Credit Cards: A, V.

Adonías   ★★

*C. Santa Nonia, 16, (south from the Pl. de Santo Domingo on C. Independencia for one
block until it forks, with C. Santa Nonia going right)* ☎ *20 67 68.*
Closed Sunday.

A pleasant dining experience waits up the stairs in the green dining room with
sturdy wood tables and ceramics on the walls. Regional cooking is done with care,
and the service is friendly. It takes some consideration in ordering to avoid the
expensive range. Credit Cards: A, D, M, V.

Casa Pozo   ★★

Pl. de San Marcelo, 15, ☎ *22 30 39.*
Closed Sunday night, the first half of July and Christmas week.

Owned by the brother of the proprietor of Adonías, there are those who consider
this better and those who consider it not as good as Adonias. We find each different—this one is less formal and the food a touch more earthy—but hard to choose
between. The bread is terrific. Located directly opposite the Casa Botines. Credit
Cards: A, D, M, V.

Directory

Information

Located at *Pl. de Regla, 3,* across from the front of the Cathedral. Open Mon.–Fri.
from 9 a.m. to 2 p.m. and from 4–6:30 p.m. Open Sat. from 10 a.m. to 1 p.m.
☎ *23 70 82.*

Trains and Buses

Five trains a day connect Madrid with León for a trip of 4–5 hours and a cost of
about 2000 ptas. Connections between León and Burgos (a two and one-half-hour
ride), Valladolid (two hours), Oviedo (two hours), and Barcelona (10-11 hours) are
also convenient. One train per day goes to Salamanca. The station is located at *Av.
Astorga, 2.* This is about five blocks west of the Pl. Santo Domingo along Av.
Ordoño II, which changes its name to Av. de Palencia after it crosses the river and
runs into Av. Astorga, perpendicular to it. ☎ *22 02 02.*

Most buses leave from Paseo Ingeniero Saenz de Miera *(* ☎ *21 10 00).* Prices and
times match the train.

Excursions

A car is required to get to **San Miguel de Escalada** ★★, 25 km outside of León, but,
as the finest Mozarabic monument extant, it is worth the short ride.

*From the Pl. de Santo Dominigo head east on Generalissimo Franco past
the Cathedral to N-601. Take N-601 south toward Valladolid for 17 km to
the outskirts of Mansilla de las Mulas. A sign that should be larger points*

right to S. Miguel de Escalada in 12.5 km. Apply to the caretaker in the small shed in front.

Ruins of a monastery complex are scattered around, though only this church survives intact. It was constructed in the 10th century by Christian refugees from Córdoba, and is the best preserved Mozarabic building in Spain. These refugees had learned their crafts and trained their eyes under the Moors to built a Christian monument with Moorish elements. The porch added in 1050 rests Moorish arches on polished columns. But an elegant Moorish window cut through the covered side of the porch contrasts oddly with a sloping roof. Inside, two aisles covered with wooden vaulting line the nave, separated from the apse by three arches and a balustrade of panels carved with Visigothic birds and Moorish foliage designs. Architecturally the church is a mishmash of Romanesque, Visigoth and Moorish, but in the end its charm wins out.

Peñafiel Castle

See Valladolid excursions.

Peñaranda de Duero

See Burgos excursions.

Salamanca ★ ★ ★ ★

Population: 167,131
Zip code: 37001; area code: 923

*From **Madrid** take A-6 north for 37 km to exit 1 for N-VI to avoid the toll, or to exit 4 at Villacastin for a faster ride. In either case, take N-110 in 83 km at Villacastin west toward Ávila for 29 km, changing there for N-501 for Salamanca 98 km further along. The trip covers 210 km. From **Ávila** take N-501 northwest for 98 km. From **Segovia** take N-110 west for 63 km to Ávila and follow the directions from Ávila. From **Valladolid** take N-620 (A-80) southwest through Tordesillas and to Salamanca in 115 km. From **north** of Valladolid, follow directions to Valladolid and then follow those to Salamanca.*

Salamanca is truly ancient. In the early third century B.C. Hannibal attacked an important Iberian settlement here. A story goes that after the town had been successfully stormed and the men disarmed, the townswomen smuggled arms to their men in hideouts in the hills. Their bravery so impressed Hannibal that he invited the men to return. The town flourished under the Romans, but was repeatedly invaded by the Moors after Spain became Christian. In 1055 it was recaptured by the Christians for good, although little was left after three centuries of destructive warfare.

In 1218 Alfonso IX founded the second university in Spain here, which soon swallowed up the first in nearby Palencia, and Salamanca flourished as a university town. From this center Europe received the fruits of Arab science, which awakened it from the Dark Ages.

Salamanca became a kind of company town with the university as its prime employer and builder. It grew quickly, with most construction occurring from the 15th through the 16th century so it presents a remarkably homogeneous face. Indeed, it is a museum of Plateresque architecture, that curious Spanish appliqué of stone on plain facades, all heightened by the warm tones of the local sandstone.

By the first centennial after its founding the university had risen to be the second largest in Europe, overshadowed only by the University of Paris. It was large enough to contain both the Cambridge and the Oxford of its time, and possessed a better reputation than either. In this era the town was home to two great medieval painters who worked on its Cathedral. Fernando Gallego was born here, and Juan of Flanders settled here. Unlike most towns in Europe, Salamanca did not raze or renovate its former cathedral when it added a newer one in the 16th century, but built the new one adjoining the old, thus preserving one of Spain's great early churches.

In the 17th century, Salamanca was home to a family of altar makers named Churriguera, who turned to the business of architecture and gave their name to an original style called *churrigueresque*, the Spanish version of the baroque. The Plaza Mayor, one of the most interesting in Spain, is their work, as is the altar in the church at St. Esteban's Monastery.

During the 18th century, Salamanca fell on hard times. The university suffered as Spain grew paranoid about the dangers of Protestantism, demanding orthodoxy above inquiry which subverted educational standards. During the Peninsular War with Napoléon, the French destroyed many of Salamanca's buildings to fortify the town against Wellington's approach.

More recently, Salamanca served as the headquarters of the Nationalists during the early years of the Civil War. One night the university faculty was harangued by the Nationalist General Millán Astry about the necessity for blood and violence to purify the soul. After this diatribe, Miguel de Unamuno, rector of the university and renowned philosopher of religion, rose uninvited to rebut Millán's views as contrary to the principles of western civilization. The audience, with Generalissimo Franco in attendance, was offended by Unamuno's disagreement with a Nationalist hero. Soon after, Unamuno was fired from his position and placed under house-arrest for life.

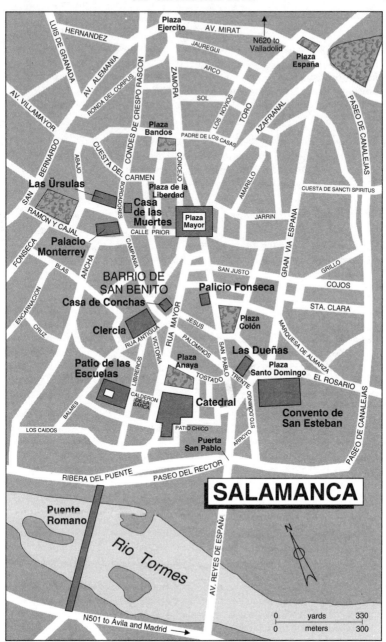

LUIS DE GRANADA
HERNANDEZ
Plaza Ejercito
AV. MIRAT
JAUREGUI
N620 to Valladolid
Plaza España
ARCO
AV. VILLAMAYOR
AV. ALEMANIA
RONDA DEL CORPUS
CONDES DE CRESPO RASCON
ZAMORA
SOL
LOS NOVIOS
TORO
AZAFRANAL
PASEO DE CANALEJAS
CUESTA DEL
ABAJO
Plaza Bandos
PADRE DE LOS CASAS
AMARILLO
CUESTA DE SANCTI SPIRITUS
SAN BERNARDO
CARMEN
CONCEJO
Las Ürsulas
Plaza de la Liberdad
Casa de las Muertes
Plaza Mayor
JARRIN
RAMON Y CAJAL
BORDADORES
CALLE PRIOR
GRAN VIA ESPANA
FONSECA
Palacio Monterrey
CAMPANA
GRILLO
BLAS
ANCHA
BARRIO DE SAN BENITO
SAN JUSTO
COJOS
ENCARNACION
CRUZ
Casa de Conchas
Palicio Fonseca
STA. CLARA
Clercia
RUA ANTIGUA
VICTORIA
RUA MAYOR
JESUS
Plaza Colón
MARQUESA DE ALMARZA
Patio de las Escuelas
LIBREROS
PALOMINOS
SAN PABLO
Las Dueñas
EL ROSARIO
Plaza Anaya
Plaza Santo Domingo
BALMES
CALDERON DE LA BARCA
TOSTADO
TRENTE
LOS CAIDOS
Catedral
Convento de San Esteban
PASEO DE CANALEJAS
PATIO CHICO
STO. DOMINGO
ARROYO
Puerta San Pablo
RIBERA DEL PUENTE
PASEO DEL RECTOR
SALAMANCA
Puente Romano
Rio Tormes
AV. REYES DE ESPAÑA
N
N501 to Ávila and Madrid →

| 0 | yards | 330 |
| 0 | meters | 300 |

Yet his spirit infuses the revitalized university today, for it thrives again, numbering 16,000 students, about twice its Renaissance complement.

Salamanca remains very much a university town with a youthfulness that fits oddly and nicely into its atmosphere of age. Because its medieval quarters had all been destroyed, it did not have to site buildings in warrens of streets as did so many Spanish towns, instead arranging them around plazas connected by thoroughfares. With its golden buildings amid the unhurried pace of academe, Salamanca is a most inviting city. UNESCO considers it a world treasure.

A circular road, variously named, leads around the old hilltop section of Salamanca. You funnel into this road from whichever direction you arrive. Salamanca is sufficiently spread out that it does not have any one place for parking hundreds of cars, and parking in the old town is difficult for anyone unfamiliar with its system of one-way streets. Follow the circular road to reach the side along the river Tormes where parking on the street is usually possible, and a short, but steep, three-block walk up the hill brings you to the Cathedrals and university.

What to See and Do

With its sumptuous entrances, old classrooms, halls and collection of art, the **university** ★★★★ is fascinating. The combination of the primitive **Old Cathedral** ★★★★ and the neoclassic **New Cathedral** ★★★ should not be missed. Nearby, **San Esteban Monastery** ★★ combines Gothic and Plateresque details in an interesting way. The **Plaza Mayor** ★★★ is among the most striking in Spain, and can be combined with a pleasant walk to see Plateresque mansions that dot the old city. One full day will do it all.

In the environs of Salamanca stand a number of picturesque towns that make for pleasant excursions: **La Alberca** ★★★ , **Miranda del Castañar** ★ , **Ciudad Rodrigo** ★ , and **Alba de Tormes** ★ , where Saint Theresa is buried. Then there is a short and unusual excursion in the surrounding countryside to **Buen Amor castle**, which is not an overwhelming architectural monument, but interesting for being a castle actually lived in.

Begin in the Patio de Las Escuelas for a lesson in the Plateresque. If climbing the hill from the river, this plaza is off the left side of C. Libros, which is the second true street—excluding an alley—going left.

The University   ★★★★

Patio de Las Escuelas, ☎ *29 44 00.*
Hours open: Mon.–Sat. 9:30 a.m.–1:30 p.m. and 4–7 p.m. Open Sun. and holidays 10 a.m.–1 p.m.
This patio dates from the dawn of the 16th century, a gift of Ferdinand and Isabella by unknown architects. On first entering the plaza the larger **Escuelas Mayores** is right, and the smaller **Escuelas Menores**, a kind of preparatory school of the main university, is to the left rear.

Above the double doors of the Mayores rises a great Plateresque work. The central medallion in the first register shows the benefactors, the Catholic Monarchs, with Isabella's face unidealized enough to be a genuine portrait. The middle register makes much of the double eagle crest of Carlos V, who reigned when the carving was finished, flanked by the visage of the Emperor and his wife. From the top peer early founders and teachers of the university, flanked by Venus, Hercules and the Virtues. The carving deepens as it goes up to compensate for its greater distance from the viewer. The whole is a brilliant composition almost hidden by all the detail.

The slightly later frieze above the portal to the Menores school is simpler and more elegant, though not so daring or seminal. On the bare walls next to the Menores, red-painted names can still be discerned. These are the graffiti of Renaissance graduates, said to be written in bull's blood.

Through the portal of the Mayores, where the ticket of admission to both schools is purchased, one penetrates the sixth oldest university in the Western World. The Copernican system was taught first at this university, and Isabella sent Columbus here when she wanted scholarly judgment about his proposed trip. (Incidentally, the professors concluded that Columbus' ideas were based on faulty assumptions, as indeed they were.) (See "Historical Profile: Columbus and the Conquistadores" on page 369.)

Salamanca employed the first known woman professor—Beatriz de Galindo—who taught Queen Isabella Latin. Famous students included the son of Isabella and Ferdinand, and the son of Felipe II, who suffered a concussion from falling down stairs in pursuit of a maid. Hernán Cortéz attended for one year before quitting to conquer Mexico. St. Ignatius Loyola, founder of the Jesuits, and Lope de Vega, one of Spain's greatest writers, both received degrees from Salamanca, and many say that Cervantes attended. At its height in the 16th century the university consisted of 25 departments and about 7000 students.

Enter the 15th-century cloisters covered by an original wooden ceiling of Mudejar work. Around the arcade ancient classrooms lead off. Proceeding left around the cloister, the first two rooms may readily be skipped. The next, in the corner, is called the **Hall of Fray Luis de León**, after an early famed teacher.

Fray Luis had been arrested by the Inquisition for the "crime" of translating the Song of Solomon into Spanish. He returned to this classroom after five years in jail and began his lecture with the words "As we were saying yesterday...". The room remains as it was in the 16th century to show what lecture halls of the time were like. Note the pulpit with a roof which served as a sounding board for projecting the teacher's voice, and note the rough, scarred logs on which students sat, a luxury in days when it was normal for students to squat on the floor. Along the right hand wall are more comfortable seats for professors who wished to hear a lecture.

Next is the **paraninfo**, or assembly hall, still used for solemn ceremonies such as the opening of the academic term and the conferring of doctorates. Arches sweep across the room with timbered ceiling between. Two 17th-century tapestries hang on the end wall framing a canopy flying a standard donated before his death by Don Juan, the student son of Isabella and Ferdinand. There is a portrait, after a design by Goya, of Carlos IV.

The next hall is a 19th-century meeting room. One passes a doorway with a lovely Moorish ceiling above, then three rooms of little interest, followed by the **chapel**. Most arresting is its splendid ceiling, despite the fact that a large part of the original has been removed to a museum in the Menores School. Small though the room may be, it was the first library of the university. Today it is redone as a baroque chapel with attractive marblework from the 18th century. Incidentally, Fray Luis is buried here, as his cenotaph on the right-hand wall indicates.

Next comes a wonderful Plateresque **staircase** with elegant "star" vaulting above. Scenes carved on the balustrade change at each flight—from pages, knights and jesters, to matrimonial scenes, to, at the top, jousts and bull baiting. The second floor gallery retains a fine ceiling and lets into an old **library** with a rich frieze high up.

On the ground floor again, one room remains to inspect—the **Hall of Francisco Salinas**. He was a famed teacher of music in the 16th century and his hall is still used by music students. Fragments of a painting by Juan of Flanders remain in this memory-filled room.

At the nearby **Escuelas Menores**, after passing through a Plateresque-topped portal, you enter a lovely, quiet patio, the small forerunner of every modern university's Quad. The scalloped arches, called **Salamancine**, that seem to reverse the expected figure and ground, are unattractive enough to be a style peculiar to this one town in Spain. To the right is a library with the finest Mudejar ceiling left in the university complex. Across the patio a modern building serves as a sort of **museum**. It houses the remainder of the ceiling from the Mayores' chapel, along with some nice primitive paintings, sophisticated works by Francisco Gallego, and, at the far end, part of a magnificent 15th-century frescoed ceiling of the *Zodiac*, a grand Renaissance work by native son Fernando Gallego. *Admission: 200 ptas.*

By retracing a few steps back up the C. Libreros to the first street going left, in one block is reached the Old Cathedral, right, and the New Cathedral adjoining, left. Along the way, note the walls topped with merlons, whether to keep students in or out is unclear.

New Cathedral and Old Cathedral

Pl. Juan XXII, ☎ 21 74 76. The entrance to the New Cathedral is on its northern face. The entrance to the Old Cathedral is from the first bay on the south inside the New Cathedral.

Hours open: daily 9:30 a.m.–1:30 p.m. and 3:30–6:30 p.m. (the Old Cathedral closes at 6 p.m. in winter).

Before rounding the **New Cathedral** to enter from the north side, it is impossible to avoid admiring the front, which is as extravagant a piece of late Gothic carving as ever you'll see. Pierced stone carving, minute designs, friezes and balustrades which mark the Cathedral's lines, culminate in an overflow of decoration around the portal. Yet the main structure is massive in appearance, despite literally hundreds of small spikelike spires and countless tiny projections to lighten the look.

The foundation for the church was laid in 1513, and work finished 50 years later, though some additions were made as late as the 18th century after an earthquake weakened the cupola. Most credit for the design belongs to the late Gothic architect Gil de Hontañon and his son Rodrigo, an early exponent of the Plateresque. Together they produced an interior that stuns with its harmony and lovely proportions after the riot outside.

A narrow, lofty nave accompanies sweeping aisles on either side, divided by piers carved into delicate columns that rise to an elegant vaulted ceiling. Atop arches joining the piers runs a lovely balustrade punctuated by delicate medallions. Altogether this is an imposing church exhibiting both Gothic and Plateresque influence, without quite being the one or the other. The **coro** contains flamboyant choirstalls designed by one of the Churriguera brothers, while the **trascoro** was designed by another. But the main monument to the Churriguera family, the **cupola** and its drum with baroque painted scenes of the life of the Virgin, is the work of both brothers together. The altar loses drama because of the distraction of two galleries that cross above it. A chapel in the apse at the right side displays a beautiful painted **Pieta** by Salvador Carmona.

A door from the first chapel on the south side leads to stairs descending to the **Old Cathedral**. Called the Old Cathedral because it was consecrated in 1160, it remains a museum of the Romanesque.

The contrast with the New Cathedral is extreme. Undeniable elegance in the New Cathedral pales beside that of the Old, which had no need for the device of a narrow, high nave impossible at such an early date. Subtly pointed arches on simple columns, with higher columns dividing each, rise to equally simple groining in the ceiling. The eye is drawn along the height and length by light from a lantern at the transept. All these features were innovations for the Romanesque style. And how lovely is the execution—see the charming, unobtrusive carvings on and above the capitals.

At the altar stands a sublime early 15th-century **retable** of 53 paintings, each in a frame. The bottom row is attributed to Francisco Gallego. Above, in a half dome, an amazing fresco of the Final Judgement leaps out of a striking black background. The statue of the Virgin on the altar is from the 12th century. Look up to the unusual lantern with its tiers of windows and flamboyant ribbing, an artwork on its own.

The **St. Martin Chapel** at the west end of the nave retains delicate 14th-century frescoes on its walls. In the south transept are a series of recesses holding delightful Gothic effigies.

From the south transept a door leads to the **cloister**, largely reconstructed, from which chapels radiate. These were used as classrooms until the University Mayores was built in the 15th century. On the east side is the **Chapel de Talavera**, for those who still followed the church rites practiced in the time of the Visigoths. The practitioners were primarily Christians in Moorish lands who had long been cut off from the Christian community—hence the name Mozarabic (almost Arab) rites. The Mudejar dome is admirable as is the altarpiece by Alonso Berruguete.

Next comes the **Santa Barbara Chapel** in which theology students took their final examinations, one at a time. The chair is original and much squirmed upon. Tradition had the students place their hands on the effigy of Bishop Lucero for inspiration and luck. What a dandy the Bishop is, with rings on every finger and fancy shoes.

The Council of Castile once met in the **Santa Catalina Chapel**, which now displays lovely paintings. The original **chapterhouse** contains a Diocesan museum and more paintings. Note the **Santa Catalina altar** by Gallego, a lovely small gold picture of *San Pedro y San Pablo*, and the *Virgin with a Rose* tryptic. On the second floor is a fine **altar** for St. Michael by Juan de Flanders, among other works.

The **Anaya Chapel** on the south side of the cloister is dedicated to San Bartolome. Here are founders' tombs of the finest 15th-century carving and a remarkable ceiling. Also in this chapel is an organ from the 14th century that may well be the oldest such surviving instrument, with lovely Mudejar inlay. *Admission: 200 ptas., to the Old Cathedral.*

Exit from the churches is into the peaceful Pl. de Anaya. The street going left, C. Tostado, downhill, leads to the wide C. San Pablo. Continuing straight on C. Concilio de Trento and passing the end of a large building on the left, the Las Dueñas Convent is reached.

Convento de las Dueñas   ★★

Pl. del Concilio de Trento, ☎ 21 54 42.
Hours open: daily 10 a.m.–1 p.m. and 4–8 p.m. (until 7 p.m. in winter.)
The building was a palace donated to house a nunnery for women of the highest rank, hence the name Dueñas. The convent church is faced with a nice Plateresque doorway, through which one enters the cloister, the only part of the convent open to the public. But this is not an ordinary cloister. Constructed in the 16th century in the form of an irregular pentagon, the capitals of the second story gallery are carved with a profusion of grotesques from Dante's hell to excite our imagination and admiration. *Admission: 100 ptas.*

The large Convento de San Esteban, across the plaza, rises above a flight of stairs. Its facade is oddly shaped and luxuriantly carved.

Convento de San Esteban   ★★

Pl. del Concilio de Trento, ☎ 21 50 00.
Hours open: daily 9 a.m.–1 p.m. and 4:30–8 p.m. (until 6 p.m. in winter.)
The original church was assigned to the Dominicans when a flood destroyed their previous home. One of the brothers, Fra Alava, designed the present church in 1524 at the height of the Plateresque movement. Planned to present its elaborate front as dramatically as possible, it lacks towers which might distract and leaves the sides bare. Above the portal is a round arch framing the stoning of St. Stephan, all contained in a huge recessed curved arch, with Christ on the cross at the top. Note

the delicate upper frieze of children and horses. The portico to the right of the facade is elegant Renaissance.

Entrance to the church is through a door at the end of the portico which lets onto a cloister, then the church. The interior dates to the 17th century and is unusually simple, heavy and dark. The one note of brightness and the center of attention is the high altar by the most famous of the Churriguera family, José. Massive gilt circling vines with grapes twist their way up wood columns, so massive that they almost hide figures of prophets and angels. On high is a painting by Claudio Coello of the Martyrdom of St. Stephen. It is said that 4000 pine trees died for this altar. Nothing is easier to criticize today than such a riotous excess of gilt, but it must be confessed that from a distance the altar makes a dramatic statement. *Admission: 150 ptas.*

Return by C. Concilio de Trento on which you came for one block to the large straight C. San Pablo. A right turn brings you in two blocks to **Fronseca Palace** ★, *now the Diputacion, on the left side. This was built for the Fronseca family in the first half of the 16th century by Rodrigo de Hontañon who helped his father design the New Cathedral. Inside, if it is possible to steal a peek, is a pleasant patio with lovely carved consoles supporting the upper gallery. Continue for three blocks more along C. San Pablo to the* **Plaza Mayor**.

Plaza Mayor   ★★★

Designed in part by the Churriguera brothers, who created the churrigueresque baroque style, and finished in 1733 (though the most imposing building, the Ayuntamiento on the north side, was added in 1755), many people consider this the most beautiful plaza in Spain. One wonders whether they have ever been to Santiago de Compostela. In any case, the plaza is more harmonious than most, with a unity of design that offers a reasonable solution to the problem of placing three stories of building above an arched arcade. However, this is one of those structures that the sun affects with its shadows by doubling the architectural details and making the whole too busy. On a cloudy day or early evening it is indeed lovely. The growth holding bells on top of the Ayuntamiento was a mistake added a century later. Attractive cafes and shops ring the plaza.

Mansion Walk   ★★★

C. Prior lies outside the southwest corner of the Plaza Mayor. At the second crossing street turn right onto C. de Bordadores, in a few steps reaching the **Casa de las Muertes** ★ on your right. Here is one of the earliest examples of what came to be called Plateresque, attributed to the great architect Gil de Siloé, and more formal than later, more developed examples would become. The house belonged to the Archbishop Alonso de Fonseca whose portrait is carved over the window. When he died his nephew had tiny skulls carved just under the top window jambs, lending the present name "Death" to the house.

Across the street and a few steps farther along is a statue to the philosopher **Unamuno** in front of the house, now a museum, in which he died under house arrest imposed by Gen. Franco. Directly opposite the Casa de las Muertes, set back in a square is the **Convent of Las Ursulas** ★, with an octagonal turret topped by an elaborate balustrade. The convent was founded by the same Archbishop Fonseca who owned the Casa de las Muertes. He is buried inside in an elegant tomb by Gil de Siloé.

Back up the C. Prior is the **Monterrey Palace ★**. Turn right to see the elegant facade framed by two corner towers and topped by an openwork balustrade. The palace (now owned by the Duke of Alba) was built for the Count of Monterrey, who through marriage was connected to all the best families, including the Fonsecas of the Casa de las Muertes. The Count displayed the coats of arms of all these connections on his home. Across the street is the **Iglesia de la Purisima Concepcion ★**, founded by the same Count of Monterrey. Inside is a wonderful Ribera *Immaculate Conception* over the altar, and the tomb of the Count.

Continue along C. de Bordadores which now changes its name to C. de la Compañia. The second street to the right leads into the **Barrio de San Benito** in which mansions of old Salamanca families surround the church of San Benito. During the Renaissance era these families formed bands that fought and killed each other in vendettas. Most of the tombs inside the church hold bodies that did not die of old age.

Back on C. de la Compañia one block further is the famed **Casa de las Conchas ★** (House of the Shells). After the owner was appointed Chancellor of the Order of Santiago he was so proud that he placed 400 scallop shells, the symbol of the order, on the walls of his house. The main door is surmounted by a Salamancine arch in which lions hold a shield with a fleur-de-lis field, the crest of the owner. The shield is repeated at the house corner. Second-story windows are as elegant as can be and the first-story windows are protected by fine Plateresque grills, each unique (with more scallop shells).

On the opposite side of the street is the **Pontifical University**, also known as the Clerecia. This is a Jesuit College begun in 1617 and finished a century and a half later. It is a fine example of baroque design.

Return around the side of the Casa de las Conchas to enter the large Rua Mayor going northeast to the Pl. del Corralillo in two blocks that contains the **Iglesia San Martin ★**. The building was erected in the 12th century, though many additions were added later, such as the Plateresque front. Inside is some lovely vaulting and nice Gothic tombs.

Where to Stay

Salamanca provides abundant hotel choices, including one of our favorites in Spain.

Expensive ($100–$200)

Hotel Residencia Rector   **R1st-class ★ ★ ★ ★ ★**

Paseo del Rector Esperabe, 10, Salamanca (on the river side of the circular road, just past the "Roman" bridge), ☎ *21 84 82, FAX 21 40 08.*

The Rector is almost too good to be a hotel. In fact, until 1990 it was a private mansion, when the owners decided to open the lower floors to the public. As it happens, the Ferran family who own it and their architect have utterly exquisite taste. They planned rooms in which you can stay, but so beautiful and comfortable that it demeans them to apply hotel standards. They are huge, decorated in perfect taste with no thought to saving costs anywhere. Since the establishment is small and family-run it does not offer the services of larger hotels, and is thus called a *residencia*. You will think you have reached heaven when you see your room (unless you happen to view the one suite, and then you will know you are still a step below). No restaurant is on the premises, but a bright nook serves for breakfasts. Of course the service is impeccably gracious. If this sounds like your kind of place, reserve well ahead since it is small indeed. *13 rooms, plus one suite.*

Parador de Salamanca   1st-class ★ ★ ★

Teso de la Feria, 2, Salamanca (from the circle road turn left at Puerto San Pablo, crossing the river on Av. Reyes de España; go left around the traffic circle on the other side, then take the first right), ☎ *26 87 00, FAX 21 54 38, Telex 23585.*

This is not what most people expect of a parador for it is a modern building. In fact, it is one of the first of the modern paradors, and beginning to show its age. It is also too far outside of town for walking. However, the reception is very professional and helpful, and the spacious rooms include enclosed balconies with lovely views of the city. So, it is a relaxing place to stay, if you don't mind a mile walk or taxi ride to town. *108 rooms.*

Gran Hotel   1st-class ★

Pl. Poeta Iglesias, 5, Salamanca (opposite the southeast corner of the Pl. Mayor), ☎ *21 35 00, FAX 21 35 00, Telex 26809.*

Grand it is not, although renovations in 1991 improved it. Service is lackadaisical, yet it charges more than any hotel in town. The location, however, is good and it offers parking for a fee. *136 rooms.*

Monterrey   1st-class ★

Azafranal, 21, Salamanca (three blocks northeast of the Pl. Mayor), ☎ *21 44 00, FAX 21 44 00, Telex 27836.*

This is the sister to the Gran Hotel, and also charges too much in our opinion. It is in dire need of renovation, caters mainly to tours and the service can be icy. *89 rooms.*

Moderate ($50–$99)

Amefa   3rd-class ★ ★ ★

Pozo Amarillo, 8,Salamanca (two blocks northeast of the Pl. Mayor on the street parallel to C. Azafranal), ☎ *21 81 89, FAX 26 02 00.*

Renovations have just been completed with great care in this family-owned hotel. Polished wood and stone run throughout the small-scale public areas. Rooms are modest, but decent in size and outfitted comfortably. The full bathrooms sparkle. You cannot do better in Salamanca for anything close to this low price. Service is willing and friendly, though English-speaking staff are not always available. *33 rooms.*

Condal   3rd-class

Pl. Santa Eulalia, 3, Salamanca (opposite the Monterrey Hotel), ☎ *21 84 00.*

The lobby is seedy, but the rooms are adequate. This is just a place to stay, and inferior to the inexpensive choices below. *70 rooms.*

Inexpensive (Less than $50)

Gran Via   3rd-class ★ ★

Rosa, 4, Salamanca (near the Amefa above, one block further northeast), ☎ *21 54 01.*
Nicely maintained and attractive, this would be your best bet in the low price range
if the Amefa is full. *47 rooms.*

Milán   4th-class ★

Pl. del Ángel, 5, Salamanca (behind the Gran Hotel), ☎ *21 75 18.*
The clean bright rooms are smaller than what one might like, and many of the baths
are only quarter tubs, so usable only for showers. If that is not a problem for you,
this hotel should suit. Its location is very good and the prices are rock bottom. *25
rooms.*

Emperatriz   3rd-class ★

C. Compañia, 4, Salamanca, ☎ *21 92 00.*
The building is medieval but the rooms are new and clean. About half have showers
only, and most are a bit bare, though attractive enough. *61 rooms.*

Pensión Marina   2nd-class

C. Doctinos, 4, Salamanca (on the side street going east from C. Compañia), ☎ *21 65
69.*
We seldom list accommodations without private bathrooms, but this is an exception
because the price is so attractive and the public bathroom is so large and clean. Keep
thinking of all the money you are saving (it costs less than $20), when nature calls.
This place is hard to miss because it is upstairs from the Communist Party headquarters, proclaimed by a banner above its street-level office.

Where to Eat

Roast lamb and suckling pig, specialties of Old Castile, are served up well at several restaurants, but the treat that only Salamanca offers is a special restaurant which marries
French to Spanish cuisine. Also, as expected in a university town, there is a wide variety
of better-than-average restaurants as well as numerous inexpensive dining places (some
serving food only a student could love). The Pl. Mayor contains a number of stylish bars
with outdoor seating for a drink, sandwich or tapas munch.

Expensive ($30+)

Chez Victor   ★★★★

*Espoz y Mina, 26 (Pl. de la Liberdad is a small park a few steps due north of Pl. Mayor,
at whose west end is the restaurant),* ☎ *21 31 23.*
Closed Sunday night, Monday, and August.

Chef Victoriano learned his craft in France and brought the lessons home to produce some of the most sublime cooking in Spain. The restaurant itself is just a rectangle leaving all focus on ample tables set attractively with fine linen and china. All
waits for the final decoration—food as exquisite to the eye as to the palate. When
his duties allow, Victoriano circulates with the most infectious smile, leaving orders
and recommendations to his attentive, multilingual wife, Margrit. The experience is
close to perfect (if only the lighting were a little less bright). The cuisine tastes closer
to French than Spanish, but is a true invention of the chef. Entrees change with the
season, but if rape (skate of lovely chewy texture), or magrite of duck are available

they deserve serious consideration. Appetizers are constant and both the *hojaldre de verduras y foie-gras con salsa de trufas* and *crab crepe* are outstanding. Desserts can be sublime and include exquisite chocolate mousse, sinful chocolate tart and delicate ice creams and sherbets. Reservations are strongly recommended. Credit Cards: A, D, M, V.

Moderate ($15–$30)

Le Sablon ★★
Espoz y Mina, 20 (next to Chez Victor), ☎ *26 29 52.*
Closed Tuesday, and July.
Its neighbor Chez Victor gets the attention, but this is a quality restaurant too, with an attractive interior of fruitwood and pink damask. The food is prepared with care and the prices are more than fair. Credit Cards: A, D, V.

Rio de la Plata ★★
Pl. del Peso, 1 (just south of the Pl. Mayor, across from the Gran Hotel), ☎ *21 90 05.*
Closed Monday, and July.
Cozy with dark wood and a fireplace, and usually crowded—a good sign—the menu ranges over Castilian dishes but excels in seafood. Ordering sea creatures, however, can push your bill into the expensive range. Credit Cards: M, V.

La Posada ★
C. Aire, 1 (a few steps east from the Pl. Mayor C. Pozo Amarillo runs northeast to let into a square in three blocks, from which the restaurant is a few steps to the right, opposite the tall Torre del Aire), ☎ *21 72 51.*
Closed the first three weeks in August.
Fortunately the cooking surpasses the decor. A neon sign announces the restaurant whose interior lives up to the expectations of such a welcome. But, if game is in season, it is well worth a try, and prices are reasonable. Credit Cards: A, D, M, V.

Inexpensive (Less than $15)

El Bardo
C. Compañia, 8 (by the Casa del Conchas), ☎ *21 90 89.*
Closed Monday and October.
The students come for the low priced menus, but the à la carte selections are generally better prepared. Prices are rock bottom.

Directory

Information
Pl. Mayor. Open Mon.–Fri. from 9:30 a.m. to 1:30 p.m. and from 4:30–7 p.m. Open Sat. from 10 a.m. to 2 p.m. and Sun. from 11 a.m. to 2 p.m. ☎ *21 83 42.*

Trains and Buses
Four trains most days connect Madrid with Salamanca, via Ávila, for a trip of about three hours. Service is more frequent to Valladolid, one and one-half hours away. Two trains go to Barcelona (14 hrs.), and four to León (three and one-half hrs.). Two trains daily deliver passengers to Porto in Portugal (almost nine hrs.). The train station is located a half-hour walk to the northeast of town on Puerto de la Estación de Ferriocarril (☎ *22 57 42*). A RENFE office is at Pl. Liberdad, 10 (in front of the Chez Victor restaurant). ☎ *21 24 54.*

Buses run frequently to Madrid, Ávila and Zamora. Two per day visit León, four reach Valladolid and five go to Cáceres in Extremadura. Two buses each day take the 11-1/2-hour trip to Barcelona, though they charge more than the train. The station is located on *Av. Filiberto Villalobos, 79* (☎ *23 67 17*), a thirty minute walk northwest following C. Ramon y Cajal, the street that passes the Casa de las Conchas.

Post Office and Telephones

C. Gran Via, 25 (two blocks north of the tourist office), ☎ *24 30 11*. Telephones are available at *Pl. Peña Primera, 1* (two blocks past Casa de las Muertes and right).

Police

In the Ayuntamiento in Pl. Mayor. ☎ *21 96 00* (*091*, for emergencies).

Excursions

Buen Amor Castle is close and amusing to see because a family lives inside. **Alba de Tormes ★** lies just southeast of Salamanca and preserves most of the body of Saint Theresa in a quaint and lovely town. Atmospheric, old **La Alberca ★★★** lies at the end of a scenic ride, with **Miranda del Castañar ★** along the way. Beside the Portuguese border, in the same area, **Ciudad Rodrigo ★★** is a town full of history with a nice cathedral and castle. Not far north, **Zamora ★★** and **Toro ★★** both have Romanesque churches reminiscent of the Old Cathedral in Salamanca. Zamora has a castle besides. From Zamora and Toro **Valladolid ★★★** is less than 100 km away on N-122. (See "Valladolid" below for a description.)

Buen Amor Castle

Travel around Salamanca by the circular road until reaching the north side to turn onto Paseo Dr. Torres Villarroel. Signs direct you to Zamora and N-630. At 21 km is a small sign for the castle, directing to an unpaved private road on the right. Note: on recent trips this road was a mass of potholes.
Hours open: daily 10 a.m.–2 p.m. and 3:30–8:30 p.m. (until 7:30 in winter).

The building began as a fort which Ferdinand and Isabella used as a headquarters during their war with Isabella's niece La Beltraneja over the right to wear the crown. It was transformed into a palace in the 16th century by the same Archbishop Fronseca who owned the Casa Muertes in Salamanca. Today it is privately owned and a working farm.

You ring the bell on the front door and the housekeeper who speaks only Spanish lets you in. Admission is free, but you are asked to buy a postcard of the castle for 200 ptas. Speaking slow Spanish, much of which will communicate, she shows you around, then turns you over to her husband who completes the tour. It is not the most splendid castle in Spain, but visiting it is one of the more unusual experiences.

La Alberca ★★★ and Miranda del Castañar ★

Follow directions for the Salamanca parador, but instead of turning left at the traffic circle across the river, continue through to take the following left, opposite the pedestrian "Roman" bridge. In one block turn left again following signs for C-512 and Veciños. Follow C-512 for 83 km to Santibañez de la Sierra. Turn right on C-515 for 10 km, turning left for **Miranda del Castanar** *two km away. For* **La Alberca** *continue for three km past Miranda at which point the right forking road winds for 14 km to La Alberca.* **Ciudad Rodrigo** *can be included by returning past Miranda del Castanar to C-515 and turning left which brings you in 73 km, the first third being quite curvy but scenic, to Ciudad Rodrigo.*

Miranda del Castañar ★ remains a reasonably unspoiled hilltop village consisting of houses with spreading eaves and flower-bedecked balconies. The Romanesque church and castle are worth a look.

After the winding trip to **La Alberca** ★ ★ ★ it is easy to understand why this village remained isolated for so long, retaining a provincial character that most towns have lost. It was, however, discovered by tourists in the 1960s when the entire town was designated a national monument and since then has become a bit taken with itself. Even so, it remains a beautiful little town. There is little to do but wander the twisting streets to the arcaded Plaza Mayor past houses built of stone up to an adobe second story marked by overhanging wood balconies bright with flowers in season. The day to come is Sunday when everyone gathers in the square in traditional dress.

Ciudad Rodrigo ★ ★

Population: 14,776

From Salamanca, the most direct route is N-620 (E-80) for 89 km. To access N-620 follow directions for the Salamanca parador, but instead of turning left at the traffic circle across the river, continue to take the following left, opposite the pedestrian "Roman" bridge. For a route that includes La Alberca, see above.

Atop its hill, the city still looks like the frontier outpost it always was, with circling ramparts and a square-towered castle. Its name "Rodrigo City" comes from Count Rodrigo Gonzalez Giron who repopulated the town after defeating the Moors who had held it for centuries.

A grand **Cathedral** ★ begun in the late 12th century received its last addition, the apse, in the 16th. The fine west portal contains quaint carvings of the Last Supper. Pleasant sculpture and strikingly grotesque choir stalls decorate the solid interior. The cloister off the north side consists of columns whose capitals represent fine Romanesque work. A pure Plateresque door opens at the east.

The **Plaza Mayor** is picturesque, with a former 15th-century mansion, now the Ayuntamiento, using towers to anchor its arcade. Near the northern rampart is the long 15th-century **Palace of Los Castros** ★, faced by Plateresque twisted columns. The severe 14th-century **Alcázar** now houses a small parador that may be entered for a look. From there the 18th-century city **ramparts** ★ can be climbed.

Alba de Tormes ★

Population: 4106

Cross the river on the south side of the circular road, turning left where signs direct you to N-501, the Airport and Ávila. On the outskirts of Salamanca turn onto C-510 for Alba de Tormes in 23 km.

This town on the banks of the Tormes River once was owned by the Dukes of Alba, hence its name. Today it is quiet, but with remains that shows it once was a seat of power. The Dukes were patrons of Saint Theresa and invited her to establish one of her new convents here. It was her last work; here she died.

Immediately after the lovely **Medieval Bridge** ★, turn left to climb to the Pl. Mayor. On the left is **San Juan church** ★. The front portal and central apse of brick are 12th century Mudejar, the rest is 18th-century. A curious 11th-century sculpture of the Apostles stands in the apse.

An alley to the right leads down to the **Church of the Encarnación** ★, the last Carmelite convent founded by St. Theresa. Over the door on the façade is a too precious Plateresque scene of an angel visiting the Saint. Inside, the church is simple and stately, with the Saint's tomb at the high altar. Her heart and one arm are inside a black marble urn. To the left, funerary stones from successive tombs where she was buried before being interred here are displayed, as one person or town after another claimed her mortal remains, thought to be capable of miracles, before their final rest. At the rear of the church is a reconstruction of the cell in which she died.

High on the hill is the keep from the former castle of the Alba's, all that is left of it.

Zamora ★★ and Toro ★★
Population: 59,734 and 9,781, respectively

From Salamanca follow the directions for Buen Amor Castle, continuing on N-630 past its turnoff for a total of 62 km to Zamora. Toro is 33 km further east of Zamora on N-122 (E-82). For Valladolid (see description under its own heading), continue east past Toro on N-122 for 97 km.

Turn left immediately upon crossing the Duero River on Av. del Mengue. Parking is available after the road curves north by the ruins of a castle surrounded by imposing ramparts. The **castle** ★ last belonged to Urraca, daughter of Fernando I. It seems she lured one brother, who had succeeded his father to the throne, here to kill him so that another, whom she favored, could rule instead.

The gem of Zamora lies across the park—the **Cathedral** ★★★. Do not be misled by the neoclassic north front; this is a 12th-century Romanesque beauty. Travel to the south end to see its original appearance. Inside the nave rises on characteristic massive piers, but uncharacteristic light streams onto the altar from a lantern at the transept crossing, an idea borrowed from the Old Cathedral in Salamanca. Also interesting are the choir stalls, from the 15th century. Though expected Biblical scenes cover the backs, the arms and misericords contain burlesques of cloistered life and fantastic animals. Stairs from the neoclassic cloister lead up to a museum with fine tapestries.

If you like the Cathedral, there is more of the same. Head northwest along C. Notarios leading away from the rear of the Cathedral. In three blocks you come to **Santa Magdalena** ★ church on the left, noted particularly for its *south portal* with elaborately decorated recessed arches.

Returning to the street by which we came, continue on it until it becomes C. Ramos. One block later brings a park with a lovely Renaissance palace on its right side. Today it is the city's parador, but it was a **palace for the Dukes of Alba** ★ in the 15th century. A lovely courtyard is decorated with medallions and coats of arms. One short block farther lies the **Plaza Mayor**. One block northeast is the **Casa de los Momos** with attractive windows, and the next right brings you to **Santiago del Burgos** ★, another lovely Romanesque church. Two more—**Santa Maria de la Horta** and **Santo Tomé**, lie due south.

Nearby Toro is also full of Romanesque churches, most built of brick. One in particular is noteworthy, the limestone **Iglesia del Colegiata** ★ ★, which boasts a glorious and almost perfectly preserved *Gothic west portal*, repainted in the 18th century to suggest its original appearance. (Open daily 10:30 a.m. to 1:30 p.m. and 5–7 p.m., until 8 p.m. in summer.) The figures of the Celestial Court and those in the Last Judgment scene are expressive as only the stiff Romanesque can be. Inside is another wondrous lantern, plus nice polychrome statuary at the nave end. The sacristy contains a painting of *The Virgin of the Fly*. Note the realistic fly on the Virgin's robe.

Santo Domingo de Silos Monastery

See Burgos excursions.

Segovia ★ ★ ★ ★ ★

Population: 53,237
Zip code: 40001; area code: 911

> From **Madrid** take A-6 northwest to Exit #3 in 61 km, switching to N-603, past lovely landscapes, for 30 km to Segovia. The total trip is 91 km. From **Ávila** take N-110 northwest for 66 km. From **Burgos** take N-1 south, toward Madrid, for 137 km, to three km past Cerezo de Abajo where you switch to N-110 heading west for Segovia in 57 km more. The trip covers 194 km. From **Valladolid** take N-601 south toward Madrid for 109 km to Villacastin, switching to N-110 for 37 km to Segovia, a total of 146 km. From **Salamanca**, follow directions to Ávila, and the directions above from there.

Take a ride around Segovia's perimeter following signs designating the "Ruta Panorámica" before entering the town. The circuit shows the unusual situation of the old city, thrust precipitously above the surrounding plain in a slender ellipse. Its appearance has often been likened to a ship, with the Alcázar at the prow and the towers of the Cathedral at the stern, while the original city walls run around most of its length. No city in Spain presents such a dramatic appearance, not even Toledo.

Segovia began as Sogobriga, a major town of the Celts. The Romans captured it in 80 B.C. and it grew into one of their most important Spanish cities which they favored with a great engineering feat by constructing an aqueduct two thirds of a mile long to lift water up from the Rio Riofrio.

What is remarkable is that the elevation of the city required the aqueduct to rise 95 feet (ten stories) above the ground. Miraculously, the aqueduct remains in perfect condition 2000 years later and could still be used today to supply the city's water.

After reconquest from the Moors, Segovia became the royal capital for a brief period. Its greatest moment occurred when the grandees of Spain met in the Alcázar to designate Isabella monarch after her half-brother Enrique IV died, passing over his heir, La Beltraneja, as illegitimate. By this time the Alcázar was centuries old, stretching back to Moorish times if not to the age of the Romans.

Segovia also boasted of a Romanesque Cathedral, as did so many cities in the area at this time, but in the succeeding reign of Carlos V the citizens of Spain rose up against their new king for his foreign ways and burned their own cathedral. This revolt, called the "Comuneros," since it was an uprising of towns, not of nobles, found one of its leaders in Juan Bravo from Segovia. In the end he was hung, though Segovia by then was cathedral-less. The city fathers hurriedly built another in the 16th century, while the Plateresque aesthetic was at its height, but for some reason favored a design in the old-fashioned Gothic style. Thus Segovia today possesses the most recent Gothic cathedral in Spain, and one of the largest.

Segovia is a city that once was important but could not find continued reasons to remain so. Though by no means poor, its population today is less by 20 percent than at its height in Renaissance times. Tourism is the main revenue producer.

Parking is an unsolved problem, especially in summer when hordes descend. Little space is available on the hill, and none at all in the main plaza below, Pl. Azoguejo (with the aqueduct). All we can suggest is to keep eyes peeled for any spot as you near the hill and to be prepared to walk some distance. Our tour of the old city starts in the Pl. Azoguejo, so we direct you there.

From **Madrid** *turn right onto Carretera de San Rafael at the major intersection where four large avenues converge. After passing the bullring, go left onto Av. del Padre Claret, which brings you to the large Pl. Azoguejo with the aqueduct in a few blocks. From* **Ávila** *and* **Salamanca** *no changes of road are necessary. Unless you turn away, you will end up in the Pl. Azoguejo. From* **Burgos** *or* **Valladolid** *no changes of road are necessary either; unless you intentionally deviate, you will end up in the Pl. Azoguejo.*

You cannot help looking at the **aqueduct** ★★ and admiring its age and simple but functional construction. The **Alcázar** ★★★, once viewed from a distance, ranks at the top of every list of what to see. The **Cathedral** ★★ is

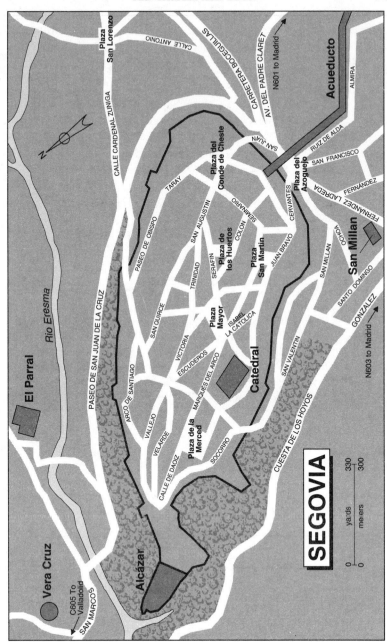

SEGOVIA

well worth a visit for its imposing effect. Then there are assorted **mansions** and churches on the hill, which being less than a mile long and narrow, can be walked from end to end. Off the hill two exceptional Romanesque churches—**Vera Cruz ★★** and **San Millán ★★**, should not be missed, and the monastery of **El Parral ★** contains rich decoration. One day would be adequate to see all this, unless you add the following excursions. About ten miles south of Segovia are two 17th-century palaces: **La Granja ★★★** with glorious gardens and fountain display, built by a king nostalgic for Versailles, and **Riofrio ★**, an overgrown hunting lodge for royalty.

Outside the Walls:
Vera Cruz, San Millán, El Parral

Go southwest from Pl. Azoguejo on Av. Fernández Ladreda, following signs to N-110 and Ávila. In three blocks the small church of **San Millán** *with a side porch, set back in its tiny square is passed. After San Millán continue on Av. Ladreda to the second street going right, Paseo Ezequiel González, which runs beside the elevated old town and provides lovely views. When it crosses the river, turn right for a moment onto C-605 heading to Segovia, and take the second left to* **La Vera Cruz** *sitting atop a hill. Return to C-605 again toward Segovia, which is named Paseo de San Juan after it crosses the river. The first left across the river takes you to* **El Parral** *Monastery.*

San Millán   ★★
Av. Fernández Ladreda, ☎ 43 43 88.
Hours open: daily 9 a.m.–1 p.m. (only for services in winter).
San Millán is the oldest (perhaps 11th century), purest Romanesque church in Segovia and one of the more charming designs in Spain. The porch outside was a place where important meetings were held; the Mudejar tower is an 11th century addition. Instead of thicker walls, external columns supporting the bays of the apse become architectural features—a local peculiarity of other Romanesque churches in Segovia. Inside, massive columns are topped with capitals carved in lively Biblical scenes. Newer baroque decoration has just been removed, uncovering marvelous Romanesque frescoes.

Vera Cruz Chapel   ★★
Carretera de Zamarramala, ☎ 43 14 75.
Hours open: Tues.–Sun. 10:30 a.m.–1 p.m. and 3–7 p.m. (until 6 p.m. in winter). Closed Mon. and holidays.
From the outside one can see that this is an unusual church—a polygon instead of the expected rectangle or cruciform shape. It was erected by the Knights Templar in the 13th century as a place for their rites, many of which were secret. In 1226 Pope Honore gave the church a piece of the True Cross, so it changed its name to La Vera Cruz. Inside, one finds a central chamber, circular in shape and two stories tall. Stairs lead up to the second story in which novice knights performed vigils while overlooking the altar. The surrounding nave is plain, except for faded 13th-century

frescoes. The place has a lovely feel of age. Stairs beside the altar lead up the tower for nice views of Segovia. *Admission: 125 ptas.*

El Parrel Monastery   ★

C. de Marqués de Villena, ☎ *43 12 98.*

Hours open: Tues.–Sun. 10 a.m.–1 p.m. and 3–7 p.m. (until 6 p.m. in winter.) Closed Mon. and holidays.

The facade, never completed, shows two unusual soaring columns with clustered niches at the bottom still waiting to be filled by statues. The church was built in the middle 15th century by Juan Pacheco in homage to the Virgin for her help in winning a duel. The Plateresque interior contains a sensitive reredo of Juan Pacheco praying on one side, his wife on the other. In the transept rests a Gothic effigy of his illegitimate sister beside a lovely flamboyant door to the sacristy.

Aqueduct   ★★

A channel in the Sierra de Fuenfria, over 11 miles away, starts water on its way to Segovia. But the land descends into a valley as it approaches the heights of the old town, so the Romans raised the water with an aqueduct to carry it up to the hill. The structure of massive granite blocks secured by physics, not mortar, was completed in the first century B.C., during the reign of the Emperor Trajan (who was born in Spain). Each block contains indentations for gripping by pincers to raise them into place. The aqueduct runs for two-thirds of a mile, reaching its greatest height of 95 feet in the Pl. del Azoguejo. It no longer functions, despite claims by the tourist authorities, but looks as if it could.

Inside the Walls

From the Pl. del Azoquejo ascend the hill by the pedestrian walk C. Cervantes, running northwest. As it goes slightly right at the top entering C. Juan Bravo, the strange **Casa de los Picos** lies left. This 14th-century fortified mansion was studded profusely with faceted protrusions a century later to produce an armored effect. C. Juan Bravo continues past the 14th-century palace of the **Condes de Alpuente**, set back left, with nice windows and plaster decoration, then past a restored former public granary down stairs to the left, before entering the **Pl. San Martin** ★.

Facing the plaza, opposite his statue in the center, is a Gothic house reputed to be that of **Juan Bravo** who led the uprising of the Comuneros in the 16th century. Other mansions surround the square, most interesting for their entrances. The house of the **Marqués de Moya** places intricate stucco designs around an utterly plain Romanesque door of massive stones; the Palace of the **Marqués of Lozoya** presents a Romanesque arched doorway fit for a church; and the **Palace of Quintanar** has an arched door surmounted by a row of curious helmets. In the center stands the 12th-century Romanesque **San Martin** ★, framed by a fine porch, and with nice carving on the front portal toward the west.

Continue on Juan Bravo pass the 18th-century prison, now the archives for the city. One block later pass the 16th-century church of **San Miguel** to the left, then take the right fork into the **Plaza Mayor** (a.k.a. Plaza José Antonio), lined with cafes. On its west side stands the Cathedral.

Cathedral   ★★

Pl. Mayor, ☎ *43 53 25.*
Hours open: weekdays 9:30 a.m.–1 p.m. and 3–6 p.m. Open weekends and holidays 9:30 a.m.–6 p.m. Open in summer daily 9 a.m.–7 p.m.
When their old Cathedral near the Alcázar was burned in the 16th century, the city fathers hired the Hontañons, father and son, who had achieved success with their neoclassical New Cathedral in Salamanca, but instructed them to design a Gothic building. This the architects did with flair, producing the last great Gothic church but with occasional Plateresque gestures. The entrance to the Cathedral is from the Plaza Mayor into the north transept. For some reason the western front of the church, with an open court that allows a fine view of the sober façade, is no longer used.

The Cathedral impresses with soaring spaces, perfect lines, nice vaulting and light, though the trascoro is nothing but a distraction. Moreover, the flamboyantly decorated chapels are not of great merit, with the exception of a nice retablo by Juan de Juni and a triptych in the La Piedad chapel, first off the south aisle.

A door in the south transept leads to the cloister, reconstructed stone by stone from the cloister of the former cathedral. As you enter, step over the tombs of the Hontañons who designed the Cathedral. The chapterhouse off the cloister has a late Mudejar ceiling in striking white and gold. Dramatic 17th-century Brussels tapestries are displayed, most of them designed by Rubens. *Admission: 200 ptas., for the cloister and museum.*

Facing the front of the church, head right down c. Daoiz, lined with souvenir shops, to number 9.

Museo de Holográfica   ★

C. Daoiz, 9.
Hours open: Tues.–Sun. 10:30 a.m.–2 p.m. and 4–7:30 p.m. Closed Mon. and holidays.
Three-dimensional holographs of scary creatures are appropriately presented in a 15th-century cellar. Kid enjoy the experience almost as much as their parents. *Admission: 220 ptas.*

Follow c. Daoiz to its end, then right past San Andres along R. Socorro which brings the gardens of the Alcázar 4 blocks with the castle itself ahead.

Alcázar   ★★★

Pl. de La Reina Victoria Eugenia, ☎ *43 01 76.*
Hours open: Mon.–Sat. 10 a.m.–7 p.m. (until 6 p.m. in winter.) Closed Sun. and holidays.
Though it looks the archetypal medieval castle, the interior today is mainly artifice. In the 14th century a former Moorish Alcázar, probably a modification of a Roman fort, was made into a Christian castle. Here Princess Isabella was first proclaimed queen of Spain. Most of Spain's medieval kings stayed at least a while; Prince

Charles of England, later King Charles I, enjoyed a visit; and the fourth marriage of Felipe II was celebrated inside. But in 1862, after Carlos III turned the old palace into an artillery school, a fire gutted the interior. Today, except for the entrance tower, the inside is a fanciful 19th-century reconstruction. If taken with a grain of salt, it remains fun to wander through.

Inside, furniture of the period, much armor, and some nice frescoes of medieval themes are displayed. The "King's Bedroom" is evocative and gives a sense of how tapestries were used to insulate cold stone walls, showing the profusion of colors in a medieval castle. The throne room is a 19th-century fantasy of how state rooms should look. *Admission: 350 ptas.*

From the Alcázar gardens go straight for a few steps, then follow C. de Velarde, the left fork, which wends for three blocks before changing its name to C. Pozuelo as it bends left to enter the Pl. de San Esteban. **San Esteban ★** is yet another lovely Segovian Romanesque church with a beautiful side gallery. It is the latest (13th century) of Segovia's Romanesque churches, and perhaps the most harmonious of all, prefaced by an elegantly thin front tower. The **Bishop's Palace** opposite is covered with curious reliefs.

Continue across the plaza to pick up C. Vitoria heading east, passing the **Casa de los Hierro**, with an intricate 16th-century entrance and grotesques, in one block on the left. The street changes its name to C. Valdelaguila as, on the left, it passes the **Casa de Hercules**, a Dominican convent named for the mighty figure on its tower. A block later the street changes its name to C. Trinidad as it passes the open and austere **San Trinidad**, yet another Romanesque church. One block later the street passes through the Pl. de Guevara, merging in another block with C. San Augustin. Then it passes a 16th-century mansion housing the **Museo Provincial del Bellas Artes**, before entering, two blocks later, the **Pl. del Conde de Cheste ★**, surrounded by mansions.

The **Disputacion** is on the left, while opposite is the **Casa de las Cabezas**. Across the plaza, left to right, are the large **Palacio del Condes de Cheste**, the **Casa de Lozoyo** (with parts from the 12th century) and **Casa de Moya**. To the right is the **Palacio Quintanar**, followed by the **Casa de las Cadenas**, both 15th-century. Behind them is the **Iglesia San Sebastian**, yet another of Segovia's Romanesque churches, past which is the aqueduct's end and stairs descending back to the Pl. Azoguejo.

Where to Stay

Segovia's selection is sparse, since most visitors day-trip from Madrid, but there are choices in every price-category.

Expensive ($100–$200)

Parador de Segovia   Deluxe ★ ★ ★

On Carretera N-601, three km north of Segovia (From the Pl. del Azoguejo take the cen-
ter of three roads fanning east, following signs to N-601 and Valladolid. Look for the
parador sign.), ☎ *44 37 37, FAX 43 73 62, Telex 47913.*

This is one of the modern paradors that tries to impress with design by looking like
an overgrown Swiss chalet. The spacious public areas are landscaped with contemporary sculpture and crafts, and the staff is efficient, organized and helpful. All is
clean, if somehow institutional. The ample rooms all overlook Segovia for fine
views, and it possesses every facility from swimming pool to new tennis courts, but
is situated half a mile from the old town *113 rooms.*

Moderate ($50–$99)

Los Linajes   2nd-class ★ ★ ★

C. Dr. Velasco, 9, Segovia (stairs descend east of the Pl. de San Esteban), ☎ *43 04 75,*
FAX 46 04 79.

The facade is 11th-century, a former palace of nobles named Falconis. Inside it is
attractively decorated and has the cozy feel of small spaces. All rooms present glorious views over the countryside, and the staff could not be more helpful. Without
question this is the best place to stay in Segovia. Parking is provided for a fee at the
foot of the hotel outside the city walls, but is hard to find. *55 rooms.*

Las Sirenas   2nd-class ★ ★

Juan Bravo, 30, Segovia (opposite Pl. San Martin, a few doors past Juan Bravo's pur-
ported house), ☎ *43 40 11, FAX 43 06 33.*

The hotel is lovely and bright, much better than its rating or charges. Attractiveness
starts with a spacious lobby and continues to a public room with a fireplace for relaxing. Bedrooms are comfortable, if unmemorable, but include TVs and go for a price
that edges on the inexpensive. *39 rooms.*

Infanta Isabel   1st-class ★ ★

Isabel la Católica, 1, Segovia (on the main square, facing the Cathedral), ☎ *44 31 05,*
FAX 43 32 40.

Inside a remodeled turn-of-the-century mansion, these rooms contain TVs and
minibars, and are decorated with charmingly hand-painted furniture. All told, you
get more than usual for this price. *29 rooms.*

Los Arcos   1st-class ★ ★

Paseo de Ezequiel González, 24, Segovia (one block south and another east of San
Millán), ☎ *43 74 62, FAX 42 81 61, Telex 49823.*

This well-run modern hotel is of the business traveler sort, with many amenities. It
incorporates the most elegant restaurant in town. However it is situated a good six
blocks away, and a steep hill-climb up to the sights. *59 rooms.*

Acueducto   2nd-class ★

Av. del Padre Claret, 10, Segovia (two blocks east of the Pl. del Azoguejo), . ☎ *42 48*
00, FAX 42 84 46.

Though outside the walls, the location is close enough to walk easily, if uphill, to
the sights. The hotel, however, fronts the major traffic thoroughfare of the town.

This is a modern hotel with the expected services of its class, nothing more. *78 rooms*

Inexpensive (Less than $50)

Plaza **Hs3rd-class ★**

C. Cronista Lecea, 11, Segovia (beside the Don José María restaurant, a short block on the street leading east from Pl. Mayor), ☎ *43 12 28.*

Small, undistinguished, but with a great location and very reasonable prices, this *hostale* is clean, the rooms tidy and the service considerate. Some rooms lack bathing facilities. *28 rooms.*

Where to Eat

Segovia is the place for roast suckling pig and suckling lamb served in three superior restaurants and others besides—so many that the restaurants begin to seem pleasantly alike. This is not to disparage the food, only to note its limited variety.

Expensive ($30+)

Mesón de Cándido **★★**

Pl. Azoguejo, 5, ☎ *42 59 11.*

Thanks to the showmanship of its former owner, this is one of the most famous restaurants in Spain. It is lodged in an old inn parts of which are 15th-century and consists of small timbered rooms with fireplaces, which display the memorabilia of years. The specialty is Castilian roasts of piglet or milk-lamb whose tenderness is proved by slicing the carcass with a dinner plate. The meat is truly flavorful, but it could only be so tender if overcooked. The trout is tasty, as is the garlic soup, and the house wine is quite good. Reserve on weekends. Credit Cards: A, D, M, V.

José María **★★**

C. Cronista Lecea, 11 (a short block on the street leading east out of the Pl. Mayor), ☎ *43 44 84.*

This time the restaurant is modern, but it still does a mean suckling pig cut with a dinner plate as at Cándido and Duque. The difference is that the chef here does other things well too. Frogs' legs and fish are good, as are the blood sausage, or the special eggs as appetizers. The house red wine is delicious, the white more ordinary. For dessert order an orange and watch the waiter cut it artfully before you are transported by the taste. The raspberry cream with walnuts isn't bad either. Reservations recommended. Credit Cards: A, D, M, V.

Mesón del Duque **★★**

C. Cervantes, 12 (at the entrance to the old town at the top of the street running up from Pl. Azoguejo), ☎ *43 05 37.*

Clearly modeled on Cándido (see previous listing) with a similar old look, though more studied, this is the same type of place. It is hard to choose between the two. This one offers a reasonably priced special menu, however. Credit Cards: A, D, M, V.

Moderate ($15–$30)

La Oficina **★**

C. Cronista Lecea, 10 (across the street from Restaurante José María)., ☎ *43 16 43. Closed Monday in winter and all of November.*

This is the lower-priced version of the foregoing, also with an azulejo tiled dining room. The choices are restricted, but cover the compulsory roast sucking pig, et. al. If you order from the special menu, your meal can be very reasonable. Credit Cards: A, D, M, V.

La Taurina ★

Pl. Mayor, 8, ☎ *43 05 77.*

Yes, this is yet another place for roasts like the preceding, with an attempt at the same ambience, though at even lower prices. Ordering from the special menu can make this an inexpensive meal, and the food can be very good. Credit Cards: A, D, M, V.

Directory

Information

Located at Pl. Mayor, 10. ☎ *43 03 28.* Open weekdays from 10 a.m. to 2 p.m. and from 4:30–7 p.m. Open Sat. from 10 a.m. to 2 p.m.

Trains and Buses

The train station is located at Paseo del Obispo Quesada, a 20-minute walk due south from Pl. Azoguejo. The #3 bus from the Pl. Mayor goes to or from the station. Nine trains each weekday travel to and from Madrid in two hours, and two go to Valladolid. One train goes to León and Salamanca, three times per week. ☎ *42 07 74.*

The bus station is located at Paseo de Ezequiel González, 10. Take Av. Fernández Ladreda southwest from the Pl. Azoguejo for five blocks, just past San Millán, to the Paseo and turn right. ☎ *42 77 25.* A dozen buses per day go to La Granja (under 100 ptas.). Service is excellent to and from Madrid, and better than the train to Ávila and Valladolid.

Post Office and Telephones

Located at Pl. del Dr. Laguna, 5 (head east out of the Pl. Mayor on C. Cronista Lecea, taking the right fork in one long block onto C. Serafin for 2 blocks). ☎ *43 16 11.* Open weekdays from 9 a.m. to 2 p.m. and from 4-6 p.m. Open Sat. from 9 a.m. to 2 p.m. Telephones are available at Pl. de los Huertos, 8 (next to the post office).

Police

C. Guardarrama (☎ *42 12 12).*

Excursions

Two enjoyable Segovia excursions take in neighboring 17th-century palaces—**La Granja ★ ★ ★**, with lovely gardens and extravagant fountains, and **Riofrio ★**, the most elegant hunting lodge anywhere. The other remarkable excursion is to **Coca Castle ★ ★** one of the most characteristic in Spain. See its description and directions under the Coca Castle listing above in this chapter.

La Granja de San Ildefonso ★ ★ ★

From Pl. Azoguejo take the southernmost of the two streets forking east, Av. del Padre Claret, following signs to N-601 and Madrid. As the bullring comes into view, stay left. In 11 km signs lead you to San Ildefonso and La Granja.

For **bus** *transport, see the "Directory" listing.*

La Granja Palace

Hours open: daily 10 a.m.–1 p.m. and 3–5:30 p.m. (Sun. closes at 2 p.m.) Gardens: open daily from 10 a.m. to sunset. Check with the Segovia Office of Tourism for the time of the fountain show (in summer, usually at 5:30 p.m.).

When, at the beginning of the 18th century, Felipe V, cousin to the King of France, received the Spanish throne, he built this reminder of home, his Versailles. With classic Gallic understatement, he named it La Granja, "the farm." Name aside, it looks very much the French palace, especially from the back, and overlooks splendid gardens, both formal and wild, that stretch to the horizon past a series of fountains that provide about the best waterworks display you'll ever see.

Unfortunately the interior of the palace suffered from fire at the beginning of our century. The reconstructed results are still worth a look for their Versailles-like vistas through room after room and for the vast tapestry collection. In the chapel, which also suffered fire damage, are the tombs of Felipe V and his queen, Isabel Farnese. *Admission: 500 ptas.*

But the main attraction is the gardens and, in summer, the incredible sunset display when the fountains go on, one by one, until Fuente La Fama, the last, shoots water 130 feet in the air. *Admission: 300ptas.*

Riofro Palace ★

See the directions to La Granja above.

Riofro Palace

Hours open: same times as La Granja.

When her husband died and her son replaced her with his own queen, Felipe V's wife, Isabel Farnese, tried to outdo the La Granja palace with this one nearby. It is huge but so simple that it seems more the hunting lodge it later became, though in a pink color appropriate for its first occupant. The courtyard is grand and monumental stairways lead to sumptuous apartments. Recently much of the palace has been turned into a Museum of the Chase, with curious but sometimes interesting exhibits. *Admission: 500 ptas.*

Soria

See Burgos excursions.

Toro

See Salamanca excursions.

Valladolid ★ ★

Population: 330,242
Zip code: 47001; area code: 983

> From **Madrid** *take A-6 north for 37 km to exit 1 for N-VI, to avoid the toll, or to its end at exit 6, for a faster ride. In either case, take N-601 north at Adanero after 122 km. You come to Valladolid in 82 km for a trip of 204 km. From* **Ávila** *take N-110 toward Villacastin for 29 km, turning north on N-VI for 27 km, then switching at Adanero for N-601 and 82 km more. The trip is 140 km. From* **Salamanca** *take N-620 (E-80) northeast for 85 km through Tordesillas, continuing on the same road for 30 km more. From* **Segovia** *take N-110 west for 37 km to Villacastin, turning north on N-VI and continue with the Ávila directions, for a trip of 148 km. From* **León** *take N-601 south for 139 km. From* **Burgos** *take N-620 (E-80) west for 125 km, skirting Palencia.*

The unusual name for the city derives from the Arabic *Belad Walid*, "Land of the Governor," showing that the Moors considered it an important town. Valladolid prospered due to its position in the center of miles of wheat farms. For centuries it functioned as a second capital for the kings of Castile and León, and when Isabella decided against the wishes of her king to marry Ferdinand from Aragón, the two eloped to Valladolid to wed in a mansion there, subsequently torn down. After the conquest of Granada, Isabella and Ferdinand appointed Valladolid the capital of the country. Although the future Felipe II was born in Valladolid, he moved the capital permanently to Madrid in 1560, leaving Valladolid with only 60 years as Spain's capital.

During its brief prominence, Columbus settled to spend his last years, and Cervantes resided for a while. Befitting its capital status, a college was established in 1496 in the exuberant style called Isabelline, the forerunner of the Plateresque. But when the court moved to Madrid, Valladolid declined. It regained momentary importance when Napoléon made it his headquarters during the Peninsular War, though he and his soldiers stripped the buildings of their treasures and shipped them to France. After Napoléon's departure, Valladolid turned to economic pursuits to recover some of its former importance, and today is a major industrial town.

Industrial success means that Valladolid is not the loveliest of cities. What the French did not destroy, the city fathers did by favoring development over historical preservation. Valladolid presents miles of factories, high-rise apartment and office buildings. Some modern Spanish cities manage to remain attractive, but Valladolid is not one of them. That is not to say the city is unbearably ugly, just that Spain spoils us to expect more.

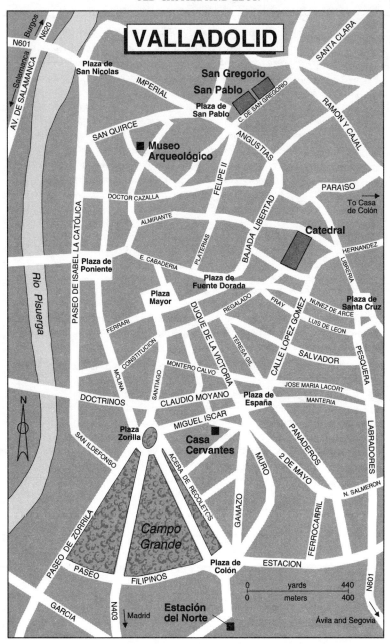

VALLADOLID

Burgos
N620
N601
AV. DE SALAMANCA
Salamanca

Plaza de
San Nicolas

IMPERIAL

San Gregorio
San Pablo

C. DE SAN GREGORIO

SANTA CLARA

RAMON Y CAJAL

Plaza de
San Pablo

SAN QUIRCE

ANGUSTIAS

■ Museo
Arqueológico

FELIPE II

PARAISO

To Casa
de Colón

DOCTOR CAZALLA

ALMIRANTE

PASEO DE ISABEL LA CATÓLICA

E. CABADERIA

PLATERIAS

BAJADA LIBERTAD

Catedral

HERNANDEZ

LIBRERIA

Plaza de
Poniente

Plaza
Mayor

Plaza de
Fuente Dorada

Plaza de
Santa Cruz

Río Pisuerga

FERRARI

DUQUE DE LA VICTORIA

REGALADO

FRAY

NUÑEZ DE ARCE

CALLE LOPEZ GOMEZ

LUIS DE LEON

SALVADOR

PESQUERA

CONSTITUCION

MCLINA

SANTIAGO

MONTERO CALVO

TERESA GIL

JOSE MARIA LACORT

MANTERIA

N

DOCTRINOS

CLAUDIO MOYANO

Plaza de
España

MIGUEL ISCAR

PANADEROS

LABRADORES

SAN ILDEFONSO

Plaza
Zorrilla

Casa
Cervantes

ACERA DE RECOLETOS

MURO

2 DE MAYO

N. SALMERON

PASEO DE ZORRILLA

Campo
Grande

GAMAZO

FERROCARRIL

PASEO

FILIPINOS

Plaza de
Colón

ESTACION

GARCIA

N403

Madrid

Estación
del Norte

0   yards   440
0   meters   400

N601

Ávila and Segovia

Route **N-601** *becomes Av. Segovia which ends at the park, Campo Grande. Turn left, then right at its end onto Paseo de Zorrilla, with a center divider, which lets into the large Pl. Zorrilla at the other end. Continue through the plaza to head in the same direction on C. Santiago which lets into the Pl. Mayor in five blocks for underground parking. From* **Salamanca** *on N-620 you reach the River Pisuerga. Turn right across the third bridge. On C. Doctrinos take the second left onto C. Santiago which leads in four blocks into the Pl. Mayor and underground parking. From* **León** *on N-601 you travel on Av. de Gijon to the river. Turn right on Av. de Salamanca. At the third bridge after that turn, turn left across the river and follow the Salamanca directions above. From* **Burgos** *on N-620 you reach the river on Av. de Salamanca. Cross the river and turn left three bridges later to follow the Salamanca directions.*

What to See and Do

The sight that makes a trip to Valladolid worthwhile is the former **College of San Gregorio** ★ ★ ★ ★ , for Isabelline decoration and even more for its great museum of polychrome sculpture in which Spain excelled. A few steps away is the lovely facade of **Colegio Santa Cruz** ★ ★ . The nearby **Archaeology Museum** ★ is worth a visit. Valladolid's neoclassical **Cathedral** ★ ★ , which should be seen, was designed in the style of Herrera who built much of El Escorial. The **University** ★ opposite has an unusual facade. For most visitors **Columbus' House** ★ ★ is a must, and **Cervantes' House** ★ ★ is evocative. One day covers it all.

From the Pl. Mayor, former site of bullfights and autos-da-fe, head north beside the Ayuntamiento, past the Post Office, and northwest along C. Correos. Walk north one block to **San Benito church** ★ , *fortresslike, but with a monumental porch. Opposite is the* **house of Alonso Berruguete**, *whose work will be admired in the Sculpture Museum. Walk one block further north to the church of* **San Miguel** ★ *which contains an elegant patio. Turn left passing the* **Palace of the Marquesses de Valverde**, *on the left, with stately decoration, to arrive at the Archaeology Museum, on the right.*

Museo Arqueológico   ★

Pl. Nelli.

Hours open: Tues.–Sat. 10 a.m.–2 p.m. and 4–7 p.m. Open Sun. 10 a.m.–2 p.m. Closed Mon. and holidays.

Beside unexceptional Roman and Iberian objects, the museum contains an interesting collection of 14th-century frescoes from a church in Peñafiel. Also interesting are oriental textiles found in the tomb of the son of Sancho IV, and Renaissance tiles. The paintings vary in quality. *Admission: 200 ptas.*

After passing a park, turn left to C. San Quirce, where a right turn leads to the space of Pl. de San Pablo in two blocks. On one side is the **Capitana General**, *a former royal palace that Napoléon appropriated for a time; on the* *other is the imposing facade of* **San Pablo**. *Past the right side of San Pablo, in the rear, waits the extraordinary* **Colegio de San Gregorio**.

Iglesia San Pablo ★★

Pl. San Pablo, ☎ *35 17 48.*
Hours open: daily 8 a.m.–1 p.m. and 5–9 p.m.

Here is a facade of astonishing richness. It is also not quite right, because the lower part, up to the arch over the door, is Isabelline from 1463, while the top three registers are later Plateresque. It presents a study in the differences between these styles. Despite ornateness, the top is orderly and static, laid out in classical squares and circles, but the bottom half is a riot of twisting, curling forms barely contained in compartments that fruitlessly try for system.

The interior of the church was destroyed by the French, though retaining lovely tombs and two handsome doorways leading off each transept, both transitional between the Isabelline and Plateresque styles.

Colegio de San Gregorio ★★★★

C. Cadeñas de San Gregorio, ☎ *26 79 67.*
Hours open: Tues.–Sat. 10 a.m.–2 p.m. and 4–6 p.m. Open Sun. 10 a.m.–2 p.m. Closed Mon., and holidays.

The entrance is sumptuous Isabelline, with foliage popping out in unexpected places. Above are heraldic motifs amid more twisting foliage. Almost certainly the great Gil de Siloé was the artist. Inside, the first court contains a window with lovely Mudejar stuccowork, followed by a court of incredibly dense lacy decoration on the fences and arches of the second-story gallery. A frieze surmounted by gargoyles displays the yoke and arrow emblems of Ferdinand and Isabella.

Right from this arcade is the entrance to the famed **Museum of Polychrome Sculpture**. Of course Germans and others excelled at medieval and Renaissance wood carving, but no one outdid the Spanish, and there is no better collection in the country than here. Some find the works too cloyingly realistic, but none can fault the virtuosity. Arrows and room numbers ensure that all will be seen in proper order.

The first exhibit is not surpassed; this is a huge retablo by Alonso Berruguete done in 1532 for the San Benito church. The dismantled work requires three small rooms to display it all. It is shown at a height where it can be appreciated, instead of at its original elevation and distance behind an altar. Berruguete studied Michelangelo's work in Florence before returning home to produce the most evocative Spanish sculpture, culminating in this his largest and finest work. Note the large bishop with the tortured face and gnarled hands, which is Berruguete's signature. The piece goes on and on, with one masterly detail after another, leaving the viewer breathless. After room #3, a stair leads to displays above, permitting a pause to rest one's eyes.

The first rooms upstairs contain minor, early works, with some nice choir stalls, but room #15 brings Juan de Juni's **Christ's Burial**, a splendid composition, and fine Flemish retablos from the Convent of San Francisco. After completing the second floor circuit, not failing to see Pedro de Mena's **Mary Magdalene**, an early baroque work, it is back to the ground floor and the work of the consummate master of polychromed sculpture, Gregorio Fernández, in rooms #4 and #5. The issue in Fernández' case is whether realism goes too far, becoming the sole consideration. Certainly this is true for those influenced by Fernández. His heritage is poor, but the master himself offers sensitivity amid excessive drama. See his *Pieta, Baptism, Recumbent Christ, and Sta. Teresa*, and decide for yourself.

Through the small garden to the chapel, with its fine vaulting, are some moving funerary pieces, in addition to Berruguete's first recorded altar, badly restored. *Admission: 200 ptas.*

Go east on the street fronting San Pablo, which becomes C. de las Angustias after the intersection, to pass the brick house in which Felipe II was born. The street angles left. In three blocks pass **Nuestra Senora de las Angustias** ★ *in which there is a superb altar by Juan de Juni at the end of the south transept, and pieces elsewhere by Fernández, if your appetite for sculpture survives. Turn left at the next opportunity, reaching a square with the rear of the Cathedral on the right and Santa María la Antigua to the left.* **Sta María la Antigua** ★ *is the oldest remaining church in Valladolid—the tower and portico being Romanesque; the rest is elegant Gothic (only open during services). Continue around to the Cathedral entrance.*

Cathedral ★★

Pl. de la Universidad, ☎ *30 43 62.*
Hours open: weekdays 10 a.m.–2 p.m. and 4:30–7 p.m. Open weekends and holidays 10 a.m.–2 p.m.
Although work commenced during the reign of Felipe II, it is questionable whether Herrera, his favorite architect, had much of a hand in the design. In the end the question is moot because the style is obviously Herreran neoclassical, whether or not by him personally. The facade, especially the upper part, is not one of Alberto Churriguera's better efforts. But power exudes from the massive austere interior. The brilliantly colored and gilded altarpiece by Juan de Juni seems out of place amid the neoclassicism, though the figures are lively. *Admission: 200 ptas.*

Across the park, to the east of the Cathedral, is the **University** ★ *. Its flamboyantly baroque front by Diego Tomé, exhibits the style that succeeded the Plateresque. A walk along the University's east face on C. Libreria brings another park, on the east side of which is the lovely* **Colegio Santa Cruz** ★ *. Begun in the Gothic style in 1487, by its completion the Plateresque had taken over, making this building one of the first in that style. Note the "classical" later windows and how they suit this precocious new design. The inner courtyard is elegant. C. del Cardinal Mendoza goes east, then turns north to become C. Colón which leads in two blocks more to the Casa Colón on the left.*

Casa Colón ★★

C. Calón.
Hours open: Tues.–Sat. 10 a.m.–2 p.m. and 4–6 p.m. Open Sun. 10 a.m.–2 p.m. Closed Mon., and holidays.

Those who remember reading how Columbus was abandoned when his patron Isabella died or how, during the last years of his life, he sued in vain for what had been promised if he discovered new lands, will expect to find his last accommodations impoverished. Instead his final home for his last two years was a mansion, all in stone. The present structure is rebuilt, but retains the original dimensions. There is something eerie about walking through these rooms to make our ideas of a legend conform to the reality of a person. In truth the museum is not much, but the experience is. *Admission: free.*

The final stop is a less pretentious house 15 minutes away that conforms more with expectations—that of Miquel de Cervantes. Retrace steps back along C. Colón and around the Pl. de Santa Cruz, following C. Fray Luis de León west for two blocks. Turn left (south) onto C. Lopez Gomez which leads to the Pl. España in two more blocks. Turn right (west) across the south end of the plaza on C. Martinez Villergas to C. Miguel Iscar. In one block turn right past a garden to arrive at Cervantes' door. Or, take a taxi.

Casa de Cervantes ★★

C. del Rastro, ☎ *30 88 10.*
Hours open: Tues.–Sat. 10 a.m.–4 p.m. Open Sun. and holidays 10 a.m.–2 p.m. Closed Mon.
When Valladolid became the capital for a short time, Cervantes bought a tract house hastily put up by a speculator. He moved in with his family and assorted hangers-on to fill 13 rooms above a tavern in what was then a seedy part of town. Here he spent a few years waiting for publication of his famed **Don Quixote**. While here, Cervantes was arrested after a nobleman, wounded by some assailant, was brought into the house and died. What you see today is fancifully reconstructed to a better condition than when Cervantes resided, but it is a nice presentation of a 17th-century house with its furnishings. *Admission: 200 ptas.*

Where to Stay

There are no wonderful hotels in Valladolid, although comfortable accommodations do exist. Consider staying in a pine forest along the road to Salamanca only 30 km west near Tordesillas. We list two nice places. Valladolid's greatest lack is inexpensive places to stay. Numerous *pensions* and *hostales* thrive in the area south of the university, but are suited only to undemanding students.

Expensive ($100–$200)

Olid Meliá   1st-class ★★

Pl. San Miguel, 10, Valladolid (Take C. Felipe II south from the east end of Pl. San Pablo. Turn right in two blocks onto C. de San Blas for a short block to arrive at the hotel on the right.), ☎ *35 72 00, FAX 33 68 28, Telex 26312.*
This hotel is modern, large and situated in a nice area convenient to most sights. It is probably the most comfortable hotel in town, though not in any way remarkable. Only the public spaces have been renovated in recent memory, but charges are barely expensive. Parking is available for a fee. *203 rooms, plus 7 suites.*

Moderate ($50–$99)

On N-620, 5k south of Tordesillas, 30 km west of Valladolid:

El Montico

2nd-class ★ ★ ★

Carretera de Salamanca, N-620, Tordesillas (At Tordesillas, take N-VI south for two km to connect with N-620 west toward Salamanca for five km more), ☎ *79 50 00, FAX 79 50 08.*

Just a mile from the parador below, this hotel occupies the same peaceful forest, but is a restored old farmhouse of some charm. It includes a good restaurant, a pool and tennis court, all contributing to relaxation. *51 rooms.*

On N-620, two km south of Tordesillas, 30 km west of Valladolid:

Parador de Tordesillas
2nd-class ★ ★ ★

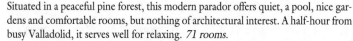

Carretera de Salamanca, N-620, Tordesillas (At Tordesillas, take N-VI south for two km to connect with N-620 west toward Salamanca for two km more), ☎ *77 00 51, FAX 77 10 13.*

Situated in a peaceful pine forest, this modern parador offers quiet, a pool, nice gardens and comfortable rooms, but nothing of architectural interest. A half-hour from busy Valladolid, it serves well for relaxing. *71 rooms.*

In Valladolid:

Roma
3rd-class ★

Héroes del Alcázar de Toledo, 8, Valladolid (Walk south of the Pl. Mayor on C. Santiago for a block, then right.), ☎ *35 47 77, FAX 35 54 61.*

Homey is the word for this small hotel convenient to most sights and to the activity in the Pl. Mayor. *38 rooms.*

Imperial
3rd-class ★

Peso, 4, Valladolid (From the Pl. Mayor walk a very short block along the west side of the Ayuntamiento, then turn right), ☎ *33 03 00, FAX 33 08 13, Telex 26304.*

The location is just a bit better than the Roma, but for a hotel without its homey feeling. Still, the rooms are comfortable and the staff tries hard. *81 rooms.*

Youth Hostel

Albergue Juvenil Rio Esgueve

Camino Cementerio, Valladolid (a long walk, or a short ride on a number 1 or 8 bus from the Pl. Mayor to the end of the line), ☎ *25 15 50.*

Open only during July and August when reservations are imperative. Charges are low: 800 ptas.

Where to Eat

Valladolid possesses one exceptional restaurant, along with a number that provide satisfying food.

Expensive ($30+)

Mesón La Fragua

★ ★ ★ ★

Paseo de Zorrilla, 10 (on the avenue with center divider that runs along the west side of the Campo Grande park), ☎ *33 87 85.*
Closed Sunday night, Monday and August.

Without question this is the finest restaurant in town, as patronage by Spanish royalty attests. The decor is traditional with more elegant touches. Here you can order traditional Castilian roasts, superbly done, but such things are available elsewhere. This is a place to let the chef charm you with more inventive dishes. Try the Rape

Gran Mesón (braised skate). The wine list is choice. Reservations are necessary. Credit Cards: A, D, M, V.

Mesón Panero ★★★

Marina Escobar, 1 (just west of Casa Cervantes), ☎ *30 70 19.*

Closed Sunday in July and August, Sunday night during the rest of the year.

La Fraqua gets more attention, and deservedly, but this place stands a good cut above the other restaurants in town. The chef is innovative and committed—even to hosting a gastronomic festival each February. All the fish is good, stuffed partridge is superb and the rabbit delicious. The *sopa Castellano* is not prepared better anywhere. Reservations are required. Credit Cards: A, D, M, V.

Moderate ($50–$99)

El Figón de Recoletos ★★★

Acera de Recoletos, 3 (this street angles southeast of the Pl. Zorrilla, where the tourist office is located, five blocks south of the Pl. Mayor), ☎ *39 60 43.*

Closed Sunday night and from the middle of July through the middle of August.

In decor and range of dishes this is a rather typical Castilian restaurant, but the food is much better than most of this type. The lamb, especially, is very good, and for the quality, prices are more than fair. Credit Cards: M, V.

Directory

Information

Located at *Pl. Zorrilla, 3* (the large plaza at the north end of the Campo Grande, five blocks south of the Pl. Mayor). It provides a much needed map. Open Mon.–Fri. from 9 a.m. to 2 p.m. and from 4–6 p.m. Open Sat. from 9 a.m. to 2 p.m. ☎ *35 18 01.*

Trains and Buses

The train station is located on C. Recondo, one long block south of the southern end of the Campo Grande. ☎ *30 35 18.* Valladolid is a rail hub for Old Castile. There is frequent service to Madrid, and reasonable service to all the major cities of Old Castile. The RENFE ticketing office is located at *C. Divina Pastores, 6.* ☎ *30 48 00.*

Buses depart from *C. Puente Colgante, 2* (in front of the bullring four blocks south of the Campo Grande off Paseo de Zorrilla, which passes along its west side). ☎ *23 63 08.* Buses are better than the train for long distances, but not as good for Old Castile.

Post Office and Telephones

Located in the Pl. de la Arrinconada, two short blocks north of the Pl. Mayor. ☎ *33 06 60.* Telephones are available at *C. Gondomar, 2,* one block north of Colegio de San Gregorio and west.

Police

Located on *C. Felipe II, 10,* which runs south from the Pl. San Pablo. ☎ *25 33 44.*

Airport

Located 14 km west of town off the León highway (N-601) with few direct flights, but connections throughout Spain (☎ *25 92 12*). The local office of Iberia is on *C. Gomaza, 17*, which runs due south from the Pl. España. ☎ *30 06 66.*

Excursions

East of Valladolid sits the massive 14th-century castle of **Peñafiel ★ ★**, lofty on its hill.

Follow the east side of the Campo Grande park. At its end turn left onto C. Estación. C. Estación soon follows railroad tracks west. After seven blocks turn right onto C. San Isidro, following signs to Soria and N-122. Peñafiel lies 93 km east of Valladolid.

Peñafiel ★ ★

From a distance, the imposing fortress can be seen sitting atop a steep hill, guarding the valley below as a fortress should. On the way up pass through a surprisingly large Pl. Mayor ringed with wooden houses whose balconies are made for watching bullfights.

The castle was constructed at the beginning of the 14th century, although a massive square keep topped by turrets was added two centuries later. Two still-solid perimeter walls defended the castle from attack. Today they help compose a perfect picture of an early medieval fortress. (Hours open: *Tues.–Sun. 11 a.m.–2:30 p.m. and 4–8 p.m.; closes at 6 p.m. in winter; admission: 200 ptas.*)

Zamora

See Salamanca excursions.

ANDALUSIA

A typical Andalusian lane in San Roque.

Historical Profile:
Moors and the Reconquest

Spain is unique among European nations because of its Islamic heritage. And what a heritage! Christian and Moor lived together, for almost 900 years, twice as long as the 400 years that have passed since the last Moor sailed away. Beyond doubt, the most important episode in all of Spanish history was the coming of the Moors, the imposition of their culture and the arduous effort by the Christians to win their country back.

How did this all come about? The arrival of Muslims in Spain is well documented; why they came is less clear. Early in the seventh century the Prophet Mohammed preached conquest as a religious duty and let plunder add its own incentive until, a century later, Mohammed's successors had vanquished all the lands in a broad belt from India in the east, through Morocco in the west. By the beginning of the eighth century, the quandary of the Muslim high-command was whether to continue the conquest from Morocco south through Africa, or north across 12 miles of water to Spain and Europe. Rumors of Spanish riches settled that issue and the invasion began. This is one explanation.

Spanish chronicles written during the Islamic domination, although centuries after the initial invasion, offer a different version. A man named Rodrigo had been elected by the nobles as the king of Spain, thereby depriving Akhila, the heir of the former king, of his expected inheritance. Soon after, Count Julian, a vassal of this King Rodrigo, sent his fair daughter Florinda to the new court to be educated. One day King Rodrigo saw Florinda bathing in the Tagus and, overcome by lust, had his way with her. Count Julian vowed revenge for his daughter's dishonor. He went to Musa, the Muslim governor of Morocco, to tell him where he could land troops unnoticed, how the Spanish army was disposed and, in general, to convince him to invade Spain. Musa sent his lieutenant Tarik Ibn Zeyad with 7000 men across the straits to reconnoiter. Reinforced by a further 5000 troops, Tarik engaged Rodrigo's much larger army. Incredibly, the left and right wings of Rodrigo's force were commanded by brothers of Akhila, the man who Rodrigo had deprived of the throne. When the battle began, these brothers stood aside, leaving Rodrigo's men to fight the Muslim army alone. It was a rout; Rodrigo's dusty saddle was found on the field, but his body was never recovered. Thus, the Spanish chronicles attribute the defeat to treason and treachery, to anything but an honest drubbing.

The facts are that a Moorish commander named Tarik first landed on Spanish soil in 711, on a mountain peninsula projecting off the coast. Ever since, the peninsula has borne his name—Gebal (mountain of) Tarik—Gibraltar. With only a small force, for his orders were merely to explore, he engaged and defeated the army of King Rodrigo near the coastal city of Algeciras. After Rodrigo's troops scattered, Tarik moved north to the capital of Toledo and took it easily.

Musa, Tarik's superior back in Morocco, grew concerned that his lieutenant had exceeded his orders and that spoils were falling to others. He embarked the next year for Spain with 18,000 men, met Tarik at Toledo and, after slapping him on the head with his riding crop, took personal command. In two years Musa conquered most of Spain. The caliph of Damascus then ordered his governor Musa to report in person on the events of the invasion.

With an immense baggage of riches and a retinue of hundreds of hostage sons of Spanish nobles, Musa paraded to Damascus where he was arrested, tried as an embezzler, and imprisoned for the rest of his life.

His son carried on the conquest, seizing all that remained of Spain except a pocket here and there in the foothills of the Pyrenees, terrain not worth a fight. The whole conquest took less than seven years.

Musa's son then married King Rodrigo's widow. He was murdered soon after in Seville's mosque, probably on orders from the caliph in Damascus who had received reports of affecting a crown and throne, and possibly of converting to Christianity. Thus ended the conquest of Spain and the family of the conqueror.

For several decades Spain was ruled by a succession of governors, known as *amirs* (commanders), appointed by the caliph in Damascus. They tested the strength of southern France with numerous raids. In 732, a major force of Muslims sacked Bordeaux then turned northeast for Paris. Near Tours, in the center of France, a large Frank army under Charles Martel blocked their advance and finally defeated them. This event did not end the raids, but it established the high watermark of the Muslims in Europe. Spain would be sufficient. In fact, one caliph concluded that Europe was indefensible so the Muslims should abandon Spain. He died before his order could be executed.

The Muslims proceeded to create an Islamic civilization in Spain with Córdoba as their capital. They called their territory *al Andalus*, the origin of the present name "Andalusia." Probably the word derives from the Arabic equivalent of "Vandal's land," although the derivation is controversial.

Of course there remained those pockets of territory in the north that had never been subjugated where the spirit of the native Spanish endured, preserving memories of their kings and a time of Christian rule. The Spanish date their attempt to win back the country to 722 when Pelayo, a noble from Asturias, defeated a Muslim force near Covadonga. It was the first victory for the indigenous people of Spain; to the Arabs it seemed nothing. In their chronicles they said:

> *...a wild ass reared up against the Muslims; they defeated his army time and again, until nothing remained of it but thirty men and two women. What harm can thirty wild asses do to us.*

Quoted by Edwin Hole,
Andalus: Spain under the Muslims

It would have been more accurate to view the Spaniards as mules, for they were outstandingly stubborn. They pushed for almost eight centuries to regain what they had lost in seven years.

Thirty years after the Muslims conquered Spain, a revolution in Damascus replaced the former ruling dynasty of Umayyads. Surviving members of the royal family were systematically hunted down and killed. Only Abd er Rahman, a grandson of the former caliph, escaped to make his way to Moroccan kinsmen of his mother, and from there he jumped to Spain. Civil war surrounded him because he was the sole remaining descendent of the usurped but legitimate ruling house of Islam. By 755 he gained control of *al Andalus*. From this time forth *al Andalus* constituted an independent kingdom, no longer subject to Damascus. Abd er Rahman unified the quarreling Muslims, raised the first stage of the great mosque in Córdoba, and founded the original dynasty of Muslim rulers in Spain.

But when Abd er Rahman began imposing autocratic rule on formerly independent governors, the Muslim governor of Zaragoza appealed to King Charlemagne in France to help him stay independent. Charlemagne marched across the Pyrenees with an army only to find the gates of Zaragoza closed against him because the governor had changed his mind. Furious, Charlemagne set siege to the city, but a rebellion at home soon forced his return. The French retraced their steps through the Pyrenees pass of Roncesvalles. Their rear guard, commanded by Roland, the Count of Brittany, was harried by attackers all the way until his force was exterminated to the last man—an event immortalized by the medieval poem *The Song of Roland*. It was Basques in the Pyrenees who accomplished the deed, despite the poem's blame of Muslims.

At the end of the ninth century, a Spanish miracle occurred. In a field in the northwest corner of Spain, shepherds observed bright lights pointing to an ancient tomb containing a miraculously preserved body. The local bishop pronounced the bones those of St. James the Apostle. Soon a church rose over the grave and the place was named Compostela, a possible corruption of *campus stella* (field of stars). After Rome, it became the holiest place in Europe, and the most important pilgrimage for Christians after Jerusalem. Spain was transformed into a sacred place to defend, while the 100,000 Europeans visiting each year on pilgrimage produced an infusion of European cultures. The rallying cry for the growing spirit of Reconquest became "Sant Iago," Saint James. No matter that the Bible says James died in Jerusalem.

The event was little noticed in *al Andalus*, poised for its time of greatest glory. Abd er Rahman III succeeded to the emirate in 912, and proclaimed himself *caliph*, "successor" to the Prophet Mohammed. His Córdoba, with a quarter of a million inhabitants, was the largest city in Western Europe, trailing only Baghdad, Constantinople and Peking in the world. It boasted the largest library extant—some 400,000 volumes—900 public baths, and sublime architecture. Abd er Rahman III constructed a sumptuous palace in the countryside, named Medinat al Zahara after a favorite wife. If it still survived, it would put even the Alhambra to shame.

Abd er Rahman III was blue-eyed with fair hair. He was descended from the Arab Abd er Rahman I, but his mother had been a Frank and his grandmother a Basque princess. Except for the royal blood in his veins, he was typical of those the Europeans called Moors, who were not at all the dusky blacks Shakespeare passed down to us. Fewer than 50,000 Muslims crossed to Spain during their conquest, and rather than Arab, most of them were Berbers—a race of blue-eyed, fair-skinned North Africans who still populate most of Morocco and Tunisia today. Indeed, the total of all those who came to *al Andalus* from Africa over the centuries probably amounted to, at most, a few hundred thousand in a population of almost six million Spanish. Intermarriage was frequent between conqueror and conquered, so that after a few centuries, the Muslims had infinitely more Spanish than Arab in their blood.

Al Andalus, according to the Muslims, was an earthly paradise. By their legend, when God created the world, he gave five wishes to each new country. *Al Andalus* asked for a clear sky, a beautiful sea filled with fish, ripe fruit and fair women, all granted by God. The fifth wish was for good government which God refused because that would have made it a heaven on earth.

At least one part of the legend was true, for *Al Andalus* ranked as the most prosperous area in Europe, thanks to the Muslims' introduction of crops—such as oranges, rice, cotton and silk—that had not previously existed in Europe. They expanded the possibilities of the written word by employing the art of manufacturing paper, so a man could write a book without killing a flock of sheep for vellum pages. They revived the important art of glassmaking which had died with the Romans. Their architecture brought new comfort to the hot and dusty Mediterranean for they built houses surrounded by blank outer walls, while rooms inside centered on a cool courtyard open to fresh air and sky. Such houses still dominate the south of Spain. The Moors also appropriated the horseshoe arch from the Visigoths and raised its use to high art in public buildings, inside of which they worked so sensitively with stucco, glazed tile and patterned designs that the world will never again see their equal.

But knowledge was the most important gift of the Muslims. The ninth through the eleventh centuries in Europe have been aptly named the Dark Ages, for the light of wisdom attained by the ancients dimmed and was lost. The Muslims nurtured this lore and passed it on to Europe. They preserved the works of the Greek mathematicians, physicians and philosophers, especially Aristotle. They introduced the science of algebra, as well as the numbers we use today (which we call Arabic, though they were merely transmitted by the Arabs from India). Nor were they messengers only. Córdoba was a center for invention and learning where the great Jewish philosopher Maimonides was born and the Muslim philosopher Averröes wrote brilliant commentaries on the master, Aristotle.

But however brightly *al Andalus* glowed, the denial of the legend's fifth wish for good government would give the Christians their chance. When the successor of Abd er Rahman III died, he left an 11-year-old heir. The reins of government fell to the vizier, a man of sufficient vigor and intelligence to seize the throne for himself. The dynasty of Abd er Rahman had ended. The usurper was dubbed *Almanzor,* "The Conqueror," for he harried the Christians as never before. He ranged through the north, sacking the Cathedral of Compostela, and brought its doors and bells to hang in the Córdoba mosque. But he left no clear successor, and *al Andalus* fell apart into twenty separate states, called *taifas,* as the 11th century dawned.

Now the Christians in the north were free from the pressure of unrelenting Muslim attacks, and grew apace. By the start of the 11th century, Asturias, the last bastion of the Spanish, had added to itself the provinces of León, Castile and Galicia. All were united in the person of a man who styled himself King Fernando I. But when he died, the usual Spanish policy of dividing the kingdom among sons was followed, which had the effect of overturning the work of uniting a large territory in the first place. This policy was to prove the bane of the Christians. To his favorite son, Alfonso VI, he gave León, and to his eldest son he bequeathed Castile, with Galicia given to his youngest boy. Alfonso VI and his older brother were soon at war over their shares to the detriment of the younger brother, who was forced into exile. The elder brother, however, did not sufficiently reckon on their sister Urraca. It seems she felt more than sisterly affection for Alfonso and hired an assassin to remove the elder sibling in his way.

After his brother's death, Alfonso VI claimed Castile in addition to León, but first the nobles forced him to swear that he bore no complicity in his brother's murder. Rodrigo Diaz de Vivar, commander of the army of León, spoke for the nobles in this affair, and matters were never cordial between Alfonso and Rodrigo Diaz thereafter. Although they cooperated in the capture of Toledo, the greatest victory up to that time by the Spanish, it was not long before Alfonso found a pretext to exile Rodrigo.

Homeless, Rodrigo Diaz became the greatest hero in Spanish history—el Cid, the mighty robber baron. He first offered his services to the *taifa* of Zaragoza, but when Alfonso arrived to attack Zaragoza, el Cid refused to take up arms against his king. He left, moving south to Valencia to help Muslims defeat the Spanish count of Barcelona. But when the Muslim governor of Valencia demanded that, as his work was finished, el Cid must leave, el Cid turned on him and conquered his territory. Thereby he gained control of 15 percent of modern Spain. Twice, mighty Muslim armies attacked el Cid, but each time he turned them away. Later he was reconciled with his king and his daughters married royalty. The *Poem of My Cid*, written by an unknown author about a century after the hero's death from yet another Muslim attack, commemorate his exploits forever. The poet makes much of the dark beard of el Cid, who was "born in a good hour."

In the meantime, after the capture of Toledo, Alfonso VI and his army swooped south. He raided throughout *al Andalus*, finally setting his foot in the sea at the end of Spain. Now the rulers of the petty *taifas* knew Spanish power at first hand and, fearing for their civilization, they cried to Morocco for help.

There had been a revolution in Morocco shortly before this call by a puritan sect committed to cleansing other Muslims of the sin of luxury. Known as the people of the *rabat* ("monastery"), these Almoravids were so fundamentalist that even their men wore veils. So it was with trepidation that the pleasure-loving governors of the *taifas* of *al Andalus* sought their aid. One explained by saying that he "preferred to herd camels for the Almoravids than to guard the pigsty of Alfonso VI." [Quoted by Joseph F. O'Callaghan, *A History of Medieval Spain.*]

The Almoravids came and, together with the governors of the *taifas*, defeated Alfonso VI. Then they returned to Morocco. They came again when Alfonso VI once more threatened; this time the *taifas* did not contribute any support. A year later, in 1090, they returned in sufficient force to conquer the *taifas* and rule *al Andalus*. Only Valencia held out, thanks to el Cid, but it too fell three years after his death when his widow no longer could defend it.

For a century, the ascetic Almoravids ruled *al Andalus* until its bounty seduced them. They fell into petty factions and began to learn the love of luxury at the same time their subjects chafed under their severe rule. Across the straits in Morocco a new fundamentalist sect, called the *Almohids* ("Unitarians"), looked upon these events with grave displeasure. In 1146 the Almohids swept in to again purify the faithful of *al Andalus*.

The Christian Spanish had always used civil unrest in *al Andalus* to increase their territory, but now they faced a serious unified enemy. The Almohids set out to win back every inch of the territory their brethren had lost, declaring a *jihad*, a holy war. Alfonso VIII (1158–1215), then king of Castile, met a huge Muslim force just south of Toledo at Alascos, and suffered the most complete defeat yet for the Spanish. His problem was that he and his territory of Castile stood alone for Spain. Aragón and the other kingdoms promised aid they did not deliver. Instead they rushed to press territorial demands on the now-weakened king of Castile. Disunity in the Spanish camp would never succeed against unified Muslims.

At this darkest hour the pope saved the day. He called for a crusade against the Infidel, a union of Christian kingdoms to oppose their own holy war against the Muslims. In 1212 a large Christian army composed of one part Crusaders from other European countries, one part the army of Aragón, and one part the army of Castile marched south from Toledo. They were soon confronted by a Muslim force equal to their own at Las Navas de Tolosa. For two days the armies stared at each other, uncertain of what to do. On July 16 the left and right side of the Christian forces commenced a pincer movement while Alfonso VIII charged the center. The Muslim lines broke, and when the caliph fled, defeat became a rout. Alfonso VIII, who had suffered the most serious Spanish defeat, had orchestrated its greatest victory. This battle tipped the scales; never again would the Christians be seriously threatened by Muslims. In remembrance, a tapestry from the field tent of the defeated caliph hangs today in Alfonso VIII's former palace, the monastery of Las Huelgas, near **Burgos**.

Three years after his great victory, Alfonso VIII died, leaving an 11-year-old son as his heir. Fortunately he also left an older daughter, Berenguela, to enforce his wishes, for the son's guardian soon grabbed control of the government and, when the child was accidently killed while playing, the protector hid news of the death so he could retain his power. Berenguela discovered the cover-up and sent for her own son, then living in Aragón. Although Berenguela had the best claim to the throne, she yielded the rights to her boy. This new king, Fernando III, would conquer most of *al Andalus.*

By the time the new king gained his majority, chaos reigned in *al Andalus.* The calif, Ibn Hud, controlled most of the Islamic territory, but he faced a rebellion by his vassal Ibn al Ahmar. In this confused situation Muslims were as likely to seek Christian help as to ask for aid from their coreligionists. When Muslims inside Córdoba let a band of Castilian soldiers into the suburbs of the city, Fernando III, aware of an opportunity, hurried with an army to lay siege. Although Ibn Hud raised a force to relieve Córdoba, an alliance between the rebellious Ibn Ahmar and Fernando III frightened him sufficiently to turn him back before reaching the city. In 1236 Córdoba, the capital of *al Andalus,* capitulated to the Spanish. Fernando III carried the bells of Santiago Cathedral home again.

After Ibn Hud was assassinated by a lieutenant, the rebel Ibn Ahmar moved to Granada and began constructing the palace we call the Alhambra. As never before, a vacuum of power existed in *al Andalus.* Fernando III took town after town, finally moving on Seville. Since the city had access to the sea through the river Guadalquivir, he collected the first Spanish navy to blockade seaborne supplies before settling down for a siege. Seville could look nowhere for relief and capitulated in 1248. When, independently, the king of Aragón captured Valencia, the Reconquest was almost complete. All that remained was Granada.

The words of the poet al Rundi describe the Muslim situation at this juncture:

> *Where is Córdoba, the seat of great learning,*
> *And how many scholars of high repute remain there?*
> *And where is Seville, the home of mirthful gatherings*
> *On its great river, cooling and brimful with water?*
> *These centers were the pillars of the country:*
> *Can a building remain when the pillars are missing?*
> *This misfortune has surpassed all that has preceded,*
> *And as long as time lasts, it can never be forgotten.*

> **Quoted by Joseph F. O'Callaghan,**
> *A History of Medieval Spain*

Fernando III had done his part at warfare. Before he died, he founded a university, promoted Castilian as the official language of Spain, and revitalized the institution of the *Cortes* (Parliament).

Then for two centuries and a quarter—from 1252 to 1482—the Reconquest stopped, daunted by the remaining task of conquering Granada. Although less than 10 percent of modern Spain remained in Moorish hands, the area was swollen with refugees entrenched in fortified towns. This was a time in the history of warfare when defense had the upper hand; a fortified town stood virtually impregnable. The best tactic available to the offense was a starvation-threatening siege that required vast reserves of food for the besieging army, along with the financial resources sufficient to keep troops in the field for six months or more. Nor did great incentives exist for the Christians. The Moorish king of Granada owed an allegiance to the king of Castile that included substantial yearly tribute. For more than two centuries no Christian ruler emerged with the vigor or the singleness of purpose to assume so difficult a task for such small advantage.

First, the Christians had to set their own house in order. They were forever dividing kingdoms by inheritance and warfare at times when unified resources were demanded. Fernando III was succeeded by Alfonso X, known as *el Sabio*, "the Wise." He earned this soubriquet for the scholarship he encouraged and the works of literature and law that emanated from his palace. But his name would have been entirely different if it had been based on his political ability. His father had married a granddaughter of Frederick Barbarossa, the Holy Roman Emperor. Alfonso emptied his treasury in an election campaign to win the title of the Holy Roman Emperor for himself. So dismayed were the nobles of Castile at this profligate waste that some rebelled while others renounced their citizenship to live among the Moors. Eventually everyone abandoned him, including his son, who usurped the throne.

Castile seemed bent on obeying the adage that things have to get worse before they improve. The worst was Pedro I, the Cruel. His father had a beloved mistress with whom he sired several children, behavior that did not please his wife, Pedro's mother. As soon as Pedro's father died, she revenged herself by killing the former mistress. This act set the tone for Pedro's reign that began in 1350 when Pedro was fifteen. One of Pedro's first royal acts was to kill one of his two illegitimate half-brothers, but the wrong one. Enrique of Trastámara, the other illegitimate son of Pedro's father and mistress, was the one he should have been watching. Enrique fled to Aragón before Pedro could catch him.

Pedro soon became engaged to the daughter of the duke of Burgundy, but, while waiting for his fiancée to arrive, he fell in love with a woman named María de Padilla. It was too late to stop the wedding, so Pedro went through with the ceremony then imprisoned his wife in the Alcázar of Toledo for eight years. Sadly, his beloved María died at 28, one of the few natural deaths in his reign. Pedro then poisoned his legal wife and declared that ten years earlier he had secretly married María, his mistress, thus making their four children legitimate.

Once his own house was in order, Pedro turned to his favorite occupation—war. He foraged south when he heard that the king of Granada, his vassal, faced a Muslim revolt, ravaging the terrain and populace along the way until those who had revolted threw themselves on Pedro's mercy. This was not a man overflowing with mercy—he killed them all. Then he began a ten-year war with Aragón. The commander of the army of Aragón was Pedro's illegitimate half-brother, Enrique of Trastámara, who had found refuge there from Pedro. War opened with Castilian successes, then settled into a stalemate, and ended in a papal truce. Each side then sought allies to tip the balance in its direction. The Aragonese enlisted French mercenaries who had been ravaging the south of France. Pedro allied himself with Edward of Wales, the Black Prince. The two augmented armies came together near the Castilian border where Pedro and the Black Prince won a resounding victory. But, when Pedro wanted to kill all the captured rebels, the Black Prince refused further cooperation and left.

On his own again, Pedro was no match for Enrique of Trastámara, who marched into Castile and was recognized as king by most of the large cities. Enrique moved on Toledo while Pedro set out from Andalusia to its defense. The two clashed outside the fortress of Montiel where Pedro was beaten, retreated to the safety of the fortress, and then offered a huge bribe to one of Enrique's lieutenants to help him escape. The lieutenant informed Enrique of his dealings before inviting Pedro to slip into his tent under cover of night. Enrique burst into the tent and struck Pedro in the face with his dagger. The two struggled and fell, with Enrique stabbing Pedro again and again until he lay still. Pedro was dead at 35.

Enrique of Trastámara, bastard son of a former king, began a dynasty in Castile from this date of 1369. One of his descendents was Isabella. Through marriages, his blood also entered the veins of the kings of Aragón and thence to Ferdinand. Spain had to wait one more century for Isabella and Ferdinand to appear, had to endure the ravages of wars among the separate kingdoms, the scourge of the Black Death, and bloody pogroms against the Jews. But in the end, Isabella of Castile united herself and kingdom with Ferdinand of Aragón.

It was Isabella who brought the singleness of purpose to complete the Reconquest. She was filled with Christian fervor. Ferdinand contributed a calculating mind that could see beyond the intimidating costs of a major war. Their marriage united the Christian states in one formidable pair.

Ironically, the Moors precipitated their own downfall. Hassan Ali, the king of Granada, seized the Christian border city of Zahara in 1481, which was equivalent to hurling a gauntlet. On hearing the news, prescient fakirs (holy men) in Granada moaned that "the ruins of Zahara will fall on our own heads." [W.H. Prescott, *Isabella and Ferdinand*, Vol. I. p. 318.] Don Rodrigo Ponce de León (grandfather of the discoverer of Florida), one of the mightiest nobles of Andalusia, made a surprise attack in response on Alhama, just six miles from Granada, and won the fortress in a bloody battle. The question was whether he could hold the town against the inevitable Muslim counterattack. He called for assistance to Henrique de Guzmán, the duke of Medina Sidonia, another mighty noble and a man with whom Don Rodrigo had waged private war for a decade. Whether because of patriotism or for the promise of half of the spoils, Don Henrique heeded the call. He arrived to find Christian forces in the city girded by a Muslim force. But the Moors, fearful of being trapped between the enemy in the city and his reinforcements behind them, left the field.

So far the war had been conducted on the Christian side by nobles; it was not a national effort. Alone they could not hold a salient deep in Moorish territory. Ferdinand and a pregnant Isabella hastened to Córdoba to expand this one success into a major campaign. Ferdinand mounted a frontal attack on Alhama's neighbor Loja, to diffuse pressures concentrating on Alhama. But, after initial success, the Spanish situation deteriorated until nothing remained except ignominious retreat. From this example, Ferdinand learned the necessity of adequate preparation and the advantages of siege over frontal attack.

Just at this moment, a revolution in Granada further weakened the Moors. Sultana Aisha, the principle wife of Hasan Ali, formed a cabal against her husband on behalf of her son. Hasan Ali fled to Málaga, which split the territory of the Moors into two opposing parts: Hasan Ali ruled the western half and his son the east, including Granada. The Christians referred to the son, Abu Abdallah, as "Boabdil," which shows how little they understood Arabic.

Ferdinand and Isabella raised the stakes by announcing a crusade. The pope confirmed the undertaking and supplied ecclesiastical revenues in support. From the corners of Europe crusaders poured into Spain to join in arms against the infidel. The campaign opened with a march against Málaga in the west. To reach Málaga, the Christian army had to cross mountains down to the city, and needed local guides who knew the terrain—Moors. In these rocky defiles the flower and pretension of Spanish chivalry were cut to pieces in a surprise attack by el Zagal, "the Valiant," brother of Hasan Ali.

Heartened by his rival's victory, Boabdil chose to attack the western Christian forces himself. Ominously, his lance broke against the arch of the gate of Elvira as he left Granada. He was defeated in a close fight at Lucena. Leaving the field, however, hemmed in by Christian forces at their rear and a river ahead, the Moors panicked. Boabdil hid, but was discovered in the bushes by a common soldier and carried prisoner to Córdoba. Boabdil agreed to pay a huge tribute in gold for his release and sign a treaty providing for two years truce.

Time was on the Christians' side. They used this respite to prepare for a final push. They built foundries for producing cannon in quantity, trained corps of engineers to mine fortified positions and developed a new military strategy. Swiss mercenaries in the Christian camp taught the Spanish a method of fighting that would make the Spanish infantry the finest in the world. The Swiss wore no armor on their backs, since they never thought of retreating, while they menaced their enemy with pikes three times the length of a man. These pikes signaled the end of knights as a military force, for such weapons could stop a charge of heavily armored cavalry.

War reopened in 1487. The Christians first captured Málaga according to a plan to close the Muslims off from the sea. Two years later they raised an army of 50,000 men to besiege the stronghold of Baeza. After seven difficult months it fell, although the Spanish lost 20,000 men mostly to disease. With the loss of this major position, el Zagul, who had replaced his brother as king, surrendered the rest of his territory. Only Granada under Boabdil remained in Muslim hands.

In March of 1491, 50,000 Christians came to Granada vowing not to leave until it fell. Wooden houses were erected against the coming cold of winter, instantly creating the third largest city in Spain, named by Isabella *Santa Fé*,

"Holy Faith." Then they waited, for Granada was then the largest fortified city in the world.

After eight months of starvation, a negotiated settlement promised Granada to the Christians 60 days hence to allow time to pack for those wishing to leave. But insurrection in the city hastened the day of capitulation. On January 2, 1492, a small party led by the archbishop of Spain carried a cross through the gates of Granada. When the Christians saw the cross silhouetted atop the Alhambra hill, they knew the city was theirs. Ferdinand, Isabella and all the troops knelt on the ground to thank God. Then the nobles and the king and queen of Spain entered the city, dressed in Moorish clothes.

After completing a ten-year campaign, probably not a single Spaniard regretted its final success. But many should have mourned the passing of a large part of the variegated society of the peninsula. They would sorely miss the intellectual accomplishments of the Moors, as well as countless examples of good things that the Moors had provided. When the Spanish court first saw the Alhambra they marvelled—here was a style of living light years in advance of their own. They should have mourned themselves, too, because their treatment of the Moors was dastardly. In the treaty they promised that all Moors who wished to could remain in their land with complete religious freedom. Within ten years Christians began forcibly converting Moors, and then brutally expelled them from Spanish soil.

Most of the architectural legacy of the Moors can be found in Andalusia, their home for almost eight centuries. **Granada's** Alhambra captures everyone's heart both for its accessible beauty and for evoking the Moors' style of life. One of the world's great mosques still stands in all its glory in **Córdoba**, and there too a 10th-century Moorish pleasure-city is under excavation at its outskirts. Although **Seville** retains little that was built for the Moors, it preserves two wonderful buildings that were sumptuously decorated by them— the Alcázar and the Casa de Pilotes. All these are monumental works in which everyone can see the stamp of the Moors, but their legacy extends as well to every whitewashed house that hides a flowered courtyard behind a solid facade to seal out the heat, with rooms surrounding this central open patio in which a fountain plays while flowers perfume the air.

Andalusia

Andalusia is archetypical Spain, thus not wholly characteristic of the rest. Bullfighting, flamenco and the guitar originated here, and although each of these has become woven through the fabric of all of Spain, nowhere else are they so prominent and pervasive as in Andalusia. Here too, gypsies, rare in the rest of the country, thrive. What makes Andalusia archetypical is that it was ruled by the Moors longest—for more than 700 years. They bequeathed to Andalusia a legacy of citrus fruits, whitewashed houses with beautiful interior patios, and, after the Christians expelled them, their palaces and mosques. Thanks to the Moors, Andalusia possesses the greatest sight in Spain—the Alhambra—along with a mosque and numerous alcázars (Moorish fortresses). If there is only time to visit one area of Spain, it should be Andalusia.

You will not be the first. Andalusia has received foreign visitors since ancient times. Phoenicians came to mine and trade, followed by neighbors from Carthage. War between the Spanish Carthagenian Hannibal and Rome next brought Romans to attack his lines of supply and stay on to rule. When Rome weakened in the fourth century A.D., "barbarian" Vandals breasted the borders of the Empire to take the south of Spain for their own. Visigoths followed a century later, pushing the Vandals across the straits into Africa, though the Visigoths continued to refer to the south as "Vandalsland." When Moors landed near Gibraltar in 711 to conquer Spain, they called their new territory *al Andalus*, approximating Vandalsland as best their language could.

When the Moors last stronghold was captured, in 1492, Christians wept along with Moors, aware that a civilization superior to their own had been destroyed. *Al Andalus* had possessed the greatest library in the world, and had nurtured the Jewish philosopher Maimonides and the Aristotelian philosopher Averröes. It had developed and maintained both sewage systems and public baths, none of which existed elsewhere in Europe. The Christians made a virtue of their deficiencies by arguing that cleanliness was ungodly, but in their hearts they acknowledged a culture superior to their own. Ferdinand and Isabella chose lovely Granada for their place of final rest. Their grandson and heir picked the Alhambra for his honeymoon. Christians all over Spain hired Moors or Mozárabs (Christians trained under the Moors) to design and decorate their homes and palaces.

The Moors had introduced citrus trees and rice. They cultivated the olive—first brought to Spanish shores by the Greeks—still Andalusia's most important crop. They appropriated the Roman horseshoe arch for major buildings, and adopted Roman ideas in domestic architecture to produce the typical—then as now—Andalusian house. Though the last Moors were ex-

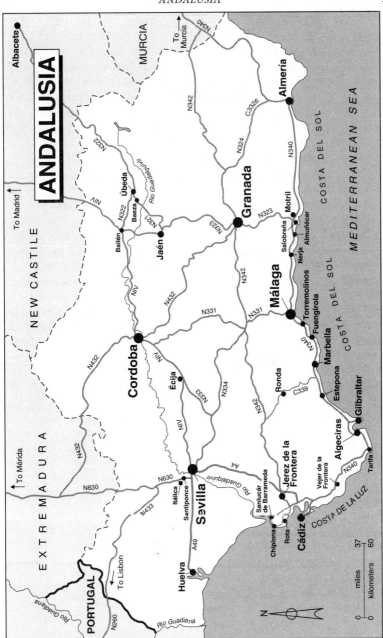

ANDALUSIA

pelled in 1609, their spirit remains alive in every Spanish whitewashed house and patio, every palace and alcázar maintained through the ages.

What lured ancient visitors—Romans, Moors, Germans and northern Christians—was the fertile land and balmy climate of Andalusia. Hemmed by the Sierra Nevada range containing the highest peak in Spain (11,242 feet), the coast is tempered by the Mediterranean Sea for winter warmth and summer breezes. Despite insignificant rainfall, the land is well watered by the Guadalquivir (from the Arabic for "Great River Valley"), allowing two crops each year.

Andalusia presents the happy paradox of mountains and beach, along with Moorish and Christian monuments. Spain's problem is that because Andalusia contains enough attractions to engage all of a tourist's time, the rest of the country is left comparatively touristless. Although we may mourn the situation, we agree that Andalusia draws the tourist because of the wealth of its offerings.

Granada ★ ★ ★ ★ tenders the Alhambra, which ranks with the greatest tourist sights in the world, in addition to the lovely Capilla Real where Ferdinand and Isabella still rest. **Córdoba** ★ ★ ★ ★ retains a great mosque, plus a medieval quarter and ruins of a pleasure city built by Abd er Rahman III in the outskirts. **Seville** ★ ★ ★ ★ ★, itself a beautiful city, offers a sumptuous cathedral, an alcázar and a private mansion sumptuously decorated by the Moors. In addition, the hundreds of miles of beaches constituting the **Costa del Sol** ★ ★ and **Costa de la Luz** ★ ★ are playgrounds for the European masses. Andalusia also contains the Renaissance towns **Baeza** ★ ★ and **Úbeda** ★ ★, the spectacularly situated village of **Ronda** ★ ★, and the home of sherry, **Jerez de las Frontera** ★.

Andalusia offers special foods and entertainments, as well. The famed gazpacho soup was created here, probably from a Moorish recipe, as was a less well-known white cold soup—*ajo blanco*. Tapas originated in Seville, and remain among the best in Spain. Deep-fried fish is a staple and, when fresh, as it generally is, can be subtle indeed. Although flamenco is a dying art, despite great efforts to keep it alive, Seville remains the best place to see the real thing. If you are lucky in the performers and their mood on the night you come, you will never forget the experience.

Baeza ★ ★

Population: 14,799
Area code: 953; Zip code: 23440

From **Madrid** *take A-4 (E-5) south toward Ocaña. The highway becomes N-IV. Continue for 292 km to Bailén. (eight km before*

Bailén a road east leads to **Baños de la Encina** *in four km, with a fine Moorish fortress.) At Bailén take N-322 east toward Úbeda for 20 km, exiting south on C-326 for 20 km to Baeza. To combine with a visit to nearby* **Úbeda**, *don't exit from N-322 after Bailén, arriving in Úbeda in 40 km. Afterwards, take N-321 west for nine km to Baeza. When finished with Baeza, N-321 takes you toward Jaén in 48 km, just before which N-323 heads south to Granada in 93 km. Or return to Bailén, from which N-IV heads west to Córdoba in 108 km.*

From **Granada** *take N-323 north toward Jaén for 88 km. Change to N-321 east toward Úbeda just before Jaén. Baeza is 48 km along N-321. From* **Córdoba** *take N-IV west toward Andujar and Bailén for 108 km. Follow the Madrid directions from Bailén.*

Why is tiny Baeza, off all beaten tracks, so full of Renaissance mansions and churches? Baeza was the first Andalusian city recaptured by the Christians during the Reconquest (in 1239), and before then was the capital of a Moorish *taifa*, or principality. For two centuries it served as the base from which the Christians pushed their Reconquest south, supplying shelter for royalty and the nobles of the army of Castile and growing rich off them. After the Reconquest was complete, Baeza sat astride the main southern route, enjoying trade and prosperity. Wealthy citizens put up grand mansions in the 16th and 17th centuries, and the city added a university in 1595. But when the town of Jaén to the southwest developed into a major city, the road moved to head directly into Jaén, bypassing Baeza and turning it into the quiet town it remains today.

From **C-326** *you arrive on Acera de la Magdalena and pass a large park. Take the first right a block after the park's end onto C. José Burell. In two blocks comes another fork. Take the right hand road, C. San Pablo, which lets onto the Paseo de la Constitución and parking. From* **Úbeda** *you travel on C. José Burell. Follow the directions above for parking.*

Baeza offers a proper **cathedral** ★, a small **palace** ★ and various **Renaissance buildings** ★ with lovely façades. It has old **fountains** ★, squares and a 16th-century university. All are located near the Paseo de la Constitutión to be seen in an hour's pleasant walk.

Go southwest through the large arcaded Paseo de la Constitución, noting the early 18th-century **Casas Consistoriales Bajas** on the north side, providing comfortable seating for officials during ceremonies in the square.

A few steps after the southwest end of the Paseo comes the attractive **Plaza de los Leones** on the left, named for the **fountain** ★ in its center. The fountain is composed of genuine antiques—the lions seem to be Roman, and the female atop the pillar is either Celtiberian or Carthagenian, bearing a likeness, according to some, of Hannibal's wife. The imposing building to the east is the 16th-century **Antigua Carnicería** ★ (Old Butcher's Shop), with a lovely coat of arms for Carlos V. Moving south through the plaza we come to an arch, the **Jaén Gate**, erected in 1526 to mark the passage of Carlos V on his way to marry in Seville. Then comes the **Casa de Pópulo**, the former courthouse, with elegant Plateresque windows and medallions. Its six doors formerly led to six notaries' offices, but now it serves as the **Office of Tourism** and can provide a worthwhile map.

Exit from the south end of the plaza along Cuesta de San Gil, taking the first left onto C. Callejon to enter the Pl. Santa María. The walls of the former 17th-century **seminary** on the left are covered with faint red names of graduates painted with bull's blood. Right (south), across the plaza, is an unusual late **Gothic fountain** ★ in the form of a small arch, with the former **Cathedral** beyond. Before entering the Cathedral, notice the **Casas Consistoriales Altas** with an imposing pair of coats of arms—of Juana the Mad, Ferdinand and Isabella's daughter, and her husband, Philip the Handsome, the parents of Carlos V.

Cathedral

Pl. de la Fuente de Santa María.
Hours open: daily 10:30 a.m.–1 p.m. and 4–6 p.m.
Technically this is not a cathedral since, after 60 years as a bishopric, the prelate left for Jaén. The building is the same, however, as when the bishop presided. Fernando III, who first conquered the city, raised the present church on the site of a former mosque. In the 16th century the interior was extensively remodeled and redecorated, but the main portal on the west front, the Puerta de la Luna with a horseshoe arch, remains from the early church. Inside are flamboyant chapels, and arches from the former mosque in the cloisters.

Head north along Cuestra San Felipe, arriving after one block at the remarkable Renaissance **Palacio del Marqueses de Jabalquinto** ★. The golden facade is covered with Isabelline decoration—every feature seems to sprout something. Though impressive, it is more admirable in detail than overall conception. Inside what today is a seminary stands a more somber patio with two charming lions guarding a grand baroque stairway. Opposite the palace is the attractive Romanesque church of **Santa Cruz** ★, the only complete church dating to the time of Baeza's liberation in the early 13th century. It remains a gem, still with some frescoes inside. North of the church stands the former **university**, dating from the late 16th century. A fine patio hides behind the plain facade, and a lovely Mudejar ceiling crowns the amphitheater.

By heading along the long west face of the university, then across its front, and turning left for a few feet then right along C. San Pablo, in half a block you pass the 16th century **Alhondiga** (grain exchange), with an arched portico. Next turn left across the Pl. del Constitutión to round the arcaded Paseo for a closer look at the **Casas Consistoriales Bajas** to the north. Continue along its east face on C. Gaspar Becerra for one block to the **Ayuntamiento** (city hall), a former prison, transformed in the 16th century into a sample of everything Plateresque. The arms of Felipe II are proudly displayed.

Where to Stay

With a parador in Úbeda 9 km away, and with Córdoba and Granada an hour farther, offering much more to do, few people spend the night in Baeza. Accommodations are, however, available in the quiet of this small town.

Inexpensive (Less than $50)

Juanito   2nd-class ★

Av. Puche Pardo, 43, Baeza (on the main road to Úbeda reached from Av. San Pablo along the south end of the Pl. España), ☎ *74 00 40, FAX 74 23 24.*
Closed the first half of November.
This is the best restaurant in town as well as the best value in hotels. The accommodations are simple, although some rooms contain TVs, but comfortable and clean. *35 rooms.*

Where to Eat

Two restaurants can be recommended, one more enterprising, the other truly inexpensive.

Moderate ($20–$50)

Juanito   ★

Paseo Arca del Agua (on the main road to Úbeda that begins at the Pl. de los Leones), ☎ *74 00 04.*
Closed Sunday and Monday nights.
The chef uses the freshest ingredients in traditional specialties of the region, including *cordero con habas* and *revuelto de setas*, both recommended. Credit Cards: none.

Inexpensive (Less than $20)

Sali

Passaje Cardenal Benavides, 15 (on the street going east from the Ayuntamiento), ☎ *74 13 65.*
Closed Wednesday night and from the middle of September through the first week of October.
Ingredients are also first rate at this unpretentious place, and, when ordered from the special menus, meals are truly inexpensive. Credit Cards: A, D, M, V.

Directory

Information

Located in the Casa del Pópulo in the Pl. de los Leones. ☎ *74 04 44.*

Trains and Buses

The nearest train station is Linares-Baeza, 13 km out of town, which serves both Baeza and Úbeda ☎ *65 02 02.* A bus connects with most trains.

Buses leave from Av. Puche y Pardo, 1 uphill on C. San Pablo (☎ *74 04 68*). Service to Granada, Jaén and Úbeda is frequent, but a change is necessary at Jaén or Úbeda for elsewhere.

Post Office and Telephones

Located a short block north of the Ayuntamiento.

Excursions

Úbeda is the natural excursion from Baeza, described under its own heading. Of course, **Granada** is only 88 km away, and **Córdoba** and **Seville** not much farther. See directions under those headings.

Cádiz ★

Population: 157,766
Area code: 956; Zip code: 11000

On N-340 from the **Costa del Sol***, the highway divides just before reaching Cádiz. Signs adequately instruct you how to proceed. Cádiz is 123 km from Algeciras, 50 km from Conil. From* **Seville** *A-4 (E-5), a toll road, or N-IV which runs beside it, bring you quickly to Cádiz in 97 km or 109 km, respectively. From* **Granada** *take N342 (E-902) west to Antequera, then continue to Jerez de la Frontera for 155 km, where the toll road A-4 (E-5) completes the journey in 39 km more. From* **Córdoba** *it is best to go first to Seville, then follow the directions above.*

Although Cádiz belongs to the Costa de la Luz, its city beaches are best left undescribed. There are fine sands a ferry-ride away across the bay, however, and more inland on the isthmus. Spain's largest port retains a romantic feeling and offers sights to see, so it is not a bad place to settle for a day or two of rest.

Cádiz is truly old. It was founded as a port named Gadir by the Phoenicians, and a port it has remained for 3000 years, for it is situated on an isthmus that carries the city three miles out into a fine bay. In time it became the main depot for treasure ships from the mines of the New World, and it prospered, although prosperity also made for temptations. Barbary corsairs raided, as did Francis Drake during preparations for the Great Armada. In Napoléon's time, the French fleet was bottled up in Cádiz by Admiral Nelson. The fleet broke through the gauntlet of English ships only to sail to defeat off the Cape of Trafalgar a few miles south.

Cádiz defies most expectations of a port. It is not grey, dirty, seedy or frightening. This is the Andalusian version—whitewashed houses, with turrets, lining narrow streets that let into lovely squares. Along the sea, north and east, gardens invite promenades. While none of the sights in Cádiz are remarkable, the walking is most pleasant.

Cádiz is famed for religious devotion. Its celebrations of Holy Week are renowned through Spain and televised across the country and even in Portugal.

POLLUTION ALERT

The beaches in the city of Cádiz are unsafe for bathing at last report.

From whichever direction you set out for Cádiz, the narrow isthmus funnels all roads to the old town at the tip. Parking is a challenge, but when N-IV ends at the large Pl. de la Constitución, go through the city walls and turn right onto Cuesta de las Calasas, which becomes Av. Ramon de Carranza in three blocks at the train station and parking.

Walk north along Av. Carranza for half a mile to the Pl. de España. Take C. Antonio Lopez going left, just past the Disputacion, which, in four short blocks, brings you to the palms of the lovely **Plaza de Mina**, the former garden of a convent. The **Office of Tourism** is located at the north corner of the plaza at *C. Calderon de la Barca, 1* (open Mon.-Sat. 9 to 2 p.m.) where a map is available for navigating the maze of Cádiz' streets. Head northwest along C. Calderon de la Barca for two blocks to the ramparts and gardens for lovely views. Return to the east side of the plaza for the **Museo del Bellas Artes y Arqueológico**.

Museo del Bellas Artes y Arqueológico ★

Pl. de Mini, ☎ *21 43 00.*
Hours open: Mon.-Fri. 9 a.m.–p.m. and 5:30–7:30 p.m. Open Sat. 9 a.m.–1:30 p.m.
As its name describes, this building combines two separate museums. The archaeological collection, consisting of local finds, is not outstanding, but there is a headless Roman female statue which was worshiped for a while as a Virgin and a nice Roman sarcophagus. It is the paintings in the fine arts section, however, that make a visit worthwhile. There are canvases by Rubens, Cano, Murillo and Ribera, and an extraordinary collection of Zurbaráns. The Zurbaráns come from a group of saints he painted for the Monastery at Jerez, and form one of his few remaining intact series. In all there are 21, some sublime. *Admission: 250 ptas., to both museums.*

For Goya frescoes, head two blocks along C. Rosario, which leaves the south end of the plaza, to **Santa Cueva**, *a late 18th-century church.*

Leaving from the west end of the Pl. de Mina, C. San José goes southwest to the Pl. San Antonio in one block and a jag right. The main shopping street, C. Ancha, heads southeast. Southwest on C. San José is the **Church of San Felipe Neri** (open only during services). It was in this church that the First Republic was proclaimed, although King Fernando VII promptly renounced its constitution when he returned to the throne. On the east side, adjacent to the church, is the **Museo Historico Municipal** ★ with an admirable ivory and mahogany model of Cádiz as it looked at the end of the 18th century. The city presents much the same appearance as today, if more battered by time and weather *(open Tues.-Fri. 9 a.m.–1 p.m. and 4–7 p.m.; open weekends 9 a.m.–1 p.m.; admission: free).*

To see a modern grand building in the exuberant Mudejar style, head west along C. Sacramento that runs beside the museum for two short blocks to the **Teatro Manuel de Falla**. Otherwise, take C. Sacramento southeast for five blocks into the Pl. Castelar. Across the plaza, at the southeast corner, C. de Santiago leads past the baroque **Iglesia Santiago** and into the Pl. de la Catedral, after two blocks more. To the west of the Cathedral with its golden dome stands a medieval town gate.

Cathedral   ★

> *Pl. Catedral,* ☎ *28 6154. Entrance on C. Acero.*
> *Hours open: Mon.-Sat. 10 a.m.–1 p.m.*
>
> The mass of the Cathedral was in place by the middle of the 18th century, though it was not finished until a century later. Its baroque facade leads to an interior of lovely proportions. Manuel de Falla, whose music incorporated so much Andalusian folklore and songs, is buried in the crypt. The museum contains about as much silver and gold as one is ever likely to see, and a monstrance (portable reliquary) that may outdo all the rest in Spain, which is saying a great deal. There are some decent paintings by Ribera and Zurbáran, among others. *Admission: 250 ptas., to the Cathedral museum.*

Where to Stay

A hotel development is rising on the thin strip of isthmus leading to the old city. But if you want to stay out of town, there are nicer places elsewhere along the coast. We recommend accommodations in the old town.

Moderate ($50–$99)

Parador Atlántico   1st-class ★ ★

> *Duque de Nájera, 9, Cádiz (off the circular road around the old town, at its most western end),* ☎ *22 69 05, FAX 21 45 82, Telex 76316.*
>
> This six-story, clean, white modern structure is more reminiscent of nice motels in the States than of a parador, but, like all paradors, the rooms are comfortable and, in this one, most windows offer pleasant views across the bay. Situated in the Parque Genoves, at the tip of the peninsula, one feels surrounded by country quiet in the heart of town. *139 rooms, plus 10 suites.*

Francia y Paris   2nd-class ★

> *Pl. de San Francisco, 2, Cádiz (one block due south of the Pl. de Mina along C. Rosario),* ☎ *21 23 19, FAX 22 24 31.*
>
> This former town house has been thoroughly and tastefully modernized inside. However, while the rooms are certainly adequate, one gets the feeling that the public spaces got more than their share of the decorating funds. The location is conve-

nient to all the sights and quiet, but without ocean views. You do save a third over the parador, however. *69 rooms.*

Where to Eat

It is hard to better Cádiz fried sardines whether from stalls along the harbor in the southeast corner of the old town or in almost any local restaurant. We list two fancier restaurants. Naturally, both specialize in seafood, and seafood is not inexpensive.

Moderate ($15–$30)

El Faro ★★

C. San Félix, 15 (at the southwest tip of the old town, a block north of the sea wall), ☎ *21 10 68.*

The owner hangs hams in an Andalusian decor to let you know he is serious about food. Here you do not need to stick to plain seafood; sauces and marinades are tastefully done, and the chef knows meat as well. This is a popular place, so reservations are advised. Credit Cards: A, D and V.

El Anteojo ★

C. Alameda de Apodaca, 22 (directly north of the Museo de Bellas Artes, near the sea wall), ☎ *22 13 20.*
Closed Monday and from the first three weeks of February.

Views across the bay from the terrace are so lovely that the food does not have to be good. In fact the food is at least good, especially if you stick to the always fresh seafood, simply prepared. Credit Cards: A, D and V.

Inexpensive (Less than $15)

El Sardinero ★

Pl. San Juan de Dios (this large plaza is two blocks east of the Pl. de la Catedral along C. Pelota), ☎ *28 25 05.*
Closed Sun. dinner.

A number of decent seafood restaurants line this square, so it is fun to walk around and choose, though el Sardinero's Basque chef elevates it above the rest. This is the proverbial simple place where good food is served. Credit Cards: A, D and V.

Directory

Information

Located on C. Calderon de la Barca, 1, which actually is on the Pl. de Mina, at the north end (☎ *21 13 13*).

Trains and Buses

The station (☎ *25 43 01*) is located on Av. del Puerto, off Plocia Calesas, just north of where the old town begins. You can get anywhere from this station. Frequent service chugs to Jerez and Seville, less often to Granada and Málaga. To Madrid the *talgo* saves two hours but costs 50 percent more than the 10 hour *expresso*.

Buses to Seville are frequent, but only leave once or twice a day for Granada and Córdoba. The station is just east of the Pl. de España in Pl. de Hispanidad. ☎ *21 17 63.* A different bus line serves the nearby coast towns: Transportes Los Amarillos is located on Av. Ramón de Carranza near the parking place. ☎ *28 58 52.*

Boat to Puerto Santa María

The fine beach across the bay at Puerto Santa María is served by four boats per day in season. They leave the harbor near the train station for a 150 ptas. trip, each way. Information is available at the tourism office.

Córdoba ★★★★

Population: 284,737
Area code: 957; Zip code: 14000

*From **Madrid** take A-4 (E-5) south toward Aranjuez, which becomes N-IV. At Bailén, after 298 km, N-IV turns west to Córdoba 108 km further away. From **Granada** take N-432 to Córdoba in 163 km. From **Seville** take N-IV (E-5) to Córdoba for 142 km.*

As their capital, Córdoba rose with the Moors to glory, but it was an important city long before the Moors came. Eight hundred years before, the Romans had made it the seat of their southern province of Baetia, as they called Andalusia. Córdoba became the largest city in Roman Spain, and here the great Latin writer Seneca the Elder was born. Later, its archbishop Hosius presided over the Church Council of Nicea, from which emanated the famous creed.

Under the Moors Córdoba glowed as the shining light of medieval Europe. By the 10th century its population had reached half a million—double its size today—at a time when neither London nor Paris approached 100,000. The streets were paved and lighted, public baths were open to all, 50 hospitals served the sick, and a third of a million mansions, houses and stores filled the city. Nor was Córdoba merely large and modern for the times. While the Dark Ages eclipsed science in the rest of Europe, Córdoba served as its reservoir of learning. Córdoba's library housed a quarter of a million volumes at a time when books elsewhere in Europe were rare as hen's teeth and only one Christian in a hundred could read. Of course the Moors had an advantage—they knew how to make paper while the rest of Europe wrote on costly sheepskin—and Córdoba sent its children to 29 public schools. The great Jewish philosopher Moses Maimonides was born and lived in Córdoba, as did the great Aristotelian scholar Ibn Rushd, known to the West as Averröes. Later his works were translated into Latin to produce the scholastic thought which Abelard, Duns Scotus and Thomas Aquinas developed to lift Europe into the Renaissance. Even algebra and Arabic numbers were disseminated from Andalusia to the rest of the continent. Without the Moorish culture in Andalusia—indeed, without Córdoba—the west would have remained in its Dark Ages for centuries longer, with unpredictable results.

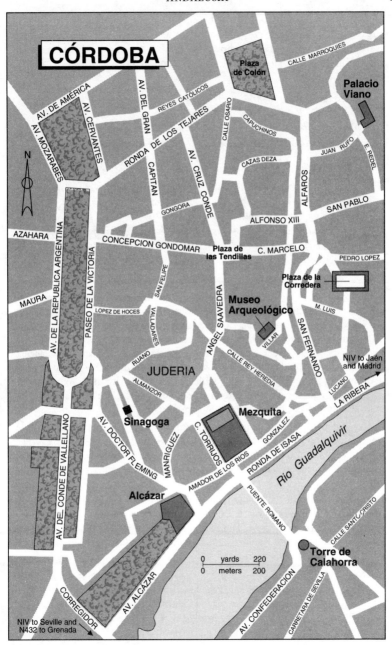

CÓRDOBA

N

Plaza de Colón

Palacio Viano

CALLE MARROQUIES

AV. DE AMÉRICA

AV. CERVANTES

AV. MOZARABES

AV. DEL GRAN CAPITAN

RONDA DE LOS TEJARES

REYES CATÓLICOS

CALLE OSARIO

CAPUCHINOS

JUAN RUFO

E. REDEL

AV. CRUZ CONDE

CAZAS DEZA

ALFAROS

SAN PABLO

AZAHARA

GONGORA

ALFONSO XIII

CONCEPCION GONDOMAR

Plaza de las Tendillas

C. MARCELO

PEDRO LOPEZ

AV. DE LA REPUBLICA ARGENTINA

PASEO DE LA VICTORIA

SAN FELIPE

Plaza de la Corredera

MAURA

LOPEZ DE HOCES

VALLADARES

ANGEL SAAVEDRA

Museo Arqueológico

M. LUIS

VILLAR

SAN FERNANDO

RUANO

CALLE REY HEREDIA

NIV to Jaén and Madrid

JUDERIA

ALMANZOR

LUCANO

LA RIBERA

AV. DE CONDE DE VALLELLANO

AV. DOCTOR FLEMING

Sinagoga

MANRIGUEZ

C. TORRIJOS

Mezquita

GONZALEZ

Rio Guadalquivir

AMADOR DE LOS RIOS

RONDA DE ISASA

Alcázar

PUENTE ROMANO

| 0 | yards | 220 |
| 0 | meters | 200 |

Torre de Calahorra

CALLE SANTO CRISTO

CORREGIDOR

AV. ALCÁZAR

AV. CONFEDERACION

CARRETARA DE SEVILLA

NIV to Seville and N432 to Grenada

Christians captured Córdoba in 1236, ending its preeminence. Even after the reconquest, Córdoba retained fame for its tooled, embossed and colored leatherwork, so desired throughout Europe that "cordovan" became a common noun in English for special leather. But never again would the city shine as it had once.

Arriving from **Madrid** *or from the direction of* **Jaén**, *travel along Paseo de la Rivera beside the Guadalquivir River. After passing the gardens of the Alcázar you arrive at a "T." Continue right onto Av. de Conde de Vallallano. Stay along the boulevard gardens on Paseo de la Victoria, though if a spot for parking presents itself, as it usually does, take it. Otherwise continue to the circle, taking Ronda de los Tejares northeast. At the third right, turn onto C. Cruz Conde, whose second right onto C. de Robledo leads to parking. From both* **Seville** *and* **Granada** *you arrive at a large traffic circle and proceed northwest to cross the bridge over the Guadalquivir River, which funnels into Av. de Conde de Vallallano. Then follow the directions above.*

What to See and Do

The sight for which Córdoba is world-famous is the **mezquita ★ ★ ★ ★ ★**, or mosque, one of the greatest raised by Islam. It is located a short block north of the Guadalquivir River. Around the mosque crowd remains of the old medieval quarter, a twisting maze of streets called the **Judería ★ ★** that extends five blocks north of the mosque, two blocks west and one block east. A medieval **synagogue ★** and an **archaeological museum ★** lie within the Judería, and lovely flowered patios can be glimpsed through doorways and grills. On its west side rise the remains of old city **walls**. An **alcázar ★** overlooks the river one block southwest of the mosque, and a block upstream is the so-called **Puente Romano**, little of which is Roman any more.

There should be more to see in Córdoba, given its former splendors. But the mosque alone repays a trip; other sights are concentrated in a small area, and everywhere orange trees perfume the air. In addition, evocative ruins of a pleasure city built by Caliph er Rahman wait at **Medinet Azahara ★ ★ ★**, 10 km outside the city. One day does justice to it all.

The best approach to the mosque is through the medieval quarters, the Judería, to acquire some feel for life as it was then. Make your way to the grand boulevard of Córdoba, the gardened Paseo de la Victoria. Head a few blocks south to reach the beginning of the reconstructed town walls. Follow these walls to their gate, the **Puerta de Almodovar**, watched over by a statue of Seneca.

Judería ★ ★

Turn immediately right through the town gate to hug the walls along C. Maimonides. Whitewashed houses, many with lovely interior patios and flowers, line the lanes. In one long block is the **Synagogue ★**, on the right (open Tues.–Sat. 10 a.m. to 2 p.m. and 3:30–5:30 p.m., opening and closing an hour earlier in winter;

closed Mon. as well as Sun. afternoons; admission: 75 ptas.). Along with the two in Toledo, this is one of the last surviving synagogues in Spain. It dates to the 14th century and is tiny, though with attractive Mudejar stuccowork along the upper walls and balcony.

Across from the synagogue is a touristy, reconstructed **Zoco** (souk, "market"), interesting only for a look at the building with craftsmen working around an open patio, which contains a museum of bullfighting (dedicated to locally born Manolete). Turn east across its southern face, first passing a statue of Maimonides and then the **Capilla de San Bartolome** on the right, with vaulting and Mudejar work inside. At the end of C. Cardenal Salazar, C. Almanzor Romero leads southeast to the corner of the **Mezquita** ★ ★ ★ ★ (mosque). Along its northern face, beside the bell tower, is its normal entrance. See the description below.

After the Mezquita, head east along its north face to take the alley going left, just before the corner of the walls, called C. Velázquez Bosco. Almost immediately take the right that leads past beautiful **flowered patios** ★ on either side and into an alley heading south, called the Calleja de las Flores. Córdoba takes great pride in its patios, holding a contest during the first two weeks of May. The alley lets into C. Encarnación which goes east for a block to C. Rey Heredia. Jag right, then left onto Calle Horno de Cristo which leads to the **archaeological museum** ★, also described below.

Mezquita ★ ★ ★ ★ ★

C. Cardenal Herrero, ☎ *47 05 12.*
Hours open: daily 10 a.m.–7 p.m. (in winter 10 a.m.–1:30 p.m. and 3:30–5:30 p.m.).
Approximately one-third of the present structure was completed by Abd er Rahman I in 785, after he purchased a Christian church on the site and razed it to erect a mosque in one year. He saved pillars from the former church, which the Christians had in turn appropriated from earlier Roman and Visigoth buildings, to incorporate in the structure. This earliest stage of the mosque covered half of a football field—75 yards by 25 wide—and employed the innovation of creating aisles by superimposing two tiers of arches for height and spaciousness. Over the next 200 years three additions were made, each incorporating the idea of superimposed arches, to quadruple the original size to 200 yards long (counting 50 yards of courtyard) by 130 wide.

When finished, Córdoba had one of the largest mosques in the world and one of the very finest, not excepting those in Cairo, Istanbul or Mecca. The plan, however, is typical of mosques the world over. First comes a courtyard with a basin for ritual ablution, followed by the mosque proper—a rectangular building with a special niche, called a *mihrab*, in its far wall that indicates the direction of Mecca. Toward this niche the congregation bows in prayer. What is unique about this mosque is the addition, made in the 16th century, of a cathedral inside. At that time, all aisles of the mosque but two were sealed off, depriving the mosque of its original open feeling, and the flat, carved and painted wooden ceiling was replaced by vaulting. (A portion of this original ceiling has been restored near the mihrab.) Today the building is the most incongruous of structures—an Oriental mosque encasing a Gothic

cathedral. Upon seeing the intrusive cathedral, Carlos V, who initially had autho-
rized its construction, berated the city fathers saying, "You have built here what you
might have built anywhere else, but you destroyed what was unique in the world."
(Ironically, this same king destroyed sections of the Alhambra to make room for his
own palace there.)

The Puerta del Perdón entrance was added to the enclosing walls in the 14th century, though in a style—except for the coats of arms of Córdoba and Spain high on
the outer side—suitable to the mosque. The side facing the courtyard is wholly
Moorish in flavor and lovely. The courtyard itself, with rows of shading orange trees
and a large ablution basin near the long wall, looks much as it would have in the
10th century. (Incidentally, the oranges are as bitter as can be.) Directly across from
the Pardon Gate is the entrance to the mosque proper.

Inside stands a magical forest. Pillars like trees stretch in every forward direction into
the distance. Originally 850 of them, all different—of marble, jasper, porphyry and
breccia—supported arches that alternated limestone and brick to form red and
white stripes. About half the pillars—the rest were displaced by the Cathedral—
remain, enough to produce an effect like no other building in the world. They came
mainly from looted older buildings in Spain, but some were shipped from Carthage
in North Africa and a few from as far as Constantinople. Having been appropriated
from different buildings, the pillars varied in height and required bases of individual
elevations to even them out. The vast majority of the capitals are concrete replicas,
with a few marble originals bearing traces of gilt near the mihrab.

The route to the mihrab is straight ahead against the south wall of the mosque,
although it involves passing the Cathedral (as quickly as possible). The **Villavicosa
Chapel** is situated just in front of the mihrab. Unfortunately it has been sealed off
recently, though it is possible to peer through the grill. This chamber was remodeled in a Mudejar style in the 14th century as a Christian chapel with a lovely dome
reminiscent of that prefacing the mihrab. Adjoining, on the left, is the **Capilla Real**,
again a 14th-century chapel addition of harmonious Mudejar work. Directly ahead
is the **mihrab**.

The mihrab was constructed in 965 using Byzantine craftsmen, probably from
Greece, hence the glittering mosaics. The mihrab proper is the tiny closet through
the horseshoe arch. Preceding it are three bays forming an enclosure for the caliph
and his family. The wooden ceiling prefacing this enclosure is the only remainder of
the tenth-century original that once covered the whole mosque. Three domes
above the caliph's enclosure are original designs of intersecting arcs that form an
octagonal center, all inlaid with mosaics to present arabesques on a gold field. Brilliant mosaics make the walls rich, but the most splendid are the arabesques framing
the archway to the mihrab. That octagonal chamber, which you cannot enter, consists of carved marble walls and a dome formed by an elegant plaster shell. So successful was the design of this mihrab that it became the standard throughout the
Muslim world.

The **Cathedral**, insistently placed in the midst of this oriental splendor, cannot be entirely ignored. It is a mishmash of every ornate style from Gothic to baroque, as if competing with the elegance of the mosque by overwhelming the viewer. On its own it is impressive, if overblown, with fine workmanship throughout. Ignoring the gilded stucco roof, the coro encloses fine baroque choir stalls, and the pulpits are baroque masterpieces in mahogany—note the bull who cranes to hear the sermon. But nothing can excuse the travesty of placing this florid Christian structure inside one of the world's greatest works of architecture. Some say that the mosque is large enough and sufficiently grand to absorb the Cathedral without loss, but most will find the Cathedral so disturbing that the experience of the mosque is undermined. Carlos V's assessment is sadly accurate. *Admission: 800 ptas.*

Museo Arqueológico Provincial ★

Pl. Jerónimo Páez, ☎ 47 40 11.
Hours open: Tues.–Sat. 10 a.m.–2 p.m. and 6–8 p.m. (until 7 p.m. in winter). Open Sun. 10 a.m.–1:30 p.m. Closed Mon. and holidays.
The museum is housed in the 16th-century palace of Jerónimo Páez, with a rich Renaissance portal, though the patio gained through it is simple. Exhibits are arranged chronologically. Rooms to the right present prehistoric material, including several endearing Iberian lions. Farther on are interesting Roman mosaics. The second floor presents a Moorish collection, mainly excavated from Medinat Azahara nearby. Amid lovely capitals, the star is a bronze inlaid stag, donated to the caliph by the emperor of Constantinople removed from a fountain in Medinat Azahara. *Admission: 250 ptas.*

Walk due south to the river and the so-called **Roman bridge**. *The bridge does rest on Roman foundations, though its present form derives from Moorish construction in the eighth century, much restored since. On the opposite bank is the* **Torre de Calahorro**, *from the 14th century. It was recently taken over by an artist and made into a museum of models of ancient Córdoba with inane verbal descriptions. (It closes at 7 p.m. in summer, 6 p.m. in winter, all day Sun. and Mon., and costs 350 ptas.) A model of the mosque when new almost makes a visit worthwhile. Downstream in two blocks is the Alcázar.*

Alcázar

Amador de los Rios, ☎ 47 20 00.
Hours open: Tues.–Sat. 9:30 a.m.–1:30 p.m. and 5–8 p.m. (until 7 p.m. in winter). Open Sun. 9:30 a.m.–1:30 p.m.
The original alcázar of the Moors stood east of the present structure—where the present bishopric faces the mosque. In the 13th century Alfonso X the Wise built a palace in the gardens of the original alcázar, which was substantially modified in the succeeding century to what exists today. Later the building served as the office of the local Inquisition and its prison until the 19th century. Although the interior is not of great interest, there are some nice mosaics inside and Moorish baths. The gardens with pools, flowers and cypresses make for peaceful strolling. *Admission: 300 ptas.*

Palácio de Viana ★★★

Pl. Jerónimo Páez, ☎ 48 22 75.

Hours open: Mon., Tues., Thurs., and Fri. 9 a.m.–2 p.m. and 4–6 p.m. (Opens and closes an hour earlier winter afternoons). Closed Wed.

The simplest course is to take a taxi, which should not cost more than $3 for the mile ride from the mosque. Normally one hardly bothers with an 18th-century palace in Spain, unless it was built by a king, but the reason for seeing this one is its dozen patios, in some ways the loveliest in this city of fine patios. In addition, there are nearly 50 rooms open to the public to show how the very rich once lived. *Admission: 300 ptas.*

Where to Stay

Córdoba serves nicely as a place to spend a night or two, with good choices in every price category. The problem is that the city does not have any excess of hotels which can be a problem in busy seasons. It is best to reserve ahead at those times.

Expensive ($100–$200)

El Conquistador   1st-class ★★★★

Magistral González Francés, 15, Córdoba (facing the east wall of the mosque), ☎ 48 11 02, FAX 47 46 77.

All white in the style of a new Moorish villa, the elegance of the decor and the beauty of its patio make it unrivaled in Códoba. In addition, the hotel is attentively run. But it demands of guests that they solve the difficult problem of choosing between a room facing the lovely interior patio and one facing the mosque. Incidentally, since this area is brightly lit at night, sleep will be more peaceful in an interior room. Parking is available for a fee. *103 rooms.*

Amistad Córdoba   Deluxe ★★

Pl. de Maimónides, 3, Córdoba (beside the synagogue in the Judería), ☎ 42 03 35, FAX 42 03 65.

Newly opened, a stone's throw from the mosque, the Amistad is constructed from two 18th-century townhouses to provides the most pleasant stay in the Judería. Rooms are eminently comfortable, and a mudéjar decorated patio sets a lovely tone. Further, prices hover on the line between expensive and moderate. *69 rooms.*

On the Carretera de El Brillant, four km north of Córdoba:

Parador de Córdoba   Deluxe ★★

Av. de la Arruzafa, Córdoba, ☎ 27 59 00, FAX 28 04 09, Telex 76695.

This is a modern parador, looking too much like a Miami Beach hotel of the second or third class. Of course it is clean and well maintained, but its best feature is lovely gardens to provide peace and quiet, albeit outside of town. A swimming pool and tennis courts are available. *94 rooms.*

Husa Gran Capitán   1st-class

Av. de América, 5, Córdoba (the avenue runs across the north end of the Victoria Gardens), ☎ 47 02 50, FAX 47 43 48, Telex 76662.

If you are part of a tour, you probably are staying here already; otherwise you probably wouldn't want to. Overrated is a term invented for such establishments. The rooms are large but uninviting and overlook either an ugly, noisy street or an unattractive courtyard. The staff tries. Parking is available for a fee. *100 rooms.*

Meliá Córdoba   **Deluxe**

Jardines de la Victoria, Córdoba (located at the southern end of the gardens that begin
where the city walls end. See the arrival directions.), ☎ *29 80 66, FAX 29 81 47, Telex*
76591.

This is supposed to be the grand hotel of Córdoba, but it does not come close. The
decor reminds one of the fifties; the lobby is dreary, and the building is situated by
a simple park that few of the rooms overlook. *142 rooms, plus four suites.*

Moderate ($50–$99)

González   **3rd-class ★ ★ ★**

Manriquez, 3, Córdoba (on the street running west from the northwest corner of the
Mosque), ☎ *47 98 19, FAX 48 61 87.*

A delightful hotel at most reasonable prices, this one is heartily recommended. The
lobby is white with light wood, punctuated by antiques, especially the lovely chandelier. Altogether this hotel feels perfectly Andalusian, clean and fresh, and is situated on an equally lovely street and offers parking for a fee. *16 rooms.*

El Califa   **R2nd-class ★ ★**

Lope de Hoces, 14, Córdoba (a block north, and short block east, of the Meliá Córdoba
and the gate to the Judería), ☎ *29 94 00, FAX 29 57 16.*

The street on which the hotel resides is lovely, filled with orange trees. The building
is attractively modern with an elegant granite reception area. Rooms are tastefully
decorated; the service is good; and parking is available for a fee. *66 rooms.*

Maimónides   **R2nd-class ★**

Torrijos, 4, Córdoba (opposite the east side of the mosque patio), ☎ *47 15 00, FAX 48*
38 03.

We remember happier days for the Maimónides. Actually it probably remains the
same, while over the years other hotels improved. It still enjoys a perfect location
and views of the mosque from front rooms, but is in need of sprucing up. Parking
is available for a fee. *83 rooms.*

Albucasis   **R2nd-class ★**

Buen Pastor, 11, Córdoba (in the Judería, one block north from the northwest corner of
the mosque and another block northwest), ☎ *47 86 25, FAX 47 86 25.*

It should cost more for marble floors, comfortable rooms and a charming patio, all
contained in a nicely restored little mansion. Everything is bright, touched with
green and intimate at the same time. We don't think there will be complaints about
the low prices. *15 rooms.*

Marisa   **R2nd-class ★**

Cardenal Herrero, 6, Córdoba (along the north wall of the mosque), ☎ *47 31 42, FAX*
47 41 44.

This hotel is simple and pleasantly, if not memorably, decorated. The small size
lends a homey feel, and the location is just as good as much more costly alternatives.
28 rooms.

Los Gallos Sol   **2nd-class**

Av. Medina Azahara, 7, Córdoba (two blocks north and one west of the Meliá Córdoba),
☎ *23 55 00, FAX 23 16 36, Telex 76566.*

This hotel is a good ten years overdue for a facelift, still looking 70s modern. It is a pleasant enough place, but nothing outstanding and a walk to the sights. *115 rooms.*

Selu   **R2nd-class**

Eduardo Dato, 7, Córdoba (a block due north of the el Caliph hotel), ☎ *47 65 00, FAX 47 83 76, Telex 76659.*

This is a functional modern hotel recently renovated with very low prices. Parking is available for a fee. *118 rooms .*

Inexpensive (Less than $50)

Serrano   **3rd-class ★★**

Pérez Galdós, 6, Córdoba (just off the right side of the Av. Gran Capitán which runs due north of the Judería, a block south and two east of the hotel Gran Capitán), ☎ *47 01 42, FAX 48 65 13.*

Modern without being stark, this hotel is a charmer. It is situated on a quiet street of pleasant art galleries. The five-block walk to the Judería is not too much to ask for such pleasing accommodations, especially at this price. *64 rooms.*

Senica   **HsR4th-class ★**

Conde y Luque, 7, Córdoba (the street runs east-west two blocks north of the mosque), ☎ *47 32 34.*

Clean as a whistle and with a lovely courtyard for breakfast what more can you ask for a low price? A room with bath costs extra, and some rooms are on the small side, but breakfast is included. Reservations are a must. Note: no credit cards. *12 rooms, half with bathrooms.*

El Triunfo   **Hs3rd-class**

Cardinal González, 79, Córdoba (at the southwest corner of the mosque, near the river), ☎ *47 55 00, FAX 48 68 50.*

Just a tad higher-priced than the foregoing and not on as pleasant a street, but recently renovated with TVs and convenient to the sights. Noise sometimes becomes a problem, however. Reserve to avoid disappointment. *60 rooms.*

Youth Hostel

Residencial Juvenil Córdoba

Pl. Judas Levi, Córdoba (behind the Episcopal Palace just west of the mosque), ☎ *29 03 66, FAX 29 05 00.*

New, clean, great location but noisy. Advanced reservations with confirmation is essential. No curfew at all, but prices start at 1000 ptas. per person.

Where to Eat

One can eat well in Córdoba, although it is difficult to dine cheaply. The regional specialty is a somewhat thicker, more garlicky version of gazpacho called *salmorejo* in which ham and eggs are included. The other specialty is *rabo de toro*—oxtail stewed in heavy tomato sauce—which no one should disparage without trying.

Expensive ($30+)

Mesón Bandolero   **★★**

Torrijos, 6 (next door to the hotel Maimonides), ☎ *48 51 76.*

The room is lovely, with brick arches forming intimate dining areas, and a patio filled with palms for outdoor eating. Tables are set with linen and sparkling brass serving plates. None of this elegance is surprising, given that this restaurant is affiliated with the tasteful hotel El Conquistador. Although the food is carefully prepared and covers specialties of the region, this recommendation is for the beauty of the place more than the food. Credit Cards: A, D and V.

El Caballo Rojo ★★
Cardenal herrero, 28 (opposite the northwest corner of the mosque), ☎ *47 53 75.*
Dining is upstairs in a huge 50s kind of place that is noisy because hordes of people are enjoying themselves. The menu claims dishes based on ancient recipes, some of which are tasty indeed, such as *ajo blanco* and *rape mozárabe*. A complimentary sherry aperitif settles you in, and ordering from a special menu can hold prices down. Reservations are strongly advised. Credit Cards: A, D, M, V.

El Blasón ★★
José Zorrilla, 11 (near the hotel Andalucia), ☎ *48 06 25.*
Upstairs, past an inviting patio, silks and candelabra produce a Belle Époque feeling of quiet luxury. Service is excellent and the dishes are innovative. There is a reasonably-priced special menu, plus a more expensive *menu de degustación* to put the chef through his paces. Credit Cards: A, D, M, V.

El Churrasco ★★
Romero, 16 (the street heading northwest from the northwest corner of the mosque), ☎ *29 08 19.*
Closed August.
Again, white walls with brick arches characterize this restaurant, this time with iron chairs and an indoor garden under a skylight. Upstairs is a more formal room. The specialty after which the restaurant is named is a kind of spicy barbecued pork that, along with other grilled dishes, draws a crowd. The *salmorejo* soup is delicious as well. Reservations are strongly recommended. Credit Cards: A, D, M, V.

Inexpensive (Less than $15)

Mesón El Burfaero ★★
Calleja La Hoguera, 5 (this alley angles of C. Deanes, which leaves the northwest corner of the mosque; or, walk through El Caballo Rojo restaurant, cited above), ☎ *47 27 19.*
Closed the second half of Nov.
Although good inexpensive food is hard to find in Córdoba, here it is served either outside in a small outside patio or inside on checkered tablecloths surrounded by stuffed trophies. For the price, there is no better, more authentic food to be found in the city. Credit Cards: A, D, M, V.

El Triunto ★
Cardinal González, 79 (at the southwest corner of the mosque, near the river), ☎ *47 55 00.*
The restaurant of this hostale noted above serves very simple, low-cost meals.

Directory

Information
On C. Torrijos, which frames the west side of the mosque, at number 10 in the Palácio de Congresos y Exposiciones. The staff is helpful with information on Andalusia in general, as well as on Córdoba. ☎ *47 12 35.*

Trains and Buses

The train station is located one mile north of the mosque on *Av. de América, 130.*
For information: ☎ *49 02 02.* Córdoba is a rail hub for the area so service is excellent, including the AVE to Seville for under an hour, rather than the usual two hour trip. Service is also frequent to Madrid, Málaga and Valencia. The RENFE ticket office is at Ronda de los Tejares 10, which cuts across Av. Gran Capitán about six blocks north of the Judería. ☎ *47 58 84.*

There is no central area for bus departures because the routes are divided among several companies. The tourist office provides information and schedules. For Madrid, Barcelona, Seville, Granada, Málaga and Jaén call ☎ *47 23 52;* for southern Andalusia the number is ☎ *23 64 76.*

Post Office and Telephones

The post office is at *15 C. Cruz Conde,* which runs north from the large conflux of streets at the Pl. de las Tendillas, just north of the Judería. Telephones are located in this same plaza at number 7.

Police

Campo Madre de Dios, 5, a wide street about ten blocks east along the river. ☎ *25 14 14;* for emergencies 091.

Excursions

Medina Azahara, located about 11 km from Córdoba, is an excavated pleasure city built by the first caliph of al Andalus, Abd er Rahman III. It is atmospheric and contains some lovely buildings reconstructed from the ruins.

> *From the hotel Meliá Córdoba, make a circuit around the north end of the Victoria garden heading south. Take the first right on Av. Medina Azahara, which becomes C-431. In eight km, bear right as a sign directs to reach the ruins in three km more.*

Medinet Azahara   ★★★

Carretera Palma de Río, ☎ *32 91 30.*
Hours open: Tues.–Sat. 10 a.m.–2 p.m. and 6–8 p.m. (opening and closing two hours earlier on winter afternoons). Open Sun. and holidays 10 a.m.–1:30 p.m. Closed Mon.
Caliph Abd er Rahman III, mightiest of the Moors, began work in 936 on a city terraced on a hill to afford beautiful views. He named it for his favorite wife, az Zahara. Records tell of construction crews numbering in the tens of thousands, of a garrison to lodge a 12,000-man army, and lovely gardens with a zoo. It must have been an Arabian Nights place, perhaps rivalling the Alhambra, and certainly surpassing it in size and age. Yet it endured for less than a century because it was razed by Berbers who felt betrayed by one of Abd er Rahman III's successors. Over the ensuing centuries the site was looted for building materials by Christian kings and aristocracy for their own building projects.

Excavations began in 1944, and reconstruction—still underway—commenced a decade later. The area contains a small city, and the Spanish government is in no hurry. The grand gate to the town and **plaza** inside have been reconstructed enough to give a sense of their design, but most impressive is the **Salon Rico**. Its walls have been re-erected, some of the original carved stones replaced, and the floor reconstructed. It is an imposing structure. The carved designs in stone are interesting for their more realistic portrayal of nature, compared to the abstraction of later Alhambra stucco. The **mosque** nearby is also worth a look. The site is a place to wander through and dream of other times and worlds. *Admission: 250 ptas.*

Costa de la Luz ★ ★

These are the beaches left to the Spanish after Europeans appropriate the rest. So do not come here expecting excitement and international flavor— stick with the Costa del Sol for that. What you will find is good sand, much better than on the Costa del Sol, and villages that retain their character. Beginning from the middle of July through August, you will also find a large part of Spain on holiday here. Accommodations are difficult to obtain during that time, but even then enough beach exists that quiet places can be found for communing with the sea. At other times accommodations should pose no problem, and the beach remains warm well into October.

Over 200 km in length, the Costa de la Luz extends west from Gibraltar to the Portuguese border. Naturally such a large area includes much variation, but to generalize, the beaches improve the farther west they go, while the atmosphere turns transparent earning the name "Coast of Light."

We describe the towns beginning in the east and going west. The first half, to Cádiz, is traversed by N-340 (E-5) west, beginning from Gibraltar (described under its own heading). Decent roads connect all the towns, though traffic can crawl in August. It is also possible to cover the route using local buses, but with much transferring involved.

Algeciras

Population: 86,042
Area code: 956; Zip code: 11200

Located across the bay from Gibraltar, 13 km distant by the road around Algeciras bay, the port of Algeciras affords the best views of the Rock and offers transportation by car-ferry to both Tangier and Ceuta in Morocco. The city itself is grey overall, though with nice public gardens inside the first perimeter wall. It contains a decent cathedral and ruins of a Moorish fort, but no beaches.

Tarifa ★

Population: 15,220
Area code: 956; Zip code: 11380

N-340 goes right into town, 21 km southwest from Algeciras.

Tarifa is the southernmost part of Spain, not excepting Gibraltar, hence only 15 km off the coast of Morocco—visible on clear days. It is also exposed to ocean winds that make it a windsurfer's dream and, because of blowing sand, often a beach sitter's nightmare. However, the beaches stretching west for 10 km from the town are lovely. The old town still retains parts of its Moorish walls and gates, and the feel overall of a North African town. On the sea, just east, are remains of a Moorish castle from the 10th century with a later fortified tower.

> *17 km west from Tarifa, a turn left down a small road toward the ocean leads to the fine beach of* **Bolonia** *with bars and eating places, and extensive ruins of the Roman town of Baelo Claudia (closed Sun. afternoons and all Mon.; guided tours on the hour: 100 ptas.).*

Where to Stay

The nicest Tarifa accommodations wait outside town on N-340, with a few cheaper places in town.

Moderate ($50–$99)

Balcón de España   2nd-class ★ ★ ★
La Peña 2, (Northeast eight km on Carretera de Cádiz; mailing address: Apartado 57),
☎ *68 43 26, FAX 68 43 26.*
Open only from April 15 to the end of Oct.
Stay in the main house or in bungalows, in either case this lovely little place provides a pool and tennis all situated in a peaceful park. It is also a popular place so it must be reserved well in advance. It is near good beaches, and even its meals are special. *38 rooms.*

La Codorniz   3rd-class ★
6.5 km on Carretera de Cádiz (N-340), ☎ *68 47 44, FAX 68 34 10.*
This is the best choice after the Balcón. It is equally clean, recently remodeled, friendly and also near good beaches. During high season it too fills up weeks in advance. *35 rooms.*

Where to Eat

Try fried fish at any stall for delicious, inexpensive eating. For inexpensive sit-down-meals, visit the line of restaurants just west of the city walls. At the next higher price level there is the **Balcón** hotel mentioned above, and the attractive **el Rincon de Manolo**, on the same highway, about one km closer to town.

Zahara de los Atunes ★

Population: 1891
Area code: 956; Zip code: 11393

> *30 km from Tarifa, turn left on the small road with a sign for the town, 11 km toward the coast.*

This little fishing town, just being discovered, owns a long, lovely beach that is seldom crowded.

Where to Stay

New hotels will probably change the situation, but for the time being choices are few.

Expensive ($100–$200)

Sol Atlanterra **Deluxe**

Four km east on the road to Atlanterra, ☎ *43 90 00, FAX 43 30 51, Telex 781 69.*
Open May through Oct.
Huge, and Miami-Beach looking, the hotel offers every service in a compound all
its own. The question is why someone would come all the way to Spain to stay in a
compound. *281 rooms.*

Moderate ($50–$99)

Antonio **3rd--class ★**

One km east on the road to Atlanterra, ☎ *43 91 41, FAX 43 91 35.*
Closed Nov.
This hotel is heavily booked, and with good reason. Here you are not part of a herd,
the views are lovely, and good meals are available on the terrace. *30 rooms.*

Where to Eat

Fried fish from stalls near the port are wonderful, but full meals can be had at the **Antonio** hotel, mentioned above, with lovely views, or from **Cortijo de la Plata**, about four km from town along the same east road.

Vejer de la Frontera ★★

Population: 12,100
Area code: 956; Zip code: 11150

Just off N-340, 71 km from Algeciras, or 50 km from Tarifa.

This is one of the most beautiful villages remaining in Spain—whitewashed
houses atop a hill encased by ramparts, from which views of the countryside
are stunning. Partially restored ruins of a **Moorish fortress** share the hill with
the Gothic and Mudejar **Iglesia de San Salvador** above a labyrinth of a **Medieval Quarter** laying against the ramparts. There is no beach here, but the
golden sands of Conil are only 12 kilometers away.

Where to Stay

Only one accommodation is worth considering, and that one is not only special but
also reasonably priced

Moderate ($50–$99)

Convento de San Francisco **2nd-class ★ ★ ★**

La Plazuela, ☎ *45 10 01, FAX 45 10 04.*
The restoration of this 17th-century convent has been painstakingly and tastefully
done by the family who owns it. Do not be put off by the entrance or lobby, nor by
the fact that such a small establishment does not offer every service. You are here for
the rooms—lovely large bedrooms constructed from former monks' cells. Although
not air-conditioned, night breezes usually encourage sound sleep. *25 rooms.*

Conil de la Frontera ★★

Population: 13,289
Area code: 956; Zip code: 11140

Past Vejer on N-340 in 14 km is a left turn to the coast and Conil in two and one-half km.

This town is transforming quickly from a quiet fishing port into a resort, and the reason for the change is golden beaches that stretch to the horizons in both directions lining an exceptionally calm Atlantic. Hotels have begun to charge resort prices.

Where to Stay

We list three small hotels, each with some character, unfortunately with prices higher than their official classification would lead one to expect.

Moderate ($50–$99)

La Gaviota   **A2nd-class ★**

Pl. Nuestra Señora de las Virtudes, ☎ *44 08 36, FAX 44 09 80.*
Open Feb.–Oct.
At least for the price you get a suite with cooking facilities. This is your place if you intend to dine in. The apartments are booked well before the high season. *15 rooms.*

Don Pelayo   **3rd-class ★**

Carretera del Punto, 19, ☎ *44 20 30, FAX 44 50 58.*
In a quiet area, and with nice sized rooms, this is your best choice, unless the idea of an apartment appeals. *31 rooms.*

Tres Jotas   **3rd-class**

C. San Sebastian, ☎ *44 04 50, FAX 44 04 50.*
This is a functional place with good service and prices a tad lower than those above. But it is a tad less nice as well. *36 rooms.*

Cádiz ★

See the description under that heading.

El Puerto de Santa María ★

Population: 61,032
Area code: 956; Zip code: 11500

From Cádiz head south along N-IV, splitting off to follow signs to Puerto Real, as it wraps north around the bay to el Puerto in 22 km.

The Rio Guadalete splits the town in two with **sherry bodegas** lining the south bank—offering tours and free samples in the mornings (but not during August harvest-time)—and a fishing harbor lining the north. Also on the north bank is a lovely promenade leading to a restored **Moorish castle** with an attractive mansion beside it, as well as a pair of nice churches. About a ten-minute walk north along the water, or a short drive, is the **Playa Puntillo**, a long stretch of fine beach.

Where to Stay

Hotels are pricey.

Expensive ($100–$200)

Monasterio de San Miguel   Deluxe ★ ★ ★ ★
C. Larga, 2, ☎ 54 04 40, FAX 54 26 04.
This 18th-century convent recently was made over with luxury trappings as a hotel.
It provides the extra features of an elegant cloister and church. This one is deluxe all
the way, yet, despite all its atmosphere, barely expensive. *137 rooms, plus 13 suites.*

Moderate ($50-$99)

Puertobahía   1st-class ★ ★
Av. La Paz, 38, in Valdelagrana (on the beach), ☎ 56 27 00, FAX 56 12 21.
For its beach location and moderate price, you have to like the Puertobahía. It adds
a pool and tennis court, if you can tear away from the lovely beach. But, when all is
said and done, the rooms are just rooms. *330 rooms.*

Los Cántaros   2nd-class ★
Curva, 6, ☎ 54 02 40, FAX 54 11 21.
The staff treats the clients well at this homey place. Prices are fair for what is offered.
39 rooms.

Where to Eat

Walk along the C. Ribera del Marisco for fresh fish from any outdoor bar, but for a
more special experience, see El Patio.

Moderate ($15–$30)

El Patio   ★
Rufina Vergara, 1, ☎ 54 05 06.
A treat for the eyes, this restaurant on a quiet square is a former 18th-century inn
arranged around a lovely patio. The food is good, without attaining excellence, but
at fair prices. Credit Cards: A, D, M, V.

Rota

Population: 25,291
Area code: 956; Zip code: 11520

From Puerto de Santa María head north along the coast on C-441
for 21 km, turning south at the sign for Rota, six km away.

There is a large U.S. naval base just outside the town which has resulted in
fast food restaurants, cheap souvenir shops and resentment among the citizens that sometimes flares into protests. On the other hand, a series of truly
lovely beaches runs for miles north of the town. But all this hardly matters
because accommodations are almost impossible to get and expensive when
gotten.

Chipiona

Population: 12,500
Area code: 956; Zip code: 11550

*A lovely coast road goes north from Rota to join C-441 in seven km,
for another eight km to Chipiona.*

Chipiona is famous for curative waters which are piped into the fountain of
the **Iglesia de Nuestra Señora de Regla**. In general, it attract an older Spanish
crowd. Otherwise, this is a basic charming resort community with miles of
lovely beaches constituting the **Playa de Regla** that runs south of the lighthouse from Av. Regla. But decent hotels are scarce.

Sanlúcar de Barrameda ★

Population: 48,390
Area code: 956; Zip code: 11540

Nine km east of Chipiona on C-441.

Sanlúcar has grown a grey band of boring houses around the older part of
town, but retains character in the center. At the mouth of the Guadalquivir,
it enjoys a nice river beach beside the warmest of waters. This also is the port
for shipping manzanilla sherry, so bodegas offer free tours and tastes. There
are enough interesting churches and two palaces to occupy one's time.

Where to Stay

Accommodations are difficult to find since most of the hotels are small, though pleasant.

Moderate ($50–$99)

Palácio de los Duques de Medina Sidonia   ★★★★★

Conde de Niebla, 1, ☎ 36 01 61.
The Medina Sidonia family is one of the most illustrious in Spain—their ancestor
commanded the Great Armada. The present duchess lets out a few rooms to us
commoners in the renovated barn of their local mansion. Each suite has a fireplace
and magnificent views. With only three rooms to rent, reservations are essential and
the Palácio does not offer the services of a proper hotel. But if you are one of the
lucky ones, you will talk about it for years. *Three Suites.*

Posada del Palácio   3rd-class ★ ★ ★

Caballeros, 11, ☎ 36 48 40, FAX 36 50 60.
Closed Jan. and Feb.
A true find and newly renovated, the location is fine, the hotel has character and the
clients are treated as guests. *13 rooms.*

Tartaneros   R2nd-class ★ ★

Tartaneros, 8, ☎ 36 73 61, FAX 36 00 45.
This is a very comfortable hotel with a few extras in the rooms, such as a TV, to justify its prices. *22 rooms.*

Los Helechos   R3rd-class ★

Pl. Madre de Dios, 9, ☎ 36 13 49, FAX 36 96 50.
Here the hotel feels like home, because it is a house made into a hotel. Homey
touches endear it. Parking is available for a fee. *56 rooms.*

Where to Eat

Two good choices are on the Bajo de Guia beach. Both are well known and packed during high season, when reservations are essential.

Moderate ($15–$30)

Bigote   ★

    Bajo de Guia, ☎ *36 26 96.*

    Little work went into the decor, but someone spends a lot of time searching for the freshest fish. Order any seafood, simply done, and you'll be gratified. Credit Cards: A, V, M.

Mirador Doñana   ★

    Bajo de Guia, ☎ *36 42 05.*

    Closed from the middle of Jan. through the middle of Feb.

    The terrace offers views of the scene. Seafood is perfectly done. The large shrimp called *langostinos* are memorable, though not cheap. Credit Cards: A, D, M.

The coast immediately north of Sanlúcar consists of the huge **national park of de Doñana ★★**, with no public roads, so coastal passage northward is impossible. One has to circle the park by traveling north to Seville and then west. However, the beaches farther west have little to offer compared to those discussed.

    From Sanlúcar C-441 east toward Lebrija reaches Las Cabezas de San Juan in 47 km, where the toll road N-IV heads speedily to **Seville**, *39 km away.*

Costa del Sol ★★

The Costa del Sol is an international playground in which the Spanish are vastly outnumbered by British and German visitors. What originally drew all the foreigners was the promise of warmth through seemingly limitless sunny days. They came in huge numbers, as did both older Americans and British to retire in the sun, forming compounds where most of the inhabitants speak no Spanish. Now miles of high-rise hotels line both the beaches and hills behind. The 120 mile stretch between Motril on the east and Gibraltar on the west that forms the heart of the Costa del Sol can no longer be described as attractive. Its beaches are shale, pebbles or grey grit, not the golden sands we all dream of, and the waters can be more than a little polluted. (Search for areas flagged with "EC," which indicates that the water attains European Community cleanliness standards.)

Why then does the Costa del Sol continue to be one of the most popular vacation spots in the world? The answer is simple: people come because it is where the people come. In high season it is an exciting, three-ring circus of crowds and activities, by night a constant round of parties and clubs. It is a people-place, not a scenic or historic spot.

Of course the coast is not uniform. **Málaga** ★, the largest city in the area, roughly divides the Costa del Sol in half. It serves most people as a place to land or detrain then quickly leave, although it possesses some attractions. The towns to its east are the least crowded of the Costa del Sol resorts and remain more Spanish than international. West of Málaga is a different story beginning with **Torremolinos** ★★, the package vacation capital of the coast, to which young, working-class English flock in endless streams. Think of it as a Fort Lauderdale, with all the crowds and excitement that implies. Yet ten kilometers west is the family resort of **Fuengirola**, and twenty kilometers farther is **Marbella** ★★★ and its neighbor **San Pedro de Alcantara** ★, resorts for the beautiful people, yachts, golf and astronomically expensive luxury hotels. At the extreme west end stands unique **Gibraltar** ★, still as British as it can be.

During July and August every beach, hotel and restaurant is crowded, and hotels raise their prices to twice what they charge in other seasons. At other times accommodations are more reasonable, though the reason for coming—the excitement—pales. The entire coast is serviced by highway N-340 which traverses every village and town and slows summer traffic to a crawl. Predictably, this highway sets the record every year for the most accidents in Spain. Local buses also connect the entire coast, as does an electrified train. Flights land at Málaga, in the center, or at Gibraltar 120 km away on the western end.

We describe the locales starting from the quieter eastern end of the Costa del Sol and make our way west.

Salobreña ★★

Population: 8119
Area code: 958; Zip code: 18680

> *From* **Granada** *N-323 reaches Salobreña after a 65 km ride of lovely mountain views. From elsewhere, get to Granada and follow that same road.*

The town hangs on a steep hill two km inland from a nice beach (by the standards of the area), but offers charm and views to repay the walk uphill and down. Mountains rise behind the town and a plain stretches in front to the sea, while sugarcane plantations spread all around. Uphill is a fine restored **Moorish castle** which offers shaded **walks** and concerts in the summer.

Where to Stay

Unfortunately accommodations are scarce in town, although two quiet places sit just outside.

Moderate ($50–$99)

Salobreña   **2nd-class ★**
> *On N-340 4 km west toward Málaga,* ☎ *61 02 61,FAX 61 01 01.*

The hotel is not terribly attractive, but it offers a pool and tennis courts at a very reasonable price for the area (although they do save on air conditioning), and the views are attractive. *130 rooms.*

Inexpensive (Less than $50)

Salambina   4th-class ★ ★ ★

On N-340 1 km west toward Málaga, ☎ 61 00 37, FAX 61 13 28.
This charmer presents lovely views over cane fields to the sea. Rooms should be booked well ahead for this little place in high season. *14 rooms.*

Almuñécar ★

Population: 16,141
Area code: 958; Zip code: 18690

A 15 km drive west from Salobreña on N-340.

The bad news is the beach (shale) and the water (less than crystal clear). The good news is that the old center of town retains charm and history and a nice promenade along the beach, unfortunately lined by high-rises. And prices have not risen as high here as elsewhere along the coast. Extensive remains of a Roman aqueduct lie a half-mile west.

Where to Stay

Quite a number of moderate and inexpensive hotels are available, from which we offer a selection.

Moderate ($50–$99)

Helios   2nd-class ★

P. de las Flores, ☎ 63 44 59, FAX 63 44 69.
Such large, modern establishments are seldom anyone's favorite, but the price of this one is so agreeable that we include it. Pleasant views go some way to make up for the lack of character. *232 rooms.*

Inexpensive (Less than $50)

Goya   R3rd-class ★

Av. de Europa, ☎ 63 05 50, FAX 63 11 92.
Closed from the middle of Jan. to the middle of Feb.
Little balconies add character to most of the rooms for a price that is a steal. The hotel is well maintained by staff that put themselves out to make your stay pleasant. *26 rooms.*

Playa de San Cristóbal   R3rd-class ★

Pl. San Cristóbal, 5, ☎ 63 11 12.
Open from the middle of March to Oct.
This is an endearing little hotel, family run, with homey touches. *22 rooms.*

Carmen   R4th-class ★

Av. de Europa, 8, ☎ 63 14 13.
Through pleasant halls after a bright, planted entry wait comfortable rooms and very nice baths. Prices are amazingly low. *24 rooms.*

Nerja ★★

Population: 12,012
Area code: 952; Zip code: 29780

22 km west on N-340 along a lovely stretch of road.

By the not so remarkable expedient of keeping developments outside town, Nerja has been able to combine popularity and attendant crowds while preserving its attractiveness. Nerja is most famous for its **Balcón de Europa**, a clifftop promenade above the sea, so dubbed by King Alfonso XII when he paused to admire the view. Four kilometers east is a series of remarkable caves, the **Cuevas de Nerja**, large enough to hold summer concerts inside. *(Open 9:30 a.m. to 6 p.m. in summer; from 10 a.m. to 1:30 p.m. and from 3–6 p.m. the rest of the year. Admission: 400 ptas.).*

Where to Stay

Good choices are unfortunately few.

Expensive ($100–$200)

Parador de Nerja   1st-class ★ ★ ★
> *Playa de Burriana-Tablazo,* ☎ *252 00 50, FAX 252 19 97.*
> This is a modern-style parador but with exposed wood beams and traditional tile floors. Its lovely garden provides views almost as fabulous as those from the Balcón de Europa. A few of the rooms partake of this view, but most overlook a central patio and pool. An elevator descends to the sandy beach, and tennis courts are available. *73 rooms.*

Moderate ($50–$99)

Mónica   1st-class ★ ★
> *Playa de la Torrecilla,* ☎ *252 11 00, FAX 252 11 62.*
> This is the new guy in town (1986) all spanking modern, white marbled and Moorish in feel. The bedrooms are plenty comfortable and offer balconies. It is the tour buses and their cargo we could do without. *234 rooms, plus 1 suite.*

Balcón de Europa   2nd-class ★
> *Paseo Balcón de Europa, 1,* ☎ *252 08 00, FAX 252 44 90, Telex 79503.*
> This modern businessperson-type hotel would not be noteworthy were it not for its glorious situation atop the cliffs. Bedrooms take advantage of the views and there is a private beach below. *105 rooms.*

Inexpensive (Less than $50)

Portofino   4th-class ★
> *Puerta de Mar, 4,* ☎ *252 01 50.*
> *Open March through Oct.*
> Better known for its restaurant, this establishment offers a few nice rooms and the same view from the clifftop that the other hotels charge a bundle for. *12 rooms.*

Where to Eat

Nerja is fortunate in restaurants, two of which are favorites.

Expensive ($30+)

Casa Luque ★★

Pl. Cavana, 2 (the main square behind the church), ☎ 252 10 04.
Closed Monday.

The house is charming and the decor is elegant, although the dining room is small. The food is authentic elevated Spanish with a Basque touch and runs to meats more than fish, although the fish is fresh and delicious. For the style of the place and savory cooking, prices are more than fair. Reserve. Credit Cards: A, M, V.

Moderate ($15–$30)

Portofino ★

Puerta del Mar, 4 (directly below the Balcón de Europa, down stairs), ☎ 252 01 60.
Dinners only; closed in Winter.

The views alone would make this worth a visit, but it adds good, traditional Spanish food (including paella) to make itself irresistible. Credit Cards: M, V.

Málaga ★

See the description under its separate heading below.

Torremolinos ★★

Population: 29,000
Area code: 952; Zip code: 29620

Some refer to this as the Costa del Sol for lower classes. If true, then these are the people who have the most fun. The city thrives on a mix of British, Americans, Germans and Scandinavians, who span a range from bank tellers, to secretaries, to outright crooks (since British extradition laws make Spain a partial asylum). Most of this crowd wear very little and/or something outrageous. Shops that run from the most camp souvenir galleries to eccentric shops, as well as restaurants and hotels, have sprung up to service the motley crew. Here you can drink or eat in English pubs, dine on authentic smorgasbord and sauerbratten, and dance until dawn, when it is time to squeeze into a spot on the body-to-body beach. The experience is entirely bizarre and fun if in the proper mood.

Where to Stay

Hotels deal mainly in package tours which means their standards are below what the individual traveler expects. Of course, if vacancies exist, hotels are willing to rent to individuals at a higher price. There is little to choose between establishments, except price, so we list the relevant information by category.

Expensive ($100–$200)

Meliá Torremolinos Deluxe

Av. Carlotta Alessandri, 109, ☎ 238 05 00, FAX 238 05 38, Telex 77060.
279 rooms, plus two suites.

Pes Espada 1st-class

Via Imperial, 11, ☎ 238 03 00, FAX 237 28 01, Telex 77655.
205 rooms.

Sol Don Pablo   1st-class

> *Paseo Maritimo,* ☎ *238 38 88, FAX 238 37 83, Telex 77252.*
> *443 rooms.*

Moderate ($50–$99)

Alhoa Puerto-Sol   1st-class

> *Salvador Allende, 55,* ☎ *238 70 66, FAX 238 57 01, Telex 77339.*
> *372 rooms.*

Don Pedro   2nd-class

> *Av. del Lido,* ☎ *238 68 44, FAX 238 37 83, Telex 77252.*
> *289 rooms.*

Isabel   2nd-class

> *Paseo Maritimo, 97* ☎ *238 17 44, FAX 238 11 98.*
> *Closed from Dec. through Feb.*
> *40 rooms.*

Meliá Costa del Sol   1st-class

> *Paseo Maritimo,* ☎ *238 66 77, FAX 238 64 17, Telex 77326.*
> *540 rooms.*

Sidi Lago Rojo   2nd-class

> *Miami, 5,* ☎ *238 76 66, FAX 238 08 91, Telex 77395.*
> *144 rooms.*

Fuengirola

Population: 30,606
Area code: 952; Zip code: 29640

> *16 km west along N-340.*

This town is a lesser version of Torremolinos without the compensations of liveliness and camp. Move on.

Marbella ★★★

Population: 67,882
Area code: 952; Zip code: 29600

> *27 km west of Fuengirola, and 43 km west of Torremolinos.*

The contrast between the two previous towns and this one could not be greater. Its name comes from *mar bella*, "beautiful sea," which is a slight exaggeration, but Marbella has grown into a haven for the rich and for those living richly for a week or two. The average income here ranks with the highest in Europe during the summer, and society pages the world over report on summer happenings. Hotels and villas line the beach for ten miles in each direction, and the huge yacht basin of Puerto Banús, seven km west, is filled all summer with almost 1000 impressive boats. Befitting the clientele, everything is expensive, although if money is not an object, one can live as well here as anywhere in the world.

Where to Stay

Marbella possesses the most luxurious hotels in the world, some with one or more world-class golf courses, others with every sport imaginable, some that act as spas that pamper, and others combining all of the above. But the cost of a double commonly breasts $200 per-night. Hotels do exist at more reasonable levels, however.

Very Expensive ($200+)

Puente Romano   Deluxe ★ ★ ★ ★ ★

On N-340 going west toward Gibraltar, three and one-half km outside of town, ☎ *277 01 00, FAX 277 57 66, Telex 77399.*

From kings to Stevie Wonder, this hotel has seen them all. They come for ever so tasteful rooms housed in separate buildings that dot lush grounds and, most of all, for the feeling of quiet intimacy. The gardens are tropical and full of unexpected paths and waterfalls. Yes, there is a small Roman bridge on the premises. Service and accommodations are deluxe in every way, and the tennis pro is Manolo Santana. *142 rooms, plus 67 suites.*

Los Monteros   Deluxe ★ ★ ★ ★

On N-340 going east toward Málaga, five and one-half km outside of town, ☎ *277 17 00, FAX 282 58 46, Telex 77059.*

Deluxe in every way, including its own private beach and a simply superb restaurant with French flavor. The atmosphere, on the other hand, is very quiet, intimate and British, but the rooms are bright and happy. *160 rooms, plus nine suites.*

Marbella Club   Deluxe ★ ★ ★

On N-340 going west toward Gibraltar, three km outside of town, ☎ *277 13 00, FAX 282 98 84, Telex 77319.*

This was the first of the grand hotels in the area, the one that turned Marbella into the haunt of the jet set. The surrounding grounds could hardly be more lovely, but the rooms are a mixed lot—from fabulous to barely adequate. Considering its prices which are the highest in the area, the place needs some work. *66 rooms, plus 24 suites.*

Expensive ($100–$200)

Hotel Don Carlos   Deluxe ★ ★ ★ ★

On N-340 going west toward Gibraltar, 10 km outside of town, ☎ *283 11 40, FAX 283 34 29, Telex 77481.*

Can you call a compound of 130 acres that rents rooms a hotel—or is it an estate, or even a small country? The hotel proper rises on pylons in a forest facing gardens that run for glorious square miles down to the loveliest beach in the Marbella area. While this one lacks the intimacy of the choices above, there is plenty of room for solitude in the gardens. *223 rooms, plus 15 suites.*

Moderate ($50–$99)

Naguele   R4th-class ★ ★

On N-340 going west toward Gibraltar, three and one-half km outside of town, ☎ *77 16 88.*

Open March through Oct. 15.

The irony is perfect: this hotel is just yards away from the two previous choices whose guests pay almost ten times as much. Of course you do not get their gor-

geous gardens, private beach or luxury rooms, but you do get the same quiet location. Note the small number of rooms, however—reservations are a must. *17
rooms.*

Inexpensive (Less than $50)

Lima   R2nd-class ★

Av. Antonio Belon, 2, ☎ *277 05 00, FAX 286 30 91.*

The architecture is not memorable, but these comfortable rooms are within two
blocks of the beach. *64 rooms.*

Where to Eat

Per square kilometer, Marbella offers more superb restaurants than anywhere else in
Spain. Though such fine meals are not inexpensive, prices tend to be fair and less than
what the hotel rates might lead you to expect. Nor do you have to dine elegantly to eat
well. **Mesón del Pollo**, across from the Hotel El Fuerte, does delectable chicken in a variety of styles for a pittance.

Expensive ($30+)

La Fonda   ★★★★

Pl. Santo Cristo, 10, ☎ *277 25 12.*
Open for dinner only, and closed Sun.

The restaurant is situated on a lovely square in a lovely old house filled with lovely
things—all contributing to the romance. The food ranges over French, Spanish and
Austrian (the nationality of the owner, who runs the famous Horcher in Madrid).
Every dish is close to perfect, and the desserts defy description. Reservations are
required. Credit Cards: A, D, M, V.

La Hacienda   ★★★

Nine km east along N-340 and an additional one and one-half km north, ☎ *283 12 67.*
*Closed Mon. (except in Aug.), Tues. (except in July and Aug.), and from the third week
of Nov. to the last week of Dec.*

The restaurant is housed in an elegant villa overlooking the sea. The food is sublime.
The chef is Belgian, and his lamb matches the best we ever tasted. Reservations are
required. Credit Cards: A, D, M, V.

Estepona ★

Population: 24,261
Area code: 952; Zip code: 29680

28 km west of Marbella on N-340, and 84 km west of Málaga.

Although the town itself is drab and developers have arrived in force, a
pleasant flowered promenade remains beside the pebble beach, and town
plazas retain their charms. The main business of Estepona is fishing. It maintains the largest fleet on the coast.

Where to Stay

In and around this town wait some of the best values along the coast.

Expensive ($100–$200)

Atalaya Park   Deluxe ★ ★ ★

12 km east along N-340 to Marbella, then turn at the sign, ☎ *288 48 01, FAX 288 57 35, Telex 77210.*
This is a huge complex that justifies consideration because it offers every facility you can imagine, including two golf courses, and because of its glorious gardens. *416 rooms, plus 32 suites.*

Moderate ($50–$99)

Santa Marta   3rd-class ★ ★ ★

11 km east along N-340 to Marbella, ☎ *278 07 16.*
Open April through Oct.
The hotel consists of bungalows around a beautiful garden, similar to some of Marbella's very, very expensive hotels. Although the rooms are by no means grand, and some are fading, the setting is as quiet and almost as lovely as what the expensive hotels provide at a small percentage of their price. *37 rooms.*

Inexpensive (Less than $50)

Buenavista   P2nd-class ★

Paseo Maritimo, 180, ☎ *80 01 37.*
Nothing grand here, but basic accommodations at fair prices add up to a good deal. There are even TVs in the air-conditioned rooms. Highway noise can be a problem, however. *38 rooms.*

Where to Eat

Inexpensive (Less than $15)

Benamara   ★

11 km east along N-340 to Marbella, one km before the turn to the Atalaya Park Hotel above, ☎ *288 37 67.*
Closed for lunch except Sun.
This is a simple roadside place that serves Moroccan dishes, and good ones at that. The couscous hits the spot, especially after a steady diet of Spanish food.

From Estepona N-340 goes west to San Roque in 35 km, the last part of which is scenic. Signs direct to La Linea, seven km south, the border for Gibraltar, and the end of the Costa del Sol.

Gibraltar ★ ★

Population: 28,339
Area code: 956; no zip code

From **Seville** *take either N-IV or the toll road A-4 (E-5) south toward Jerez in 84 km. Continuing past Jerez toward Cádiz, pick up N-340 at San Fernando in 38 km N-340 takes you to La Linea, the border, in 119 km. From* **Granada** *take N-342 for 92 km to exit #1 at Salinas, where you pick up N-351 to Málaga for 60 km. From Málaga follow the slow coast road N-340 for 120 km to the border. From*

Córdoba *take N-331 for 116 km to N-334 for one km east before pick-*
ing up N-331 again for a 57 km ride to Málaga. The slow coast
road, N-340, leads to the border in 120 km.

The "Rock," which natives refer to as "Gib," does indeed look like the
Prudential logo. It is a spit of land four miles long by half a mile wide, 90
percent of which is taken up by precipitous mountain. This was one of the
two ancient Pillars of Hercules, paired with the comparable peak of Gebel
Musa directly across the straits. It was the Phoenicians who promoted the
legend that the world ended at these straits in order to frighten others away
from their colonies farther west. The name "Gibraltar" comes from *Gebel
Tarik*, "Tarik's Mountain" in Arabic, named after the leader of the first
Moorish incursion into Spain. It was seized by the English in 1704 during
the War of Spanish Succession, ostensibly on behalf of the Hapsburgs, but
more likely so the British could control a base in the Mediterranean. Ever
since, this British colony has been a sore spot in Spain's side.

For decades the Spanish tried to isolate Gibraltar by barring entry from
Spain. But in 1985 the border at La Linea was opened and now is crossed by
thousands of tourists, many attracted by Gibraltar's freeport status for duty-
free liquor and VAT-free goods. Officially the currency is the British Pound
Sterling, but Spanish pesetas are accepted everywhere. Gibraltar has pleasant
beaches on its east side, the town on its west side and the Rock in between
with its caves and "apes." Half a day covers everything.

From the border at La Linea you cross the end of the airport field and funnel into Main Street, lined with pubs and duty free shops. At the end of the
street is the **cable car** ★★★ station *(closed Sun.)* for a ride to the top of the
rock. Buy a one-way ticket and walk to additional sights on the way down.
Halfway to the top the cable car stops at the **Apes' Den** ★★. The half-tame
monkeys, called apes because they are tailless, are a mischievous lot, so watch
cameras and anything loose they might grab. Feedings are at 8 a.m. and 4
p.m. The top of the Rock presents unrivaled views overlooking Europa Point
where the Atlantic and Mediterranean Oceans meet. On clear days Morocco
is visible 11 miles away.

From the top take Saint Michael's Road south to **Saint Michael's Cave**. This
was a hospital during the Second World War but now serves as an eerie au-
ditorium where summer concerts are held. Follow Queen's Road north to its
end for Upper Town Road and the **Gibraltar Laser Experience** ★ *(closed Sun.)*
which recreates World War II events and displays paraphernalia, all in a tun-
nel used for shelters during that war. Below it are the remains of a **Moorish
castle** from the 14th century. Steep alleys lead to the northern end of Main
Street. At Bomb House Lane on the right is the **Gibraltar Museum** (*closed
Sun.*), with exhibits depicting the history of Gibraltar, as well as some nicely
preserved Moorish baths. Opposite the museum stands the **tourist office**. The

Governors' Residence is at the next Main Street corner. Here, on special days of the year, one of those **Changing of the Guard** ★★ ceremonies is presented as only the British do them.

Where to Stay

Hotels tend to be expensive on Gibraltar, though there are a few moderate accommodations. But, the British reduced their military garrison by half in 1990 and it remains to be seen what impact that will have on the hotel situation.

Expensive ($100–$200)

The Rock Hotel   Deluxe ★★★★

3 Europa Road, ☎ *730 00, FAX 730 13, Telex 2238.*
This is the luxury hotel of Gibraltar, looking as a British colonial hotel should, with a huge terrace and ceiling fans. Refurbishing in pinks and oranges was completed recently to sustain its preeminent position on Gib. It overlooks the town from a lovely garden with views over town and sea. *143 rooms.*

Caleta Palace   1st-class ★★

Catalan Bay Road (on the west side of the isthmus), ☎ *765 01, FAX 710 50, Telex 2345.*
Here is a hotel for relaxing in style near some of the best beach on the isthmus. Every room presents beautiful sea views. *153 rooms.*

Moderate ($50–$99)

Bristol   2nd-class ★★

10 Cathedral Square, ☎ *768 00, Telex 2253.*
Located by the Cathedral in the heart of town, with a nice garden, this hotel manages to convey the sense of a colonial hotel. Wood paneling helps, as does the comfortable furniture in ample rooms. However, the prices were pushing the "moderate" limit when last we visited, and may have passed it by the time you arrive. *60 rooms.*

Queen's Hotel   3rd-class ★

1 Boyd Street, ☎ *740 00.*
Easy to find, next to the cable car station, this hotel has little character, but a game room, sun deck and agreeable service. The bedrooms are clean as a whistle and nicely decorated. *24 rooms.*

Where to Eat

None of the more expensive places seem worth their charges, but the pubs and fish-and-chips places lining Main Street remain fun for a meal or two.

Directory

Information
Located in Cathedral Square, near the governor's residence. ☎ *764 00.*

Post Office and Telephones
The post office is at *102 Main Street,* four blocks north of the governor's residence.

Police
The main station is on Irish Town Street, ☎ *725 00.*

Granada ★★★★★

Population: 262,182
Area code: 958; Zip code: 18000

> *From **Madrid** A-4 (E-5) runs south to Ocaña in 63 km, where N-IV (E-5) continues south to Bailén in 235 km more. From **Bailén**, N-323 (E-902) reaches Granada in 130 km, for a total trip of 427 km. From **Córdoba** N-432 goes directly southeast to Granada in 166 km. From **Seville** N-334 east toward Antequera changes its designation to N-342 at Salinas before completing a trip of 251 km.*

Only Granada in all the world presents the Thousand and One Nights in palpable reality. Granada did not stand among the major cities of the Moors during most of their 700-year reign in Spain, but as their last capital it constituted the culmination of an artistry so impressive that Christian conquerors could not bear to destroy it. For this reason the last palace of the Moors, the Alhambra, remains standing today.

Granada first attained prominence when Jaén was captured by the Spanish in 1246, forcing the Moorish ruler of the principality to move his capital southward. He chose Granada, which thus became the final capital of the dynasty of Nasrids, for his family name was Ibn el Ahmar Nasir. He learned from his defeat to deal with Christians rather than fight them. His successors used diplomacy to stave off the Christians, even allying with them to capture Seville, and by doing so prospered. But the Christians seized piece after piece of the rest of the Moorish empire, until Granada stood alone. Swollen with refugees from lost domains, Granada grew to 200,000 souls by the 14th century, about four times the London of those times, and construction began on the Alhambra Palace.

Toward the end of the 15th-century revolt weakened Granada. Caliph Muley Hassan fell in love with a Christian woman named *Zoraya* (Morning Star), who had converted to Islam. This love affair threatened the position of his principal wife who fled with her young son before the caliph could repudiate her. She marshalled supporters by citing the caliph's severe tax policies, then returned to depose the old caliph and placed her son Abu Abdallah, known to the Christians as Boabdil, on the throne. Granada's rule had fallen to a child-king who reigned over subjects divided into those supporting the young new caliph and those favoring the previous one. It was a perfect time to attack; Isabella and Ferdinand declared war. Twice Boabdil sallied forth with his army, and each time was captured and forced to cede territory. After the second loss, he vowed never to leave Granada again.

By 1491 the Christians had cut Granada off from the sea and all other avenues of supply, and settled in for a siege. Eight months later, on January 2,

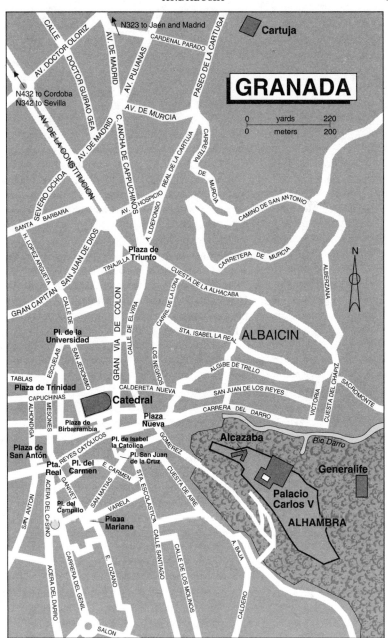

GRANADA

1492, the city surrendered and Boabdil marched away forever with tears in his eyes. The Catholic monarchs entered the city dressed in Moorish clothes to seal the end of 781 years of Moorish domination.

Within decades the Christians expelled the Moors from Spain and burned most of Granada, including all its mosques. Only the Alhambra remained untouched for its beauty lent it a sanctity. Although Ferdinand and Isabella chose this city as their final resting place, decline continued. The last blow was the expulsion in 1609 of the Moroscos, people of Moorish descent, depleting Granada of most of its population. By the 18th century the city numbered less than 50,000 citizens. But through good times and bad, the stream of visitors never abated. The most famous tourist was Washington Irving, who lived for three months in the ruins of the Alhambra Palace and there began his evocative *Tales of the Alhambra*. Today both tourism and revitalized agriculture have again brought prosperity to Granada.

Situated in the low foothills of the Sierra Nevada, the city encompasses three peaks in a row—the Alhambra sits on the middle and highest, north of which the smaller hill of Sacromonte rises, and Monte Mauror stands to its south. Most of the city proper lies in the valley below these hills and west, although the Albaicín, the old quarter, nestles between the two hills of the Alhambra and Sacromonte. Unforgettable views from the lower city show the Alhambra shining atop its hill against a backdrop of the snow-clad Sierra Nevada.

Note: Granada also retains a significant Gypsy population, as visitors discover. The women sell flowers, while the men hover around. They can be very insistent; and valuables should be carefully watched.

Parking is available on the Alhambra hill, but parking in the city below is far from the sights. The best course is to begin at the Alhambra, walk or taxi down, then taxi back up to your car.

*From **Madrid** and north, Granada is entered on Av. de Madrid, which arrives at a traffic circle just after passing the University on the left. Take Av. de la Constitución to the left. At the next intersection, in one very long block past a park, go left on Av. del Hospicio, then right at the first opportunity onto Av. Andaluces. Round the circle at Pl. del Triunfo to continue out the opposite end on C. Elvira. Elvira ends in about ten blocks at C. Reyes Católicos. Turn left here into the Pl. Nueva, and take the first right onto the narrow Cuesta de Gomerez, which leads through the gate to the Alhambra precinct. Signs direct to the Alhambra Palace and parking.*

*From **Córdoba** and west Granada is entered on Av. de la Constitución. After passing a large park on the left, follow the directions from Madrid above. From the **Costa del Sol** and south traffic funnels* *into Acara del Casino which ends at the large Pl. Puerta Real. Take the large street right, Reyos Católicos, for about eight blocks to the Pl. Nueva. The right at the far end of the plaza, the narrow Cuesta de Gomerez, leads in six blocks through the gate to the Alhambra Precinct. Signs direct to the Alhambra Palace and parking.*

The **Alhambra Palace** ★★★★★ ranks at the top of any list of the most beautiful and fascinating buildings in the world. As a bonus the **Alcazaba** ★, a 13th-century fortress, stands beside it, the stunning Renaissance **palace of Carlos V** ★★ abuts it, and the lovely summer palace of the Moors, the **Generalife** ★★★, perches above. The Alhambra Precinct alone requires rushing to complete in half a day. In the city proper below the Alhambra is the moving and elegant **Capilla Real** ★★★, the burial place of Ferdinand and Isabella, beside an impressive **Cathedral** ★. The old quarter of the **Albaicín** ★ is worth exploring, for it is a maze of whitewashed houses with beautiful patios that afford lovely views of the Alhambra above. Two churches merit a look—the **Carthusian Monastery** ★, north of the city center, and **San Juan de Dios** ★, not far from the Cathedral. By hurrying and hitting only highpoints, Granada can be covered in a day, but is much more enjoyable in two.

Alhambra Precinct

Puerta de las Granadas, ☎ *22 75 27.*

Hours open: Mon.–Sat. 9 a.m.–8 p.m. (closes at 6 p.m. in winter). Open Sun. 9:30 a.m.–6 p.m. Illuminated in the summer on Tues., Thurs. and Sat. nights from 10 p.m.–midnight (in winter on Sat. 8–10 p.m.), for a separate charge of 625 ptas.

A steep climb begins before passing through the entry gate to the precinct. This gate, the *Puerta Las Granadas* (Pomegranates' Gate) was erected by Carlos V in 1536 on the site of a former Moorish portal. Past this entrance waits an enchanted forest where everything suddenly quiets in stands of stately elms, planted by the duke of Wellington in the 19th century. Signs direct pedestrians to the **Puerta de la Justicia**, their entrance, and cars to the **Puerta de Coches**, by a roundabout but scenic route. One combined ticket serves all the sights, but the proper order in which to visit the various sights is an issue. The best course is to see the palace of Carlos V first, for it pales after the Alhambra, and the same point holds for the Alcazaba. Then see the Alhambra, followed by the lovely walk to the gardens of the Generalife. However, this timing is made difficult by the fact that tickets now prescribe set times of entry to the Alhambra and palácio. Do not miss your appointed time, for the ticket is invalid thereafter. If possible, go early in the day before the crowd collects. *Admission: 625 ptas. for the Alhambra Palace, Alcazaba, Generalife and palace of Carlos V; free after 3 p.m. on Sun.*

Note: The government now limits the number of visitors per day. Go early in the day to ensure admittance.

The palace of Carlos V lies directly ahead, if entering from the Puerta de la Justicia, or to the left, if entering from the Puerta de Coches.

Palácio de Carlos V

Because he so loved the site, Carlos V wanted a palace of his own adjoining the Alhambra, though his love was not so pure that it prevented him from destroying about a third of the Alhambra Palace—all the private royal rooms—to gain space. As his architect he used the Italian Machuca, who had trained with Michelangelo, to plan a severely neoclassical structure. The design is wholly elegant, so much that it seems too austere to inhabit, although it delights as pure design.

The plan is a circle inside a square. The outer face emphasizes two stories with rows of regular windows distinguished by alternating piedmonts and circles above, and separated by Ionic pilasters on the upper story. Inside comes the shock of a huge open circular patio formed of simple Doric columns below and Ionic columns above, with recesses intended for statues. On at least one occasion a bullfight was held in this patio. The original plan included a huge dome to cover the central patio, but the building was never finished and seems never to have been inhabited, in fact, by Carlos V or by anyone else.

To the left, on the ground floor, is the **Museo de Art Hispano-Musuleman** *(open Mon.–Fri. 10 a.m. to 2 p.m.; admission: 250 ptas.)*. It contains objects found in the Alhambra area, including pieces of original decoration, a cistern with lions attacking gazelles and a huge blue 14th-century pitcher almost as tall as a person. On the second floor is the **Museo de Bellas Artes** *(open Tues.–Sun. 10 a.m. to 2 p.m.; admission: 250 ptas.)*. It displays works by Granada artists, including paintings by Cano, but also a fine Limoges enamel triptych of the Crucifixion from the early 16th century.

Alcazaba

To the left (west) of the Palácio de Carlos V is an open area known as the Pl. de los Aljibes (cisterns). The reservoir beneath was constructed by the Catholic monarchs to collect water, for the Christians did not know how to work the existing Moorish water system. The Alcazaba stands to the left (west) of this plaza.

A fortress (*alcazaba*) has existed on this eminently defensible site since the 10th century, though the present structure dates from the 13th. The fortress adds a 12-foot thickness of wall to that surrounding the entire Alhambra precinct. Sturdy square towers gave defenders secure places from which to fire down on attackers. The one in the northwest corner, called the **Torre de le Vela**, was that from which Cardinal Mendoza, sent ahead to ascertain that the town was safe, raised the flag of Christian Spain to signal that the city was theirs at last. Today it offers splendid views over the city and the Alhambra Palace, with the Sierra Nevada behind. A plaque nearby quotes the haunting lament of a Moorish poet: Nothing is sadder than to be blind in Granada.

Alhambra Palace

Ibn el Ahmar Nasir (a.k.a. Muhammad I), founder of the Nasrid dynasty, began a palace on this site in the 13th century, but little of the original remains. Of what survives, the Court of Myrtles was built for Yusuf I in the middle of the 14th century, the Court of the Lions for Muhammad V near the end of that century and the Tower of the Infantas for Muhammad VII at the close of the 14th century.

The facade is of no architectural interest, for Islamic palaces are intended as private places, and hide all luxury from public view. Further, tradition called for each new ruler to add rooms of his own, rather than occupy his predecessor's quarters. Thus, the palace is a compound consisting of numerous rooms, rather than a unified structure. However, the Alhambra did separate into three distinct areas. One contained the living accommodations for the caliph. That part was destroyed to build Carlos V's palace. Another consisted of public rooms for ceremonies—such as audiences with the caliph or his ministers—and for music, or other entertainments. Several of these survive—the Mexuar, Hall of the Ambassadors, Kings' Chamber, Hall of the Two Sisters and Abencerrajes Gallery. A final part sheltered the close staff of the caliph, most importantly his harem. Note that the names today applied to the rooms are generally fanciful and give little indication of original names or uses.

No consideration was given to permanence or future generations in designing these rooms, they served only for the enjoyment of one owner. Construction was of brick, wood and, especially, stucco, molded and carved into the most intricate designs then painted and gilded, but eminently perishable. In 1591 gunpowder exploded outside the walls near the Court of the Lions, causing great damage. In the 19th century French troops left explosives when they retreated from bivouac here, which fortunately did not go off. But in general, centuries of neglect exacted a heavy toll on such fragile materials.

Reconstruction has been under way for almost a century. If what you see looks too new to be original, that is because it is, but all has been restored with the greatest authenticity to suggest the original.

Still, the feeling of these rooms would have been quite different from what you see today, for they would have been furnished, Persian carpets would have lined the floors, metal and glass lanterns would have bounced soft light off brightly painted decorative wood and stucco. The miracle of the Alhambra is that despite reconstruction and the loss of furniture and paint it still captivates as few other buildings can. Very likely its appeal is for the way of life this architecture presents, so different from anything Western. There is no attempt to awe with size, only with beauty. No room is farther than a few feet from an outdoor patio playing water for both its sight and sound, and gardens are never more than a step away. Nature and artifice cohabit more intimately than in our western buildings.

Entrance is into the **Mexuar**, from the Arabic *Mashwar*, "audience chamber." Its balcony was added when Isabella and Ferdinand remodeled this room as a chapel and still bears traces of 15th-century painted design. At the end of the room Isabella and Ferdinand added an oratory which involved lowering the original floor, for Christians preferred to stand to look out of windows, while Moors sat. The exit door on the left was cut through the walls for us tourists.

That doorway leads to the **Patio de Cuarto Dorado**, redecorated in Mudejar style after the Reconquest but with an elegant low fountain. Across the patio is the facade of the **Palace of Comares**, from 1370, which serves as a fine sample of the Alhambra aesthetic. Simple rectangular portals are surrounded by the most refined carved stucco designs. Windows above are fitted with intricate wooden screens, *mashrabia*, to allow the ladies of the court to look out without being seen. The left portal leads to royal apartments; the right once admitted to administrative offices, no longer existing.

Take the left portal into a small room then go left again into the glorious **Patio de Los Arrayanes** (Court of the Myrtles). A central reflecting pool is lined by Myrtle bushes. By reflection the pool doubles the arcades at both ends to emphasize the harmony of simple arches and ornate decoration. The center arch is higher than the others to display a more ornate arch behind it that leads into an end room. Around the sides of the pool repose four sets of chambers for wives, with alcoves for their divans, but little surviving decoration. The room at the far end (south) was destroyed to construct the palace of Carlos V.

Before entering the near end, notice the fine carved design of its original doors. They lead into the apartment for the caliph, the **Sala de la Barca**, with alcoves on either end for divans showing that it served as a bedroom. A lovely wood ceiling above places a half dome on either end so the caliph could see "stars" as he closed his eyes. At the rear is the magnificent **Solón de Embajadores** (Room of the Ambassadors), the audience chamber of the palace. Here the caliph would sit in the recess of the center window, framed and made dazzling by its light, to receive embassies. Decoration on the walls of amazing complexity would have been even more startling with original paint, and almost prevents the eyes from rising to an astonishing ceiling that ascends to a dome symbolizing heaven.

Return to the Patio de los Arrayanes and follow the left side to the next to last portal, the open one. Before going though to one of the great wonders of the Alhambra, enter the end arcade for a look at the basement of the palace of Carlos V, just to remember how cold Christian architecture became two centuries after the Alhambra. It seems altogether inhuman after a taste of the Moors.

Through the portal, after a small chamber for a caliph's wife, comes the **Sala de los Mozárabes**, whose ceiling was once highly praised before it suffered great damage from an explosion.

But it is difficult to concentrate on this room when the **Patio de los Leones** beckons. The hall opens to a pavilion of slender columns with unique capitals supporting stalactite arches and domes. Across the way, past the fountain, is the pavilion's twin. The fountain rests on the backs of twelve charming lions who give the patio its name. Various state apartments ring the patio with entrances off a columned arcade.

In the center of the right side is the **Sala de los Abencerrajes**, named for a clan who supported Boabdil and his mother in their rebellion against the reigning caliph. Tradition says the former caliph murdered the leaders of this family before ceding his throne and sees remains of that blood in stains on the floor. The doors are lovely and the stalactite ceiling is a wonder.

At the far end of the patio is the **Sala de los Reyes**, three rooms in a row named for the painting of ten seated Moors over the central room. (The Christians believed that Moors had kings.) Given Islamic strictures against painted figures, these 14th-century paintings on leather probably were executed by Christians.

Off to the left side of the patio is the **Sala de las Dos Hermanas** (Two Sisters), fancifully named for two marble slabs in the pavement, although the room may indeed once have formed part of the harem. It possesses the most amazing of the surviving stalactite, or honeycombed, domed ceilings said to contain 5000 individual cells. How it manages to be beautiful amid the incredible detail is one of art's mysteries. The walls too are rich in decoration. The Arabic inscription that looks so elegant, actually commemorates the circumcision of a caliph's son. Opposite the entrance, a window retains the only surviving Moorish shutter in the palace, although most windows originally had them.

A portal at the rear lets into the **Sala de los Ajimeces**, named for the windows of its porch that give a lovely view of the **Patio de Lindaraja** below, originally with a reflecting pool like the other patios. Once more the ceilings are worth admiring.

A corridor at the end leads across the patio to rooms remodeled by Carlos V. It was here that Washington Irving stayed to study the beauties and myths of the Alhambra. At the far end of these apartments a modern corridor runs to the **Tocador de la Reina** (queen's dressing room) in a tower, remodeled by Elizabeth of Parma, wife of Felipe V, and hung with paintings.

Stairs descend to a patio with four cypresses where a sign points to **baños** (baths). These were the original *hamman*, or bath, of the palace, today in the form of a remodeling by Carlos V.

Cross the Patio de Lindaraja to enter the main gardens of the Alhambra. Ahead and to the left is the **Torre de las Damas**, the oldest surviving part of the palace—dating from the beginning of the 14th century—and not in the best condition. The pool is watched over by two Moorish lions rescued from a hospital in the city below. The pavilion now is simple, since columns have replaced the original carved stucco piers in the rear wall, but the tower retains some fine workmanship inside.

Several other towers in the Alhambra walls are worth visiting, especially the **Torre de la Captiva** (Imprisoned Woman), a miniature palace three towers farther along the walls, and the **Torre del las Infantas** (Princesses), next in line and late in period but sumptuously decadent.

From the Torre de las Infantas, it is worth a minute to return in the direction of the palace to visit the **Parador de San Francisco** in the center of the gardens. Once this was a convent in whose chapel the bodies of Isabella and Ferdinand rested while waiting completion of their tombs in the lower town. Return to the Torre de las Infantas where a gate, a little farther along the wall, lets out to a cypress-lined walk up to the Generalife.

Generalife ★★★

Its present name is a distortion of the Arabic *Jennat al Arife*, "Garden of the Architect." This was a summer retreat for the caliph and his court, placed higher on the

Alhambra hill to capture breezes. Originally, it would have been rustic and a working farm, though today it has been reconstructed into formal gardens. The building is arranged around a central court in which, as usual for the Moors, water flows. Both short sides of the building contain graceful pavilions. A gallery for views over the Alhambra Palace runs along the near long side. On the far side were apartments for the caliph and his entourage, but compared to the luxuries of the palace, the Generalife is simple and fresh.

While a taxi back to the city is not expensive, it is pleasant to walk from the Alhambra hill if feet are not too tired. Simply head downhill. After a couple of hundred yards to the gate of Puerta las Granada, Cuesta de Gomerez leads to the Pl. Nueva in about five blocks. A left turn onto the large C. Reyes Católicos brings the busy Pl. de Isabel la Católica in five blocks more. Head right along Gran Via de Colón to take the second left down C. de los Oficios. The **Palácio Madraza** *is passed on the left, with painted 18th-century facade. It was Granada's university under the Moors. Inside is an octagonal Mudejar room with nice decoration and dome, and the Sala de Babildos with a fine ceiling. (Open 9 a.m. to 2 p.m.; admission is free.) On the right, a little farther along the alley, is the entrance to the* **Capilla Real***, and still farther along is the* **Cathedral***.*

Capilla Real   ★★★★

C. de los Oficios, ☎ *22 92 39.*

Hours open: daily 10:30 a.m.–1 p.m. and 4–7 p.m. (until 6 p.m. in winter).

In her will Isabella asked to be buried with Ferdinand at whichever place he chose. Ferdinand selected Granada, the site of his greatest victory. In 1506, two years after Isabella's death, a mausoleum was begun by Enrique de Egas under Ferdinand's direction and finished in 1521, five years after Ferdinand's death. The art this chapel contains, the beauty of the tombs and their historical importance makes this one of the most moving sights in Spain.

Behind an uninspired facade lies an interior composed of every element of the developed Isabelline style. Emblems of the Catholic monarchs are everywhere, including their well-known arrow and yoke motif (the first letter of the Spanish word for arrow and for yoke was the same as the first letter in Ferdinand and Isabella's name). Entry is through the sacristy—two simple rooms made splendid by the art inside them.

The paintings are the original collection of Isabella and demonstrate both her deep religious devotion and surprisingly refined aesthetic sense. Here are some masterpieces, seldom reproduced, from the 15th century and earlier. Paintings include a wonderful *Cristo Muerto* by Roger van der Weyden, a very interesting Botticelli, a fine *San Juan Evangelista* by Berruguete, and four spectacular Memlings, among others. Also on display are Isabella's crown and scepter, some needlework by her own hand, and the sword of Ferdinand. Adorning the walls are banners flown by the Christian army during the conquest of Granada.

The adjoining chapel seems surprisingly small for figures that loom so large in history. Near the entrance, in the finest Italian marble, are the effigies of Ferdinand and Isabella. Farther back and standing slightly higher are effigies of their daughter, Juana the Mad, and her husband, Philip the Handsome—the parents of Carlos V. The carvings of Ferdinand and Isabella hold the greatest interest for the personages represented, and suggest true if idealized likenesses of that famed pair. However, the faces are difficult to see without a ladder—climb the pulpit for the best look. Nonetheless, the other pair of carvings—of Juana and Philip—are artistically superior, the masterpiece of Bartolome Ordoñez. In the crypt below lie the actual lead coffins, unadorned, each under its corresponding effigy. The small fifth casket holds a niece of Juana's.

The retable at the altar is among the first in the Plateresque style, and its panels depict the capture of Granada and conversion of the infidels. Kneeling painted statues of Ferdinand and Isabella that seem to be true portraits, by the great Diego de Siloé, flank the retable. *Admission: 200 ptas.; Sun. free.*

Cathedral ★

Gran Via de Colón, ☎ 22 29 59.
Hours open: same hours and ticket as the Capilla Real; Sun. free.
After finishing the Capilla Real, its architect Egas was commissioned by Carlos V to design an adjoining cathedral. To Carlos the chapel was not sufficiently impressive to memorialize his illustrious grandparents. Seven years later the great architect Diego de Siloé took over the job, though the Cathedral was not finished until 1714. Given its purpose and the talent that worked on it, the Cathedral should be wonderful. Unfortunately, it is not a success, although interesting in its parts.

The main facade is due to Granada's great artist, Alonso Cano (buried inside). It is simple in design but heavy in feeling. Inside, soaring ceilings seem to bear down on too massive piers. What is original about the interior is the main altar, set in a huge circular niche with arches cut through to a circling ambulatory. The effect, though interesting, detracts from the importance of the altar. The upper gallery in the rotunda above the altar contains some fine paintings by Cano, and the stained glass higher up is the finest 16th century work. But the loveliest part of the Cathedral is the doorway in the south transept. This was the original door to the Capilla Real and is harmonious Isabelline work.

The streets south of the Cathedral are known as the **Alcaicería***. They formed the silk bazaar under the Moors, but it burned in 1843. Today it is reconstructed as a warren of souvenir shops. The baroque church of* **San Juan de Dios** *is nearby, and the charming quarter of the* **Albaicín** *is not far. For the church, follow C. San Jerónimo that goes north from the middle of the north face of the Cathedral. In about eight short blocks, turn right on the large C. San Juan de Dios for two blocks to the church on the left.*

San Juan de Dios ★

C. San Juan de Dios, ☎ 27 57 00.
Hours open: daily 10 a.m.–1 p.m. and 2–6 p.m.

Juan de Robles was a Portuguese of Jewish descent who devoted his life to the sick and needy. He was canonized for founding the Order of the Knights Hospitallers and the adjoining hospital was established in his memory in 1552, two years after his death. The church was added in the 18th century. Its facade is admirable and the inside is a glittering baroque fantasy, culminating in the churrigueresque high altar. Behind the altar is Juan's tomb. The patio of the still-functioning hospital that precedes the church is a painted Renaissance beauty. *Admission: 150 ptas.*

For the Albaicín, return to the Pl. Nueva.

Albaicín   ★★

Covering the slope facing the Alhambra is the Albaicín, the surviving part of Moorish Granada. Still a maze of twisting alleys and whitewashed houses—some dilapidated, some with splendid patios inside, and some veritable mansions—the Albaicín offers something worth seeing at every step.

Head east along the Pl. Nueva, passing the early 16th-century **Audiencia** in the northwest corner. The **Pl. Santa Anna** is reached in one block, containing a church by Diego de Siloé from 1548 with a graceful tower and fine portal. From the north side of the church Carrera del Darro leads east along the banks of the tiny Darro River. The Albaicín hugs the north side of the steeply rising hill.

After the second bridge, **Moorish baths** (*Baños Arabes*) stand at number 31 (open 10 a.m. to 2 p.m. and 3–6 p.m.; admission free). Nothing of the decoration remains except star-shaped ceiling vents that once contained colored glass. About two blocks farther on the left is the **Convent of Santa Cataline de Zafra** from 1540 which incorporates a Moorish house. The **Casa de Castril** from 1539 follows at number 43, with a splendid facade of scallop shells and a phoenix. The house belonged to Bernardo Zafra, a treasurer to Queen Isabella, and today is the local archaeological museum (open Tues.–Sat. 10 a.m. to 2 p.m.; admission: 200 ptas.). The patios inside are lovely, although the collection is of minor interest. Opposite is **Santos Pedro y Pablo** with a fine Mudejar ceiling from 1576.

Walk five short blocks along the continuation, called the Paseo de Padre Manjon, pausing for awesome views of the Alhambra walls on high. At the end, Cuesta del Chapiz goes left. The **Casa de Chapiz** at number 14 is a 16th-century Morosco (a Moor who converted to Christianity) house with lovely garden. Going right, the Camino del Sacromonte leads up the hill of that name. Here Gypsies inhabit these caves furnished as homes. None still live in these caves, but they are preserved as tourist traps. The homes are interesting to see, but beware the Gypsies—carry no more cash than you can afford to lose.

Otherwise, continue along Cuesta de Chapiz to the first true street going left. It winds up to reach the church of **San Nicholas** in about three blocks, from whose terrace are the finest views of the Alhambra. Then wander back through the Albaicín to admire patios fortuitously glimpsed through vestibules and gates along the way.

La Cartuja is two km north of the center of town and reached by driving west from the Pl. Nueva along Carrera del Darro. After the street changes its name to Passeo del Padre Manion, it turns north and changes its name again to Cuesta del Chapiz. It bends left, then turns right and changes its name, for the last time, to C. Pages, before ending at a "T." Go left on Carretera de Murcia as it winds up the hill to the monastery.

La Cartuja ★

Caomp de Añfácar, ☎ 20 19 32. Bus number 8 from the front of the Cathedral goes here.

Hours open: daily 10 a.m.–1 p.m. and 4–7 p.m. (closes at 6 p.m. in winter).

This church was redecorated in 1662 at the height of the baroque period and stands as one of the finest examples of that exuberant style, a constant surprise to the eye. In a way it brings you back to Europe after a visit to the Moorish Alhambra. The altar is a swirl of brown and white marble, frosted by molded stucco, beneath a painted dome. The sacristy is admirable for its marquetry doors, vestment chests and walls inlaid with silver, tortoiseshell and ivory. In the monastery proper hangs a series of paintings by a former monk—martyrdoms that luxuriate in blood. *Admission: 250 ptas.*

Where to Stay

Granada provides a good selection of hotels, but it is also heavily visited so it is wise to reserve ahead in busy seasons. Your choice will be between staying on the Alhambra Hill, for its quiet and views, or sleeping in the city below. In the city proper ask for rooms in the back of hotels to minimize noise.

On the Alhambra hill:

Expensive ($100–$200)

Parador de San Francisco   1st-class ★ ★ ★ ★

Alhambra, Granada (in the palace precinct, follow signs), ☎ 22 14 40, FAX 22 22 64, Telex 78792.

This was a monastery built at the end of the 15th century and for its first two decades employed the monks in watching and praying over the bodies of Ferdinand and Isabella while awaiting permanent tombs in the Capilla Real. Today's parador faces its own lovely patio on one side and the Alhambra gardens on the other. A better location can hardly be imagined. Rooms in the original wing have character, antiques and very expensive prices; those in the new wing are more ordinary at lower charges. This is the most heavily booked parador in Spain with a long waiting list. Reserve very early if you want to ensure getting a room. *38 rooms.*

Alhambra Palace   Deluxe ★ ★ ★

Pena Partida, 2, Granada (continue on the main road through the Alhambra hill to the circle where signs direct you left for the Alhambra, but turn right), ☎ 22 14 68, FAX 22 64 04, Telex 78400.

The hotel was done at the turn of the century in Moorish style with arches, bright tiles, and wooden ceilings that make it a fantasy appropriate to its location. The terrace bar faces the Sierra Nevada and rooms overlook either the town or the same beautiful mountains. The rooms are large and comfortably designed, although the public spaces are showing signs of wear. Indeed deterioration has reached the point where the only acceptable accommodations are those on the top floor, which provide spectacular views as well. We have also heard complaints about sloppy service and mis-additions on the bill. This is *not* a deluxe hotel. *132 rooms.*

Moderate ($50–$99)

América   4th-class ★ ★

Real de la Alhambra, 53, Granada (fifty feet south of the Parador), ☎ *22 74 71, FAX 22 74 70.*

Open Mar.–Nov. 9.

This flower-bedecked gem beats the location of the government parador by 50 feet. It is an utterly charming place to stay, but already discovered so its few rooms must be booked months in advance. *12 rooms, plus one suite.*

Alixare   1st-class ★

Av. de los Alixares, Granada (continue straight when signs for the Alhambra Palace direct you left), ☎ *22 55 75 FAX 22 41 02 Telex 78523.*

At the furthest reaches of the Alhambra hill, this hotel offers quiet and a pool. It is otherwise undistinguished and often filled by package-tour groups. *168 rooms, plus one suite.*

In the city proper:

Expensive ($100–$200)

Princesa Ana   1st-class ★ ★ ★

Av. de la Constitución, 37, Granada (on the main street into the city, opposite the bull-ring and just before the train station, about one mile northwest of the Cathedral), 5☎ *28 74 47, FAX 27 39 54.*

Although modern (built in 1989), white marble and peach-pink decorative tones make this easily the most elegant hostelry in town. The bedrooms are lovely, the prices are correct and a taxi solves any problem about the distance from the sights. *nine rooms, plus one suites.*

Moderate ($50–$99)

Victoria   1st-class ★ ★ ★

Puerta Real, 3, Granada (this main plaza of the city is a few blocks east of the Cathedral along C. de Reyes Católicos), ☎ *25 77 00, FAX 26 31 08, Telex 78427.*

This Granada establishment that never was the best in town has acquired charm with the years. The location is first rate, although on a very noisy square, and the unassuming lobby hides more interesting, rather posh, public spaces and rooms recently redone. For its character and location, it's a better choice than the Meliá below. *69 rooms.*

Meliá Granada   1st-class ★ ★

Angel Ganivet, 7, Granada (due south of the Cathedral on a street running southeast from the large Pl. Puerta Real), ☎ *22 74 00, FAX 22 74 03, Telex 78429.*

A modern, businessperson's hotel that is professionally managed, pristine and charges fair prices. *191 rooms, plus six suites.*

Inglaterrra   2nd-class ★

Cetti Meriem, 4, Granada (this street is directly behind the rear of the Cathedral, off C. Gran Via de Colón), ☎ *22 15 58, FAX 22 71 00.*

Brand new in 1992, the place sparkles with good taste. Bedrooms are comfortable and sufficiently large. *36 rooms.*

Inexpensive (Less than $50)

Kenia   2nd-class ★ ★

C. Molinos, 65, Granada (at the southeast extreme of the city), ☎ *22 75 06.*
Ensconced in a former small mansion located in a quiet part of town, the rooms are simple, but the garden is lovely. Antiques dot the public rooms and the prices are low, although pushing the inexpensive limit. As it is some distance from the sights, it is best for those with a car. *16 rooms.*

Macía   3rd-class ★ ★

Pl. Nueva, 4, Granada, ☎ *22 75 36, FAX 22 35 75.*
This sparkler of a reasonably-priced hotel is located on the pleasant Pl. Nueva, central to the sights of the Alhambra above and the town below. Floors are marble, the rooms light and airy, most are air-conditioned and the prices are low. *40 rooms.*

Sacromonte   3rd-class ★

Pl. del Lino, 1, Granada (Walk away from the facade of the Cathedral on C. Marqués de Gerona for three blocks to C. Alhondga, then turn left for two blocks.), ☎ *26 64 11, FAX 26 67 07.*
This very pleasant hotel is located in the heart of town on a quiet plaza. Rooms are white with pink bedspreads and somewhat spartan for our taste. *33 rooms.*

Hostal-Residencial Lisboa   **P3rd-class**

Pl. del Carmen, 27, Granada (this is the plaza off C. de los Reyos Católicos just before the Pl. Real), ☎ *22 14 13.*
This one is very inexpensive so anything you get is a plus. What you receive is a decent sized room with a pleasant bath. Forget the furniture. *28 rooms.*

Youth Hostel

Albergue Juvenil Granada

C. Ramón y Cajal, 2, Granada (from the train (or bus) station walk west (or east) to the wide Camino de Ronda, then north to the gravel path at its end), ☎ *27 26 38, FAX 28 52 85.*
Newly renovated, and there are nothing but double rooms for the reasonable price of 1000 ptas. There is no curfew.

Where to Eat

Granada has a reputation as a dining wasteland. In fact there are several fine restaurants in town and outside; it is only the average that could stand improving.

Expensive ($30+)

Ruta del Veleta   ★ ★ ★

Carretera de Sierra Nevada, 50; six km southeast of Granada (from the Pl. Real head south along Carrera del Genil, left on Paseo del Salón, then continue on Paseo de la Bomba following signs to "Pico del Veleta and Sierra Nevada"), ☎ *48 61 34.*
Closed Sun. eve.
Granada's loveliest restaurant is this large one, outside the city. The dining room spreads blue and white ceramics around and overhead to lend both elegance and hominess. The food is first rate—from grilled meat to fish—the wines superb, and the service polished. Reservations are strongly advised. Credit Cards: A, D, M, V.

Sevilla   ★ ★

Oficios, 12 (in the alley opposite the Capilla Real), ☎ *22 88 62.*

Closed Sun. evening.

This is the most famous restaurant in Granada, as celebrity pictures indicate, although not particularly touristy. It is charmingly decorated with tiles lining intimate dining rooms. This is the place to try Andalusian specialties, such as *sopa sevillana* (with fish), *cordero al la pastoril* (spicy lamb stew) and *rape a la granadina* (monkfish in a shrimp and mushroom sauce). Reservations are advised. Credit Cards: A, D, M, V.

Cunini   ★★

Pescaderia, 9 (two short blocks south of the Cathedral front, in the Alcaicería), ☎ *25 07 77.*

Closed Mon.

The decor is simple but precise, and seafood is perfectly prepared. Without question this is the best seafood restaurant in town, try the fritura to prove it. Credit Cards: A, D, M, V.

Moderate ($15–$30)

Alcaicería   ★

Placeta de la Alcaicería (down an alley to the left off C. de los Oficios), ☎ *22 43 41.*

Three lovely dining areas surround a patio, all white and green and light. The good taste extends to the food.

Inexpensive (Less than $15)

Mesón Andaluz   ★

Elvira, 17 (across Gran Via de Colón, 2 blocks east of the Cathedral), ☎ *25 86 61.*

Closed Tuesday and the second half of February.

Inexpensive restaurants line this street, but this mesón is the best. It looks perfectly Andalusian inside and serves imaginative food for this lower price-range. Credit Cards: A, D, M, V.

Directory

Information

Located at *Pl. Mariana Pineda, 10* (☎ *22 66 88*). From the Cathedral head two blocks south to Pl. Isabel la Católica, then right onto Reyes Católicos for five blocks to Puerta Real. Take Ángel Gariver, the hard right, for three blocks. Open Mon.-Fri. 10 a.m. to 1 p.m. and 4-7 p.m., Sat. from 10 a.m. to 1 p.m. The trip is worth it for the free map of the Alhambra and city.

Airport

 A small airport (☎ *44 70 81*) 17 km outside of town serves Madrid and Barcelona twice per day (only once on Sunday) and provides the same service to Barcelona. The Iberia office is at *Pl. de Isabel la Católica, 2*, one block south of the Cathedral along Gran Via de Colón (☎ *22 75 92*). A shuttle bus runs from here to the plane.

Trains and Buses

The train station at the end of Av. Andaluces can be reached by following Gran Via de Colón north for a mile and a half (☎ *27 12 72*). Trains connect with Madrid two times a day, taking from seven hours on the fastest, which costs about 5000 ptas., to eight and a half hours on slower trains for half the price. Málaga in the Costa del Sol can be reached by three trains. Seville is served three times a day for

1500 ptas., and connections are possible for other destinations. The downtown RENFE office is at *C. de los Reyes Católicos, 63* (☎ *22 71 70).*

Several bus companies divide the available routes, which means that the place of departure depends on the destination. Alsina Gráells handles most of the Andalusia destinations, at *Camino de Ronda, 97,* a mile due west of the Cathedral (☎ *25 13 58).* More distant routes are the domain of Bacoma on *Av. Andaluces, 12,* near the train station (☎ *28 42 51).* A trip to Madrid costs as much or more than the low cost train fare, but is faster. Bus #11 goes to both bus stations and the train from Gran Via Colón and Puerta Real.

Shopping

The Alcaicería is a warren of souvenir shops where you will see examples of the local blue and white ceramic. However, the top quality is sold at *Ceramica Arabe* (☎ *20 12 27)* in the *Pl. San Isidro, 5.* This square is located a half mile north of the Cathedral, past the Hospital Real, a block east of Av. de la Constitución.

Post Office and Telephones

The main post office is at Puerta Real, the main traffic plaza south of the Cathedral. Telephones are available at *C. de los Reyes Católicos, 55.* It remain open until 10 p.m.

Police

The main station is in Pl. del Carmen, the northeast corner of the Puerta Real (☎ *091,* for emergencies).

Excursions

Granada is a good base from which to visit **Úbeda** and **Baeza**, both described under separate headings in this chapter. The **Costa del Sol**, described earlier, is also near. The natural tour is to visit **Córdoba**, less than two hours northwest, and/or **Seville**, three hours due west. The scenic town of **Ronda** is another good trip. Descriptions can be found under the respective headings in this chapter.

Italica

See "Excursions" under Seville

Jerez de la Frontera

See "Excursions" under Seville city listing

Málaga ★

Population: 503,251
Area code: 952; Zip code: 29000

From **Madrid** *either head for Granada or Córdoba and follow directions from there. From* **Granada** *take N-323 south toward*

*Motril, but at Salobreña in 65 km go west along N-340 for 92 km. From **Córdoba** take N-331 south toward Antequera for 116 km. Go east on N-321 for eight km to pick up N-331 south again for 35 km more. From **Seville** take N-334 east for 159 km to Antequera and follow the preceding directions.*

In ancient times the quarries of Málaga were famed far and wide, even supplying some of the stone for the great basilica of Sancta Sophia in Constantinople. Under the Moors, Málaga served as the port for Granada and thus became a major target for Ferdinand during his efforts to seal off Granada from reinforcements and supplies. Naturally the Moors had fortified the Málaga securely against such a possibility, but Ferdinand captured it anyway in 1487 after a difficult siege. To send a message to Granada, he killed all its defenders with ceremony.

Málaga's cloudless skies had made it a garden lauded by Arab poets. Wine, apricots, oranges and later sugarcane, helped keep Málaga rich. But those who tended the garden were Moors, so when they were expelled in the 16th century Málaga fell on hard times. In the 18th century demand for Málaga's sweet wine helped it recover, though the city suffered again when tastes in the next century turned to drier French vintages. Tourism in recent days has helped, but Málaga remains a poor city with a high crime rate for Spain.

Málaga also boasts of a famous native son, Pablo Picasso, although his family moved away when he was ten.

Málaga is the major city of the Costa del Sol. Since it has no beaches to speak of, most people use it as a transit hub without bothering to look at the town. The city may not be attractive overall but it contains handsome sights, certainly worth part of a day to explore. Be alert in the evening, however, because street robberies are too prevalent.

One should see the ruins of the Moorish **Alcazaba** ★ and nearby **Gibralfaro** with quiet walks and gardens, the **Cathedral** and **Museo de Bellas Artes**. All lie within an area of five blocks. Málaga is split, on a north-south axis, by the River Guadalmedina. Most places of interest cluster to its east. In fact the sights all center around the Puerto (Port), along which runs a pleasant park with underground parking at its eastern end in the Pl. de la Marina.

*From the **Airport** and from the **western Costa del Sol** watch for signs to Av. de Andalucia as you approach one of the rare clover leafs in Spain. Head east to the Pl. de la Marina and parking. From **Granada and north** one-way streets complicate matters. The city is entered on Av. de Jorge Silvela along the Guadalmedina. At the second bridge one-way streets force the crossing of the river. Take the first left to parallel the river, but at the next bridge, go right for one block on C. Marmoles, taking the next left to a large traffic circle. Go left* *again along Av. de Andalucia, which enters the Pl. de la Marina and parking. From the* **eastern Costa del Sol** *the city is entered on Paseo de Marítimo which reaches a large traffic circle after passing the hospital. Head left along the Paseo del Parque, at the end of which is the Pl. de la Marina and parking.*

Additional parking lies two blocks north along Cortina del Muelle which runs east.

From the Pl. de la Marina walk north to the edge of the park. There C. Molina continues north for two blocks to the Cathedral. Or take the next main street to the east, C. Marqués de Larios, which also heads due north. This is the main shopping street of Málaga, bordered by interesting stores. The **office of tourism** *is on the right in about three blocks. An alley going right, just past the office of tourism, leads to the Cathedral.*

Cathedral

Pl. Obispo, ☎ *221 59 17.*
Hours open: daily 10 a.m.–1 p.m. and 4–5:30 p.m.
Original designs for the Cathedral were drawn by the famed Diego de Siloé in 1528 in a neoclassical style, but the single completed tower shows that it is not finished yet. Money ran out. Some would say that funds were cut off when the church elders saw what it looked like, for this is not the most attractive of cathedrals, although interesting enough for a look. The interior is overly dark, as could be said for many others in Spain, but the massive Corinthian columns make an impact with their girth. The various chapels and altar hold little of interest, but the choir is quite another story. The stalls consist of the finest wood carving by masters of that genre—by Pedro de Mena (buried nearby) and Alonso Cano, among others—admirable for exquisite details. *Admission: 100 ptas., to the choir and treasury.*

From the front of the Cathedral walk due north beside the baroque **Bishopric**. *At the end of the Pl. turn right (east) along C. Cister by the* **Sagradio**, *formerly the site of the city mosque, now with a nice Isabelline north face. At its west end C. San Agustin heads northeast for two blocks to the Museo de Bellas Artes.*

Museo de Bellas Artes

San Augustín, 6, ☎ *221 83 82.*
Hours open: Tues.–Sat. 10 a.m.–1:30 p.m. and 5–8 p.m. (closes an hour earlier in winter). Open Sun. 10 a.m.–1:30 p.m. Closed Mon.
The building itself is interesting—the former palace of Buenavista. Inside waits a varied collection, from Roman mosaics, to paintings by Zurbarán and Ribera. The paintings are on loan from the Prado, and thus not of the first class, but childhood drawings by Picasso are simply wonderful. *Admission: 250 ptas.*

Turn right after the museum for two blocks to the **Pl. de la Merced**, *passing the church of* **Santiago** *with a Mudejar tower on the way. The buildings around the plaza with peeling shutters harken to the turn of the century. A* *plaque at number 15 on the north edge of the plaza marks the house where* **Picasso** *was born. Go south from the plaza along C. Alcazabilla, passing remains of a* **Roman theater** *on the right. At the end of the street stands the large* **Aduaña**, *from the end of the 18th century. To the left is the* **alcazaba**.

Alcazaba   ★

Pl. de la Aduana, ☎ *221 60 05.*
Hours open: Mon.–Sat. 11 a.m.–2 p.m. and 5–8 p.m. (closes an hour earlier in winter). Open Sun. 10 a.m.–2 p.m.

Although restored from the foundations up, the buildings and, especially the gates and fortifications, are evocative, a kind of second-rate Alhambra. The walls were built in the 11th century and show clever tactics to concentrate attackers in a winding entrance. Inside, a small inner palace, built over the course of the 11th-14th centuries, remains admirable in reconstruction. It contains a museum of material from the Visigothic era through the Moorish, including fine ceramics. The double fortress wall leads steeply up to the **Gibralfaro** (mountain lighthouse), actually ruins of a castle from the 14th century. The parador stands beside it. The gardens are lovely with bougainvillea and views of the town and its setting are striking. *Admission: 100 ptas.*

Where to Stay

Since few people stay overnight, the choices usually prove adequate.

Expensive ($100–$200)

Málaga Palacio   1st-class ★

Corina del Muelle, 1, Málaga (off the northeast corner of the Pl. de la Marina), ☎ *221 51 85, FAX 221 51 85.*
The glitter has faded from this older hotel, but it still retains its fine location and views of the park from the rooms that face it. *205 rooms, plus 16 suites.*

Moderate ($50–$99)

Parador de Málaga-Gibralfaro   2nd-class ★ ★ ★

On the Gibralfaro hill, Málaga, ☎ *222 19 03, FAX 222 19 02.*
Although this is a modern building, its ivy covered stone lends an older look, but it is the views over the town and sea along with the quiet, that makes this an excellent choice. Renovations underway will add rooms, a/c and freshen faded rooms. A minibus goes up and down from the city. **Note:** when we last visited, the Parador was closed for repairs. It should reopen by the time you arrive, but check. *17 rooms.*

Los Naranjos   2nd-class ★

Paseo de Sancha, 35, Málaga (about one half mile due east of the Paseo del Parque), ☎ *222 43 19, FAX 222 59 75, Telex 77030.*
The name comes from the small orange grove in front, a nice touch that heralds the attention given throughout this admirably run little hotel. And there is a decent beach nearby. *41 rooms.*

Las Vegas   2nd-class

Paseo de Sancha 22, Málaga (just before Los Naranjos), ☎ *221 77 12.*
The building is nothing remarkable, but the garden around the pool is nice. If you get a room at the back with ocean views, you will enjoy your stay. *107 rooms.*

Inexpensive (Less than $50)

Victoria   **P3rd-class ★**

C. Sancho Lara, 3, Málaga (on a side street off the main shopping street C. Marqués de Larios), ☎ *221 77 12.*
The location is super and the price is right. Rooms are not memorable, but they are squeaky clean. *13 rooms.*

Where to Eat

Think fried fish and walk to the east end of the Paseo del Parque, then a block further for the area known as Pedragalejos. Here unassuming places serve delectable fried fish for a pittance.

Expensive ($30+)

Café de Paris   **★ ★**

C. Vélez Málaga, 8 (east of the Paseo del Parque and a soft right onto Paseo Canovas del Castillo), ☎ *222 50 43.*
Closed Sun and the first half of Sept.
No question that this is the best food in town, owned by a former chef at some of Spain's finest restaurants. Try the *menu de degustación* to sample his wares. Seafood is the star, of course, and prepared with care. Reservations and jacket and tie are required. Credit Cards: A, D, M, V.

Antonio Martín

Paseo Marítimo, 4 (a block south of the Cafe de Paris), ☎ *222 21 13.*
Closed Sun. eve.
The ocean view from the terrace makes this old institution a pleasure. Fish simply prepared is your best choice, for the kitchen can be erratic with sauces. Reservations are strongly advised. Credit Cards: A, D, M, V.

Inexpensive (Less than $15)

La Cancela

C. Denís Belgrano, 3 (C. Molina Larios is the street that passes the facade of the Cathedral and ends a block later at C. Granada. The restaurant lies down an alley off C. Granada.), ☎ *222 31 25.*
Closed Wed.
Two eclectically decorated small dining rooms immediately make you feel relaxed. The food is standard, but hearty, and modestly priced.

Directory

Information

Located on *Passaje de Chinitas, 4,* off C. Marqués de Larios, the main shopping street that heads due north from the Pl. de la Marina. ☎ *221 34 45.*

Trains And Buses

The train station is west of the port, across the river on C. Cuarteles *(☎ 231 25 00).* The RENFE office is at C. Strachan, 2 (just west of the southern face of the Cathedral (☎ *221 31 22)).* Connections can be made almost anywhere in Spain.

The central bus terminal is at Paseo de los Tilos, just past the train station. This is a large hub for bus routes and offers frequent service to most destinations *(☎ 235 00 61).*

Post Office and Telephones

A post office branch is located across the street south from the front of the Cathedral, but the main office is just across the river on Av. de Andalucia (☎ 235 90 08). Telephones are available across from the Cathedral at Calle Molina Larios, 11.

Police

The telephone number is ☎ 221 50 05.

Airport

Ten flights (☎ 224 00 00) arrive daily from Madrid and there are four daily flights to Barcelona. No carriers from the U.S. land here, but a change-over can be made at Madrid. Electric trains (Ferrocarril) go the 10 km to and from the airport every half hour. The best stop is the Centro/Alameda station, located a block north and slightly west of the Pl. de la Marina. Buses also make the trip on the same schedule, leaving from the Cathedral. The Iberia office is at Molina Lario, 13 (☎ 221 82 04).

Excursions

The **Costa del Sol** is the natural excursion from Málaga. See a description under that heading.

Ronda ★ ★

Population: 31,383
Area code: 952; Zip code: 29400

*From **Seville** the fastest route, though not the most direct, is to go south either on the toll road A-4 (E-5) or on the free N-IV to Jerez for 90 km, then east on N-342 to Algodonales for 70 km, where C-339 heads south for lovely views and some hairpin curves along 43 km of road. From **Córdoba** head south on N-IV for 12 km, where N-331 splits off. Follow N-331 to just short of Antequera in 116 km, then west for three km along N-334 and an exit onto N-342 to Algodonales in 90 km. Take the scenic C-339 south to Ronda in 43 km. From **Granada** take N-342 west past Antequera, switch to N-342 for 90 km to Algodonales. Take C-339 south for 43 km to Ronda.*

Ronda is one of those special places that almost everyone loves. It could hardly be more unusual in its situation. The old city stands on a bluff with precipitous drops on three sides, and the fourth side is separated from the newer part of town (post-Reconquest) by an incredible slice of 300-feet-deep gorge. From this aerie, views over the valley and distant hills are nothing short of stupendous.

Everyone, beginning with the Celts, made a stronghold of the impregnable old city, but it was the Moors who left the most lasting remains. Only surprise and the use of metal cannonballs for the first time in Spain allowed Ferdinand to capture it in 1485. Ronda became the center of a revolt by the Moors against forced conversions to Christianity a decade after the fall of

Granada. The insurrection was put down with great difficulty and loss of life. Then the Moors were expelled to quelled such threats in Ronda. The remaining citizens turned to banditry, safe in their fortress fastness, causing two centuries of problems for the police.

Little Ronda had a seminal impact on the sport of bullfighting. A corporation was founded here in 1493 to supervise such events, which at the time still pitted mounted men against the bulls. In the beginning of the 18th century, the local Romero family invented a new way to fight—on foot using capes and a team of assistants, and killing the bull at the end with a sword thrust. The modern, stylized form of bullfighting was thus invented in Ronda. At first fights were held in Ronda's Pl. de la Ciudad by sealing off the streets, then a special ring for the purpose was built in 1785, the second oldest in Spain (after Seville).

Being close to Gibraltar and enjoying cool summer breezes, Ronda has always been a favorite of the English. Hence, the very British hotel Reina Victoria was built here in 1906 for officers vacationing with their families. Here Rainer Maria Rilke, the great German poet, stayed for several months in 1912 recovering from an illness, and began his *Spanish Elegies*. Hemingway visited frequently, and the substantial ashes of Orson Welles are buried on a bull farm outside of town. Today, tourists throng on weekends, but weekdays remain serene.

The town is entered on C. de Sevilla. To cross the Puente Nuevo into the old town a turn must be made at some time to the parallel street to the right, C. Jerez, which changes its name to San Carlos. Across the bridge the name again changes to C. Armiñan. Parking is where you find it. If all else fails, city parking is just to the right of the Puente Nuevo in the Mercadillo, or new town, side.

The old town, called the Ciudad, is less than half a mile long by a quarter wide, so no one can get lost by too much. On the other hand, it conforms to a Moorish layout of winding streets and alleys so everyone gets lost at least a little. That is to say, it's a place for wandering. Start at the far (southern) end of the Ciudad, at the **Alcazaba**.

Not that there is much to see of the old Moorish fort, for the French demolished it in 1809, but it is a romantic site with nice views. Follow the main street, called C. Nuñez at this point, back in the direction of the new town for two blocks. As the street bends right go left into the main square, the **Pl. de la Ciudad** ★. It was here that the modern form of bullfighting was first practiced. At the north end of the plaza stands the church of **Santa María la Mayor** ★ (open at the caretaker's whim; 100 ptas. donation). This is a mosque done over with the trappings of a 17th-century Christian church, as the recently uncovered mihrab in the vestibule shows (now with a statue of the Virgin inside). The church tower originally was the minaret. Inside, a Gothic nave hovers above a gilded baroque high altar.

Leave by a small street running from the east side of the church. Go east to a "T" where C. Ruedi de Gameros goes north for one block to the **Mondrag-on Palace** ★, imposing with twin graceful turrets. This is a Renaissance re-building on the site of the former Moorish palace in which Ferdinand and Isabella stayed while Isabella gave birth to a daughter. Today it houses exhi-bitions, so you can enter to admire its two handsome patios with glazed tiles and Mudejar stucco tracery. Do not miss the gallery in the rear with lovely artesonado ceiling and dramatic views of the valley. *(Open weekdays 9 a.m.–2 p.m.; admission: 200 ptas.)*

Retrace steps back to the church and go east to the main street, here called C. Armiñan, but take the first right into a pretty square with a striking little **minaret** standing alone to show that there once was a mosque nearby. Take C. Marqués de Salvatierra from the northeast corner of this plaza for two blocks to the **Casa del Marqués de Salvatierra** on the right. The Renaissance facade displays "savages" over the portal and may be visited *(open daily, ex-cept Thurs., 10 a.m.–1 p.m. and 4–7 p.m.; admission: 200 ptas., for guided tour).*

Downhill to the right one passes two bridges, the first on Roman founda-tions, the second claimed to be Moorish. Further down the ravine are some of the finest **Moorish baths** ★ remaining in Spain *(open Tues.–Sat. 10 a.m.–1 p.m. and 4–7 p.m.; open Sun. 10 a.m.–1 p.m.; admission: free)*. On the return up the hill, continue past the Casa del Marqués de Salvatierra toward the Puente Nuevo, and pass the **Casa del Rey Moro**. Although called the House of the Moorish king, it obviously dates from the early 18th century.

Continue to the Mercadillo (new town) over the Puente Nuevo, a spectac-ular 18th-century bridge, then along C. San Carlos to the **Pl. de Toros** ★, the bullring, in two blocks. It was completed in 1785, and surely is the most charming in Spain—which is why it has so often been featured in movies *(open daily 10 a.m.–6 p.m.; admission to the museum: 200 ptas.)*. One block farther on C. San Carlos brings the lovely gardens of the **Alamenda Tajo** on the left. From here a dramatic walk along the cliffs leads to the Victorian hotel with the apt name of **Hotel Reina Victoria**, worth looking in and walking through the gardens in the rear.

Where to Stay

To fully experience Ronda one has to spend the night in the **Hotel Reina Victoria**. But if $100 in season is too much, there is a less expensive option.

Expensive ($100–$200)

Reina Victoria   1st-class ★★★★★

Av. Dr. Fleming, 25, Ronda (on entering town take the first right to the hotel), ☎ *287 12 40, FAX 287 10 75.*

Built in 1906 by an English company for British guests, there is nothing so charmingly colonial anywhere in Spain. It truly does seem Victorian, with the grace, charm and decor of that era. Today it is run by the Husa chain, caters to tour groups and has recently been completely renovated, but it still retains its old feeling. The gardens are lovely, with views that cannot be matched. Try very hard to get a room at the back with a balcony overlooking the valley. One more plus—it is just barely on the wrong side of the expensive range. *89 rooms.*

Parador de Ronda   1st-class ★★★

Pl. de España, Ronda (this plaza is where the Puente Nuevo disgorges in the new part of town), ☎ *287 75 00, FAX 287 81 88.*

The 18th-century Ayuntamiento (City Hall) has just been made over as one of the newest paradors. It is a crisp place with some character, but, best of all, with fabulous views over the gorge and countryside. *71 rooms.*

Inexpensive (Less than $50)

Virgen de los Reyes   R2nd-class ★

C. Lorenzo Borrego, 13, Ronda (turn left at the end of the gardens onto C. Padre Mariano Soubirón, for two blocks, then a right and another right), ☎ *87 62 36.*

For a rock-bottom price you get A/C and a comfortable room that is spotlessly clean *67 rooms.*

Where to Eat

Although there are a number of inexpensive restaurants in the Mercadillo (new town), none stands out compared to two moderately priced places, also in the Mercadillo, serving better food.

Moderate ($15–$30)

Don Miguel   ★★

Pl. de España, 3 (at the Puente Nuevo), ☎ *287 10 90.*
Closed Sun., and the middle two weeks in Jan.

Two terraces offer such spectacular views of the Tajo Gorge that they may be too much for diners subject to vertigo. If bothered, feast your eyes on the milk-fed baby lamb lying your plate and all will be well, for it is good. Reservations are advised on weekends. Credit Cards: A, D, M, V.

Pedro Romero   ★

Virgen de la Paz, 18 (opposite the Pl. de Toros), ☎ *287 11 10.*

Named after the founder of modern bullfighting, naturally the restaurant is decorated with memorabilia of the bullring. Somehow it is attractive and homey (if you can ignore the stares of dead bulls). Of course you should try the *rabo de toro* here, and for dessert there is a special caramel custard *al coco* (with coconut) that should not be missed. Credit Cards: A, D, M, V.

Directory

Information

Located in the Pl. de España at number 1, which is the plaza just before the Puente Nuevo. Open Mon.-Fri. from 10 to 2:30 p.m. ☎ *287 12 72.*

Trains and Buses

The train station (☎ *287 16 73*) is on Av. Andalucia in the northeast corner of the Mercadillo. Ronda connects directly with Seville, Algeciras, Málaga and Granada. A change at Bobadilla is necessary for other destinations.

The bus station is off the same avenue four blocks west, at Pl. Concepción García Redondo, 2 ☎ *287 22 64.* However, different companies with different routes and schedules use the building. Service is more frequent by bus.

Post Office and Telephones

The post office is located at *C. Virgin de la Paz*, 20, opposite the Pl. de Toros.

Police

In the Pl. de la Ciudad in the old town (☎ *287 32 40*; emergency: ☎ *091*).

Seville ★★★★★

Population: 653,833
Area code: 95; Zip code: 41000

> *From* **Madrid** *aim either for Córdoba or Granada and follow the directions from there. From* **Granada** *take N-342 west for 92 km past Antequera, then take N-334 northwest for 159 km to Seville. From* **Córdoba** *take N-IV (E-5) southwest for Seville in 142 km.*

Seville does not boast the best art museum, cathedral or Moorish architecture, but it is second best in all these arenas and, thus, places high on total points. Since it is a beautiful city replete with lovely vistas, a cosmopolitan city where orange and palm trees line streets punctuated by quiet parks, it is a tourist's delight. For better or worse, it is also, however, the hottest city in Spain.

Seville has been important since the time of the Iberians, thanks to its safe situation inland along the Guadalquivir River that provided an easy road to the sea. Julius Caesar himself fortified it in 45 B.C. and it grew into one of the most important Roman towns in Spain, as still impressive ruins at nearby Italica attest. In fact, it bred two Roman Emperors—Trajan and Hadrian. Seville was the first capital of the Visigoths, before Toledo took over that position. Under the Moors, Seville stood second behind Córdoba until 1023, when the kingdom split into principalities and Seville's independence left it free to surpass the former capital. For two centuries her prosperity was unrivaled, then, in 1248, Seville was conquered by the great Christian warrior Fernando III, later sainted for his accomplishments. Saint Fernando was buried here in 1252.

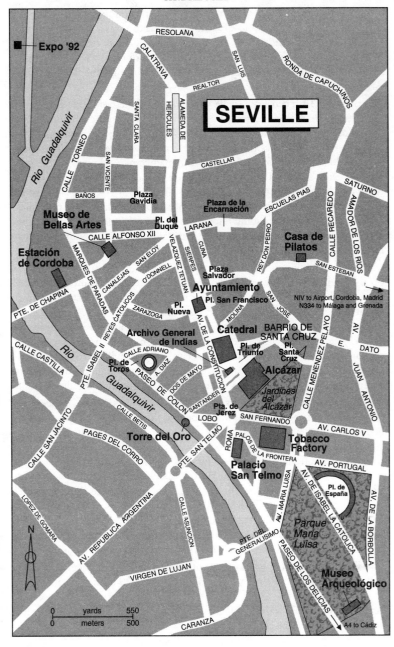

Naturally many Moors fled Seville after this early conquest. Their property was divided among Fernando's followers, to create a class of Andalusian nobles whose wealth and power were (and in some cases remain) immense. Thus arose, for example, the dukes of Medina Sidonia, one of whom almost financed Columbus' first voyage, and another of whom admiralled the Great Armada.

In the early 14th century, Seville was favored by the notorious king Pedro the Cruel, who remodeled the palace of the Moors into the striking Alcázar we see today. Later, riches from the New World brought great prosperity to Seville, for this was the port to which the treasure ships sailed to unload their silver, gold and tobacco, much of which remained in local pockets. Carlos V came to Seville to meet and marry his bride, Isabel of Portugal, remodeling rooms in the Alcázar for his honeymoon suite. But, in 1647, a plague broke out, ran rampant for five years and reduced the population by one third. This, combined with declining trade from the New World, began a slide that was climaxed by the silting up of the Guadalquivir River, handing preeminence thereafter to Cádiz as Spain's New World port.

Nonetheless, life continued in Seville. Spain's finest artist, Velázquez, was born here in 1599, as was Murillo in 1618. Zurbarán became an adopted son. The French writer Beaumarchais visited in 1764, and wrote a story about a Seville roué named Don Juan that inspired Mozart's *Don Giovanni*. Mozart followed with *The Marriage of Figaro*, inspiring Rossini's *Barber of Seville*. Later Prosper Merimée wrote a story about a Gypsy in Seville who enchanted a soldier, which became Bizet's *Carmen*. Seville's Tobacco Factory served as the model for Carmen's place of employment. In the present century, textiles and metallurgy have returned prosperity to Seville.

Seville is famed in Spain for its Easter festivities, when nightly processions of hooded and robed penitents march behind floats of bejeweled and flower-bedecked Saints and Virgins. Bands and bystanders break out into song as the processions pass. This is followed two weeks later by the April Fair, a week of celebrations. Tents are set up outside the town to which Sevillanos ride on horseback in costumes like those in *Carmen* and celebrate with food, wine and parties throughout the night. In association with these festivities are a month of bullfights involving the finest matadors, as well as impromptu nightly dancing, including flamenco and the local dance called the Sevillano. It is a festive and memorable time to visit, but a period when all hotels are booked full at prices twice their usual charges.

Seville also hosted the World's Fair of 1992, Expo '92. In fact this was the city's second World's Fair. Its first, celebrated in 1929 as the Ibero-America Exposition, was rather a dud because of the world financial collapse that year. The recent fair occupied the island of La Cartuja, just north of the city-center. Some pavilions and rides remain.

Arriving from the north or east on **N-IV**, *or from the* **Airport**, *one travels along Av. Aeropuerto which becomes Av. de Kansas City (yes, that is its name) as it goes through the city. When it ends in a "T," go left along Av. Luis Morales which changes its name to Av. San Francisco Javier near the university on the right. Take the next right along C. Enramadilla, which narrows, then widens, and is called Av. Carlos V. As it passes the bus park, parking is available to the right.*

Arriving from **Málaga** *on* **N-334** *enter the city along Av. de Andalucía, passing through one huge, clover-leafed intersection and then two other major intersections. At the third intersection, with the Soccer Stadium visible to the right, turn right along Av. Luis Morales, and follow the rest of the directions above.*

Arriving from **Cádiz** *or* **Jerez** *on N-IV from the south along Av. de Jerez, the corner of the large Parque de Maria Luisa is soon reached. Turn right at the park onto C. Muñoz León, which follows the edge of the park under the new name of C. Borbolla. Continue for one block past the park's end, make a left onto Av. Carlos V, and parking to the left in two blocks.*

From **Mérida** *traffic is funneled across the Guadalquivir River on Av. de Cristo de Expiración. Take the first right after the bridge, along a street that soon is named Paseo Cristobal Colón. Bear left at the Torre del Oro, the polygonal stone tower, onto Almirante Lobo which feeds in one long block into the busy circle called the Puerta de Jerez. Continue through the circle to take the large street opposite, C. San Fernando, by the gardens of the Alcázar. At the end of the gardens, continue through the traffic circle onto Av. Carlos V. Parking is available at the second right.*

Seville offers an abundance of interesting things to see set in one of the most beautiful cities in the world. The **Alcázar** ★★★★ and the **Casa de** **Pilatos** ★★★ both are wonderful hybrid Moorish palaces, built for Christians by Moorish artisans—Mudejars. The **Cathedral** ★★★ is among the finest in Spain, and the largest. Seville's **Museo de Bellas Artes** ★★★ houses the second best art in Spain, including remarkable Zurbaráns and one of Velázquez' finest paintings. The **Museo Arqueológico** ★ displays finds from nearby Roman Italica. The **Barrio Santa Cruz** ★, the old quarter, retains lovely plazas, flowered patios and elegant houses. There are admirable buildings—the **Archivo General de Indias**, the **tobacco factory**, the **Ayuntamiento** ★ and the complex called the **Pl. de España**. Last, but not least, the remains of **Expo '92** on the island of La Cartuja have been turned into an amusement park. It is quite impossible to see Seville in less than two days.

Proceed west along Av. de Carlos V from the parking lot to cross the Pl. de Juan de Austria. Across the plaza the still westward street is renamed C. San Francisco. Pass the gardens at the rear of the Alcázar on the right by the huge building on the left. This was the former **tobacco factory**, *famed as the model for Carmen's place of employment. At one time 10,000 workers rolled Cuban cigars here, but now it constitutes a part of the University of Seville and only the carving of the story of tobacco around the main door betrays its former function. At the end of the street stands the grand* **Hotel Alfonso XIII**. *Turn right along C. San Gregoro into the* **Pl. de Contratación**, *the hub of numerous sights. The* **Office of Tourism** *is down the alley to the right. The square building to the left is the* **Archivo General de Indias**, *and ahead is the* **Cathedral** *with the* **Giralda Tower** *visible above its west side. To its right is the* **Alcázar**, *and between the Cathedral and Alcázar is the entrance to the* **Barrio Santa Cruz**.

The Cathedral Area

Cathedral and Giralda Tower   ★★★

Pl. del Triunfo, ☎ *421 28 00.*
Hours open: Mon.–Sat. 11 a.m.–5 p.m., Sun. 2–4 p.m. Closed Jan. 1 and 6, May 30, Aug. 15, Dec. 8 and 25.

After conquering Seville, the Christians first used the mosque of the Moors for religious services, but in 1401 decided to build a cathedral of their own, and finished the project in the remarkably quick time of a century. A member of the original building committee is said to have exclaimed: "Let us build a cathedral so immense that everyone who sees it will take us for madmen." What they constructed was the largest Gothic cathedral in the world, save perhaps the still unfinished Saint John the Divine in New York, and the fourth largest cathedral of any sort. They razed the mosque to build it, though left its Patio of Oranges for a cathedral cloister and its minaret for a bell tower. The main portal of the present facade is modern, surrounded by two others of the period.

On the east face of the Cathedral, to the rear, rises the **Torre Giralda** ★★ (Weathervane Tower). Beside it waits the entrance to the Cathedral and the ticket counter.

The tower is actually the minaret from the mosque of 1198. When the Cathedral went up, a bell tower was added to the top of the minaret surmounted by a statue which turned in the wind and symbolized Faith. Altogether, the tower stands over 300 feet high, as handsome and harmonious a structure as can be imagined up to the place where the arcade of the belfry begins. (Use a hand to block the top and its harmony will be apparent.)

The tower may be climbed by walking up interior sloping ramps (of course these were never meant for horses, as many of the guidebooks say) for the best view of the Cathedral and surrounding city. Note that each bell in the clarion is named.

When the Cathedral is entered, its vast size is not initially apparent. The light is dusky because the stained glass windows are unusually high, the piers seem less massive because they are formed into smaller columns, and the doubling of the aisles on each side of the nave is not obvious at first. Further, as with so many Spanish cathedrals, the central coro blocks any grand view down the nave. Nonetheless, the cathedral is a football field long, almost equally wide and the vaulting above the nave soars 135 feet into the air.

Entering by the south transept one confronts the impressive **tomb of Christopher Columbus**. The coffin is carried by four figures representing the original four kingdoms of Spain—Castile, Aragón, Navarre and León. The work was cast in the 19th century. However, whether Columbus' body actually lies in the coffin is a subject of controversy. It is known that he died in Valladolid and that his body was carried to Santo Domingo for burial. The Spanish say that the corpse was disinterred, taken to Havana, then returned here to prevent capture during the Spanish-American War. In Santo Domingo they claim that Columbus' remains never left.

The **high altar** is fronted by an ornate Plateresque gilt screen which seems to double the gilt of the awesome Gothic retable, the largest in Spain. Its details are difficult to study from a distance. In the apse behind the high altar is the large **Capilla Real**, a Plateresque marvel. High up, Fernando III, the conqueror of Seville, is shown receiving the keys to the city. On the chapel altar stands a silver and bronze shrine for the king's remains. His body proved incorruptible, so Fernando was declared a saint and is still carried in processions during Easter week. Above the shrine stands a small Virgin, said to be a gift from Louis IX of France that Fernando carried with him in battle. To the left is the effigy of King Alfonso X, the Wise, Fernando's son, and opposite is Fernando's wife, Beatrice of Swabia. The striking dome above radiates heads of martyrs spiralling to the apex.

Stairs in the chapel lead to a vault below (generally closed) in which coffins hold Pedro the Cruel and his "wife" Maria de Padilla. Ironically, resting beside Pedro is his half-brother Fadrique Trastámara, who Pedro killed, and whose brother avenged the death by killing Pedro before founding the dynasty that bred both Isabella and Ferdinand.

To the left, facing the Capilla Real is a chapel with a retable by Zurbarán. To the right, in the corner, is a lovely oval room with a fine frescoed ceiling, the **Chapterhouse**. Church vestments are displayed adjoining. Further along is a neoclassical **Sacristy** with a painting by Zurbarán, and an adjacent **treasury** displaying numerous relics, including the actual keys to the city presented to St. Fernando—silver gilt by the Moors, iron gilt by the Jewish community.

In the center of the nave stands an ornate **coro** with fine Gothic choirstalls. Between the coro and the front door to the Cathedral lies a **tombstone for Columbus' son Hernando**.

Before one finishes with the Cathedral, a quiet treat awaits through a door on the right side that gives access to the **Patio de los Naranjos**, the courtyard for the former mosque. Inside is the original basin for the mosque, perhaps appropriated from a Visigothic fountain. The chapel to **Our Lady of Granada** carries a fine Mudejar ceiling, and up red marble stairs is stored the **Columbus Archives** of books owned by the discoverer, many annotated in his hand, which were donated to the Cathedral by his son Hernando. *Admission: 550 ptas., to the Cathedral and Giralda Tower.*

Alcázar   ★★★★

Pl. del Triunfo, ☎ *422 71 63.*

Hours open: Tues.–Sat. 10 a.m.–5 p.m. Open Sun. 10 a.m.–1 p.m. Closed Mon.

Across the Pl. de Triunfo south from the Cathedral, past square battlement towers and through an unassuming gateway with a tiled lion above, is the entrance to the Alcázar. These walls are all that remain of a Moorish palace from 1176. In 1366 Pedro the Cruel replaced that palace with a smaller one of his own. But he so admired the Moorish aesthetic that he borrowed artisans from the Caliph of Granada to construct it. Here Pedro lived with his "wife" Maria de Padilla. (See "Historical Profile: Moors and the Reconquest" on page 267.) And here he murdered Fadrique of Trastámara, his half-brother. On another occasion he invited the emir from Granada to dinner and killed him for his jewels, one of which, a giant uncut ruby, found its way into the British royal crown. Later Isabella gave birth to her only son while she and Ferdinand resided here. Carlos V, their grandson, married his wife in the Hall of the Ambassadors. A hundred years later, Velázquez' patron Felipe IV, restored the Alcázar, although an earthquake and fire in the 18th century did substantial damage and restoration has been crude at times. Nonetheless, this is the oldest continually occupied palace in Europe (the present king and queen often stay), and the finest surviving example of Mudejar architecture.

Through the gate one enters the **Patio de Montería**. On the left is the **Sala de Justicia** with plaster coats of arms around the walls, and a remarkable wooden ceiling above. Farther left, though presently closed, is the lovely **Patio de Yeso**, one of the few remaining parts of the original Moorish palace. From the Patio de Montería, three **stone arches** (possibly Roman) straight ahead lead to the **Patio de Leones**, with patterned pavement and the handsome **Palace of Pedro the Cruel** across the way.

The main façade, with its arcaded wings on two sides, presents an almost Byzantine look due to a deep overhanging eave above the entrance. Below the eave, blue tiles bear an Arabic inscription saying that there is no conqueror but God, a kind of putdown by the Moorish craftsmen of their Christian master who could not read Arabic. The right-hand wing was built by Ferdinand and Isabella as a center to deal with matters concerning the New World.

Starting in this Isabelline wing, a vestibule hung with nice tapestries leads to a room for audiences and finally a small **chapel** with ornate coffered ceiling. The picture above the altar shows Mary protecting dim figures of Native Americans under her cloak. The blond-haired figure beside her on the right is thought to be Columbus.

Outside, at the far end, a grand stair leads to **royal apartments** on the second floor. Left of the landing is the intimate **Oratory of Isabella** with a remarkable tile depiction of Mary visiting her cousin St. Isabella. Rooms of varying styles and age follow, including the **banquet hall** with a lovely ceiling, built by Carlos V for his wedding feast. But the finest of the rooms is **Pedro the Cruel's bedroom** with intricate carving in perfect Mudejar style, and an alcove for his bed.

The treasure of the Alcázar is Pedro's palace. Enter through the main portal into a **vestibule** that presents an elegant vista of horseshoe arches. Bright tiles (unfortunately modern) line the walls halfway up, intricate painted stucco runs along the high walls and through the arches, and a complex coffered ceiling hangs overhead.

Turn left from the vestibule into the **Patio de las Doncellas** (Maids of Honor), the center of the palace. If only Carlos V had not added the classical second story to the patio it would be a perfect jewel. Ignore that second story and enjoy the multilobed arches, brilliant tiles and the rhythm of the arches, not ignoring the ancient original doors. Of course there is a fountain in the center for the sound of water, and vistas through the patio sides of surrounding rooms.

Cross to the right side to see the so-called **Salón de los Reyes Moros**, which of course was intended for Christian, not Moorish kings. In any case it displays nice woodwork, fine wooden doors and alcoves for beds.

Cross to the far side to enter the **Salón de Carlos V**, with a fine coffered ceiling that replaced the original Mudejar one. This is followed by a long room that ends at the triple arches of the **Peacocks**, named for the tiled birds above the arches, a fantasy of pattern on pattern.

Through the peacock arches waits the most splendid room in the Alcázar, the **Salón de Embajadores**, in which Carlos V is said to have held his wedding. The room seems more a jeweler's work than that of tilers or plasterers, for the complexity of the intricate designs stretches belief. Above is a dome that has no equal in the world. Throughout there is the surprise of western motifs—seashells over the arches, castles and lions above portraits of the kings of Spain around the ceiling—that makes sense in a room designed for Christians by the Moors.

Off this room and through another for Felipe II, the small **Patio de las Muñecas** (dolls) is entered, named for two tiny faces on the capital of one of the columns. For many this is the favorite of all the Alcázar rooms, because of its human scale, despite the intricacy of designs which seem to rise to the heavens. On one side is a room called **Isabella's bedroom**, on another, the bedroom for her new baby, **Don Juan**.

Return through the vestibule to the Patio de Leons. Turn right along a gallery to the **Patio de María de Padilla**, the site of a Gothic palace older than Pedro's, though much remodeled. Here are a suite of rooms known as the **Palace of Carlos V**.

The **Emperor's Room** with non-Moorish tiles halfway up the walls and groined vaulting above seems rather a mishmash, but the **Tapestry Room** displays an amazing series of tapestries depicting a battle that Carlos fought in Tunis. Two hundred years later Felipe V ordered copies made of all the tapestries, which is our good fortune, because the originals disappeared and today you see these perfect copies.

What would a Moorish palace be without gardens? The Alcázar has its own in the rear planted with exotic trees and dotted with ornamental waterways. Directly behind the Alcázar, first passing the aptly named **Grotesque Gallery** to the left, is the beautifully tiled **Carlos V Pavilion**. After the gardens, the Alcázar is exited through a garage in which two 17th-century carriages are parked. Note the use of leather straps as shock absorbers. *Admission: 600 ptas., exact change.*

Archivo General de Indias

Pl. Archivo de Indias, ☎ *421 12 34.*

Hours open: Mon.–Sat. 10 a.m.–1 p.m. Closed Sun.

On its own square between the Cathedral and Alcázar, this impressive building was designed in 1572 by Herrera, the architect of the Escorial. Originally it was an exchange where merchants conducted business, but it was remodeled in the 18th century into an archive for the masses of material relating to the discovery, administration and trade of New World. Almost 40,000 files, going back to Columbus' time, are stored on the second floor, along with changing exhibits of maps and documents of general historical interest. It is worth the climb for a look. *Admission: free.*

Barrio Santa Cruz   ★

This quarter is what remains of the Moorish layout of Seville, crowding houses along meandering alleys. Located next to the Alcázar and the mosque, this would have been the most densely populated part of the city during the time of the Moors. Long after the Moors and Jews who lived here had been expelled, this area again became a desirable place to live. Today the quarter's real estate is expensive and the glistening whitewashed houses are perfectly maintained. The barrio is a place for strolling past cafes, artisans' shops and lovely patios to come unexpectedly into charming squares. The whole area can be explored in a half hour's leisurely ramble.

The barrio begins alongside the east face of the Alcázar complex, extending in a rectangle for about five blocks east and north. Exit from the Alcázar to the right around the building, following its east face, to arrive in one block at the **Pl. Elvira**, with fountain and benches. Continue along the Alcázar side, turning right at the wall that borders the Alcázar gardens to follow Callejon del Agua past some of the nicest houses in the barrio. A short left turn at the end of the wall brings the attractive **Pl. Alfaro**. This is where Figaro supposedly serenaded Rosina on her balcony (a dozen other houses, however, claim that honor as well). To the right of the plaza a short street lets into the attractive **Pl. Santa Cruz**. From here you can wander north and west again to see more of the barrio, or retrace your steps to the Alcázar for the next sight.

West of the Cathedral

Covering about four blocks to the west of the Cathedral are a few nice things to see—the **Hospital de la Caridad**, *the* **Torre del Oro**, *and the* **Pl. de Toros**.

The wide Av. de la Constitución runs along the west side of the Cathedral. Head south along it, turning right on C. Santander just after passing the Archivo de Indias. Turn right at the next corner on C. Temprado to view the **Hospital de la Caridad** on the right. It was founded in 1674 by Don Miguel de Manara who decided, after spending the first part of his life in pleasure and debauchery, to devote his remaining time to helping the poor. Some claim he was a model for the character Don Juan. The building is subdued baroque in style and its church contains a series of paintings by Murillo, along with two gruesome canvases by Leal. Manara is buried in front of the altar of the church. *(Open Mon.–Sat. 10 a.m.–1 p.m. and 3:30–6 p.m.; Sun. 10 a.m.–1 p.m.; admission: 200 ptas.).* On the opposite side of the street is the **Teatro de la Maestranza**, Seville's new opera house.

Back on C. Santander continue for one block to its end at Paseo de Cristobal Colón and the river. Left is the impressive **Torre del Oro**, so named for gold hued tiles that used to decorate its sides. It was built in 1220, along with a twin across the river (no longer standing), to control river traffic. At night a chain between the two towers could be raised to close the river. The smaller tower on top and steeple are later additions. Today the structure functions as a naval museum *(open Tues.–Fri. 10 a.m.–2 p.m.; weekends to 1 p.m.; closed Mon.; admission 100 ptas.).*

Two blocks north along Paseo Cristobal Colón is the **Pl. de Toros de la Maestranza ★**, Seville's bullring. Built in 1763, it is the oldest and most beautiful in Spain. Across the river C. Betis, a riverfront street with the feeling of a resort, is festive with cafes, restaurants and shops.

North of the Cathedral

Two worthwhile sights lie north of the Cathedral area. Each is eminently walkable—at a distance of roughly half a mile—though the **Museo de Bellas Artes** *is west and the* **Casa de Pilatos** *is east, which makes the combined trip closer to a mile. If the walk sounds too long, take a taxi for one leg of it. We describe the entire walk from the Cathedral but it can be followed in the reverse direction, of course.*

From the northern face of the Cathedral either Av. de constitución or the smaller C. Hernando Colón leads due north for one block into the Pl. San Francisco. Running along the left side of the plaza is the most unusual **Ayuntamiento ★**, completed in 1564. The façade is a riot of Plateresque decoration, so much adorned that the building seems too slight to bear it. The surprise is the other side, barely embellished at all. That side was re-done in the 19th century when styles had changed.

Running away from the north end of the plaza is the pedestrian shopping street of C. Sierpes, lined with attractive stores. Where it begins a bust of Cervantes marks the spot of the former debtors' prison in which the writer began *Don Quixote*.

One block along C. Sierpes, down an alley to the left, is the church of **San José** (1766), a gaudy little structure with the most baroque of altars. Returning to Sierpes and continuing across it on C. Sagasta for a block to the west, the attractive plaza and church of **San Salvador** presents itself. The church was completed in 1712 on the site of the first great mosque of Seville. Its bell tower is the former minaret from 1079, and the facade incorporates original arches of the mosque. Only a foot or two of the arch columns show, demonstrating how much the ground has risen in nine hundred years.

For the **Casa de Pilatos** (see the description that follows) continue across the plaza and due west for five blocks.

Return to C. Sierpes and continue north for two blocks to the **Palacio de la Condesa de Lebrija**, on the right. The interior is not of the first order, but it has three patios with mosaics from nearby Roman Italica and a rather nice artesonado ceiling over the stairs. C. Sierpes ends in one block more when it reaches the busy C. Martín Villa. Slightly right is the department store el Corte Inglés. The **Museo de Bellas Artes** (see description that follows) is left along Martín Villa, which becomes C. Campaña for a block, then becomes C. Alfonso XII before reaching the museum three blocks later.

Casa Pilatos   ★★★

Pl. Pilatos, 1, ☎ *422 50 55.*

Hours open: daily 9 a.m.–6 p.m.

On the right day, when the crowds are small and the mood is right, this can be one of the most memorable sights in Spain. But it should not be viewed through the aesthetics of the Moors. Theirs was an ornate look of patterns heaped upon patterns but always with lightness and elegance. This palace for the Marqués of Tarifa was completed in 1540, and partially modelled on the House of Pontius Pilate which the Marqués had visited in Jerusalem. You will not notice any Roman or near-eastern features, but you will see a riot of Mudejar design. Here are the elements of Moorish architecture—vibrant patterned tiles, carved stucco filigree and textured wood ceilings—all taken to their extreme. The result is brash compared to the Moor's delicacy, but wonderful on its own terms.

Past a Plateresque portal and entrance courtyard, the drama begins with the central patio—Moorish arches on the lower level, Gothic balustrade and arches above, bright tiles on the walls and Roman statues inhabiting the corners. In the center stands a fountain, not a low, unassuming water trickling device, but a strong architectural statement. The fantasy continues in rooms leading from this patio, culminating in the southwest corner in the stairway to the upper floor with its remarkable ceiling. The second floor is more prosaic, with rooms of varying later periods and some antiques. Only part can be visited, because the present owner, the Duque de Medinaceli, still lives in one wing. *Admission: 10000 ptas.*

Museo de Bellas Artes   ★★★

Pl. del Museo, ☎ *422 18 29.*

Hours open: Tues.–Fri. 10 a.m.–2 p.m. and 4–7 p.m.; Sun. 10 a.m.–2 p.m. Closed Mon.
This is the second best art museum in Spain, which still leaves it far removed from the Prado. The art is housed in a former convent with three delicate patios constructed in 1612, but thoroughly restored in the early 19th century. Its collection of works was rescued from nearby convents during the 19th century when many religious orders were suppressed in Spain. Extensive remodeling was still under way at our last visit, with no end in sight.

The collection is weighted heavily toward artists from Seville, including some of the finest work of her adopted son Zurbarán. Room IV displays a fine El Greco portrait of his son Jorge Manuel. In the same room a canvas by Pacheco, teacher and father-in-law of Velázquez, of a man and woman praying is worth a look. Pacheco is universally condemned as a journeyman artist, with good reason, but this work is inspired.

The Zurbarán collection, in Rooms V-VII, rivals that of the Prado. *Saint Hugh and the Carthusian Monks at Table* is interesting, *The Apotheosis of Saint Thomas Aquinas* is a miracle of perspective and design (with Zurbarán himself peering at the viewer, behind the kneeling Carlos V), and the *Virgin of the Caves*, in which those magical white Zurbarán monks kneel to a Virgin with astonishing pink roses at her feet, is unforgettable.

Upstairs in Room X are the two Velázquez' owned by the museum, and one, *The Portrait of Cristobal Suarez de Ribera*, by itself repays the admission charge. It is among the most profound portraits ever done.

Subsequent rooms display a nice Goya *Portrait of José Duarzo*, and a fine statue of *Saint Bruno* by Montañes, as lifelike as wood can be. There are some charming 19th- and early 20th-century works by local artists as well. The museum owns an extensive collection of Murillo (in Room VIII) and of Valdés Leal (in Room IX), a Sevillano taken with Ruben's historical style. *Admission: 250 ptas.*

South of the Cathedral

South of the Cathedral past the baroque **Palacio de San Telmo** *an imposing arc of buildings borders a canal at the* **Pl. España**, *built for the aborted 1929 Seville World's Fair. The lovely* **Parque de Maria Luisa** *harbors the* **Museo Arqueológico, Museo de Atres y Costumbres Populares** *and the* **Pabillon Real**.

Av. de la Constitución runs south from the west side of the Cathedral and ends in the traffic circle of Puerta de Jerez. Continuing south past the Hotel Alfonso XIII, Av. de Roma arrives in one block at the **Palacio de San Telmo** whose churrigueresque portal is admirable. This was the residence of the dukes of Montpensier who donated their palace grounds—now the Parque de María Luisa—to the city. They also donated this palace, although the city has not yet decided what to do with it.

Around the end of the palace, head southeast along its remaining gardens to Av. del Peru. In two blocks after passing the **Teatro Lope de Vega**, one of the buildings of the 1929 World's Fair, you arrive at Av. María Luisa, across which is the **Parque de María Luisa**. Walk south through the park, part wild, part formally arranged, to the south end past attractive villas left over from the 1929 World's Fair. Just before the end, comes the **Museo de Artes y Costumbres Populares** ★ with interesting exhibits of crafts, furniture and costumes *(open Tues.–Sun. 10 a.m.–2 p.m.; admission: 250 ptas.)*. In a few yards more the park ends, facing the **Museo Arqueológico** across the street.

Museo Arqueológico   ★

Pl. de América, ☎ 423 24 01.
Hours open: Tues.–Sun. 10 a.m.–2 p.m. Closed Mon.
In the basement reside artifacts from pre-Roman cultures, including a famous hoard of sixth century B.C. gold found at Carambola, fine Phoenician statues and ceramics. The ground floor displays Celtiberian statuary, although none as wonderful as in Madrid, with the exception of some charming bulls and lions. Here too are lovely Roman mosaics and statuary from nearby Italica. *Admission: 250 ptas.*

Head east then north along the eastern edge of the park on Av. de Isabel la Católica, to pass the monumental **Pl. de España**. *This was Spain's pavilion for the 1929 World's Fair, and is a fantasy worth viewing. By continuing along Av. de Isabel la Católica, you return to the huge university building (the former tobacco factory), past which are the gardens of the Alcázar and the Cathedral area again.*

Discovery Park, Isla de la Cartuja   ★

Isla de la Caruja, ☎ *446 16 16. This island is in the Guadalquivir north of the Cathedral square, opposite the Museo de Bellas Artes.*

Hours open: in summer and during holidays Tues.–Thurs. 8 p.m.–2 a.m., Fri.–Sun. noon–1 a. m. (pavilions close at midnight, or 8 p.m. on Sun. Open in winter Fri.-Sun. noon-midnight (pavilions close at 8 p.m., or midnight on Sun.).

Here are remains of the 1st-Class World's Fair of 1992 in case you missed it. The fair commemorated the 500th anniversary of Columbus' discovery of the New World, and its theme was "The Age of Discovery." For this mammoth event, a lake was dug on the island to provide natural air conditioning. Now it is all a huge theme park that can be fun and educational for children of all ages.

The exhibition centers on the 15th-century monastery of **Santa Maria las Cuevas**, where Columbus reputedly explained his theories to the monks. From here begins the Way of Discovery, that includes a **Pavilion of the 15th Century** to show what life was like in Columbus' time in various parts of the world. The **Discovery Pavilion** presents the great inventions and discoveries that formed the modern world, including an audiovisual presentation in which the seats move. The **Navigation Pavilion** traces the history of maritime exploration, and lets you "walk on water." The **Puerto de Indias** reconstructs a 15th-century port with shops, taverns and crafts of the era. There are miles of nature sights and cable cars, catamarans and a circus, ending with an impressive fireworks and laser show at night. *Admission: 500 ptas. for entry; 4000 ptas. for adults or 3000 ptas. for children and senior citizens for all pavilions.*

Where to Stay

A rush of hotels arrived for the 1992 Seville World's Fair so that now, during normal times, Seville has sufficient beds for all her guests. But not for Easter week or the *fiera* that follows it. You are already too late for lodgings for these events, though you can commute to them from Madrid, Málaga, Córdoba or Granada. At any other times beds should be available, although at prices almost a third higher than usual for Spain. Inexpensive and moderately priced rooms are hard to find. A clutch of fabulously atmospheric hotels also rings the city. Consider driving 20 miles or less into town from one of the three listed below, instead of staying in the city.

Very Expensive ($200+)

Alfonso XIII   Deluxe ★ ★ ★ ★

San Fernando, 2, Sevilla (on its own grounds opposite the rear of the Alcázar gardens), ☎ *422 28 50, FAX 421 60 33, Telex 72725.*

Utterly deluxe and among the most atmospheric hotel in Spain, the Alfonso was built so that aristocrats would have a place to stay while visiting the 1929 World's

Fair. The style is Mudejar with elegant glazed tiles, marble and mahogany everywhere, all surrounding a central patio that offers as lovely a spot for a drink as anyone could wish for. Of course the hotel location is perfect, and it is managed by the CIGA chain, which speaks well for the quality of service. It is, however, very expensive, approaching 40,000 pesetas for a double, though handsome discounts are given for stays of two nights or more. *122 rooms, plus 19 suites.*

In Sanlúcar la Mayor, 27 km west:

Hacienda Benazuza   1st-class ★ ★ ★ ★ ★

Virgén de las Nieves, Sanlúcar la Mayor (take exit 6 off A-49 to Huelva to N-431 to Sanlúcar for signs), ☎ *570 33 44, FAX 570 34 10.*
Closed from the middle of July through August.
Be a caballero for a night or two in this luxury hacienda, parts of which date to the 10th century. It's majestic, evocative and supplies every luxury including some of the best food in Spain for a memorable total experience. Chef Eric Del Gallo of the hotel's La Alqueria Restaurant is French trained, but composes his own dishes, such as hot shrimp salad, saffron potatoes and squab with truffles and cabbage. *26 rooms, plus 18 suites.*

In Seville:

Las Casas de la Judería   A1st-class ★ ★ ★

Pl. Santa Maria la Blanca, Sevilla (This plaza runs north-south at the eastern end of the Barrio Santa Cruz. The hotel is a block north.), ☎ *441 51 50, FAX 442 21 70.*
Four houses near the Barrio Santa Cruz were combined and gutted to produce a small number of comfortable apartment suites. In addition to one, two or three bedrooms each has a dining room and kitchen, including clothes washer and dryer. The furniture includes fine antique reproductions, and many rooms overlook lovely internal patios. For a party of travelers who would need more than one hotel room, a suite with two or three bedrooms could actually prove a bargain. *31 suites.*

Expensive ($100–$200)

In Carmona, 33 km east:

Casa de Carmona   1st-class ★ ★ ★

Pl. de Lasso, 1, Carmona (take N-IV east toward Écija to the first exit for Carmona. At the entrance to town.), ☎ *414 33 00, FAX 414 37 52.*
This is a 16th-century palace outfitted as a luxury hotel. The courtyard with its orange trees is sufficient reason to stay, that is, if you can leave the magnificent sitting room with elegant antiques and its starry ceiling. Bedrooms are cozy with delicate floral designs. There is even a pool. *29 rooms, plus one suite*

Parador Alcázar del Rey Don Pedro   1st-class ★ ★ ★

Carmona 41410 (outside of Carmona, follow signs through town), ☎ *414 10 10, FAX 414 17 12, Telex 72992.*
Pedro the Cruel used Moorish craftsmen to build the Seville Alcázar then sent them to renovate a fortress high on the Carmona hill into his summer palace. Now his 14th-century palace has been remodeled once more into a comfortable parador in which history seeps from every stone. Take a gander at the baronial dinning room, then retreat to your comfortable bedroom to dream of days gone by. *63 rooms.*

In Seville:

Tryp Colón   Deluxe ★ ★ ★

Canalejas, 1, Sevilla (two blocks south of the Museo Bellas Artes), ☎ *422 29 00, FAX 422 09 38, Telex 72726.*

This is the other grand old hotel of Seville, also built for the 1929 World's Fair. The lobby is dramatically lit by a stained glass dome and the hotel has been recently remodeled to maintain its place near the top. However, it is not the Alfonso XIII either in luxury, location or romance, although it does save half the pesetas. *211 rooms, plus seven suites.*

Doña Maria   1st-class ★ ★ ★

Don Remondo, 16, Sevilla (head to the east end of the Cathedral and go northeast along C. Don Remondo for less than half a block), 5 ☎ *422 49 90, FAX 422 97 65.*

This gem of a small hotel is as conveniently located as a hotel can be—you can hit the Cathedral with a rock. The decor is lux and homey at the same time and each bedroom is different, which means that some are better than others. This is a most pleasant change from big hotel monotony at a price that is barely expensive. *nine rooms, plus two suites.*

Raddisson Príncipe de Asturias   Deluxe ★ ★ ★

Isla de la Cartuja, Sevilla (on the Expo '92 island), ☎ *446 22 22, FAX 446 04 28.*

This was the major hotel project for the Expo '92 World's Fair. During the fair you had to be a head of state to stay, now its three rings of circular corridors are filled with the rest of us. The attraction is the ultramodern style and being the only hotel on an island that is its own three-ringed circus. A five-minute taxi ride whisks you to the sights. *288 rooms, plus seven suites.*

Inglaterra   1st-class ★ ★

Pl. Nueva, 7, Sevilla (this lovely plaza fronts the west side of the Ayuntamiento, a block due north of the Cathedral), ☎ *422 49 70, FAX 456 13 36, Telex 72244.*

This is a staid hotel, with an atmosphere that belies its modern architecture. The service is superior and the rooms are eminently comfortable, but it seems expensive for what it provides. *109 rooms, plus four suites.*

Meliá Sevilla   1st-class ★ ★

Av. de la Borbolla, 3, Sevilla (just east of the northeast end of Parque de Maria Luisa), ☎ *442 15 11, FAX 442 16 08, Telex 730 94.*

This is a modern high-rise hotel, all gleaming metal and polished stone, and thoroughly impersonal. The rooms are comfortable, but it is a bit of a hike to the sights. A room costs half that of the Alfonso XII, and the buffet breakfast includes champagne, however. *365 rooms, plus five suites.*

Bécquer   2nd-class ★

Reyes Católicos, 4, Sevilla (This street runs away from the Puente Triana, a.k.a. Isabel II, the bridge just north of the Pl. de Toros. The hotel is at the beginning of the street.), ☎ *422 89 00, FAX 421 44 00, Telex 72884.*

The hotel dates from the 60s, and is beginning to gain the charm that comes with age and good maintenance. Marble and dark woods in the lobby provide some elegance, and the service is more than adequate. If only the rooms had a little more character and the prices were less. *120 rooms.*

Moderate ($50–$99)

La Rábida   2nd-class ★

Castelar, 24, Sevilla (from the northwest corner of the Cathedral go west along C. Garcia de Vinuesa for one block, then right for two blocks along C. Castelar), ☎ *422 09 60, FAX 422 43 75, Telex 73062.*

This is a converted townhouse with atmosphere with low rates. A pleasant patio resides inside, which some of the rooms overlook. The bedrooms are modern and comfortable, a good choice that would be even better if the staff cared more. *87 rooms.*

Alcázar   2nd-class

Meléndez Pelayo, 10, Sevilla (across the street from the northeast end of the Alcázar gardens), ☎ *441 20 11, Telex 72360.*

This is a modern hotel of no distinction except that the location is convenient to the sights and the bedrooms are larger than most. *96 rooms.*

Inexpensive (Less than $50)

Murillo   3rd-class ★ ★

Lope de Rueda, 9, Sevilla (Located in the heart of the Barrio Santa Cruz where no car can go. A porter will carry your luggage from the Pl. Santa Cruz, however.), ☎ *421 60 95, FAX 421 96 16.*

This lovely little hotel is beautifully decorated in the character of Andalusia. The public areas are warm with dark woods though the bedrooms could be brighter. *57 rooms.*

Hostal Goya   P2nd-class ★ ★

Mateos Gago, 31, Sevilla (the street goes due east from the east face of the Cathedral and reaches this hotel in two blocks), ☎ *421 11 70.*

This would be a find, if it hadn't already been found, with so few rooms that it is essential to book in advance. The building with its gay awnings is charming, the rooms are clean and there is a garden on the roof. The location is as good as that of the Alfonso XIII for about a sixth of its price. Of course you don't get air conditioning, and no credit cards are accepted. *20 rooms, half with bath.*

Youth Hostel

Albergue Juvenil Sevilla

C. Isaac Peral, 2, Sevilla (several km southeast of the center; take bus 34 from Pl. Nueva or in front of the Office of Tourism), ☎ *461 31 54.*

This is a heavily booked hostel that imposes a three-day limit on stays. But there are no curfews, the cost is 1000 ptas. and there are palms to overlook in the yard.

Where to Eat

Seville's reputation is that it serves the best food in Andalusia. Here tapas were invented, and some of the best can still be found—eating is one of Seville's genuine treats. On a fine afternoon or evening, a pleasant outing can be made across the river over the bridge near the Torre del Oro and turning right along C. Betis. The atmosphere is that of a summer resort and restaurants, many with views of the river and the sights, serve quite good food. For recommendations look for the C. Betis address in the selections below. If feeling in a picnic mood, have a cup of gazpacho to go from **Gaspaciaria** at C. Hernando Colón, 7, just north of the Cathedral.

Expensive ($30+)

Egaña Oriza ★★★★

San Fernando, 41 (at the southeast tip of the Alcázar Garden), ☎ *422 72 11.*
Closed Saturday at lunch, Sunday, and August.

This restaurant is the most innovative and acclaimed in Seville. The bar at the entrance serves sublime tapas. The dining room is comfortably large, modern and tan, brightened by light from a two-story glass wall. The food is Basque nueva, unique and subtle. How does quenelles of duck on a potato nest sound? Game is a specialty. Here you are in the chef's hands and they are good hands indeed. Reservations are essential and prices are very high, a bit too high in fact, but almost worth it. Credit Cards: A, D, M, V.

Pello Roteta ★★★

Farmacéutico Murillo Herrera, 10 (across the river, three blocks behind C. Betis), ☎ *427 84 17.*
Closed Sunday and from the middle of August through the middle of September.

Roteta got better and better to the point where its quality was acknowledged by a Michelin star, then it fell back on its laurels. The dining room remains elegant without overpowering, for it is the food that counts here. The accent is Basque, mainly practiced on seafood. Try the heavenly blanquette of monkfish (rape) with crayfish tails. Whatever you do, save room for the gelatine of fresh fruit. Prices remain low for the quality of this cuisine which still makes this a special place. Credit Cards: A, D, M, V.

In Sanlucar la Mayor, 27 km west:

La Alquería Restaurant at Hacienda Benazuza ★★★

Virgén de las Nieves (take exit 6 off A-49 to Huelva to N-431 to Sanlúcar for signs), ☎ *570 33 44, FAX 570 34 10.*
Closed from the middle of July through August.

This luxury hacienda in acres of countryside currently serves some of the best food in Spain. Chef Eric Del Gallo of the hotel's La Alqueria Restaurant is French trained, but composes his own dishes, such as hot shrimp salad, saffron potatoes and squab with truffles and cabbage. In addition there are special menus to keep the cost down. Lunch is a buffet for about 2000 ptas. Credit Cards: A, D, M, V.

La Albahaca ★★

Pl. Santa Cruz, 12 (in the Barrio Santa Cruz, one block north of the eastern end of the Alcázar Gardens), ☎ *422 07 14.*
Closed Sunday.

This is the intimate, romantic place people imagine in Seville, all tiles and greens in an elegant small mansion. The food and service will not disappoint. Sea bass with fennel and bonito are just two specialties, and how does tangerine mousse sound for dessert? Credit Cards: A, D, M, V.

Asador Ox's ★★

C. Betis, 61 (opposite side of the river, opposite the Cathedral), ☎ *427 95 85.*
Closed Sunday in summer, Sunday night in winter, and August.

Although the chef is Basque, the restaurant specializes in grilled fish and meats, all perfectly done. Installed in a small townhouse, the light decor lends a fresh feeling. Credit Cards: A, D, M, V.

La Isla ★★

C. Arfe, 25 (cross Av. de la Constitución at the southern end of the Cathedral and take the first right down C. Arfe, little more than an alley), ☎ *421 26 31.*
Closed Monday, and from the middle of August to the middle of September.

In an ancient building but newly decorated in salmon and white with black lacquer furniture, this is the best pure seafood restaurant in Seville. Start with the house paella, followed by the fish of your choice, and you will hardly notice that the service lacks a certain graciousness. Credit Cards: A, D, M, V.

Florencia ★

Av. Eduardo Dato, 49 (this avenue runs due east from the northern tip of the Alcázar Gardens, though the street begins with the name of C. Demetrio de Rios, a walk of about four long blocks), ☎ *453 35 00.*
Closed August.

The dining room, done in peach and light greys is the most elegant in the city. The menu tends to the novelle, with a menu de degustación to sample the chef's proudest wares. While the food is quite good, it falls short of its setting. Credit Cards: A, D, M, V.

Rio Grande

C. Betis, 61 (opposite Ox's), ☎ *427 39 56.*

The view from the terrace is the thing here, especially at night when lights sparkle on the river. Although the menu ranges over international dishes, we suggest sticking with Andalusian ones, such as paella and gazpacho which are done reasonably well. Credit Cards: A, V, D, M.

Moderate ($15–$30)

Los Alcázares ★

C. Miguel de Manara, 10 (la few steps west of the Alcázar front, across from the Archivo de Indias), ☎ *421 31 03.*
Closed Sunday.

The decor is typical Andalusian and the menu covers the expected, but the bill will be less. For the price and basic Spanish food, this is a good place. Credit Cards: A, D, M, V.

Modesto ★

C. Cano y Cueto, 5 (C. Santa Maria la Blanca forms the eastern border of the Barrio Santa Cruz. The restaurant's street runs east from its southern end), ☎ *441 68 11.*
Closed Wednesday.

This is a popular, unassuming place that serves superior tapas in great variety. If you're in the mood for a full meal, the dining room upstairs is pleasant with white walls and blue-and-white tiles, more intimate than the tables outside. Fried fish is delectable, as are the specials. Credit Cards: A, D, M, V.

Inexpensive (Less than $15)

Hostería del Laurel

Pl. Venerables, 5 (this plaza is exactly in the center of the Barrio Santa Cruz), ☎ *422 02 95.*

The outside looks like a mesón should, and the inside continues the theme with hanging hams and garlic above heavy wooden tables. The food is standard Spanish cuisine, but agreeable and inexpensive. Credit Cards: A, D, M, V.

Pizzeria San Marco   ★

C. Betis, 66 (just south of Ox's), ☎ *428 03 10. Closed Mon.*

Yes it is a pizzeria, but all modern and shining and heavily patronized by the locals. The most expensive pasta is less than $10, and tasty.

Evenings Out

Seville is the best place to see flamenco and maintains three permanent *tablas* for the art. Each is a small place, seating an audience of 50 or fewer, so reservations are always a good idea and can be arranged by most hotels.

Los Gallos

Pl. Santa Cruz, 11, ☎ *421 69 81.*

Too intimate for comfort, but Gallos puts on the most authentic flamenco, and prides itself on the best performers.

El Arenal

Dos de Mayo, 26, ☎ *421 64 92.*

Will serve you dinner, or not, as you wish, and the show is often good.

El Patio Sevillano

Paseo de Colón, 11, ☎ *421 41 20.*

Mixes other kinds of folk dance and songs with flamenco for mainly tour groups.

Understand that pure flamenco can be very intense. The aim is to throw one's soul to the audience; performers are judged by the depth of their feelings. It is part dance, part guitar music, part singing and part rhythmic clapping. The dancing should be familiar, but the singing is strangely guttural and as earthy as the human voice can become. Guitarists can be amazing virtuosos, and the clapping incredible. Given a good group of performers, the experience will be unforgettable. Current prices are 3000 ptas., which includes one free drink. In summer there usually are three shows, one at about 7:30 p.m., another at 10 p.m., the last at midnight, but check. In winter the second and final performance will be at around 10 p.m.

Directory

Information

Located on Av. de la Constitución, 21B, just south of the Cathedral. Open Mon.–Sat. from 9:30 a.m. to 7:30 p.m. and Sun. from 9:30 a.m. to 2 p.m. ☎ *422 14 04.*

Airport

Seville's San Pablo Airport (☎ *451 61 11*) connects with major European cities and most Spanish airports, but few overseas destinations. It is located 12 km east along N-IV. A taxi should cost about 2000 ptas. Currently, seven flights per day travel to Madrid and five to Barcelona. Iberia is located at *Almirante Lobo, 3 (* ☎ *422 89*

01). This street runs to the river from Puerta de Jerez, the plaza at the western corner of the Alcázar gardens. Buses connect from there with flights.

Trains and Buses

The train station is Santa Justa (☎ *454 02 02*) at the intersection of José Laguillo and Av. Kansas City, about one mile northeast of the Cathedral. Six high speed AVE trains connect with Madrid in under three hours (6000–9000 ptas.), half the time and twice the price of other types of trains. The AVE also goes to Córdoba 10 times per day in under an hour (about 3000 ptas.). Slower trains double the time and halve the price. Only three trains go to Granada per day for a trip of almost five hours. Málaga is also served three times per day. Four trains daily take the 10–13 hour trip to Barcelona for 9000 to 7000 ptas. The RENFE office is on *C. Zaragoza, 29,* about three blocks north of the Pl. de Toros (☎ *421 79 98).*

Seven different bus companies split up the routes, and depart from two different stations. Plaza de Armas (☎ *490 80 40)* at the junction of Puente Cristo de la Expiración (opposite the Expo '92 island) serves longer distances. Plaza de San Sebastián (☎ *441 71 11)* at C. José María Osborne (just east of the Alcázar gardens) handles Córdoba, Granada, Málaga and other nearby areas with frequent service. See the office of tourism for schedules and the various companies.

Post Office And Telephones

The main post office is at *Av. de la Constitución, 32,* west of the Archivo de Indias. Telephones are available at the *Pl. Nueva, 3,* which is on the west side of the Ayuntamiento, and open weekdays to 10 p.m., though closed for lunch. Sat., it closes at 2 p.m.

Police

The main station is at the *Pl. de la Delicias* (☎ *461 67 76;* ☎ *091* for emergencies).

Shopping

Among the best buys in Spain are ceramics made in Seville, partly because their prices are low, partly because the quality of work and design is high. You can get a taste of the wares by walking along the pedestrian mall of C. Sierpes. At #30 is **Cerámica Sevillano**, with fine designs, and at #66 **Sevillarte**, equally good. **Martian** at #6 sells thicker, more folk-like pieces. If you like what you see, there is a larger selection at **Cerámicas Sevilla** on Pemiento, #9, which runs beside the wall to the Alcázar Gardens in the Barrio Santa Cruz. This outlet continues around the corner, at Gloria, #5. The wares are part gold-rimmed which are Moorish-inspired and part Renaissance blues on white and blues and greens on white. The supply is so large this shop seems to be a factory, but it is not. For the true factories and their outlets, you have to cross the river over Puente Isabel II, the bridge just north of the Pl. de Toros. Directly off the bridge you come to C. San Jorge and the heart of the ceramic outlets. Prices are incredibly low, and most companies will ship. Try **Cerámica Santa Ana** at #31, **Cerámica Ruiz** at #27, and **Cerámica Montalvan**, especially for tiles, around the corner at Alfareria #21.

Interesting too are the fans, including some very expensive hand-painted antiques, at **Casa Rubio** on C. Sierpes, #56. Farther down Sierpes at #73 is a leather shop named **Bolsos Casal** with copies of expensive name bags for women at modest prices. For the horsey set there is a superb leather store, **El Caballo**, on *C. Antonio Diaz, #7*, at the end of the street on the east side of the Pl. de Toros. You can also get those flat brimmed Spanish riding hats. A nice branch of **Artespaña** displays well-made furniture and accessories in the Pl. de la Gavidia, just north of the **el Corte Inglés** department store at the end of C. Sierpes.

Yes, there is a **flea market**. It opens every Sunday morning along C. Alameda de Hercules, which is north of the Museo de Bellas Artes.

Excursions

Roman remains at **Itálica** lie nine km north, for a half day of exploring. **Jerez de la Frontera**, the home of sherry, waits an hour south for a pleasant half day of free or inexpensive samples. Of course, magical **Córdoba** and **Granada** are within a few hours east, and described under their respective headings in this chapter. For an excursion of two or three days, consider the area of **Extremadura**, due north, which has not yet become flooded with tourists and is described in a later chapter. Also, the Portuguese border and beginning of the Algarve beaches are 175 km to the west; Lisbon is 417 km distant.

For **Itálica** *cross the river on the Puente de Chapina, the third bridge north of the Cathedral area, to travel west along C. Ordiel on the west bank. Follow signs to Santiponce and Mérida. About three km outside of town turn north on N-630. Follow signs one km past Santiponce for Itálica.*

Buses leave every 30 minutes or so from the Pl. de Armas bus station on the river next to the bridge to Expo 92.

For the **Algarve** *follow the directions for Itálica but do not turn north on N-630. Continue west instead on A-49 (E-1). After three km, switch to N-431, just before Huelva in 92 km, and a farther journey of 63 km to Portuguese border.*

For **Lisbon** *follow the directions to Itálica and continue past it along N-630. Just before Zafra in 134 km turn west on N-432 (E-102) to Badajoz in 79 km at the border. West from Badajoz on N-4 (E-90) brings you to Cruzamento de Pagoes in 152 km. There go south on N-10 (still E-90) to Setubal in 35 km and the highway E-1 to Lisbon 50 km away.*

For **Extremadura** *follow the directions to Itálica and continue past it along N-630. You arrive at Mérida in 194 km.*

For **Jerez** *follow Av. de la Palmera leading south from the southern end of the Parque de Maria Luisa. You are given the choices of the toll road A-4 or the free N-IV toward Cádiz, reaching Jerez in about 70 km.*

ITÁLICA   ★

Satiponce, ☎ 439 27 84.
Hours open: Tues.–Sat. 9 a.m.–5:30 p.m., Sun. 10 a.m.–4 p.m.

This Roman town was among the earliest in Spain for it was founded in 206 B.C. by Scipio Africanus as a place of retirement for his veterans who defeated Hannibal. By the second century A.D. it had grown to a population of 10,000 and stood among the most important towns in Spain. Two emperors were born here—Trajan and Hadrian. Prosperity ended with the arrival of the Visigoths who favored nearby Seville. Itálica then became a quarry for marble and stone materials, even for mosaics, to use as decoration in later Christian mansions. The surprise is that anything remains, and quite a bit does, though only a quarter of the site has been excavated so far.

There is a huge amphitheater that once seated 40,000, a theater, two baths, a forum and a network of streets. Here and there some remaining mosaics are fenced off, but the major works and all the statuary are carted off to museums in Madrid and Seville as soon as they are uncovered. *Admission: 250 ptas.*

Jerez de las Frontera ★

Population: 176,238.

Area code: 956; Zip code: 11400.

Arrival is along Av. Alcalde Alvaro Domecq, though at C. Guadalete one-way signs force a right onto C. Beato Juan Grande, which becomes Alameda Cristina in one block. Continue one block and turn slightly left. Then one-way signs again force a right fork onto C. Larga. Again comes a fork and a right on C. Lanceria to the garden of the Pl. del Arenal. Turn right then left around the garden, take the first right into the Pl. Monti. Turn left at the end of the plaza past the gardens of the Alcázar. Follow them to their end for parking beside the Alcázar.

NOTE... *Almost all bodegas close Aug., and are closed on weekends.*

The Arabs corrupted the Roman name *Caesaris* to *Xerex*, which the Spanish in turn corrupted to Jerez. Then an English corruption gave us "sherry." Jerez is a rather quiet and pleasant town, a place to see a nice Alcázar, some mansions, a sherry bodega or two, and even some elegant dressage similar to the Viennese Lippizaners. As to the bodegas, most open only weekday mornings between 10 a.m. and 1 p.m., or so, close all of August, and most charge an admission of between 250 and 400 ptas. For this you get a tour of almost an hour and samples. Most of the tours are in English.

After a look at the restored **Alcázar**, a stop can be made at the oldest bodega in Jerez, **Gonzalez Byass** (needs a reservation), at *C. Manuel Maria Gonzalez, 12* (☎ *34 00 00*), the street west of the Alcázar. Return to C. Manuel Maria Gonzalez and follow it north. As it bends east around the gardens, take the first left to the **Colegiata church ★** with a fine baroque stair and portal. In the sacristy hangs Zurbarán's *Sleeping Girl*, a worthwhile work seldom seen or reproduced. North of the church we arrive in the Pl. del Arroyo, a.k.a. Pl. de Domecq. At its west end C. San Ildefonso runs north to the bodega of **Pedro Domencq**, one of the largest shippers. In this instance reservations are required *(☎ 33 19 00)*, but the visit is free. At the east end of the Pl. Arroyo is the huge **Palacio de Marquesse de Bertemati**. Following its south side for a block brings the charming **Pl. del Asunción**. At its south end is the **Casa del Cabildo Vieja**, late 16th-century with an ornate facade. A small archaeological museum is housed inside. On the east side of the plaza is **San Dionisio**, a redone Moorish-Gothic church, still with a nice Mudejar tower and fine artesonado ceiling above the nave. Four or five blocks northeast of the plaza is the house of the discoverer of Florida, **Ponce de León** (1537), with a pretty patio.

For more bodegas stop by the **office of tourism** for a map and information. It is located two blocks north of the Pl. Arenal gardens at *C. Alameda Cristina, 7 (☎ 33 11 50)*.

You need a cab to get to the **Real Escuela de Andaluza de Arte Equestre** on Av. de Duque de Abrantes, 11 *(☎ 31 11 11)* to see Lippizaner-like dressage. Shows are Thurs. from noon to 1:30 p.m. and tickets are available at the box office, which opens at 11 a.m., for 1800–2300 ptas., depending on seats (children pay less). Dress rehearsals happen on Mon., Wed. and Fri. at 11 a.m. for less than half the full-dress charge.

Úbeda ★ ★

Population: 28,717
Area code: 953; Zip code: 23400

From **Madrid** *take A-4 (E-5) south toward Ocaña. Along the way the highway becomes N-IV. Continue for 292 km to Bailén to take N-322 east toward Úbeda for 40 km. To combine with* **Baeza,** *close by, take N-321 west for nine km to Baeza. After Baeza, N-321 wends to Jaén in 48 km, just before which N-323 heads south to Granada in 93 km. Or, return to Bailén, from which N-IV heads west to Córdoba in 108 km.*

From **Granada** *take N-323 north toward Jaén for 88 km, changing to N-321 east toward Úbeda just before Jaén. Úbeda is 57 km along N-321. From Córdoba take N-IV west toward Andújar and Bailén for 108 km. From Bailén take N-322 east toward Úbeda for 40 km.*

Like its sister city Baeza, Úbeda was taken early by the Christians during their Reconquest and became wealthy as a staging post for the battles farther south. In the 16th century, it invested those profits on monuments and palaces, unfortunately just as a new road to thriving Jaén was about to turn Úbeda into a backwater. These lovely building are spread around, but one perfect concentration in the Pl. Vázquez de Molina constitutes one of the finest single assemblages of Renaissance architecture in Spain.

The city does its part to accommodate tourists by clear signs directing traffic to the *Zona Monumental,* the major sights within the old city walls. Úbeda also offers crafts in a Gypsy quarter nearby. All can be seen in two hours.

The place to begin is the harmonious open Pl. Vázquez de Molina. Due north is the **Casa de las Cadenas**, now the city hall, named for the chains around the forecourt, and built for a secretary to Felipe II. Its front is imposing with classical columns and surprising, out of place, caryatids. Wander around the back for a look at its lovely patio and a stop at the **tourist office** next door for a fine brochure and map.

In the Pl. Molina again, the mansion next to the Casa de las Cadenas is the **Palacio del Condestabal Dávalos** ★, a 17th-century renovation of a structure a century older. Its long, restrained front is made harmonious by two elegant lines of windows. This is one of the first historic buildings made into a parador, in 1930, and is still splendid inside. Opposite, to the south of the plaza, is the church of **Santa Maria de los Reales Alcázares**. Behind it are remains of the Moorish **Alcázar** for which it is named, but the church is mainly 16th-century inside with notable painted ironwork and unusual ceilings of arabesques painted blue.

At the east end of the plaza stands the unusual **Capilla del Salvador**. (If closed, apply to the first door on the right.) This church once formed part of a great palace designed for Carlos V, but only it and some ruins behind remain. The front is a truly original design by the architect Vandelvira from plans by Gil de Siloé. Two round towers at the corners seem much too low, until the eye rises to the triangular pediment above, and grasps the triangular design. The portal is styled as a Roman arch with scenes carved around and above. The inside suffered great damage during anticlerical raids at the outbreak of the Spanish Civil War, including the destruction of most of the church treasures and art, but has been reconstructed to its original neoclassical look. A theatrical high altar behind fine ornamental ironwork contains what remains of Berruguete's original retable, and the sacristy is a glorious Italianate masterpiece of coffered ceiling, medallions, graceful caryatids and atlantes.

Walk north from the front of the chapel up C. Horno Contador passing the **Casa de los Salvajes** on the left in one block. The reason for the name is evident in the men dressed in animal skins holding the coat of arms of a local bishop. A short block further brings the Pl. Primero de Mayo, the main square. Across, well displayed, sits the church of **San Pablo** ★. The west front portal is accomplished 13th-century work; the south portal is a lovely Isabelline design. Inside, the chapels command attention with fine iron grillwork, stucco vaults and doorways.

Continue from the rear of the church northeast along C. Rosal. The **Casa Canastero**, in a short block, was a bishop's mansion, with two carved soldiers bearing the owner's coat of arms. More mansions line the previous street, C. Montiel. Ahead stand the city walls and a 14th-century **Mudejar gate**. Outside the walls the street is renamed Cuesta de la Merced, and changes its name again after going through a square to C. Valencia. Here is the Gypsy quarter and crafts of pottery, ironwork and esparto grass.

If time permits, the huge **Hospitale de Santiago** at the intersection of C. Obispo Cobos and the road to Jaén is worth seeing. It was built in 1575 by the architect who executed the Capilla el Salvador. A large statue of St. James as the Killer of Moors rises above the entrance, and inside is a classical colonnaded patio with a grand staircase covered by original frescos.

Where to Stay

While there is no need to stay the night in Úbeda with Granada and Córdoba an hour away, there is no reason not to enjoy the lovely parador either, or some less expensive accommodation.

Expensive ($100–$200)

Parador Condestabal Dávalos   1st-class ★ ★ ★

Pl. Vázquez de Molina, 1, Úbeda, ☎ *75 03 45, FAX 75 12 59.*

This parador, installed in the 16th-century palace of the commander-in-chief of Castile's army, is one of the loveliest small ones, and situated on a pretty square. The patio is elegant, the common spaces are homey with working fireplaces, the stairway to the rooms is grand, and the ample rooms have wood ceilings and commodious baths. *31 rooms.*

Inexpensive (Less than $50)

La Paz   3rd-class ★

Andalucia, 1, Úbeda (at the northeast corner of the old city walls), ☎ *75 21 46, FAX 75 08 48.*

The hotel is modern and the rooms are simple, but with homey touches. This place sparkles because of a renovation in 1994. A stay here also provides an opportunity to investigate the city walls. *51 rooms.*

Where to Eat

Pickings are slim for a town of this size, with only one place we can recommend. Of course, there is always the parador.

Moderate ($15–$30)

Cusco

Parque de Vandelvira, 8, ☎ *75 34 13.*

Closed Monday night and from the middle of July through August.

The place is simple and so is the food, but it is prepared with some care. And the bill will not shock. Credit Cards: A, V.

Directory

Information

Pl. del Ayuntamiento, 2, next to the rear of the Ayuntamiento. ☎ *75 08 97.* Open Mon.–Fri. 10 a.m. to 1:30 p.m. and 6–8 p.m. Open weekends 10 a.m. to 1:30 p.m.

Trains And Buses

Buses leave the central C. San José nine times a day for the train station at Linares-Baeza 20 km away. Buses are frequent to Baeza (less than $2) and connect less frequently with Córdoba, Seville and Madrid.

Post Office and Telephones

On C. Trinidad, just north of the walls. ☎ *75 00 31.*

Police

In the Ayuntamiento. ☎ *75 00 23.*

Excursions

The natural excursion is to Baeza. Granada, Córdoba and even Seville are an hour or two away. See the respective descriptions under separate headings in this chapter.

EXTREMADURA

After 2000 years the Roman bridge at Mérida still stands.

Historical Profile:
Columbus and the Conquistadores

Christopher Columbus was born Cristoforo Colombo in Genoa, Italy in 1451, the son of a master wool weaver. Attracted more by the tales from sailors in this seaport town than by the prosaic looms to which he was apprenticed, he grew into a romantic, dreaming of fabled kingdoms. Physically, he was tall, with high cheekbones, an aquiline nose, a ruddy complexion and striking red hair—that turned white by the age of 30. It is likely that the blood of an ancient barbarian who had invaded Italy flowed somewhere in his veins.

The first records of Columbus at sea occur only after the sale of his family's house and business in 1473, when he was 22. Columbus apparently worked for his father, as youths of the time generally did, until something caused the family business to fail, setting Columbus free. The next year Columbus sailed to North Africa as a deckhand, and a year after to the Aegean. In 1476, he joined a merchant convoy to Portugal, but his ship was attacked off the Lisbon coast by pirates and sunk. Columbus swam to shore and made his way into the city, which was then a center for maritime exploration. After a quick return to Genoa, he set off for Lisbon again to begin a new life.

He resided for eight years among a community of Genoese in Lisbon where he and his brother sold maps. Here he taught himself Portuguese, Spanish and Latin. Columbus was devoutly religious, so it was not surprising that he first met Felipa Perestrello e Moniz, the daughter of a deceased aristocratic sea captain, in a chapel near his shop. They fell in love and were married in 1479. Diego, their first son, was born the next year.

Soon after, Columbus sailed with Felipa for a stay with her relatives in Madeira, and later—probably thanks to friends of her father—joined an expedition sailing to West Africa's Gold Coast. These voyages sent Columbus to farther reaches than all but a handful of his contemporaries.

Felipa's contacts gained Columbus an audience with the king of Portugal in 1484, to whom Columbus proposed his grand plan to sail west to Cathay, to Cipango (Japan) and India to trade there for precious spices, pearls and gold. Although the Portuguese king declined to support this expedition, he left open the possibility of reconsideration. However, when word arrived that Bartholeme Dias had rounded Africa, the king no longer had reason to explore a westward course to India, for one of his own captains had opened an eastward route.

There is no mystery about how Columbus came to the idea of reaching the Indies by sailing west. Educated people of the time all knew these lands lay somewhere across the Atlantic, for even then, belief in a flat earth was confined to the ignorant. Columbus differed only in his assessment of the practicality of such a trip. He thought the East lay 2400 miles west of the Azores, the westernmost lands known to Europeans—a voyage of less than three months—while conventional wisdom estimated the distance at daunting 10,000 miles. It was one thing in those times to cruise along a coastline for a month or more, quite another to sail for long periods out of sight of land. Although the astrolabe existed, its use required data from prior voyages, so uncharted waters could only be traversed by imprecise compass dead-reckoning. The longer the voyage, the farther off course errors would take a ship.

and errors were unavoidable. Educated people believed that Columbus' project was possible, but, if the distance was 10,000 miles, too risky to undertake.

Because Columbus placed Japan a thousand miles closer to Europe than most cartographers, he figured that the Indies were one quarter as distant as the others thought, for, by decreasing the size of each degree of latitude, he lowered the scholarly estimate of the world by 25 percent. Of course, Columbus was wrong: 2400 miles west of the Azores lay the Virgin Islands in the Caribbean, not Japan.

Felipa died in 1485, leaving Columbus to raise his five-year-old son. Unable to generate interest in his plan at the Portuguese court, Columbus sailed to Spain. On landing, he placed his child in the monastery of la Rabida, near modern Huelva, a step that would prove crucial to making his eventual voyage possible. In Seville he met Enrique de Gúzman, the Duke of Medina Sidonia, a hero of the Reconquest. Enrique agreed to underwrite Columbus' voyage, but then engaged in a private quarrel that caused the king and queen to exile him from the city. Columbus next turned to Luis de la Cerda, the Duke of Medina Celi, who owned a merchant fleet, and gained his support. Columbus required no more money than a wealthy person of the time could afford—less than $100,000 by today's standards—and unfailingly convinced those who heard his arguments. Only scholars resisted him. But Luis thought the enterprise should have royal approval, so he asked permission of the queen.

Queen Isabella invited Columbus to explain his proposal in person, and they met in nearby Córdoba. She was interested enough to consider royal sponsorship, but first submitted the matter to a commission of scholars for study. In the meantime, she provided Columbus with housing and a stipend. Columbus waited for six years, as the royal stipend dwindled away, until the commission issued its report: the enterprise was indeed possible, but it was based on factual errors that made it impractical.

A desolate Columbus returned to the monastery of la Rabida to collect his son, intending to sail for France or England to try for other sponsorship. But first he told his tale to the abbot of the monastery, Juan Perez, and created another convert. The abbot, who had once been confessor to the queen, asked Isabella to reconsider. She sent for Columbus, supplying a mule and money for his transport to Santa Fé, outside of Granada which she was then besieging.

Presumably this recall meant that Isabella had changed her mind and was now willing to support Columbus, yet after their meeting she dismissed him again. The suspicion is that, after gaining approval in principle, Columbus cooled the queen's ardor by asking for excessive rewards. We know he demanded that he be raised to noble rank, named Admiral of the Ocean Seas (the highest maritime office in Spain), appointed governor-general of any lands he should discover, and receive one-tenth of all the profits realized from his explorations.

As Columbus rode off on his mule, the royal treasurer Santangel changed Isabella's mind once again by pointing out that the necessary funds were available in a dormant account. The titles and percentages should not be a sticking point, he suggested, since they would be granted only if Columbus were successful and in that event would be merited. Isabella sent for Columbus one last time and agreed to underwrite his expedition.

Columbus sped to Palos de la Frontera, beside the monastery, for that city had been fined for a communal misdeed and owed the crown the services of two caravels. These were the *Niña* and the *Pinta*. Each was about 70 feet long by 23 wide, the size of a modern coastal yacht. Columbus bought another vessel, the *Santa María*, which was 50 percent larger although less seaworthy, for his flagship. The *Niña* and *Pinta* carried crews of 24 and 26 respectively, while the *Santa María* carried 40. Sailors consisted primarily of men from nearby towns, and included a sailor sentenced to death for killing a man in a brawl and three of his friends caught engineering his jailbreak. One *converso*, (former Jew) was hired because Columbus thought his knowledge of Hebrew and Arabic would be helpful in conversing with the Great Khan of China.

Preparations were completed by August 2, 1492, but Columbus waited one day more because, on this deadline for all Jews to leave Spain, the seas were congested with ships. On August 3rd his tiny armada set sail for the Azores, where they restocked before entering uncharted waters. Throughout the voyage Columbus kept two ship's logs, a real one and another—for the eyes of the crew—that shaved 10 percent from the distance traveled to make the men feel less far from home. As it happened, the fake log proved the more accurate.

After two months they arrived at the place where Columbus had assured the crews that Japan lay. No land was sighted. The sailors, whose fears had been calmed by Columbus' certainties, now threatened mutiny. If they sailed much farther, their provisions would not last the return trip. Columbus talked them into continuing for two days more. The next day signs of land were spied—a floating log and a carved stick. The second day, October 12, a sailor caught sight of one of the islands of Bermuda.

Columbus sailed around the Caribbean looking for China and Japan, and seeking gold. He landed on Cuba and at the Dominican Republic. Then he returned home, hitting the Azores by superb dead-reckoning. After reprovisioning, he sailed to Portugal, but left hurriedly, fearful of poisoning by the king whose eastern monopoly to India was threatened by Columbus' discoveries. Thirty-two weeks after he had set out, he docked again at Palos, then crossed Spain with six captured Indians (as he called them), colored birds, masks and trinkets of gold. When Columbus arrived in Barcelona, where the court was then in residence, the king and queen wept with him in joy over his success.

Columbus captained three subsequent voyages to explore, colonize and bring Catholicism to the New World. On the second voyage, he carried horses, cows and pigs, none of which existed in the New World. In return his men brought back 500 slaves and syphilis to Europe, although not without first leaving smallpox and measles behind. He sighted the mainland of South America on his third voyage, the first European to do so. But he had no inkling that he had discovered a new continent, assuming that all major land masses must already be known by the enlightened times of the 16th century.

With each succeeding voyage Columbus' star, which had shone so brightly at his first success, grew more tarnished. Colonization had not succeeded: one village was obliterated by Indians, another by disease. Under his command, but not always by his order, natives were killed, enslaved, tortured and raped. He had to contend with the wildness of the terrain, the natives and his own men, a combination that would test any governor's ability. On his third voyage, based on stories from jealous lieutenants, Columbus was arrested in Santa Domingo and carted to Spain in chains, only to be forgiven by his sovereigns in person. The worst ignominy was his return from his fourth voyage to no fanfare at all, in part because his benefactor, Isabella, lay dying.

After Isabella died, King Ferdinand rescinded many of the honors and much of the money that she had promised Columbus. The last years of Columbus' life were spent petitioning for what he had originally been assured. On May 20, 1506, the severely arthritic Columbus died. The coat of arms he personally designed said simply: To Castile and León, a New World given by Columbus.

This New World still remained to be conquered. Mexico and Peru contained Indian kingdoms that would test any European power, but the Spanish conquistadores were extraordinary men who performed what can only be called miracles. Most of them came from Extremadura, on the Portuguese border—hard men bred by a harsh environment.

In 1519, an expedition set out for Mexico under the command of Hernán Cortés. Five hundred men, 15 horses and two cannons landed on the island of Cozumel, then ferried to the mainland. This force was able to hold off and defeat thousands of Indians at a time, thanks in part to the Indians' fear of horses, which they had never seen, in part to legions of Indians who rebelled against the Aztecs and in part to a prophecy that their god Quezalcoatl would return as a white man flying over the sea. Cortés burned his ships to force resolve on his men, then marched to the capital where he invited Montezuma, the emperor of Mexico, to visit, captured him, then defeated his armies. Hundreds of pounds of gold and an empire were gained in the process.

Cortés was born in **Medellin** in Extremadura, to a family of lesser nobility. A sickly child, he studied law for two years at the University of Salamanca before quitting to his parents' grave displeasure. He was a strong-willed young man, determined to win fame as a soldier, so he signed on for a war in Italy. Before embarking, tales about the New World turned his head, however, leading him to spurn his commission for a sail westward instead. After his conquests, he retired to Medellin where he lived for 11 years more, dying at the ripe old age of 63.

In 1512 an ill-fated Spanish expedition landed near modern Panama. Indians killed most of the force; the rest were left under the command of a young lieutenant named Francisco Pizarro. But reinforcements arrived, including a young stowaway named Vasco Núñez de Balboa who was fleeing creditors. After convincing the soldiers to appoint him their leader, Balboa set off into the jungle and discovered the Pacific Ocean. In full armor he walked into the sea to take possession for Castile. Balboa also had been born in Extremadura, in the town of **Jerez de los Caballeros**. Unfortunately, his triumph was short-lived. Envy of his discovery and charges of theft caused the Governor-general of the Americas to order Pizarro to arrest and behead Balboa in 1530.

Pizarro thus became the commander of Central America, an uncharted jungle that held no excitement for him. At age 50 he turned his attention south to modern-day Peru. Using trickery, he captured the ruling Inca and, by governing the country through him, conquered an empire the size of Europe with a population of five million—all with an army of 180 men and 27 horses. The Inca ruler offered one of the world's great bribes for his freedom—enough gold and silver to fill a room 17 feet by 12, as high as Pizarro could reach. Pizarro accepted 13,000 pounds of gold and 26,000 pounds of silver, then burned the Incan ruler at the stake. Later, Pizarro was repaid in kind—assassinated by masked Spanish soldiers.

He too was an Extremaduran, from **Trujillo**. Born illegitimate to a hidalgo captain of infantry and a humble mother, he was raised with the captain's legitimate offspring and took one half-brother with him to Peru. The brother survived to bring riches home to Trujillo, along with an Inca princess wife.

With such conquests came unheard-of fortunes. American silver and gold mines annually supplied the equivalent of the Spanish royal income from all other sources combined, although, unforgiveably, millions of natives perished from starvation and disease to excavate this treasure. The great irony is that Spain was not enriched by her new wealth at all. She had become embroiled in a decades' long war in the Netherlands that consumed all her resources. The gold and silver unloaded from galleons in Seville was immediately transported north to fund Spain's army. All in vain, for Spain lost the war.

Extremadura

The name of the province means "Beyond the Duero (River)." Like its name, the land conjures up extremes. The area is generally poor, though three great rivers course through it. The problem is that their tributaries do not spread far from their main beds, a millennia-old condition that the Spanish government began correcting in the 1950s with dams and canals. The hard land of Extremadura produced hard men—as exemplified by the Spanish adventurers who conquered the great Indian civilizations of the New World. These men seized any opportunity to leave rather than face the prospect of scratching a living from unproductive fields. Hernán Cortés, conqueror of the Aztecs and Mexico, came from Medellin; Francisco Pizarro, conqueror of the Incas and Peru, came from Trujillo; and many of their less famous soldiers emigrated from other Extremaduran villages and towns.

Extremadura comprises the western edge of Spain. Geographically it would be natural for Extremadura to belong to Portugal. Mountains block it from the rest of Spain in the north, east and south, yet it blends unbroken with the land across its western border. The Romans ignored the border in the early centuries of the Christian era and placed their capital of Lusitania, as they called later-day Portugal, at Mérida in Extremadura. There the finest Roman ruins in Spain still survive. When Portugal became a nation by breaking away from Spain in the 11th century, it seized what land it could but was unable to control Extremadura, leaving it in Spanish hands where it remains.

The southern half of Extremadura presents an exotic landscape of flat land strewn with huge boulders that look like Celtic dolmans and menhirs. A white and chalky soil supports acres of olive groves standing immobile around these prehistoric rocks, with an effect that is mystical. Hills emerge in the north, leading to mountains, where the land grows greener and scenic in more standard ways. Extremadura is the least populous area of Spain, as the difficulties of scraping a living would suggest, and thus is more given over to wildlife than elsewhere else. Here you see buzzards, falcons and hawks circling the air and storks by the score settled on rooftop nests. The sounds of castanets heard in many towns are merely storks conversing.

Extremadura is the part of Spain least visited by tourists, which means it is less spoiled and bustling than the rest. Yet, there are sights enough here to repay a two-day pause on the way to or from Andalusia. **Mérida ★★** preserves a Roman theater of elegant design beside a Roman arena. A new museum dramatically presents some of the best Roman art in Spain. The medieval walls of **Cáceres ★★** enclose the most complete and homogeneous assemblage of Renaissance mansions in Spain. Charming **Trujillo ★★**, the home of Pizarro, offers its own Renaissance mansions above a lovely Plaza Mayor, along with castle ruins and history. **Guadalupe ★★★** perches

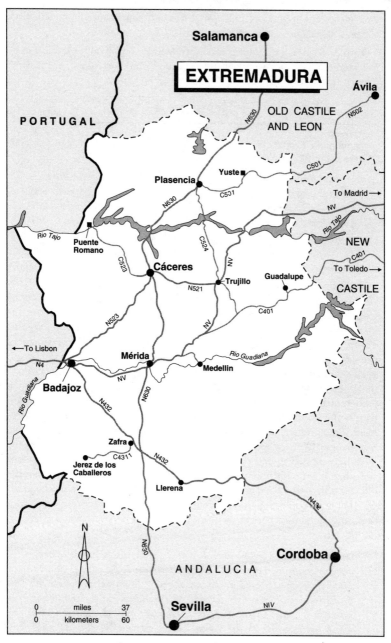

its atmospheric monastery loftily atop a mountain. Inside the famed Black Virgin resides amid riches endowed by the Conquistadores.

From Andalusia, a pleasant route north toward Toledo and Madrid can be followed that includes Mérida, Cáceres, Trujillo and Guadalupe, or the route may be traversed in reverse.

Cáceres ★ ★

Population: 71,852
Area code: 927; zip code: 10000

From **Madrid** *N-V southwest runs straight to Trujillo in 261 kilometers. From* **Trujillo** *head west on N-521 for 49 kilometers to Cáceres. From* **Mérida** *N-630 leads north to Cáceres in 71 kilometers. From* **Andalusia** *see the directions to Mérida. From* **Guadalupe** *C-401 leads to Zorita in 53 kilometers. Go north on C-524 for 28 kilometers to Trujillo, and follow the directions from there. From* **Toledo** *follow the directions to Guadalupe.*

The Romans called it Colonia Norbensis Caesara which the Spanish shortened to Cáceres. It was an early and persistent battleground fought over by Christians and Moors. Here the nucleus of the famed Order of Santiago, the most distinguished society in Spain, was formed in 1170 to muster knights devoted to the Reconquest. By 1229, when Christians had taken control of the city for good, Cáceres was producing company after company of soldiers—first to fight against the Moors, later to conquer the Indian civilizations in the New World. Soldiering proved lucrative for some of these men who returned from campaigns, and they erect houses proclaiming their wealth and status to all. By the end of the 16th century, when no worlds remained to conquer, Cáceres ceased raising mansions, indeed ceased to grow. The happy result for today's visitor is that the old part of the town is the most homogeneous, best preserved Renaissance quarter in Spain. The mansions had been built primarily in the most privileged area—that within the old city walls—and filled those two acres so densely that few stores or modern buildings could find room. Thus, although not especially beautiful or imposing, an almost perfect picture of the Renaissance survives in Cáceres' old quarter.

From **Madrid** *or* **Trujillo** *turn left at the bullring. Be careful to obey one-way signs as they funnel arrivals into the large Pl. del General Mola in front of the old walls and parking. From* **Mérida** *follow Av. de España with its center island. At its end, the street changes its name to C. San Antón. Take the next right onto C. Donoso Cortés which lets into the Pl. del Santa Clara, against the old city walls.*

Turn a hard left, almost doubling back, to follow the walls into the large Pl. del General Mola and parking.

Purple signs saying "Ciudad Monumental" point the way.

What to See and Do

The preeminent sight of Cáceres is the **Renaissance Quarter** ★ ★ ★ contained inside the old walls. Outside, the **church of Santiago** ★, where the Order of Santiago was founded, is worth seeing for a fine retable.

From the spaciousness of the Pl. de General Mola the old **walls** present an imposing face. Although substantially restored now, the foundations are Roman, parts are Moorish, and the remainder date to the 15th century. Towers protrude from the walls so that defenders could shoot back at an enemy storming the town. Of the two towers on either side of the main gate, that on the left rests on Roman foundations, and that on the right in adobe derives from 12th-century Moors. The curving stairs and gate, called the Arco de la Estrella, were designed by a member of the Baroque Churriguera family in the 17th century. The **Office of Tourism** lies to the right, where an essential map is available.

A short block through the gate brings the 16th-century **Episcopal Palace**, on the left, with medallions of the Old and New World, interesting for depictions of geography as it was then known, flanking its portal.

We have entered the Pl. de Santa María. To the right stands the large **Mayoralgo Palace** with elegant windows and a nice patio inside. More awaits in the plaza, but first turn left down C. Conilleros to the **Casa de los Toledo-Moctezuma**, with an unusual domed tower. Now a municipal archive, the house once belonged to a lieutenant of Cortés who married the daughter of the Aztec emperor Montezuma and built this edifice with her dowry. Go south along the walls to the **Torre de los Espaderos** (Armorers) on the right at the next corner. Like most of the towers in the city this one was truncated by Isabella to lessen violent feuds among the city's families, each of which had raised a tower for defense.

Exit the walls through the Scorro Gate for a look at the church of Santiago by following C. de Godoy, which heads northwest. In one block the **Palácio de Godoy** is passed, with a fine corner balcony, to enter the **Plaza de Santiago**.

During the 12th century, in an earlier church on the site, the forerunner of the Order of Santiago was established. So prestigious did it become that 400 years later Velázquez would devote his time and effort to try to gain membership in the order. The present church is 16th century, built by Rodrigo Gil de Hontañon, the last great Gothic architect. Inside, a splendid retable in high relief by Berruguete surrounds Santiago Matamore (St. James, the Slayer of Moors) with scenes from the life of Christ. Note the anguished faces and elongated bodies that are Berruguete's signature. Return through the walls again, and head directly west along C. Tiendas to return to the Pl. de Santa María.

Passing the **Torre de Carvajal**, on the left, cross to the **Catedral de Santa María**. Sixteenth-century Gothic, the church is elegant within and without. The retable consists of refined figures, difficult to discern in the interior gloom. Head along the north side of the cathedral to exit the plaza from the west and enter the Pl. de San Jorge.

On the left is the **Palácio de los Golfines de Abajo**, one of two palaces in the quarter owned by this family. The façade becomes elegant through Mudejar designs, especially the windows and their surrounds, and Plateresque intricacy in the griffins along the roof edge. Its owner was permitted to display the coats of arms of Ferdinand and Isabella after they had enjoyed his hospitality.

Continue west across the plaza to pass the **Residencia de Luisa de Carvajal**, on the left, and walk around the north face of the **Iglesia de San Francisco Javier**, with an imposing 18th-century façade. Pass the **Torre del Sol**, from the 15th century, with a nicely carved family crest over the arch, to reach the rear of the church of San Mateo. Along its south side stands the 15th-century **Casa de las Ciqüeñas** (House of the Storks), now occupied by the military, retaining the only intact tower that Isabella permitted. If the guard allows, peek into the patio to see its delicate arches.

To the left is the former **Casa de las Veletas** (House of the Weathervanes). It houses a small museum of archaeological exhibits—the costumes and utensils for everyday use are especially interesting, as is a 12th-century cistern from the original Moorish Alcázar that serves as its basement. *(Open Tues.–Sun. 9:30 a.m.–2:30 p.m. and 5–7 p.m. Closing on Sun. at 2:30. Admission: 200 ptas.)*

Return north to view the 15th-century **church of San Mateo** with its striking tower. In the austere interior rest the noble families of the city. Walk north along the church façade to the **Casa de Ulloa** and turn left (west) down the typical C. Ancha. In less than a block on the left is the **Casa do Comendador de Alcuescar**, with a Gothic tower, nice window decoration and a fine balcony. Beside it stands the former **Casa de Sanchez de Paredes**, now a parador, which may be entered for a look around.

Turn right at the walls at the end of the street, and right again at the next corner onto C. del Olmo. At the end of the block on the left is the other house of the Golfines family, the **Palácio dos Golfines de Arriba**, with an imposing tower. Both this and the **Casa Adanero** opposite have lovely patios. Go left around the Palácio dos Golfines to reach the walls and turn right to come to the **Casa de la Generala** in one more block. Another block brings a return to the Arco de la Estrella from which the tour began.

Where to Stay

The hotel situation in Cáceres is tight. The area does not see enough foreign tourists to warrant substantial hotel construction, though the Spanish arrive on weekends to fill the available beds. Choices are few so reservations are advised.

Expensive ($100–$200)

Meliá Cáceres   1st-class ★ ★ ★

> Pl. San Juan, 11, Cáceres (the plaza just south of the Pl. del G. Mola by the entrance to the old town), ☎ 21 58 00, FAX 21 40 70.
> Like the parador (above), this hotel is lodged in a Renaissance palace, but it is brighter, larger and more comfortable than the parador. *86 rooms.*

Parador de Cáceres   1st-class ★ ★

> C. Ancha, 6, Cáceres (inside the walls at the middle of the west wall—entrance from the Pl. de Santa Clara), ☎ 21 17 59, FAX 21 17 29.

Here you can sleep in one of the mansions you came to see. The house was built in the 15th century, became a restaurant a century ago, and in 1989 was transformed into a parador. It is stark inside, but quiet. Patios abound, as do suits of armor. *27 rooms.*

Moderate ($50–$99)

V Centenario   Deluxe ★★

Carretera de Salamanca, one and one-half km west (head west from the major traffic circle of Pl. de América, following signs for N-630 and Plasencia), ☎ *23 22 00, FAX 23 22 02.*
This modern structure offers every facility from tennis to swimming in a full-service hotel of the deluxe-class for prices as low as any we've seen for this level. The bedrooms are eminently comfortable. *129 rooms, plus nine suites.*

Extremadura   2nd-class ★

Av. Virgen de Guadalupe, 5, Cáceres (This street is the continuation of N-521 from the north, as it bends south. The hotel is opposite the large Parque del Príncipe.), ☎ *22 16 00, FAX 21 10 95.*
This is a pleasant hotel of the modern sort, fronted by the rough stone of the old city. It has a swimming pool and has just been renovated. Service is good and the prices are more than fair. *68 rooms.*

Alcántara   2nd-class

Av. Virgen de Guadalupe, 14, Cáceres (opposite the Extremadura Hotel), ☎ *22 89 00, FAX 22 87 64.*
This hotel loses in the competition with its sister across the street. It has seen better days, but not for a while, and has the audacity to charge more. *67 rooms, plus three suites.*

Inexpensive (Less than $50)

Almonte   Hs3rd-class ★

C. Gil Cordero, 6, Cáceres (a few steps west of the Pl. de America), ☎ *24 09 26.*
Attractive and with enough rooms that at least one should be available and at a sinfully low price, this hotel also provides parking for a fee. *90 rooms.*

Where to Eat

In general Extremadura is not a place for gastronomes. However, two of the best restaurants in the province are located in Cáceres to stand as exceptions to that rule. The area is known for game, pork and ham.

Expensive ($30+)

Atrio   ★★★

Av. de España, 30 (actually the restaurant is a jag north from this main street with center island.), ☎ *24 29 28.*
Closed Sun. night.
Located in a shopping mall cul de sac, Atrio blends into the shadows in forest green. The interior is yellow and white, sleek, and surprisingly elegant for provincial Spain. The chef tries to make everything special to justify high prices, adding truffles to most dishes. Still, the service is professional and the quality of the food is astonishingly good. Credit Cards: A, D, M, V.

Moderate ($15–$30)

El Figón de Eustaquio ★★

Pl. San Juan, 12 (This quiet plaza is one block from the west end of the Pl. del General Mola.), ☎ *24 81 94.*

Many consider this the best restaurant in the province, forgetting the more luxurious dishes at Atrio (above). There is nothing nouvelle about the food, but local dishes are inventively and tastefully prepared. Prices will be expensive, if ordering à la carte, but moderate if one of the special menus is selected. The restaurant is attractive, consisting of a number of rooms of intimate scale. At lunchtime it is extremely busy, and reservations are required. Credit Cards: A, M, V.

Directory

Information

Located to the right of the main city walls' gate at Pl. del General Mola, 33. Although English is not spoken, the staff is willing. Weekday hours run from 9 a.m. to 2 p.m. and 6–8 p.m., opening and closing an hour earlier on winter afternoons. Sat. 10 a.m. to 2 p.m. (☎ *24 63 47*).

Trains and Buses

The train station (☎ *22 50 61*) is located on Av. Alemania, three km south of town on the road to Mérida. Though the station is small, service is good to and from Madrid and includes Talgos because Cáceres lies on the main line to Portugal. There are three daily runs to Mérida. One slow, early morning train goes to Seville.

The bus station is located across the street from the train station. Service is surprisingly good for a city of this size, with most cities on the western side of Spain accessible. ☎ *24 59 54.*

Police

Av. Virgen de la Montaña, 3, just east of the Av. de España. ☎ *22 60 00.*

Excursions

From Cáceres, **Trujillo**, **Mérida** and **Guadalupe** each are an hour or two away. See the descriptions under separate headings in this chapter. **Lisbon** is 349 km west.

Guadalupe ★★★

Population: 2765
Area code: 927; zip code: 10140

*From **Madrid** take N-5 southwest to Talavera de la Reina in 131 km. Turn south on N-502 to Guadalupe in 106 km. From **Cáceres** take N-521 to Trujillo in 49 km. From **Trujillo** take C-524 for 28 km to Zorita, and go east on C-401 for 51 km to Guadalupe. From **Mérida** take N-V northeast to Miajads in 51 km and then C-401 for 75 km.*

Legend has it that at the beginning of the 13th century a shepherd found a cow, apparently dead, in the mountains beside the Guadalupe River. As he knelt to examine the beast, Mary suddenly appeared exhorting him to summon the priest, for a sacred image of herself lay buried beneath the animal. The cow revived, and a blackened three-feet-high image of the Virgin Mary holding Jesus soon was unearthed—the Black Virgin of Guadalupe.

Alfonso XI invoked the aid of this icon during a crucial engagement with the Moors 50 years later. After victory, he built a grand monastery for her sanctuary which became a famous pilgrimage center. Here Isabella and Ferdinand signed the documents authorizing Columbus' explorations, and Columbus brought Indians from the Americas to be baptized in the fountain in front of the church. In gratitude for their successes, the Conquistadores heaped riches on the church of this Virgin to make it the most richly adorned in Spain. Yet, by the 19th century the monastery was abandoned by the monks who had inhabited it, and it naturally fell into disrepair. Franciscan friars took it over at the start of the present century to restore it to its former glory. Once again it has become a center of pilgrimages as the symbol of *hispanidad*, the cultural ties linking Spain with Latin America.

Part of the allure of the Virgin and her monastery is their remoteness high on a peak of the Sierra de Guadalupe. Though access in this day of motor transport is no effort, the rugged scenery is wondrous and the final sight of the monastery clinging to its mountain puts the traveler in the proper frame of mind. Though there are no monuments to see other than the monastery and its church, the village surrounding the monastery has been famed for copper-work for centuries. Products are on sale in numerous little shops.

Monasterio Guadalupe ★★★

Pl. de Santa Mará de Guadalupe, ☎ *36 70 0.*
Hours open: daily 9:30 a.m.–1 p.m. and 3:30–7 p.m.

Although the core of the building is late 14th-century, additions were made though the 18th. The complex is a jumble because geography crowded each addition within a limited perimeter.

The **fountain** in the middle of the picturesque Pl. Mayor in front of the church was used to baptize the first Americans brought to Europe. The church facade is flamboyant 15th-century Gothic. Two towers in rough stone with crenulated battlements guard either side, and fortress walls surround the whole. Bronze doors from the 15th century illustrate the events of Mary's life.

The church may be toured on one's own for free; the tour of the monastery requires a guide and fee. Entrance for the monastery tour is through the arcade to the left.

The **church** proper was built in the 14th century, and is among the oldest monastery churches in the country. The interior retains its original proportions and dimensions, but almost hidden under later decorative additions such as the 18th-century balustrade at the top of the nave and 16th-century wrought iron grille facing the sanctuary. The classical retable is 17th-century work by El Greco's son and another artist.

In a splendid dress (changed daily), the Black Virgin, the reason for all this show, looks down from on high, illuminated by spotlights.

The tour of the **monastery** comes first to a 15th-century Mudejar-style cloister with two stories of horseshoe arches. A tiled brick fountain in the center wears a complex spire. The former rectory displays a collection of extravagant church vestments, all sewn by the former Hieronymite monks with exquisitely rich and ornate handwork. A fine Gothic cloister lies beyond. Although not normally included in the tour, it can be seen from the hotel Hospederia next door.

The Chapterhouse, with fine artesonado ceiling, stores medieval choirbooks, some with delicate illustrations. Paintings are displayed as well, including small panels by Zurbarán. The tour passes through the church next, along the second floor choir (note the organ cases), to enter a splendid 17th-century sacristy.

Here is the only series of Zurbarán's paintings remaining in the place for which they were designed—a truly remarkable group of eight works. The room itself is sumptuous with mirrors and gilt and shows the simplicity of these paintings in a far different way than would the plain walls of a museum.

The tour then wends through a series of chapels, each more ornate than the last. In the first is another fine Zurbarán, after the next comes an octagonal room with ornate reliquaries. Rich jasper stairs lead up to a room with interesting full length paintings of Biblical figures by the 17th-century Neopolitan, Luca Giorano. Finally the tour enters the closet-sized 17th-century Camarin. A garish marble dais from 1953 spins, and the Virgin herself is there. *Admission: 300 ptas., for the guided tour in Spanish of approximately one hour.*

Where to Stay

Other than on feast days, the few hotels prove sufficient as most tourists hurry on to their next stop. Although there is little to see other than the monastery, those who rush away miss two of the more interesting hotels in the country.

Moderate ($50–$99)

Parador de Guadalupe   1st-class ★ ★ ★

C. Marqués de la Romana, 10, Guadalupe (opposite the monastery), ☎ 36 70 75, FAX 36 70 76.

Pilgrims have slept here since the 15th century. Isabella stayed too, signing her contract with Columbus in these rooms. The surviving Mudejar decorations are lovely, as is the patio, but bedrooms have been decorated more recently in a restful Moorish style. The hotel is quiet, provides fine views of surrounding mountains and valley below, and offers a pool. *40 rooms.*

Hospederia del Real Monasterio   2nd-class ★ ★ ★

Pl. Juan Carlos I, Guadalupe (at the rear of the monastery, opposite the church), ☎ 36 70 00, FAX 36 71 77.

This hotel is installed in former rooms of the monastery, and surrounds the lovely Gothic cloister—which may be entered from the bar. The shock is that the monks run it. Accommodations are eminently comfortable, much of the furniture was made by the brothers, and the wood beams in the rooms are ancient. Prices are also very reasonable—a third less than the Parador, which itself is reasonably priced. *46 rooms, plus one suite.*

Inexpensive (Less than $50)

Cerezo   **Hs3rd-class ★ ★ ★**
Gregorio López, 12, Guadalupe (about a block east and uphill from the monastery), ☎ *36 73 79, FAX 36 75 51.*
There are no better accommodations at these prices in the country. Rooms are comfortable, clean, many with scenic views, and the owners are true hosts. Even the food is good, and inexpensive. *15 rooms.*

Where to Eat

Guadalupe offers two of the least expensive restaurants serving decent food in all Spain. Try the monk's cooking at the Hospederia for under $20, or walk up to the hotel Cerezo to spend even less.

Directory

Information
There is no office as such, nor the need in such a small village, but the Ayuntamiento can answer questions. It is uphill along Av. Don Blas Perez, the main street of the village.

Trains and Buses
No trains, but buses leave from below the village for Madrid (at 9 a.m. and 3:30 p.m.), Trujillo and Cáceres (at 6:30 a.m. and noon).

Police
Located in the Ayuntamiento. ☎ *36 70 06.*

Excursions

Trujillo, **Cáceres** and **Mérida** are easily reached from Guadalupe. See directions and a description under the appropriate separate heading in this chapter. **Toledo** is less than 200 km away on C-401 and described in the "Madrid and New Castile" chapter.

Mérida ★ ★

Population: 41,783
Area code: 924; zip code: 06800

*From **Seville** take N-630 north for 197 km. From **Cáceres** take N-630 south for 71 km. From **Trujillo** take N-V south for 88 km.*

Mérida was founded by soldiers from Caesar Augustus' Spanish campaigns in 23 B.C. as their retirement village. They called it Emerita Augusta (Augustus' Veterans), from whose first half the present name evolved. Augustus' son-in-law donated a theater to the new town that seated 6000, and the citizens added two aqueducts and a racecourse plus an arena for chariot races and sea battles that could hold 14,000 cheering spectators. Mérida prospered at the crossroads from Salamanca to Seville, and from Toledo to Lisbon. It also administered the large Roman territory of Lusitania, which encompassed latter-day Portugal. Under the Visigoths and Moors it remained an important city, but lost that importance when Portugal broke away from Spain. Indeed, one of Mérida's claims to fame is that it is one of the few cities in Spain that Isabella and Ferdinand never visited.

Today Mérida seems more a large village—albeit with a certain vitality—than a city. All seems ordinary until one reaches the top of the hill and looks on the remains of ancient Rome. The Roman **theater** ★ ★ is probably the most elegant anywhere and the **arena** ★ is imposing. In addition, Mérida has just completed a lovely **museum** ★ to house some of the finest Roman art in Spain. Ruins of Mérida's Moorish **alcazaba** are evocative. From its walls you can view a still-functioning **Roman bridge**.

> *From the south and* **Seville**, *cross the River Guadiana on the old Roman Bridge. A left turn on the far bank brings parking.*

> *From* **Cáceres** *follow Av. Via de la Plata until the small Albarregas river (more a stream) is crossed, passing a Roman aqueduct on the left to arrive at a fork. Take the right fork and continue on C. Calvario for three long blocks until it ends at C. Almendralejo. Turn right to the bank of the Guadiana, then go left at the circle onto Av. del Guadiana and parking.*

> *From* **Trujillo** *comes an interchange at the outskirts of town. Take Av. Juan Carlos I, heading southwest. In about five blocks (passing faint remains of the Roman racecourse on the left) this ends. Go right on Av. de Extremadura, which changes its name to C. de Almendralejo and leads to the banks of the Guadiana River. Go left at the circle there along Av. del Guadiana for parking.*

What to See and Do

Alcazaba

Pl. de España, ☎ *31 73 30. Walk downstream along the river (south) for approximately one block. The entrance is on the north side, away from the river.*
Hours open: Mon.–Fri. 9 a.m.–2 p.m. and 4–7 p.m. (closes an hour earlier in winter). Open Sat. 9 a.m.–2 p.m.

The Romans built a substantial fortress here which they constructed so stoutly that successive Visigoths and Moors had only to repair and maintain it. After the Moors, it fell into disrepair and suffers now from 1000 years of neglect exacerbated by a French gutting in 1808. What you see today is the fortress walls and the cistern, the rest being mainly a dusty field. It is worth a climb down dank stairs to the Moorish cistern added in the 10th century. It descends to the depth of the river so its water table would keep the cistern filled during a siege. Note the Roman-style vaulting in the passageway, Corinthian capitals top Visigothic columns, and Visigoth pillars used as lintels. A walk on the walls gives nice views of the river—often with sheep and cattle gently grazing nearby—and of the long Roman bridge with 64 arches. *Admission: 200 ptas.; ticket good for the Roman precinct as well.*

Walk left from the Alcazaba entrance to the Pl. de España at the corner, the main square of the town surrounded by shops and restaurants. Here, at the west end of the plaza is the **Hotel Emperatriz***, a former 16th-century palace with a huge interior patio. Walk along the near side (south) of the plaza to C. Santa Eulalia, the major shopping street. In two and a half blocks, turn right on C. Francisco to see the Roman* **Temple of Diana***, with a nice Corinthian peristyle. Continue for two more blocks up C. Santa Eulalia, turning right onto C. José Ramon Melida, where stores are passed that sell local red incised pottery and handsome reproductions of Roman blue and green glass. The attractively modern brick building in two blocks is the* **Museo Nacional de Arte Romano***. At its end lies the precinct of the* **Roman ruins***.*

Museo Nacional de Arte Romano ★

C. José Ramón Melida, ☎ *31 16 90.*
Hours open: Tues.–Sat. 10 a.m.–2 p.m. and 4–6 p.m. Open Sun. 10 a.m.–2 p.m. Closed Mon., and holidays.

For Spain this is a daringly modern building in which to display ancient art, and it suits almost perfectly one of the best Roman collections in the country, all excavated from this area. The ground floor shows statues, including a lovely Ceres taken from the Roman theater (a copy stands there now in place of this original). The next floor is for less interesting ceramics, glassware and coins. The top floor houses some nice mosaics and several fine busts. In the basement are original Roman *thermae* (steam-baths). *Admission: 200 ptas.*

Monumentos Romanos ★★

C. José Ramón Melida, ☎ *31 25 30.*
Hours open: Same hours as the Roman Museum above.

The theater is surely Spain's most beautiful remembrance of Rome. Most of it dates to A.D. 23, including the seats for 6000, the entranceways formed of stones so carefully fitted that they required no mortar, and a pit in the front for the chorus. The elegant towering stage wall was added in the second century A.D. Beyond the stage reposes a garden and portico where the audience could stroll during intermission. It all seems so civilized. Today, classical plays are still performed during summer evenings. (Check at the Office of Tourism for times and prices.)

North of the theater stands a large arena that held 14,000 spectators at chariot races, gladiatorial combats and mock sea battles (for which the floor was flooded). A low wall protected the spectators in the front row, the most expensive seats, from wild animals sometimes employed as contestants during gladiatorial bouts. The cavern in the center of the arena floor presumably held the machinery for producing such shows. *Admission: 200 ptas.*

C. Francisco, on which the Temple of Diana is situated, would lead to the local parador if followed north, away from the temple. The **parador** *inhabits a former baroque convent. C. de Almendralejo, at the rear of the parador, leads east in five blocks to the small* **Iglesia de Santa Eulalia***, beside the train station. This 13th-century church was built upon a 6th-century original and* contains Visigothic pillars in its nave from the earlier church. Nearby are several Roman houses under excavation.

Where to Stay

Mérida provides surprisingly few hotels for a town of its size and tourist interest.

Expensive ($100–$200)

Parador Via de la Plata   1st-class ★ ★

Pl. de la Constitución, 3, Mérida (signs direct you), ☎ 31 38 00, FAX 31 92 08.
The outside of this former 16th-century convent is unassuming, but the interior adds baroque decorative touches to combed whitewashed walls for a nice effect. The former chapel is now a restful lounge and there is a simple patio in the center. Bedrooms are comfortable and pleasant; the service is attentive; here is private parking and a lively restaurant. *80 rooms, plus two suites.*

Moderate ($50–$99)

Tryp Medea   1st-class ★ ★ ★

Av. de Portugal, Mérida (three km south of the town center, along the old N-V), ☎ 37 24 00, FAX 37 30 20.
This is Mérida's newest (1993) most modern hotel in town, glistening with marble and mirrors. A comfortable room is assured along with saunas and such, but it is a twenty minute walk to the sights. *126 rooms.*

Nova Roma   2nd-class ★ ★

Suárez Somonte, 42, Mérida (on the hill with the Roman ruins this street runs west for a long block to this hotel), ☎ 31 12 61, FAX 30 01 60.
After the Tryp Mérida these are the best modern accommodations in town. Comfortable but sparsely furnished accommodations leave you a stone's throw from the Roman ruins. *55 rooms.*

Cervantes   3rd-class ★

C. Camilo José Cela, 8, Mérida (just off the north corner of the Pl. España), ☎ 31 49 01, FAX 31 13 42.
Although the rooms are nothing special, the hotel is centrally located and professional. *30 rooms.*

Emperatriz   2nd-class

Pl. de España, 19, Mérida (The plaza is one block from the Roman bridge.), ☎ 31 31 11, FAX 30 03 76.
This is an unusual place. It is a former huge mansion from the 16th century, inside of which stands an awesome, soaring patio with rooms rising through three stories around it. In the past the hotel had been unbelievably seedy, incorporating a disco and arcade games which disturbed the guests. Renovation is complete now to transform this dowager into a serious hotel with comfortable bedrooms. *41 rooms.*

Where to Eat

Mérida locals enjoy a meal out, so they keep several good restaurants in business.

Moderate ($15–$30)

Nicholás   ★ ★

Félix Valverde Lillo, 13 (this street runs parallel to, and to the west of, the main shopping street, C. Santa Eulalia), ☎ 31 96 10.

Closed Sun. night, and the middle three weeks in Sept.

In its own town house, this is easily the prettiest and the most elegant restaurant in town. The cuisine is that of the region—partridge with truffles and good pork. The fixed-price menus usually include good choices at moderate prices. Credit Cards: A, D, V.

Inexpensive (Less than $15)

Briz   ★★

C. Félix Valverde Lillo, 5 (near Nicholás), ☎ *31 93 07.*

This is an unassuming place that serves very good food at very reasonable prices. Hearty food is the thing here—either lamb or partridge stew, for example, or good sausage. The house wine is hearty as well. Credit Cards: A, D, V.

Casa Benito   ★

C. Santa Eulalia, 13, ☎ *31 55 02.*

As with the other restaurants in town, the menu covers hearty regional dishes. This place is especially popular at lunch for its reasonable fixed-price menus, but goes à la carte at night.

Directory

Shopping

Mérida sells inexpensive reproductions of blue and green Roman glass goblets and vases. On the street leading to the Roman precinct, C. José Ramon, **Reproduciones** **Romanes** at #40 and **Copias Romanes** at #20, both provide nice selections, especially the latter. They also sell the local incised brown-red pottery. **Greylop** #24 has the best pottery selection. Across the street at number 13, **Mascara** sells endearing puppets and other high quality crafts.

Information

Located by the Roman precinct on C. María Plano. ☎ *31 53 53.*

Trains and Buses

The train station is located on C. Cordero, north of Santa Eulalia Church. ☎ *31 81 09.* Service is frequent to Cáceres, Badajoz on the Portuguese border, Seville and Madrid. Otherwise, it's spotty.

The bus station lies one kilometer across the Roman bridge on Av. de la Libertad. Buses serve more cities, more frequently, than do the trains. ☎ *37 14 04*

Post Office and Telephones

Located in the Pl. de la Constitución, where the parador is. ☎ *31 24 58.*

Police

The offices are in the ayuntamiento in the Pl. España. ☎ *38 01 00.*

Excursions

Cáceres, **Trujillo** and **Guadalupe** are the main Spanish sites of interest nearby. Each is described under its own heading in this chapter. **Seville** lies three hours south.

Trujillo ★ ★

Population: 9445
Area code: 927; zip code: 10200

*From **Madrid** N-V going southwest runs (fairly) straight to Trujillo in 261 km. From **Guadalupe** take C-401 west to Zorita in 51 km, then join C-524 going north to Trujillo in 28 km. From **Cáceres** N-521 goes straight to Trujillo in 49 km. From **Seville**, follow directions to Mérida. From **Mérida** N-V goes east to Trujillo in 88 km.*

Trujillo is said to have spawned 20 American nations. While that is an exaggeration, this village contributed far more than its share to the conquest of the Americas, for it was the home of Francisco Pizarro. Pizarro, an illegitimate son of a noble family, left his dead-end job as a swineherd to seek a fortune in the New World. When he reached Peru, he followed the strategy that Cortés had employed in Mexico. Under the protection of a truce, he captured the Inca Atahualpa, and ruled his empire through him until he was strong enough to grab the reins himself. Thereby he accumulated riches that are incalculable in modern terms. However, rivalry with a lieutenant led Pizarro to kill him, only to be murdered in turn by friends of the dead man. Pizarro's half-brother Hernando and various compatriots from Trujillo survived the death to return with sufficient treasures to make their hometown wealthy for a while.

Trujillo had been an unimportant village before the Conquistadores left to seek their fortunes. When they returned, each built a mansion as impressive as his booty would allow. However, this new wealth provided only a one-time injection into the economy of the town, which settled back into obscurity after its building boom in the 16th and 17th centuries. Today Trujillo offers mansions similar to those of Cáceres, though less densely and—thanks to their whitewashed facades—less austerely. They surround one of the most pleasant, expansive plaza mayors in Spain. Above the plaza, majestic ruins of a 12th-century Moorish fortress look down. Trujillo is an engaging village.

*From **Madrid** and **Guadalupe** the road funnels into the Pl. del General Mola. Go straight through onto C. San António, which enters the Pl. San Miquel in one block. Continue through to C. Sofrago, which changes its name to C. Silleria, then enters the Pl. Mayor, where parking should be available. From **Mérida** Trujillo is entered along Carretera de Badajoz. Continue across the large Av. de la Encarnación, following the side of a park along C. Pardos. Continue straight through the small Pl. de Aragon along C. Romanos, which is named C. Parra when it bends right, and leads into the Pl. Mayor for parking. From **Cáceres** the town is entered along Av. Ramon y*

Cajal. Bear left at the park onto C. Ruiz de Mendoza. Angle left at the small Pl. de Arágon onto C. Romanos, which is named C. Parra when it bends right, and leads to Pl. Mayor for parking.

What to See and Do

Begin in the lovely **Plaza Mayor ★**. The plaza is irregular in shape, although almost forming a triangle. Varying levels are linked by broad flights of stairs for variety. At the north center strides a powerful bronze **statue of Francisco Pizarro**, sculpted in 1927 by two American artists. Its twin resides in Lima, Peru, the city Pizarro founded. To the left (west), in an arcade, is the **Office of Tourism** which provides a map.

At the northeast side of the plaza stands the 16th-century Gothic church of **San Martín**, with a soaring nave and numerous Renaissance tombs. An arcade on its south side once served as a communal meeting place. Opposite is the **Palacio de San Carlos**, from the early 17th century, now a convent. The bell at the door will bring a nun (if rung at any normal Spanish museum hour) to show off an arched inner court storing Visigothic fragments, and interesting vaults of the basement. (A donation is in order.)

South around the plaza is the mansion of the **Marquesa de Piedras Alba**. At the southwest corner of the plaza stands the **Palácio de la Conquista**. De la Conquista was the Marquis' title conferred on Francisco Pizarro's brother Hernando, who survived to return wealthy from Peru. Once home, he built this mansion with an extraordinary number of grilled windows. At the corner balcony is a series of busts of the family. On the left are Francisco with his wife, Yupanqui Huaynas, daughter of the Inca. On the right are Hernando and his bride, Francisca (Francisco's daughter).

Proceeding west by the mansion, you reach the former **ayuntamiento** (town hall), from the 16th century, with an old reconstructed triple arcade. Through the central arch the **Palácio de Pizarro de Orellana**, now a school, preserves a fine patio with an elegant plateresque upper gallery.

Passing the front (south), follow C. Almenas due west to the restored town walls and one of the original seven gates, the **Gate of San Andres**. Once through and past San Andres Church, the remains of **Moorish baths**, now a stagnant reservoir, are faced. Turn right into the quiet, almost abandoned old town, then left along C. de la Paloma going north, and prepare for a climb.

In two blocks you arrive at the Gothic **Santa María**, restored in the 15th century. The bell tower remains from the original Romanesque structure. (If closed, apply at the house to the right of the steps.) Inside, the church is pristine Gothic, with lovely vaulting. The retable at the altar is a Spanish masterpiece by the great Fernando Gallego from Salamanca. A hundred peseta coin is necessary to illuminate it. All around are the tombs of the great families of the city. The upper choir is fronted by an elaborate balustrade with coats of arms of Ferdinand and Isabella at each end to indicate their seats, should they be in residence.

Follow the church facade to the east side, and walk north to its rear, across from which is the **Pizarro Museum**. Although it was closed for repairs at our visit, it should be reopen for yours. (Open daily 10 a.m.–2 p.m. and 4–6 p.m.; closed on holidays; admission: 250 ptas.). This is the former home of Francisco Pizarro's father. It is unlikely that the illegitimate Francisco was born here, though he did spend some of his childhood playing with his legitimate brothers in this place. Some of the rooms are nice, although the so-called museum has little to show.

The steep lane continues up to the top of the hill to massive twelfth-century crenelated walls of the **Castillo** (Castle). So far only the Moorish curtain-wall with its square towers has been restored. The area is a peaceful place to wander, watch the birds and look over the countryside.

Return down C. Santiago that runs from the southwest corner of the fortress walls. In a long block you reach the town walls and, prefaced by two stately towers, the **church of Santiago** built into the walls. Pass through the Santiago gate in the walls to return to the Pl. Mayor.

Where to Stay

Trujillo is a pleasant place to spend a night since it has enough life and activity, yet not too much. Unfortunately, the town offers few hotel rooms.

Expensive ($100–$200)

Parador de Trujillo   1st-class ★ ★ ★

Pl. de Santa Clara, Trujillo (two blocks due east of the Pl. Mayor), ☎ *32 13 50, FAX 32 13 66.*

This time the parador is installed in a former 16th-century convent. Befitting its convent heritage, it is less formal than many paradors and correspondingly more inviting and relaxed. Half of the rooms are in the convent and focus on a simple central cloister, providing a pleasant atmosphere; the other half are in a new wing surrounding a pool. Antiques are spread around. *46 rooms.*

Moderate ($50–$99)

Las Ciqüeñas   2nd-class ★

Carretera N-V, Trujillo (about two km east of town), ☎ *32 12 50, FAX 32 13 00.*

This is a clean, modern hotel with extra facilities, yet modest prices. *78 rooms.*

Inexpensive (Less than $50)

Mesón la Cadena   Hs3rd-class ★ ★

Pl. Mayor, 8, Trujillo, ☎ *32 14 63.*

The building is a 16th-century mansion. Rooms above the mesón are pleasant and comfortable, with views of the plaza and town walls. Such an attractive hotel at these prices is a find, indeed. *Eight rooms.*

Where to Eat

You can dine reasonably well in this town for very little money.

Moderate ($15–$30)

Hostal Pizarro   ★ ★

Pl. Mayor, 13, ☎ *32 02 55.*

This restaurant is an institution, not only of Trujillo, but of all Extremadura. The chef and waitress are two sisters who inherited this place long ago from their father. Together, they serve the most authentic Extremaduran home cooking. Partridge casserole is delicious and the roast lamb is quite good. The prices will please you almost as much as the food does. Credit Cards: M, V.

Inexpensive (Less than $15)

Mesón la Troya

Pl. Mayor, 10, ☎ *32 13 64.*

Over a hundred years ago this was a stable, but now humans chow down some of the best tasting food for the money in Spain. Every dish is authentic, hearty and good. An omelette and salad arrive to keep you happy while you peruse the short menu. Give the *prueba de cerdo*, a heavily garlicked pork casserole, serious consideration. Credit Card: V.

Mesón la Cadena ★

Pl. Mayor, 8, ☎ *32 1463.*

Whitewashed walls are made charming by local ceramics, creating an atmosphere far more deluxe than the prices. While à la carte selections can bring the bill above the inexpensive category, numerous *platos tipicos* fit comfortably within it. Credit Cards: A, M, V.

Directory

Information

Installed in an arcade on the left of the Pl. Mayor. Its hours are variable.

Buses

The station is at Carretera a Badajoz, four or five blocks south of the Pl. Mayor. ☎ *32 12 02.* It serves the towns of Extremadura and offers frequent trips to Madrid.

Police

In the Pl. Mayor. ☎ *32 01 08.*

Excursions

Cáceres, **Mérida** and **Guadalupe** are all short excursions from Trujillo. See the respective descriptions in this chapter.

GALICIA, ASTURIAS AND CANTABRIA

The Plaza Obradoiro, Santiago de Compostela, invites contemplation.

Historical Profile:
Religion and the Inquisition

Spain's Catholic roots are old and deep. Even before the pope bestowed the title *los Reyos Católicos* (the Catholic Monarchs) on Ferdinand and Isabella in the 15th century, Spain had taken pride in being a Catholic country. By the sixth century its Visigothic rulers had converted to Catholicism, and even after the Moors conquered most of Spain in the eighth century, the mass of the population remained steadfastly Catholic under an Islamic government. Those Moors were tolerant of other religions, freely allowing Jews, persecuted by much of the Christian world, to make homes in their territory, so as the Christians regained land throughout the reconquest, they inherited a Jewish and Moorish minority, making Spain a melting pot of religions. The story of religion in Spain is the tale of how this country changed from the most tolerant in Europe into the least.

Until the end of the 15th century, religion neither qualified nor disqualified anyone for a vocation. Despite the proximity of three religions, unlike more homogeneous France and Germany, Spain bred no Christian heresies. Then, at the end of the 14th century, pogroms exploded throughout the south of Spain and in Barcelona to the northeast. Christian mobs, either jealous of Jewish economic success or frightened by tales of Jewish atrocities, killed thousands of Jews. As a result of these religious massacres, a small percentage of fearful Jews converted to Christianity, becoming known as *conversos*.

Anti-semitism was far from sanctioned by the government. A Jew in the 15th century could still occupy an important position—one, in fact, was in charge of supplying Ferdinand's troops during the Granada campaign, and another served as Isabella's court physician. Isabella had stated publicly "all the Jews in my realms are mine and under my care and protection and it belongs to me to defend and aid them and keep justice." [Henry Kamen, *Inquisition and Society in Spain*, p. 12.] Yet, by 1478 she had instituted the Spanish Inquisition, and 20 years later signed an edict expelling all of the Jews in Spain.

What changed Isabella's attitude and why did she order an inquisition? While it is clear that clerics urged their monarchs to impose an inquisition, Isabella and, even more, Ferdinand did not always do what Rome's clergy directed. Circumstantial evidence suggests Ferdinand as the driving force behind the Inquisition, with Isabella following his lead.

Because an ongoing inquisition had existed in Aragón before Castile's more infamous one, Ferdinand of Aragón had firsthand acquaintance with its operation, while Isabella of Castile did not. Since Ferdinand's character was one of shrewdness, while Isabella was more other-worldly and sentimental, the fact that the Spanish Inquisition was instituted immediately before Castile began its costly war against Granada looms with significance. It seems likely, in fact, that the Spanish Inquisition was instituted by Ferdinand as an economic policy. Strikingly, over 90 percent of those tried by the Inquisition were former Jews, although they constituted only a few percent of the population. The reason for such concentrated persecution could not have been that former Jews committed 90 percent of all heresies, but rather that they controlled a disproportionate amount of the country's wealth.

During the early years of the Inquisition, all seized assets became the property of the Crown, a policy which contributed substantially to the national revenue. In fact, in 1482 the pope issued a bull stating:

> ...that in Aragón, Valencia, Mallorca and Catalonia the Inquisition has for some time been moved not by zeal for the faith and the salvation of souls, but by lust for wealth, and that many true and faithful Christians, on the testimony of enemies, rivals, slaves and other lower and even less proper persons, have without any legitimate proof been thrust into secular prisons, tortured and condemned as relapsed heretics, deprived of their goods and property and handed over to the secular arm to be executed, to the peril of souls, setting a pernicious example, and causing disgust to many.

Quoted by Kamen, *op. cit.*, p. 34

Whatever the causes, in 1478, granting a petition signed jointly by Ferdinand and Isabella, Pope Sixtus IV issued a bull establishing the Spanish Inquisition in Castile. Two years later it was announced that the first tribunal was en route to Seville. Four thousand households fled before the inquisitors arrived, confirming, at least in the minds of its proponents, the need for such measures.

The Spanish Inquisition was modeled after earlier inquisitions in France. It consisted of itinerant tribunals acting as courts of law, overseen by a supreme council under the direction of an Inquisitor General. The first Inquisitor General was Isabella's former confessor, Tomás de Torquemada. Because prevention of heresy was the expressed purpose of the Inquisition, only Christians could be tried. But the true "purpose of the trial and execution [was] not to save the soul of the accused but to achieve the public good and put fear into others." [Contemporary source quoted by Kamen, *op. cit.*, p. 161.] That is, the goal was not justice, but discipline—both for the accused and for the community.

A tribunal would arrive at a town and call for a high mass, which the populace was required to attend. There townspeople all swore an oath to support the Inquisition's business. After reading a long list of heresies, an invitation was then extended to the audience to denounce themselves or their neighbors. In the early days of the Inquisition a 30-day grace-period was extended during which immediate confessions were lightly punished. Usually enough denunciations were received to give the tribunal sufficient work.

Heresy included sacrileges of the slightest sort. One man was arrested for smiling when a friend said the words "the Virgin Mary;" another for urinating against the wall of a church; yet another for shouting during cards that "even with God as your partner you won't win this game." [Kamen, *op. cit.*, p. 162.] The slightest suspicion that a citizen practiced Judaism caused his arrest. Wearing finery on Saturday, the Jewish Sabbath, could do it, as could refusing pork when dining out, or even washing on a Jewish holiday. Sex was another area of concern to the tribunals. Five percent of all those convicted by the Inquisition were convicted of bigamy; homosexuality and bestiality were crimes; but even saying that sex was no sin served as grounds for arrest.

Once testimony against an accused person had been obtained, the evidence was sent to theologians to determine if the offense constituted a heresy. If it did, the accused was arrested and imprisoned. Upon his arrest an inventory was made of his assets so they could be seized until his case had been decided. Although the Inquisition resorted to torture to force confessions, it should be noted that all European criminal courts of the time did likewise, and the Inquisition was more sparing of this device than was civil justice. Torture was used only on those accused of the most serious heresies, about one third of the cases.

Three forms of torture were employed. The *garrucha*, or hoist, involved being hung by the wrists with heavy weights tied to the feet, then raised and dropped until abruptly caught by the rope. The *toca*, water torture, involved stuffing a towel in the mouth, then pouring containers of water down the open throat. The *potro*, or rack, consisted of progressively tightening cords around the accused's body. According to the rules of the Inquisition, a confession gained through torture did not count as truth unless the subject repeated his confession on the day following. All details of a torture session were meticulously recorded.

One account of a woman accused of refusing pork and of changing her bed linen on Saturdays runs as follows:

> She was ordered to be placed on the potro. She said, "Señores, why will you not tell me what I have to say? Señor, put me on the ground—have I not said that I did it all?" She was told to tell it. She said "I don't remember—take me away—I did what the witnesses say." She was told to tell in detail what the witnesses said. She said, "Señor, as I have told you, I do not know for certain. I have said that I did all that the witnesses say. Señores, release me, for I do not remember it." She was told to tell it. She said, "Señores, it does not help me to say that I did it and I have admitted that what I have done has brought me to this suffering—Señor, you know the truth—Señores, for God's sake have mercy on me.

Kamen, *op. cit.*, p. 176.

Trials were conducted in secret. Anyone arrested was presumed guilty since the evidence had already been heard and judged heretical—the accused

could only try as best he could to prove
he did. Yet, as the above account indicates,
against him or even who had brought them. T
possible, and only after someone confessed could
appointed by the tribunal. The judicial process was, i
diences broken up by periods of prison confinement, rath
ous trial, and the normal period from incarceration to a resolu
was three years, though there were cases that pended for 20.

At the end waited the *auto da fé*, or "ceremony of faith." Public *aut*
were popular ceremonies, consisting of colorful processions through
main streets of town by the members of the tribunal, followed by guards,
then all the accused. The dress was striking, looking like nothing so much as
brightly colored Klu Klux Klan outfits—except for the black worn by those
sentenced to die.

After stirring speeches by members of the tribunal and public confessions
by the accused, sentences were read. Four different sentences were possible.
First, an accused person could be acquitted. But since this amounted to an
admission that the tribunal had made a mistake, its usual form was to sus-
pend the judicial process without acknowledging the innocence of the accused. A second sentence was penance, which could encompass anything
from a fine to a prison term, to enforced wearing of a *sanbenito*, a yellow
robe with crosses that marked the wearer as a former heretic. The third type
of sentence was reconciliation, reserved for more serious crimes. Punishment
could include banishment, service as a galley slave, seizure of one's assets, or
public flogging—in any combination. Relaxation was the most serious sentence, reserved for those who did not repent of their crimes or who had re-
lapsed into evil ways. About two percent of the accused were "relaxed." The
penalty was to be tied to a stake then roasted alive unless the criminal confessed at the last moment, in which case he was strangled before the burning.

Not every Spaniard supported the Holy Office, as the Inquisition was
called. A contemporary wrote:

> *Those newly converted from the Jewish race, and many other
> leaders and gentry, claimed that the procedure was against the
> liberties of the realm, because for this offence their goods were con-
> fiscated and they were not given the names of witnesses who testified
> against them.*
>
> *As a result the conversos had all the kingdom on their side, in-
> cluding persons of the highest consideration, among them Old
> Christians and gentry.*

Kamen, *op. cit.*, p. 37.

that some people in high places,
the Inquisition, but he is surely
was against it. A truer description
mporary who said that "it is only
this war against the Holy Office,
ommon citizens never attacked the
their common voice against it; they
and was not disbanded until 1834.
church leaders, it must have had

wns rose against the Inquisition. In
against the tribunal, causing the In-
zens. In response, the clergy of Teruel
but were set upon by Ferdinand with
nit.

Perhaps the most .... ion occurred in 1485 when the inquisitor Pedro Argües was assassinated as he knelt in prayer. The deed was probably arranged by *conversos* and was not unexpected, since Fra Argües wore chain mail beneath his robes and a steel helmet under his clerical hat. However, the murder only strengthened the inquisitors' resolve and increased the numbers of their adherents.

Effects of the Inquisition ran deep through Spanish society. Although it began as an attack on former Jews, Jew and non-Jew alike were at risk, for anyone at all could be accused. The Inquisition gave rise to the concept of *limpieza de sangre*, purity of blood, that caused everyone to rush to geneologists to prove the absence of Jewish ancestors in every limb of his family tree. In almost every case this involved deception, for it was rare for a family of any standing in Renaissance Spain to be without a drop of Jewish blood. A royal secretary reported that all the noble lines of Castile, including Isabella and Ferdinand, had *converso* ancestors, along with half the high government officials and four Spanish bishops in Aragón. [Kamen, *op. cit.*, p. 19.] Even the first Inquisitor General, Tomás de Torquemada, and Saint Teresa of Ávila came from *converso* families.

The effect of the Inquisition has been long. Even today it is not uncommon for a Spaniard to take pride in the "attribute" of not having Jewish blood.

Galicia, Asturias and Cantabria

These three ancient provinces top the western half of Spain in a belt 500 miles long, but, in parts, only 30 miles deep. Although each province is different, all offer a similar range of attractions to the tourist. The whole area borders an Atlantic lined with rocky inland peaks, and receives more rainfall than anywhere else in the country—thereby earning the name "Green Spain." Its population stems from ancient roots, and both the folklore and languages differ from the rest of Spain.

Ancient **Galicia**, tucked into the northwest corner of Spain, sits atop Portugal. Bordered by the Atlantic on two sides, it is the wettest part of Spain (though the inland remains relatively dry through most of the summer). Galicia is green and wooded. Because it sits on a rift in the earth that caused prehistoric folding and splitting, hills and mountains cover most of the terrain, and the coast is crinkled into inlets with hills on either side, like Norwegian fjords or Scottish firths. Overall, Galicia presents landscapes more associated with Scotland than with Spain, and the comparison is not inaccurate.

In the eighth century B.C., Celts from northern France migrated to Galicia, perhaps even before another group migrated to Britain to become the Welsh and early Scottish. They named the area Gaelia (from which Galicia derives), the root word for both "Gaul" and "Wales." They brought musical instruments, similar to bagpipes, and legends, including that of the Holy Grail. Romans made fast work of their territory, however—conquering, then leaving, with little permanent imprint. So isolated was Galicia that the Moors barely stopped by when they were conquering the rest of Spain, permitting the area to be the earliest to return to Christian ways. In the beginning of the ninth century shepherds found an uncorrupted body reputed to be Saint James (Sant' Iago). The site of Santiago de Compostela and this body became a great pilgrimage center in the Middle Ages, and remains so today.

Galician cuisine emphasizes the products of the sea, reputedly better and fresher from its coasts than anywhere in Spain. The favored accompaniment is a *vina verde*, a "green" wine, so called not for its color but for the fact that the grapes are picked young. There wines are very light and dry, and often produce a hint of sparkle on the tongue.

Asturias, the center province of this northern belt, is considered the first kingdom of Spain. The Visigoths, chased to this extremity by the Moors, began their Reconquest from here. Thus, the Asturian city of Oviedo may be called the first capital of modern Spain. Within its confines is located the pantheon of the earliest kings; and on its outskirts stand the oldest palace, the remodeled church of Santa Maria del Naranco. But the area is infinitely more ancient than this. The cave of Altamira and others nearby contain paleolithic paintings from 15,000 years ago. Asturian food is hearty and "peasant" in character. Beans in great variety and sauces, often with sausages added, are staples.

Cantabria province is the Basque homeland. The origin of these people and their language is unknown, although it is clear that they hunted whales off the coast of Greenland as early as the ninth century. They are proud of their ancient heritage, traditions and language, and are fiercely independent. Basque industriousness contributes to the prosperity of the region, aided by rich deposits of iron ore. Their chefs are renowned. And their beautiful coast, with the elegant resorts of Santillana del Mar, Santander and Donostia (San Sebastián) is evidence of the good fortune of the Basques.

Simply put, Basque cooking is the best in the country. Perfectly done fish are the stars, either simply broiled (as with heavenly sardines) or in a green sauce (especially hake). Although meats are not plentiful, when offered they will be of first quality. To accompany their meals Basques favor cider or *txakoli*, a young fresh wine of which the whites are best. Both the cider and txakoli should be young. Look for *idiazabal* cheese, made from sheep milk, which is creamy when young and slightly sharp when aged.

In Galicia many people speak Gallego, a language akin to Portuguese. Basque (Euskera) is spoken in Asturias and Cantabria. Though Spanish is understood and spoken by all, in some instances town names on road signs will not be written in Spanish. In this text we use the place-names a traveler is most likely to see.

The premier sight of the area is the Romanesque Cathedral of **Santiago de Compostela** ★★★★★ in Galicia. Galicia also offers lovely beaches—the **Rias Altas** and **Rias Bajas** ★★—which are generally uncrowded and infinitely more scenic than their Mediterranean counterparts. Asturias provides competition with the beaches of its **Costa Verde** ★, in addition to offering prehistoric paintings in **Altamira** and nearby caves ★. It offers the quiet sophistication of **Oviedo** ★★, incorporating the oldest civilian Christian works in Spain. Cantabria provides the elegant resorts of the **Basque Coast** ★★★—**Santander** ★, **Santillana del Mar** ★★, and beautiful **Donostia** ★★★ (San Sebastián).

Basque Coast ★★★

Sweeping around the French border, the Bay of Biscay forms 250 km of Basque Coast. "Biscay" is a corruption of *Vizcaya*, the Spanish word for

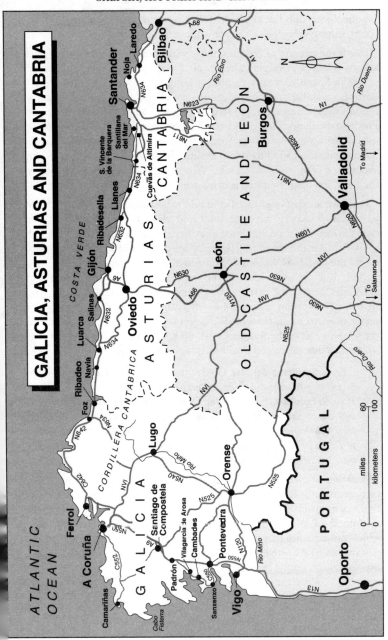

Basque. Steep cliffs line the bay, broken by estuaries. Where they find shore-room, fishing villages face the sea while green hills climb behind.

This is the country of Basques, those who speak Euskera, a language of no known relatives or origin. The people are notoriously independent—place names in Spanish are spraypainted overnight with Basque equivalents. The Basque separatist movement claims several political murders each year, though such violence is supported by only a small proportion of the people. Fortunately, the danger for visitors is slight, as the target is always the Spanish government or its agents, not ordinary citizens or tourists. Though the political situation will be evident because of omnipresent painted slogans, it should not otherwise affect a visit. What is more likely to be remembered is the food, for Basque cuisine is extraordinary.

The Basque coast might well contain the best beaches in Spain, in addition to beautiful scenery, superior food and elegant resorts—all with smaller crowds than will be encountered elsewhere. What it lacks is the stark light of the south, for the days are frequently misty. Instead a mellow atmosphere shows the dark blue sea and deep green hills to dramatic effect. The coast is anchored at the west end by the expensive and sophisticated resort of Santander, and at the east end by beautiful and elegant Donostia (San Sebastián). In between, a score of lovely villages wait patiently for those who prefer quiet to sophistication. We begin our description with Santander at the western end of the Basque Coast, 30 km from Santillana del Mar, where the **Costa Verde** (discussed below in this chapter) ends.

> *From* **Santillana del Mar** *C-6316 west joins N-611 in 8 km for a 17 km trip to Santander. From* **Burgos** *take N-623 north for 123 km. From* **Valladolid** *take N-620 for 58 km to Palencia, then N-611 for 209 km to Santander. From* **Madrid** *follow the directions to Burgos, then follow the Burgos directions. From* **Pamplona** *take N-240 north to Tolosa in 64 km, changing there for N-I north for 22 km to Donostia (San Sebastián), then follow the route below backwards.*

Santander ★ caters mainly to Spanish seeking elegance and such sophisticate entertainment as theater and dance. It has a casino for gambling, beautiful ocean promenades and fine beaches, but does not offer old buildings, quaintness or charm. A tornado in 1941 threw the ocean upon the city which caused a fire that destroyed most older buildings, so today the town glistens newly. An intelligent ordinance passed after this cataclysm imposed a five-story limit on the height of buildings and set aside land for gardens and walks, to produce the modern, attractive city of almost 200,000 citizens.

Santander spreads in a line along the bay leading out to Magdalena Point. Almost a century ago its citizens subscribed together to build a **palace** to attract Alfonso XIII, whose summer residency did much to popularize the resort. Now the palace the citizens built is an annex of Menéndez Pelayo International University, providing summer classes in Spanish for foreigners. The best beaches ring this point. Fine beaches also line the northern area called El Sardinero, the home of the **Gran Casino del Sardinero**. Golf is across the bay at Pedreña; an airport lies seven km south of the city.

Where to Stay

Very Expensive ($200+)

Real   **Deluxe ★ ★ ★ ★**

Paseo Perez Galdos, 28, Santander (in el Sardinero, but on Los Peligros beach), ☎ *(942) 27 25 50, FAX (942) 27 45 73, Telex 39012.*
Without question this turn-of-the-century hotel with splendid views of the bay from spacious bedrooms is the premier hotel in the city, but its prices are correspondingly high—over 30,000 pesetas per night. *116 rooms, plus nine suites.*

Moderate ($50–$99)

Rhin   **R1st-class ★ ★**

Av. Reina Victoria, 153, Santander (at the southern end of el Sardinero beach), ☎ *(942) 27 43 00, FAX 27 86 53.*
You can stay three nights here for the cost of one at the Hotel Real. The accommodations are comfortable, the views lovely and the beach is across the street. *95 rooms.*

Inexpensive (Less than $50)

México   **2nd-class ★**

C. Calderón de la Barca, 3, Santander (opposite the bus station), ☎ *(942) 21 24 50.*
Tasteful decor makes this hotel special. That, and the moderate prices, make it a find. However, it is quite a walk to el Sardinero beach and prices only dip into the inexpensive range outside July and August. *35 rooms.*

Where to Eat

Expensive ($30+)

El Molino   **★ ★ ★ ★**

In Puente Arce, 13 km southwest, ☎ *(942) 57 50 55.*
Closed Sun. night, and Mon. except in summer.
Though installed in a 17th-century mill in gardens beside a stream, the renovation is utterly elegant. The food is of the first order—expensive, but worth every peseta. Oh, that sea bream braised with thyme! Credit Cards: A, D, M, V.

Moderate ($15–$30)

Bodiga del Riojano   **★ ★**

Rio de la Pila, 5 (off C. Santa Lucia, four blocks north of the port), ☎ *(942) 21 67 50.*
Closed Sun., the last week in June and from the last week in Oct. to the last week in Nov.
Atmospheric with dark woods and old wine barrels, this restaurant serves wholesome terrific fish at modest prices and the wines are unusual and good. Credit Cards: A, D, M, V.

From Santander take N-634 east. It cuts inland across the Ajo Cape to reach lovely **Laredo** *in 48 km. However, by avoiding the cape* *one misses* **Noja** ★ , *10 km deeper in the cape, with a spectacular beach called Playa Ris. If interested, look for the turn-off about 38 km after Santander and the pleasant hotel below.*

Where to Stay

Moderate ($50–$99)

Montemar   3rd-class ★ ★

On the Ris beach, Noja, ☎ *(942) 63 03 20.*
Open from the middle of June through the middle of Sept.
Located on the beach, this restful, comfortable hotel with its own tennis court cannot be bettered for its moderate price. *59 rooms.*

Laredo ★ was once a sleepy fishing village that happened to have a wonderful beach to its west. Today it has grown into a true resort with an August population swollen to ten times the 10,000 off-season population. High-rise buildings now line the beach, which remains as fine as it ever was, although less scenic, of course. On the last Friday of August Laredo holds its "Battle of the Flowers," when flowered floats parade through the mass of winding streets that constitute the town.

Where to Stay

Moderate ($50–$99)

Risco   2nd-class ★ ★

Alto de Laredo, Laredo (one km south on the old road to Bilbao), ☎ *(942) 60 50 30, FAX 60 50 55.*
The restaurant is closed on Wed., except in July and Aug.
What makes this a special place are spectacular views from a bluff overlooking the village. Surprisingly, prices are moderate, plus, the restaurant is the best and most inventive in the area, not even discounting its modest prices. *25 rooms.* Credit Cards: A, D, M, V.

Ramona   4th-class ★

Alameda José Antonio, 4, Laredo, ☎ *(942) 60 71 89.*
The restaurant is open from the middle of June through the middle of Sept.
It is the moderate prices—of both the rooms and food—that make this hotel stand out. Despite their modest prices, the accommodations are most comfortable, and the food savory. *10 rooms.*

28 km of beautiful drive further west along N-634 brings picturesque **Castro Urdiales**.

The quiet village of **Castro Urdiales** ★ ★ huddles on a peninsula around castle ruins and a 14th-century church, all framed by mountains that sweep around the beach and bay. The site is lovely. The town retains a less assuming character than others nearby, except for copying Laredo with its own Battle of the Flowers on June 24.

Where to Stay

Moderate ($50–$99)

Miramar 2nd-class ★

On the beach, Castro Urdiales, ☎ (942) 86 02 00, FAX 87 09 42.
The views are lovely and the accommodations comfortable at this moderately priced establishment. *34 rooms.*

After Castro Urdiales comes a boring stretch of road leading to **Bilbao**, *a city of half a million holding little interest for a tourist. The city can be skirted by joining highway A-8 going east. Exit at Amorebieta (exit 18) to take C-6313 toward* **Gernika** *for a bit of history.*

When squadrons of German planes carpet-bombed Gernika (Guernica) during the Spanish Civil war it became an international symbol of atrocity. Gernika was neither a military center nor of strategic importance. It was, and remains, merely a symbol for the Basques. Whether for this reason, or simply to practice their bombing, German planes killed hundreds of civilians and their animals during a surprise raid on April 26, 1937. Thus, there is little that is old in Gernika, but the stump of the original Oak Tree, under which the Basque parliament traditionally met to have their rights acknowledged by Spanish sovereigns, remains in the town plaza beside a newer tree planted after the bombing.

Leaving Gernika, take C-6212 northeast toward **Gauteguiz de Arteaga**, *with a restored 15th-century castle. From Arteaga the coast road going north presents lovely views and passes by the resort of* **Playa de Laida**, *then peaceful* **Elanchove** *in a fine bay, before reaching* **Lekeitio** *(Lequeitio) in about 35 km.*

What could be more picturesque than a village tucked into a bay cut into the foot of a small mountain? Suppose we add a fleet of brightly colored boats, and two wide beaches spreading to either side of the harbor? For good measure throw in a flamboyant 15th-century church with flying buttresses standing atop other buttresses, and you have the postcard-village of **Lekeitio ★★★**.

Where to Stay

Moderate ($50–$99)

Beitia 3rd-class ★

Av. Pascual Aboroa, 25, Lekeitio, ☎ (94) 684 01 11.
Open from Apr. through the second week in Oct.
This is a clean and restful moderately priced hotel with a serene patio, set in the most picturesque of fishing villages. *30 rooms.*

12 km west along C-6212 brings **Ondárroa ★**, *which is hardly less picturesque than Lekieto, on a spit of land jutting out into the sea.* **Matriku** *(Motrico), four km farther on, is losing its attractiveness to* *modern developments.* **Deba** *(Deva), in another four km, retains a fine beach.*

Where to Stay

Moderate ($50–$99)

Miramar   2nd-class ★

C. Arenal, 24, Deba, ☎ (943) 60 16 60.

Views of the coast are lovely, the rooms are comfortable and clean, and the prices are moderate. *60 rooms.*

*At Deba pick up the larger road, N-634, for nine km to **Zumaya** (Zumaia), with surf. South of the town C-6317 bears left toward Zestoa and **Azpeitia**, in 16 km, for an excursion to the birthplace of San Ignacio de Loyola, founder of the Jesuit Order.*

The 16th-century church in the town of Azpeitia retains the baptismal font from an earlier building at which Inigo Lopez Recade was baptized. After a decade of killing, he joined the priesthood and adopted the name Ignacius of Loyola. Still later he founded the Society of the Jesuits. Several noteworthy mansions surround the church, but west of the town is the site of the saint's birth, now the **Sanctuary de Loyola**, a monastery. The monastery encloses the house of his family, the Santa Casa. Important rooms—such as the one in which he was born, the one where he convalesced from wounds, and the one in which he experienced his conversion, have been made into chapels.

*From Zumaia N-634 leads east to **Guetaria** ★ with a street of medieval houses leading to a lovely 15th-century church. **Zarauz** ★, a fashionable resort, is three km further east. Lovely villas with gardens line the beach, and two nice Renaissance palaces stand in the village.*

Where to Stay

Moderate ($50–$99)

Alameda   3rd-class ★

Gipuzkoa, Zarauz, ☎ (943) 83 01 43, FAX 13 24 74.

This is a professionally run place that soothes with a lovely terrace for tranquil views. Moderate prices are reasonable, given all this hotel offers. *38 rooms.*

Where to Eat and Stay

Expensive ($30+)

Karlos Arguiñano   ★★★★

Mendilauta, 13, Zarauz, ☎ 13 00 00, FAX 13 34 50.
The restaurant is closed Sunday night and Wednesday.

Here is as splendidly gracious a place to sleep and eat as any in Spain. The food is elevated in design and preparation, served most professionally in an elegant dining room. After a special dining experience, we often wish that we could simply walk upstairs to bed. Here you can. Every bedroom is large and most offer beautiful sea views. The food and the rooms are expensive, to be sure, but you'll count the money well spent for the pampering. *12 rooms.* Credit Cards: A, D, M, V.

Three km after Zarauz the express E-10 is joined for a 13 km trip to Donostia (San Sebastián), the jewel of the coast.

Donostia ★ ★ ★ (*San Sebastián*, in Spanish) nestles between two small mountains that face a bay of elegant proportions, looking something like a scallop shell. It is a *Belle Époch* resort, much frequented by the French. Nonetheless, it was an Englishman who, in 1896, built the Miramar Palace for Queen María Christina that first brought cachet to the city. Intelligent planning since that time created a city of elegant walks, parks, bridges and buildings, that never ceases to delight the eye. Add the fact that there are more superb restaurants in this city of under 200,000 than in all of Madrid, and you get an almost perfect resort—although at a cost, for elegance is expensive.

Resting atop a hill at the foot of Mount Igueldo, the **Miramar Palace** is under renovation today, but its fine gardens are open for strolling. The palace faces the mile-long curve of **La Concha beach** that must be counted among the most beautiful in the world. At the west end of the beach towers Monte Igueldo, with splendid views from the summit. At the east end stands Monte Urgull, at the tip of a peninsula. A lovely promenade lines the length of the beach for pleasant walks. Most sights, however, cluster near Monte Urgull.

Where La Concha beach ends on the east, a garden grows around the present **Ayuntamiento**. The building was formerly the city casino, built before the turn of the century. But, during the time of Franco when games of chance were banned, the unused structure was taken over by the city. Inside it is a glittering mass of marble and glass. At the end of the gardens of this Parque Alderdi Eder, the elegant shopping street of **Av. de la Libertad** runs east-west. Two blocks north of the park, and one block east, is the main square of the town, the **Pl. de la Constitución**. It is a friendly place, busy with groups of strollers. Some balconies still retain numbers from the days when bullfights were held in the plaza and balconies were rented to fans. Three blocks north of the Pl. de la Constitución is the city museum—**Museo San Telmo** ★. Formerly it was a monastery, now it houses a nice collection of Basque art through the ages, along with paintings by El Greco, Goya and others. (*Open in summer Mon.–Sat. 9 a.m.–9 p.m.; Sun. 9 a.m.–1 p.m. Other seasons, 10 a.m.–1 p.m. and 3:30–7 p.m.; Sun. 10 a.m.–1 p.m. Admission: free.*)

Beside the museum stands the 18th-century church of **Santa María**, with a sober interior and inebriated chapels. A steep path northwest of the church leads upwards to the fortress of **Castillo de Santa Cruz del la Mota**, which guards the summit of Monte Urgull. The castle, from the 16th century, illustrates how buildings changed from secure places of lodging for important persons to fortresses designed to withstand heavy bombardment by cannon. A military museum inside provides little of interest.

Proceeding east, then north, from the Museo San Telmo brings the **Paseo Nuevo**, an attractive promenade around the peninsula of Ugull. At its end is the **Palacio del Mar**, an oceanographic museum. *(Open daily 10 a.m.–1:30 p.m. and 3:30–7:30 p.m., to 8 p.m. in summer; closed Mon. from the middle of Sept. to the middle of May. Admission: 300 ptas.)* East of the museum, in three short blocks, is the Urumea River, spanned by four ornate **deco bridges** from the turn of the century. Near the first of these, the Puente de Kursaal, a park surrounds the **Victoria Eugenia Theater** and the **María Cristina** Hotel, both Victorian palace-like structures from early in our century.

The sights do not endear Donostia to the traveler as much as its elegant, peaceful ambiance—even when the city is filled with summer crowds. There is a style here seldom encountered today.

Where to Stay

Very Expensive ($200+)

María Cristina   Deluxe ★ ★ ★ ★

Paseo República Argentina, Donostia, ☎ (943) 42 49 00, FAX 42 39 14, Telex 38195.
This is a hotel for the aristocracy, built with the finest materials at the turn of the century—mahogany woodwork, onyx baths and Carrera marble columns. It is situated in an extensive park and remodeled throughout in 1988. This is one of the world's great hotels. Aristocracy comes at a price, however—about 40,000 pesetas per night. *109 rooms, plus 27 suites.*

Expensive ($100–$200)

De Londres y de Inglaterra   Deluxe ★ ★ ★

Kalea Zubieta, 2, Donostia (just south of the Parque Alderdi Eder, where the ayuntamiento is located, facing La Concha beach), ☎ (943) 42 69 89, FAX 42 00 31, Telex 36378.

Views of the sea, the gorgeous beach and two hills that anchor each end of the bay are unrivaled from this elegant hotel. Want more? There is a casino next door. The views and elegance are not inexpensive, but cost about half as much as the María Cristina. *133 rooms, plus 12 suites.*

Moderate ($50–$99)

Niza   R2nd-class ★ ★

Kalea Zubieta, 56, Donostia (west of the Hotel de Londres, facing the beach), ☎ (943) 42 66 63, FAX 42 66 63.
Here you enjoy the same magnificent views offered by the Hotel Londres for a moderate price. You do not partake of as much elegance, but do get a comfortable room. *41 roooms.*

Inexpensive (Less than $50)

Hostal Residencia Easo   Hs3rd-class ★

Kalea San Bartolome, 24, Donostia (two blocks south of La Concha beach, behind the hotel Niza), ☎ *(943) 46 68 92.*

Clean, comfortable, largish rooms, close to the beach, makes this hotel a true bargain at its extremely inexpensive rates. *11 rooms.*

Where to Eat

Eating in Donostia represents one of life's more difficult choices. Four or five of the finest restaurants in Europe await. Which one(s) will it be?

Expensive ($30+)

Arzak   ★★★★★

Kalea Alto de Miracruz, 21 (east of the city, on the way to Hondarribia), ☎ *(943) 27 84 65, FAX 27 27 53.*

Closed Sun. night, Mon., the last half of June to the second week of July, and the middle three weeks of Nov.

The only question about this restaurant is whether it is the first or second best in all Spain. When you eat here, however, the issue seems settled in Arzak's favor. It was Chef Jean Arzak who created Basque *nueva cucina*, and he presents a menu of dishes every one of which is innovative and perfect in its way. To start, blow the budget on crayfish or save a little with fish soup that will spoil you for this dish forever. Chef Arzak's renowned favorites are listed on the back menu. Save room for orange flavored flan. Considering the succulence of the food and the elegance of service, prices are correct, though, of course, very expensive. Reservations weeks in advance are a must. Credit Cards: A, D, M, V.

Akelarre   ★★★★

Passeo del Padre Orcolaga, 56, in the barrio de Iqueldo (east of the city on the slopes of Mount Iquedlo), ☎ *(943) 21 20 52, FAX 21 92 68.*

Closed Sun. night, Mon., Feb., the first week of Oct.

Anywhere else this restaurant would stand above all others, but Donostia has Arzak too. Views are exceptional from the slope of Mount Igueldo and the food is sublime. Start with mushrooms and asparagus spears. Some justly rave about the *lubina* (sea bass with green peppers), but the *salmonetes* (red mullet) create a choice between two utterly wonderful options. Prices are in the expensive range, but a tad below those at Arzak. Reservations are absolutely required. Credit Cards: A, D, M, V.

Panier Fleuri   ★★★★

Paseo de Salamanca, 1 (at the mouth of the Urumca River), ☎ *(943) 42 42 05, FAX 42 42 05.*

Closed Sun. night, Wed., the first three weeks in June.

Since the chef was recently named the best in the country, this restaurant would be a standout in any part of Spain, but here the competition keeps every establishment on its toes. There is a definite French accent to the Basque food here, but every dish is utterly delectable. We still can taste the sole with spinach. As with the preceding, prices are well into the expensive range, and reservations are required. Credit Cards: A, D, M, V.

Moderate ($15–$30)

Alotza   ★ ★

Kalea Fermin Calbeton, 7 (just south of the Pl. de la Constitución), ☎ (943) 42 07 82. Closed Wed.

While this establishment is not close to the elevated league of the preceding, its prices are moderate and its food remains innovative, witness peppers stuffed with crab. The atmosphere is less formal too, for a relaxed meal. Credit Cards: A, D, M, V.

N-1 leads east of Donostia in 20k. to **Hondarribia** ★ *(Fuenterrabía). This lovely town overlooks Hendaye across the French border. Because of its border location, it is fortified by 15th-century walls. Several blocks of Renaissance mansions survive in splendor along C. Mayor, ending at the Palacio de Carlos V, finished in the 16th century, now a handsome parador.*

Where to Stay

Expensive ($100–$200)

Parador el Emperador   2nd-class ★ ★ ★

Pl. de Armas del Castillo, Hondarribia, ☎ (943) 64 21 40, FAX 64 21 53.

This castle presents a monolithic face of awesome power. It had to be strong when built in the 11th century, situated as it was on the border with France. Carlos V renovated it early in the 16th century, and the Spanish government remodeled the inside into a parador 20 years ago to convey the atmosphere of medieval times as no other parador. Although it costs in the expensive range, it is a very special place to spend a night. The French and Spanish know this well, reserve far in advance. *36 rooms.*

Where to Eat

Expensive ($30+)

Ramón Roteta   ★ ★ ★

In Irun, 3 km south of town, ☎ (943) 64 16 93.
Closed Sun. evening and Thurs., except in summer; the last half of Nov., and Feb.

Lodged in an elegant mansion, this restaurant serves food elevated both in style and price. Poached eggs with truffles are sublime, and the rice with vegetables and clams is simply outstanding. Credit Cards: A, M, V.

Costa de las Rias (Galician Coast) ★ ★

Rias are deep cuttings in the coast carved by river estuaries. Since the sea's pounding hammers the land down, views can be remarkable from surrounding hills. Here are beaches (often of fine sand, sometimes littered with shells) without the crowds of the Costa del Sol, though swimming in the Atlantic tests all but New Englanders. The southernmost rias, called the Rias Bajas, provide more temperate bathing and are unquestionably the most attractive, for here the coast rises high for grand panoramas. From the latitude of Santiango de Compostella south to the Portuguese border five separate rias shape the southern Galician coast into the thumb and fingers of a hand. We describe these five rias from north to south.

C-550 follows their contours and makes for a scenic day's trip by car. This road was much in need of repair on our last visit; proceed carefully, if driving. Surprisingly good bus service visits all the coastal towns.

From Santiago de Compostela take N-550 west for 18 km to Padrón.

Padrón stands at the head of the Ria de Arousa where, according to legend, winds blew Saint James, Spain's Santiago, ashore to began a seven-year sojourn in Spain. In the Church of Santiago, beside a bridge over the Sar, the stone where the ship is supposed to have moored sits beneath the altar.

From Padrón, a turn west on C-550 goes to the Ria Muros y Noia, with good beaches and few tourists, or a turn south on C-550 goes to four other rias over a route that provides more interest along the way.

Ria Muros y Noia:

C-550 wends with little scenic interest to Ribera, a fishing town at the end of a cape in 42 km. The road then cuts across the cape to Porto do Son. Do not miss the romantic **Castro de Barona ★** *on the way. This is an ancient Celtic fortress on a small isthmus, with lovely surrounding beaches that generally are deserted. Noia, at the head of the ria, is 20 km further on.*

In **Noia**, the picturesque 14th-century **Santa María a Nova** stands amid an ancient cemetery that contains some 10th-century tombstones inscribed with runes. **San Martin**, facing the sea, wears some nice statues on its facade. There are decent beaches around Noia, but better ones lie further on.

The most scenic area is the north side of the ria. Fine beaches surround Muros, 36 km away, entered across a 14th-century bridge.

Charming **Muros ★** is a fishing village divided by alleys, with arcaded streets and the pretty Gothic church of **San Pedro**. Fine beaches line Point Louro.

Where to Stay

Moderate ($50–$99)

Muradana   **R2nd-class ★**
Av. Marina Española, 107, Muros, ☎ *(981) 82 68 85.*
A pleasant-enough place at a low moderate price, offers very inexpensive meals besides. *16 rooms.*

A visit to **Cabo Finisterre ★***, the westernmost part of Europe and the end of the world to the ancients, is a scenic excursion. Continue north from Muros on C-550 along a lovely stretch of coast to*

Corcubion, 42 km away. The village of Finisterre is 13 km west, and 2 km further is the windswept cape, with its lighthouse overlooking the sea. The beaches are gorgeous.

Ria de Arousa:

From Padrón, C-550 going southwest reaches **Villagarcia de Arousa** *in 25 km, with a green promenade along the sea, plus a special restaurant with rooms to rent.*

Where to Stay and Eat

Expensive ($30+)

Chocolate ★ ★ ★

Av. Cambados, 151, Vilaxoan (actually in the town of Vilaxoan), ☎ (986) 50 11 99, FAX 50 67 62.

Closed Sun. nights.

This is a delightful restaurant, serving some of the finest food in Galicia for deservedly expensive prices. It also offers 18 tastefully decorated rooms at inexpensive rates. *18 rooms.* Credit Cards: A, M, V.

Cambados ★, *in 10 km, is a lovely town with an unforgettable square, two sides of which are formed by the 16th-century palace of Fefiñanes. There is a lovely parador, but no beaches.*

Where to Stay

Moderate ($50–$99)

Parador del Albariño 2nd-class ★ ★

Paseo de Cervantes, Cambados, ☎ *(986) 54 22 50, FAX (986) 54 20 68.*

This parador is almost rustic, built in the style of the manor houses of the area around a courtyard. It is a relaxing, homey place to stay and prices are moderate. *63 rooms.*

Pazo el Revel 2nd-class ★ ★ ★

Camino de la Iglesia, Vilalonga, ☎ *(986) 74 30 00, FAX 74 33 90.*

Open June through Sept.

This hotel is installed in a 17th-century manor house, with a lovely garden behind for quiet, containing a pool and tennis courts. You cannot do better for a moderate price. *21 rooms.*

This matter is taken care of in 15 km at **O Grova** *(El Grove)* ★*, and the gorgeous pine island of* **A Toxa** *(La Toja)* ★*, off its coast. Beaches are plentiful in this favored resort area. The island of A Toxa has recently been subjected to large-scale hotel development, even a casino.*

Where to Stay

Expensive ($100–$200)

Louxo 1st-class ★ ★ ★

Island of A Toxa, ☎ *(986) 73 02 00, FAX 73 27 91.*

The hotel sits in a magnificent park with views, near the casino, and offers every sports facility. Although it charges in the expensive range, it is half the price of the Gran Hotel nearby and provides more attractive rooms. *112 rooms, plus three suites.*

Moderate ($50–$99)

Mar Atlántico   2nd-class ★ ★ ★

In San Vincente del Mar, nine km south of O Grove, ☎ *(986) 73 80 61, FAX 73 82 99.*
Set in a sylvan pine forest, here you feel the cares of the world fall away not impeded by charges barely in the moderate category. *34 rooms.*

Where to Eat

Moderate ($15–$30)

La Posada del Mar   ★

C. Castelao 202, in O Grove, ☎ *(986) 73 01 06.*
Closed Sun. eve (except in Aug.), and from the second week of Dec. to the end of Jan.
The dining room offers views across the channel to the pretty island of A Toxa. Seafood is fresh as can be, and prices are moderate.

Ria de Pontevedra:

C-550 proceeds south through the resort village of **Sanxenxo** *(Sangenjo), and the more typical fishing village of* **Combarro**, *before which is a comfortable place to stay.*

Where to Stay

Moderate ($50–$99)

Stella Maris   2nd-class ★

On C-550, before Combarro, ☎ *(986) 77 03 66.*
This is a pleasant little hotel with some views at an attractively low moderate price. *27 rooms.*

Pontevedra *arrives in 35 km. Alternatively, you can drive directly to Pontevedra from Padrón along N-550, a fast 37 km.*

Pontevedra is a sleepy town of some size (65,137 population) that does well as a base for exploring the rias. It preserves an old section in a small area opposite the Burgo Bridge. Here is **Santa María la Mayor**, a late 15th-century Plateresque church for fishermen. (Note the reliefs at the rear of the west end.) The **Museo Provincial**, five blocks southeast on the Pl. de Lena consists of two former mansions tied together by an arch. The pre-Roman—especially the Celtic—material is most worthwhile. This museum tries hard to interest by reconstructing parts of famous ships, and modeling antique kitchens *(open daily 11 a.m. to 1:30 p.m. and 5–8 p.m.; admission: 200 ptas.).* Near the northeast edge of the Jardines Vincenti are romantic ruins of the 14th-century convent of **Santo Domingo**.

Where to Stay

Moderate ($50–$99)

Parador Casa del Barón   1st-class ★

Pl. de Maceda, Pontevedra, ☎ *(986) 85 58 00, FAX 85 21 95.*
This parador is a remodeled 18th-century mansion, which was never attractive, but
bedrooms are spacious and charges are moderate. *47 rooms.*

Where to Eat

Expensive ($30+)

Doña Antonia   ★★★★

Soportales de la Herreria, 9 (the second floor), ☎ *(986) 84 72 74.*
Closed Sun.
This restaurant is a gourmet's dream. Oh, that lamb coated in honey cooked over a
wood fire! All the food is superb and served with elegance at a cost that will only
hurt for a little while. Credit Cards: V, D, M, A.

Casa Solla   ★★★

Carretera de La Toya (2 km west of town), ☎ *(986) 85 60 29.*
Closed Sun. eve, Thurs. eve, and Christmas week.
Pity the person who must choose between this restaurant and Doña Antonia. This
one is more sylvan, with a lovely garden, but the food is no less spectacular. Want
proof? Try the creamed oysters. Nor will you suffer if you order the lamb here. Credit
Cards: A, V, M.

*Still on C-550, now going southwest, quickly pass Marin, then miles
of beaches to reach* **Hio** ★ *near the end of the cape in 28 km, with a
fine Romanesque church and more miles of nice beach.*

Ria de Vigo:

*South of Hio the scenery grows more lovely with each kilometer until
reaching the outskirts of Vigo in 51 km. This industrial city can
readily be skirted for the scenic 18 km ride to* **Panxón***, a charming
fishing village.* **Playa América** *is a modern resort lining the bay with
its ribbon of fine sand beach.* **Baiona** *(Bayona), at the west end of the
bay, lodges its popular parador in the former 16th-century fortress of
Monte Real, atop a hill with magnificent views.*

Where to Stay

Expensive ($100–$200)

Parador Conde de Gondomar   Deluxe ★★★

1.5 km outside Baiona, ☎ *(986) 35 50 00, FAX 35 50 76, Telex 83424.*
This luxury parador is built to look like an 18th-century mansion and is located
inside the walls of a genuine ancient castle. It offers swimming, tennis and romantic
views of the sea. For all this it costs just a touch more than the average parador. *124
rooms.*

Fine beaches continue to Cape Silleiro. There is little scenery south of this place, though **Tui** *(Tuy)* ★ *in 61 km, at the Portuguese border, is a charming town with nice mansions and a fortress-like 13th-century Cathedral.*

Costa Verde ★

This Asturian coast is as pretty as any in Spain, and beloved by the Spanish. Bluffs line a shore broken by clean sandy inlets for protected bathing. The coast is long, extending from Ribadeo at the border of Galicia for 300 km east to San Vincente, where the Basque Coast begins. However, we describe a route that extends past these political boundaries for 50 km on either side. It does not seem proper, for example, to bring you to within 30 km of beautiful Santillana del Mar, then not mention it. The coast is roughly divided in two by Gijon, from which either the less spoiled western half or the more elegant eastern half can be explored. As the coast is so long, we divide our description into these western and eastern routes.

From **Oviedo** *the toll road A-66 leads to Gijon in 29 km. From* **León** *follow directions to Oviedo. From* **Santiago** *it is possible to come from the western end of the coast by taking the toll road A-9 north to Betanzos for 57 km, then taking N-VI east to Baamonde for 47 km, and, finally, N-634 northeast to Ribadeo in 90 km.*

Western Costa Verde

Gijon is a city of a quarter of a million people bordering a wide bay. It consists largely of modern buildings, since the Civil War destroyed most of its older structures. Today it prospers as one of the main ports for shipping the coal from mountains to its south, and from manufacturing steel in its outskirts. While it offers fine sand beaches, surprising to come upon after the commercial bustle of the rest of the city, they can grow polluted during the height of summer.

Where to Stay

Expensive ($100–$200)

Parador El Molina Viejo   1st-class ★

Parque Isabel la Católica, Gijon (east of the center of the city), ☎ *(98) 537 05 11, FAX 537 02 33.*

This parador is installed in a cider mill from the 18th century amid a lovely garden, but for all its first-class rating, provides simple accommodations. The rooms overlooking its extensive park are preferred. The beach is near and prices are barely expensive. *38 rooms, plus two suites.*

Where to Eat

Moderate ($15–$30)

Casa Victor ★

C. Carmen, 11 (near the train station, by the port), ☎ *(98) 534 83 10.*
Closed Sun. and Nov.

The restaurant looks like many a mesón in the area but serves the best seafood in town. Victor, the owner and something of a culinary legend, is a thoughtful restaurateur who modifies the traditional fare of the region with his nueva touches. Credit Cards: A, D, M, V.

Head west from Gijon on N-632 (or avoid Gijon altogether by taking the west branch of A-8) to **Avilés** *in 25 km. Once Avilés ranked with the prettiest towns in Spain, but large steelworks put an end to that. Three km farther the village of* **Salinas** ★ *emerges from the pines. It is an attractive resort town with the longest beach on this coast.*

For an excursion to prehistoric cave paintings, at Soto del Barco west on N-632 in 13 km, take N-633 south in the direction of Cornellana. Following signs for **San Román** *in 13 km. The cave is above the town, and contains a lovely painting of a wounded stag and yellow horse.*

West on N-632, after Avilés, comes **Cudillero** *in 20 km, after taking C-2 north for one km. The village is picturesque and proud of its castle, though there are no worthy beaches. Next on N-632, in about 30 km, comes* **Cadavedo**, *a pretty small town with nice beaches, but few accommodations. 30 km more, as the road changes designation to N-634, brings lovely* **Luarca**.

Luarca ★ lines the mouth of the Rio Negro, where it opens into a lovely bay in the sea. The town consists of charming whitewashed slate roofed houses set along cobbled alleys. At the end of the estuary is a lighthouse, a church and a fascinating cemetery, while a path leads above the bay for fine views. A decent beach borders the cliffs.

Where to Stay

Moderate ($50–$99)

Gayoso 2nd-class ★ ★

Paseo de Gómez, 4, Luarca, ☎ *(98) 564 00 50, FAX 564 16 42.*
Closed Nov. through Apr.

This hotel is seasoned and atmospheric, the rooms large, and wooden balconies add just the right touch. It also remains pleasantly within the moderate price category. *33 rooms.*

Inexpensive (Less than $50)

Casa Consuelo   3rd-class ★

On N-634, 6 km west, ☎ *(98) 547 07 67, FAX 564 16 42.*
Closed from the middle of Sept. through the first week in Oct.
Situated nicely, with fine views, this hotel is an exceptional buy for its inexpensive
price. As a bonus the associated restaurant serves excellent food, although at higher
prices. *35 rooms.*

Where to Eat

Expensive ($30+)

Leonés   ★ ★

Paseo Alfonso X el Sabio, 1, ☎ *(98) 564 09 95.*
The decor is best described as "quaint," but the food is special. We think often of
the scrambled eggs with shrimp, spinach and a hearty tang of garlic, not to mention
the apple sherbet. It is an expensive little place, however. Credit Cards: A, V, D, M .

Signs to La Coruña return you to N-634 going west. **Navia** *in*
20 km is a new town and fishing port. **Tapia de Casariego** ★*, in*
20 km more, presents a splendid beach with good surfing to the west of
this sleepy fishing village.

Where to Stay

Moderate ($50–$99)

Palacete Pañalba   1st-class ★ ★ ★

C. El Cotarelo, in Figueras, two km from Casariego, ☎ *(98) 563 61 25, FAX 563 62 47.*
This is a luxurious *modernista* mansion of delicate proportions, made into a hotel
that is tasteful, reserved, quiet and costs in the moderate range. In fact, it is more a
museum than a hotel, having been declared a national artistic monument. *10*
rooms, plus two suites.

In 10 km, after crossing the Rio Eo, we arrive at **Ribadeo**.

Technically **Ribadeo** ★ sits across the border in Galicia, and it is a more
substantial town than its population of under 10,000 would suggest. It offers a quaint fisherman's quarter, a lighthouse, a castle, a parador and an attractive beach. On the hill two km outside the town is the Hermitage of
Santa Cruz, and fine views of the coast. Northwest of Ribadeo range miles of
fine beach and few tourists.

Where to Stay

Moderate ($50–$99)

Eo   2nd-class ★

Av. de Asturias, 5, Ribadeo, ☎ *(982) 10 07 50, FAX 10 00 21.*
Open mid June-mid Sept.
The modern parador in town offers no charm and falls second to this restful, well-
run place. When you add the fact that this establishment charges in the low-moder-
ate range—so you pay a third less than at the parador—the choice is clear. *24*
rooms.

Where to Eat

Moderate ($50–$99)

O Xardin   ★

C. Reinante, 20, ☎ *(982) 10 02 22.*
Closed Mon. in winter, and from Christmas through Jan.
Aptly named "The Garden," this is a relaxed, bistro place that serves inventive, well-prepared food at a moderate price. Credit Cards: D, M, V.

From Ribadeo N-634 meets N-642 going north in 19 km toward Foz. In about three km signs direct to **San Martin de Mondoñedo** ★★*, a church from the beginning of the 12th century. It is all that remains of a former monastery. The style is the earliest form of Romanesque, with a timber roof, and outer buttresses. The capitals inside are carved in charming scenes and the stone retable is endearing.* **Foz** ★ *is a busy little port with two fine beaches separated by a headland. More white sand beaches, this time amid lovely scenery, lie 40 km north around the town of* **Vivero***. Unfortunately, accommodations here are scarce. We found one nice place, however.*

Where to Stay

Moderate ($50–$99)

Ego   2nd-class ★

At the Playa de Area on C-642, two km north, ☎ *(982) 56 09 87, FAX 56 17 62.*
This is a well-maintained hotel that provides beach and ocean views for a moderate price. *29 rooms.*

Eastern Costa Verde

From Gijon (see above), head east on a pretty stretch of N-632 to **Villaviciosa** ★ *in 30 km. This village of charming streets is the cider capital of Asturias, with a nice church in the Pl. Mayor and restaurants from which refreshing cider is available. 18 km more brings* **La Isla** ★ *on a huge bay ringed with numerous beaches.*

Where to Stay

Moderate ($50–$99)

Astuy   2nd-class ★

On the beach, three km east of La Isla ☎ *(942) 67 95 40, FAX 67 95 88.*
Closed from mid Jan. to mid Feb.
This hotel sits opposite a lovely beach and charges a low moderate price for clean and comfortable accommodations. *53 rooms.*

In 21 km comes **Ribadesella**.

Ribadesella ★★ offers pleasant accommodations and a splendid beach. On the outskirts a marvelous cave called **Cueve Tito Bustillo**, contains paleolithic paintings of the age of Altamira, and, in some cases, of that quality. (Open

10 a.m. to 1 p.m. and 3:30–6:30 p.m.; closed Mon., and summer weekends; admission: 200 ptas. Only four hundred people are allowed inside per day.)

Where to Stay

Expensive ($100–$200)

Grand Hotel del Sella   1st-class ★ ★

Paseo de la Playa, Ribadesella, ☎ (98) 586 01 50, FAX 585 74 49.
Open Apr.–mid Oct.
Views of the town and bay from the rooms facing the sea are lovely. Other rooms are contained in an 18th-century mansion. A tennis court and pool are available, and prices are correctly expensive. *82 rooms.*

Moderate ($50–$99)

Ribadesella Playa   2nd-class ★

Paseo de la Playa, 34, Ribadesella, ☎ (98) 586 07 15, FAX 586 02 20.
Closed Jan.
The views are as lovely from this former mansion as from the Grand Hotel down the beach, but at a low moderate price. This hotel is less grand, but very comfortable. *17 rooms.*

Five km west of Ribadesella, just before Nueva, N-632 feeds into the better N-634. From Nueva to Santillana del Mar almost 100 km west, fine beaches line every kilometer of the route. The first town worthy of note along the way is **Llanes** ★ *, a quiet resort with good beaches dotted with interesting rock formations, a nice church and a castle.*

Where to Stay

Moderate ($50–$99)

Don Paco   2nd-class ★ ★

Posade Herrera, 1, Llanes, ☎ (98) 540 01 50, FAX 540 26 81.
Open June-Sept.
The hotel is a former 17th-century palace beside the town ramparts. Rooms facing the sea provide beautiful views, and are comfortable, though showing wear, with prices securely within the moderate range. The restaurant is truly grand, though the food is less so and inexpensive. *42 rooms.*

After 15 km of road bordered by shore and mountains comes the village of **La Franca** ★ *, on the outskirts of which a lovely cliff frames a fine beach.*

Where to Stay

Moderate ($50–$99)

Mirador de la Franca   3rd-class ★ ★

On the beach, one km west of La France, ☎ (985) 41 21 45, FAX 41 21 53.
Open April through the end of Sept.
This is a lovely little place beside a fine beach, offering views and quiet at a moderate price. *52 rooms.*

In another 18 km comes **San Vincente de la Barquera**.

San Vincente de la Barquera ★ ★ is blessed with a huge beach that led to quick development as a resort, somehow without losing its attractiveness. The town is filled with old arcaded houses and has several nice mansions, a castle and interesting remains of a 13th-century convent.

Where to Stay

Moderate ($50–$99)

Residencia Miramar   R2nd-class ★ ★

In Barquera, one km north of San Vincente, ☎ (942) 71 00 63, FAX 71 00 75.
Open Mar. through the middle of Dec.
Views of the ocean and surrounding mountains are stunning from this charming little hotel. All this, and quiet too, comes at a moderate price. *21 rooms.*

A few kilometers outside of San Vincente turn left onto the coastal road C-6316, which brings **Comillas** *in 10 km.*

Comillas ★ has long been a resort attracting visitors of the ilk of King Alfonso XII. The town is attractive with a charming Plaza Mayor and fishing port. It also contains a set of neo-Gothic buildings from the end of the 19th century, including a Moorish style **pavilion by Gaudi** (now a restaurant). To all this it adds miles of beaches to the west, five km outside of town.

Where to Stay

Moderate ($50–$99)

Josein   3rd-class ★

C. Manuel Noriega, 2, Comillas, ☎ (942) 72 02 25.
Open Apr.-Sept.
The views of the beach and sea are worth more than the moderate price charged. Rooms are comfortable and clean. *23 rooms.*

Hosteria de Quijas   3rd-class ★ ★

On N-634 near Reocín, ☎ (942) 82 08 33.
Closed from the last week in Dec. through the fourth of Jan.
The hotel reposes in an elegant 18th-century mansion that makes one feel like a baron. There is a pool, though the beach is some distance away. This is the way to live, and at a moderate price. *13 rooms.*

Where to Eat

Expensive ($30+)

El Capricho de Gaudí   ★

Barrio de Sobrellano, ☎ (942) 72 03 65.
Closed Mon. (except in summer), and from the 2nd week in Jan. through the 2nd week in Feb.
To be frank, the food is not extraordinary and on the expensive side, but the building is a treat and the service is elegant. It was designed by Gaudí in 1885 as a summer pavilion in a style composed of Moorish elements carried to their extremes. You can peek in, of course, without dining. Credit Cards: A, D, M, V.

Continue west on C-6316 for 19 km to elegant **Santillana del Mar**.

Santillana ★ ★ ★ has been called the prettiest village in Spain and well it might be—except on weekends when the tourists descend. Exception must be taken to its name however, for it is several kilometers from the sea. At the northern end of the main street stands the late 12th-century **Collegiate Church of Santa Julliana** (whose corrupted name denominates the village). The façade is elegant Romanesque on the east end, and the interior contains interesting vaulting. In the choir four lovely Romanesque statues hide inside a 17th-century Mexican silver altarfront. The cloisters are quietly moving. Throughout the length of the village stand elegant **mansions** from the 15th-17th centuries. Half a mile to the south is a **zoo** which presents several European bison exactly like those depicted on the ceiling of **Altamira Cave**. That cave lies two km southwest, but can be entered only by official permission that takes months to secure.

Where to Stay

Expensive ($100–$200)

Parador Gil Blás   1st-class ★ ★ ★

Pl. Ramón Pelayo, 11, Santillana del Mar, ☎ *(942) 81 80 00, FAX 81 83 91.*
This parador is situated amid noble Renaissance mansions, and is one itself, from the 17th century. Baronial in every way, the edifice oozes atmosphere. Prices barely crest the expensive range, which is one reason the rooms are heavily booked. Note that the hotel has a modern annex across the way that offers none of the character you are paying for. Demand a room in the manor house, or go elsewhere. *56 rooms.*

Moderate ($50–$99)

Altamar   2nd-class ★ ★

C. Cantón, 1, Santillana del Mar, ☎ *(942) 81 80 25, FAX 84 01 03.*
Here you also get to stay in a baronial mansion, also from the 17th century, but at a solidly moderate price that makes up for the fact that the mansion is a little smaller and the service not as grand as at the parador. *32 rooms.*

Eight km to the west C-6316 joins the better N-611 for a speedy 25 km trip to **Santander** ★. *See the Basque Coast for a description.*

Oviedo ★ ★ ★

Population: 190,123
Area code: 985; zip code: 33003

From **León** *take N-630 north for 115 km. The road winds through scenic mountains, and can consume three hours, if there are trucks—and there always are. Alternatively, one can take N-120 west for eight km to pick up the toll road A-66 north to save almost an hour. From* **Gijon** *on the Cantabrian coast take A-66 west, then south for 29 km.*

Oviedo, situated over a pass through the Cordillera Mountains and less than 20 miles from the sea, was established as a defensive outpost to bar the Moors from the little territory remaining to the Spanish Christians. Nonetheless, by the middle of the eighth century the Moors had utterly destroyed the town. Alfonso II, one of the earliest Spanish kings, then rebuilt the city and moved his court there in 810. Thus Oviedo is one of, if not the, oldest capitals of the kings of Spain. Alfonso built two churches when he moved into town. One, Santullano, survives in its original form. In the other, Alfonso built a special shrine to contain the sacred relics of the Visigoths that they had managed to carry away from Toledo when the Moors seized that capital. Centuries later, this old church was replaced by a Gothic Cathedral but the original shrine was preserved in the newer structure, and survives still. Alfonso's successor, Ramiro I, built a summer palace on the slopes of Mount Naranco nearby. One hall of that palace remains today in the somewhat altered form of a church. Thus, Oviedo was on course to become a proper capital when Christians captured León, to the south, to which the court moved, never to return. Since 1388, however, the heir to Spain's throne has been designated Prince of Asturias, in remembrance of the historical importance of this province and Oviedo.

The city languished until the 19th century when coal deposits in the Cordillera Mountains began to be exploited, bringing prosperity to the area. Oviedo again became what it had been centuries before, a kind of capital of the Asturian region—this time more an economic than a political center. Today Oviedo exudes an attractive comfort and, despite its largish population, seems a small town. The city centers on a lovely park, the Parque de San Francisco, filled with ponds, fountains, flowers, aged trees and strolling people. Along its north side runs an avenue of attractive stores and banks; a block back from its west side stands the elegant town parador; and a block from its east corner stretches the small old quarter that contains many of the sights for tourists.

Come to relax in Oviedo. The distances to sights are eminently manageable on feet, the park calls for strolls and leisurely rests, and the food is good. What is worth seeing will take no more than half of one day, but most visitors are in no hurry to leave.

The most interesting sight in Oviedo is **Santa María del Naranco ★★**, the former hall of King Ramiro's palace. It is four km northwest of town on a mountainside with lovely views. A hundred feet away is **San Miguel de Lillo ★**, an equally ancient church. The Gothic **Cathedral ★★** is one of the highlights of the city proper, for inside is preserved the Cámera Santa, a ninth century shrine of hoary Christian relics. Renaissance mansions surround the Cathedral. The **Archaeological Museum ★** nearby is worth a stop, as is the **Museo de Bellas Artes de Asturias**. Several blocks northeast stands

Santullano ★, a 9th-century church. West of the park is the Renaissance Hospital of the Principality of Asturias, now a special **parador** with an elegant baroque facade.

> *Arriving from* **León** *and* **south** *on N-630 the town is entered on Av. León. Continue straight as the street changes its name to Calvo Sotelo. It passes along the edge of the large Parque de San Francisco on the left. Parking lies at the end of the park, down the first left across C. Fruela straight ahead.*
>
> *From the* **north** *on A-66 continue straight onto C. Victor Chavarn, which changes its name to Alcalde G. Conde and enters a plaza in one block. Take, not the acute left, but the gentle left which brings C. Arguelles in one block. Turn right and take the first left to parking, just before the park.*
>
> *From the* **northeast on N-634** *C. Jovellanos winds and changes its name to C. Arguelles. Take the first left to parking, just before the park.*

Head east from the northeast corner of the park along C. San Francisco. In one block the 17th-century **Old University** stands on the right. A jag left, then immediately right, brings the attractive plaza of Alfonso II. Immediately left is the 17th-century **Valdecarzana Palace**, and at the southwest corner stands the **Casa de la Rua**, a 15th-century house. Proceed ahead to the Cathedral.

What to See and Do

Cathedral ★★

Pl. de alfonso II, ☎ *522 10 33.*
Hours open: Mon.–Sat. 10:15 a.m.–1 p.m. and 4–7 p.m. (to 6 p.m. in winter). Open Sun. 4–7 p.m.

The original Cathedral was begun in 781 and finished in 802. In 1388 the city decided to replace that church with a larger Gothic structure that was not completed until the 16th century. Of the early church, two pieces still remain today. South of the present facade stands San Tirso, which is just a window frame from the 9th-century church; and inside the present Cathedral is the Cámera Santa (Holy Chamber).

The facade is blackened with a grime that adds to the feeling of age, if not attractiveness. The soaring south tower is a Gothic masterpiece, but the incomplete north tower and empty niches around the portals lend an air of incompleteness to the whole.

The interior seems small but well proportioned and light. Overall, this is a most sedate flamboyant Gothic church. Chapels lining both sides of the nave are later baroque additions, as is the ambulatory which displays photographs of the reconstruction of the Cámera Santa. Poorly restored, the 16th-century retable looks better from the length of the nave than close at hand. The north transept (left) contains a fine late Gothic chapel to house remains of some of the earliest kings of Spain in marble sarcophagi so eroded that the names and decoration can no longer be discerned.

The south transept (right) leads to the Cámera Santa. This "Holy Chamber" was built in 810 by Alfonso II to house sacred relics the Visigoths carried away when the Moors conquered Toledo and most of the rest of Spain. In the 12th century the Cámera was masterfully redecorated in the Romanesque style. During the Spanish Civil War the chapel was bombed, then faithfully reconstructed afterwards. In 1977 thieves stole its most priceless treasures, though the culprits were apprehended on their way to France and the treasures regained. The Cámera Santa consists of one doorway and a tiny apse displaying treasures, housed in the former cloister which currently serves as a gallery of revolving art exhibits, though also displaying some medieval tombs.

Cámera Santa: The vault of the main chamber rests on Romanesque statues of apostles serving as columns. They compare with the great work of Master Mateo in Santiago, whose influence is probable. A sublime figure of Christ watches over the doorway. In the tiny apse, more a large niche, reside the priceless treasures for which the Cámera, indeed the Cathedral, were erected. Precautions to prevent a recurrence of the 1977 robbery prevent any close viewing of these artworks. But there in the center is the Cruz de los Angeles, a bejeweled Maltese cross from 808, probably used for ceremonies during the reign of Alfonso II. To the side rests the Cruz de la Victoria, from 910, actually a sheath to protect the oak cross carried by Pelayo in the first Christian victory over the Moors. There is also a coffer covered in silver with Arabic writing, early reliquaries, ivory diptyches and silver and gold plate. *Admission: 300 ptas. to the Cámera Santa and cloisters.*

South past **San Tirso**, which is simply a 9th-century window, comes the 18th-century palace of Velarde housing the **Museo de Bellas Artes de Asturias**. Although not of the first rank artistically, the paintings inside form a charming collection of unfamiliar works. Continuing south would bring the Pl. Mayor and the picturesque **Pl. de Daoiz y Velarde**, the town market, west of it.

Returning to the Cathedral and walking behind, leads to the **Provincial Archaeological Museum** ★, housed in an 18th-century convent. (Open Tues.–Sat. 10 a.m.–1:30 p.m. and 4–6 p.m. Open Sun. 11 a.m.–1 p.m. Admission: free.) What is special about this museum is its display of fragments and reproductions of early Asturian art, preparing for the Asturian art you see in the Cámera Sancta and the churches at Naranco.

North from the front of the Museum brings C. Martinez Vigil heading northeast for five blocks to Santullano at the end of a small park.

Santullano   ★

Hours open: Tues.–Sun. 10 a.m.–1 p.m. and 4–6 p.m. If closed, apply at the Presbytery on the left.

This church is among the oldest in Spain, dating from the early tenth century, the times of the Asturian kings. The exterior is charming, with a wide porch in front and three square apses in the rear. The inside is small but elegant and preserves traces of 10th-century frescoes on the walls, reminiscent of late Roman work. *Admission: free.*

A block west of the west end of the Parque de San Francisco is the city's imposing **parador** *housed in the former Antiquo Hospital del Principado from the 18th century. The harmonious, almost classical front is surmounted by a baroque extravaganza of a coat of arms above the door.*

Santa María del Naranco ★★

El Monte Naranco.
Hours open: daily (Mon.–Sat. in winter) 10 a.m.–1 p.m. and 3–7 p.m. (until 5 p.m. in winter).

On the precipitous slopes of the hill of Naranco Alfonso II built a summer palace early in the ninth century to catch breezes and lovely views. He erected a small church, San Miguel de Lillo, a hundred feet north. Over the centuries the palace fell to ruin and disappeared, all except for one part that was made into a second church. Today, two ancient churches stand on this hill, though one, Santa María, began life as the hall of an Asturian palace.

To reach Naranco take C. Calvo Sotelo along the eastern edge of the park for four blocks past the park. At the large intersection take Av. del Padre Vinjoy going right. Follow the second right onto the major thoroughfare of Av. Hernandos Menéndez Pidal, which changes its name to Av. de Colón, after a park. Cross a bridge over train tracks, continuing straight along the smaller C. Ramiro I. In two short blocks a sign directs left up Av. de los Monumentos to Naranco in less than four km.

The first impression of Santa María is of a building with too many architectural elements for its tiny size. Gradually one becomes aware that this is caused by an unfamiliar aesthetic, not by detail, for the building is harmonious. Remodeling from a palace into a church occurred in the early tenth century and consisted of adding some religious carving inside and outer walls where needed, for the hall was neither the front nor back of the palace. Thus, the present structure retains architectural elements from the time when it was the palace audience hall, providing a glimpse of the life-style of the rich in the ninth century.

The structure conveys a sense of strength despite its size. Constructed of local stone with buttressing pilasters strengthening the long walls, the main room stands over a low first floor, probably to raise it above the damp. Outer porches at either end provide fresh air and peaceful views. Inside, note the cradle vaulting of the ceiling, the medallions hanging around the top of the walls, and the pillars carved in twisted columns. This building prefigures the Romanesque, but with elements such as the foregoing, that are unique contributions to architecture.

A hundred feet further up the hill is the original church for the palace, **San Miguel de Lillo**, also dating to the ninth century. Its plan is simple: a narrow nave to emphasizes the height. The window tracery is exceptional, as are carvings on the entrance door jambs and column bases. *Admission: 250 ptas.*

Where to Stay

Oviedo is not equipped for tourists as much as some Spanish cities; instead its hotels cater mainly to business people at a rate they can afford. There are abundant hotel choices at the expensive level, but few at lower rates.

Expensive ($100–$200)

De La Reconquista   **1st-class ★ ★ ★ ★**

C. Gil de Jaz, 16, Oviedo (one block west of the west end of the Parque de San Francisco), ☎ *524 11 00, FAX 524 11 66, Telex 84328.*

This is one of our favorite hotels in Spain. The outside is stately yet with a touch of humor in the gigantic baroque coat of arms affixed to the front. The interior is elegant through and through with a huge central patio that expansively invites. Bedrooms are large, tastefully decorated and comfortable; the bathrooms are luxurious. All this and service that is close to perfect too—attentive, helpful but not obsequious. Unlike other paradors this one is managed by the Italian CIGA company, which owns and manages some of the grand hotels of Europe. There is always a rub, of course—the charges are expensive, over 20,000 pesetas per couple per night. Is that too much for accommodations you won't forget? *132 rooms, plus 10 suites.*

Moderate ($50–$99)

Principado   **1st-class ★**

C. San Francisco, 6, Oviedo (east of the east corner of the Parque de San Francisco), ☎ *521 77 92, FAX 521 39 46, Telex 84003.*

This hotel offers no history or stunning architecture, but provides a comfortable place to rest at half the price of La Reconquista. Its rooms were nicely renovated in 1990. *62 rooms, plus four suites.*

Inexpensive (Less than $50)

Favila   **3rd-class**

C. Uria, 37, Oviedo (one block north of the Hotel Reconquista; one block south of the train station), ☎ *525 38 77, FAX 527 61 69.*

As mentioned, accommodations below the expensive level are difficult to find in this city. This hotel is not special, but stands in a pleasant area and has the advantage of lower rates than most, low enough to be considered inexpensive. *24 rooms.*

Where to Eat

Catering to businesspeople has a happy effect on Oviedo's restaurants. The town boasts two that serve exceptional food and one that is pure fun.

Expensive ($30+)

Casa Fermín   **★ ★ ★**

C. San Francisco, 8 (west of the northwest corner of the Parque de San Francisco), ☎ *521 64 52, FAX 522 92 12.*
Closed Sun night.

Relaxing pinks and greys provide a background for greenery and bright skylights in this most elegant of Oviedo's restaurants. It serves the best food in town. Because the owner is a promoter of the food of his region, the menu consists of *fabada* (beans in a tomato sauce with ham), clams with fois gras *en papillote* and seafood. Everything is prepared with care and style, and the prices are fair. Reservations are advised, especially weekends. Credit Cards: A, D, M, V.

Trascorrales ★★
Pl. de Trascorrales, 19 (two blocks south of the Cathedral in the marketplace), ☎ *22 24 41.*
Closed Sun, and the second half of Aug.
Although the decor is rustic with dark wood and copper pots, it is tasteful. The food is aggressively *nueva cucina*, and inventiveness abounds. Strawberries in a sauce of sugar and pepper is not something that would occur to most, but try them and be transported. Reservations are recommended. Credit Cards: A, D, M, V.

Moderate ($15–$30)

El Raitan ★
Pl. Trascorrales, 6 (opposite the restaurant Trascorrales), ☎ *21 42 18.*
Closed Sun. eve.
This looks like a rustic inn, and waitresses dress appropriately so that everyone relaxes and has a good time. You don't even have to make a single choice. From wine and soups through dessert, everyone is served the same eight-or nine-course meal (we lost count), with family style service allowing seconds and thirds. Some of the bean dishes seem a little too similar to others, but do not worry. In an instant that dish will be taken away and replaced by something different. Be hungry. Reservations advised. Credit Cards: A, D, M, V.

Inexpensive (Less than $15)

Cabo Peñas ★
Melquiades Alvarez, 24 (one long block south of the train station, or two blocks northwest of the north corner of the park), ☎ *522 03 20.*
While this restaurant may look like a fast-food kind of place, the food outdoes that impression. Go to the back room for the genuine Asturian article, which, when ordered from one of the special menus, is nicely inexpensive. Credit Cards: A, D, M, V.

Directory

Information
The office is located at Pl. Alfonso II, one block west of the park (☎ *521 33 85*). The staff is helpful and speak English.

Trains and Buses
The RENFE station is located on C. Uria (☎ *524 33 64*). The station is three long blocks northwest of the park. RENFE trains go south to León and Madrid (three trains per day), and west to Barcelona (two per day) and points between. FEVE, a different railway company, serves the north. The FEVE station is on Av. Santander (☎ *528 01 50*), a two minute walk left of the RENFE station.

There are also two main bus companies. ALSA, which serves the south, is located in the lower level of a shopping mall on Primo de Rivera, 1 (☎ *528 12 00*). It is three blocks due north of the park. More frequent service to more places is provided than the train does. EASA on C. Jerónimo Ibrán, 1 (☎ *529 00 39*) is located near the RENFE train station, and serves much of the north.

Post Office and Telephones

The main post office is at *C. Alonso Quintanilla*, which is two blocks north of the park. Telephones are available in Pl. de Porlier, behind the University, a long block east of the park.

Police

The main police station is on *C. General Yague, 5* (☎ *521 19 20*), which is a distance from the center of town.

Airport

Oviedo uses the Gijon airport, 47 km away. The Avianco office is located on C. Uria, two blocks northeast of the park (☎ *524 02 50*).

Excursions

From Oviedo the **Verde** and **Basque Coasts** both are within 75 km. See the descriptions earlier in this chapter. **León** lies 115 km south on N-630, with the rest of Old Castile following. See the descriptions in the "Old Castile and León" chapter.

San Sebastián (Donastia)

See the description under "Basque Coast."

Santander

See the description under "Basque Coast."

Santillana del Mar

See the description under "Costa Verde."

Santiago de Compostela ★ ★ ★ ★

Population: 93,695
Area code: 981; zip code: 15700

*The best route from **Madrid** is N-VI all the way to Lugo, 453 km to the northwest. Be alert near Benavente, lest you lose the road. At Lugo head west on N-547 for 107 km to Santiago. From **León** take N-120 west for 38 km to Astorga, where N-VI is picked up going northwest to Lugo, 169 km away. There take N-547 going west for an additional 107 km. From **Oviedo** take N-634 west, which follows the coast for 81 km then heads inland to Lugo, 71 km farther. At Lugo take N-547 going west to Santiago in 107 km. From Portuguese **Porto** the coast road N-13 is the more scenic route. It reaches the border at Valenca do Minho in 128 km, though requires a short span on*

N-113 going north. From the border take N-550 to Santiago in 105 km.

Legend tells of a sea voyage by the Apostle Saint James whose boat was driven by storms to the mouth of the Ulla river. He anchored in the present city of Padrón and began preaching Christianity to the locals. Seven years later he returned to Jerusalem where he was killed by Herod. According to the legend, however, disciples brought James' body back to Spain and buried it near the place where his ship had originally landed. Through the troubled times of invasions by Visigoths and Moors the location of the body was forgotten, until 813 when a shining light drew shepherds to the spot. A cult grew around the venerated remains. Thirty years later, during an engagement between a band of Christians and Moors, a knight mysteriously appeared whose standard bore a red cross on a white field. He routed the infidels, then disappeared as mysteriously as he had come, but several knights claimed to recognize him as Saint James—Santiago. This event fixed the epithet *Matamoro*, "Slayer of Moors," to Saint James, and made him the patron saint of the Reconquest.

By the 11th century, pilgrims by the hundreds of thousands (two million, in the record year) from all the corners of Europe walked as far as 1000 miles to visit those sacred remains. They came to atone for some sin or to receive help for a personal problem, and wore a kind of uniform. Enclosed by long hooded cloaks, they carried a stave taller than a man, tied a gourd for water to the stave and sported a broad hat with three scallop shells attached. Such shells were the symbols of the saint, so the pilgrims were referred to as those who "took the cockleshell." The route was hard and unfamiliar, so in 1130 a monk named Aimeri Picaud wrote history's first guide book to describe the roads, climate and sights, as well as the manners and customs of people along the way. Monasteries and hospitals sprang up along the route to offer simple accommodations for weary pilgrims. Among the famous pilgrims were Charlemagne, el Cid and Saint Francis of Assisi.

In the 16th century because of Spanish wars against France, Holland and England, the number of pilgrims declined drastically. In 1589 Francis Drake raided La Coruña, 50 miles from Santiago, frightening the Bishop of Santiago so much that he hid the sacred relics for safety. Incredibly, afterward no one could remember where. It was not until 1879 that they turned up again, were duly certified as authentic by the pope, and the pilgrimages began again. In any year when the Feast of Saint James (July 25) falls on a Sunday, special indulgences are granted to pilgrims. At that time, they arrive in numbers that pass one million.

The entire area around the Cathedral of Santiago is a national monument. A newer town surrounds it, heavily populated by university students. On weekends, as a kind of initiation rite, male students in ancient capes roam the plazas serenading women. If a woman is pleased, she contributes a bright ribbon the student pins to his cape; if displeased, she douses him with water. All the sights lie in a radius of a few blocks of the Cathedral.

> *Parking is an unsolved problem in Santiago, compounded by one-way streets, unmarked dead-ends and a lack of direction signs.*

> *From **Lugo**, the **airport** and **east** the city is entered on C. Concheiros which is soon renamed San Pedro. At Puerto de Camino turn left onto C. Virgen de la Cerca. As it bends right the street receives the name C. Fuente de San Antonio and reaches parking in the Pl. de Gelmirez Galicia on the right in three blocks. The lot is four blocks due south of the Cathedral. For additional parking closer to the Cathedral, continue straight, though the street changes its name to C. Mola. In two blocks a park is reached. Go right, then left along its border, C. Pombal. Take the first right which forks off from Pombal. When the street bends right, parking lies both left and right in one block.*

> *From **Portugal** and **south** N-550 continues straight on Av. Rosalia de Castro until reaching the end of a park. Turn left and left again to follow the park, now on C. Pombal. Take the first street that forks right from Pombal. When this street bends right, parking lies to both on the left and the right in one block.*

What to See and Do

Cathedral of Santiago ★★★★★

Pl. de Obradoiro, ☎ 58 35 48.
Hours open: Mon.–Sat. 10 a.m.–1 p.m. and 4–7 p.m. Open Sun. 10 a.m.–1:30 p.m.

A church was erected to protect the remains of Saint James immediately after their discovery in 813. It was enlarged a hundred years later, only to be destroyed during a raid by the Moors in 997. The present edifice was begun in the 11th century and finished by the 13th, although a new front was added in the 18th century. Plazas surround the front, back and most of both sides to show off this cathedral better than any other in Spain.

No plaza in Spain can match the spacious **Pl. de Obradoiro** (Work of Gold) ★★★★ in front of the cathedral. Opposite the cathedral stands the ornate former **Palacio de Rajoy** from 1772, now the ayuntamiento. To the west is the imposing façade of the **Hospital Real** ★★, a pilgrim hostelry from 1511, now Spain's grandest parador. Its Plateresque façade was added in 1687. To the East is the **Colegio de San Jerónimo**, in the Romanesque style but from the 17th century. And to the north is the cathedral, rising two flights above the Plaza to dominate everything else. In between, a vast field space keeps these magnificent buildings at a slight distance, both in space and time.

The so-called Obradoiro façade of the cathedral is perhaps the most successful example of the churrigueresque style. Though replete with twistings, intricate knobs, spikes and vines, as the style dictates, the strong thrust of the two towers' rising, creates an effect like flames shooting up to the sky. The façade was added to the original front of the cathedral by Ferdinand Casas y Novoa in 1750. Fortunately, the original front was not torn down to make way for the new. It remains inside, protected from the elements as any great work of art should be.

A 12th-century Romanesque cathedral resides beyond the facade. Inside the entrance is the original front of the Cathedral, one of the masterpieces of Western art. It is known as the **Door of Glory** and consists of a series of statues and scenes by a sculptor named Mateo who died in 1217. The central shaft which presents the figure of Santiago above the Tree of Life, shows Mateo himself kneeling at the base. Centuries of pilgrims, thankful to have completed their pilgrimage, wore away the impress of five fingers in this central pillar. Above the main door is *Christ in His Glory*, surrounded by an orchestra of church elders. The arches are supported by Apostles, and the columns rest on monsters. (Traces of painting, visible here and there, are newer—16th century.) The left door presents the tribes of Israel, and the right, the Last Judgement. Choose your own entry, after admiring both the reserve of the presentation of these most passionate of religious themes and the simple elegance of their execution.

The interior is surprisingly plain and dark to those used to Gothic and later cathedrals. The Romanesque order lacks the gallery of windows known as the clerestory which let light into later churches. Nor does it employ pointed arches and rising ribs in the vaulting to carry the eye upwards, or carved columns or balustrades to add variety. It takes but a moment, however, for the utter simplicity and huge scale of this Cathedral (300 feet long, 100 feet high at the dome) to work its magic.

A portal to the right leads to the Plateresque **Reliquary Chapel**, with effigies of the earliest kings and queens of Spain. To its right is the **Treasury**. Amid countless crucifixes, the bejeweled bust of Santiago Alfeo stands out. But the reason for the church lies ahead at the end of the nave. The high **altar** is lit by a dome added in the 15th century from which a huge silver censer, called the **botafumeiro**, is swung on special days through the energies of eight men. The 18th-century altar contains a 13th century seated statue of Saint James, elaborately attired. Ascending stairs on the right side allow the faithful to kiss the hem of his gown. Descending stairs on the right side lead to a plain **crypt** in which rests the body of Saint James and two of his disciples. This crypt actually is part of the foundation of the original ninth century basilica. Excavations have shown that beneath it lies an ancient Roman and Swabian necropolis, which suggests that the name Compostela, instead of being a corruption of *campus stella* (field of stars), comes directly from the Roman *compostela* (cemetery).

In the right hand transept is the entrance to the cloister. But first study the tenth-century depiction of Santiago Matamoro to its right above a door leading to the sacristy. This is the earliest portrayal of Santiago as the Slayer of Moors. The plain **cloister** is late Gothic by Gil de Hotañton. Across it waits the entrance to the Cathedral **museum**. Its library displays the huge Botafumeiro, while the chapterhouse shows 17th-century and earlier Spanish tapestries, and allows fine views of the plaza and its buildings. There too is the papal letter certifying that the remains in the crypt indeed are those of Saint James. In the basement are various archaeological bits, some excavated from earlier churches on the site. *Admission:300 ptas., to the museum and cloisters.*

Exit from the south transept through the **Puerta de las Platerias** (Goldsmith's Door) ★. This too is an early 11th-century Romanesque work, without the elegance of the Door of Glory but with exuberance to take its place. Unfortunately some of the carving is obscured by additions on either side of the portal. Ahead and slightly left is the **Casa de la Canonica** (Canon's House), now a monastery. Rounding the rear of the Cathedral we come to the **Puerta Santa**, a door added in the 17th century which incorporates far older sculpture by Mateo originally intended for the Cathedral choir. We now are in another lovely square, the **Pl. de la Quintana**. Stairs lead up to a baroque 17th-century mansion on the right, the **Casa de la Parra**, now a gallery rotating exhibits of modern art.

Ahead, across the Pl. de la Inmaculada, stands the **Convento de San Marin Pinario** ★. The facade facing the plaza, completed in the 18th century, sends massive classical columns to the roof. Further north, its church is more ornate. A decaying interior remains dramatic with a wide nave covered by a daring coffered vault. The churrigueresque retable is by the architect of the Cathedral facade, Casas y Novoa. The choirstalls are lovely 17th-century work.

Continuing the circuit of the Cathedral, pass along the alley of the Passaje Gelmirez, which goes under an archway to return to the Pl. Obradoiro. To the left of the arch is the **Palacio Gelmírez** ★, the former Bishop's Palace. Parts are as old as the 12th century. Several rooms may be visited, including the kitchen, Salon de Fiestas, and the huge Salon de Synod. A visit is most worthwhile. (Open daily through the summer Mon.–Sat. 10 a.m.–1 p.m. and 4–7 p.m.; admission: 100 ptas.)

In the plaza, the huge building forming the north side is the **Hotel de los Reyes Católicos** ★★, a former hospice for pilgrims built by Ferdinand and Isabella in gratitude for their victory over the Moors. The design of the building is a cross within a square which affords four lovely patios, each different from the other. A nice chapel sits decorously in the center. The Plateresque facade with stunning doorway and harmonious window moldings was added in 1678. Today it is the most luxurious of all the paradors. (Free tours available daily 10 a.m.–1 p.m. and 4–6 p.m.)

Calle Franco ★ heads south between the cloisters of the Cathedral and the San Jerónimo College across the plaza. Old buildings and new shops and restaurants run for six blocks down to the pleasant Pl. del Toral, with its fountain. A return to the Pl. Obradoiro can be made along **Rua del Villar**, which runs parallel to C. Franco, also with old houses and interesting shops.

Santa María del Sar   ★

R. do Castrón d'Ouro. The church is located about one and one-half km southeast of the old town. South of the circular road, Av. Fuente de San Antonio, C. Castron d'Ouro becomes C. de Sar. As it passes beneath the bypass road, the church lies to the right. Hours open: Mon.–Sat. 10 a.m.–1 p.m. and 4–6 p.m. Closed Sun.

This is a church of the same 12th-century era as the Cathedral. Incongruous buttresses were added in the 12th century, for reasons that become evident as soon as you step inside. Before doing so, however, look at the remaining cloister gallery with elegant carved small paired arches. There reside the tombs of priors through the 15th century.

The inside startles, because the pillars of the nave all lean inward. The reason is that this ground near a river could not support the burden the pillars carried, hence the need for outside buttresses. The effect is strange indeed. *Admission: 100 ptas.*

Where to Stay

There are beds in Santiago in every price category. If our selections should be full, C. Franco and Rua del Villar, mentioned above, each has numerous *hotel residencias* for low prices.

Expensive ($100–$200)

Reyes Católicos   Deluxe ★ ★ ★ ★ ★

Pl. de España (Obradoiro), Santiago de Compostela, ☎ 58 22 00, FAX 56 30 94, Telex 86004.

This is the most deluxe of all paradors. If you are lucky enough to get a room in the front overlooking the plaza, you'll never want to leave. But if you are among the less fortunate, your room will look onto one of four lovely patios, which requires no sympathy. The only problem with this hotel is that it is expensive, passing 20,000 pesetas per night in high season, although worth every centavo. Simply wandering the halls and patios is a pleasant excursion. It is amusing to think that the elegant dining room served as a maternity ward when the hotel was a hospital in the 18th century. *130 rooms, plus six suites.*

Araguaney   Deluxe ★ ★

Alfredo Brañas, 5, Santiago de Compostela (the street runs parallel to the park, ten short blocks roughly south of the Cathedral), ☎ 59 59 00, FAX 59 02 87, Telex 86108.
This is the opposite of the Reyes Católicos—as modern as the other is venerable—but deluxe, nonetheless. It is all chrome, marble and glass, with a heated swimming pool whose glass bottom forms the ceiling of a trendy discotheque. Bedrooms are comfortably sized. The problem is that prices almost match Reyes Católicos. *65 rooms.*

Moderate ($50–$99)

Hogar San Francisco   2nd-class ★ ★ ★

Campillo de San Francisco, 3, Santiago de Compostela (follow C. San Francisco, the street along the east side of Los Reyes Católicos, for one long block north), ☎ 58 16 00, FAX 57 19 16.
What could be more appropriate than staying in a convent in Santiago? This hotel is installed in the Convent of San Francisco, although the cells have been modernized into comfortable rooms. The public rooms, however, retain some of their rich 18th-century decoration. This is a special hotel, for a price that makes it more enjoyable. *71 rooms.*

Windsor   Hs1st-class ★ ★

República de El Salvador, 16-A, Santiago de Compostela (directly behind the Araguaney, a block further south), ☎ 59 29 39.

Dark woods and floral prints make this an inviting little hotel. True, it is located on a busy shopping street and caters to tour groups, but the service is considerate, and prices are low compared to others in this category. *50 rooms.*

Compostela   **1st-class ★**
Calvo Sotelo, 1, Santiago de Compostela (at the corner of Av. Fuente de San Antonio and C. Horno, seven blocks directly south of the Cathedral where the new town begins), ☎ *58 57 00, FAX 56 32 69, Telex 82387.*
This is a bit of a dowager today, needing sprucing up. Certainly it does not merit its official rating. But the prices are those of a second-class hotel and it is a professional establishment. Are its lights dim to save on electricity? *98 rooms, plus one suite.*

Gelmírez   **1st-class ★**
C. Horneo, 92, Santiago de Compostela (this street runs due south from the end of the old town), ☎ *56 11 00, FAX 56 32 69, Telex 82387.*
Although the lobby is not memorable, the bedrooms are pleasant and good sized. Furnishings are fairly new; the decor covers a lot of browns and greens. Being a largish hotel, the service can be spotty, but prices are low for this class. *138 rooms.*

Inexpensive (Less than $50)

Mapoula   **Hs2nd-class ★ ★**
C. Entremurallas, 10 "third floor," Santiago de Compostela (at the southern edge of the old town, just before Av. Fuente de San Antonio), ☎ *58 01 24, FAX 58 40 89.*
Fortunately, there is an elevator to carry you four flights up to what the Spanish call the third floor (the ground floor is not counted). You will find white rooms, bright and clean. There are no special views, but the location is good, the price is right as rain and the decor is pleasant. The only problem is that the hotel is often full, as one would expect. *12 rooms.*

Universal   **R2nd-class ★**
Pl. de Galicia, 2, Santiago de Compostela (at the east end of the street with the Hotel Araguaney), ☎ *58 58 00, FAX 58 57 90.*
This is a step up from the usual low-priced hotel. The bedrooms are larger, as are the bathrooms, and the furniture has some style. But the prices are higher too, stretching the inexpensive category. *54 rooms.*

Suso   **Hs2nd-class**
Rua do Villar, 65, Santiago de Compostela (parallel to C. Franco), ☎ *58 66 11.*
This little second floor hotel is located close to the Cathedral in an old building. The rooms are modest, but comfortable. Service is willing, but there is a bar to take care of in addition to the rooms. Prices are genuinely inexpensive. *Nine rooms.*

Where to Eat

Galicia is known for octopus and shellfish, for a hearty vegetable soup called *caldo gallego,* and for *empanadas,* a sort of turnover. By all means try a *viño verde,* a "green wine," with seafood. As an alternative to our recommendations you can wander down C. Franco, and Rua del Vilar parallel to it, both of which are lined with small attractive restaurants.

Expensive ($30+)

Toñi Vicente   **★★★★**
Av. Rosalia de Castro, 24 (this artery is a kind of continuation of C. Franco),. ☎ *59 41 00, FAX 59 35 54.*

Closed Sun., the middle two weeks of Jan. and the last two weeks of Aug.
This comet just landed on the restaurant scene in Santiago. It is as elegant as anyone could wish and the food is truly spectacular. Baked sea brill is sublime and the desserts are memorable. Seafood is the specialty, so the prices must be considered bargains for such sublime food. Credit Cards: A, D, M, V.

Anexo Vilas   ★★

Av. Villagarcia, 21 (C. Marinez Anido runs along the south side of the Herradura park in the new town. It changes its name to C. Rosalia de Castro before coming to a large intersection. The right-hand road, Av. Romero Donallo, arrives at this restaurant at its first left), *59 86 37.*
Closed Mon.
The second best food in town is served at this Santiago institution. Sr. Vilas, the owner, tirelessly promotes the cooking of Galicia. After you try the sardinas *Mama Sueiro*, sardines with peppers and garlic, you may well become a promoter too. Credit Cards: A, D, V.

Don Gaiferos   ★

C. Nueva, 23 (the street that goes south from the Pl. de la Quintana, behind the Cathedral cloisters), *58 38 94.*
Closed Sun. and the last week in Dec.
The decor was the most tasteful in town before Toñi Vicente blew everyone else away. The cooking is more international than regional, and competent, but not exceptional. Credit Cards: A, D, M, V.

Moderate ($15–$30)

Reyes Católicos   ★

Pl. Obradoiro, 1, *58 22 00.*
This recommendation is not for the hotel restaurant but for the bar and the platos combinados it serves. These are the most expensive and best we've had. A bill for two with wine will push $30. For the money you will be served a plateful of simply done food of high quality, and get to wander through the elegant hotel. The bar is left from the entrance, through the huge lounge. Credit Cards: A, D, M, V.

Nova Gallihea   ★

C. Franco, 56, *58 27 99.*
This is a restaurant for locals, with no concessions to tourists. The decor is nothing much, the restaurant tiny, but the food is authentic home cooking if your home is in Galicia. Ordering one of the special menus will keep costs moderate.

San Clemente   ★

Pl. San Clemente, 6 (this little plaza is downstairs at the south end of the ayuntamiento from the Pl. Obradoiro), *58 08 82.*
Closed Sun. eve.
Seafood is what makes this restaurant special and seafood is not inexpensive, but the crowds here demonstrate that the quality is good and the prices are fair. Credit Cards: A, D, M, V.

Alameda   ★

Puerta Fajera, 15 (at the bottom of C. Franco, bordering the park), ☎ *58 66 57.*

The restaurant is its own sylvan building, all in green and white, situated by the park, with tables outside for views. The food is good and there are special menus to hold down the cost. Credit Cards: A, D, M, V.

Inexpensive (Less than $15)

O'Sotano ★

C. Franco, 8 (in the basement), ☎ 56 50 24.

The biggest problem with this restaurant is its popularity—which can lead to both crowding and noise. There are no complaints about how good the food is for the price. In fact, prices are low enough that you can order à la carte, instead of being restricted to special menus.

Directory

Information

The main office is located on R. del Vilar at number 43. ☎ 58 40 81. There is a smaller office at the north end of the Ayuntamiento in the Pl. Obradoiro.

Trains and Buses

The train station is at R. Gen. Franco, just south of the main circular road, Av. de Lugo, a 15 minute walk south of the Cathedral. ☎ 52 02 02. Two trains per day travel to Madrid in eight hours, others cover most destinations in the area.

The bus station is at C. San Cayetano, a 20-minute walk northeast of the Cathedral. Service to sights in Galicia is good, but slow for longer distances. ☎ 58 77 00.

Airport

Santiago Airport (☎ 59 74 00)is 11 km east of town on N-547, the road to Lugo. There are direct flights to European capitals, and good connections with all of Spain. Buses to Santiago meet the flights. The Iberia office is located on C. General Pardiñas at 36, which is west of C. Horno, the main street of the new town. Buses leave here for the airport. ☎ 57 20 24.

Post Office and Telephones

Located to the right of C. Franco, two blocks from the Pl. Obradoiro. ☎ 58 12 52.

Police

Located behind the Post Office. ☎ 58 22 66.

Excursions

A pleasant day can be spent at the beach at a nearby scenic ria—a sea inlet, like a Norwegian fjord. See descriptions under the **Costa de las Rias** heading above.

For garden fans, **Pazo de Oca** is a country estate 25 km south open to the public.

South on N-525 toward Orense (Ourense) for 27 km, a sign directs a right turn for Valboa and the Pazo de Oca just after crossing the Ulla River.

Pazo de Oca ★

Hours open: 9 a.m.–1 p.m. and 4–8 p.m. Opens and closes an hour earlier in winter.
At the end of the road stands a typical manor house of the area. Behind it, terraces descend to a lily pond and a still lake on which a stone boat seems to float. Deep greens, rust colored moss and eerie stillness pervade. *Admission: 200 ptas.*

NAVARRE AND ARAGÓN

Quaint Gothic sculpture prefaces the Holy Sepulcher in Estella.

Historical Profile:
From Habsburgs to Bourbons

When the ascetic, industrious Felipe II (see "Historical Profile: World Power and the Great Armada—Felipe II" on page 99) passed the scepter to his son, the monarchy changed completely. Felipe III was as profligate with his person and court as his father had been abstemious, and he lacked all common sense.

439

Disdaining such realities as a bankrupt treasury, Felipe III attempted to conquer England—which his father had been unable to accomplish with vast financial resources. He sent 50 ships toward the British Isles in 1599, only to see them dispersed by a tempest. In 1601, 33 Spanish galleons landed in Ireland, where their troops were defeated easily by the English. The reduced numbers in these flotillas show Spain's changed fortunes from the glorious days of Felipe II's 136-ship Invincible Armada. However, these particular follies of Felipe III ceased in 1603 when England's Queen Elizabeth died, for her successor, James II, as a Catholic was no enemy.

Felipe III turned next to Portugal where he, through a complete lack of sensitivity, began undermining the union forged by his father who had sworn that only native Portuguese would fill important Portuguese offices. Felipe III appointed Spaniards to the governing council of Portugal, as well as to vacant Portuguese bishoprics. When he traveled to Portugal for his first and only visit in 1619, he billed the extravagant cost of the trip to the Portuguese. This insult, when added to Portugal's loss of a rich empire in the Far East to the Dutch and English (who the Portuguese viewed as enemies of Spain, not of themselves), bred resentment that erupted into revolution and Portuguese independence in the next reign.

Felipe III also expelled the Moroscos—Moors who had converted to Christianity. Because the half-million Moroscos were hard-working farmers who made Andalusia and Valencia bloom, their eviction cost Spain a significant decline in its agricultural production in addition to five percent of its population. All told, Felipe III proved ruinous for an already ailing Spain. In fact, one of Felipe's seemingly inconsequential acts would prove fatal to the Habsburg dynasty he headed. He arranged a marriage between his son and the daughter of the King of France, thereby introducing French blood into the Spanish royal line to give France a future claim on the throne.

In 1622, 16-year-old Felipe IV succeeded his father. He stood tall and thin, and looked more resolute than he was because of his thrusting Habsburg jaw. Both he and his French bride, Isabel de Bourbon, loved spectacles. The two delighted in *autos-da-fě*, theater performances, bull fights, and parades. Often one or the other would play childish tricks, such as turning snakes loose into the audience.

When Felipe was a child, his tutor had been the Duke of Oliveres, and their friendship grew as the youngster matured. Oliveres assumed the position of chief minister in Felipe's new government.

Oliveres' principle policy was to centralize Spanish power in the monarchy, a goal that ran counter to ancient currents of separatism throughout a country still comprised of independent provincial *cortes* (parliaments), laws and taxations. Oliveres brought Felipe IV to the cortes of Aragón and of Valencia to exhort concessions against their own independence. But he could make no headway against Catalonia, and when the French invaded the Catalan territory of Rousillon, the citizens of Barcelona refused even to billet Spanish troops on their way to win it back. This spark set off a civil war in 1640.

But first there was revolution in Portugal. Portugal's most powerful noble, the Duke of Bragança, owned one third of the country and was feared by Oliveres, who once tried to kidnap him. Switching tactics, Oliveres sought Bragança's loyalty by bribing him with power by giving him command of the Portuguese army. Oliveres' mistrust of Bragança proved prescient when, in 1640, the Duke turned his troops against the Spanish and liberated the country in 24 hours, thus ending Spain's 60-year union with Portugal.

While Felipe's energies were focused on Portugal, Catalonia asked France to become its protector. The French jumped at the chance and, when the Spanish army returned from Portugal, the French routed it at Lerida.

Oliveres' policies had cost Spain Portugal and precipitated civil war, leaving Felipe IV no choice but to fire his friend, who died insane three years later.

In 1646, Baltasar Carlos, Felipe's heir, died. Felipe, who had lost his first wife, married his deceased son's betrothed, Marianna of Austria. Although the loss of Portugal bothered Felipe IV greatly, the occupying French army in secessionist Catalonia was more serious. It cost a decade of civil war before Felipe's troops finally recaptured Barcelona in 1651. Another decade of preparation was required before Felipe felt ready to invade Portugal. But, by that time, the Duke of Bragança, now calling himself King, had formed an alliance with England that had brought an English wife and army to his defense. In 1663, his combined forces decisively defeated the Spanish.

News of the defeat hastened Felipe's own death, which went unmourned by his people. In fact, were it not for the long association between Felipe IV and his friend the painter Velásquez, few would remember this king. Instead he seems more real than any other Spanish monarch because the canvases of the great Velásquez immortalized the sad king and vacuous family.

Felipe IV left a four-year-old cretin as his heir. Carlos II suffered from premature senility, never learned to speak or eat normally, but survived against all expectations to reign for 35 years. With this king the line of Habsburgs had run dry, for although Carlos II married, he was incapable of siring children. All Europe now eyed Spain rapaciously, knowing that some non-Spaniard could eventually acquire the crown. On his deathbed, Carlos named Philip of Anjou, the grandson of Louis XIV of France as his heir.

Thus the 18th century began with a Bourbon king on the Spanish throne, known to the Spanish as Felipe V. But the Habsburg family was not yet ready to concede. Archduke Charles, of the Austrian branch of the Habsburgs, supported his competing claim with an army that landed at Barcelona in

1702. This opened the War of Spanish Succession in which Austrians, aided by opportunistic England, fought the Spanish for almost a decade. In the first battle, Felipe V was defeated at Barcelona, then the English entered Spain from Portugal to capture Madrid. Felipe rushed back, retook the capital, then returned east to defeat the Austrians at Almansa. In his absence, Madrid was again taken, so he wheeled and recaptured it. Thus were battles both won and lost during this war, but neither side could gain any decisive victory. Hostilities ended in 1711, simply because the combatants were exhausted.

Felipe had survived the attack on his throne, losing only the peninsula of Gibraltar to the English, but the tired Spanish king retired in 1724 to La Granja, a model of Versailles he had built to remind him of home. His rest lasted only seven months, for his heir died of smallpox, forcing the old king back on his throne for another 20 years. He died, deranged, in 1746.

Felipe V's second son and successor, Fernando VI, demonstrated that Bourbons could administer as well as defend their country. He promoted Spanish political neutrality and simplified an overly complex tax structure to allow the economy to recover from decades of war and its burdening costs. Unfortunately, Fernando carried a Bourbon proclivity for mental illness and died in 1759. His half-brother, Carlos III, carried on.

Carlos III was 43, robust and ruddy, when he came to the throne. His passion was hunting, and he dressed so as to be ready in a moment to grab a gun and chase after wolves. Yet he proved an able king. One of his first concerns was the lawlessness rampant in Madrid, both robberies and crimes of passion. The very apparel of the time made arrest and prosecution difficult— men walked in street-length black cloaks and wide-brimmed slouch hats, which concealed their identities and whatever weapons they might carry. Carlos outlawed the long cloaks, sending out police armed with knives to reduce illegal lengths on the spot. In response, the citizens rebelled and chased the king from Madrid. But when Carlos made such cloaks and hats the uniform of the Royal Executioner, street fashions changed immediately.

Carlos also followed the lead of France and other European countries in expelling the Jesuit Order. This allowed him to modernize university curricula, controlled until then by clerics and grown archaic under their direction. He also decreed it was no disgrace for *hidalgos* (noblemen) to work, a revolutionary step. In Spain one man in three considered himself an hidalgo and, however impoverished, maintained his status by never dirtying his hands. New businesses, including weaving, received government assistance under Carlos, whereas before Spain had sent its abundant wool to England and Flanders for weaving, buying the finished product back at higher prices. Carlos' measures so invigorated the economy that the population of Spain increased by one sixth. He died at age 72, in 1788, of a depression that the Bourbons seemed heir to.

Carlos IV was entirely unlike his father. Dull and amiable, he was a creature of his more enterprising wife. She, in turn, was smitten by a soldier of the Royal Guard, Manuel Godoy. Godoy was dubbed a duke at 25, and soon after named prime minister of Spain.

In 1789 the world's crowned heads trembled at the news of the French Revolution. The bumbling Spanish king, his shrewish wife and immature prime minister decided to play at war to right matters and restore the French monarchy. When the French executed their king, Godoy invaded France. A quick and humiliating defeat, however, left Godoy no option but to sue for peace. For failing at generalship Godoy was awarded the title "Prince of the Peace" by his adoring queen. Then France and Spain joined in arms against England. Godoy, with the help of 15,000 French troops, invaded England's ally Portugal and conquered it in three weeks. He sent his queen an orange branch from her new territory to earn the name "War of the Oranges" for the campaign. But Spain paid dearly for this victory, for off the coast at Trafalgar Lord Nelson sank the combined French and Spanish fleets to the bottom of the sea.

Nor was Spain's alliance with France going well. Napoléon sent 100,000 troops to Spain, ostensibly to protect it from attack, but actually to surround the garrisons of major northern cities. When Napoléon demanded that northern Spain be ceded to him, even Carlos could see that he was about to be reduced from an ally to a subject. He fled with his court to Aranjuez. There his son Fernando stirred up the citizens to ransack Godoy's mansion in search of the architect of the foreign policy that threatened Spain's independence. Although Godoy escaped by hiding in a rolled carpet in his attic, the mob moved to the Aranjuez palace where a frightened Carlos IV abdicated in favor of his son. However, son Fernando found the French in control of the capital, Madrid, so he crossed the border into France to seek Napoléon's recognition and assistance. Once the mob disbursed, Carlos reconsidered his abdication and, independently, with his queen and Godoy, set out to visit Napoléon as well. All the contestants for Spain's crown now called on the Corsican General to adjudicate between them. Napoléon's judgment was that Fernando should renounce his claim and Carlos should do so as well, so that his own brother Joseph could rule instead. Then he arrested the lot.

Spain received the news that a Frenchman was now their ruler on the second of May, 1808. On this day, the *Dos de Mayos*, the citizens rose up against their invaders. With Spain's royal family away in France, juntas of private citizens organized defenses and raised militias, hounding Joseph from Madrid in ten days. It took the presence of Napoléon backed by 300,000 French troops to reinstate him. Still the citizens fought, not major battles which they could not win, but little wars—*guerrillas.*

Eventually, England sent Wellington with enough troops to win Portugal, although insufficient to threaten the French in Spain. But when Napoléon left for his ill-fated invasion of Russia in 1810, Wellington was able to hammer successfully at the French, finally chasing them north of the Pyrenees three years later. Wellington followed the retreating French to defeat Napoléon at Belgium's Waterloo in 1814.

Now Spain was free again, but without a king for the first time since the era of the Visigoths. Delegates from Spain, the Philippines and all the American colonies met in Cádiz to draw up the first constitution in her history. The delegates offered Fernando VII the office of constitutional monarch, but when he returned to Spain to accept the crown, he revoked the constitution and arrested every delegate he could find.

Fernando remarried late in life, producing one child, a daughter. To ensure the continuation of his line he altered the laws of succession so that a woman could inherit the throne. Nonetheless, civil war broke out after his death in 1833 between partisans of Isabella II and those favoring Fernando's brother, Don Carlos ("the Carlists"). Five more years of strife left Isabella II in control. During her reign she followed her father's lead in suppressing all liberality and constitutional government, although her preference was for sexual adventures above governing. In 1868, a putsch of the navy and army ended her rule.

Isabella left a 12-year-old son. After an interim reign and a Second Carlist War over his succession, Alfonso XII was summoned from England's Sandhurst College to be crowned king at age 17. He died at 27, in 1886, leaving a pregnant wife. Alfonso XIII was thus born a king.

As Alfonso grew, he watched the last of Spain's overseas possessions fall away. A mysterious explosion had sunk the United States battleship Maine in the harbor of Havana, provoking the United States to declare war on Spain. Within a year, Cuba was independent and the Philippines were a protectorate of the United States. Spain managed to avoid the horror of World War I by neutrality, but the radical political parties that unbalanced Europe in the first part of the 20th century—communist, anarchist and socialist—came to infect Spain as well. See "Historical Profile: The Spanish Civil War" on page 469. The time of monarchies had passed. In 1931, elections showed that Alfonso XIII had lost the support of his people. He abdicated and moved to France.

Navarre and Aragón

Navarre, tucked between the Basque counties and northern Aragón, is tiny. Not 100 miles long in any direction, Aragón could contain it five times over. However, size is the major geographic difference between the two states. Both border the Pyrenees, are precipitously mountainous at their northern ends, descend to plains in the south, and suffer climates that are perhaps the worst in Spain. Since both are landlocked, away from the tempering influences of the sea, they see snow in winter and burn from a searing summer sun.

Despite geographic similarities and a shared history up to the 11th century, the two states later separated for 400 years before reunion by Ferdinand in 1512. Surprisingly, smaller Navarre during the time of its greatest hero, Sancho III, dominated not only Aragón but all of Christian Spain. Having conquered kingdoms from Catalonia through Aragón, along with Old Castile and León, Sancho called himself "King of the Spains." On his deathbed in 1035, however, Sancho willed Aragón to one son, Navarre to another, Catalonia to a third and Old Castile to a fourth. After much jockeying among these four powers, Old Castile merged with León, while Aragón dominated Navarre and Catalonia. Navarre retained enough authority, however, for its king to arrange a marriage in 1191 between Berengaria, daughter of King Sancho VI, and Richard the Lionheart.

From the 13th through the end of the 14th century, Aragón played a major role in European politics. Aragón's control of Catalonia brought suzerainty over its territories in southern France between Rousillon and Nice. Then, in 1282, Sicily, which ruled Italy south of Naples, offered its crown to the king of Aragón to prevent French usurpation. By the end of that century the armies of Aragón had completed the reconquest of the eastern coast of Spain as far south as Valencia. Thus, Aragón controlled one third of Spain, almost one quarter of France, and half of Italy. But when its King Ferdinand married Isabella, the monarch of Castile, in 1469, the identity of Aragón submerged in a larger confederation. By that time Navarre had broken away.

How had tiny Navarre managed to seize independence from powerful Aragón? The king of Navarre had died childless in 1234, and the citizens of Navarre voted that his nephew, the French count of Champagne, be offered the throne. For three centuries after, Navarre's crown—the prize of marriage alliances—was passed among various French nobles, ending with Jean, Duc d'Albret, in 1512. These transfers of power were orchestrated by kings of France anxious for a friendly neighbor on their southern border, an area controlled by archrival Spain. On their side, the Navarrese, hoping to avoid digestion by Aragón and Castile, had happily seized on a strong protector. In

1512, Ferdinand ended Navarre's independence when his conquering army engulfed it en route to war with France.

Although the provinces of Aragón and Navarre cover more than 10 percent of Spain, they contain less to attract tourists than their size would suggest. Of course Navarre's capital of **Pamplona ★** is best known for its running of the bulls during the feast of San Fermin. Although a city of no particular attractiveness, it does contain a Gothic cathedral and an interesting museum of Navarrese art. Since the French controlled Navarre during the Middle Ages, hundreds of thousands of French pilgrims passed through this little kingdom on their way to Santiago de Compostela, leaving behind ancient Romanesque monasteries built for their convenience. **Olite ★**, **La Oliva ★ ★** and **Leyre ★ ★** survive, as does one town so filled with medieval buildings as to still convey the atmosphere of those times—**Estella ★ ★**, nicknamed "La Bella." As for Aragón, its vast expanse is more likely to be driven through by tourists on their way to Barcelona than stopped at for sight-seeing. Aragón does offer **Zaragoza ★ ★**, a major city which contains the Moorish palace of Aljaferia and a splendid Cathedral. There is a truly ancient monastery situated amid spectacular scenery at **San Juan de la Peña ★ ★** and a perfect ancient castle at **Loarre ★**. In addition, **Ordesa National Park ★ ★** offers miles of rugged scenic beauty, while the palace where Ferdinand was born still stands in **Sos del Rey Católico ★**.

Estella ★ ★

Population: 13,086
Area code: 948; zip code: 31200

> From **Pamplona** take N-111 west by following C. Bosquecillo that cuts between the Jardines de la Taconera and the gardens of the Ciudadela. **Puente la Reina**, in 24 km, presents a fine Romanesque church from the 12th through 14th centuries on the town outskirts. Estella is 21 km further. From **elsewhere**, follow the directions to Pamplona in its section below, and then follow the directions above.

The town, which pilgrims dubbed "Estella la Bella," grew overnight. In the 11th century the king of Navarre offered tax-free status to anyone who would settle this spot, for he needed bodies in the southern part of his territory to oppose Moorish attacks. Ordinary people came, as did merchants, and a town of separate quarters, or parishes, sprang up in which emigrés migrating from the same area of Spain lived together. When the kings of Navarre took up residence during the 12th century, Estella became a royal town and the host to hordes of pilgrims on their way to Santiago de Compostela. Competing parishes vied with each other to raise ever more splendid churches, a contest whose results remain for our appreciation.

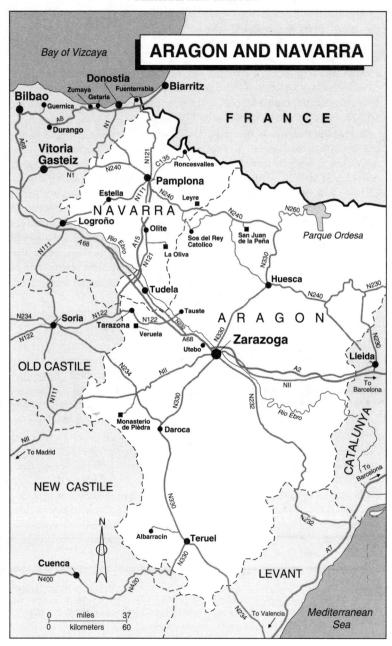

Cross the tiny Rio Ega, following signs to the main, though small, plaza of the town—**Plaza de San Martín**. This is the heart of the ancient *barrio franc*, or French Quarter. To the right, dating from the 12th century, is the **Palacio de los Reyes de Navarra**, one of the oldest secular structures in Spain. Although much restored, it contains one fine Romanesque capital (main facade, left pillar) depicting Roland in battle with the Moorish giant Farragut. It also houses the **Tourist Office**. On the opposite side of the plaza stands the 16th-century former **ayuntamiento** emblazoned with a coat of arms.

Elegant **San Pedro de la Rua** ★ overlooks the plaza (tours arranged by the tourist office; admission: 100 ptas.) The church is 12th-century Romanesque, fronted by a lovely portal of Mudejar design. Instead of crowds of holy figures, delicate arabesques surround an unusual scalloped arch. Inside, Gothic elements compete with the Romanesque design in three separate apses. At the church center rises a charming column of entwined serpents. A baroque chapel on the left is devoted to a relic of Saint Andrew, preserved from 1270. The second bay on the right leads to remains of a wonderful cloister with masterfully carved columns. Sadly, half of this cloister was blown up by mistake when Felipe II destroyed an adjacent castle that he feared would serve as a stronghold of the Navarrese independence movement.

Santo Sepulcro, at the end of the street, presents a pure Gothic portal with a moving *Last Judgment*.

On the other side of the river, beside C. Mayor (over the bridge, then left, then right) is the quarter settled by Navarrese, which still retains much medieval atmosphere. The quarter's proudest possession is the 12th-century Romanesque **Iglesia de San Miguel Arcangel** ★. The north portal is as intensely Christian as can be, serving as an antidote to the "foreign" flavor of San Pedro. Scores of Biblical figures crowd for room around the doors. Note especially the statue columns carved in high relief.

Outside of Estella, 3 km south as directed by a sign from N-111, stands the massive **Monastery of Irache** ★. Its foundation is truly ancient, dating from the tenth century. Later, Cistercian monks built one of the first pilgrim hospitals here, and in the 16th century Benedictines founded a university that functioned for almost 300 years. The church is open for guided tours (*Tuesday-Sunday 9:30 a.m.–1 p.m. and 3-7 p.m. admission: 100 ptas.*). Its facade is 17th-century, as is the cupola inside that prefaces an apse from the 12th century. The Plateresque cloister seems somehow cold.

Where to Stay

Irache   **R2nd-class ★**

Carretera Pamplona-Logroño, N-111, km 43 (1 km west on N-111), ☎ *(948) 55 11 50.* This is the only good choice in the neighborhood. It is moderate in price, modern, clean and comfortable, and supplies tennis courts and a pool. *74 rooms.*

Where to Eat

Navarra ★

C. Gustavo de Maeztu, 16, ☎ 55 10 69.
Closed Sunday evening, Monday, and the 2nd half of December.
The attractiveness of the place justifies its expensive prices. It is decorated as a medieval inn surrounded by a pretty garden. The trout Navarra is delectable. Credit Cards: A, V.

La Oliva Monastery ★★

From **Pamplona** *take N-121 south toward Zaragoza by following Av. de Zaragoza as it leaves the large hub of the Pl. del Principe de Viana. In 40 km comes* **Olite** *with its fine castle. 17 km south of Olite take C-124 east for an attractive drive of 18 km through the countryside.*

French monks completed this Cistercian monastery, the first built outside their homeland, in the 12th century. From its inception it counted as a major missionary center in Spain. Cistercian buildings are characterized by their simplicity, foregoing the decorative embellishments of the Romanesque and Gothic styles, and the simplicity of La Oliva became intensified after abandonment in the 19th century when its treasures were stripped away. Today the Cistercians have returned to restore it. (*Open daily 9 a.m.–8 p.m., until 6 p.m. in winter; admission: 100 ptas.*)

The plain facade is enhanced by a single band of sculpture above the central portal. Austerity inside produces a solemn effect. Pointed arches are a surprise in a 12th-century structure, either a peculiarity of this particular Romanesque design or the first example of the Gothic in Spain. The adjacent cloister is an interesting mishmash of 15th-century architecture grafted onto an older structure.

See "Olite" for accommodations and dining.

Leyre ★★

From **Pamplona** *take N-121 south toward Zaragoza by following Av. de Zaragoza as it leaves the large hub of the Pl. del Principe de Viana. Five km outside the city take N-240 heading east. In 35k C-127 heads south for* **Sangüesa** *and* **Sos del Rey Católico**, *a detour of 24 km. (both described below). Continue on N-240 for Leyre, looking for the turnoff to Monasterio Leyre in 16 km.*

On the way to the monastery of Leyre, Sangüesa and Sos del Rey Católico are worth a stop. Tiny **Sangüesa**, seven km along C-127, is filled with mansions. Beside the town bridge stands **Santa María la Real**, a former royal chapel from the 13th century. The present *Ayuntamiento* was formerly the **Palace of the Princes of Viana**, and the main street is lined with attractive classical houses, leading, two streets after the bridge, to the imposing Baroque **Palace of Vallesantoro** on the right.

Seven km east is the birthplace of Francis Xavier. Born Francisco **Javier** in 1506, he cooperated with Ignatius Loyola in founding the Order of Jesuits. Later he traveled to Japan, becoming one of its first Western missionaries, and personally converted several hundred thousand Buddhists. He died as he was about to enter China on a similar mission. In the 16th century, soon after his death, the house in which he was born was replaced by a castle that contains some nice murals. It may be toured daily 9 a.m.–1 p.m. and 4–7 p.m. A simple *Son et Lumiere* is presented Sat., Sun. and holidays at 10:30 p.m., during June and July. Admission: 100 ptas., for the sound and light show.

Sos del Rey Católico lies a further 13 km south on C-127. This walled village, all of which has been declared a national monument, remains under restoration. There are a number of lovely mansions to be seen along with the **Palacio de Sada** in which Ferdinand was born—although substantially altered a century later. There is also a modern parador charging moderate prices:

Parador Fernando de Aragón   1st-class ★ ★

    Sos Rey Católico, ☎ *(948) 88 80 11, FAX: 88 81 00.*
    65 rooms.

The ancient **monastery of San Salvador de Leyre**, just off N-240, is beautifully situated beside a valley reservoir framed by rocky hills. It was the spiritual center of medieval Navarre. A great Romanesque church, consecrated in 1057, served as the royal pantheon for her kings and counted most of Navarre among its dominions, providing revenue. In the 13th century, however, Aragón gained control of Navarre and favored San Juan de la Peña as a religious center, diverting revenues from Leyre. Nonetheless, Cistercian monks undertook the job of enlarging the church with a grand Gothic vault. By the 19th century the site was abandoned, but Benedictines have been in residence since 1954 restoring the convent.

The western portal of the church from the 12th century is justly famous. Carvings cover every inch. The figures are archaic, but possess great charm. The most imposing part of the church, however, is the crypt below it. Entry is forbidden, but 100 ptas. will illuminate it so you can see it through the grille. It was built in the 11th century to provide a foundation for the original church, and is composed of large rough-hewn blocks that form a cavern of arches. Massive columns buried deep into the earth for support show only a foot or so above the floor.

In the church above, the most striking feature is the later (13th-century) high Gothic vault. The first several bays, however, remain from the earlier church. A modern chapel contains the pantheon of the earliest kings of Navarre, formerly interred in the crypt. The bones of ten kings and queens lie in wooden caskets inside.

Loarre Castle

See "San Juan de la Peña" for a description and directions.

Olite ★ ★

Population: 2,829
Area code: 948; zip code: 31390

From **Pamplona** *take N-121 south toward Zaragoza by following Av. de Zaragoza as it leaves the large hub of the Pl. del Principe de Viana. Olite is reached in 40 km. (See also "La Oliva Monastery" and "Leyre".)*

Charles III, king of Navarre, ordered a castle built here in 1406. Charles was also the count of Evreux in France, so he employed French architects. What arose was a fantasy that blended solid stone walls for strength with the elegant apartments of a palace. From that time until Ferdinand conquered Navarre in the 16th century, Olite was the main fortress of the Navarrese kings. Dominated by this castle, the entire village today retains a medieval atmosphere, not yet spoiled by crowds of tourists.

The village is entered through an arched gateway; then the turrets of the **castle ★** come into view. Fifteen towers mark the perimeter walls. Originally the castle inside contained a roof garden, a lions' den, an aviary and a small courtyard used for bullfights. It has been much remodeled over the centuries and today houses a parador for which some original stuccowork and painted marquetry ceilings have been restored. *(Open Mon.–Sat. 10 a.m.–2 p.m. and 4 p.m.–7 p.m., closes an hour earlier in winter; open Sun. 10 a.m.–2 p.m.; admission: 100 ptas.)*

The Gothic **Santa María la Real**, formerly the royal chapel, stands beside the castle with a fine 14th-century facade. Nearby **San Pedro**, in many ways artistically superior to Santa María, although in the Romanesque style, has a richly carved 12th-century portal.

Where to Stay

Moderate ($50–$99)

Parador Principe de Viana   **2nd-class ★ ★ ★**
Pl. de los Teobaldos, 2, Olite, ☎ *(948) 74 00 00, FAX: 74 02 01*

This parador conveys more of the feeling of a castle than any other. There are grand halls, hidden stairways, parapets, tapestries and suits of armor—all a great deal of fun for a price below the expensive line. Note that most rooms are housed in a modern addition; reserve to secure one of the 12 castle rooms. *43 rooms.*

Casa Zanito   3rd-class

C. Mayor, 16, Olite (second floor), ☎ *(948) 74 00 02.*
Closed from the last week of December through the first week of January.
The accommodations are comfortable and unassuming, if a little small, but their price hugs the low end of the moderate category, and a decent moderately priced restaurant waits downstairs. *15 rooms.*

Where to Eat

Try Casa Zanito, above, for a moderate meal, or, for a memorable dining experience at prices that barely climb into the expensive, read on:

Moderate ($15–$30)

In Tafalla, 5 km north of Olite on N-121:

Tubal   ★★★

Pl. de Navarra, 2 (on the second floor), ☎ *(948) 70 08 52.*

Closed Sun. night, Mon., and from the last week of Aug. through the first week of Sept.

This unassuming restaurant may be the best in Navarre, and is unquestionably the best for the price. Every dish is prepared with exquisite taste. If the cod with garlic and crab does not make your mouth water, the partridge salad should. Save some room for fresh ice cream. Credit Cards: A, D, M, V.

Ordesa National Park ★★

From **Zaragoza** *take N-350 north toward Huesca, and past it to Sabinanigo, for a total of 141 km. Then take N-260 north to Biescas, for 15 km, at which point N-260 turns east for a lovely 23 km drive to Torla and the entrance to the park. From* **Pamplona** *take N-121 south toward Zaragoza by following Av. de Zaragoza as it leaves the large hub of the Pl. del Principe de Viana. Five km outside the city take N-240 heading east. In 113 km Jaca is reached. Continue east on N-330 for 18 km to Sabinanigo. Go north on N-260 for 15 km to Biescas, staying on N-260 as it turns east for 23 km to Torla and the entrance to the park.*

Although Spain maintains a number of parks and wildlife preserves, Ordesa is its most dramatic, recognized since 1918 as a natural treasure. The park cannot be driven through; it consists of a number of well-marked hiking trails that cover its most attractive sights. These trails range from easy walks to demanding hikes, though most lie within the abilities of the average person. The scenery is breathtaking—waterfalls, gorges, caves, precipitous peaks, mountain meadows and stands of fir and beech. Chamois, boar and mountain goats share the beauties. The park includes a restaurant serving inexpensive meals, a tourist office nearby (open July and Aug.) and a modern parador:

Parador de Monte Perdido 2nd-class ★ ★

  Valle de Pineta, 22350 Huesca, ☎ *(974) 50 10 11.*
  This modern, moderately-priced parador wins no design awards, but the point is the spectacular scenery. Its restaurant is more adventurous than most and the fireplace is convivial. *24 rooms.*

NOTE*...The trails are passable only from May through Sept., with the first and last of these months unpredictable. Check with the Oficina de Turismo de Huesca* ☎ *(974) 22 57 78).*

The Circo Soaso walk covers most of the dramatic scenery. Hiking is not difficult, though the complete circle covers 28 miles. It begins at the Cadiera refuge.

Pamplona (Iruñea) ★

Population: 183,126
Area code: 948; zip code: 31000

The most direct route from **Madrid** *is A-2 west toward Guadalajara, which receives the designation N-II after Alcalde Henares. In 151 km, at Medinaceli, take N-111 north to Soria. Passing through Soria and around Logroño, N-111 reaches Pamplona in 281 km more. From* **Burgos** *take N-1 west toward Gasteiz (Vitoria) for 115 km and continue on the same road for 72 km past Gasteiz to Pamplona. From* **Segovia**, **Valladolid**, **León**, *and* **Salamanca**, *follow directions to Burgos in the "Old Castile" chapter, and the directions from Burgos above. From* **Donostia** *(San Sebastian) take N-240 south for 86 km. From* **Zaragoza** *take N-232 or the toll road A-68 west toward Logroño. The toll road splits just past Murchante in 86 km. Take N-15 north to Pamplona in 78 km. By N-232, connect with N-121 outside Castejon, which is followed north to Pamplona for 85 km. From* **Barcelona** *follow directions to Zaragoza, then the Zaragoza directions above.*

The city's Spanish name derives from Pompey, for he refounded the city by settling Basques here in 77 B.C. Both Goths and Francs captured it during the fifth and sixth centuries. Then the Moors held it for 50 years until it was liberated by Charlemagne in 748. Angered because he did not receive sufficient pay for this service, Charlemagne sacked the city and tore down its walls. In retribution, the citizens attacked his rear guard at the pass of Roncesvalles as he was returning to France, massacring it to the last man, and giving rise to the medieval epic *The Song of Roland*.

By the ninth century Pamplona was chosen capital of the county of Navarre, which became a kingdom under Sancho I. Though small, the kingdom and its capital prospered until 1512 when Ferdinand conquered it to incorporate Navarre into the larger political entity of Spain. In 1521 a French force came to besiege Pamplona. Although the siege was successfully resisted, one of the defenders, Iñigo Lopez de Recalde, was wounded with momentous consequences. During the time spent recovering from his wounds, Iñigo was struck with the idea of an army for Christ. As St. Ignacio de Loyola he went on to found the Jesuit Order.

The best fact best known about Pamplona is its running of bulls, made famous by Ernest Hemingway in *The Sun Also Rises*. This takes place during the annual festival of San Fermin in the second week of July, which commemorates the martyrdom of a local third-century saint. Bullfights occur every evening during the festival. Every morning at 7 a.m. a rocket announces that the bulls for the evening's fights have been loosed from their corral to run 1000 yards through the barricaded streets of the city to the ring. Brave and foolhardy citizens wearing traditional red and white neckerchiefs test their courage by running ahead of the herd, ducking into building entries as bulls near. During the festival the population of Pamplona triples, as do the prices of the hotels, although the price hardly matters, since all the rooms have been booked months before.

The rest of the year Pamplona is a quiet city, except for occasional boisterous students from the local university. Although it is lined by grand avenues, the city is not particularly attractive. It does retain a small old quarter, whose character has been all but obliterated by restaurants and shops. Considering everything, Pamplona is probably better visited than stayed in, especially with such wonderful accommodations as those at Olite, less than 40 km away.

The bullring borders an old quarter that is less than half a kilometer square. Here are the city **Cathedral** ★, imposing enough for a visit, and the **Museo Navarra** ★, with a fine collection of murals. Of course the **Plaza de Toros** ★ should be seen, along with the ruins of the walls of the city fortress, **La Ciudadela**. Half a day suffices.

*From **Madrid** and from **Burgos**, Pamplona is entered on Av. Bosquecillo which runs through the large park of the Ciudadela. Take Av. del Ejercito right at the end of the park, which in two long blocks presents parking on both the left and the right. From **Zaragoza** you arrive on Av. de Zaragoza, which leads into a large traffic circle called Pl. del Principe de Viana. Take Av. del Conde Oliveto that* *leaves the plaza going west. At the next large intersection, in two short blocks, parking can be found both to the left and to the right. From* **Donostia** *(San Sebastian), after leaving the river Arga, drive through the Jardines de la Taconera along Recta de Taconera. When this street turns slightly right and changes its name to Yaques, parking is available in one block farther on both its left and right sides.*

The parking lots border the citadel called **La Ciudadela**. This pentagonal fort was built in the 16th century by Felipe II. Now it is surrounded by acres of gardens. A walk west for four blocks along the attractive Paseo de Sarasate, planted in the center, leads to the heart of the city at the **Pl. del Castillo** with the large **Disputacion** (Provincial Council Building) at its south end.

To its north are a maze of twisting streets that constitute the old quarter of Pamplona. From the northern corner of the plaza, C. Chapitela leads to the Pl. Mercaderes in one block. C. Santo Domingo leads from its northwest corner to the **Museo Navarra ★** in two blocks. Along its side are remains of the **town walls** that provide nice views of the river Arga and the city. Behind the museum stands the corral where the bulls are kept before letting them run the streets to the bullring. From the west end of the Pl. Mercaderes, C. Curia leads to the **Cathedral ★** in three short blocks. Two blocks south and one block west of the Pl. del Castillo is the famed **bullring** of Pamplona.

What to See and Do

Museo de Navarra ★★

Cuesta de Santa Domingo, ☎ 22 78 31.

Hours open: Tues.–Sat. 10 a.m.–1:30 p.m. and 5–7 p.m. Open Sun. for the morning hours.

The museum is housed in a 16th-century building, once the charity hospital of Misericordia. Its exhibits are a little different from most museums, hence interesting.

The museum displays Roman mosaics found in the area. Most are purely geometric, the carpets of the time, but the third gallery contains a fine depiction of the Cretan fable of Theseus and the Minotaur. Gallery four presents the Romanesque period in the form of elegant capitals from the 12th-century Cathedral of Pamplona, torn down in favor of the present one. Capitals in the center of the room are masterpieces of composition and detail.

The second floor presents early paintings. The first three galleries reconstruct the Palace of Oriz to show its unusual 16th-century monochrome wall panels. Succeeding galleries present a collection of stately murals from the 13th through 15th centuries, taken from various churches in the area surrounding Pamplona. Furniture occupies the third floor, along with a few paintings, including a fine Goya of the Marqués de San Andrian. Do not miss the fine second-century mosaic in the courtyard. *Admission 200 ptas.*

On the way to visit the Cathedral, turn west for a few steps from the Pl. Mercaderes to see the church of **San Saturnino**. *The Last Supper carved on the north door of this Romanesque church is remarkable.*

Cathedral ★

Pl. de la Catedral.
Hours open: daily in summer 8 a.m.–1:30 p.m. and 4–8 p.m. Open in winter 8–11:30 a.m. and 6–8 p.m.

This Cathedral was built over the course of the 14th century, to replace an earlier Romanesque edifice. However, at the beginning of the 18th century, a front was added that combined baroque decoration with a classical design, producing the present disconcerting look.

Inside, however, the church is pure Gothic, of a style peculiar to Navarre. The nave does not soar as high as other Gothic churches, and the choir has been removed to allow a view down to the altar, while ceiling ribs are plain and the walls are bare. The altar is faced by an intricate iron grille, before which stands an elegant marble tomb of Carlos III, the last great king of Navarre, and his wife, carved by a Frenchman.

The cloister is elegant Gothic. On its east side is the Barbazan Chapel with lovely vaulting, named for the bishop entombed in it. On the south side is an unforgettable door, carved all around with precious Biblical scenes. The 14th-century refectory of the Cathedral now is the diocesan museum, worth seeing for its medieval kitchen as well as for a collection of polychromed statuary. *Admission: 150 ptas., to the Museum and cloister, open only in the summer.*

Bullring ★

Passeo Hemingway.
The structure suggests the Coliseum in Rome. Appropriately, fronting the entrance is a bust of "Papa" Hemingway, who did more than anyone to bring renown to this city.

Where to Stay

Higher-classed hotels in Pamplona tend to charge more than their services merit, and during the Feast of San Fermin all prices triple. The best values are in lower-priced establishments, for Pamplona is not a city of hoteliers. As an alternative to staying in Pamplona, consider Olite (described previously). There you can spend the night in a medieval castle converted into a parador while a wonderful restaurant waits nearby. Or consider Zaragoza for less costly sleeping (see its own entry).

Expensive ($100–$200)

Tres Reyes 1st-class ★ ★
Jardines de la Taconera, Pamplona(at the north border of the gardens surrounding the Ciudadela), ☎ *22 66 00, FAX: 22 29 30, Telex: 37720.*
Most rooms overlook a pleasant garden. They are eminently comfortable, and the service is good, yet the hotel is modern with no special charm. Still, the rooms are fair values at just over $100 a night. *168 rooms.*

Maisonnave 1st-class ★
C. Nueva, 20, Pamplona (two blocks west of the Pl. del Castillo), ☎ *22 26 00, FAX: 22 01 66, Telex: 37994.*

The location is superior, the hotel modern, and the rooms comfortable, but there are more rooms than the small staff can handle and, as the most expensive hotel in town, the prices are way out of line. *152 rooms.*

Moderate ($50–$99)

Europa   R1st-class ★ ★ ★

C. Espoz y Mina, 11, Pamplona (one block south of the Pl. del Castillo, beside the tourism office), ☎ *22 18 00, FAX 22 92 35.*

These tastefully modern large rooms are located on the second floor above one of Pamplona's best restaurants. The location is prime and the rooms approach the deluxe for a moderate price. *25 rooms.*

Yoldi   2nd-class ★

Av. San Ignacio, 11, Pamplona (three blocks south of the Pl. del Castillo), ☎ *22 48 00, FAX 21 20 45.*

Recent renovations have made this one of the more attractive hotels in town. It has always been a comfortable, quiet place to stay. *48 rooms.*

Eslava   R3rd-class ★

Pl. Virgin de la O, 7, Pamplona (beside the Jardins de la Taconera), ☎ *22 22 70, FAX 22 51 57.*
Closed Christmas week.

If you get one of the rooms overlooking the valley, you will be pleased indeed. Even if you don't get the view, the room will be attractively old with wood-beamed ceilings. The hotel is quiet and reasonably priced. *28 rooms.*

Ohri   3rd-class ★

C. Leyre, 7, Pamplona (a block and a half south of the bullring), ☎ *22 85 00, FAX 22 83 18.*

The location is good, the rooms comfortable, and its small size allows individual attention for each guest, but it overcharges, in our opinion. *55 rooms.*

La Perla   2nd-class

Pl. del Castillo, 1, Pamplona, ☎ *22 77 06.*

The location is wonderful—on the main square in the heart of town. This hotel is the city's oldest and was a favorite of both Hemingway and Henry Cabot Lodge. But time has passed and the hotel has not kept up—now it is seedy and uncomfortable. As best we can determine, this year will be the 25th anniversary of its last full renovation. Front rooms, however, provide good views of the running of the bulls. *68 rooms.*

Where to Eat

Food can be good in Pamplona, after all this is Basque country. Dishes range from stews to simply grilled fish and meat. During the Festival of San Fermin, the loser of the previous evening's contest (when it is the bull) is available around town in stews.

Expensive ($30+)

Europa   ★ ★ ★

C. Espoz y Mina, 11 (1 block south of the Pl. del Castillo, beside the tourism office), ☎ *22 18 00; FAX: 22 92 35.*
Closed Sun.

Your choices for the best food in Pamplona are Europa, and Josetxo and Hartza described below. Each serves truly wonderful food. The other two win on ambiance; Europa wins on prices which are 20 percent less than their's. As to the quality of the food, the choice is very difficult. The other two may be slightly more original in their creations, but we like the Europa best for succulent flavors. We confess that doing the comparing was no chore at all. Credit Cards: A, D, M, V.

Josetxo ★★★

Pl. Principe de Viana, 1 (on the major traffic circle, four blocks south of the Pl. del Castillo), ☎ *22 20 97.*

Closed Sundays, and Aug.

This formal and elegant restaurant bears a long-standing reputation as the best in Pamplona and charges prices accordingly. Today Hartza, below, provides stiff competition as does Europa, above, but Josetxo remains first-rate. Fish are the specialties, including crab (especially a superior soup) and omnipresent hake, but the pigeon should not be overlooked. Reservations are advised. Credit Cards: A, D, M, V.

Hartza ★★

C. Juan de Labrit, 19 (opposite the bullring, to the north), ☎ *22 45 68.*

Closed Sunday evening, Monday, August, and Christmas week.

Elegant enough in its lovely townhouse, nonetheless, this restaurant is a little less "stiff" than Josetxo. Its menu tries fewer selections, but each is exceptional—ingredients are exceptional and the chef's touch is delicate. Reservations are strongly advised. Credit Cards: A, D, M, V.

Moderate ($15–$30)

Otano ★

C. San Nicolas, 5 (one block along the street that leaves the west side of the Pl. del Castillo), ☎ *22 70 36.*

Closed Sunday evening.

The restaurant is located above the bar and decorated as everyone imagines a Spanish eatery should be. The food is hearty and features regional specialties. Although this is a perfectly decent restaurant, for less than twice the price you get more than twice as enjoyable meals at the three superstars above.

Inexpensive (Less than $15)

Café Iruna ★

Pl. del Castillo, 44, ☎ *22 20 64.*

The art deco decor is gorgeous, and the hearty food can be inexpensive if one is careful in ordering. This is an in spot for evening tapas.

Directory

Information

Located on *C. Duque de Ahumada, 3,* a short block east of the Pl. del Castillo. English is spoken, travel information is current, and the staff will help with hotel accommodations. *22 07 41.*

Airport

Aeroporto de Noaín, the local airport (☎ *31 75 82*), is 7 km south of the city, and provides service to large Spanish cities. Two weekday Avianco flights arrive from Madrid and one from Barcelona. There is no airport bus.

Trains and Buses

The Estación de Rochapea (☎ *13 02 02*) is located on *C. Rochapea*, 2 km from the center of town. The number nine bus goes there for 75 ptas. from the Paseo do Sarasate, the wide boulevard running west of the Pl. del Castillo. Train service is spotty to both Madrid and to Barcelona at three per day. Service to Donostia is three times daily and to Zaragoza nine.

Buses depart from *Av. Conde Oliveto, 4*, which is one block west of the main traffic circle, Pl. del Principe de Viana. Buses beat the train in frequency, time of travel and cost. ☎ *21 36 19*.

Post Office and Telephones

Located at *Paseo Sarasate, 9*, the wide boulevard running west of the Pl. del Castillo. ☎ *22 12 63*. Telephones are available around the corner from the Tourist Office at C. Cortes de Navarra.

Police

The municipal police are located on *C. Monasterio de Irache, 2*, which is outside the center of the city. ☎ *25 51 50*.

Excursions

Pamplona is a center around which monasteries and castles from the early Middle Ages congregate. The medieval town of **Estella** ★ ★, filled with churches and mansions, is less than 50 km southwest. (See the separate description.) **La Oliva** ★ ★ is an elegant 12th-century monastery readily combined in a half-day tour with the nearby town of **Olite** ★ and its splendid castle. (Each is separately described above.) **Leyre** ★ ★, 50 km east, is a 12th-century monastery favored by the kings of Navarre that houses their remains. Nearby are **Sangüesa**, filled with medieval mansions, **Sos del Rey Católico** ★, with the palace in which Ferdinand the Catholic was born, and **Javier**, the birthplace of Saint Francis Xavier. (All three are described above under the heading of "Leyre.") Another 50 km in the same direction is the oldest monastery of all, **San Juan de la Peña** ★ ★, on an astonishing site, along with the truly romantic **castle at Loarre** ★. (Both are described below under "San Juan de la Peña.") For a change of pace, a national park at **Ordesa** ★ ★ provides opportunities for hikes with incredible scenery (described above under its own heading).

San Juan de la Peña ★ ★

*From **Zaragoza** take N-350 north toward Huesca, then past it to Sabinanigo, for a total of 141 km. Follow N-330 east for 18 km to Jaca. Continue east, now on N-240, for 11 km. Turn south on C-134 for a final five km to San Juan. From **Pamplona** take N-121 south toward Zaragoza by following Av. de Zaragoza as it leaves the large*

*hub of the Pl. del Principe de Viana. Five km outside the city take N-
240 heading east. In 92 km Puenta de la Reina de Jaca is reached.
10 km further east take C-134 south for a final five km to San Juan.*

For the **Castillo de Loarre ★** , one of the most atmospheric in Spain, continue nine km south to Bemues. There take N-330 south to join N-240 south
for 25 km to Ayerbe. Turn east as a sign directs for seven km to the village of
Loarre.

Monastery of San Juan de la Peña   ★★★

*Hours open: Tues.–Sun. 10 a.m.–2 p.m. and 4–7 p.m. (opening and closing an hour ear-
lier in winter). Closed Mon. (closed Tues. in winter).*

Sometime during the ninth century a hermit named Juan chose a barely accessible
cliff (Peña) for his hermitage. He must have had an eye for scenery. A full-fledged
monastery existed by the 10th century, along with a lower church built into the cliff
wall. In the 11th century the monks adopted the Cluniac reforms and built another
church in an early Romanesque style above the first. The order grew to become
considered the holiest in Aragón, conducting the burial of its kings from the 11th
to the 14th centuries. In the 17th century rich revenues and growing membership
led to another church being erected higher up the mountain. The French pillaged
this third church in 1809. Fortunately they left the earlier churches intact.

The crypt, partly underground, is actually the original 10th century church on this
site. The Sala del Concilio served as the monks' dormitory and is massive. The
church itself is unique, a design of *Mozárabs* (Christians taught by the Moors). Two
aisles are demarcated only by great arches and lead to dual apses that are mere niches
cut into the mountain rock. Remains of 10th-century murals can be detected on the
walls and undersides of arches.

Stairs lead to an upper story and courtyard that constitute a pantheon of early Aragonese nobility. The tombs, which line the left wall, are marked by simple plaques
surrounded by a border of balls. Only coats of arms indicate the occupants who
range from the 11th-century founder of the Kingdom Aragón, Iñigo Arista (with a
cross and four roses), through 14th-century nobles.

The upper church was built in the late 11th century in the earliest Romanesque
style. Living rock forms part of the roof over a single aisle. Off the north wall a
chapel decorated in the 18th century serves as a pantheon to the kings of Navarre
from the 11th through the 14th centuries. Outside, a lovely Romanesque cloister is
bordered by the face of the cliff on one side and a sheer drop on the other. The capitals are carved in a seminal Romanesque style and depict biblical history through
the time of the Evangelists. On the left side reposes a 15th-century chapel, sorely
out of place.

From Ayerbe, four km of rocky road and hairpin curves are rewarded at the
end by a castle aerie, with serene views.

Loarre Castle   ★★

This aerie was built into the cliff face at the end of the 11th century by Sancho
Ramirez, the king of Aragón and Navarre. Later a religious order was installed

inside. Fronted by almost a third of a mile of stout wall that follows the curving mountainside, this fortress meets all expectations. A massive keep leads by a covered stairway to a magnificent chapel with elegant columns. The rest of the castle is a maze of winding passageways, with battlements that are brilliantly designed defensive structures. All it needs is King Arthur.

Zaragoza ★ ★ ★

Population: 590,750
Area code: 976; zip code: 50000

*From **Madrid** take A-2 west toward Guadalajara, which receives the designation N-II after Alcalde Henares. In 328 km Zaragoza is reached. From **Burgos** take N-1 west toward Logroño for 89 km. After Miranda, turn south on N-232 toward Logroño, continuing past Logroño to Zaragoza in 170 km more. From **Pamplona** take either N-121 or the toll road A-15 south for 85 km to Castejon. There take either N-232 or the toll road A-68 south for 95 km more. From **Barcelona** take A-7 south toward Tarragona. After 62 km take N-2 west toward Lleida (Lerida) which brings you to Zaragoza in 234 km.*

The flat plains of southern Aragón, well watered by the Ebro river, grow miles of wheat and corn. Zaragoza is the commercial center for this vast region. Romans first founded a town on the site in 25 B.C., which they named Caesar Augusta, from the sound of which the present name derives. Fifteen years later, according to tradition, the Virgin Mary appeared to Saint James beside the river, standing on a pillar of jasper, which she left behind to mark the event for some reason. Soon a church rose around the pillar, still preserved, although now it resides inside Nuestra Señora del Pilar, an 18th-century rebuilding of the earlier church. In the second week of October, the city celebrates its "Pillar" festival with parades, lantern-lit processions, and, of course, bullfights.

In the eighth century the Moors captured Zaragoza. By the 11th century it had became a rich and important *taifa* (principality) within the Moors' domain. Its ruling family of Benihud built a palace, like that of the Alhambra, only more substantial for these colder climes. This *Aljaferia*, after much remodeling through the ages, has been restored to something of its former state, and is a wonder. In the first part of the 12th century, however, Alfonso I recaptured Zaragoza for the Christians. Zaragoza remained the capital of Aragón from that time until the end of the 15th century when Ferdinand married Isabella and Aragón ceased to exist as a separate kingdom.

During the Peninsular War against Napoléon, the French attempted to capture Zaragoza, but the citizens held firm through a two-month siege.

The city still refused to capitulate when the French, after reinforcements, stormed the walls. Fighting turned hand to hand and proceeded through the town, house by house. Only by dynamiting most of the buildings were the French able to quell the citizens. By that time the city lay in ruins with half of its 100,000 citizens dead.

Zaragoza's recovery from this ruin is remarkable. The population has grown to ten times the number the French left living, and the city has expanded to several times its 19th-century size. Although much that was historical and interesting has been lost, today Zaragoza is a thriving commercial center that preserves a few treasures for us tourists.

The sight that makes Zaragoza worth a stop is the **Aljaferia ★★★**, which preserves marvelous Moorish stuccowork and ceilings. A complex beside the river consists of a huge **Cathedral ★**, **Nuestra Señora del Pilar ★** containing the venerated pillar and a rare example of a Renaissance secular building—the **Lonja ★**. In addition, the tasteful **Museo Camón Aznar ★** is well worth a look.

> *From* **Madrid** *the city is entered on Av. de Madrid. As the avenue emerges from a tunnel, the Aljaferia is on the left, and parking should be available on the streets around it. From there take Av. Conde de Aranda for about eight blocks until it ends at the large Av. Cesar Augusto. Take this avenue left for six blocks until it enters the Pl. del Pilar. Arriving from* **Pamplona** *on* **A-68***, go left when it ends at the Pl. del Toros. If arriving from Pamplona or* **Burgos** *on* **N-232***, keep left to travel along Av. de Navarra which ends at the Pl. del Toros. In both cases, in one block a left will bring the Aljaferia, a right will follow Av. Conde de Aranda for eight blocks until it ends at the large Av. Cesar Augusto. A left on this avenue for six blocks brings the Pl. del Pilar. From* **Barcelona** *the city is entered on Av. Cataluña. After crossing the Rio Ebro, you'll find the Pl. del Pilar is on the right.*

Along the huge rectangle of the Pl. del Pilar are **Nuestra Señora del Pilar** and the **Lonja**. The **Cathedral** is due west in a continuation of the plaza. One block south of the plaza at C. Espoz y Mina, 23, is the interesting **Museo Camón Aznar**. The **Aljaferia** is a distance from the plaza. To get there, head south from the extreme west end of the plaza along Av. Cesar Augusto for six blocks. Then turn left on Av. Conde de Aranda for eight blocks more, a total of about one km.

What to See and Do

Nuestra Señora del Pilar ★

Pl. del Pilar, ☎ *39 74 97.*
Hours open: daily 9:30 a.m.–2 p.m. and 4–7 p.m.

The present structure, replacing a much older church, was built in 1680 to house the sacred pillar and image of the Virgin. It was designed by the son of Felipe II's great architect, Herrera. The son did not inherit his father's genius but designed an innovative structure nonetheless. His quadrangular plan features a huge dome surrounded by smaller tiled cupolas added a century later. From a distance it looks like a Turkish mosque.

Inside, columns seem excessively massive, as if the architect, unsure of his calculations, made them overly safe. The most interesting feature is the ten frescoed cupolas—the one in the center of the north nave was painted by the young Goya, who was born nearby. Ornate chapels line the aisles leading to the high altar backed by a fine marble retable by Damian Forment.

Beside the altar is the Santa Capilla surrounded by marble columns. In a niche on the right above altars stands the sacred pillar covered in silver supporting an extravagantly robed Virgin. Her attire is changed daily. Columbus is said to have taken a piece of the pillar with him for luck on his first voyage to The New World. The pillar is kissed by the faithful from outside the chapel rear. Three bombs that landed on the chapel during the Civil War (but did not explode) hang nearby to demonstrate the pillar's power. *Admission: 200 ptas., to the museum.*

To the east of N.S. del Pilar is the huge reconstructed **Ayuntamiento** *with ornate eaves. To its west is the* **Lonja**.

Lonja ★

Pl. de Catedral.
Hours open: during exhibitions only 10 a.m.–1 p.m. and 5–8 p.m. Open Sun. and holidays during exhibitions from 11 a.m.–2 p.m.
Most medieval commercial towns provided a central building where commodities could be brokered. This is one of the few surviving, to give a sense of civil architecture in the 16th century. The hall is a Gothic structure with Plateresque decorative elements. Twenty-four columns surmounted by grotesques support the ceiling, surrounded by a frieze that records the raising of the building. *Admission: free.*

West of the Lonja is the huge **Palace of the Archbishop** *and the Cathedral.*

Cathedral ★

Pl. de Catedral, *29 12 38.*
Hours open: daily 9 a.m.–2 p.m. and 4–6 p.m.
The Cathedral is most notable for its size. A baroque façade was added in the 18th century to cover a Gothic interior. Today all architectural styles from the Gothic to Mudejar, through the Plateresque and churrigueresque sprinkle the inside. In a most unusual touch, the marble floor below depicts the vaulting overhead.

To the left of the altar and its retable of fine Gothic work is a tomb of Archbishop Juan of Aragón, the brother of Ferdinand the Catholic. A slab in black stone nearby marks the location of the heart of Don Baltasar Carlos, the son of Felipe IV who Velásquez painted often and whose death left the Spanish throne to the French Bourbons. The Parroquieta Chapel holds a fine 14th-century tomb carved in Burgundian style, covered by a lovely Mudejar ceiling.

Paintings in the Treasury include works of Ribera, Zurbarán, and Goya, while the adjacent Tapestry Museum displays a grand collection of Gothic and later works. The *Betrothal of Anne of Brittany* is a masterpiece. *Admission: 200 ptas., for the Treasury, and the Tapestry Museum.*

Museo Camón Aznar ★

C. Espoz y Mina, 23, ☎ 39 73 28.
Hours open: Tues.–Sat. 10 a.m.–1 p.m. and 5–9 p.m. Open Mon. 10 a.m.–1 p.m. and Sun. 11 a.m.–2 p.m.
In this former Palace of Pardo is stored the art collection of a famous art historian with impeccable taste. The works include an Andrea del Sarto of *Four Saints,* an unusual El Greco still-life, a fine Zurbarán crucifixion, along with works by Ribera, Ribalta, Rembrandt and Van Dyck. Most captivating are a rare Velázquez sketch and a profound Goya self-portrait. *Admission: 150 ptas.*

Aljaferia ★★★

C. Los Diputados, ☎ 28 95 28.
Hours open: Tues.–Sat. 10 a.m.–1:30 p.m. and 4:30–6:30 p.m. Open Sun. 10 a.m.–2 p.m. Closed holidays.
The Moorish governor of Zaragoza built this palace in the 11th century. After Zaragoza was reconquered by the Christians, it became the palace of the kings of Aragón, with much remodeling of rooms and decor. Later it served as an administration center and courts for the local arm of the Inquisition; later still, as an army barracks. The huge building recently underwent extensive restoration, resulting in a Moorish first floor and a Gothic and Renaissance second floor. All told, this building contains some of the more exquisite rooms to be seen in Spain.

Of exceptional interest on the first floor is the *musallah,* private mosque, a jewel that rivals parts of the mosque in Córdova. The *mihrab* is a gem, as is the stucco filigree. A magnificent staircase from 1492 leads up to the Christian apartments. Of the former throne room only an elaborate ceiling remains, containing the entwined initials of Ferdinand and Isabella. A fine ceiling crowns the room where Santa Isabel (Isabel of Portugal) was born, above an altogether charming room. The juxtaposition of Moor and Christian architecture just a floor apart provides much food for thought. *Admission: free; 200 ptas. for the guided tour.*

Where to Stay

As a major city, Zaragoza includes a full complement of hotels. Since it is not a major tourist stop, however, most hotels represent good values.

Expensive ($100–$200)

Gran Hotel Deluxe ★★★

C. Joaquin Costa Canalejas, 5, Zaragoza (twelve blocks south of N.S. del Pilar), ☎ 22 19 01, FAX: 23 67 13, Telex: 58010.
For once the name fits—this Belle-Époque hotel has been declared a national monument. Its rotunda is a deco marvel. Long in need of renovations which have finally been completed, any last quibbles have now been laid to rest. Prices reflect that fact, but service is exceptional. *140 rooms.*

Moderate ($50–$99)

Goya   1st-class ★

C. Cinco de Marzo, 5, Zaragoza (on the first street to the west along the grand avenue
Paseo de la Independencia, due south of N.S. del Pilar), ☎ 22 93 31, FAX: 23 47 05,
Telex: 58680.

This hotel offers quiet and professional service but without the atmosphere of the
Gran. It charges less as well for rooms as large, and is located more conveniently for
the sights. *148 rooms.*

Ramiro I   1st-class ★ ★

C. Coso, 123, Zaragoza (C. San Vicente de Paul heads south from the west end of the
Cathedral. In four blocks C. San Jorge goes west one block to this hotel.), ☎ 29 82 00,
FAX 39 89 52, Telex: 58689.

This hotel charges less than normal for its class. It is an older establishment with
most conveniences, although it is somewhat understaffed. Still, the rooms are comfortable and a good value. *104 rooms.*

Inexpensive (Less than $50)

Conde Blanco   3rd-class ★ ★

C. Predicadores, 84, Zaragoza (this street goes west from the Mercado de Lanuza, the
market a block south of the west end of the Pl. del Pilar), ☎ 44 14 11, FAX 28 03 39.

The locale is quiet and attractive, conveniently situated between the sights of the Pl.
del Pilar and those of the Aljaferia. The hotel is modern and professionally run.
Please do not tell the management its prices are too low. *87 rooms.*

Youth Hostel

Residencia Juvenil Baltázar Gracián

C. Franco y López, 4, Zaragoza (follow Av. César Augusto from the Lonja until it forks,
taking Av. Valencia for one km to this street), ☎ 55 15 04.

Renovations should be complete when you arrive, but were ongoing at our last visit.
All should be fresh and clean.

Where to Eat

Zaragoza possesses a large number of good restaurants but has lost its one shining star.
The best meals will merely be pleasant, but the figures on the check will satisfy.

Expensive ($30+)

La Mar   ★ ★

Pl. Aragón, 12 (this large plaza lies at the south end of the wide Av. Independencia, which
begins a short eight blocks south of the Pl. del Pilar), ☎ 21 22 64.
Closed Sunday and August

For starters, the decor is elegant and lovely, the nicest in town. Specialties, of
course, are denizens of the sea, cooked well here. Service is gracious, though slow.
The bill should be a pleasant surprise, for the charges are barely expensive for food
that tastes like much more. Credit Cards: A, M, V.

La Matilde   ★ ★

Casta Alvarez, 10 (The large Pl. de Lanuza with a covered market is west off the Pl. del
Pilar. Alvarez leaves the west side of this plaza.), ☎ 44 10 08.
Closed Sunday, holidays and August.

No elegance here, this is a mom and pop place that serves unusually refined food, the sort of place that may become a gourmet mecca. The crowds will come for the truffle paté. So far the food is richer than the charges. Credit Cards: A, D, M, V.

Moderate ($15–$30)

El Asador de Aranda

Arquitecto Magdalena, 6 (go south along Av. Independencia from the Pl. de España for one block, then left for two blocks along San Miguel to take a right turn on this street), ☎ *22 64 17.*

Closed Sunday night and August.

The trip to this local place is worth the effort. Here, in cheerful surroundings, you will be served delectable food for reasonable costs. Game dishes are good as are roasts. Credit Cards: M, V.

Inexpensive (Less than $15)

Tres Hermanos

C. San Pablo, 45 (turn west on block south of the Mercado de Lanuza, the market a block south of the west end of the Pl. del Pilar), ☎ *44 10 85.*

Closed Tuesday.

We cannot guarantee gastronomic heights but can assure that cost will be low. The sign outside translates as "Economical Meals," and those are what you get. The restaurant is downstairs and generally crowded.

Directory

Information

Located in the Torreón de la Zuda-Gloneta Pio XII, which is at the west end of the Pl. del Pilar. The staff is helpful and speaks English. ☎ *20 12 00.*

Airport

Zaragoza's airport (☎ *34 90 50*) is nine km west of the city on N-232. It's a substantial terminal serving the major cities of Spain. Ebrobuses, for under 100 ptas., connect with the Pl. de San Francisco. The Iberia office is located at *C. Canfranc, 22-24* which goes west from the Pl. de Aragón at the southern end of the Paseo del la Independencia (☎ *21 82 59*).

Trains and Buses

Estación Portillo (☎ *28 02 02*) is located on Av. Clave, four blocks south of the Aljaferia. As the major city in the region, Zaragoza offers convenient schedules to most of Spain, including 14 daily trains from Madrid and 16 from Barcelona. The RENFE office (☎ *23 38 02*) is located at *C. Clemente, 13*, a street which leaves the grand boulevard Paseo de la Independencia heading east.

There is no central bus terminal, a host of independent companies and service is not as convenient as the train anyway. If interested, see the tourist office for details.

Post Office and Telephones

Located on the grand boulevard *Paseo de la Independencia, 33* (☎ *22 26 50*).

Police

☎ *59 30 88*; emergency: ☎ *091.*

Excursions

All the excursions from Pamplona described above are as easily visited from Zaragoza. See the description under "Pamplona excursions" to make a choice. Descriptions of the individual sights include directions from Zaragoza.

CATALONIA AND THE LEVANT

Casa Batlló in Barcelona is Gaudí's exercise in blue–green tiles.

Historical Profile:
The Spanish Civil War

The Civil War of 1936-39 was perhaps the blackest event in Spain's history. Starting as a military putsch, it degenerated into atrocities of such unprecedented proportions that no Spaniard can speak impassively about them half a century later.

The stage for civil war had been set by a century of army coups. From the time of Napoléon's defeat in 1813 through the Spanish-American War in 1898, 37 relatively bloodless overturns had been attempted—12 successfully—as one general seized power after another. Because each new government tried to appease only conservative constituencies—land owners and the Spanish Catholic Church—Spain entered the 20th century as the least-liberal, least developed country in all of Western Europe. Industry was negligible; land magnates controlled vast acreage; the Church owned a third of the nation's wealth; the army, with one general for every 100 troops, barely functioned.

Miguel Primo de Rivera, the last in this series of dictators, seized the government in a coup in 1920 and ruled as a dictator for ten years until the army withdrew its support. King Alfonso XIII formed the first new government in a decade just as world depression hit Spain, creating even greater unemployment and social unrest. The next year, civil turmoil compelled the king to call for general elections. Most of the votes went to candidates who supported the monarchy, due largely to the urgings of Catholic priests and the strong-armed tactics of large landowners coercing thousands of peasants. Nonetheless, all the large cities except Cádiz voted against the king. Realizing that a country cannot be governed without the cooperation of its cities, the army withdrew its support from Alfonso, who abdicated and rode off into exile.

Thus, amid economic depression and growing unrest, the tragic Second Republic began, the heir of a morass of problems. Over a million farm workers lived in near slavery, hiring out for the pitiful wages decreed by mammoth farm owners. Most of these people had never in their lives tasted meat. Decades of outlawed unionism fostered resentment among a million urban laborers who knew that workers in other countries enjoyed better conditions than theirs. At the same time, various regions of Spain, especially Catalonia and the Basque region, resented government attempts to diminish their *fueros*—ancient rights of independence.

Grievances varied. Some cried for agricultural reform, the division of 10,000-acre farms into smaller plots for starving farmers. Some opposed the centrism of the national government, preferring regional autonomy. Still others objected to the stranglehold of the Spanish Catholic Church on education and morals—although Spain was the least Catholic of all the Catholic countries with only one citizen in five regularly attending mass.

It was an era of political upheaval worldwide, disturbing old certainties. Communists revolutionized Russia, while fascists marched in Germany and Italy. Everywhere politics had polarized into left or right. In Spain, the largest organization on the left was the anarchists, who resented all forms of government, believing that people would cooperatively work out problems on their own. Many laborers and teachers agreed with the anarchists, but a large number instead followed the socialists, who argued that raising wages, providing health needs and offering proper education were primary duties of any government. The next largest group on the left were the Marxists, introduced into Spain by Paul Lafargue, Marx's own son-in-law. Marxists believed in communally-owned enterprises instead of private property. However, because Marxist theory gave little weight to the political power of peasants while encouraging a centrist state, most Spaniards felt it offered no solution to their problems. Finally, there were communists, divided into those who followed Trotsky and those who followed Stalin and took orders from Russia. In 1931, perhaps 10,000 Spanish considered themselves Stalinists.

The largest party on the right was the CEDA, the Catholic party. Next came the Carlists, who supported a return to monarchy under Prince Don Carlos. Last was a small group, called the Falange Español, "Spanish Phalanx," led by José Antonio Primo de Rivera, the son of the former dictator. His was a paramilitary organization, schizophrenically supporting anti-capitalist social reforms along with fascist ideals of cleansing society through the shedding of blood.

At the beginning of the Second Republic the temper of the government was mainly socialist. One of its first acts was to separate the church from the state. The prelate of Toledo responded with a sermon calling for the return of the monarchy; radical leftists answered by burning 20 churches. On the question of regional autonomy the new government agreed to permit home rule for the Catalans, but not for the Basques. Headway on the grave issue of agricultural reform was imperceptible. It was not a great surprise, therefore, when, after an election was called in 1933, opponents of the regime won a majority of seats. This second republican government immediately overturned all the policies of the first. Basques rose in Asturias, demanding autonomy, but were violently put down by soldiers. Thirty thousand political prisoners soon crowded the jails, for frustration had turned into anger and violence.

To increase their political clout, both the left and right formed "fronts," coalitions of individual parties from the same end of the political spectrum. In 1936, the Popular Front—consisting of socialists, Marxists and communists—won the third general election, even though the single party that elected the most delegates was the monarchists. A liberal government was formed, while the right called for a coup d'état. After police shot a Civil Guard who threw a bomb at the president of the Republic, the Guard's funeral erupted into a running gun battle between Falangists and socialists. Falangists encouraged such violence. They attempted to assassinate the deputy speaker of the Cortés; then they tried to kill the most prominent socialist in

Catalonia. When they machine-gunned laborers in Madrid, the government had had enough. It closed the offices of the Falange and arrested its leader, José Antonio.

This arrest, and massive strikes in Madrid and in Barcelona helped anarchists and socialists increase their popularity. But the Spanish Army, worried about anarchy, a dissolution of the country into independent states, and a departure from Catholic ideals, grew agitated.

At this time the army consisted of 30,000 hardened troops protecting territory that Spain controlled in northern Morocco, as well as untrained home forces. Francisco Franco y Bahamonte, the son of a Galician naval paymaster, had chosen the army over his father's service because so few ships and opportunities survived the Spanish-American War. He had risen to the rank of general in charge of the Spanish Foreign Legion, whose motto was *Viva la Muerte* ("Long Live Death"). Franco, a small man with a pot belly and squeaky voice, was brave, but always cautious. Because his loyalty was questionable, the government posted him in the Canary Islands far from Spain.

An army rebellion rose in Spanish Morocco on July 18, 1936, after months of plotting. The next day an English pilot flew Franco to Morocco to lead the army over the straits to Spain, but the sailors of the fleet refused to transport their brothers in arms. Instead, in the first major airlift in history, the army was carried by German and Italian airplanes to Spain. On the mainland, meanwhile, garrisons of troops attempted to seize Spain's major cities. The government was helpless with its army in rebellion, but private citizens defied the troops, and succeeded more often than not, so that by the end of the first week, only Seville, Cádiz, Jerez and Algeciras in the south, and Pamplona, Burgos, Valladolid, and the territory of Galicia in the north, were held by the army. As a putsch the uprising was a failure, now it was a case of surrender or war. So far the army held only a horizontal strip across the north, minus the Basque region, and a small area in Andalusia.

Except for police of questionable loyalty, the Republican government commanded no forces. All the major parties—anarchists, socialists and communists—demanded weapons, but the government feared the anarchy of a country in arms. People acquired weapons by force or purchase anyway, and formed themselves into militia.

If it was to be war, Franco's troops would need supplies. He turned to Italy and Germany. Mussolini, favoring a fascist regime in Spain to oppose the British Mediterranean fleet, supplied planes and troops. A total of 50,000 Italian troops entered the fray by the end. Hitler, too, desired a fascist regime in Spain, viewing it as a strategic threat to France's southern border and a needed southern base for German U-boats. Also, civil war in Spain would provide an opportunity to field-test new equipment and soldiers. Hitler supplied the latest German aircraft to make up the infamous Condor Legion, along with tanks, artillery and a host of military advisers.

The Republican government needed supplies from other countries, too, because Spain had no substantial war industry. Initially, France sold the government outmoded materials at inflated prices, but soon closed its borders to further sales. The socialist Prime Minister of France, Léon Blum, should have sympathized with the kindred government of Spain, but his shaky administration feared antagonizing the French rightists and Hitler. The British maintained a facade of neutrality, as their Prime Minister, Anthony Eden, argued that aiding the Republic would only lead to increasing German and Italian supplies for the rebels. In fact, high-ranking members of the British government maintained close social ties to the Spanish nobility and openly preferred fascism to liberal policies. In the end, Eden sent the English navy to support Franco. Although the United States Neutrality Act prevented aid to any belligerent, Ford and General Motors sent 10,000 trucks to Franco, none to the Republic, and DuPont delivered as many bombs. Because of Franco's pro-Catholic views, the rebels gained the support of Joseph Kennedy, who exerted a powerful influence in the U.S. on their behalf. In the final analysis, the leaders of the free world feared a "red menace" more than fascism, since leftists were intent on doing away with class privileges.

With nowhere else to turn, the Republic petitioned Stalin for supplies. His image required that he not refuse, but, feeling weak because he had just purged his army, he feared the consequences of Hitler's displeasure. So he dribbled insufficient aid with great fanfare. Still, as the Republic's only supplier (except for Mexico), Russia strengthened the hand of the Spanish Stalinists, who gradually gained control of both the government and its armed forces. By refusing aid to the Spanish Republic, the democracies pushed it further left.

Both sides commenced a propaganda campaign to gain international approval. Franco's army started to refer to itself as Nationalist, and its adherents claimed that Republicans killed 20,000 priests and raped nuns by the hundreds over the course of the war. Later, the number was reduced to 7937 killed, and no rapes were substantiated. But, undeniably, genuine atrocities were committed by the Republican side—army officers were executed as they left their homes, businessmen and priests were murdered, all during the early days of the war when the passion for retribution was most intense. Conflicting propaganda makes the truth elusive, but an estimate of 10,000 civilian murders by Republicans is generally accepted.

Nationalist atrocities were of a different order. Its soldiers killed at least ten times as many civilians as the Republicans, doing so systematically over the course of the war less from rage or the intent to punish than to exterminate all liberals. "Your women will give birth to Fascists," their graffiti boasted.

The war opened with a Nationalist attack on Madrid. By November 8, 1936, the city was virtually surrounded, its fall imminent, for no one expected citizens with guns to match professional soldiers. The Nationalists concentrated their attack on the western suburbs, around the University, where Madrileños had been reinforced by an army of Barcelona anarchists and the first of the International Brigades that would eventually number 35,000 troops. These primarily working-class people—enlisting to fight fascism—had been recruited throughout Europe and America by the communists, but included as many non-communists as party members in their ranks. By substituting determination for military training, this motley collection of untried troops, against all expectations, held off the Nationalists.

The Republican government was as surprised as anyone at this valiant defense—its members had fled to Valencia anticipating the fall of the capital. The battle for Madrid settled into a stalemate, and, when the Nationalists tried to bomb the city into submission, the first such attempt in history, resistance only hardened.

Yet Madrid would have fallen had Franco not diverted his forces for a propaganda expedition. When the army garrison of Toledo failed to capture that city in the first days of the revolt, they were chased into the Toledo Alcázar by the citizens and besieged. Eleven hundred defenders and 500 civilian sympathizers fighting to stay alive grew into a symbol of Nationalist steadfastness. Franco's first priority was relieving the Toledo garrison, an action that delayed his arrival in Madrid by three weeks. By then Republican reinforcements had arrived.

Blocked at Madrid, the Nationalists planned to conquer the rest of the country, causing Madrid to fall from lack of support. As 1937 began, the Nationalists commanded 100,000 army troops and an equal number of Carlist and Falangist militia, plus 10,000 German and 50,000 Italian regulars. Republican troops comprised 320,000 men and women, though at any given time half of these irregular troops were away on leave. The Nationalists aimed first at the northern Basque region.

Their campaign went smoothly except for one horrible incident at Guernica. That city was a Basque symbol of no military importance, and lay a good six miles behind the military front. On April 26, between 4:30 and 7 p.m., wave upon wave of German planes systematically destroyed the town. First came a carpet of high explosive bombs, then strafing, and finally a torrent of incendiary shells. The carnage, illuminated by burning houses, was the most horrifying the world had seen. One third of the citizens suffered injuries; 1654 people died. Miraculously, one of the few survivors of the raid was the sacred oak tree of the Basques under which their treaties had traditionally been signed. The Nationalists publicly disavowed responsibility for the massacre, pointing their fingers at German pilots. Indeed, it is quite possible that

Hitler was trying a new concept of saturation bombing as an experiment. In Paris, the Spanish painter Picasso immortalized the horror in his *Guernica*, considered by many experts the greatest modern painting.

By 1938 armies on both sides had grown to 700,000. The Nationalists drove toward the sea on the east and reached it with ease, cutting off Catalonia and its capital of Barcelona. Madrid formed an isolated pocket in the west.

Generally in war defense is less costly of lives and material than offense. In defending their homes, the Republicans proved to be staunch fighters, but the Republican government was anxious for the publicity of major victories and time and again used their untrained troops in ineffective offensive campaigns. In defense of Barcelona, the Republicans threw nearly 200,000 men at the Nationalist circle around the city. Initial success was followed by a slowing and finally a complete stoppage of the advance. Bogged down, the citizen-soldiers became fodder for an uncontested Nationalist air force and artillery, and by the time they retreated back to Barcelona, the Republicans had lost almost half of their troops along with tons of irreplaceable equipment. A quarter of a million Republicans now remained to defend Barcelona, sharing only 40,000 rifles. The Pope urged Franco to wait until after the Holy Season to attack, but on December 23, Franco entered Barcelona behind 300,000 well-armed troops, while half a million refugees fled before him into France. Madrid fell on March 31, 1939, and Franco announced the official end of the Civil War on April 1. Now Spain was Franco's problem.

Generalissimo Franco, *El Caudillo* ("The Leader"), immediately enacted the Law of Political Responsibilities, which made criminals of all persons guilty of subversive activities from October 1, 1934 to July 18, 1936, as well as those who opposed the National Movement, either actively or passively. By this law, everyone who opposed the coup, in word or deed, and those who simply lived in a community that was against it was guilty of a serious crime. Franco bragged that he possessed a list of a million liberal criminals. Two hundred thousand people were executed over the first five years of his regime, and a like number were imprisoned and used as forced labor to reconstruct the battered country. In Franco's new Spain, a man could be fined for walking the streets without a hat or jacket, a woman for bared arms in public. Everyone went to church, for not to do so was grounds for arrest.

Since all electoral candidates were members of Franco's FET party, he ruled until his death on November 20, 1975. His Spain, with its subsidized hotels, cheap food from a depressed economy and trains that almost always ran on time, was a haven for tourists. Although he supplied Hitler with Spanish ores to repay the cost of German supplies during the Civil War, Franco kept Spain officially neutral during World War II. He cut crime to minuscule proportions by jailing suspects along with the guilty. Throughout his reign he warned of the anarchy that only he could keep at bay. After his death, the Third, and present, Republic commenced peaceably and orderly. The Spanish economy blossomed, but then so did crime, as it seems to in all democracies.

Catalonia and the Levant: The Sights

However natural it may be to think of Spain as culturally homogeneous, that conception is frequently misleading and never more so than in Catalonia's case. Catalonia (called "Catalunya" locally) is the most European part of the Iberian peninsula. It has as much in common with the south of France as with the south of Spain—as well it should, for the two were joined throughout much of their history.

Catalonia was the second place in the Iberian Peninsula to receive foreign settlers. The Greeks colonized Empúries, north of latter-day Barcelona, in the sixth century B.C., and there introduced the olive into Spain. Two centuries later Carthagenians followed. Their attack on the Roman colony at Segunto, in the second century B.C., brought Roman armies to Spain in retaliation to destroy the bases of their Carthagenian enemy Hannibal. The Romans stayed to conquer the peninsula. Tarragona, south of Barcelona, functioned as the Roman headquarters in Spain until Goths stormed it in the fifth century. Then Moors followed in the eighth century. Unlike their sojourn in the rest of Spain, however, the Moors held Catalonia for only a short time.

To rid itself of Moors, Catalonia appealed to the great King of the Franks, Charlemagne. He sent his son Louis le Debonair, Count of Toulouse, who freed Catalonia from Moors in 801 and united it with his territory in southern France. Charlemagne organized the combined territories into what he called the Spanish Marches, merging Catalonia with the part of France later known as Languedoc (from "Language of Oc," for the non-Parisian tongue spoken there). But, less than a century later, Catalonia turned the tables when Wilfred the Hairy, the first Count of Barcelona, took Toulouse. In 987, as the rest of France united in recognizing the usurper Hugh Capet as its new king, Barcelona and its French territory refused to acknowledge his claim, thereby declaring itself separate from the rest of the kingdom of France.

These Catalan and southern French territories remained united for 700 years, preserving their independence by playing off the neighboring powers of France and Aragón against each other. Indeed, for a golden three centuries it was Catalonia that controlled Aragón, rather than the other way around. When an Aragonese king died childless in 1137, his brother was forced to abandon monastic life to rule the kingdom. He betrothed his daughter Petronila to Ramón Berenguer IV, the Count of Barcelona, then returned to his cloistered existence. Berenguer IV thus became Regent of

Aragón and, when the monk-king died in 1172, Berenguer's 10-year-old son was crowned Alfonso II, the King of Aragón.

At the time both Castile and Aragón were separately attempting to reconquer territory from the Moors. It would sometimes happen that both kingdoms had designs on the same city, but it would not do for one Christian king to rescue a city from the Moors only to have to defend it from another Christian king. In 1179 Alfonso II, negotiated a treaty with the King of Castile that drew a vertical line from Logroño in the north through Alicante in the south to demarcate separate east-west spheres of conquest. Two reigns later, Jaume I earned the name "Conqueror" by taking Valencia, thereby giving Catalonia and Aragón control of the entire eastern coast of Spain. Catalonia had established itself as a power in Europe.

Jaume's successor Pedro III married the only child of King Manfred, ruler of Sicily which at that time controlled all of Italy south of Rome. When the French attempted to impose claims on Sicilian territory, the Italians rose against them, and Pedro came to their aid with an army. Since he was in Italy with troops, he seized the throne of Sicily for Catalonia. Now Catalonia controlled the south of France, one third of Spain and half of Italy. Catalan troops next went to the aid of Constantinople, beleaguered by the Turks. In return, the pope granted them the territory of Turkey, though in name only, since the Turks who actually controlled the country did not agree. A small force also landed in Greece and were ceded Athens by the pope.

Catalonia's Mediterranean dominance lasted only 50 years. Pedro IV left two sons when he died, both of whom expired childless, so the throne reverted—never to return to Catalonia—to an Aragonese in 1410. Turks soon regained control of Greece and the Catalans came home from Turkey.

Yet Catalonia continued to govern substantial territory in the south of France for two centuries more. The two areas shared a language, customs and cuisine. Provençal, as it is known in France, or Catalan, as the related tongue is known in Spain, was the favored tongue of the troubadours during the Middle Ages for it lent itself superbly to poetry. Catalonia considered itself a Mediterranean country facing east, rather than west into Spain, and fought fiercely to remain independent of the hegemony that powerful Castile created throughout the rest of the peninsula, resisting every effort to impose Castilian Spanish as its language. When forced to recognize Castilian Kings, the Catalans swore an oath that was a model of noncommitment: "We, who are as good as you, swear to you, who are no better than us, to accept you as king and sovereign lord, provided you observe all our liberties and laws—but if not, not."

In 1639 France invaded Catalonia's French territory and Catalans enlisted to fight alongside troops from the rest of Spain. But when the Spanish King

**CATALUNYA AND
THE LEVANT**

ordered the people of Catalonia to billet his troops in their houses, they took the command as an affront to their rights, declaring war on Spain and inviting the French to join them.

Too strong for Felipe to expel, French troops occupied Catalonia and much of Aragón for over a decade. But the Catalans soon tired of their new overlord, and were as jealous of rights that the French usurped as they had been of those that the Spanish tried to. As local support eroded, the French saw the handwriting on the wall and agreed to leave Catalonia. However, the 1669 treaty that ratified the French departure ceded them those Catalan territories that today form the south of France.

As late as the 1930s, during the Spanish Civil War, Catalonia fought against the Nationalists and Franco as much for independence from the rest of Spain as against dictatorial government. Franco made them pay dearly. He imposed Castilian as the official language on all of Spain, and made writing Catalan a prisonable offense. Today, Catalonia is a semi-autonomous territory of Spain, similar to a state in the U.S., and its official language is the old, French-sounding, Catalan.

Beautiful **Barcelona** ★★★★★ is the treasure of Catalonia, and for most people one of the highlights of Spain. One reason it is so enjoyable is that its entertainments are so varied. It offers a well-preserved medieval quarter and fine Cathedral in the Barri Gòtic, an exceptional museum of medieval art in the Museo de Arte de Catalunya, fine museums for the modern art of both Picasso and Miró, and the eccentric, lovable architecture of the genius Gaudí. There is more to Catalonia than the capital, however. **Empüries** ★★ preserves rare Greek ruins, and **Tarragona** ★★ displays extensive Roman remains. **Poblet** ★★★ and **Santa Cruz** ★★ monasteries are grand medieval edifices. Beaches of great appeal line 600 miles of coast—the scenic **Costa Brava** ★★, the golden Costas **Azahar** ★★ and **Dorada** ★★, and the sandy stretches of the **Costa Blanca** ★★. South in the Levant is the major metropolis of **Valencia** ★★, with enough variety to repay a day's visit while staying on the Costa Azahar to its north, or the Costa Blanca to its south.

Barcelona ★★★★★

Population: 1,754,900
Area code: 93; zip code: 08000

From **Perpignan** *in France both the toll A-9, and the free N-9, reach the Spanish border at La Jonquera in 20 km. There they continue in Spain under the new names of A-7 and N-II and reach Barcelona after 160 km. From* **Zaragoza** *the toll road A-2 east joins A-7 in 137 km for a further trip of 62 km. Alternatively, there is the* *free N-II which reaches Llerida (Lérida) in 142 km and Barcelona in a further 156 km. From **Pamplona**, **Madrid**, **Valladolid**, and west, follow directions to Zaragoza, and the directions from that point above. From **Valencia** the best routes are the parallel coast roads A-7 (toll) and N-340. They reach Barcelona in 331 km. Note that N-340 can be slow going when beach towns are crowded in summer.*

Legend has the city founded by Hannibal's father, the Carthagenian general Hamilcar Barca, and derives the city's name from Barca's. In reality the city is newer, descending from a Roman colony established in the time of Augustus, named Faventia Julia Augusta Paterna Barcino. Shortened to Barcino, the name transmographied over time into "Barcelona." The original town comprised a low hill just inland from the sea—the present Barri Gòtic—as it would for almost 1000 years. Franks captured Barcelona from the Romans in A.D. 263, and when the Romans reconquered it they surrounded the hill by a cyclopian wall that still exists in scattered pieces. In 874, after the French had expelled the Moors and annexed Catalonia in the process, Wilfredo el Velloso (the Hairy) was named the Count of Barcelona and granted independence by the ironically named French king, Charles the Bald. From that time forth, Barcelona maintained preeminence in Catalonia.

The city grew and prospered both because its location on the eastern coast made it a funnel through which most of the Mediterranean trade flowed into Spain, and because its people were singularly hard-working and blessed with sound business sense. Barcelona remains the busiest port in Spain, its second largest city, and a more substantial business center than the country's political capital, Madrid.

In both the middle of the 18th and the middle of the 19th centuries Barcelona undertook imposing urban renewals. The first entailed razing most of the ancient Roman walls to construct a wide thoroughfare along the western edge of the Barri Gòtic, primarily for promenades. The thoroughfare followed a sometime stream and permanent sewer and was named the Ramblas, perhaps from the Arabic *raml*, meaning "stream." The second project produced a great addition to the city north of the Barri Gòtic. Called the Eixample (Extension), it was a marvel of rational city planning that more than doubled the city's size. Today, Barcelona spreads both north and south of this extension, following the coastline.

The visitor will spend most of his time in the center of this sprawling metropolis, anchored by the port of Barcelona midway between the north and south halves of the city. Immediately south of the port rises the abrupt hill of Montjuïc. Here are several fine museums and arenas from the 1992 Olympic Games. Two blocks inland from the port and running for ten blocks further west is the original heart of Barcelona, the Barri Gòtic, containing the Cathedral and other medieval buildings. Its south border consist of the lovely

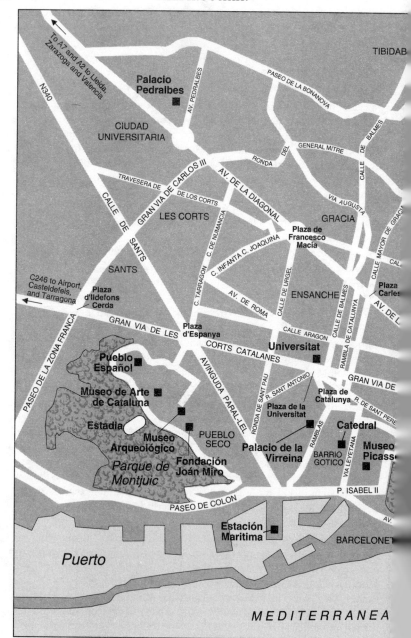

Ramblas, which changes their name every few blocks. South of the Ramblas, leading to Montjüic, is a maze of streets called the Barri Xines (Chinese Quarter), the former red-light district, now much toned down although still not the safest place after dark. North of the Barri Gòtic a park called the Ciudadela blooms where an 18th-century fortress once stood, providing space for a zoo and the Museum of Modern Art. Extending west from the Barri Gòtic, beginning at the landmark Plaça Catalunya, runs the 19th-century urban development Eixample, with boulevards, elegant stores and buildings by Gaudí.

Over all, Barcelona's atmosphere is one of industry, quiet excitement and good taste. Catalan will be the language most often overheard. It sounds something like French and many words will be understood by those familiar with that tongue. Spanish is understood by all, French by most, and English by a large number of Barcelona residents, particularly those in service industries. Street names use *Avinguda* for Avenue, *Carrer* for Street and *Plaça* for Plaza.

Convenient underground parking is generally available in a large lot under the square behind the Boquería, the main food market. It is one block west of the Rambla St. Josep, and thus near the Barri Gòtic.

From the **Airport** *22 km south of the city, C-246 feeds into the expressway Ronda del Litoral. Take exit 21, Pl. Colom/Pl. de la Pau and head west along the wide Ramblas divided by a center strip for about six blocks, until passing the Teatre del Liceu on the left. Take the next left, C. Hospital, and the first true right off it to parking.*

From **France** *and north, exit to either A-17 or A-18. Both intersect with Ronda del Besòs which becomes the Ronda del Litoral in about one mile. Take exit 21, Pl. Colom/Pl. de la Pau and head west along the wide Ramblas divided by a center strip for about six blocks, until passing the Teatre del Liceu on the left. Take the next left, C. Hospital, and the first true right off it to parking.*

From **Madrid**, **Zaragoza** *and west Barcelona stay on A-7 as it becomes the Ronda del Litoral. Take exit 21, Pl. Colom/Pl. de la Pau and head west along the wide Ramblas divided by a center strip for about six blocks, until passing the Teatre del Liceu on the left. Take the next left, C. Hospital, and the first true right off it to parking.*

What to See and Do

The pleasures extended by Barcelona encompass a wider spectrum than any other city in Spain. High on any list would be the sights of the **Barri Gòtic—the Cathedral** ★★, the **Frederic Marés Museum** ★★, the **Museum of the City of Barcelona**, the **Palau de la Géneralitat** ★, and the buildings of the **Plaça del Rei** ★. The **Ramblas** ★★ call for leisurely strolls. Nearby is the 14th-century church of **Santa Maria del Mar ★★**, off **Carrer Montcada ★**, a street of Renaissance mansions. On the summit of **Montjuïc** stands the **Museu d'Arte de Catalunya ★★★**, of wondrous medieval art, the ultramodern **Fundació Joan Miró ★**, and the **Olympic** stadia. In the newer part of the city, the Eixample, tower fantastic buildings by **Gaudí ★★**, including the incredible **Sagrada Família ★★★** church. In the Parque de la Ciutadella, northeast of the Barri Gòtic, is a **zoo**, while the extensive **Picasso Museum ★** is passed on the way. In such a large city, the most convenient plan is to visit sights by area, and we organize them that way.

> **Note:** the **Bus Turístic Cien (100)** *provides convenient transport to most of Barcelona's sights, leaving from outside the el Corte Inglés department store in the Pl. Catalunya at the west end of the Ramblas every half hour starting at 9 a.m., from mid-June until the middle of September. The bus stops at fifteen sights around the city, at any one of which passengers may get off to board again half an hour later for the next circuit. Multilingual members of the Tourist Board ride along to answer questions. The cost for a full day's ride is 1000 ptas., or 700 ptas. for half a day, payable on boarding.*

POLLUTION ALERT

Although Barcelona's beaches have been impressively restored, look for blue EC flags that indicate acceptable pollution levels before daring the water.

Barri Gòtic

This quarter is named for the dense concentration of Gothic buildings that create more of a medieval atmosphere than survives in any other city in the world. It encompasses the original city of Barcelona before its expansion, and includes traces from as far back as Roman times, pedestrian walks and a charming square.

At the corner of C. Hospital at the end of Rambla Sant Josep stands the small Pl. de la Boquería on the north side of the street. C. Boquería, more a shopping arcade than a street, heads north for a bit more than three blocks before changing its name to C. Coll and entering the charming Plaça Sant Jaume.

Plaça Sant Jaume   ★

Two Gothic buildings form the east and west borders of the plaza. On the east is the much restored **Ajuntament** (City Hall), generally with banners hanging from the second-story windows of its 19th-century facade. Its northern face along C. de la Ciutat is from the 15th-century. A dramatic black and gold mural by the 20th-century artist and architect Josep Sert resides inside, along with an impressive Gothic hall where the Consell de Cent, the ruling body of Barcelona, once met. *(Open Mon.–Sat. 9:30 a.m.–1:30 p.m. and 4:30–7:30 p.m.)* On the west side of the plaza stands the **Palau de la Géneralitat ★**, a grand 15th-century palace and, until recently, the seat of Catalonia's government. Walk west from the plaza along the north face of the palace to its entrance on C. Bisbe Irurita. Inside is an elegant

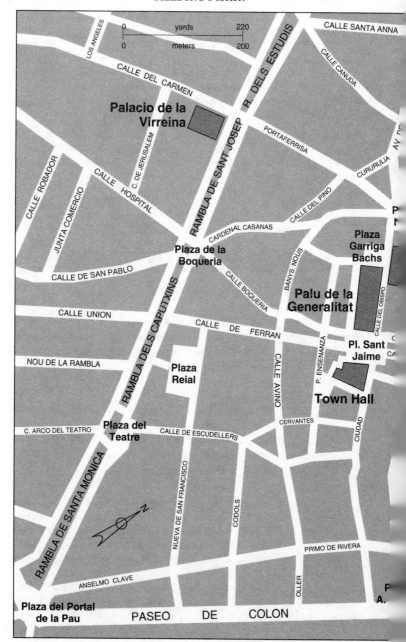

CENTRAL BARCELONA

Renaissance patio, an imposing 16th-century hall, and a lovely chapel dedicated to Saint George, the dragon-slayer—who is a patron saint of Barcelona as well as of Britain. A weathered 15th-century medallion of that saint on C. Bisbe Irurita marks the outside entrance to the patio. But you can't enter without special permission.

The narrow C. Bisbe Irurita is bordered on the right side by the **Casa de los Canonigos** *(Canons), connected to the Palau de la Géneralitat by a covered passageway overhead that looks eminently medieval, although constructed in 1926. At the end of Bisbe the plaza of the Cathedral opens,* **Plaça Nova***. Turning back to face the Cathedral, the* **Palacio de Bisbe** *on the right contains two soaring plain towers of a more weathered stone than the rest, grizzled because they remain from the fourth-century Roman walls of the town. The open plaza before the Cathedral is the place to see the local folkdance, the* Sardana*, danced to the accompaniment of fife and drum by parishioners after mass on Sundays.*

Cathedral   ★★

Pl. de la Seu, ☎ *315 15 54.*
Hours open: daily 7:30 a.m.–1:30 p.m. and 4–7:30 p.m. Cloister Museum open daily 11 a.m.–1 p.m.

Although the Cathedral was constructed in the 14th century, its facade is more recent—late 19th-century—designed to suit the Gothic interior. Inside, the church is harmonious in proportion, though wider in feeling than even normally wide Spanish Gothic churches. The whole is unfortunately dulled by blackened stone and a less spacious clerestory than eyes would wish.

In the center a trascoro in marble carved after designs by the great Bartolomé Ordoñez illustrates the martyrdom of Saint Eulalia by Romans in the 4th century. She was a native of Barcelona and is the patron saint of the Cathedral. The coro of two tiers of high stalls surmounted by individual spires is admirable. Upper tiers are emblazoned with the coats of arms of France, England, Portugal, Hungary, Poland, Sweden and The Netherlands, for here Carlos V convened kings to join his exclusive club—the Knights of the Golden Fleece.

Stairs at the foot of the altar descend to a crypt preserving remains of Saint Eulalia in a fine 14th-century marble sarcophagus attributed to Giovanni Pisano, but more likely by an unknown north Italian. The Gothic door to the sacristy and museum leads to 11th century wooden coffins of the founders of the original church on this site, Ramón Berenguer I and his wife.

Off the south transept stand an unusual cloister. Magnolias and palm trees surround a pond in which geese play in memory of their Capitoline ancestors. A small museum in the chapter house on the west side exhibits a collection of paintings. The most striking is the composition and faces of *Pieta* by Bartolomé Bermijo, with a most human-looking bespectacled priest. *Admission: 50 ptas.*

Pass around to the north side of the Cathedral to follow the narrow C. dels Contes de Barcelona along its flank. At number 10 on the left is the Frederic Marès Museum.

Museu Frederic Marès   ★★

Pl. De Sant Iù, 5-6, ☎ *310 58 00.*

Hours open: Tues.–Sat. 10 a.m.–2 p.m. and 4–7 p.m. Open Sun. 10 a.m.–2 p.m. Closed Mon.

The heart of the collection was gathered by a Catalan artist named Marès, who reconstructed the Gothic tombs of the Aragón kings at Poblet Monastery (described under that heading below). The top floor of the museum is a melange of everyday objects and advertisements that capture the spirit of design in the early part of this century. Displayed in the basement are early stone sculptures, including Roman, Moorish, Romanesque and Gothic pieces, gathered by this inveterate collector. On floors in between, beneath lovely ceilings, is a singular collection of polychromed wood sculpture—mostly from Catalonia, but also from elsewhere in Spain. *Admission: 250 ptas.*

Continue along C. dels Contes de Barcelona to take the first left into the Pl. del Rei.

Plaça del Rei   ★

Hours open: Tues.–Sat. 10 a.m.–2 p.m. and 4–7 p.m. Open Sun. 10 a.m.–2 p.m. Closed Mon.

The plaza is named for the 14th-century royal palace of the Kings of Aragón that occupies its far left, down a flight of stairs. One enters an immense arched Gothic audience hall, the Saló del Tinell, with a reconstructed wood ceiling. Among other rooms that may be visited is one with splendid murals of the Catholic Monarchs attending Columbus, for somewhere in this palace, perhaps in the Saló del Tinell, the Catholic Monarchs received Columbus after his first trip to the New World to hear the news of his amazing discoveries and weep together with joy. *Admission: free.*

Next to the palace stands its **Capilla de Santa Agata**, spare and moving with a fine altar and splendid painted wood ceiling. Its stained glass displays medieval coats-of-arms. Enter the chapel from the building on the right side of the plaza, the 15th-century Casa Padillàs, now the **Museu d'Història de la Ciutat**. The purpose of the museum is to show models of early buildings and various stages of Barcelona's growth, but, in the course of moving the building from its original site in the Eixample and digging a new foundation, Roman and Visigoth structures were discovered. So the most interesting sights reside in the basement where these ancient remains are displayed. *(Hours for the Museu are the same as for the palace; admission. 250 ptas.)*

The building on the near left side of the plaza is the 16th-century **Palau del Lloctinant**, now housing an astonishing collection of medieval records. For the average person a look in the courtyard at the grand stairway with its lovely ceiling will suffice.

Continue along C. dels Contes de Barcelona to the second left onto C. Libreteria. Take the second left again to enter the grassy Pl. Berenguer el Gran. Here is the best look at the remaining **Roman walls***, for the Chapel of Saint Agatha was built into them, and would have lost an outer wall if this* part of the Roman fortification had been torn down along with the rest. The walls were 27 feet thick in parts and 60 feet high, though not quite so elevated here. Return to the Pl. del Rei and go away from it along the apse of the Cathedral. At the end of the apse, tiny C. Paradis turns left. Where it bends right, the CEC Mountaineering Club stands at number 10. Walk inside to see the four pillars remaining from the Roman **Temple of Augustus**.

Montjuïc

Commanding both city and sea, this steep hill seems to call for a fortress. In more peaceful times its abundant land provides space for museums and athletic stadia, though it served for centuries as the cemetery of the city. The name presumably derives from *Mons Iovis*, Mount Jupiter in Latin. The best entrance, if driving, is from the Pl. Espanya. Head down the Ramblas to the sea. Turn right at the statue to Columbus and right again in one short block onto Av. del Paral-lel, which ends in about 15 blocks in the Pl. Espanya. A grand vista to the left leads up an equally grand stairway to the Palau Nacional.

Incidentally, the fountains are lighted at night and play to music on Sat. and Sun. at 10 p.m. in summer, 9 p.m. in winter. To the right of the start of the palace stairs is a reconstruction of the German Pavilion designed by Mies van der Rohe in 1929. Its Bauhaus elegance seems most ordinary today, although it caused an uproar when new because of its extreme contrast with the more traditional grandeur of the palace.

If car-less, Montjuïc is best reached by the funicular that runs from 11 a.m.–9:30 p.m. in summer, only on weekends in winter, and costs 165 ptas. Walk toward the sea along Rambla Caputxins for two blocks. Turn right on C. Nou de la Rambla for seven short blocks to Av. del Paral-lel and the funicular station. You exit on the hill near the Fundació Miró. Follow the directions below in reverse.

Palau Nacional, Museo de Arte de Catalunya   ★★★

Parc de Monjuïc, ☎ 423 71 99.

Hours open: Tues.–Sun. 9 a.m.–2 p.m. Closed Mon.

The grand boulevard leading from the Pl. Espanya, the fountains, the van der Rohe German Pavilion, and the palace itself all were built for a world's fair hosted by Barcelona in 1929. Today the palace houses the Museu d'Arte de Catalunya, one of the world's great assemblages of medieval art. Its collection of Romanesque painting is unsurpassed.

The reason for the excellence of the collection is that its works were appropriated by the government during the early 1900s from Romanesque and Gothic churches throughout Catalonia to protect the art both from thieves and natural deterioration. Although one way to amass a great collection, this seizure denuded parish churches throughout Catalunya.

Romanesque paintings alone fill 34 rooms. Special notice should be paid to the charming 12th- and 13th-century works, such as frescoes from Pedret, Bohi and

Santa María, and especially to the *Pantocrator* fresco from Sant Clemint de Taull, with a precocious use of foreshortening and a haunting gaze. Note the Byzantine feeling combined with attempts at portraiture. The Gothic period blossoms with the *Nativity* of Lluis Borrassa, and the precision of Bernat Martorell, then ascends to genius in Lluis Dalmau's *Verge dels Consellers*, and culminates in the retablos of Jaume Huguet. Although weakest in artworks from periods after the Gothic, the museum possesses paintings by Ribalta, Velázquez and Zurbarán, a fine Ribera, and lesser works by el Greco and Tintoretto. *Admission: 500 ptas.*

Poble Espanyol

Marqués de Comilias, ☎ *325 78 66. Follow the road west from the palace, Av. dels Montanyans, and turn right at the first opportunity.*
Hours open: daily 9 a.m.–8 p.m.
This "Spanish Village" is another survivor from the 1929 World's Fair. It is a collection of replicas of houses in different styles, presenting the variety found through Spain, amid a melange of souvenir and crafts shops, restaurants, and even amusement rides. Viewing these replicas obviously makes sense only for those who cannot see the real thing. The admission charge is steep, but the experience is pallid. For unfathomable reasons, the Spanish love it. *Admission: 650 ptas.*

Museu Arqueològic ★

Passaig de Santa madrona, 39-41, ☎ *423 21 49. Go east from the palace, taking the left fork along Passeig de Santa Madrona.*
Hours open: Tues.–Sat. 9 a.m.–1 p.m. and 4–7 p.m. Open Sun. 9:30 a.m.–1 p.m. Closed Mon.
This museum displays notable and rare Carthagenian jewelry discovered in the Balearic Islands, along with a fine selection of Celtiberian pieces. The collection is strong in Roman and Greek artifacts, mainly from excavations at nearby Empúries—note the bronze panther head and the *Venus of Empúries*. Interesting too are reconstructions of a Roman kitchen and atrium. The fittings of an actual Roman catapult are also on view. *Admission: 250 ptas., free on Sun.*

Fundació Miró ★

Pl. de Neptú, ☎ *329 19 08. Return along Santa Madrona back to the fork to curve around left. Turn left at Av. de Miramar for a few yards.*
Hours open: Tues.–Sat. 11 a.m.–7 p.m. Open Sun. 10:30 a.m.–2:30 p.m. Open Thurs. evening to 9:30 p.m. Closed Mon.
The all-white building designed by Josep Sert provides part of the pleasure, for it is perfectly suited to the bright colors of the art on its walls. Joan Miró was born in Barcelona, but lived in France in self-imposed exile during Franco's years. It was he who donated most of the artworks and the money to house them. The collection spans the breadth of his work, from sculptures, to tapestries, to mobiles, to precisely designed colorful paintings. The building is bright and airy, and the art makes one smile. *Admission: 500 ptas.*

Return along Av. de Miramar for the 70,000 seat Olympic Stadium, swimming pool, and other stadia. Note the covered Sant Jordi stadium of impressive Japanese design. Ahead on Av. de Miramar is the teleferique (cable car) that, for 325 ptas., rides up to the **Parc d'Atracciones***, a rather tame amuse-*

ment park, then continues up to the **castle** *at the summit of Montjuïc for 100 ptas. more. (The cable car runs weekdays from noon to 3 p.m. and from 4–8:30 p.m.; weekends from 11:30 a.m. to 8:30 p.m. In the winter it opens only on weekends.)*

Castell de Montjuïc

Parc de Montjuïc, ☎ *412 00 00.*

Hours open: Tues.–Sat. 10 a.m.–2 p.m. and 4–7 p.m. Open Sun. 10 a.m.–8 p.m., or to 2 p.m. in winter. Closed Mon.

The fortress was built in 1640 by the citizens of Barcelona during one of their rebellions against the rest of Spain. Although the English stormed it, followed later by the French and by Franco, it presents an imposing front. Unrivaled views over the city and sea are presented from the roof, but housed inside is the usual collection of military museums. *Admission: 150 ptas.*

The Ramblas ★★

The Ramblas consist of a wide pedestrian island bordered by two narrow streets that runs for just under one mile. Citizens and visitors alike love to passeo past kiosks selling newspapers, magazines, books and erotic comics, flower stalls, bird sellers, and impromptu entertainers. Every block or two the Ramblas change their name and character. None of the sights along the way are spectacular, but the walk continually presents precious surprises, and for many this will be the Barcelona remembered longest. Note that the Ramblas turn more seedy at night when they function as the city drug center. We start from the beginning of the Rambla Sant Josep, one long block west of the C. de l'Hospital, or three blocks east of the Pl. Catalunya.

On the southwest corner at number 99 stands the 18th-century **Palau de la Virreina**. Although named for his widow, it was built by a viceroy to Peru who skimmed a fortune from Peruvian silver. Today revolving exhibitions are presented, with a choice display of canvas treasures by Raphael, Van Dyke and Zurbarán on the second floor and a stamp collection on the top floor. *(Open Tues.–Sat. 10 a.m.–2 p.m. and 4:30–8:30 p.m.; open Sun. 10 a.m.–2 p.m., Mon. 4:30–9 p.m. Admission: 500 ptas.)*

Continue down Rambla Sant Josep toward the sea. On the right, half way along the block, is the entrance to a huge covered food market, called the **Boquería ★**, roofed in 1870's girdered ironwork. Walk through the market and out the rear entrance to see the 18th-century **Antic Hospital de la Santa Creu** across the parking lot. No longer a hospital, its patios are tranquil. Returning to the Rambla, a sidewalk mosaic by Miró is located near the corner.

Crossing C. de l'Hospital and the next street, C. de Sant Pau, brings the remains of the opera house of Barcelona at the next corner—the **Gran Teatre del Liceu**, one of the few buildings for true opera in Spain. A horrible fire consumed it in 1994. It had a rocky beginning too. On opening night in 1892, an anarchist threw two bombs into the audience, though performances were more ordinary afterward. Reconstruction is under way.

Now following Rambla del Caputxins, cross C. la Unio. On the left side of the street C. Colom leads into the **Plaça Reial ★**. This is a rare true plaza in Barcelona, surrounded by an arcade of homogeneous buildings. Palm trees wave and a fountain of the three graces decorates the center, whose streetlamps were designed by Gaudí. Today the square is slightly seedy with bars all around, but on Sundays it comes to life with a philatelic and numismatic market.

Continuing a few feet down the Rambla, turn right onto C. Nou de la Rambla. At number 3 is the **Palau Güell ★ ★**, an early building by Gaudí. Since it now functions as a museum (for theater memorabilia), it is the rare civil building by this eccentric architect open to the public. Don't miss it! *(Open weekdays 11 a.m.–2 p.m. and 5 p.m.–8 p.m., weekend 4–8 p.m. Admission: 200 ptas.)*

The Rambla grows less attractive from this point on. At its end stands a solemn statue of Columbus pointing over the wrong sea. To his left, the first street north, C. Banca, holds the **Museu de Cera de Barcelona**, one of those wax museums that every large European city seems to have. *(Open Mon.–Sat. 11 a.m.–2 p.m. and 5–8 p.m. Admission: 750 ptas.)*

To Columbus' right, in a barn of an old building, is the **Museu Maritim ★** . The building, called the Drassens Reials, is worth the visit. Dating from the 14th century, it is the only surviving medieval shipyard in Europe. The collection inside features an exact model of the galley *La Real*, flagship of Prince Don Juan during the great battle of Lepanto against the Turks in 1571. *(Open Tues.–Sat. 10 a.m.–2 p.m. and 4–7 p.m. Open Sun. 10 a.m.–2 p.m. Admission: 200 ptas.)* Floating in the harbor opposite the far side of the Maritime Museum is a replica of Columbus' flagship, the **caravel Santa Maria ★** . Its tiny size is a shock that evokes appreciation for the courage of those who sailed so insubstantially past the end of the known world. The ship may be toured, using the ticket from the Maritime Museum. *(Open daily 9 a.m.–2 p.m. and 3 p.m.–sunset.)*

Along the water, north of the port, stands Barcelona's latest example of urban development, constructed to serve as the 1992 Olympic village, and then to be sold for expensive condominiums. Beside the ocean stretches a wide ocean promenade and beach, yacht clubs, bars and restaurants. Here is where Barcelona's hip crowd takes a pleasant but lively passeo in the evening. Tapas tend to be good and fresh seafood is available (for suggestions, look for Moll del Gregal addresses in the restaurant reviews following).

The Eixample

The area known as the Eixample was constructed above the western end of the Barri Gòtic in the middle of the 19th century to proclaim a modern age for Barcelona. Streets run straight as arrows, intersecting at right angles to form the clean lines of a grid. Its design represented both the rationality and egalitarianism of the time through orderly homogeneity. By the original plan, each block would be a square of the same size, every 200 squares would contain a hospital, every 25 a school. However, the program was only haphazardly carried through.

The buildings raised along these streets were separately commissioned by individuals and companies, but most aimed to incorporate the latest ideas in architecture—to express the spirit of the modern. Hence, the young Gaudí found several commissions here, along other noted Catalan architects of his era. Most of their buildings no longer remain, as changing ideas of what was contemporary led to replacement by later models, but enough survive to give this area the most extensive collection of art nouveau architecture in the world.

Guided tours of *Modernista* architecture are given Tuesday, Wednesday and Thursday at 3 p.m. by the Guide Bureau at *54 Via Laietana (☎ 310 77 78)*, just east of the Picasso Museum. The tours take about two hours and cost about $7. The Bureau will arrange individual tours at other times.

Passeig de Gràcia remains the most elegant street of the Eixample. It is lined with stylish shops, banks and fancy apartments, but one side of a single block of Passeig de Gràcia retains enough early 20th-century buildings to earn the playful name "Manzana de la Discordia" ★—the Block of Discord.

Pas. de Gràcia begins at the Pl. de Catalunya with its fountains. The plaza lies four blocks west of the Pl. Nova, fronting the Cathedral. It is also the western terminus of the Ramblas, about three blocks west of the Rambla Sant José. Pas. de Gràcia leaves the northwest corner of the plaza and heads west beside the el Corte Inglés department store.

Three blocks west along Passeig de Gràcia, bordered by street lamps designed by Gaudí, C. del Consell de Cent is crossed. Here begins the "Block of Discord." Stay on the north side of Pas. de Gràcia for the full view of the buildings opposite, then cross over to inspect their details.

The principle of this early modern movement was the opposite of what governed later 20th-century design. Clean lines, smooth, even-textured materials, the simplest and straightest shapes all characterize architecture in our time, but the *modernista* movement from the late 19th-century found inspiration in the curves and irregularities of nature, not in mathematical precision. To our eyes such buildings seem playful, full of unexpected turns and details, and serve as an antidote for the uniform simplicity whose familiarity has bred, if not contempt, at least a kind of boredom. The proof that we hardly look at contemporary buildings lies in how arresting these earlier fantasies are.

First, at number 35, is the **Casa Lleó Morera**, designed by a famed Gaudí contemporary named Domènech i Montaner. Only the upper two floors remain from his design, but grow enough flowers and beasts to give a sense of how exotic and Gothic in feel it must once have been. The interior is more elegant than what the exterior leads one to expect and incorporates the finest craftsmanship. Although the building is commercial, among its clients is the Patronat de Turisme on the third floor in a stunning apartment. Perhaps some question about the promotion of tourism will occur to you; if so, call ☎ *302 06 08*.

At number 41 stands the pyramid-topped medieval-looking **Casa Amatller**, designed by another Gaudí contemporary—Puig i Cadafalch. The interior is again elegant, though not open to the public. However, the art institute on the second floor often responds to sincere inquiries to show visitors around their office. The **Casa Batlló** next door at number 43, is Gaudí's exercise in blue-green tiles. This was his interpretation of the cave of St. George's dragon, with balconies suggesting skulls, beneath the sinuous dragon of a roof. The front doors seem to undulate as if made of soft material—understandably Salvador

Dali admired them. Admission requires advance permission, but a quick peek from outside is allowed.

Two blocks farther west, occupying the corner of the south side of the street at number 92, is Gaudí's most imposing building, an apartment complex named **Casa Milà**, though known familiarly as "La Pedrera" (The Stone Quarry). The exterior looks like a massive fortress melting. Ironwork balconies are intricate assemblages of matted vegetable-like matter, each unique. Chimneys on the roof remind of the shapes children produce by dripping wet sand. In this case a free tour, at least of the roof, is available to the public. *(Tours on Tues.–Sat. at 10 a.m., 11 a.m., noon and 1 p.m. by calling ☎ 487 36 13 in advance.)*

Turn left in one block for a few steps along C. d'Aranyó to number 255. Here is the **Fundació Antoni Tàpies**, another building by Domènech i Montaner in an Islamic-influenced style. Towering over its roof is metal sculpture by the artist Antoni Tàpies, whose works the building now exhibits. *(Open Tues.–Sun. 11 a.m.–8 p.m.; Admission: 400 ptas.)*

North in 11 blocks along C. de Provence waits the incomparable Gaudí church of Sagrada Família, but a slight detour along the way presents two more *modernista* buildings. Continue along Pas. de Gràcia to turn right in three blocks to reach the **Pilau Quadras** at *Av. Diagonal 373*. This is another building by Puig i Cadafalch, whose interior with its sculpture and mosaics is stunning, and entrance is both allowed and free, for it is now a museum of musical instruments. *(Open Tues.–Sun. 9 a.m.–2 p.m.)* One block further north along the Diagonal on the opposite side of the street at 416 stands the huge **Casa de les Punxes**, like a Gothic castle.

> *Continue one block farther on Diagonal to take C. Provenca that forks off to the left. It leads in six blocks to Sagrada Família.*

Sagrada Família ★★★

C. Mallorca, 401, ☎ 455 02 47.
Hours open: daily 9 a.m.–8 p.m. (closes at 7 p.m. in winter).
Work began on a rather ordinary neo-Gothic church in 1882. Two years later the architect resigned and Gaudí won the commission to complete it. It remained his favorite project until he died in 1926. Work proceeded slowly, since funds were inadequate, and private commissions would take Gaudí away from his work on the church for years at a time. For the last ten years of his life Gaudí lived in a small room on the church grounds, for the project consumed him, and he spoke of it as needing two centuries to complete. In 1926, absentmindedly crossing a street, he was struck by a trolley and killed. Since then the issue has been whether or not to finish the church. Gaudí left an awesome, but roofless structure, too incomplete to function as a church and of a design so personal that no one could complete it as he would have. Anarchists burned all of Gaudí's plans during the Civil War. Nonetheless, work, financed in large part by admission fees, has been under way since 1979 to finish the church with an intent to be as faithful to Gaudí's conception as possible. The problem is that Gaudí himself worked from the inspiration of the moment as much as from blueprints.

Only the west façade of three envisioned by Gaudí was finished by the time of his death, but what an awesome facade it is, of a spirit recognizably Gothic translated into modern idioms. The façade represents Christ's birth in carved scenes that seem to grow from the stone around the portals. Study the fine details and wonder at the overall conception. Fear of the power of an unrestrained imagination causes some people to feel a strong aversion to the building, but most agree that the building is spiritual, awesome and playful, providing a wholly unforgettable experience. *Admission: 600 ptas.; 150 ptas. more to ride to the tower top.*

North of the Barri Gòtic

Via Laietana forms the north border of the Barri Gòtic. It can be reached either by going north one block from the Pl. Nova in front of the Cathedral, or by continuing through the Pl. Sant Jaume along C. Jaume I for four very short blocks. At Pl. de l'Angel where Via Laietana intersects with C. Jaume I, take C. de la Princesa north (straight).

Turn down the fourth right along C. de Montcada onto **C. Montcada** ★*, a street declared a national monument for all the mansions that line it. At number 15, on the right is the* **Palau Berenguer d'Aguilar***, a 15th-century mansion that houses the* **Picasso Museum***. Opposite is the 14th-century* **Palau dels Marques de Lleó***, at number 12, displaying an extensive collection of Spanish clothing and other apparel (open Tues.–Sat. from 10 a.m. until 2 p.m. and from 4:30 p.m. until 7 p.m.; admission: 200 ptas.). More 15th-century mansions stand at numbers 14, 23 and 25 (home of a branch of the French Galería Maeght run by the founder's children), ending with the baroque, forbidding* **Palau Dalmases** *at number 20.*

Museo Picasso   ★

 C. Montcada, 15-17, ☎ 319 63 10.
 Hours open: Tues.–Sun. 10 a.m.–7:30 p.m. Open Sun. 10 a.m.–3 p.m.
 Two things make this an interesting museum. Of course the first is the artworks displayed. Although this is far from the finest assemblage of Picassos, and does not contain many of the artist's more familiar works, the collection is the largest in the world, strong in childhood drawings and paintings of the seminal "Blue Period." The second note of interest is that the building is composed of two 14th-century mansions remodeled and joined. Against all expectations they provide a fine setting for the modern art on their walls. *Admission: 500 ptas.*

At the end of C. Montcada, on the right, stands the rear of the church of **Santa Maria del Mar***.*

Santa María del Mar   ★★

 Pl. de Santa María.
 Hours open: Mon.–Fri. 9 a.m.–1 p.m. and 5–8 p.m.
 Barcelona's most dramatic church was finished in the 14th century to epitomize the Gothic style as interpreted in Catalonia. Although the west octagonal tower was not added until five centuries later, the remainder of the outside is early, and celebrated for its west portal. Note the solid buttresses surrounding the church, so different

from the "flying" French versions. The interior was gutted of its baroque decoration during the Spanish Civil War, which restored its original Gothic lines. The nave is high, the vaulting unusually wide, and the adjoining aisles narrow to emphasize spaciousness. Pillars are set more widely than in any other Gothic church in order to carry the eye to the apse behind. Instead of a solid wall, the high altar is formed of soaring columns connected by narrow arches. Chapels along the aisles seem denuded, although fine stained glass windows provide their own decoration. *Admission: free.*

Return to C. Montcada and continue across on Passeig del Born to reach the beginning of the **Parc de la Ciutadella** *in four blocks.*

Parc de la Ciutadella

At the beginning of the 18th-century, after Barcelona had taken arms against the national government yet one more time, an angry Felipe V razed blocks of houses to build a fortress for cowing the citizens. A century and a half later the citizens got their revenge by razing his fortress to turn it into a lovely city park, and placed museums and a zoo within its ample confines.

The layout is as follows. Ahead on the left is the **Geology Museum**, of interest to those who know about such things. A short distance to its left stands the **Castell del Tre Dragons**, originally a modernista cafe erected by Domènech for the 1888 Exhibition held in the park, but now a museum displaying almost every kind of dead animal. The building is most interesting architecturally as a harbinger of the *modernista* movement. *(Open Tues.–Sun. 9 a.m.–2 p.m. Closed Sun. Admission: 250 ptas.)*

To the right of the Geology Museum is the **Umbraculo**, a lovely conservatory of tropical plants. Straight ahead in about two blocks' distance are the gardens and lakes of the park, including the **Font de Aurora**, a work on which Gaudí assisted. To the right of the lakes and fountains stands the **Palau de la Ciudadela**, what remains of the fortress of Felipe V after the rest was torn down. Today the palace houses the Catalan Parliament and the **Museum of Modern Art**. Pre-modern would be a more accurate name, for, despite an occasional Picasso or Miró, most of the works are by earlier Catalans. Some of the modernista furniture is appealing. *(Open Tues.–Sat. 9 a.m.–7 p.m. Open Sun. 9 a.m.–3 p.m., and Mon. 3–7 p.m. Admission: 400 ptas.)*

Continuing south (right), is the **Parc Zoológic**. While there may be larger collections of animals elsewhere, only this zoo offers an albino gorilla. His name is *Copito de Nieve* (Snowflake). The dolphin and orca show enchants everyone. *(Open daily 9:30 a.m.–7:30 p.m.; closes at 5 p.m. in winter; admission: 900 ptas.)*

Parque Güell ★

Funded by his patron Güell, Gaudí began work in 1900 on a planned community of houses—a housing development—to express his ideas of urban design. He planned a grand entrance area, spaces for 60 houses, shaded walks and a shopping plaza. Gaudí personally designed every element including furniture for the houses that were completed—nothing was bought ready-made. Such painstaking design took time, so, by the 14th year of the project, only the entrance to the park, the agora-like market, a grotto, pagoda, some walks and one house had been finished, in which Gaudí lived. Güell decided he could pour no more money into the project, so it remains in precisely that state today.

By car drive west along Pas. de Gràcia for two miles to the large green Pl. Fernando Lesseps. Turn right around the plaza along Travesera de Dalt. Take the second left onto Av. de la Muntanya. The sixth right along C. Olot crosses the entrance to the park.

By public transportation, take the green line, number 3, toward Montbau, getting off at the Lesseps stop. From there it's a six block walk uphill. Or take the #24 bus that runs along Pas. de Gràcia and goes to the park entrance.

Hours open: daily 10 a.m.–9 p.m., or to 6 p.m. in winter. The Casa-Museu Gaudí is open daily 10 a.m.–1:30 p.m. and 4:30–7 p.m.

No one would think from the entrance that it introduced a housing development. The ironwork gates are intricate, the staircase grand although bordered by homier mosaic walls, while at the top stands a classical structure of ionic columns. Walking up, one discovers that the columns are formed of mosaics guarded by a sumptuous blue dragon. The pavilion at the end, consisting of a forest of columns, was intended as a community shopping area, quite unlike any mall in our experience. Look at the undulating ceiling, a mosaic fantasy. Walks behind this pavilion lead to a square lined by Gaudí benches peacefully overlooking all of Barcelona.

Wander over bridges, elevated paths and through a grotto to the **Casa-Museu Gaudí**, at the rear of the park. Inside are many of the designs, including furniture, that Gaudí constructed for his planned community. *Admission to the park is free. The museum costs 200 ptas.*

Where to Stay

When it hosted the 1992 Olympics, Barcelona built 12 major new hotels which increased rooms in the city by a third, easing some of the hotel pressure. Just this year we are seeing prices decline in select instances by as much as a third with this increased supply. Still, room costs in Barcelona stand with Marbella as the highest in Spain and burden visitors' budgets. On the other hand, Barcelona does tender some lovely hotels.

The premier location would be on or near the Ramblas, convenient to both sights and shopping. But given that Barcelona provides a subway system, it is possible to stay outside of this center if near a subway stop, and commute. Such a location is a decided second best, however, to the Ramblas area with its opportunity for serendipitous walks.

Very Expensive ($200+)

Ritz   **Deluxe ★★★★★**

Gran Via de les Corts Catalanes, 668 (Corts Catalanes cuts across the top of the Barri Gòtic one block west of Pl. Catalunya. The hotel is one block west and three north of Pl. Catalunya.), ☎ *318 52 00, FAX 318 01 48, Telex 52739.*

If you want the best, here it is. By any measure the Ritz ranks with the finest hotels in the world. It was built in the belle époque style of 1919, and a recent face-lift has made its elegance dazzle again. The entrance—all chandeliers, gilded mirrors and flowers—is as grand as can be, but, in this case, the hotel is not merely a lobby. Its rooms are among the most spacious and beautiful in Spain. Many contain marble fireplaces (though not lit these days), and huge baths in bathrooms the size of some other hotels' bedrooms. Even if its accommodations were merely ordinary, the Ritz would still be worth a stay for the service—you will find no more attentive staff and knowledgeable concierges anywhere. Of course it costs in the 40,000 peseta range, but that is only money. *148 rooms, plus 13 suites.*

Claris   **Deluxe ★ ★ ★**

Pau Claris, 150 (one block north and two west of the Pl. de Catalunya), ☎ *487 62 62, FAX 215 79 11.*
The building is a lovely 19th-century neoclassic, done post-modern inside. Antiques abound from English, to Hindu, to French; and a Japanese garden adds just the touch for this eclectic mix. The owner collects Egyptian antiquities—thus the framed pages from the *Description d'Egypt* on the walls and a small museum of his collection. Don't worry, the bedrooms are tastefully new. As a bonus, prices drop almost 50 percent on weekends to the barely expensive. *106 rooms, plus 18 suites.*

Le Meridien Barcelona   **Deluxe ★ ★ ★**

Ramblas 111 (actually one block south of the R. bels Estudis), ☎ *318 62 00, FAX 301 77 76, Telex 54634.*
This is the latest reincarnation of a 50s hotel called the Manila. Now the up-scale Meridian chain is trying its hand at the property. The original hotel had a prime location, now it is raised up to modern snuff in conveniences and comfort. Incidently, prices dip down in the merely expensive range on weekends. *198 rooms, plus seven suites.*

Condes de Barcelona   **1st-class ★**

Passeig de Gràcia, 75 (six blocks west of the Pl. de Catalunya), ☎ *484 86 00, FAX 488 06 14, Telex 51531.*
The building is the striking 1894 former mansion of the Batllós for whom Gaudí also designed a building farther down the passeig. The renovation of the public rooms is exquisite. Its location is convenient for boutique shopping and only a six-block walk to the Ramblas and Barri Gòtic. That's the good part. The bad is that the hallways are dingy, paint is peeling in some bedrooms and, worst, some contain unpleasant odors. The annex across the street, also housed in a modernista mansion, is more spic, span and odor free. *110 rooms, plus 71 in an annex, plus two suites.*

Expensive ($100–$200)

Avenida Palace   **1st-class ★ ★ ★**

Gran Via de les Corts Catalanes, 605 (one block north of Pl. Catalunya), ☎ *301 96 00, FAX 318 12 34, Telex 54734.*
This fine hotel was built in 1952 in the grand Rococo style of an earlier era. Inside, all is marble, brass, flowers and lovely stuccowork, with a pair of elegant stairways leading up from the lobby. The rooms are very comfortable, if somewhat overdone. The location beats that of the Ritz at half the price. *147 rooms, plus 18 suites.*

Regente   **1st-class ★ ★**

Rambla de Catalunya, 76 (five blocks west of Pl. de Catalunya), ☎ *487 59 89, FAX 487 32 27, Telex 51939.*
Its townhouse-intimacy, modernista front, tastefully decorated rooms and lovely roof terrace all deserve raves. Now that it has reduced its prices by a third to the bor-

der of expensive territory, so does its value. Hooray as well for its location. But service and accessories are not quite first-class. *78 rooms.*

Rivoli Rambla   1st-class ★ ★

Rambla dels Estudis, 128, ☎ *302 66 43, FAX 317 50 53, Telex 99222.*
The slick, modern style is perfect for Barcelona; the hotel is small enough for intimacy and the location is superior. All that prevents us from praising this establishment even more is the small size of the rooms for such prices. *81 rooms, plus nine suites.*

Majestic   1st-class ★ ★

Passeig de Gràcia, 70 (five blocks west of the Pl. de Catalunya), ☎ *488 17 17, FAX 488 18 80, Telex 52211.*
Think of this as two hotels, each with a fine location for shopping, but the front rooms, in a former townhouse, are spacious and attractive, while the back rooms, in a huge extension, are drab and overlook nothing. Only the front rooms merit two stars. *328 rooms, plus one suite.*

Princesa Sofía   Deluxe ★ ★

Plaça Pius XII (opposite the university, two miles southwest of the center along Av. Diagonal), ☎ *330 71 11, FAX 330 76 21, Telex 51032.*
Of the modern hotels in Spain this one ranks with the best managed—remarkable, given the large number of rooms. And it offers every facility. Recently redecorated, the rooms themselves are both spacious and comfortably modern. However, the hotel is located too far from the center for walking (though the Maria Cristina subway stop waits a block away). On the other hand, it has just cut its prices by a third to fit into the expensive range rather than flying high above it. *481 rooms, plus 24 suites.*

Gran Derby   1st-class ★ ★

C. Loreto, 28 (Follow Av. Diagonal northwest to Pl. Francisc Macia, a circle with fountain. Take the left onto Av. J. Tarradellas, then the first right onto Av. de Sarria for a short block to C. Loreto.), ☎ *322 20 62, FAX 410 08 62, Telex 97429.*
The hotel is expensive (although barely so) and, although situated in a quiet neighborhood, is both three miles from the center of town and a fair distance from the nearest subway stop. It is recommended because the rooms are superbly tasteful and huge. All include a separate sitting room, and two-bedroom suites are available. For two couples traveling together, or for a family, such an arrangement could prove cost-effective. Don't confuse it with its more ordinary annex, called the Derby, a few doors down. *31 rooms, plus 12 suites.*

Colón   1st-class ★ ★

Av. de Catedral, 7 (across the plaza fronting the Cathedral), ☎ *301 14 04, FAX 317 29 15, Telex 52654.*
After a recent renovation, the Colón again offers comfort and style, although we feel some nostalgia for the eccentric, if threadbare, former look. We see enough Laura Ashley at home. Its location is most convenient (although the bells of the Cathedral chime outside the windows). Sixth-floor rooms with balconies over the plaza are preferred. To compensate, it has reduced its prices to mid-way in the expensive range. *138 rooms, plus nine suites.*

Moderate ($50–$99)

España   2nd-class ★ ★ ★

C. Sant Pau 9-11 (just south of the Ramblas by the Teatre del Liceu), ☎ 315 22 11, FAX
317 11 34.
The location of this old Barcelona standard is terrific, with the Ramblas just around
the corner. The elegant inside, designed by the great modernista architect
Domènech i Montaner, is a treat and the rooms were thoroughly remodeled and
upgraded for the Olympics. This is one special hotel for the price. 84 rooms.

Montecarlo   2nd-class ★ ★

Rambla dels Estudis, 124, ☎ 317 58 00, FAX 317 57 50, Telex 93345.
The look of the marble entrance and wooded reception area is the way we think of
Barcelona. Location on the Ramblas is a great plus. Accommodations are suffi-
ciently comfortable, and the prices, for a change, are fair. 80 rooms.

Gran Via   2nd-class ★ ★ ★

Gran Via de les Corts Catalanes, 642 (one block west of the Pl. de Catalunya), ☎ 318 19
00, FAX 318 99 97.
The hotel is a turn-of-the-century mansion retaining some of the original decor
including a grand neoclassic staircase and palm ringed courtyard. The breakfast area
is a hall of mirrors. Guest rooms are not quite up to the elegance of the rest of the
building, but are slowly being renovated. About half are now new and stylish, the
rest are threadbare, so look before you book. Front rooms have views, but note that
they also include noise. 53 rooms.

Rialto   3rd-class ★ ★

C. Ferrán, 42 (one block south of the Pl. de Sant Jaume in the Barri Gòtic), ☎ 318 52
12, FAX 315 38 19, Telex 97206.
This hotel, along with the Suizo and Gòtico that follow, is owned by the Gargallo
Company and similar in tasteful decors, intimacy and exceptional location. All three
would be ideal if the tour groups hadn't discovered them. 141 rooms.

Suizo   2nd-class ★ ★

Pl. del Angel, 12 (this plaza is two blocks behind the back of the Cathedral and north
beside Via Laietana), ☎ 315 41 11, FAX 315 38 19, Telex 97206.
Perhaps because it is smaller than its two sisters above, we slightly prefer the Suizo.
Like the others, the decor is charming, and the service is respectful. Go for one of
the attic rooms with skylights and parquet floors. 48 rooms.

Gòtico   2nd-class ★ ★

C. Jaume I, 14 (three short blocks north of the Pl. de Sant Jaume in the Barri Gòtic),
☎ 315 22 11, FAX 315 38 19, Telex 97206.
White walls and floors set off dark wood furniture in this elegant little hotel, other
wise similar to the Rialto and Suizo. Similar also is a location hard to better. 83
rooms.

Mesón Castilla   3rd-class ★

C. Valldoncella, 5 (at the western end of Rambla Estudis C. Tallers angles left leading to
the hotel in four blocks), ☎ 318 21 82, FAX 412 40 20.
The neighborhood is quiet and lovely, more of an asset than the rooms. Although
the location requires a four- to six-block walk to the sights, the stroll is pleasant
enough to repay the exercise. There are modernista touches to the outside, and

rooms are comfortable enough (only half are air-conditioned), though of no great distinction. *56 rooms.*

Gaudí   2nd-class ★

C. Nou de la Rambla, 12 (a few steps south of the Rambla Caputxins, opposite the Palau Güell), ☎ *412 26 36.*

This hotel is recommended for its fine location and for a unique view from rooms on the upper floors. The rooftop of the Palau Güell opposite is a fantasy of shapes that can only be seen from these hotel windows. Otherwise, this hotel is ordinary, although at the bottom of the moderate range. *73 rooms.*

Regencia Colón   2nd-class ★

C. Sagristans, 13 (a half block west of the Hotel Colón), ☎ *318 98 58, FAX 317 28 22, Telex 98175.*

This is the annex for the Hotel Colón discussed above. It lacks the charm and views of its sister, but provides a fine location and slightly dowdy comfort at a third off its price. *55 rooms.*

San Augustín   2nd-class ★

Pl. Sant Agusti, 3 (this plaza is one block south of the Rambla Sant Josep along C. de l'Hospital), ☎ *318 17 08, FAX 317 29 28, Telex 98121.*

Proximity to the Ramblas and sights make this hotel worth considering. It is also across the street from the market. Alas, rooms are ordinary. *77 rooms.*

Inexpensive (Less than $50)

Nouvel   3rd-class ★ ★ ★

C. Santa Ana 18-20 (the street goes north from the western end of Rambla Estudis), ☎ *301 82 74, FAX 301 83 70.*

This hotel is attractively decorated in a *modernista* style. Rooms have just been renovated and are ample for the price. Best of all, the service is conscientious. *55 rooms.*

Lausanne   P2nd-class ★ ★

Av. Portal de l'Angel, 24 (just east of the southern end of the Pl. Catalunya), ☎ *302 11 39.*

For the low price you get a room with some size and style, and the management is most professional. The location is good, if a few blocks from the sights. So much for the price is a true find in Barcelona. *17 rooms, half with showers.*

Rey Don Jaime I   3rd-class ★

C. Jaume I, 11 (just south of Pl. Jaume in the Barri Gòtic), ☎ *315 41 61.*

Its location in the Barri Gòtic is the most notable feature of this hostale. The staff is willing, but the rooms are undistinguished, however, the prices are rock bottom. *30 rooms.*

Cortés   3rd-class ★

C. Santa Ana 25 (across the street from the Nouvel described previously), ☎ *317 91 12, FAX 301 31 35, Telex 98215.*

Basic accommodations are provided in a neighborhood convenient to both sights and shopping. The hotel is not as attractive as the Novel above, but rooms are comfortable and even less expensive. *45 rooms.*

Residencia Australia **Hs2nd-class ★**

Ronda Universitat, 11 (the street goes north across the western end of Pl. de Catalunya), ☎ *317 41 77.*

Named for the country in which the owner lived for 20 years, this hostale exhibits exceptional concern for guests. The location is not far from the sights, adjacent to an extension of the University of Barcelona. *23 rooms, half with baths.*

Hostal Residencia Palacios **P2nd-class ★**

Gran Via de les Corts Catalanes, 629bis (opposite the Office of Tourism, one block west and two north of the Pl. Catalunya), ☎ *301 37 92.*

The rooms have more style than usual in this rock-bottom price range. Not all the bathrooms have showers, but such a room can be requested. *25 rooms, half with shower.*

Hotel Residencia Oliva **P2nd-class ★**

Passeig de Gràcia, 32, 4th floor (on the "Block of Discord" near Gaudí's Calla Batlló), ☎ *317 50 87.*

The rooms are somewhat more roomy than this price range usually provides, if a little dark, and it is fun to stay on this street of elegant shops and unusual architecture. *16 rooms, no showers.*

Youth Hostels

Albergue Juvenal Palau

C. Palau, 6 (behind the Ajundament off Pl. de Sant Jaume in the heart of the Barri Gòtic), ☎ *412 50 80.*

No youth hostel in Spain is better located. The only trouble is the small size which makes reserving imperative. 1100 ptas. buys breakfast as well.

Albergue Juvenal Mare de Déu de Montserrat

Passaig Mare de Déu del Coll, 41 (out past Park Güell; take bus 28 from the Pl. Catalunya), ☎ *210 51 51.*

As different from the Palau above as can be imagined. Out of things completely, but a villa surrounded by woods and panoramic views. Expensive at 1300 and a lot of rules, such as a five day maximum stay.

Where to Eat

By mingling French ideas with Spanish, Barcelona serves some of the best food in Spain. *Bullabesa (suquet de peix,* in Catalan), the French fish stew bouillabaisse, is available, but the specialty stew is the less elegant *sarsuela,* a "comic opera" of seafood. Since the south of France influences Catalan cuisine, Italian-style dishes migrate to Barcelona menus. *Pa amb tomàquet,* bread soaked with olive oil and spread with tomato, is the usual appetizer; pastas, such as macaroni, will often be seen. Catalans dine very late. The normal dinner hour is 10 p.m., and restaurants do not open in the evening much before that time. Although Barcelona boasts a large number of the finest restaurants in all Spain, exalted prices make it possible for a diner to pay 15,000 pesetas at the most expensive. Of course, no one is forced to splurge, for Barcelona contains modest restaurants where good meals are available for 2000 pesetas as well. And there is a McDonald's, among other inexpensive eateries.

Before dinner consider a champagne bar, called a *xampanyeria,* to sample glasses of various Spanish brands while munching *tapas.* A rather elegant one is **La Cava del Palau** at *C. Verdaguer i Callis, 10* (go north along the front of the Cathedral to Via Laietana in one block, west for a block along Laietana, right along C. Sant Pere, to the first left). Munch on cheeses, pâtés, smoked fish or anchovies. (Closed Sun. ☎ 310 09 38) A more earthy example, brightened by charming tiles, is **El Xampanyet** at *C. Montcada, 22* (head north from Pl. Jaume in the Barrio Gòtico to reach C. Prinesa which leads to the Picasso Museum in three blocks and C. Montcada). *(Closed Mon. ☎ 319 70 03.)*.

Rather than a full dinner, consider munching on tapas during a pleasant stroll along the renovated area north of the port, the Moll Olimpic. You can follow the crowd to dine where they do, or try our favorites, *Tick Tack Toe* and *El Cangrejo Loco*, which we note later in this section.

Expensive ($30+)

Neichel

> *Av. de Pedralbes, 16bis (Av. Pedralbes heads northwest from Pl. Pius XII, which is at the southern end of Diagonal. The restaurant is in the third alley on the right.),* ☎ *203 84 08, FAX 205 63 69.*
> *Closed Saturday for lunch, Sunday, Christmas week, Holy Week and August.*

To cite one restaurant as the best in Barcelona is certain to provoke argument. With some trepidation we offer this one. True, it is not as beautiful as some others, since it is installed in a modern housing complex. Also, the cooking is as much French as Spanish, since its owner hails from Alsace. But no chef in Spain is more thoughtful about his food. The *menu de degustació* is very expensive, but presents the best the restaurant offers which is exceptional indeed. Save room for extraordinary cheeses and desserts. Our only complaint is that the atmosphere is so serious and formal that it is hard to lose oneself in the pure joys of the food. Reservations are required. Credit Cards: A, D, M, V.

Can Gaig

> *Pas. de Maragall, 402 (located in the far west of the city, a 15-minute taxi ride is simplest, although the Maragal subway stop from either the 4 or 5 line brings you to within six blocks),* ☎ *429 10 17.*
> *Closed Mon., holiday evenings, Holy Week and August.*

If you want the best of pure Catalan cooking, here it is. Not prettified, not served in dramatic or romantic surroundings, just food that brings the pure pleasure of good taste. The beautiful people will be at El Dorado Petit or Via Veneto, the gourmets will be Neichel, or here if they are Catalans. Gaig's version of suquet is sublime, lobster ravioli is a delight and the pigeon roasted in its own juices is unrivaled. The chef is talented, imaginative and serious about his craft. True, the loveliness of surroundings that can add so much to the total dining experience is not offered here, but the food ranks above what those pretty places serve. Reservations are imperative. Credit Cards: A, D, M, V.

Eldorado Petit

> *C. Dolors Monserda, 51 (Located about four km northwest of Pl. Catalunya in the area known as Sarria—it is best to take a taxi.),* ☎ *204 51 53, FAX 280 57 02.*
> *Closed Sun.*

Undeniably this restaurant stands among the best in Barcelona, and many people place it at the top. The food is insistently *nueva cocina*, inventive and the most beautiful we have ever seen. Housed in a turn-of-the-century summer house with a lovely covered patio for summer dining, the decor is as elegant as the food. Mushroom and truffle salad can be followed by scallops with leeks or roast pigeon stuffed with foie gras. Prices are a bit below the exalted Neichel level. Credit Cards: A, M, V.

Botafumeiro ★★★

C. Mayor de Gràcia, 81 (Mayor de Gràcia is the continuation of Pas. de Gràcia, after it crosses Diagonal. The restaurant is located four blocks farther along the street.), ☎ *218 42 30, FAX 415 58 48.*

The restaurant is named after the giant censor swung in the Cathedral of Santiago de Compostela, for the owner migrated from Galicia. He misses home so he flies his fish in daily to Barcelona. Need we mention that this is the best pure seafood restaurant in the city, and some say the country? The decor is functional white and light wood, for this is a no-nonsense restaurant. Order *mariscos Botafumeiro*, a cascade of shellfish of every variety, and we think you will agree. Prices reach Neichel levels and reservations are advised. Credit Cards: A, D, M, V.

La Dama ★★★

Avinguda Diagonal, 423 (three blocks south of the intersection of Diagonal with Pas. de Gràcia), ☎ *202 06 86, FAX 200 72 99.*

Convenient to the boutiques of Passeig de Gràcia, this is a most elegant restaurant housed in an architectural statement—an art nouveau building that contributes to the experience. The food is first rate, getting better all the time, and *nueva* to the core—witness cream of potato soup with caviar, or roast potatoes stuffed with crayfish or crayfish flavored with orange vinegar. Prices are high, but worth it. Credit Cards: A, D, M, V.

Jaume de Provença ★★★

C. Provença, 88 (Provença cuts across Pas. de Gràcia just before Diagonal. This restaurant is 11 blocks south, near the Sants train station.), ☎ *430 00 29.*
Closed Sunday night, Monday, Holy Week, Christmas week and August.

This is a pleasant antidote to some of the trendy elegance of Barcelona's better known establishments with no sacrifice to the palate. The restaurant consists of intimate, slightly rustic rooms, emitting romantic feeling. The food is a different story. It is elegant, inventive, delicious, and merits inclusion with the best in the city. Take, for example, gratin of clams and spinach, crabmeat lasagna, codfish with saffron sauce, seabass soufflé and an orange mousse dessert that is unforgettably exquisite. Service is considerate and prices are correct. Reservations are required. Credit Cards: A, D, M, V.

Via Veneto ★★★

C. Ganduxer, 10 (heading southwest along Diagonal, turn right at the second street past the traffic circle Pl. Francesc March), ☎ *200 72 44.*
Closed Saturday lunch, Sunday and the first three weeks in August.

Via Veneto ranks among the most dramatic Barcelona restaurants—with its Belle Époque decor—and stands with the best for the caliber of its food. Despite the restaurant name, the cuisine is Catalan of the *nueva cocina* sort. Food is elegant to the eye and sublime on the palate. Reservations are required. Credit Cards: A, D, M, V.

Can Majó ★★

Almirall Aixada, 23 (Follow the port north from the Pl. Colom for about 10 blocks as it bends to enter the development of Barceloneta. This street is the fourth off of the main Pas. Joan de Barbó.), ☎ *221 54 55.*
Closed Sun. night and August.

Botafumeiro has the style and the meticulous attention to detail, but Majó serves seafood that can be just as enjoyable in more relaxed surroundings. What Majó is not, however, is attractive. Come for a convivial atmosphere and fresh fish perfectly done, or for paella (*pelada*) that can only be bettered in Valencia. Credit Cards: A, V.

Agut d'Avinyó ★

C. Trinitat, 3 (From the Rambla de Caputxins go north along C. Ferrán, bordering the Pl. Reial. One block after the plaza turn right onto C. d'Avinyó to find this restaurant a few steps later in a cul-de-sac on the right.), ☎ *302 60 34.*
Closed Holy Week and Christmas week.

Dark wood, rush-caned chairs and white walls create the first impression of a mesón. A closer look at the venerable antiques shows the restaurant to be more elegant than that. Seating is on five small levels. The cuisine is traditional Catalan compared to the *nueva cocina* so in vogue elsewhere. Mussels in garlic cream sauce are delectable; meat and game generally are combined with some fruit sauce. The food is good, although not at the outstanding level of some others, but a convenient Barri Gòtic location and comfortable surroundings entitle it consideration. Reservations are advised. Credit Cards: A, D, M, V.

Moderate ($15–$30)

Siete Portas ★★

Passeig Isabel II, 14 (in the port, two blocks left of the end of Via Laietana), ☎ *319 30 33.*

Seven doors do indeed front the street, opening onto a large mirrored, marble-floored dining area. The specialty is seafood which is amazingly reasonable for the quality and quantity. Fish paella and the house version of *sarsuela* are excellent and bountiful enough to share. Note that this area is not safe at night, so commuting by taxi is recommended. Reservations are advised. Credit Cards: A, D, M, V.

Senyor Parellada ★★

C. Argentería, 37 (the street leads northeast from Via Laietana, just north of the Pl. Jaume), ☎ *315 50 94.*
Closed Sunday and holidays.

The restaurant is dignified without being stuffy, surrounding a leafy atrium, and serves well-prepared Catalan dishes at fair prices—an excellent value all around. Credit Cards: A, D, M, V.

Brasserie Flo ★★

C. Jonqueres, 10 (C. Jonqueres heads southwest off Via Laietana west of the Cathedral. The restaurant is located a block south of the back of the el Corte Inglés department store beside Pl. Catalunya.), ☎ *319 31 02.*

Opened by a group of expatriate French who missed home-cooking, this is a most authentic brasserie installed in an old warehouse that somehow feels French. Pâtés and the choucroute are the real thing. Reservations are advised. Credit Cards: A, D, M, V.

El Cangrejo Loco

Moll del Gregal, 29-30 (along the new beach esplanade just north of the port), ☎ *221 17 48.*

This is a convivial and popular place that serves good, moderately priced seafood. Blow the budget on a menu degustación for about $20. and you should be both full and happy. Credit Cards: A, D, V.

Tick-Tack-Toe ★

Moll del Gregal, 20-21 (along the new beach esplanade just north of the port), ☎ *221 00 66.*
Closed Wed, and Sun. eve.

Along with El Cangrejo Loco above these neighbors present a pleasant choice. Tick-tack-toe for tapas, Cangrejo for a sit-down meal, or both. As a matter of fact, you can also sit down here, but we slightly prefer the meals at Cangrejo. Credit Cards: A, D, V.

La Caracoles ★

P. Escudellers, 14 (the street runs east from the Pl. Reial at the end of Rambla Caputxins), ☎ *302 31 85.*

This venerable Barcelona institution is much favored by tourists. Despite its popularity, the rustic surroundings are relaxed and it serves hearty Catalan food prepared well. Of course, try the snails (caracoles), but fried fish, roast chicken, mussels and paella are tasty too. Reserve, but there still may be long waits. Credit Cards: A, D, M, V.

Font del Gat

P. Santa Madrona (on Montjuïc between the Fundació Miró and the Museu Arqueològic), ☎ *424 02 24.*
Closed Mon., except for holidays, and winter.

This is the place for lunch while visiting Montjuïc. The restaurant is nicely styled inside, but dining on the terrace is the most pleasant. Even if the food is ordinary, the views are special. Credit Cards: A, D, M, V.

Inexpensive (Less than $15)

Agut

C. Gignas, 16 (follow C. Ciutat from the north side of the Ajuntament in Pl. Jaume in the Barri Gòtic to C. Ample just before reaching the port. Jag left then right.), ☎ *315 17 09.*
Closed Sunday evening, Monday, and the month of July.

This one is almost too good to be true. It offers fantastic value for food that is genuinely well prepared—and has done so for 75 years. It looks as it should, incorporating a kind of fifties decor in a place that is older. Of course nothing is perfect. The neighborhood should be walked with caution at night No reservations. Credit Cards: A, M, V.

Egipte

C. Jerusalem, 12 (directly behind the Boquería market off Rambla Sant Josep), ☎ *317 74 80.*
Closed Sunday.

No frills here, just good food of the homey Catalan variety. The reason for the Egyptian motif is anyone's guess. There are crowds at lunch, but also numerous low-priced special menus. Things grow quieter in the evening. Being practically a part of the market, the fish are always fresh. Prices are very fair, and no reservations are taken. Credit Cards: none.

Raim D'or Can Maxim ★

C. Bonsucces, 8 (Bonsucces goes south from the west end of Rambla Etudis), ☎ *302 02 34.*
Closed Sunday.
This place is always crowded because the food is good and the prices low. The gazpacho is heavenly, although only served at lunchtime. Credit Cards: A, M, V.

Pitarra ★

C. d'Avinyó, 56 (d'Avinyó runs east from C. Ferrán halfway between the Rambla Caputxins and the Pl. Jaume in the Barri Gòtic), ☎ *301 16 47.*
Closed Sunday.
The food is good, flavorful and remarkably inexpensive. Credit Cards: A, M, V.

Les Corts Catalanes

Gran Via de les Corts Catalanes. 630 (a block west of the P. Catalunya), ☎ *301 03 76.*
This is the place for the vegetarians among us, but the food is good enough for carnivores to enjoy it too. The empanadas in particular are tasty. Credit Cards: V.

Burger King

Rambla de Canaletes, 135 (near the Pl. de Catalunya), ☎ *302 54 29.*

Kentucky Fried Chicken

C. Ferrán, 1-3 (on the Rambla de Caputxins), ☎ *412 51 54.*

Shopping

Barcelona is the best shopping city in Spain—for selection, trendiness and lovely avenues made for walking. That is not to say everyone will buy, for it is not—with some exceptions—a city of bargains. What it is is a city well designed for the activity. Store hours generally run from Mon.–Fri. from 9am to 1:30 p.m. and from 4 or 5–8 p.m. Many stores open Saturday for the morning hours, but do not reopen in the afternoon. They close on Sunday.

Fine **boutiques** for clothing, leather, jewelry and shoes, many on the cutting edge, are concentrated in a rectangle bordered by Pas. de Gràcia on the east, Rambla de Catalunya to the south, Pl. Catalunya to the north and Diagonal nine blocks west. It is perfectly possible to cover the whole area in a leisurely late afternoon and early evening.

The area begins with a branch of **El Corte Inglés** department store, for moderate-priced clothing, at the Pl. Catalunya. **Loewe's** extravagant leather stands at *Pas. de Gràcia, 35.* At *53-55* a mall, called **Boulevard Rosa**, contains over 100 fine boutiques. Also at *55* is **Centre Permanent D'Artesana**, displaying works by artisans from around Catalunya. **Rodier** is at *66,* **Fiorucci** at *76.* **Adolfo Domíngues**, the designer who gave Don Johnson his look on *Miami Vice*, has a shop at *89,* with clothes for women as well.

Turn west (left) on C. Mallorca for some special stores. At the corner of Rambla de Catalunya, at *100,* is **Groc**, an outstanding designer for men. Across the street at *C. Mallorca 242* stands **José Tomas**, another fine men's designer. Turning left down Ramblas de Catalunya brings **Artespaña** *at 75,* a government store for superior craft furniture and accessories, and they ship.

Returning to C. Mallorca, further along is an extraordinary showplace of houseware and furniture design. **B.D. Ediciones de Diseno**, at *291*, is run by architects who sell museum-quality designs by the greats, living and deceased, such as chairs and furniture fittings by Gaudí. The building that houses the store is a monument too, designed by the *modernista* architect Domènech i Montaner. At number *258 on C. Còrsega*, which is the last street along Passeig de Gràcia going south before Diagonal, is a shop named **Urbana** which stocks fixtures reclaimed and restored from *modernista* buildings. It sells everything from light fixtures to mantels, armoirs and door knobs, each an artwork. Return to *Pas. de Gràcia at 96* for **Vincón**, another superior furniture and houseware vendor.

Different goods can be found in other areas. For **trimmings and costume jewelry** at great prices, walk from the Rambla Sant Josep to the Pl. Jaume along C. Boquería, which changes its name to C. Call. This is the wholesale trimmings and accessories area with store after store, though only a few sell to retail buyers.

There are two areas for **antiques**. One is in the Barri Gòtic in the area just south of the Cathedral along the tiny streets of C. Banys Nous and C. del la Palla. Art nouveau jewelry can be surprisingly affordable in some of these tiny shops. For fine **lace**, try **L'Arca de l'Avia** at *Banys Nous, 20*. Behind the Cathedral on C. Franseria is **Grafiques el Tinell**, for **prints** from old woodblocks and etchings, some handcolored. *On Baixada de la Libreria, 2*, the next street to the east, is **Papirum** which sells antique and handcolored **paper** and end-papers.

The second antique area is just west of the Barri Gòtic on C. Montcada. From the Pl. Jaume in the heart of the Barri Gòtic go north through the Pl. Angel to follow C. Princesa. The fourth right is C. Montcada, with the **Picasso Museum** selling a large selection of **prints**, **shirts**, etc., on the corner. For four short blocks antiques shops line both sides of Montcada going south. Also on this street is a fine shop for **handcrafts** called **1741** *at number 2*, and an outlet of **Fondacion Maeght**, the great French **art gallery**, *at 25*. Lastly, an **antiques market** is held in the Pl. del Pi, just west of the Pl. de la Boqueia, on Thurs. from about 10 a.m. until 2 p.m. or so.

Espadrilles, the traditional rope-soled canvas shoes of Catalonia, can be purchased at **La Manual Lapargalera** on C. d'Avinyó, just after it turns east from C. Ferrán on the way to the Pl. Jaume in the Barri Gòtic.

Yes, there is a large **flea market** in Barcelona. It consists of more junk than jewels, but you never know. It is called **Els Encants**, and takes place in the Pl. de les Glòries Catalanes which is on Gran Via Corts Catalanes about 15 blocks north and one block west of the Pl. Catalunya. The red line 1 metro from Pl. Catalunya toward Santa Coloma stops at the Glòries station right at the spot. Markets take place Mon., Wed., Fri. and Sat. beginning at dawn. Note: there has been talk recently of moving this market. Check at the tourist office before making the trip.

All day Thursday (except in Aug.) the Mercado Gòtic de Antiquedes takes over the Pl. Nova (in front of the Cathedral) for antiques and personal treasures galore.

Directory

Information

There are several convenient branches of the Office of Tourism. All provide a map and a complete list of Barcelona hotels. One office is located at the airport, another on Gran Via del Corts Catalanes, 658 (one block west and two north of Pl. Catalunya), another at Pl. Porta de la Pau (where the Ramblas ends at the port) The telephone numbers are: ☎ *478 47 04, 301 74 43, 412 26 40*, respectively. All are open Mon.–Fri. 9 a.m. to 7 p.m. and on Sat. from 9 a.m. to 2 p.m. In summer the Ajuntament in Pl. Sant Jaume in the Barri Gòtic (☎ *402 72 62*) will also take inquiries and supply a map, as will the Palau de la Virreina at Rambla 99.

City Tours

Both Julià Tours at *Ronda Universitat, 5* (☎ *317 64 54*) and *Pullmantur at Gran Via, 635* (☎ *318 12 97*) offer half-day tours of Barcelona for about 3500 ptas. The Palau de la Virreina at Rambla 99 rents cassettes for walking tours of the city.

Currency Exchange

Banks in the Eixample give good rates, as does American Express and El Corte Inglés department store. If you need to change money when such establishments are closed, beware of currency exchanges on the Ramblas which charge exorbitant rates, go instead to the Estació de Sants train station where bank rates are offered after bank hours (until 10 p.m. everyday, except for a siesta from 2–4 p.m. on Sun.)

U.S. Consulate

Pas. Reina Elisenda, 23 (☎ *280 22 27*).

Canadian Consulate

Via Augusta, 125 (☎ *209 06 34*).

American Express

Pas. de Gràcia, 101 (☎ *217 00 70*).

Airport

International and domestic flights all arrive at El Prat de Llobregat Airport, 14 km south of the city (☎ *478 50 00*). TWA flies directly to the U.S., others change somewhere in Europe. A taxi will cost about 2500 ptas. and take half an hour. An *Aerobús* outside the door from customs travels to the central Pl. Catalunya every 15 minutes or so for 450 ptas. Trains leave to and from the airport every 30 minutes for a 20-minute trip that costs 300 ptas. The Barcelona terminus is Estació Central De Sants, well-connected by metro, and finally to the central Pl. de Catalunya. Iberia has an office at *Pas. Gràcia, 30* (☎ *401 33 84*). An airport shuttle bus leaves from there every hour or so.

Trains and Buses

Long distance domestic trips and travel to other European countries is handled by the newly modernized Estació de França (☎ *490 02 02*). The station is located on Av. Marqués de L'Argentina, near the water by Ciutadella park and the zoo. Sixty trains go daily to Madrid, eight to Seville, 14 to Valencia. All the domestic trains also go through Estació Central De Sants, located at Pl. Països Catalanes, in the southwest. Lines red 1 and green 3 of the metro both stop at Sants-Estació. The downtown RENFE office is at Pas. de Gràcia, 13 (☎ *322 41 42*).

Barcelona is served by five different bus companies, with as many terminals. There is no system to the separation of routes. Check with the Office of Tourism, or try the largest terminal, Estació del Nord (☎ *265 65 08)* at C. Ali-bei, 80, half way between the Pl. Cataluny and the Pl. Glòries.

Post Office and Telephones

The main post office is at the end of Via Laietana near the port at Pl. d'Antoni Lopez (☎ *318 38 31)*. Telephones are available at *C. de Fontanelle*, 4, at the east end of el Corte Inglés by the Pl. Catalunya.

Police

The Centro de Atencion Juridico Polcial (☎ *301 90 60*) where English is spoken is at *C. de la Ramblas, 43*, which runs west from Rambla Caputxins.

Excursions

The closest good beach is at lively, lovely **Sitges**. See the description under **Costa Dorada** ★ in this chapter. Charming beaches also lie north about 100 km along the **Costa Brava** ★★, also described in this chapter. Extensive Roman ruins have been excavated at **Tarragona** ★ and **Empúries** ★, which has rare Greek ruins as well, while **Santes Creus** ★ and **Poblet** ★★ are two extraordinary medieval monasteries. Each is described under its own heading below.

For **Sitges** *and the* **Costa Dorada** *head toward the sea along the Ramblas to enter the expressway Ronda del Litoral at its end. Go southwest toward the airport. Past the airport the road becomes the coastal C-246 which reaches Sitges in 43 km. The fastest route to* **Tarragona**, **Santes Creus** *and* **Poblet** *is to go to the port along the Ramblas, head south on the expressway Ronda del Litoral. Follow signs to Tarragona after 84 km. For Poblet and Santes Creus, after 49 km change to A-2 toward Llerida. At exit 11, Vila-Rodona, leave the highway for Santes Creus. For Poblet leave the highway at exit 9, Monblanco, and take N-240 toward Llerida for six km. For the* **Costa Brava** *and* **Empúries** *take the Ramblas to the port and enter the expressway Ronda del Litoral going north and west, which becomes the Ronda del Besòs in about one mile. In about another mile take A-17 toward Girona, then A-7 toward Girona. For the Costa Brava take exit 9 at Videres and aim for the coast and Sant Feliu de Guixols along C-253 and C-250. For Empúries continue past Girona to exit 5 at Viladamat, then 16 km toward the coast to L'Escala with Empúries on its outskirts.*

Trains to **Sitges** *leave frequently from Estació De Sants. The trip takes less than an hour and costs about 350 ptas., round trip.* **Tarragona** *is served very frequently by train for an hour and a half trip costing 450 ptas.* **Poblet** *is reached by train to Llerida for a trip of three-plus hours and a cost of 850 ptas., then by bus for an hour.* **Santa Creus** *is further along that same bus route. Two buses per day travel the two-and-a-half-hour trip to* **Empúries** *for* *about 1000 ptas. They are operated by Sarfa (☎ 265 11 5894 34) in the Estació del Nord, between the Pl. Catalunya and Pl. Glòries.*

Costa del Azahar ★★

Perfumed by acres of orange groves, the resorts of the Costa del Azahar begin 175 km south of Barcelona where the Costa Dorada ends (see the description below), and stretch south past Valencia to the Cabo de la Nao, covering a distance of 260 km. These resorts are a mixed lot—some charming, some overdeveloped—but their sand beaches are the finest in Spain. We describe the coast beginning at Benicarló and work our way south past Valencia. N-340 follows the coast.

Benicarló

Population: 16,587
Area code: 964; zip code: 12580

Benicarló is on N-340, 28 km south of San Carles de la Rápita at the end of the Costa Dorada.

Once attractive, the town is today overbuilt, although it does offer a parador, a small port and decent beaches.

Where to Stay

Moderate ($50–$99)

Parador de Benicarló   1st-class ★★

Av. del Papa Luna, 5, Benicarló, ☎ 47 01 00, FAX 47 09 34.

Hotel gardens run down to the sea to produce a feeling of peaceful quiet. The hotel itself is modern and of no special distinction, but tennis and a pool are provided for a price that is barely moderate. *108 rooms.*

Peñiscola ★★★

Population: 3,077
Area code: 964; zip code: 12598

South of Benicarlo seven km along the scenic unnumbered coastal road.

On a small peninsula (which is what the town's name means) Peñiscola snuggles tiny whitewashed houses against a solemn castle on a hill. Cars are not allowed in the narrow twisting streets. The village is charming, and the **castle**, which was the home of the antipope Luna during his exile in the 15th century, is worth a look. What is less charming is the stretch of high-rises that line the beach on either side of the peninsula. However, finer, whiter sand beaches do not exist elsewhere in Europe and they run for miles.

Where to Stay

Moderate ($50–$99)

Hostería del Mar   1st-class ★ ★ ★

*Carretera de Benicarlo, Peñiscola (on the road to Benicarlo, one km north of the penin-
sula),* ☎ *48 06 00, FAX 48 13 63.*

This hotel is affiliated with the national paradors and outdoes most of the modern
ones in style. White wall and dark wood lend a Castilian look, but most dramatic are
the views over the sea and peninsula. Tennis is available. *85 rooms, plus one suite.*

Inexpensive (Less than $50)

Marina   4th-class ★

Av. José Antonio, 42, Peñiscola, ☎ *48 08 90, FAX 48 08 90.*
Open from April–October.

No views, but restful, comfortable rooms should satisfy most people, and the prices
will fit anyone's budget. *19 rooms.*

Alcocéber ★★

Population: 2703
Area code: 964; zip code: 12579

*From Peñiscola CS-500 leads away from the coast to N-340. After
16 km on N-340 a small road leads to the beach.*

Don't tell anyone about this place, for it has yet to be fully discovered. The
town quietly nestles between two fine crescent beaches with empty spots.

Where to Stay

Moderate ($50–$99)

Aparthotel Jeremías-Romana   3rd-class ★ ★

One and one-half km south of town on the beach, Alcocéber, ☎ *41 44 11, FAX 41 24
11.*

The moderate price buys not a bedroom, but a suite, which is all this hotel consists
of. The aura is calm, ocean views are lovely, and the beach is super. Tennis is available. *39 suites.*

Jeremías   2nd-class ★

One km south of town on the beach, Alcocéber, ☎ *41 44 37, FAX 41 24 44.*
Open from March to the end of October.

Just as quiet, and in as lovely a spot by the beach as the Jeremías-Romana, this hotel
offers comfortable rooms at very affordable prices. Tennis is available. *38 rooms.*

Benicasim ★

Population: 4705
Area code: 964; zip code: 12560

From Alcocéber return to N-340 going south for 32 km.

Developers came in force decades ago, attracted by the spectacular setting
of wide beaches with mountains rising above them. The mountains and
beaches remain, enlivened today by crowds. Because development began in

the seventies, hotels in Benicasim are somewhat dated-looking but charge
seventies prices to make them bargains today.

Where to Stay
Moderate ($50–$99)

Intur Orange   1st-class ★ ★

Gran Avenida, Benicasim, ☎ *39 44 00, FAX 30 15 41, Telex 65626.*
Open April through October.
Looking like an overblown chalet, this huge hotel, surrounded by a lovely garden,
is only 100 yards from the sea. It lacks tasteful decor but makes up for it with bargain prices for the rooms. Ask for one with a sea view. Tennis is available, along with
most other facilities. *415 rooms.*

Voramar   2nd-class ★ ★

Passeo Pilar Coloma, 1, Benicasim, ☎ *30 01 50, FAX 30 05 26.*
Open April through September.
Though lacking the garden, this hotel otherwise is more attractive than the Hotel
Intur Orange. Bedrooms overlooking the sea have ample balconies. The hotel is on
the beach and offers tennis courts. *55 rooms.*

Sagunto ★

Population: 52,759
Area code: 96; zip code: 46500

Sagunto is 65 km south of Benicasim by N-340.

Known as *Seguntum* in Roman times, the Carthagenian siege of this town
in 218 B.C. precipitated the Second Punic War. Although Sagunto has no
beach, it has ruins enough to repay a visit of an hour or two.

Climb the hill to the Moorish **alcazaba** with excavations of Roman remains
inside. On the way is an **amphitheater** sufficiently restored to be used for festivals. The ruins are a mix of Roman, Visigothic and Moorish, and fun to sort
through. *(Open Tues.–Sat. 10 a.m.–2 p.m. and 4–6pm; open Sun. 10 a.m.–*
2 p.m.; closed Mon.; admission: 200 ptas.)

Valencia ★★

See the description under a separate heading.

From Sagunto the speedy toll A-7 whisks to Valencia in 25 km.

El Saler ★★

Area code: 96; zip code: 46012.

From Valencia take the autopista V-15 for 12 km south, then the
coast road for two km.

Despite proximity to Valencia and a dramatic location on a sandbank with
sea on one side and a huge fresh-water lagoon on the other, el Saler has so far
escaped overdevelopment. Two expensive hotels are here, one for the golf
enthusiast.

Where to Stay

Expensive ($100–$200)

Sidi Saler   1st-class ★ ★ ★

On the beach three km southeast of town, El Saler, ☎ *161 04 11, FAX 161 08 38, Telex 64208.*

This is a modern super-luxury resort that charges expensive, but fair prices, considering all the style and services—including both an indoor pool and an outdoor one, and tennis too. *260 rooms, plus 16 suites.*

Parador de el Saler   1st-class ★ ★ ★

Near the beach seven km south of town, El Saler, ☎ *161 11 86, FAX 162 70 16, Telex 610 69.*

The raison d'etre for this modern parador is the golf course it sits amid. A pine forest runs beside it and beach is near, so activities are not restricted to the links. *58 rooms.*

Gandía ★

Population: 52,646
Area code: 96; zip code: 46700

From el Saler the scenic coastal road joins N-332 in 24 km at **Cullera,** *with a beach development. 26 km further is Gandía.*

Gandía's claim to fame is that it was the duchy of the Borja family. One Borja became a pope (Alexander VI), another was his notorious son, known to us through the Italians as Caesare Borgia, still another was the pope's equally notorious daughter, Lucretia. All were born, not in Gandía but in Jativa, 20 km inland. Here, however, the great-grandson of Pope Alexander VI was born, Francisco Borja. He reversed the family reputation by becoming the vicar-general of the Jesuit order, and leading a saintly life for which he was canonized. The **Palacio del Santo Duque** in Gandía was his home, which can be toured. *(Open daily for guided tours at 10 a.m., 11 a.m., noon, 5 p.m., 6 p.m. and 7 p.m.; in winter at 11 a.m., noon, 4:30 p.m. and 5:30 p.m.; admission: 100 ptas.)* Six km east of Gandía is its port with a beach development running north.

Where to Stay

Moderate ($50–$99)

Bayren I   1st-class ★ ★ ★

Passeig Maritim Neptu, 62, Gandía (at the beginning of the beach), ☎ *284 03 00, FAX 284 06 53, Telex 61549.*

The outstanding feature of this hotel is its grand terrace with splendid sea views. Accommodations are first-class, but of no great style. Still, you get a lot for a moderate price. *153 rooms, plus 11 suites.*

Gandía is 36 km from Cape Nao, the start of the Costa Blanca, described below.

Costa Blanca ★

Located south of Valencia and running into the Costa del Sol, the Costa Blanca is endowed with fine beaches and a climate that is virtually rainless, indeed cloudless. Beginning in the 1960s, these attractions drew developers the way a dying animal lures vultures. Natural beauty that once thrilled now is covered in concrete, but the fine beaches remain along with the weather. Here and there a pocket of serenity so far has escaped the mobs. Water and air along this coast remain warm enough through October for sunning and bathing. We describe the better resorts starting in the north at Denia on Cape Nao and running southwest to Capo de Palos, a coastline of 250 km. The most scenic resorts lie at the start of this route, on Cape Nao, a craggy promontory that dives into the sea, broken here and there by coves and beaches. The cape stands only 135 km west of the island of Ibiza, and ferries run to and from Denia. The most extensive beaches, on the other hand, wait at the southern end of the coast.

*From **Valencia** the fast toll A-7 speeds south to Alicante. At exit 62 backtrack on N-332 for three kilometers to Onda, from which a road heads east to the coast in nine kilometers. From the eastern end of the **Costa del Sol** at **Almeria** N-340 winds 139 kilometers to Vera, where 11 kilometers toward Garrucha on the coast brings a scenic coastal road that reaches Agulas in the north in 38 kilometers. Follow the description of the Costa Blanca in reverse. From **Madrid** the fastest route is to go to Valencia and follow the directions above.*

Denia

Population: 22,162
Area code: 96; zip code: 03700

Denia has seen history from the Iberians on. In fact its name derives from Roman Dianium, for the goddess Diana. Nothing of this past remains on view, though there are ruins of a 13th-century medieval castle on the hill above town. This is very much a family resort, and its long pleasant beaches are highly developed. Ferries to Ibiza (☎ 578 42 00) and Formentera (☎ 578 53 62) leave the port. Afternoon hydrofoils reach Ibiza in an hour and a half (about $65), while evening ferries take five hours (about $50).

Where to Stay

Moderate ($50–$99)

Rosa 2nd-class ★

On the road to Las Marinas, two km northeast of town, ☎ *578 15 73, FAX 578 15 73. Open Mar.–Oct.*
This peaceful little place is not far from a beach and has a pleasant terrace, swimming pool and tennis court, all for a modest price. *39 rooms.*

Jávea ★★

Population: 10,964
Area code: 96; zip code: 03730

The steep and winding, but scenic, coast road reaches Jávea in 10 km.

The old town huddles around a 16th-century fortified church inside ramparts and Moorish gates, but the beach is a modern development. Wondrous grottos line the coast around Jávea and a safari park is located at Vergel a few km inland *(open 10 a.m.–7:30 p.m. in summer, until 6 p.m. in winter)*. Six km east stands Cape San Antonio with fine views to Ibiza on a clear day. A scenic coast road runs for 12 km southeast to Cape Nao, again with spectacular views of sea and promontory.

Where to Stay

Expensive ($100–$200)

Parador de Jávia   1st-class ★★

On the beach four km southeast of town, ☎ 579 02 00, FAX 579 03 08.
Paradors do find the best locations. This one is surrounded by a garden in a palm grove with beach to the north and beach to the south. The hotel itself is modern and unexceptional, but most comfortable. *65 rooms.*

Moraira ★★

Area code: 96; zip code: 03724

No good road goes directly to Moraira from Jávea. Return to N-332 and go south for six km, then follow signs east for Moraira in 9 km.

Moraira is so secluded the developers haven't found it. Hurry. A promontory to the south forms a sheltered cove. The village proper gathers around an old watchtower above a little harbor.

Where to Stay

Expensive ($100–$200)

Swiss Moraira   1st-class ★★★

Two and one-half km west of town on the road to Calpe, ☎ 574 71 04, FAX 574 70 74. Closed Jan.
Relax in the quiet of pine grove in this sleek modern hotel that tends to every care. A dramatic pool and tennis are provided, but it is a two mile drive to the beach. *25 rooms.*

Inexpensive (Less than $50)

Moradix   3rd-class ★

One and one-half km west of town, ☎ 574 40 56, FAX 574 45 25.
This is a secluded, pleasant place providing comfortable rooms, views of the sea and appealingly low prices. *30 rooms.*

Where to Eat

El Girasol   ★★★★

1.5 km on the road to Calpe, ☎ *574 43 73.*

Closed Mon. off season, and from Jan. through Feb.

Save up for this one. In the cozy dinning room of this elegantly restored villa are served the best meals along the Costa Blanca, food that need not bow to any in the country. Fish are the stars, served with a French touch—expensive, but memorable. What bowls us over, however, are the desserts. Credit Cards: A, Visa, D and M accepted.

Calpe ★★

Population: 8000
Area code: 96; zip code: 03710

Return from Moraira to N-332 for the 12 km drive south to Calpe.

The Peñón de Ifach, a miniature version of Gibraltar, rises from the sea, connected to the coast by a spit of land lined by sand beaches on both sides. So far so good. But the beaches are divided by a solid concrete row of high-rises of no appeal. Still, Calpe has that scenic rock, and is not as crowded as some other resorts.

Where to Stay

Moderate ($50–$99)

Roca Esmeralda   1st-class ★

Ponent, 1, Calpe (on the Playa Levante, along the road to Moraira, three and one-half km north of town), ☎ *583 61 01, FAX 583 60 04.*

To be sure, this is another of those characterless high-rise modern hotels, but this one at least charges bottom dollar for all its services and provides lovely views. *212 rooms.*

Inexpensive (Less than $50)

Venta La Chata   3rd-class ★★★

On the road toward N-332, four and one-half km north of town, ☎ *583 03 08.*

Closed from the middle of Nov.-the middle of Dec.

This is an utterly charming little place that charges incredibly low rates. Set behind trees and flowers, it is the perfect antidote to the modern high-rises, such as Roca Esmeralda. Accommodations are rustic, but atmospheric, and terraced gardens looking to the sea are a perfect touch. *17 rooms.*

Altea ★

Population: 11,108
Area code: 96; zip code: 03590

A gorgeous 11 km stretch of N-332 connects Calpe to Altea.

This is a romantic little fishing village of whitewashed houses surrounding a church with a blue-tiled dome. On every side except the sea, mountains shelter its tiny cove. But the developers have arrived.

Where to Stay

Inexpensive (Less than $50)

Altaya   3rd-class ★

La Mar, 115, Altea (in the port), ☎ 584 08 00.
Closed from Christmas week through Feb.
The hotel is situated in the town proper, which provides a sense of being in Spain
not offered by the expensive high-rises outside. Rooms are fairly comfortable and
their price makes them a genuine value. *24 rooms.*

Where to Eat

Monte Molar   ★★★

Take N-332 northeast for two and one-half km, then a left at the sign for one km, ☎ 584
15 81.
Closed Wed. in winter, and from the middle of Jan. through the middle of Mar.
The restaurant is absolutely gorgeous and elegant, with a pretty terrace overlooking
the sea. The food matches its surroundings—as memorable, though of course more
expensive. For seafood, try the timbale of fish with asparagus; for meat, the magret
of duck with mushrooms; and for fun, the snails with rice. Reservations are strongly
advised. Credit Cards: A, D, M, V.

Benidorm

Population: 25,544
Area code: 96; zip code: 03500

*A pretty stretch of N-332 leads to Benidorm in 10 km, which lies
two km off the highway.*

Picture a rocky promontory with a village of whitewashed houses along
twisting alleys, add two crescent white sand beaches on either side. Now picture characterless high-rise hotels all around so that the village is hidden, and
add enough beds—all full during the summer—for a third of a million package-tour vacationers. This is Benidorm. One must stay on the beach near the
old town, to see what was once attractive about Benidorm, and this guides
our recommendations.

The **Casino Costa Blanca** *(☎ 589 27 12)* with gambling is on N-332, 6 km
south of town.

Where to Stay

Moderate ($50-$99)

Cimbel   1st-class ★

Av. de Europa, 1, Benidorm (on the Playa de Levant), ☎ 585 21 00, FAX 586 06 61.
This large modern hotel is similar to others, except it is on the beach and close to
the old town. A front room is essential. *140 rooms.*

Inexpensive (Less than $50)

Bilbaíno   3rd-class ★★

Av. Virgen del Sufragio, 1, Benidorm (on the Playa de Levant, where it begins at the Pro-
mentorio del Castillo), ☎ 585 08 04, FAX 585 08 05.

Open Mar.–Nov.

For our money this is the best location in town. Facing the sea, one sees only beach and the character of the village on the promontory. Inexpensive meals are also served. *38 rooms.*

Playa de San Juan ★

Population: 10,522
Area code: 96; zip code: 0354

N-332 going west from Benidorm arrives at Alicante in 45 km, where a seven km backtrack along the coast reaches Playa de San Juan.

Fine sand and the extent of the beach makes this resort so popular. Development is still expanding, but it is hard to fill such a long expanse. Swelled by arrivals from Madrid, however, the Spanish manage to cover most of it themselves during August. There is nothing of scenic interest here except the sea, but an extensive nightlife adds interest. The sun and water make this an attractive alternative to staying in Alicante, for those who wish to see the sights of that city.

Where to Stay

Expensive ($100–$200)

Sidi San Juan   **Deluxe ★ ★ ★**

It is its own compound without a street address, ☎ 516 13 00, FAX 516 33 46, Telex 66263.

This modern compound on a private beach is surrounded by wonderful gardens. The hotel is deluxe in every way and, all things considered, well worth its expensive price for the beauty, seclusion and comfort. *176 rooms.*

Moderate ($50–$99)

Almirante Pocardy   **2nd-class ★**

Av. de Niza, 38, Playa de San Juan, ☎ 565 01 12, FAX 565 71 69.

This is the best value on the beach. The hotel is peaceful, offers sea views, a pool and tennis, along with comfortable rooms. The Pocardy restaurant ensconced inside provides tasty meals at low prices. *68 rooms.*

Alicante ★

Population: 251,387
Area code: 96; zip code: 03000

From the direction of Benidorm Mount Benacantil is soon passed, with parking just below it on the Passeo de Gomez by the beach before the port. If full, continue along the Esplanada de España for additional parking.

Alicante is the major city of the Costa Blanca. Coincidentally, given its location on the "White Coast," the city name is apt, for it derives (with a prefaced Arabic "Al") from its Roman name—Lucentum, "Place of Light."

People visit Alicante because it is a transportation hub, for the activity of a city and for castle ruins high on a hill, but it does have long beaches as well. A couple of fine churches add to the appeal.

The interesting sights lie at the bottom of, and on, Mount Benacantil, east of the port. Walk the lovely palm-lined Esplanade de España in the direction of the steep hill, turning left at its end where the sea wall begins on the right. Two short blocks lead to the **Ayuntamiento** in golden stone with twin towers. The style is churrigueresque, from the middle of the 18th century. Entry is permitted to see a rococo chapel and ornate hall. *(Open daily 9 a.m.–3pm; admission: free.)*

A short block north **San Nicolás de Bari**, a serene neoclassical Cathedral beckons with a lovely cupola. Go west for one long block on Calle Mayor, the street of the Ayuntamiento, to the church of **Santa María**. The facade is a wedding cake of swirling baroque confection. Continue along the sea side of the church, down steps to an elevator that climbs Mount Benacantil to **Castillo de Santa Bárbara ★**. The castle is an accretion from the 13th-16th centuries built on much older foundations. It has drawbridges, a moat and dungeon—as any respectable castle should—and splendid views. *(Open Sun.–Fri. 9 a.m.–9 p.m.; in winter open Sun.–Fri. 10 a.m.–1 p.m. and 5–8 p.m.; open Sat. 10 a.m.–1 p.m.; closed Mon., in winter. Admission: 200 ptas.)*

Where to Stay

Staying at the beach seven km east at Playa de San Juan (discussed above) is an option to rooming in the city, though Alicante can be a fine host too.

Moderate ($50–$99)

Residencia Palas 2nd-class ★

Pl. Ayuntamiento, 6, Alicante, ☎ *520 66 90.*
The choice between this hotel and its sister (below) is between larger bedrooms and more attractive public spaces. The public areas in the Residencia are nothing to speak of, but the bedrooms are large and comfortable. Location on the plaza is congenial, and prices of both Palas hotels are good values. *53 rooms.*

Palas 2nd-class ★

C. Cervantes, 5, Alicante (one short block east of the Pl. Ayuntamiento and a short block toward the sea), ☎ *520 93 10, FAX 514 01 21.*
Chandeliers and antiques lend an old-world aura to the public spaces. Rooms are attractive, in a regency style, though not as large and relaxing as at its sister hotel. *42 rooms.*

Where to Eat

For inexpensive dining wander the old town at the foot of Mount Benacantil. For special food, try the following recommendation.

Expensive ($30+)

Delfin

Esplanada de España, 12, ☎ *521 49 11.*

A lovely terrace looks over the port and palms of the esplanade. The upstairs dining room is bright, indeed too much so, and elegant. Cuisine is *nueva* with a distinctly French touch, and comprises both seafood and meat. Every dish is delicate, but the chef does get carried away, heaping more ingredients where less would be better. Reservations are strongly advised. Credit Cards: A, D, M, V.

Moderate ($15–$30)

Quo Vadis   ★

Pl. Santisima Faz, 3 (at the northern end of the Esplanada turn inland for three blocks),
☎ *521 66 60.*
Closed Sun. night and Mon.

Some will like this place, some will not. The decor is very Spanish with swords and shields above traditional red-checkered tablecloths that promote a friendly atmosphere. What is special about the place is that the chef tries so hard to please that most dishes become a sort of entertainment. If flambé is fun for you, you'll have a ball. Yet some of the creations are good by any standard, such as the salt-baked dorado. No reservations are accepted. Credit Cards: A, D, M, V.

Santa Pola ★

Population: 12,022
Area code: 96; zip code: 03130

From Alicante follow the water south and signs for the airport. A few km outside of the city, take N-332 along the coast. Exit 20 km from the city, as signs direct, for a one km trip to Santa Pola on the coast.

Fine sand beaches lined by pine trees, call out for bodies. People answer the siren call both for the beaches and the fish restaurants along the harbor. The offshore island of Tabarca is regularly served by ferries because it offers marvelous sand.

Where to Stay

Moderate ($50–$99)

Polamar   2nd-class ★

Playa de Levant, 6, Santa Pola, ☎ *541 32 00, FAX 541 31 83.*

Comfortable and fairly priced, this hotel offers views and a terrace, all on the beach. What else could you want? *76 rooms.*

Guardamar del Segura ★

Population: 5708
Area code: 96; zip code: 03140

N-332 reaches Guardamar in 30 km.

Guardamar seems to have infinite sand beaches, stretching both north and south of the town. That is all there is, but if beach is the priority, here it is in spades.

Where to Stay

Moderate ($50–$99)

Guardamar   3rd-class ★

Av. Puerto Rico, 11, Guardamar del Segura, ☎ *572 96 50, FAX 572 95 30.*
This is our choice for the views and comfortable rooms, although the pool seems a
gilding of the lily in this beach-town. *52 rooms.*

La Manga del Mar Menor ★

Area code: 968; zip code: 30370.

*From Guardamar take N-332 south for 59 km to El Algar, then
the coast road toward Cabo de Palos for 17 km.*

A 20-k-long sandbar forms a huge lagoon called the Mar Menor (Small
Sea) that is calm for water skiing. A resort lines the sandbar, though some of
its modern buildings have style. Spanish families love its calm waters, however, and book all the rooms for July and August by April.

Where to Stay

Expensive ($100–$200)

Sol Galua   2nd-class ★

Hacienda Dos Mares and Grand Via, La Manga, ☎ *56 32 00, FAX 56 32 54, Telex
67119.*
This comfortable modern hotel sits on a promontory with spectacular views over
both lagoon and sea. Prices are very fair for its class. *177 rooms.*

Costa Brava ★ ★

Potentially, this "Wild Coast" is Spain's most scenic. Overbuilding since its
discovery in the 1960s, however, has spoiled much of it and summer crowds
pose problems, yet parts still retain a stunning beauty. Officially, the Costa
Brava begins at Lloret de Mar about 60 km north of Barcelona, and continues north for 130 km of cliffs, secreted coves and resorts all the way to the
French border. What makes this coast special is that geography produced
small inlets that constrain resorts to intimacy rather than sprawling over acres
of beach. For the same reason, finding accommodations in August without
reservations is practically impossible, although September should prove relatively easy—and the water remains warm. May and even June see some vacant rooms. Winter, although beautiful, is chilly and few hotels remain open.
We trace a route that begins in the south above Barcelona at Lloret and ends
at the French border.

*From Barcelona take N-7 north toward Girona. Leave the highway
at Videres (exit 9) and aim for the coast and Sant Feliu de Guixols
along C-253 and C-250. Lloret de Mar is south from Sant Feliu
along 49 km of scenic, but winding, coast road.*

Lloret de Mar

Population: 10,480
Area code: 972; zip code: 17310

There is nothing quaint about Lloret. It is serious enough about being a resort to bloat by ten times in August. People come from all over Europe for the beach, which is pleasant and clean, and for the crowds. Lloret is not characteristic of the rest of the coast.

The Casino Lloret de Mar (☎ *36 65 12*) entices at the north edge of town on Carretera de Blanes.

Where to Stay

If rooms are available, Lloret offers some good values.

Expensive ($100–$200)

Roger de Flor   1st-class ★ ★ ★
C. Turó de l'Estelat, Lloret de Mar (off the Carretera de Tossa), ☎ *36 48 00, FAX 37 16 37.*
Open April–Oct.
These are the most attractive and peaceful accommodations in town, sitting amid the pines a short distance from the beach. The rooms have some character, as opposed to the modern high-rises, yet offer as much comfort. The garden is lovely, the terrace sylvan. *87 rooms, plus six suites.*

At Platja de Fanals, two km south of town:

Rigat Park   1st-class ★ ★
Platja de Fanals, ☎ *36 52 00, FAX 37 04 11.*
Closed December through the first week of January.
A magnificent expanse of park surrounds this charming modern hotel. Here there is some calm close to the activity of Lloret, and the beach is balmy. Tennis and a superfluous pool are provided. *87 rooms, plus 17 suites.*

Moderate ($50–$99)

Excelsior   2nd-class ★
P. Mossen J. Verdaguer, 16, Lloret de Mar (directly behind the beach promenade, by the gardens), ☎ *36 61 76, FAX 37 16 54, Telex 97061.*
Open Apr.–Oct.
Located right on the beach, this well-run hotel provides views to the sea from front rooms. The price is reasonable, though the rooms are standard, but this is a very popular place. *45 rooms.*

Marsol   2nd-class ★
P. Mossens J. Verdaguer, 7, Lloret de Mar (directly behind the beach promenade, by the gardens), ☎ *36 57 54, FAX 37 22 05.*
Open Mar.–Oct.
A fine location, a rooftop pool, air conditioning, and reasonable rates, all make this hotel worth considering. Views of a pleasant palm plaza may be requested. *87 rooms.*

Tossa de Mar ★★★

Population: 2969
Area code: 972; zip code: 17320

The corniche road north from Lloret to Tossa and beyond to Sant Feliu de Guixols offers an amazing variety of hairpin curves and scenery, from cliff-top views over the ocean to forests and coves. Tossa is 12 km north of Lloret.

Tossa is fortunate in its site and manages to retain its character amid numerous vacationers. The town surrounds a horseshoe bay in which a nice beach nestles, with a cape and lighthouse at one end girded by remains of 12th-century town walls. Vila Vella, the old town, was designated a national monument for charming alleys that run beside golden Renaissance walls, towers and fishermen's houses all huddling the cape.

Where to Stay

Tossa provides abundant accommodations in the inexpensive to moderate range. A few stand out.

Moderate ($50–$99)

Mar Menuda   2nd-class ★ ★ ★

Platja de Mar Menuda, Tossa de mar (at the beginning of the northern beach), ☎ *34 10 00, FAX 34 00 87.*
Closed Jan. through Feb.
This is a quiet, restful hotel with a lovely shade terrace over the sea and best beach in the town. You can't do better in this town for any price. There is even a pool and a tennis court. *50 rooms.*

Inexpensive (Less than $50)

Hotel Diana   R2nd-class ★ ★ ★

Pl. de España, 6, Tossa de Mar, ☎ *34 18 86, FAX 34 11 03.*
Closed Nov.–April.
This is a century-old townhouse with modernista details and a patio you could sit in for ever. Balconies and largish rooms are unusual for such prices. You won't find more interesting architecture for any price. *21 rooms.*

Sant March   R3rd-class ★

C. Nou, 9, Tossa de Mar (two blocks back from the bridge to the Platja Gran), ☎ *34 00 78.*
Open May–Sept.
Situated on a quiet street, this hotel offers rock-bottom comfort. *30 rooms.*

Where to Eat

Expensive ($30+)

Es Molí   ★ ★ ★

Tarull, 5 (hiding behind the church), ☎ *34 14 14.*
Closed Monday, Wednesday out of season and Feb.
Look no further for the most attractive setting and best food in town. Dine in a courtyard bordered by arches surrounding a fountain, or facing the garden. It is dif-

ficult to mention just one or two dishes, but the soups are elegant and the cascade of grilled fish is memorable.

Sant Feliú de Guíxols ★

Population: 15,485
Area code: 972; zip code: 17220

The corniche road provides 23 km of magnificent scenery and hairpin curves on the way from Tossa to Sant Feliu.

Sant Feliú is attractively circled by hills sheltering a bay. It enjoys great popularity as a resort, popularity that comes more from its conviviality than its beach, which is nothing to speak of. Instead, everyone buses to the magnificent sands of S'Agaró three km to the north. The town **church** was remodelled inside in the 14th century, but its wonderful façade with a charming arcade remains intact.

Where to Stay

Given its popularity, Sant Feliú is woefully short of hotels, which makes reservations imperative.

Very Expensive ($200+)

In S'Agaró, three km north:

Hostal De la Gavina   Deluxe ★ ★ ★

Pl. de la Rosaleda, Sant Feliú, ☎ *32 11 00, FAX 32 15 73, Telex 57132.*

Here is real style presided over by so caring a staff that they make you feel you deserve it. On its own little peninsula above the beach and surrounded by pines, this hotel can satisfy every desire for pampered quiet. All is deluxe, as befits the Relais & Châteaux chain, and the furniture is worth a fortune, considering which, a bill that stretches a little past the expensive price-range is not excessive. *74 rooms.*

Moderate ($50–$99)

Murla Park   1st-class ★ ★

Pas. dels Guíxols, 22, Sant Feliú (at the northern end of the platja), ☎ *32 04 50, FAX 32 00 78, Telex 57364.*
Closed Nov.

This hotel provides quiet and some nice views over the bay. It is efficiently run. *89 rooms.*

Inexpensive (Less than $50)

Rex I   3rd-class ★

Rambla del Portalet, 16, Sant Feliú (two streets back from the platja), ☎ *82 18 09.*
Open June–Sept.

The Rex is well managed and provides more pleasant rooms than comparable establishments at this price. *25 rooms.*

Where to Eat

Befitting its popularity, Sant Feliú supports two superior, though expensive, restaurants.

Expensive ($30+)

Can Toni   ★★★★

C. Sant Martiria, 29 (well back from the beach, near the bus station), ☎ 32 10 26.
Closed Mon. from Oct.–May.
Though lacking the grand style of Eldorado Petit, the chef here is truly talented and
creative. For informality and fine food at reasonable prices, this is one of our favorite. Credit Cards: A, D, M, V.

Eldorado Petit   ★★★

Rambla Vidal, 23 (about halfway to the beach along the Rambla), ☎ 32 18 18, FAX 32
14 69.
Closed Wed. out of season and Nov.
This is the original establishment that went big time in Barcelona. The food is
almost as beautiful and inventive here, but in more relaxed surroundings, and
although the prices are expensive, they are barely so. Credit Cards: A, M, V.

Palafrugel ★

Population: 15,030
Area code: 972; zip code: 17200

*From Sant Feliú C-255 winds north past S'Agaró and Palamos to
Palafrugel in 23 km.*

Although not on the beach, Palafrugel serves as the hub for several beach
communities within a five-k radius. One of these, **Calella**, offers a string of
adorable beaches, another, **Llafranc**, has magnificent coastal views, but **Tamariu**, surrounded by umbrella pines, is less crowded and the most lovely. Still
another beach, **Aigua Blava**, lies in a secluded cove surrounded by azure sea
and has a parador. Lastly, **Begur** offers a medieval castle. A 50 minute walk
from Calella brings the Castell i Jardins de Cap Roig, a fine botanical garden
formed of a maze of flowers and tropical plants. *(Open daily Mar.–Dec. 9
a.m.–9 p.m.; admission: 200 ptas.)* Good ceramics are produced in **La Bisbal**,
12 km along C-255 on the way back toward Girona.

Where to Stay

Each of the surrounding beach villages offers some fine accommodations.

Very Expensive ($200+)

In Peratallada:

Castell de Peratallada   Unclassed ★★★

Pl. del Castell, Paratallada (this Medieval town is six km west of Palafrugel), ☎ 63 40 21,
FAX 63 40 11.
Open only Fri. through Sun from Nov. to March. The restaurant is closed Sun. night and
Mon.

If you're fortunate to get one of the five rooms, you're in for one of the more
unusual hotel experiences. This is a true Medieval castle which is privately owned
and puts up guests. There is a lived-in castle feeling here that is missing from similar
paradors. Note, it is not a full service hotel since its business is serving meals that are
expensive purely as food, but worth it for the atmosphere. *Five rooms.*

Expensive ($100–$200)

In Aigua Blava:

Aigua Blava   1st-class ★ ★ ★

Platja de Fornells. Aigua Blava, ☎ *62 20 58, FAX 62 21 12, Telex 56000.*
Closed from the middle of Feb. through mid Nov.

This hotel wins easily over the parador nearby. The Aigua Blava is less expensive,
superbly managed and situated in a formal garden overlooking the cove. It offers a
pool and tennis, all for prices that are barely expensive. *85 rooms.*

Parador de Aiguablava   1st-class ★ ★

Aigua Blave, ☎ *62 21 62, FAX 62 21 66.*

Views over the cove and coast are nothing short of magnificent. Otherwise, this is a
modern-style parador with the expected fine accommodations and good service. *87
rooms.*

Moderate ($50–$99)

In Tamariu:

Hostalillo   2nd-class ★

C. Bellavista, 22, Tamariu, ☎ *61 02 50, FAX 61 02 17.*
Open last week in May through Sept.

Of the options in Tamariu, we prefer this one for its lovely terrace looking over the
cove. Considering that it is the best hotel in town, its prices are better than fair.
Good, inexpensive meals are served in the restaurant. *70 rooms.*

In Calella:

Sant Roc   3rd-class ★

Pl. Atlantic, 2, in Barri Sant Roc, ☎ *61 42 50, FAX 61 40 68.*
Open from Apr. through the middle of Oct.

This is peaceful little hotel above the beach with spectacular views over coast and
sea. *42 rooms.*

Garbí   2nd-class ★

Av. Costa Daurada, 20, Tamariu, ☎ *61 40 40, FAX 61 58 03.*
Open from the middle of Apr. through Oct.

Situated in a lovely pine forest, this hotel provides quiet along with generous
accommodations. *30 rooms.*

Inexpensive (Less than $50)

In Llafranc:

Casamar   3rd-class ★ ★

C. Nero, 3, Llafranc, ☎ *30 01 04, FAX 61 06 51.*
Open from the middle of Apr. to the middle of Oct.

This little gem provides splendid views over the cove at prices that are lower than
Garbí. *20 rooms.*

L'Escala ★

Population: 4,048
Area code: 972; zip code: 17300

Follow signs to **Pals** ★, *a 14th-century farming community, lovingly restored. Continue north along C-260 through* **Torroella** *with a 13th-century castle, then through flat fields to L'Escala after 27 km.*

Although L'Escala offers decent beaches, its main attraction is the extensive classical ruins nearby at Empüries. The ruins are a walkable two km from town, and are described under a separate heading in this chapter.

Where to Stay

Moderate ($50–$99)

Nieves-Mar   **2nd-class** ★

P. Martim, 8, L'Escala, ☎ *77 03 00, FAX 10 36 05, Telex 98532).*
Open April–Oct.
With a pool, tennis courts and nice views of the sea, this is the best choice in town and very reasonable for what it offers. Simple fresh fish are done well in its modestly-priced restaurant, and the fish soups are delicious. *80 rooms.*

Cadaqués ★★★

Population: 1547
Area code: 972; zip code: 17488

Head north to Castello d'Empüries, with an exceptional provincial Gothic church from the 13th century. Continue toward Roses on C-260, but in seven km follow signs left to Cadaqués, 10 km of winding scenery further on.

This is the archetypical fishing village, as pretty as the nicest postcard of quaint whitewashed houses surrounding a little harbor. The town is lively, but suffers from a beach that, though as scenic as can be, includes uncomfortable stones. The village gained international fame when Salvador Dali built a summer cottage outside of this village that attracted a collection of artists including Picasso, Utrillo and Duchamp. His house, ornamented with egg-shaped decorations, is in Lligat opposite the Port Lligat hotel. Fans of Dali, or anyone interested in the exotic or the subconscious, should take a trip to **Figueres**, 25 km inland, the town where Dali was born and died. There the pink Dali Museum is decorated with huge boiled eggs and bubble gum, preceded by a pile of tractor tires. The inside is better seen than described *(Open Oct.–Mar. daily 11:30–6pm, and July–Sept. 9 a.m.–9pm; admission: 600 ptas.)*

Where to Stay

Expensive ($100–$200)

Playa Sol   **2nd-class** ★

Platja Pianch, 3, Cagaqués, ☎ *25 81 00, FAX 25 80 54).*
Closed Jan.–Feb.
This modern hotel presents pretty views of the village. The garden is attractive and the hotel offers tennis and a pool. *49 rooms.*

Moderate ($50–$99)

S'Aguarda   2nd-class ★ ★

> *Carreteria de Port-Lligat, 28 (on the way to Port-Lligat, one km north of town),* ☎ *25 80 82, FAX 25 87 56).*
>
> *Closed Nov.*

Pleasant views and surroundings add to the comfortable, fairly-priced rooms that even include TVs. *27 rooms.*

Where to Eat

Expensive ($30+)

La Galiota   ★ ★

> *C. Narciso Monturiol, 9,* ☎ *25 81 87.*
>
> *Open July through Sept., and weekends during the rest of the year.*

In addition to being the best place to eat in town, this is the trendiest. Pictures by Dali line the walls. However, the restaurant is not pretentious either in decor or cuisine—the simplest things, such as garlicked leg of lamb, can be sublime. Reservations are strongly advised. Credit Cards: A, D, V.

The remaining 38 km of coast are breathtakingly scenic, but do not offer beach towns as pleasant as those described. **Port de la Selva**, *nine km along, is a fine natural harbor in a huge bay. Another six km brings* **Port de Llanca**, *with a long beach subject to winds. Nine km south of Llanca are the marvellous ruins of the 11th-century* **Monestir de Sant Pere de Roda** ★. *Views up and down the coast are stupendous. (Open daily 10 a.m.–2 p.m. and 4 p.m.–dusk; admission: 150 ptas.) From Llarca, 21 km along N-260 brings the French border at the town of* **Port Bou**.

Costa Dorada ★ ★

Starting just south of Barcelona, the Costa Dorada consists of mile after mile of the golden sand after which the coast is named. It starts at Castelldefels, 25 km south of Barcelona, and ends at Sant Carles de la Rápita, where the river Ebro forms a delta at the sea 150 km south. C-246 follows the northern part, changing to N-340 from Calafell south. We describe the sights starting from the Barcelona end.

> *From* **Barcelona** *take the freeway toward the airport. Past the airport you have a choice between the scenic and slow coastal C-246 or the new A-7 toll road, in either case reaching Castelldefels in 23 km. From* **Valencia** *take either the toll A-7 or the free N-340 (which crawls through coastal towns in the summer) 183 km to Tortosa and follow the description below in reverse.*

Castelldefels

Population: 24,559
Area code: 93; zip code: 08860

This and Sitges, which follows, are the two most popular resorts for Barcelonans. Both are crowded, yet retain enough attractiveness to draw visitors. Pine hills behind its enormous beach make sunning in Castelldefels particularly sylvan. The town contains a Romanesque church and the keep from a medieval castle. But since this beach is a day outing for Barcelonans and many own houses in the town, the hotel situation is terrible.

19 km farther south comes lovely Sitges.

Sitges ★★★

Population: 11,850
Area code: 93; zip code: 08870

This is one of the most appealing towns in Spain. It contains an attractive harbor, a lovely sea promenade, whitewashed houses and a long golden beach. In addition, it has a couple of nice museums including the **Casa Llopis**—for dolls and furniture. Add a very swinging nightlife, enhanced by a substantial influx of gays, and the stage shows of a casino (☎ *893 36 66*) nearby in Sant Pere de Ribes and you have about everything you could want in a resort, except seclusion.

Where to Stay

Proximity to Barcelona seems to have infected most hotels here with its high price disease.

Expensive ($100–$200)

Terramar   **1st-class ★ ★**
   P. Maritim, 80, Sitges (at the southern end of the beach), ☎ *894 00 50, FAX 894 56 04, Telex 53186.*
   Open May–Oct.
   On its own little square overlooking the beach, this is a most comfortable hotel, if largish. The views are nice and tennis is available as well. *209 rooms.*

Subur Maritim   **2nd-class ★**
   P. Martim, 72, Sitges (on the beach at the bottom of Pas. Dr. Benapres), ☎ *894 15 50, FAX 894 04 27, Telex 52962.*
   This intimate place is watched over by an attentive staff. Views of the beach and ocean are pleasant and the garden around the pool is restful. *46 rooms.*

Moderate ($50–$99)

Romantic y la Renaixenca   **4th-class ★ ★ ★**
   C. Sant Isidre, 33, Sitges (three blocks back from the northern end of the beach), ☎ *894 83 75, FAX 894 81 67.*
   Open Apr. through Oct.
   These three buildings are managed as one hotel and provide the opportunity to stay in a *modernista* house of airy halls and lovely tiles. The garden is lush and, yes,

romantic. Accommodations are comfortable, if a little cramped, but the prices are fair indeed. *55 rooms.*

Vilafranca del Penedès and Sant Sadumi D'Anoia ★

Take C-420 inland for 22 km to Penedès. Sant Sadumi lies 11 km north of Penedès on C-243.

This is an excursion for those interested in wine. Penedès is the still-wine capital of Catalonia with a wonderful museum of the grape in the **Museu dei Vi** on the Pl. Jaume. The museum occupies the ground floor of a 14th-century palace of the kings of Aragón. (*Open daily 10 a.m.–2 p.m. and 4–6pm; admission: 250 ptas.*) Tours and tastings at various bodegas are also possible, such as **Miguel Torres** on *Comercio, 22.*

Sant Sadumi seems to have nothing but champagne on its mind as sign after sign points to some *cava* producer. Tours and tastings are offered. In addition, since the town first attained prosperity at the turn of the century, it is a virtual museum-town of the *modernista* style. **Codorniu**'s cellars and the house of the family on *Caserio* are superior examples. Its facilities are so vast that visits are conducted via a tiny train.

Villanova i La Geltrú ★★

Population: 43,560
Area code: 93; zip code: 08800

From Sitges the attractive coast road leads to Villanueva in seven km.

Golden sand is framed by boulders around a bay, while olive and palm trees lend shade. An enchanting museum, the **Casa Papiol**, sits in the northern end of the town, which reconstructs living conditions for the well-to-do at the turn of the 19th century, and is fascinating for the details.

Where to Stay

A town of this size should provide more hotels, but, at least, the prices begin to decline as the distance widens from Barcelona.

Moderate ($50–$99)

Sovli 70   3rd-class ★

P. Ribes Roges, 1, Villanova i La Geltrú, ☎ *815 12 45, FAX 815 70 02.*
Closed from the second week of Oct.–mid Nov.

Here, prices are reasonable and there are views over the lovely beach. *30 rooms.*

C-246 is joined a few km south of La Geltrú and leads to el Vendrell, at which point the road is designated N-340 and reaches Tarragona in 27 km. Or join A-7 for a faster ride.

Tarragona ★★

See the description under its own heading.

Salou ★

Population: 16,450
Area code: 977; zip code: 43840

From Tarragona follow signs to A-7, but take the freeway south toward Salou, before entering the toll road. Salou is 10 km along the freeway.

Salou is much enjoyed by the Tarragonians, who cover its long expanse of sand in the high summer. Pleasant flowered promenades, lined by palms, follow the beach. A glut of building, however, has virtually swallowed up what was once a fishing port.

Where to Stay

Because Salou is accustomed mainly to day-trippers from Tarragona, its hotels are few, but reasonable.

Moderate ($50–$99)

Carabela Roc   2nd-class ★

C. Pau Casals, 108, Salou (on the platja de la Pineda, seven km east), ☎ *37 01 66, FAX 37 07 62, Telex 56709.*
Open from the second week in Apr.–Oct.
This charmer is nestled amid pines near a fine long beach. *96 rooms.*

Inexpensive (Less than $50)

Planas   2nd-class ★ ★

Pl. Bonet, 3, Salou, ☎ *38 01 08.*
Open from the middle of Apr. through Oct.
Location on the beach, fronted by a most pleasant terrace, combined with low prices, make this modest hotel stand out. *100 rooms.*

Cambrils de Mar ★

Population: 11,211
Area code: 977; zip code: 43850

The coast road N-340 covers the eight km to Cambrils.

By the few added kilometers it lies farther from Tarragona, Cambrils manages to retain more character. It includes a pretty marina, and is less developed overall. Cambrils also beckons gourmets, thanks to a family named Gatell whose various members run three excellent restaurants.

Where to Stay

Prices are more than fair.

Moderate ($50–$99)

Mónica   2nd-class ★ ★

C. Galcerán Marquet, 3, Cambrils de mar, ☎ *36 01 16, FAX 79 36 78.*
Open Mar. through Nov.

Its palm grove garden makes this choice stand out. Reasonable prices and comfortable rooms don't hurt. *56 rooms.*

Where to Eat

Expensive ($30+)

Joan Gateli/Casa Gatell   ★★★

P. Miramar, 26, ☎ 36 00 57.
Closed Sun. night, Mon., Jan. and Christmas week.
Put yourself in the capable hands of Sr. Joan. Start with his remarkable selection of *entremeses*, then move on to a fabulous seafood with rice or an excellent paella. The lobster (*bogavante*) will set you back a bit. Any good fish restaurant is going to be somewhat expensive, but this one is sure to please. Credit Cards: A, D, M, V.

Sant Carles de la Rápita ★

Population: 9960
Area code: 977; zip code: 43540

> *The next point of interest after Cambrils is 65 km south. Either join the toll road A-7 or the free N-340 heading south toward Tortosa. If travelling by A-7, exit at Amposta (exit 41), the next town after Tortosa, and take N-340 from there. In 13 km farther comes Sant Carles.*

Sant Carles perches on the edge of the Ebro delta, which is one thing that makes it special. This low land grows tons of rice, and each fall millions of migrating birds harvest the last pickings on their way to wintering in Africa. Virtually all the coastline of the delta is beach by any definition.

The second thing that makes Sant Carles special is that it is a planned community—planned in the middle of the 19th century by Carlos III who created so much of Madrid. This was to be the model port of Spain, since it was situated in a huge protected bay. Construction of a rational gridded town commenced, but the expected trade never arrived. Perhaps Spain had enough harbors already. So today it sits, all prettied, waiting for ships that will never come, receiving sun- and nature-lovers instead.

Incidentally, the best prawns in Spain are served around town.

Where to Stay

Prices are more than fair; they're downright low.

Inexpensive (Less than $50)

Juanito Platja   4th-class ★★

On Platja Miami, one km south, ☎ 74 04 62.
Open Apr.–Sept.
Quiet (because it is out of town), on the beach for lovely views, and with a terrace for lounging, this is our favorite choice in Sant Carles. *35 rooms.*

If full, take your pick between the following serviceable, inexpensively priced hotels:

Miami Park 2nd-class

   Av. Constitución, 33, Sant Carles, ☎ *74 03 51.*
   Open Apr. through Mar.
   80 rooms.

Llansola 3rd-class

   C. San isidro, 98, Sant Carles, ☎ *74 04 03.*
   Closed Nov.
   18 rooms.

Plaça Vella 3rd-class

   C. Arsenal, 31, Sant Carles 21 rooms. ☎ *77 24 53, FAX 74 43 97.*
   18 rooms.

Empuries ★ ★

One route to Empúries is described in the Costa Brava itinerary, along with accommodations. From **Barcelona** *the quickest route is along the toll A-7 past Girona to exit 5, then turning toward the coast to Viladamat and L'Escala. A sign points along a paved road to Empúries one km before L'Escala. The trip covers 145 km.*

Hours open: Tues.–Sun. 10 a.m.–2 p.m. and 3–7 p.m. From the middle of Sept.–May open from Tues.–Sun. 10 a.m.–1 p.m. and 3–5 p.m. Closed Mon.

Empúries is the one place in Spain where significant Greek remains can be explored. While the ruins are not extensive, neither are they abundant in Greece itself. The experience is heightened by the fact that the site, having drastically declined by the third century A.D. and abandoned since the eighth century, is not surrounded by modern buildings—thus freeing the imagination to humanize the stones. There are also extensive remains of a Roman city located on a gentle hill overlooking the sea, pleasant beaches and guides in togas to show you around.

Phoenicians settled first on this spot in the sixth century B.C. on what was then an offshore island, now joined to the mainland. Greeks arrived in the fourth century B.C. and built their *Neapolis* ("New Town") about an eighth of a mile south of that first settlement. It became the major Greek colony on the peninsula, from which both the grape and olive were introduced to Spain and western Europe. But the Greeks faded as upstart Rome grew aggressive.

In 49 B.C. Julius Caesar built a retirement town for his Roman veterans higher up the hill. As Roman power declined, beginning in the third century, invasions so depleted both cities that they fell readily to the Moors in the eighth century, and were abandoned thereafter.

The Greek city, lowest on the hill, is entered through a cyclopian gate south of the Museum. Immediately to the left stands its sacred precinct with remains of the Temple of Aesculapeus, the god of medicine. Just north a tall watchtower rises, from which lookouts could scan the sea. At its feet lie remains of the town cisterns, including a reconstructed water filter. Directly to the right of the gate run the colonnades of the Temple of Zeus Serapis, a combined Greek and Egyptian god of the sun and fertility. The town meeting place—agora—stands 100 yards north of this gate. Behind it is a reconstruction of the stoa, or roofed market. Ruins of a very early Christian basilica lie just to the north.

The extensive Roman town spreads up the hill and across a road. Much remains to be excavated, though two houses with mosaics have been cleared and are interesting studies as early versions of the typical patioed Spanish houses of today. The forum, lined by porticos, lies to the south of these houses. Temples and shops would have surrounded this plaza. An amphitheater can be discerned 100 yards further on. *Admission: 400 ptas. A helpful guidebook in English costs 500 ptas.*

Poblet Monastery ★ ★ ★

Poblet and **Santes Creus** *monasteries, being 30 km apart, are readily combined in one trip. From* **Barcelona** *take the toll A-7 west for 62 km, where it divides. Join A-2 toward Lleida to exit 11, Vila-Rodona. Santa Creus is three km north of Vila-Radona. For Poblet continue to exit 9, Montblanc. Go west for six km on N-240 to L'Esplung de Francoli and Poblet. From* **Zaragoza** *and west both monasteries lie on the route to Barcelona, and the directions above may be followed.*

Hours open: daily 10 a.m.–12:30 p.m. and 3–6 p.m. (or to 5 p.m. in winter).

Poblet began as an architectural masterpiece and now is the most complete example of a Gothic monastery in Spain. It has won international awards for the quality of its restoration. *Admission: 600 ptas., for guided tours.*

The monastery was founded by Ramón Berenguer IV in the middle of the 12th century to thank God for success against the Moors. He brought Cistercian monks from his territories in southern France to create a cloistered community. Poblet was favored through the 15th century by the kings of Aragón, who established a residence for retreats and made the monastery their royal pantheon. But, during the Napoleonic Wars and the anticlerical times that followed in the 19th century, Poblet was desecrated and abandoned. Cistercians returned in 1940, restoring the monastery ever since.

After passing through gates in two perimeter walls, the Romanesque Chapel of Santa Catalina, from the time of the founder, lies on the left. Directly ahead is the baroque 18th-century church front, with two tall towers. The huge, solemn adjoining cloister contains a large hexagonal fountain and pavilion.

The church interior, in the simple Cistercian style, is mainly 13th-century. Its pride is the tombs of the House of Aragón that repose on either side of the transept crossing.

Architecturally unique, the royal tombs are placed on low archways from which the sarcophagi and effigies angle down toward the viewer. They date from the middle of the 14th century. On the left are effigies of Jaume I, who reclaimed Valencia from the Moors; Pere IV, with two wives; plus Fernando I and Martin I. On the right are effigies of Alfonso II, Juan I and Juan II, with their respective wives. Because the sculpture is lovely and moving, it is a shock to learn that the originals were utterly destroyed and that what we now see are carvings by the Catalan artist Frederic Marès this century. They are, however, faithful to the original aesthetic.

The tour continues through the monastery kitchen, refectory and an elegant chapterhouse, to the huge dormitory and adjoining royal palace from 1400. A smaller dormitory nearby has been converted into a museum that shows the appalling state of the monastery before its reconstruction.

Where to Stay and Eat

Inexpensive (Less than $50)

Masia del Cadet   4th-class ★ ★
Les Masies, Poblet, ☎ *87 03 33, FAX 87 03 26.*
Although primarily in the restaurant business and serving good food on the high side of inexpensive, the Masia is a very pleasant place to stay as well. Rooms are serviceable, but by no means grand, yet the views over the countryside and to the monastery are grand indeed and well worth the stay. *12 rooms.* Credit Cards: A, D, V.

Santes Creus Monastery ★ ★

See the encompassing directions to nearby Poblet Monastery above.
Hours open: daily 10 a.m.–1 p.m. and 3–7 p.m. (to 6 p.m. in winter). Admission: 350 ptas., for guided tours.

Santes Creus was founded as an annex to Poblet monastery (described previously) by the same king at about the same mid-12th-century date, and—like Poblet—for Cistercian monks from France. Similarly, it was favored by the kings of Aragón and served as a royal pantheon for several. It too was abandoned and suffered damage in the middle of the 19th century, but restoration began in this century and continues. The lovely Gothic architecture and completeness of Santes Creus are rivaled in Spain only by Poblet.

A baroque gateway through perimeter walls lets into the principle courtyard, surrounded by outbuildings now privately owned. The former bishopric with a patio serves today both as the local ayuntamiento and the school. At the far end stands the 13th-century church, with battlements added a century later.

Entrance through the south side lets into a grand cloister. Though restored, the original liveliness of the carvings on the capitals prefigured the later, more flamboyant Gothic, and makes the cruder fountain pavilion and basin seem out of place. Tombs of the nobility of Aragón fill wall niches.

The church interior is severely simple in the Cistercian style. A high nave is raised on massive square pillars. Light is admitted through a 13th-century lantern at the transept crossing and through original rose windows at either end of the church—the one in the apse being particularly lovely. Left and right of the altar are the royal tombs. On the left, beneath a canopy, reposes Pere III. His son Jaume II and wife are to the altar's right. These effigies represent the very finest carving of the 14th century. Later, Plateresque decoration was added below them.

The adjoining chapterhouse is properly solemn, and the dormitory above forms an elegantly simple gallery surmounted by a timber roof. Outside, to the right, is a lovely cloister from the 12th century. A passage leads to the kitchens and refectory, then to the royal palace with an elegant patio and fine stairway.

Tarragona ★ ★

Population: 111,869
Area code: 977; zip code: 43000.

> *One route to Tarragona is described under the* **Costa Dorada** *heading. From* **Barcelona** *the most speedy route is to take the toll road A-7 west for 97 km. From* **Zaragoza** *and west the toll A-2 leads in 214 km to exit 11 at Valls where a connection in eight km to N-240 brings Tarragona in 16 km more. Slower, but toll-less, is to take N-II for 142 km to Lleida, where N-240 leads to Tarragona in 90 km more. From Valencia the toll A-7 speeds to Tarragona in 257 km, while the free N-340 consumes twice the time because of its route through coastal resorts.*

Today Tarragona is Catalonia's third city, but once it was the principle city of all of Spain. Caesar Augustus made it the Roman capital of that part of the Iberian peninsula controlled by the Romans and called Terraconensis, in which some find the source of the present name. But non-Roman remains of massive stone walls show that a town long preceded that Roman one. The original settlement was an Iberian town which the Carthagenians took, settled, and called Tarchon, a more likely source for the present name.

In any case, under the Romans, Tarragona prospered, enjoying a population probably twice that of today. Saint Paul is said to have visited to begin the process of Christianizing Western Europe. Tarragona became the original and primary bishopric of Spain—a primacy that lasted until passing to Toledo in the 11th century. But, in 711, the Moors razed the city so completely that it remained deserted for 300 years. It rose again to become the major city of eastern Spain, but because it served as a center for rebellions, it was repeatedly sacked—in 1643, 1705 and 1811. These assaults stunted growth, allowing Barcelona, and even Valencia and Terrasa, to eventually surpass it in importance and size.

Tarragona possesses a fine collection of Roman artifacts displayed in the **Museu Arqueològico ★**. The **Praetorium ★** is where Caesar Augustus stayed and Pontius Pilate was born. A lovely walk, called the **Passeig Arqueològic ★**, follows old city walls that are Roman with earlier remains and later additions. There are ruins of a huge **circus maximus**, and an imposing Gothic **Cathedral ★**. There is also a cemetery with sarcophagi of the earliest Christians, called the **Necropolis Paleocristia ★**; and a splendid Roman mausoleum, **Centcelles ★**, five km west of town. Tarragona, as yet undiscovered by tourists, is a pretty city with a cute port below terraced houses that well repays a half day's visit.

POLLUTION ALERT

Tarragona's beaches are not considered safe for bathing.

*From the **Costa Dorada** the city is entered on Via Augusta, which funnels into Rambla Vella after a slight right. In five blocks comes a hospital on the right, followed by the old city walls. Take the next right for parking. From **Barcelona**, **Zaragoza** and west, the city is entered along N-240 which funnels into the major traffic circle of Pl. Imperial Tarraco. Take Rambla Nova with a center strip leading out of the opposite side of the circle that was entered. In two blocks comes a major intersection where a gentle left should be made onto Av. Pau Casals. The third right, C. López Peláez leads to parking one block later on the left. From **Valencia** on A-7, cross the Francoli River along Av. Ramón i Cajal. When this street crosses the large intersection with Rambla Nova (with the center strip), continue straight across. The name of the street is now Av. Pau Casals, and the third right, C. López Peláez, leads to parking on the left in one block.*

*Rambla Vella, a few steps south of the parking place, divides the new part of Tarragona from the older section north of the Rambla. Walk a half block to the beginning of the walls and follow them northwest for two blocks to the Portal de Roser. Here begins the Passeig Arqueològic between the walls, but first pass through the gate into the Pl. Pallol to see a few remains of a **Roman forum**.*

What to See and Do

Passeig Arqueològic

Pl. de Pallol, ☎ *24 57 96.*

Hours open: Tues.–Sat. 9 a.m.–1:30 p.m. and 3–8 p.m. (to 6 p.m. in winter). Open Sun. 10 a.m.–1 p.m.

This walk along the city walls passes pretty gardens and provides views over the countryside, but it also presents an opportunity to see the different stages of the walls' construction. Of course the lowest part of the walls, composed of massive stones, is the oldest—pre-third-century B.C., and probably built by Carthage. It supports a Roman wall of regular construction built by Scipio Africanus in the third century B.C. Above are Visigothic and medieval additions. The outer wall beyond it is an 18th-century English structure. *Admission: 400 ptas.*

The walk ends at the portal de Sant Antoni, which lets into the old quarter. Following the walls south leads to the Museu Arqueològic in three blocks.

Museo Arqueològic ★

Pl. del Rei, 5, ☎ *23 62 09.*

Hours open: Tues.–Sat. 10 a.m.–1 p.m. and 4:30–8 p.m. (to 7 p.m. in winter). Open Sun. 10 a.m.–2 p.m. Closed Mon.

The exhibits all were found at Tarragona or in the surrounding area, and most are Roman. The statuary is not outstanding, but the mosaics, especially an appropriately haunting Medusa, are striking. Some smaller articles on the second floor hold interest. *Admission: 200 ptas.*

The tall Gothic building adjoining is the praetorium.

Pretori Romani/Museu d'Historia ★

Pl. del Rei.

Hours open: Tues.–Sat. 10 a.m.–1 p.m. and 4:30–8 p.m. (to 7 p.m. in winter). Open Sun. 10 a.m.–2 p.m. Closed Mon.

Though looking Gothic because of restoration in the Middle Ages, this building is a true first century B.C. palace that sheltered historical figures of a magnitude that seem mythical. Caesar Augustus is known to have slept here, and Pontius Pilate, later praetor of Judea, was probably born within these walls during his father's term as the governor of Tarragona. A thousand years later kings of Aragón also resided here. Today the building serves as a museum of the city's history, with exhibits that are of small interest. But the basement remains Roman, and includes mysterious tunnels and vaults. On the first floor is a sarcophagus of Hippolytus, salvaged from the sea and claimed to be third-century B.C. Greek. *Admission: 400 ptas.*

The Cathedral is two blocks northeast along C. Santa Anna, which crosses the front of the museum, then a left along the picturesquely arcaded C. Merceria.

Cathedral

Pl. de la Seu, ☎ *23 86 85.*

Hours open: daily 10 a.m.–12:30 p.m. and 4–7 p.m. (to 6 p.m. in winter).

This 14th-century Cathedral was raised during the transitional period between Romanesque and Gothic styles. The facade presents a lovely Gothic central portal flanked by smaller round Romanesque doors.

Entry is through the large cloister on the north side. Although the interior vaulting is Gothic, this earliest part of the church is a Romanesque frame. Moorish influence is apparent in the geometric pierced-work in arches and in the polylobed arches closest to the cathedral. In fact a 10th century mihrab penetrates the west gallery amid Roman architectural fragments. The cathedral was built on the site of a former mosque (which replaced an even earlier Roman Temple of Jupiter), from which this "prayer niche" survives. Although most of the capitals of the arcade are merely foliated, a few are charmingly carved. Everyone's favorite, in the second bay on the east, depicts a cat's funeral conducted by rats. The museum off the east gallery displays a fine collection of tapestries, including the beautiful Gothic *La Bona Vida* (The Good Life).

Dusky light inside the cathedral slowly reveals the immense size of the church—a football field in length (one of the biggest in Catalonia), seeming even higher than it is because the side aisles reach only halfway up the nave. Though severe in feeling, all the decorative work is first-rate and to be savored. Most outstanding is the intricate and delicate high altar retable by Pere Joan and Guillermo de la Mota. It depicts the life of Saint Tecla who was converted by Saint Paul then suffered persecution from everyone, including her mother. Several times she was saved from death by Divine intervention. *Admission: 300 ptas., including guide.*

After visiting the Cathedral, go around the back to see the **Chapel of Sant Pau**, *on what is reputed to be the site where Saint Paul first preached. Rebuilt in the middle of the 13th century, the chapel shows signs of much greater age.*

From directly in front of the Cathedral descend C. Mayor past antique stores to reach the Pl. de la Font, named for the fountain. This is the site of the Roman **Circus Maximus**, *still under excavation (entrance is free). When new in the first century A.D., the circus was a narrow oval, 350 feet long, seating 25,000 spectators.*

Walk to the western end of the Rambla Vella to turn right along Pas. de les Palmeres to the balcony overlooking the sea at the first corner. Called the **Balcó de Mediterràni**, *its view of city and sea are lovely. Toward the beach below can be seen a Roman* **amphitheater**. *Stairs to the left descend to the structure, in which one is free to wander. Ruins of a 12th-century Romanesque church stand in the center.*

For the **Necropolis Paleocristia** ★ *walk seven blocks northwest up the gardened Rambla Nova to its end. West along Av. Ramón i Cajal for a half mile, almost to the river, brings the necropolis on the left. This large cemetery from the earliest Christian times contains a large number of tombs, sarcophagi and urns, some reused from the pagan Romans. More are displayed* *in the museum. (Same hours as the Museu Arqueològic; admission: 200 ptas.)*

The **Centcelles Mausoleum** ★ *requires a car or taxi for the five km trip. Take Av. Ramón i Cajal across the river, following signs to A-7 and Valencia. Turn off onto the road marked for Reus. In Constanti turn right onto C. de Centcelles, unpaved, for half a mile, turning left just before the village of Centcelles. Two large buildings, monumental, but incongruously tiled in pink, stand in a modern vineyard. Inside, a large cupola is covered with wonderful mosaics depicting early Christian themes. The mausoleum belonged to a wealthy Roman of the fourth century.*

Where to Stay

Prices remain reasonable in Tarragona, although the selection is sparse and lacks character.

Expensive ($100–$200)

Imperial Tarraco   1st-class ★ ★

P. Palmeres, Tarragona (at the end of Rambla Vella), ☎ *23 30 40, FAX 21 65 66.*
This crescent of a modern hotel stands just above the Balcó de Mediterràni for postcard views over the town and sea. A room with a sea view is the whole point of the hotel, so insist on one. The rooms are comfortable, if a little bare, and include a private balcony. This is the best hotel in town and reasonably priced for its category. *155 rooms, plus 15 suites.*

Moderate ($50–$99)

Lauria   2nd-class ★

Rambla Nova, 20, Tarragona (a block from the end of the Rambla, near the Balcó de Mediterràni), ☎ *23 67 12, FAX 23 67 00.*
This businessperson's hotel is sleek, well located and back rooms provide distant sea views. Note, only about half the rooms are air-conditioned. *72 rooms.*

Inexpensive (Less than $50)

España   4th-class ★ ★

Rambla Nova, 49, Tarragona (a block north of the Hotel Lauria), ☎ *23 27 07.*
This modern townhouse with an excellent location charges attractive prices. Rooms are comfortable, and the outer ones have balconies. *40 rooms.*

Where to Eat

For the best, freshest seafood, head for the port and innumerable restaurants. Our favorite, La Puda, is described in this section. The port stands at the southwest end of the beach—by heading due south from the Rambla Nova the walk is less than half a mile.

Moderate ($15–$30)

La Puda   ★ ★

Muelle Pescadores, 25 (across from the pavilion where the fishermen dock), ☎ *21 15 11.*
Completely unpretentious with sea-blue walls and white tablecloths, this restaurant serves the freshest fish in town for fair prices. Start with an appetizer platter of the day's catch, followed by the house fish soup, or whatever claims your fancy. No reservations are taken. Credit Cards: A, D, M, V.

La Galería ★

Rambla Nova, 16 (near the Hotel Lauria), ☎ *23 61 43.*
Closed Wed. night, Sun. and Sat. and Sun. lunch in summer.
The cuisine is inventive and remarkably inexpensive. The decor is attractively Belle
Époque with artwork by the chef, who will also decorate your plate with a lovely
entree. The sauces are good. Reservations are required on weekends. Credit Cards: A,
D, M, V.

Directory

Information

A municipal Tourist Office is located at *C. Major, 39*, opposite the Cathedral steps
(☎ *24 19 53*).

Trains and Buses

The station is in the port at Pl. de la Pedrera (☎ *24 02 02*). Trains run almost continually to Barcelona, 13 per day cover the four-hour run to Valencia, and nine go
to Zaragoza, but only two do the eight-hour trip to Madrid, the same number as to
Seville. RENFE has a convenient office at *Rambla Nova, 40* (☎ *23 25 24*).

The bus station is located on Pl. Imperial Tarraco, at the top end of the Rambla
Nova (☎ *22 91 26*). In this instance, bus service is less convenient for most destinations than the train.

Police

☎ *23 33 11.*

Excursions

Tarragona stands in the middle of the **Costa Dorada**, previously described. **Barcelona**,
to the north, and **Valencia**, to the south are natural trips, described in this chapter.

Valencia ★ ★

Population: 751,734
Area code: 96; zip code: 46000

From **Barcelona** *the toll A-7 is much faster than the free N-340,
which crawls through beach resorts for the 257 km trip. From the*
Costa Dorada *the same route is preferred, covering about 200 km.
From* **Madrid** *N-III leads directly in 351 km. From Almeria at the
end of the* **Costa del Sol** *N-340 reaches Alicante in 299 km, outside of
which the toll A-7 completes the remaining 179 km.*

Valencia has been a garden since the time of the Greeks, with the usual succession of masters—Carthagenians, Romans, Visigoths, then Moors. In the
11th century Valencia declared herself an independent Moorish state, but, in
1094, El Cid gathered an army of Christians and dissatisfied Moors to seize
the heavily fortified city for himself. Over the next five years he personally
controlled this fief, one of the richest areas in Spain, and died defending it
during one of the Moor's repeated efforts to take it back. (Legend has it

that, even after his death, El Cid's troops set his dead body astride a horse to frighten enemies away.) Three years later, the Moors regained their hold, and El Cid's wife, who had assumed command of his forces, left Valencia. Moors retained the city for only a century, until Jaume I of Aragón recaptured it for the Christian side.

Through war and peace Valencia prospered, for it is Spain's most fertile region—on a huge well-irrigated plain favored by continual warm weather. Only in the 17th century did it decline, when expulsion of the Moors' descendents drained it of farmers. But decline was only temporary, for it was not long before immigrants from poorer parts of Spain replenished the lost workforce. Today Valencia is the third-largest city in Spain, spreading across a wide level landscape. It is comfortably pleasant in winter, but can steam in midsummer.

Valencia presents an unattractive face to arriving visitors. Sprawling modern suburbs and factories seem to extend forever, surrounding and hiding Valencia's attractions, almost all of which nestle in a bend in the river Turia at the core of the city. There is an interesting **Cathedral** ★, containing the Holy Grail (it is claimed), and rare civil Gothic architecture in the **Lonja de la Seda** ★★ and the **Palacio de la Generalidad** ★. The **Colegio del Patriarca** contains a choice collection of paintings (though requiring special permission). Two fine *modernista* buildings are the **Estación** and the bustling **Mercado Central** (Central Market). Not far away, beside a pleasant garden, reposes the **Museo Provincial de Bellas Artes**, one of Spain's better museums of painting. Spain's finest ceramic collection is housed in the **Palacio Marqués Dos Aguas** ★★, a building so ugly that it is not to be missed. Valencia can provide a day's enjoyment by any reckoning.

POLLUTION ALERT

At last report Valencia's beaches are not safe for swimming.

Parking is available in Pl. Zaragoza, the square in front of the Cathedral. From the **airport** *and* **Madrid** *a dry watercourse is crossed to travel along Av. del Cid. It changes its name to San José Calasanz, after crossing the perimeter road (Av. de Pérez Galdos) before entering the large Pl. España. Take C. San Vicente Martir across the plaza, going northeast to the Pl. de Zaragoza and parking in 12 blocks. From* **Barcelona** *and the* **Costa Dorada** *follow signs for "Centro" and cross the riverbed to travel along the wide Av. de Peris y Valera. Turn right on C. Sueca to reach the huge, four-lane Gran Via Germanias and turn left (a momentary right is necessary first). The street bends under the train tracks to enter the large intersection of the Pl. España. Take San Vicente Martir heading northeast to the*

Pl. de Zaragoza and parking in 12 blocks. From the **Costa del Sol** *the city is entered along Av. de Auslas March. Turn left at the intersection to follow the large Av. de Peris y Valero which bends along an elevation over the train track. At the end of the elevation take San Vicente Martir on the right to the Pl. de Zaragoza and parking in 12 blocks.*

What to See and Do

Cathedral ★

Pl. de la Reina, ☎ *391 81 27.*

Hours open: daily 10 a.m.–1 p.m. and 4–6 p.m. (in winter for the morning hours only). Most of the cathedral was built in the 14th and 15th centuries, the Gothic era. Plateresque and baroque decorations that were applied later to the interior as in so many Spanish churches, in this case have been removed to leave the simpler Gothic original. The main facade is a strange bird—remodeled in the early 18th century in a Gothic style to blend with the interior. More striking is the adjoining octagonal Gothic tower, called the Miguelete, with a pierced upper story lined with tracery. It is unique.

Inside, stripped of decoration, the revealed Gothic superstructure seems plain. The first chapel on the right with elegant vaulting is the original chapterhouse. On its altar stands a small purple agate cup surrounded by alabaster reliefs. According to legend, this is the true Holy Grail used by Christ at the Last Supper. Indeed it is an old cup, certainly dating to Roman times, that had been venerated for centuries in northern Catalonia before its donation to the cathedral. The chains nearby were captured by an Aragonese fleet in the 15th century from the port of Marseilles, though why they should be displayed in a church is a puzzle. The museum off this chapel contains a number of early Valencian polychromed sculptures, a dark Zurbarán, a lovely Caravaggio *Virgin* and two special large Goyas of St. Francisco Borja, the saintly member of that otherwise venal Borge family.

Returning to the church proper, the 16th-century high altar betrays a large debt to Leonardo da Vinci. The camborio at the crossing uses alabaster panes instead of glass. Chapels in the left aisle are interesting, with some good paintings here and there. The treasury contains much goldwork, including a piece by the master, Benvenuto Cellini. *Admission: 100 ptas. to the museum.*

Proceed around the Cathedral to view the outside. The earliest part, the south facade, is Romanesque, while the north facade is badly weathered Gothic. A huge **Archbishop's Palace** *is connected to the south face. Off the north side stretches the lovely* **Pl. de la Virgin** *with a neoclassic fountain of a reclining colossus in the center. To the right, connected to the Cathedral by an arcade, is the* **Basilica de Nuestra Señora de los Desamparados** *(Our lady of the Forsaken), with a venerated gilt statue of the Virgin inside. This building, completed in 1667, was the first Spanish lunatic asylum, and possibly the first in the world.*

To the right of the plaza, fronted by orange trees, is the Gothic **Palau de la Géneralitat ★**. In this 15th-century building the Cortés of Valencia sat to impose the "general" tax, for which the building was named. The façade is elegant, though the second tower is 20th century. Inside is a fine patio, a splendid hall with lovely tiles, 16th-century murals and an artesonado ceiling, and two tower rooms with wondrous gilt and painted ceilings. (Open weekdays 9 a.m.–2 p.m. Admission: free, but by advance permission only. ☎ 332 02 06.)

Continue along the street fronting the palace, **C. Caballeros**. The doorknockers of many mansions lining this street are high so a horseman could reach them without dismounting. Some Gothic patios (such as numbers 22 and 23) are visible through doorways. After number 41, turn left down the tiny C. Abadadia San Nicholas to **Iglesia San Nicolás**. Although this was one of the oldest churches in the city, during the 16th century it was redecorated inside and out in the most flamboyant churrigueresque style. The interior is a baroque extravaganza.

Return to C. Caballeros, to take C. Bolseria, the third left. It leads downhill in three blocks to the Pl. del Mercado. The **Mercado Central**, after which the plaza is named, is on the right—a *modernista* production of tiles and glass from 1928. Inside is a collection of over a thousand stalls, divided into two sections, one for meat and produce and another for fish.

Across from the Mercado is the Gothic Lonja de la Seda.

Lonja de la Seda ★★

Pl. del Mercado, ☎ 391 36 08.
Hours open: Tues.–Sat. 10 a.m.–2 p.m. and 4–8 p.m. Open Sun. 10 a.m.–2 p.m. Closed Mon.
Valencia became the center for the silk the Moors introduced into Spain. Late in the 15th century, to proclaim their prosperous status, silk merchants erected this building as a bourse to manage and trade their goods. The richly decorated result is one of the finest surviving examples of Gothic civil architecture. A center tower divides the façade into halves, one side with the arms of Aragón and elaborate tracery, the other with an ornate upper gallery. The large Salon de Contratación inside, where contracts were bought and sold, supports a lofty ceiling on unusual Gothic twisted columns. A stairway from the Orange Tree Courtyard leads up to the Salon de Consular del Mar (Maritime Court), covered with a wonderful carved gargoyle ceiling of the period, brought here from the former town hall. Admission: free.

Continue along the plaza, which lets into Av. Maria Cristina at the end, and leads in four blocks to the bustling garden Pl. del Pais Valenciano (a.k.a. Pl. de Ayuntamiento), with the **Ayuntamiento** on the right. Although its facade is early 20th-century, the interior is 18th. An elegant Salo de Festes is left of the entrance. There is a small museum containing miscellany along with some fine ceramics. (Open Sun.–Fri. 9 a.m.–1:30 p.m.; Admission: free.) The **Office of Tourism** with a worthwhile map is located in this building.

Two blocks ahead the imposing **Estación del Norte** *can be seen, a modernista marvel worth the walk for a closer look.*

*From the north end of the Pl. Valenciano take C. Barcas going right. Turn
left at the old theater building onto C. Poeta Querol. The second left at a
church on C. Salva brings the 19th-century university complex. To its north
stands* **Colegio del Patriarca**, *a former 16th-century seminary. Inside, around
an elegantly simple patio, are rooms with fine tiles. The second floor consists
of a choice museum with charming Valencian primitives, a superb Van der
Weyden triptych, a Caravaggio, Ribaltas and an El Greco. (Open daily 11
a.m. to 1:30 pm, but only on weekends in winter; admission: 100 ptas.)*

*Return to C. Querol, continuing north to the next corner after the church.
Here, on the left around the corner, is an unforgettable building—the Palacio
Marqués de Dos Aguas.*

Museo de Cerámica/ Palacio Marqués de Dos Aguas

Poeta Querol, 2, ☎ 351 63 92.

*Hours open: Tues.–Sat. 10 a.m.–2 p.m. and 4–6 p.m. Open Sun. 10 a.m.–2 p.m. Closed
Mon.*
Erected in the 18th century, this is the most baroque civil building in Spain. The
main portal is surrounded by an incredible assemblage, including two alabaster
atlantes pouring water in an obvious pun on the Marqués' name. Originally, the
façade was covered in murals as well. Inside is an exceptional ceramics museum,
with over 5000 pieces on display, the best collection in a country famous for that
art. It must be admitted, however, that it is difficult to concentrate on ceramics
amid the extravagance of gilt, marble and murals in the palace rooms. Such bad taste
has seldom been surpassed, and the opportunity to see it is special. *Admission: 300
ptas.*

Continue to the end of the street, and right around the Gothic church of
San Martín, *coated in baroque decoration although sporting a 15th-century
bronze equestrian statue of the saint over the door. Head toward the cathedral and along its right (south) side, this time rounding the right side of the
Archbishop's Palace to view the* **Almudín** *at its rear. This was the public granary from the 16th century and now houses a museum of paleontology.*

*Walk north to the Puente Trinidad, crossing the riverbed. On the other
side, to the right on C. San Pio V is the Fine Arts Museum.*

Museo San Pío/ Provincial de Bellas Artes

San Pio V, 9, ☎ 360 57 93.
*Hours open: Tues.–Sat. 10 a.m.–2 p.m. and 4–6 p.m. Open Sun. 10 a.m.–2 p.m. Closed
Mon.*
For the scope and quality of its paintings this museum ranks as the third best in
Spain. For the art of Valencia it is first-rate. The ground floor, however, is dedicated
to sculpture and mosaics of a secondary sort. It is the second floor that shines,
beginning with a series of rooms emphasizing medieval primitive paintings from the
area surrounding Valencia. The paintings are unrestrained in their graphic depic-

tions of blood and gore, yet refreshingly innocent. The contrast with the rampant imagination displayed by Bosch's *Los Improperios* (The Mockers) in gallery 30, drawn by a more tutored hand, is instructive. (The centerpiece of this triptych hangs in El Escorial.)

Juan Macip and Juan de Juanes represent the Renaissance well. Extraordinary canvases by Ribalta in gallery 37 lead the way to Ribera in gallery 40. One gallery is devoted to Goya, and another to a single painting—a haunting Velázquez self-portrait. *Admission: free.*

Where to Stay

Though not numerous, hotels in Valencia usually prove adequate because the number of tourists is correspondingly small. Rooms are fairly priced. In such a sprawling city, however, a location close to the sights is important and guides our selection.

Expensive ($100–$200)

Reina Victoria   1st-class ★ ★

C. Barcas, 4, Valencia (the street heading east from the Pl. Valenciano), ☎ 352 04 87, FAX 352 04 87, Telex 64755.

With its light and airy look the hotel suggests a French hostelry of the 1930s. Recently refurbished, the comfortable bedrooms all wear deep pile rugs and chintz bedspreads. Service is exemplary. *94 rooms, plus three suites.*

Moderate ($50–$99)

Inglés   2nd-class ★ ★

C. Marqués de Dos Aguas, 5, Valencia (across the street from the palace), ☎ 351 64 26, FAX 394 02 51.

The building is a former palace, but the bedrooms, though comfortable, are by no means deluxe. The location is first-rate, however. *61 rooms, plus one suite.*

Continental   R2nd-class

C. Correos, 8, Valencia (one block along the street that leaves the center of the Pl. Valencianos, heading east), ☎ 351 09 26, FAX 351 09 26.

This hotel occupies the upper two floors of a townhouse, and provides comfortable bedrooms, although not much more. *43 rooms.*

Inexpensive (Less than $50)

Bristol   R2nd-class ★ ★

C. Abadía San Martín, 3, Valencia (at the end of the street of the Palacio Marqués de Dos Aguas), ☎ 352 11 76.

This is a comfortable, intimate hotel, without frills such as AC. It is well maintained, the bedrooms are comfortable, and the location is super. *40 rooms.*

Moratín   Hs3rd-class

C. Moratín, 15, Valencia (off C. Barcas which runs east from the north end of the Pl. Valencianos), ☎ 352 12 20.

Inexpensive accommodations are in short supply in Valencia. Although this establishment is in no way special, it is clean and the service is friendly. *12 rooms.*

Youth Hostel

Albergue Juvenil Colegio "La Paz"

Av. del Puerto, 69 (half way to the port, take bus 19 from the Pl. Ayuntamiento), ☎ *361 74 59.*

Ok, you aren't paying for beauty, but the cost is under 1000 ptas. Curfew at midnight and open only from July through mid September.

Where to Eat

Valencia is the birthplace of paella, and restaurants here compete with one another for the most tasty version. This is where the rice grows, so most other specialties incorporate that grain in some form. However, the current rage is *fideuà*, almost a paella style dish that uses vermicelli in place of the rice. Produce is invariably fresh and delicious. Valencianos also love their shellfish, hence the many restaurants with *marisqueria* in their name. These will necessarily be expensive, but the quality will be high. While *nueva cocina* is available, it is generally better sampled elsewhere.

Expensive ($30+)

Oscar Torrijos ★★★

Dr. Sumsi, 4 (From the Estación del Norte go east along the bullring to take a right along P. Rusafa for two blocks to a large intersection. Take the wide Av. de l'Antic Regne de Valencia southeast for three blocks to a square on the right.), ☎ *373 29 49.*
Closed Sun. and from the middle of Aug. through the middle of Sept.

Among quite a number of good restaurants in this city, Torrijos stands out. If you want the very best of rice dishes, order *Arroz de langosta* here. There is a delicacy of flavor and intelligence of preparation rare in any restaurant that infuses most of the dishes here. The decor is attractive, but in no way memorable; the food is both. Reserve. Credit Cards: A, D, M, V.

Moderate ($15–$30)

El Plat ★★

Ciscar, 3 (one block south and six west of the eastern end of Gran Via Marqués, which is the large center divided road two blocks south of the Estación del Norte), ☎ *395 15 11.*
Closed Easter week.

This restaurant specializes in paella, serving some of the best in the city. It is an unpretentious place, but serious about food, and there are other local specialties as well, all amazingly low priced. Reservations are not taken. Credit Cards: A, M, V.

Rio Sil ★

C. Mosén Femades, 10 (take the second left from the southeast corner of the Pl. Valencianos and walk to near the end of the tiny street), ☎ *352 97 64.*
Close the first half of July.

Closer to the sights than El Plat II, this restaurant also does paella extremely well. The decor is vaguely nautical and there are tables outside. Credit Cards: A, M, V.

El Timonel ★

C. Felix Pizcueta, 13 (three blocks east of the Estación del Norte), ☎ *352 63 00.*
Closed Mon.

The interior is reminiscent of a yacht, a little hokey, but this is probably the best shellfish restaurant in town and worth the walk. Reservations are advised for dinner. Credit Cards: A, D, M, V.

Inexpensive (Less than $15)

La Romeral   ★

> *Gran Via Marqués del Turia, 62 (Gran Via Marqués is the large center divided road two blocks south of the Estación del Norte. The restaurant is situated two blocks from its eastern end.),* ☎ *395 15 17.*
>
> *Closed Mon. and Aug.*
>
> This local place serves well-prepared dishes for amazingly low prices. Credit Cards: A, D, M, V.

Directory

Shopping

Valencia is the home of the Lladró pottery works that produces those cute, pricey, glossy white figurines with a touch of blue or pink. Naturally stores all over town sell them along with Naos, the cheaper line. For the true aficionado Valencia is unique in having a Lladró factory outlet. Prices are almost half of retail. Although the pieces are seconds, usually their imperfections are so minor that only an expert can tell. The unmarked store is in a suburb of the city called Tavernes Blanques, so a taxi is the only means of getting to *C. 1 de Mayo, 32.*

Antique and **books** stores surround the Lonja. A **flea market** is held Sun. in the streets behind the Cathedral.

Airport

Valencia's airport (☎ *350 95 00*) serves European capitals as well as all of Spain. It is 10 km southwest of town. Bus #15 leaves hourly from the bus station. Iberia (☎ *352 05 00*) is on C. de la Paz, 14 (just east of the Pl. Zaragoza in front of the Cathedral).

Information

Located in the Ayuntamiento in the Pl. Valencianos (☎ *351 04 17*).

Trains and Buses

The Estación del Norte is on C. de Játiva, two blocks south of the Pl. Valencianos (☎ *351 36 12*). Service is good to most destinations in Spain.

The bus station (☎ *349 72 22*) is located at *Av. de Menéndez Pidal, 13* (across the river, north of the sights). Even more frequent service is provided than by train. Bus # 8 from the Pl. Valencianos goes there.

Police

Gran Via de Ramón y Cajal, 40 (south of the Estación del Norte). ☎ *351 08 62.*

Excursions

Valencia divides the **Costa del Azahar** from the **Costa Blanca**, its natural excursions. Both are described above. The nearest good beach is outside **El Saler**, described in the Costa del Azahar section.

THE SPANISH LANGUAGE

Pronunciation is easier with Spanish than for most languages because it is highly consistent. The only problem is that Basques talk in a separate tongue, as do Catalans, and some inhabitants of Galicia, so not all conversations or signs will be in Spanish. However, everyone can speak and understand Spanish when they choose to, and with tourists they will.

For Spanish vowels, *a* sounds like that in b*a*ck, *e* is short as in s*e*t, *i* long like pol*i*ce, *o* like n*o*te, and *u* long like r*u*le. Spanish *ei* is pronounced as if *ey*, as in th*ey*, and *ai* is pronounced as if a long *y*, as in b*y*.

Spanish consonants generally are pronounced as in English, though there are some exceptions. *H* is always silent *B* between vowels is pronounced like an English *v*. On the other hand, *V* sounds like an English *b*. *C* usually is hard as if it were a *k*, but is lisped before an *i* or *e*. Similarly, *G* usually is hard and slightly guttural as if it were the *ch* in loch, but sounds soft like English *h* before *e* or *i*. *J* always sounds like *h*. Doubled *LL* is pronounced like an English *y*, so *tortilla* is pronounced *torteeya*. *N* is normally like the English version but when surmounted by a tilde (~) becomes *ny* as in ca*ny*on. *R* is rolled and *rr* rolled even more. Spanish *Z* is pronounced like an English *th*, so Zaragoza sounds like *Tharahotha*, with the *ho* slightly guttural. Lastly, *qu* sounds like an English *h*

Normally the last syllable of a Spanish word receives the stress. If a word ends in a vowel, "n" or "s," the stress is on the next-to-last syllable. When some other syllable should be stressed an accent is placed at that point.

WORDS AND PHRASES

ENGLISH	SPANISH
Good morning (afternoon/evening)	Buenos días (tardes/noches)
Goodbye	Adios
How are you?	¿Cómo está usted?
Very well, thank you.	Muy bien, gracias.
Please/thank you	Por favor/gracias
You are welcome	De nada
Yes/no	Si/no
Pardon me	Perdón
I do not speak Spanish	No hablo español
Do you speak English?	¿Habla usted inglés?
I do not understand	No comprendo
Miss	Señorita
Madam	Señora (married), Doña (unmarried)
Mister	Señor
Open/closed	Abierto/cerrado
Entrance/exit	Entrada/salida
Push/pull	Empujar/tirar
Today/yesterday/tomorrow	Hoy/ayer/mañana
Where is...	Dónde está...?
the toilet	el baño/sanitario/lavabo
the train station	la estación de ferrocarriles
the post office	oficina de correo
How much is it?	¿Cuánto es?
Help!	¡Socorro!

NUMBERS

ENG.	SPAN.	ENG.	SPAN.	ENG.	SPAN.
1	uno	11	once	21	veintiuno
2	dos	12	doce	30	treinta
3	tres	13	trece	31	treintiuno
4	cuatro	14	catorce	40	cuarenta
5	cinco	15	quince	50	cincuenta
6	seis	16	diez y séis	60	sesenta
7	siete	17	diez y siete	70	setenta
8	ocho	18	diez y ocho	80	ochenta
9	nueve	19	diez y nueve	90	noventa
10	diez	20	veinte		
100	cien(to)	101	ciento uno		
200	doscientos				
300	trescientos				
1000	mil	2000	dos mil		
0	cero				

DAYS

ENGLISH	SPANISH	ENGLISH	SPANISH
Monday	Lunes	Friday	Viernes
Tuesday	Martes	Saturday	Sábado
Wednesday	Miércoles	Sunday	Domingo
Thursday	Jueves		

MONTHS

January	Enero	July	Julio
February	Febrero	August	Agosto
March	Marzo	September	Septiembre
April	Abril	October	Octubre
May	Mayo	November	Noviembre
June	Junio	December	Diciembre

AT THE HOTEL

ENGLISH	SPANISH
I have a reservation	He hecho una reserva
I would like...	Quisiera...
a single room	una habitación individual
a double room	una habitación doble
a quiet room	una habitación tranquila
with bath	con baño
with a shower	con ducha
with air conditioning	con aire acondicionado
for one night only	sólo una noche
for two nights	por dos noches

ON THE ROAD

ENGLISH	SPANISH
north(south/east/west)	norte(sur/este/oeste)
right(left)	derecho(izquierdo)
straight ahead	todo derecho
far(near)	lejos(cerca)
gas station	gasolinera
tires	los neumaticos
oil	el aceite
danger(caution)	peligro
detour	desvio
Do Not Enter	Paso Prohibido
No Parking	Estacionamento Prohibido
No Passing	Prohibido Adelantar
One Way	Dirección Única
Reduce Speed	Despacio
Stop	Alto
Toll booth	Peaje

A list of Spanish words for common restaurant dishes follows, arranged by the categories listed on most menus. Nonetheless, unfamiliar words are certain to be encountered in restaurants, so a pocket Spanish menu guide is most useful.

COMMONLY USED WORDS AND PHRASES

SPANISH	ENGLISH
ENTREMESES	**HORS D'OEUVRES**
Butifarra	Catalan sausage
Chorizo	hard, spicy pork sausage
Fiambres	cold cuts
Jamón serrano	paper-thin slices of cured raw ham, similar to prosciutto
Salchicha	fresh pork sausage
SOPAS	**SOUPS**
Ajo blanco	cold soup of ground almonds, garlic and grapes
Caldos	broths
Gazpacho	cold soup of tomatoes, cucumber, olive oil and garlic
Sopa de ajo	garlic soup
Sopa de fideos	noodle soup
HUEVOS	**EGGS**
Huevos cocidos (or duro)	hard-boiled eggs
Huevos escalfados	poached eggs
Huevos fritos	fried eggs
Huevos pasado por agua	soft-boiled eggs
Huevos revueltos	scrambled eggs
Tortilla patata	potato omelette
Tortilla a la flamenca	Spanish omelette
Tortilla francesa	plain omelette
PESCADOS Y MARISCOS	**FISH AND SHELLFISH**
Almejas	clams
Anguila	eel

COMMONLY USED WORDS AND PHRASES

SPANISH	ENGLISH
Bacalao	cod
Besugo	sea bream
Bonito or atun	tuna
Boquerónes	fresh anchovies
Calamares	squid
Cangrejo	crab
Gambas, camarones or cigalas	prawns
Langosta	lobster
Lenguado	sole
Mejillones	mussels
Merluza	hake
Ostras	oysters
Pez espada	swordfish
Salmonetes	red mullet
Sardinas	sardines
Trucha	trout
Vieiras	scallops
CARNE	**MEAT**
Cerdo	pork
Cochinillo	suckling pig
Cordero	lamb
Higado	liver
Lechazo	milk-fed lamb
Rinones	kidneys
Solomillo	sirloin
Ternera	veal
Vaca	beef
AVES Y CAZA	**POULTRY AND GAME**
Conejo	rabbit
Faisan	pheasant

COMMONLY USED WORDS AND PHRASES

SPANISH	ENGLISH
Pavo	turkey
Pato	duck
Perdiz	partridge
Pollo	chicken
VERDURAS	**VEGETABLES**
Aceitunas	olives
Alcachofas	artichokes
Aguacate	avocado
Berejenas	eggplant
Ensalada (verde/mixta)	salad (green/mixed)
Espinacas	spinach
Garbanzos	chickpeas
Guisantes	peas
Judias verdes	French green beans
Pepino	cucumber
Piso	fried vegetables
Puerros	leeks
Setas	mushrooms
Zanahoria	carrots
QUESOS	**CHEESES**

Most are local, so a complete list would be lengthy, but the following types are generally available.

Idiazabal	smoked
Manchego	fresh or smoked
Queso de Durgos	soft
Roncal	hard
Villalon	soft
POSTRES	**SWEETS**
Arroz con leche	rice pudding
Flan	creme caramel

COMMONLY USED WORDS AND PHRASES

SPANISH	ENGLISH
Helado	ice cream
Nalillas	pudding
FRUTAS	**FRUIT**
Cerezas	cherries
Frambuesas	raspberries
Fresons	strawberries
Higos	figs
Manzanas	apples
Melocotons	peaches
Naranjas	oranges
Peras	pears
Plátanos	bananas
Pomelo	grapefruit
Sandia	watermelon
Uvas	grapes
MISCELLANEOUS	
una botella	bottle
una mesa	table
camarero	waiter
La cuenta, por favor	The check, please

HOTEL QUICK REFERENCE LIST

(By Region)

Because dollar prices vary as the peseta floats internationally and as local ordinances change, instead of specific dollar amounts we use the following price-categories:

Very Very Expensive (VVExp) . . . .**$300+**

Very Expensive (VExp). **$200-299**

Expensive (Exp) **$100-199**

Moderate (Mod). **$51-99**

Inexpensive (Inexp) . . . . **$50 or less**

(all prices are per double per night in high season)

MADRID AND NEW CASTILE					
HOTELS	**Phone #** **FAX #**	**Class**	**Price**	**Rooms**	**Stars**
Aranjuez	*91+*				
Hostal Castilla **Carretera Andalucia, 98** **Aranjuez 28300**	891 26 27	2nd	Inexp	17	★★★★★
Madrid	*91+*				
Albergue Juvenal Santa Cruz de **Marcenado** **C. Santa Cruz de Marcenado,** **28** **Madrid 28003**	547 45 32	YH	Inexp		
Albergue Juvenil Richad Shir- **man** **Casa de Campo** **Madrid 28003**	463 56 99	YH	Inexp		
Alcalá **Alcalá, 66** **Madrid 28009**	435 10 60 435 11 05	1st	Exp	153	★★
Arosa **De la Salud, 21** **Madrid 28013**	532 16 00 531 31 27	1st	Exp	139	★★
Carlos V **Maestro Vitoria, 5** **Madrid 28012**	531 41 00 531 37 61	2nd	Mod	67	★

MADRID AND NEW CASTILE

HOTELS	Phone # FAX #	Class	Price	Rooms	Stars
Cervantes, Hotel C. Cervantes, 34 Madrid 28001	529 27 45	HR3rd	Inexp	12	
Continental Gran Via, 44 Madrid 28014	521 46 00	HR3rd	Inexp	29	
Don Diego Velázquez, 45 Madrid 28014	435 07 60 431 42 63	HR2nd	Mod	58	★
El Prado Prado, 11 Madrid 28012	369 02 34 429 28 29	2nd	Exp	47	★★
Francisco I Alcalá 2 Madrid 28012	548 43 14 531 01 88	Hs2nd	Inexp	58	★★★
G. H. Reina Victoria Pl. Santa Ana, 14 Madrid 28012	531 45 00 522 03 07	1st	Exp	201	★★★★
Hostal Auto Paseo de la Chopera, 69 Madrid 28045	539 66 00 530 67 03	3rd	Mod	24	
Hostel Residencia Lisboa Ventura de la Vega, 17 Madrid 28014	429 98 94	Hs2nd	Inexp	23	★★
Inglés Echegaray, 8 Madrid 28014	429 65 51 420 24 23	2nd	Mod	58	★
Mónaco Barbieri, 5 Madrid 28004	522 46 30 521 16 01	R3rd	Inexp	32	★
Moderno Arenal, 2 Madrid 28014	531 09 00 531 35 50	2nd	Mod	98	
Palace Pl. de las Cortes, 7 Madrid 28014	429 75 51 429 82 66	Deluxe	VExp	456	★★★★

MADRID AND NEW CASTILE

HOTELS	Phone # FAX #	Class	Price	Rooms	Stars
París Alcalá, 2 Madrid 28014	521 64 96	3rd	Mod	120	★
Regina Alcalá, 19 Madrid 28014	521 47 25 521 47 25	2nd	Mod	142	★★
Ritz Pl. de la Lealtad, 5 Madrid 28014	521 28 57 532 87 76	Deluxe	VExp	156	★★★★★
Santander, Residencia Echegaray, 1 Madrid 28012	429 95 51	R2nd	Inexp	38	★
Santo Mauro Zurbano, 36 Madrid 28014	319 69 00 308 54 77	Deluxe	VExp	37	★★★★
Serrano Marqués de Villemejor 8 Madrid 28014	435 52 00 435 48 49	1st		34	★★★
Suecia Marqués de Casa Ribera, 4 Madrid 28014	531 69 00 521 71 41	2nd	Exp	128	★★★
Tirol Marqués de Urquijo, 4 Madrid 28008	548 19 00	3rd	Mod	35	
Tryp Ambassador Cuesta de Santo Domingo, 5 Madrid 28013	541 67 00 559 10 40	1st	Exp	181	★★★
Tryp Fenix Hermosilla, 2 Madrid 28014	431 67 00 576 06 61	1st	Exp	213	★★★
Villa Magna Paseo Castellana, 22 Madrid 28046	578 20 00 575 31 58	Deluxe	VVExp	182	★★★
Villa Real Pl. de las Cortes, 10 Madrid 28014	420 37 67 420 25 47	Deluxe	VExp	115	★★★★

MADRID AND NEW CASTILE

HOTELS	Phone # FAX #	Class	Price	Rooms	Stars
Wellington Velázquez, 8 Madrid 28001	575 44 00 576 41 64	1st	VExp	258	★★

Sigüenza   91+

Parador Castillo de Sigüenza Plaza del Castillo Sigüenza 19250	39 01 00 39 13 64	1st	Exp	80	★★★★

Toledo   925+

Carlos V Calle Horno de Magdalena, 1 Toledo 45001	22 21 00 22 21 05	2nd	Mod	69	★★★
Hostal del Cardenal P. Recaredo, 24 Toledo 45003	22 49 00 22 29 91	R2nd	Mod	27	★★★★★
Imperio Calle Cadenas, 5 Toledo 45001	22 76 50 25 31 83	R3rd	Inexp	21	★★
Los Cigarrales Carretaria de Circunvalación, 32 Toledo 45000	22 00 53 21 55 46	3rd	Inexp	36	★★★
María Cristina Calle Margués de Mendigorria, 1 Toledo 45003	21 32 02 21 26 50	2nd	Mod	63	★★★★
Parador Conde de Orgaz Cerro del Emperador Toledo 45002	22 18 50 22 51 66	1st	Exp	76	★★★
Residencia Juvenil San Servando Castillo San Servando Toledo 45002	22 45 54	YH	Inexp		

OLD CASTILE AND LEÓN

HOTELS	Phone # FAX #	Class	Price	Rooms	Stars
Ávila	**918+**				
Hostale Continental Pl. de la Catedral, 6 Ávila 05001	21 15 02	Hs2nd	Inexp	54	★★
Hosteria de Bracamante Bracamonte, 6 Ávila 05001	25 12 80	2nd	Mod	18	★★
Palacio de Valderrábanos Pl. Catedral, 9 Ávila 05001	21 10 23 25 16 91	1st	Exp	73	★★★★
Parador Raimundo de Borgoña Marqués de Canales y Chozas, 16 Ávila 05001	21 13 40 22 61 66	1st	Exp	63	★★★
Rastro, El Pl. del Rastro, 1 Ávila 05001	22 12 18	Hs2nd	Inexp	14	★
Residencia Juvenal Duperier Av. Juventud Ávila 05001	21 35 48	YH	Inexp		
Burgos	**947+**				
Almirante Bonifaz C. Vitoria, 22 Burgos 09004	20 69 43 20 29 19	1st	Exp	79	★★
Condestable C. Vitoria, 8 Burgos 09004	26 71 25 20 46 45	1st	Exp	85	★★
Cordón La Puebla, 6 Burgos 09004	26 50 00 20 02 69	2nd	Mod	35	★★
Del Cid Pl. Santa María, 8 Burgos 09003	20 87 15 26 94 60	2nd	Mod	28	★★★
España Paseo de Espolón Burgos 09003	20 63 40 20 13 30	4th	Inexp	69	★

OLD CASTILE AND LEÓN

HOTELS	Phone # FAX #	Class	Price	Rooms	Stars
Fernán González C. Calera, 17 Burgos 09002	20 94 41 27 47 21	2nd	Mod	84	★★★
Palacio Landa Carretera Madrid-Irun, kilometer 236 Burgos 09000	20 63 43 26 46 76	Deluxe	Exp	42	★★★★★
La Rioja Region	**941+**				
Iturrimurri N-232 1 k south of Haro Haro 26200	31 12 13 31 17 21	2nd	Mod	36	★★
Los Augustinos San Agustin, 2 Haro 26200	31 13 08 30 31 48	1st	Mod	60	★★★★
Marixa Sancho Abarca, 8 Laguardia 01300	10 01 65	4th	Inexp	10	★
Parador Santo Domingo de la Calzada Pl. del Santo Calzada 26250	34 03 00 34 03 25	2nd	Mod	61	★★★★
León	**987+**				
Don Suero Av. Suero de Quiñones, 15 León 24002	23 06 00	Hs2nd	Inexp	106	★★
Parador San Marcos Pl. San Marcos 7 León 24001	23 73 00 23 34 58	Deluxe	Exp	200	★★★★★
Quindós Av. José Antonio, 24 León 24002	23 62 00 24 22 01	1st	Mod	96	★★★
Riosol Av. de Palencia, 3 León 24009	21 66 50 21 69 97	R2nd	Mod	141	★

OLD CASTILE AND LEÓN

HOTELS	Phone # FAX #	Class	Price	Rooms	Stars
Salamanca	*923+*				
Amefa Pozo Amarillo, 8 Salamanca 37002	21 81 89 26 02 00	3rd	Mod	33	★★★
Condal Pl. Santa Eulalia, 3 Salamanca 37002	21 84 00	3rd	Mod	70	
Emperatriz C. Compañia, 4 Salamanca 37001	21 92 00	3rd	Inexp	61	★
Gran Hotel Pl. Poeta Iglesias, 5 Salamanca 37001	21 35 00 21 35 00	1st	Exp	136	★
Gran Vía Rosa, 4 Salamanca 37001	21 54 01	3rd	Inexp	47	★★
Milán Pl. del Ángel, 5 Salamanca 37001	21 75 18	4th	Inexp	25	★
Monterrey Azafranal, 21 Salamanca 37001	21 44 00 21 44 00	R1st	Exp	89	★
Parador de Salamanca Teso de la Feria, 2 Salamanca 37008	26 87 00 21 54 38	1st	Exp	108	★★★
Pensión Marina Calle Doctinos, 4 Salamanca 37001	21 65 69	P2nd	Inexp	21	
Residencia Rector Paseo del Rector Esperabe, 10 Salamanca 37008	21 84 82 21 40 08	R1st	Exp	14	★★★★★
Segovia	*911+*				
Acueducto Av. del Padre Claret, 10 Segovia 40001	42 48 00 42 84 46	2nd	Mod	78	★★

OLD CASTILE AND LEÓN

HOTELS	Phone # FAX #	Class	Price	Rooms	Stars
Infanta Isabel Isabel la Católica, 1 Segovia 40001	44 31 05 44 32 40	1st	Mod	29	★★★
Las Sirenas Juan Bravo, 30 Segovia 40001	43 40 11 43 06 33	R2nd	Mod	39	★★★
Los Arcos Paseo de Exequiel González, 24 Segovia 40002	43 74 62 42 81 61	1st	Exp	59	★★
Los Linajes C. Dr. Velasco, 9 Segovia 40003	43 04 75 46 04 79	R2nd	Mod	55	★★★★
Parador de Segovia Carretera N-601, 3 k north Segovia 40003	44 37 37 43 73 62	Deluxe	Exp	113	★★★
Plaza C. Cronista Leccea, 11 Segovia 40001	43 12 28	Hs3rd	Inexp	28	★
Valladolid	*983+*				
El Montico Carretera de Salamanca Tordesillas 47100	79 50 00 79 50 08	2nd	Mod	51	★★★
Imperial Peso, 4 Valladolid 47001	33 03 00 33 08 13	3rd	Mod	81	★
Olid Meliá Pl. San Miguel, 10 Valladolid 47003	35 72 00 33 68 28	1st	Exp	210	★★
Parador de Tordesillas Carretera de Salamanca, N-620 Tordesillas 47100	77 00 51 77 10 13	2nd	Exp	71	★★★
Roma Héroes del Alcázar de Toledo, 8 Valladolid 47001	35 47 77 35 54 61	3rd	Mod	38	★

ANDALUSIA

HOTELS	Phone # FAX #	Class	Price	Rooms	Stars
Baeza	**953+**				
Juanito Paseo Arca del Agua Baeza 23440	74 00 40 74 23 24	2nd	Inexp	35	★
Cádiz	**956+**				
Francia y París Pl. de San Francisco, 2 Cádiz 11004	21 23 19 22 24 31	2nd	Mod	69	★
Parador Atlántico Duque de Nájera, 9 Cádiz 11002	22 69 05 21 45 82	1st	Exp	149	★★
Córdoba	**957+**				
Albucasis Buen Pastor, 11 Códroba 14004	47 86 25 47 86 25	R2nd	Mod	15	★
Amistad Córdoba Pl. de Maimónides, 3 Córdoba 14004	42 03 35 42 03 65	1st	Exp	69	★★★
Andalucia José Zorrila, 3 Córdoba 14008	47 60 00	3rd	Inexp	40	★★
El Califa Lope de Hoces, 14 Córdoba 14004	29 94 00 29 57 16	R2nd	Mod	66	★★
El Conquistador Magistral González Francés, 15 Córdoba 14003	48 11 02 47 46 77	1st	Exp	103	★★★★
González Manriquoz, 3 Córdoba 14003	47 98 19 48 61 87	3rd	Mod	16	★★★
Husa Gran Capitán Av. de América, 5 Córdoba 14008	47 02 50 47 43 48	1st	Exp	100	
Los Gallos Sol Av. Medina Azahara, 7 Córdoba 14005	23 55 00 23 16 36	2nd	Mod	115	

ANDALUSIA

HOTELS	Phone # FAX #	Class	Price	Rooms	Stars
Maimónides Torrijos, 4 Córdoba 14003	47 15 00 48 38 03	R2nd	Mod	83	★★
Marisa Cardenal Herrero, 6 Córdoba 14003	47 31 42 47 41 44	R3rd	Mod	28	★
Meliá Córdoba Jardines de la Victoria Córdoba 14004	29 80 66 29 81 47	1st	Exp	146	
Parador de Córdoba Av. de la Arruzafa Córdoba 14012	27 59 00 28 04 09	1st	Exp	94	★★
Selu Eduardo Dato, 7 Córdoba 14003	47 65 00 47 83 76	R2nd	Mod	118	
Sénica Conde y Luque, 7 Córdoba 14003	47 32 34	Hs4th	Inexp	12	★
Serrano Pérez Galdós, 6 Córdoba 14001	47 01 42 48 65 13	3rd	Inexp	64	★★
Triunfo, El Cardinal González, 79 Córdoba 14003	47 55 00 48 68 50	Hs3rd	Inexp	60	
Residencia Juvenil Córdoba Pl. Judas Levi Córdoba 14003	29 03 66 29 05 00	YH	Inexp		

Costa de la Luz

Conil de la Frontera	956+				
Don Pelayo Carretera del Punto, 19 Conil de la Frontera 11140	44 20 30 44 50 58	3rd	Mod	31	★
Gaviota, La Pl. Nuestra Señora de las Vir- tudes Conil de la Frontera 11140	44 08 36 44 09 80	A2nd	Mod	15	★

ANDALUSIA

HOTELS	Phone # FAX #	Class	Price	Rooms	Stars
Tres Jotas C. San Sebastian Conil del la Frontera 11140	44 04 50 44 04 50	3rd	Mod	36	
El Puerto de Santa María	956+				
Cántaros, Los Curva, 6 El Puerto de Santa María 11500	54 05 06 54 11 21	2nd	Mod	39	★
Monasterio de San Miguel C. Larga, 27 El Puerto de Santa María 11500	54 04 40 54 26 04	Deluxe	Exp	150	★★★★
Puertibabia Av. La Paz, 38 El Puerto de Santa María 11500	56 27 00 56 12 21	1st	Mod	330	★★
Sanlúcar de Bar- rameda	956+				
Helechos, Los Pl. Madre de Dios, 9 Sanlúcar de Barrameda 11540	36 13 49 36 96 50	R3rd	Mod	56	★
Palacio de los Duquess de Medina Sidonia Conde de Niebla, 1 Sanlúcar de Barrameda 11540	36 01 61	NR	Mod	3	★★★★★
Posada del Palacio Caballeros, 11 Sanlúcar de Barrameda 11540	36 48 40 36 50 60	3rd	Mod	11	★★★
Tartaneros Tartaneros, 8 Sanlúcar de Barrameda 11540	36 20 44 36 00 45	R2nd	Mod	22	★★
Tarifa	956+				
Balcón de España Carretera de Cádiz: Apartado 57 Tarifa 11380	68 43 26 68 43 26	2nd	Mod	40	★★★

ANDALUSIA

HOTELS	Phone # FAX #	Class	Price	Rooms	Stars
Codorniz, La Carretera de Cádiz Tarifa 11540	68 47 44 68 34 10	3rd	Mod	35	★
Vejer de la Frontera	**956+**				
Convento de San Franciso La Plazuela Vejer de la Frontera 11150	45 10 01 45 10 04	2nd	Mod	25	★★★
Zahara de los Atunes	**956+**				
Antonio Carretera de Atlanterra Zahara del los Atunes 11393	43 91 41 43 91 35	3rd	Mod	30	★
Sol Atlanterra Carretera de Atlanterra Zahara de los Atunes 11393	43 90 00 43 30 51	Deluxe	Exp	281	

Costa del Sol

Almuñécar	**958+**				
Carmen Av. de Europa, 8 Almuñécar 18690	63 14 13	R4th	Inexp	24	★
Goya Av. de Europa Almuñécar 18690	63 05 50 63 11 92	R3rd	Inexp	26	★
Helios P. de las Flores Almuñécar 18690	63 44 59 63 44 69	2nd	Mod	232	★
Playa de San Cristóbal Pl. San Cristóbal, 5 Almuñécar 18690	63 11 12	R3rd	Inexp	22	★
Estepona	**952+**				
Atalaya Park Carretera N-340 Estepona 29680	288 48 01 288 57 35	Deluxe	Exp	438	★★★
Buenavista Paseo Marítimo, 180 Estepona 29680	80 01 37	P2nd	Inexp	38	★

ANDALUSIA					
HOTELS	**Phone #** **FAX #**	**Class**	**Price**	**Rooms**	**Stars**
Santa Marta **11 k east along** **N-340 to Marbella** **Estepona 29680**	278 07 16	3rd	Mod	37	★★★
Marbella	**952+**				
Don Carlos, Hotel **Carretera B-340** **Marbella 29600**	283 11 40 283 34 29	Deluxe	Exp	238	★★★★
Lima **Av. Antonio Belón, 2** **Marbella 29600**	277 05 00 286 30 91	R2nd	Mod	64	★
Marbella Club **Carretera de Cádiz** **Marbella 29600**	277 13 00 282 98 84	1st	VExp	90	★★★
Monteros, Los **Carretera de Cádiz** **Marbella 29600**	277 17 00 282 58 46	Deluxe	VVExp	169	★★★★
Nagueles **Carretera de Cádiz** **Marbella 29600**	77 16 88	R4th	Mod	17	★★
Puente Romano **Carretera de Cádiz** **Marbella 29600**	277 01 00 277 57 66	Deluxe	VVExp	209	★★★★★
Nerja	**952+**				
Balcón de Europa **Passea Balcón de** **Europa, 1** **Nerja 29780**	252 08 00 252 44 90	2nd	Exp	105	★
Moníca **Playa de la Torrecilla** **Nerja 29780**	252 11 00 252 11 62	1st	Mod	235	★★
Parador de Nerja **Playa de Burriana-Tablazo** **Nerja 29780**	252 00 50 252 19 97	1st	Exp	73	★★★
Portofino **Puerta de Mar, 4** **Nerja 29780**	52 01 50	4th	Inexp	12	★

ANDALUSIA					
HOTELS	**Phone #** **FAX #**	**Class**	**Price**	**Rooms**	**Stars**
Salobreña	**958+**				
Salobreña Carretera de Málaga Salobreña 18680	61 02 61 61 01 01	2nd	Mod	130	★
Salambina Carretera de Málaga Salobreña 18680	61 00 37 61 13 28	4th	Inexp	14	★★★
Torremolinos	**952+**				
Alhoa Puerto-Sol Salvador Allende, 55 Torremolinos 29620	238 70 66 238 57 01	1st	Exp	372	
Don Pablo, Sol Paseo Marítimo Torremolinos 29620	238 38 88 238 37 83	1st	Exp	443	
Don Pedro Av. del Lido Torremolinos 29620	238 68 44 238 37 83	2nd	Mod	289	
Isabel Paseo Marítimo, 97 Torremolinos 29620	238 17 44 238 11 98	2nd	Mod	40	
Meliá Costa del Sol Pasero Marítimo Torremolinos 29620	238 66 77 238 64 17	1st	Exp	540	
Meliá Torremolinos Av. Carlotta Alessandri, 109 Torremolinos 29620	238 05 00 238 05 38	1st	Exp	109	
Pes Espada Vía Imperial, 11 Torremolinos 29620	238 03 00 237 28 01	1st	Exp	205	
Sidi Lago Rojo Miami, 5 Torremolinos 29620	238 76 66 238 08 91	2nd	Mod	144	
Gibraltar	*956+*				
The Rock Hotel 3 Europa Road Gibraltar	730 00 730 13	1st	Exp	143	★★★★

ANDALUSIA					
HOTELS	**Phone #** **FAX #**	**Class**	**Price**	**Rooms**	**Stars**
Caleta Palace **Catalán Bay Road** **Gibraltar**	765 01 710 50	1st	Exp	153	★★
Bristol **10 Cathedral Square** **Gibraltar**	768 00	2nd	Mod	60	★★
Queen's Hotel **1 Boyd Street** **Gibraltar**	740 00	4th	Inexp	24	★
Granada	*958+*				
Alhambra Palace **Peña Partida, 2** **Granada 18009**	22 14 68 22 64 04	1st	Exp	132	★★★★
Albergue Juvenal Granada **C. Ramón y Cajal, 2** **Granada 18010**	27 26 38 28 52 85	YH	Inexp		
Alixare **Av. de los Alixares** **Granada 18009**	22 55 75 22 41 02	1st	Mod	169	★
América **Real de la Alhambra, 53** **Granada 18009**	22 74 71 22 74 70	4th	Mod	13	★★
H-Residencia Britz **Cuesta de Gomerez, 1** **Granada 180010**	22 36 51	P3rd	Inexp	22	★
H-Residencia Lisboa **Pl. del Carmen, 27** **Granada 18014**	22 14 13	P3rd	Inexp	28	
Inglaterra **Cetti Meriem, 4** **Granada 18010**	22 15 58	2nd	Mod	36	★
Kenia **C. Molinos, 65** **Granada 18008**	22 75 06	2nd	Inexp	16	★★
Macía **Pl. Nueva, 4** **Granada 18010**	22 75 36 22 35 75	3rd	Inexp	40	★★

ANDALUSIA					
HOTELS	**Phone #** **FAX #**	**Class**	**Price**	**Rooms**	**Stars**
Meliá Granada Ángel Ganivet, 7 Granada 18009	22 74 00 22 74 03	1st	Exp	197	★★
Parador de San Francisco Alhambra Granada 18009	22 14 40 22 22 64	1st	Exp	38	★★★★
Princessa Ana Av. de la Constitución, 37 Granada 18009	28 74 47 27 39 54	1st	Exp	61	★★★
Sacromonte Pl. del Lino, 1 Granada 18002	26 64 11 26 67 07	3rd	Inexp	33	★
Victoria Puerta Real, 3 Granada 18005	25 77 00 26 31 08	2nd	Mod	69	★★★
Málaga *952+*					
Málaga Palacio Corina del Muelle, 1 Málaga 29015	221 51 85 221 51 85	1st	Exp	221	★
Naranjos, Los Paseo de Sancha, 35 Málaga 29016	222 43 19 222 59 75	2nd	Mod	41	★
Parador Málaga-Gibralfaro Monte Gibralfaro Málaga 29016	222 19 03 222 19 02	2nd	Mod	17	★★★
Vegas, Las Paseo de Sancha 22 Málaga 29015	221 77 12	2nd	Mod	107	
Victoria C. Sancho Lara, 3 Málaga 29015	222 42 23	P3rd	Inexp	13	★
Ronda *952+*					
Parador de Ronda Pl. de España Ronda 29400	287 75 00 287 81 88	1st	Mod	71	★★★

ANDALUSIA					
HOTELS	**Phone #** **FAX #**	**Class**	**Price**	**Rooms**	**Stars**
Reina Victoria Av. Dr. Fleming, 25 Ronda 29400	287 12 40 287 10 75	1st	Exp	89	★★★★★
Virgen de los Reyes C. Lorenzo Gorrego, 13 Ronda 29400	87 62 36	R2nd	Inexp	67	★
Seville	***95+***				
Albergue Juvenal Sevilla C. Isaac Peral, 2 Sevilla 41008	461 31 54	YH	Inexp		
Alcázar Meléndez Pelayo, 10 Sevilla 41004	441 20 11	2nd	Mod	96	
Alfonso XIII San Fernando, 2 Sevilla 41004	422 28 50 421 60 33	Deluxe	VExp	141	★★★★★
Bécquer Reyes Católicos, 4 Sevilla 41001	422 89 00 421 44 00	2nd	Exp	120	★
Casa de Carmona Pl. de Lasso, 1 Carmona Sevilla 41410	414 33 00 414 37 52	1st	Exp	30	★★★★
Casas de la Judería, Las Pl. Santa María la Blanca Sevilla 41004	441 51 50 442 21 70	A2nd	VExp	31	★★★★
Doña María Don Remondo, 16 Sevilla 41004	422 49 90 422 97 65	1st	Exp	61	★★★
Goya, Hostal Mateos Gago, 31 Sevilla 41004	421 11 70	P2nd	Inexp	20	★★
Hacienda Benazuza Virgen de las Nieves Sanlúcar la Mayor Sevilla 41800	570 33 44 570 34 10	R1st	VExp	44	★★★★

ANDALUSIA

HOTELS	Phone # FAX #	Class	Price	Rooms	Stars
Inglaterra Pl. Nueva, 7 Sevilla 41001	422 49 70 456 13 36	1st	Exp	113	★★
Meliá Sevilla Av. de la Borbolla, 3 Sevilla 41004	442 15 11 442 16 08	1st	Exp	370	★★
Murillo Lope de Rueda, 9 Sevilla 41004	421 60 95 421 96 16	3rd	Inexp	57	★★
Parador Alcázar del Rey Don Pedro Carmona Sevilla 41410	414 10 10 414 17 12	1st	Exp	63	★★★★
Rábida, La Castelar, 24 Sevilla 41001	422 09 60 422 43 75	3rd	Mod	87	★
Radison Principe de Asturias Isla de la Cartuja Sevilla 41092	446 22 22 446 04 28	Deluxe	Exp	295	★★★
Tryp Colón Canalejas, 1 Sevilla 41001	422 29 00 422 09 38	1st	VExp	218	★★★
Úbeda **953+**					
Parador Condestable Dávalos Pl. Vázquez de Molina, 1 Úbeda 23400	75 03 45 75 12 59	1st	Exp	31	★★★
Paz, La Andalucía, 1 Úbeda 23400	75 21 46 75 08 48	3rd	Inexp	51	★

EXTREMADURA

HOTELS	Phone # FAX #	Class	Price	Rooms	Stars
Cáceres	*927+*				
Alcántara Av. Virgen de Guadalupe, 14 Cáceres 10001	22 89 00 22 87 68	2nd	Mod	67	
Almonte C. Gil Cordero, 6 Cáceres 10001	24 09 26	Hs3rd	Inexp	90	★
V Centario Carretera de Salamanca Cáceres 10001	23 22 00 23 22 02	Deluxe	Mod	138	★★
Meliá Cáceres Pl. San Juan, 11 Cáceres 10001	21 58 00 21 40 70	1st	Exp	85	★★★
Extremadura Av. Virgen de Guadalupe, 5 Cáceres 10001	22 16 00 21 10 95	2nd	Mod	68	★★
Goya Pl. General Mola, 33 Cáceres 10001	24 99 50	Hs2nd	Inexp	15	★
Parador de Cáceres C. Ancha, 6 Cáceres 10003	21 17 59 21 17 29	1st	Exp	27	★★
Guadalupe	*927+*				
Cerezo Gregorio López, 12 Guadalupe 10140	36 73 79 36 75 51	Hs3rd	Inexp	15	★★★
Hospederia del Real Monasterio Pl. Juan Carlos I Guadalupe 10140	36 70 00 30 71 77	2nd	Mod	47	★★★
Parador de Guadalupe C. Marqués de la Romana, 10 Guadalupe 10140	36 70 75 36 70 76	1st	Mod	40	★★★★

EXTREMADURA

HOTELS	Phone # FAX #	Class	Price	Rooms	Stars
Mérida	*924+*				
Cervantes Camilo José Cela, 8 Mérida 06800	31 49 01 31 13 42	3rd	Mod	30	★
Emperatriz Pl. de España, 19 Mérida 06800	31 31 11 30 03 76	2nd	Mod	41	
Guadiana Pl. de Santa Clara Mérida 06800	31 32 07	Hs3rd	Inexp	12	
Nova Roma Suárez Somonte, 42 Mérida 06800	31 12 61 30 01 60	2nd	Mod	55	★★
Parador Vía de la Plata Pl. de la Constitución, 3 Mérida 06800	31 38 00 31 92 08	1st	Exp	82	★★
Tryp Mérida Av. de Portugal Mérida 06800	37 24 00 37 30 20	1st	Mod	126	★★★
Trujillo	*927+*				
Mesón la Cadena Pl. Mayor, 8 Trujillo 10200	32 14 63	Hs3rd	Inexp	8	★★
Las Ciqüeñas Carretera N-V Trujillo 10200	32 12 50 32 13 00	2nd	Mod	78	★
Parador de Trujillo Pl. de Santa Clara Trujillo 10200	32 13 50 32 13 66	1st	Exp	46	★★★

GALICIA, ASTURIAS, AND CANTABRIA

HOTELS	Phone # FAX #	Class	Price	Rooms	Stars
Basque Coast					
Castro Urdiales	**942+**				
Miramar Playa Castro Urdiales Castro Urdiales 39700	86 02 00 87 09 42	2nd	Mod	34	★
Deba	**942+**				
Miramar C. Arenal, 24 Deba 20820	60 16 60	2nd	Mod	60	★
Donastia	**943+**				
De Londres y de Inglaterra Kalea Zubieta, 2 Donastia 20007	42 69 89 42 00 31	Deluxe	Exp	145	★★★★
H. Residencia Easo Kalea San Bartólome, 2 Donastia 20007	46 68 92	Hs3rd	Inexp	11	★
María Cristina Paseo República Argentina Donastia 20004	42 49 00 42 39 14	Deluxe	VExp	136	★★★★★
Niza Kalea Zubieta, 56 Donastia 20007	42 66 63 42 66 63	R2nd	Mod	41	★★
Hondarribia	**943+**				
Parador el Emperador Pl. de Armas del Castillo Hondarribia 20280	64 21 40 64 21 53	2nd	Exp	36	★★★★
Laredo	**942+**				
Ramona Alameda José Antonio, 4 Laredo 39770	60 71 89	4th	Mod	10	★
Risco Alto de Laredo Laredo 39770	60 50 30 60 50 55	2nd	Mod	25	★★

GALICIA, ASTURIAS, AND CANTABRIA

HOTELS	Phone # FAX #	Class	Price	Rooms	Stars
Lekeitio	**94+**				
Beitia Av. Pascual Aboroa, 25 Lekeitio 48280	684 01 11	3rd	Mod	30	★
Noja	**942+**				
Montemar Playa Noja Noja 39180	63 03 20	3rd	Mod	59	★★
Santander	**942+**				
México Calderón de la Barca, 3 Santander 39002	21 24 50	R3rd	Mod	35	★★
Real Paseo Pérez Galdós, 28 Santander 39005	27 25 50 27 45 73	Deluxe	Exp	125	★★★★
Rhin Av. Reina Victoria, 153 Santander 39005	27 43 00 27 86 53	R1st	Mod	95	★★
Zarauz	**943+**				
Alameda Gipuzkoa Zarauz 20800	83 01 43 13 24 74	3rd	Mod	38	★
Karlos Arguiñano Mendilauta, 13 Zarauz 20800	13 00 00 13 34 50	NR	Exp	13	★★★

Costa de las Rias

Baiona	**986+**				
Parador Conde de Gondomar Baiona 36300	35 50 00 35 50 76	Deluxe	Exp	124	★★★
Cambados	**986+**				
Parador del Albariño Paseo de Cervantes Cambados 36630	54 22 50	2nd	Exp	63	★★

GALICIA, ASTURIAS, AND CANTABRIA

HOTELS	Phone # FAX #	Class	Price	Rooms	Stars
Pazo el Revel Camino de la Iglesia Vilalonga 36630	74 30 00 74 33 90	2nd	Mod	21	★★★
Combarro	**986+**				
Stella Maris Carretera C-550 Combarro 36993	77 03 66	2nd	Mod	27	★
Muros	**981+**				
Murandana Av. Marina Española, 107 Muros 15250	82 68 85	R2nd	Mod	16	★
O Grove	**986+**				
Louxo Isla A Toxa O Grove 36980	73 02 00 73 27 91	1st	Exp	115	★★★
Mar Atlántico San Vincente del Mar O Grove 36980	73 80 61 73 82 99	2nd	Mod	34	★★★
Pontevedra	**986+**				
Parador Casa del Barón Pl. de Maceda Pontevedra 36002	85 58 00	1st	Mod	47	★
Vilagarcia de Arousa	**986+**				
Chocolate Av. Cambados, 151 Vilaxoan Vilagarcia de Arousa 36600	50 11 99 50 67 62	None	Mod	18	★★

Costa Verde

Comillas	**942+**				
Hostería de Quijas Carretera N-634 Comillas 39520	82 08 33	3rd	Mod	13	★★
Josein C. Manuel Noriega, 27 Comillas 39520	72 02 25	3rd	Mod	23	★

GALICIA, ASTURIAS, AND CANTABRIA

HOTELS	Phone # FAX #	Class	Price	Rooms	Stars
Gijon	**98+**				
Parador El Molina Viejo **Parque Isabel la Católica** **Gijon 33203**	537 05 11 537 02 33	1st	Exp	40	★
La Franca	**985+**				
Mirador de la Franca **Playa La Franca** **La Franca 33590**	41 21 45	3rd	Mod	52	★★
La Isla	**942+**				
Astuy **Playa La Isla** **La Isla 39195**	67 95 40 67 95 88	2nd	Mod	53	★
Llanes	**98+**				
Don Paco **Posade Herrera, 1** **Llanes 33500**	540 01 50 540 26 81	2nd	Mod	42	★★
Luarca	**98+**				
Casa Consuelo **Carretera N-634** **Luarca 33792**	564 07 67 564 16 42	3rd	Inexp	35	★
Gayoso **Paseo de Gomez, 4** **Luarca 33700**	564 00 50 564 16 42	2nd	Mod	33	★★
Ribadeo	**982+**				
Eo **Av. de Asturias, 5** **Ribadeo 27700**	11 07 50 11 00 21	2nd	Mod	24	★
Ribadesella	**98+**				
Grand Hotel del Sella **Paseo de la Playa** **Ribadesella 33560**	586 01 50 585 74 49	1st	Exp	82	★★
Ribadesella Playa **Paseo de la Playa, 34** **Ribadesella 33560**	586 07 15 586 02 20	2nd	Mod	17	★

GALICIA, ASTURIAS, AND CANTABRIA

HOTELS	Phone # FAX #	Class	Price	Rooms	Stars
Santillana del Mar	**942+**				
Altimar C. Cantón, 1 Santillana del Mar 39330	81 80 25 84 01 03	2nd	Mod	32	★★
Parador Gil Blás Pl. Ramón Pelayo, 11 Santillana del Mar 39330	81 80 00 81 83 91	1st	Mod	56	★★★
San Vincente de la Barquera	**942+**				
Miramar, Residencia San Vincente de la Barquera 39540	71 00 75 71 00 75	R2nd	Mod	21	★★
Tapia de Casariego	**98+**				
Palacete Pañalba C. El Cotarelo, Figueras 33794	562 61 25 563 62 47	1st	Mod	12	★★★
Vivero	**982+**				
Ego Playa de Area C-642 Vivero 27850	56 09 87 56 17 62	2nd	Mod	29	★
Oviedo	*985+*				
Principado C. San Francisco, 6 Oviedo 33003	521 77 92 521 39 46	1st	Mod	66	★
Reconquesta, De La C. Gil de Jaz, 16 Oviedo 33004	524 11 00 524 11 66	1st	Exp	142	★★★★★
TFavila C. Uría, 37 Oviedo 33002	525 38 77 527 61 69	3rd	Inexp	24	
Santiago de Compostela	*981+*				
Araguaney Alfredo Brañas, 5 Santiago de Compostela 15701	59 59 00 59 02 87	Deluxe	Exp	65	★★★

GALICIA, ASTURIAS, AND CANTABRIA

HOTELS	Phone # FAX #	Class	Price	Rooms	Stars
Compostela Calvo Sotelo, 1 Santiago de Compostela 15702	58 57 00 56 32 69	1st	Mod	99	★
Gelmírez C. Horneo, 92 Santiago de Compostela 15702	56 11 00 56 32 69	1st	Mod	138	★
Hogar San Francisco Campillo do San Francisco, 3 Santiago de Campostela 15702	58 16 00 57 19 16	2nd	Mod	71	★★★
Mapoula C. Entremurallas, 10 Santiago de Compostela 15702	58 01 24 58 40 89	Hs2nd	Inexp	12	★★
Parador Reyes Católicos Pl. de España Santiago de Compostela 15705	58 22 00 56 30 94	Deluxe	VExp	136	★★★★★
Suso Rua do Villar, 65 Santiago de Compostela 15702	58 66 11	Hs2nd	Inexp	9	★
Universal Pl. de Galicia, 2 Santiago de Compostela 15706	58 58 00 58 57 90	R2nd	Inexp	54	★
Windsor República de El Salvador, 16-A Santiago de Compostela 15701	59 29 39	Hs1st	Mod	50	★★

ARAGÓN AND NAVARRE

HOTELS	Phone # FAX #	Class	Price	Rooms	Stars
Estella	*948+*				
Irache CarreteraPamplona-Logroño, N-111, k43 Ayegui 31200	55 11 50	R2nd	Mod	74	★

ARAGÓN AND NAVARRE

HOTELS	Phone # FAX #	Class	Price	Rooms	Stars
Ordesa National Park	**974+**				
Parador de Monte Perdido Valle de Pineta, Huesca 22350	50 10 11	2nd	Mod	24	★★
Olite	**948+**				
Casa Zanito C. Mayor, 16 Olite 31390	74 00 02	3rd	Mod	15	
Parador Principe de Viana Pl. de los Teobaldos, 2 Olite 31390	74 00 00 74 02 01	2nd	Mod	43	★★★
Pamplona	**948+**				
Europa Espoz y Mina, 11 Pamplona 31001	22 18 00 22 92 35	R1st	Mod	25	★★★
Eslava Pl. Virgin de la 0, 7 Pamplona 31001	22 22 70 22 51 57	R3rd	Mod	28	★
Maisonnave C. Nueva, 20 Pamplona 31001	22 26 00 22 01 66	1st	Exp	152	★
Ohri C. Leyre, 7 Pamplona 31001	22 85 00 22 83 18	3rd	Inexp	55	★
Perla, La Pl. del Castillo, 1 Pamplona 31001	22 77 06	2nd	Mod	68	
Tres Reyes Jardines de la lacoñera Pamplona 31001	22 66 00 22 29 30	1st	Exp	168	★★
Yoldi Av. San Ignacio, 11 Pamplona 31002	22 48 00 21 20 45	2nd	Mod	48	★
Sos del Rey Católico	**948+**				
Parador Fernando de Aragón Sos del Rey Católico 50680	88 80 11 88 81 00	1st	Exp	65	★★

ARAGÓN AND NAVARRE

HOTELS	Phone # FAX #	Class	Price	Rooms	Stars
Zaragoza	**976+**				
Conde Blanco C. Predicadores, 84 Zaragoza 50003	44 14 11 28 03 39	3rd	Inexp	87	★★
Goya C. Cinco de Marzo, 5 Zaragoza 50004	22 93 31 23 47 05	1st	Exp	148	★
Gran Hotel C. Joaquín Costa Canalejas, 5 Zaragoza 50001	22 19 01 23 67 13	Deluxe	Exp	140	★★★
Ramiro I C. Coso, 123 Zaragoza 50001	29 82 00 39 89 52	1st	Mod	104	★★

CATALONIA AND THE LEVANT

HOTELS	Phone # FAX #	Class	Price	Rooms	Stars
Barcelona	**93+**				
Albergue Juvenal Palau C. Palau, 6 Barcelona 08002	412 50 80	YH	Inexp		
Albergue Juvenal Mare de Déu de Montserrat Pas. Mare de Déu del Coll, 41 Barcelona 08888	210 51 51	YH	Inexp		
Australia, Residencia Ronda Universitat, 11 Barcelona 08002	317 41 77	Hs2nd	Inexp	23	★
Avenida Palace Gran Vía de les Corts Catalanes, 605 Barcelona 08007	301 96 00 318 12 34	Deluxe	Exp	165	★★★
Claris Pau Claris, 150 Barcelona 08009	487 62 62 215 79 11	Deluxe	Exp	124	★★★

CATALONIA AND THE LEVANT

HOTELS	Phone # FAX #	Class	Price	Rooms	Stars
Colón Av. de Catedral, 7 Barcelona 08002	301 14 04 317 29 15	1st	Exp	147	★★
Condes de Barcelona Passeig de Gràcia, 75 Barcelona 08008	215 06 16 216 08 35	1st	Exp	109	★
Cortes C. Santa Ana 25 Barcelona 08002	317 91 12 301 31 35	3rd	Inexp	45	★
España Sant Pau 9-11 Barcelona 08007	315 22 11 317 11 34	2nd	Mod	84	★★★
Gaudí C. Nou de la Rambla, 12 Barcelona 08001	412 26 36	2nd	Mod	73	★
Gótico C. Jaume I, 14 Barcelona 08002	315 22 11 315 38 19	2nd	Mod	83	★★
Gran Derby C. Loreto, 28 Barcelona 08029	322 20 62 410 08 62	1st	Exp	43	★★
Gran Vía Gran Vía de les Corts Catalanes, 642 Barcelona 08007	318 19 00 318 99 97	2nd	Mod	53	★★★
Lausanne Av. Portal de l'Angel, 24 Barcelona 08002	302 11 39	P2nd	Inexp	17	★★
Majestic Passeig de Gràcia, 70 Barcelona 08008	488 17 17 488 18 80	Deluxe	Exp	336	★★
Meridien Barcelona, Le Ramblas, 111 Barcelona 08002	318 62 00 301 77 76	Deluxe	VExp	205	★★★
Mesón Castilla C. Valldoncella, 5 Barcelona 08001	318 21 82 412 40 20	3rd	Mod	56	★

CATALONIA AND THE LEVANT

HOTELS	Phone # FAX #	Class	Price	Rooms	Stars
Montecarlo Rambla dels Estudis, 124 Barcelona 08002	317 58 00 317 57 50	2nd	Mod	80	★★★
Nouvel C. Santa Ana 18-20 Barcelona 08002	301 82 74 301 83 70	4th	Inexp	55	★★★
Oliva, Hotel Residencia Passeig de Gràcia, 32 Barcelona 08008	317 50 87	P2nd	Inexp	16	★
Palacios, Hotel Residencia Gran Vía de les Corts Catalanes, 629bis Barcelona 08007	301 37 92	P2nd	Inexp	25	★
Princesa Sofía Plaça Pius XII Barcelona 08028	330 71 11 330 76 21	Deluxe	Exp	505	★★
Regencia Colón C. Sagristans, 13 Barcelona 08002	318 98 58 317 28 22	2nd	Mod	55	★
Regente Rambla de Catalunya, 76 Barcelona 08008	215 25 70 487 32 27	1st	Exp	78	★★
Rey Don Jaime I C. Jaume I, 11 Barcelona 08002	315 41 61	3rd	Inexp	30	★
Rialto C. Ferrán, 42 Barcelona 08002	318 52 12 315 38 19	2nd	Mod	141	★★
Ritz Gran Vía de les Corts Catalanes, 668 Barcelona 08010	318 52 00 318 01 48	Deluxe	VExp	161	★★★★★
Rivoli Rambla Rambla dels Estudis, 128 Barcelona 08002	302 66 43 317 50 53	Deluxe	Exp	90	★★
San Augustín Pl. Sant Agusti, 3 Barcelona 08001	318 17 08 317 29 28	2nd	Mod	77	★

CATALONIA AND THE LEVANT

HOTELS	Phone # FAX #	Class	Price	Rooms	Stars
Suizo Pl. del Angel, 12 Barcelona 08002	315 41 11 315 38 19	2nd	Mod	48	★★

Costa del Azahar

Alcocéber	964+				
Aparthotel Jeremías-Romana Playa de Alcocéber 12579	41 44 11 41 24 11	3rd	Mod	39	★★
Jeremías Playa de Alcocéber 12579	41 44 37 41 24 44	2nd	Inexp	38	★

Benicarló	964+				
Parador de Benicarló Av. del Papa Luna, 5 Benicarló 12580	47 01 00 47 09 34	1st	Mod	108	★★

Benicasim	964+				
Intur Orange Gran Avenida Benicasim 12560	39 44 00 30 15 41	2nd	Mod	415	★★
Voramar Passeo Pilar Coloma, 1 Benicasim 12560	30 01 50 30 05 26	2nd	Mod	55	★★

El Saler	96+				
Parador de el Saler El Saler 46012	161 11 86 162 70 16	1st	Exp	58	★★★
Sidi Saler Playa Saler 46012	161 04 11 162 70 16	1st	Exp	276	★★★

Gandía	96+				
Bayren I Passeig Maritim Neptu, 62 Gandía 46730	284 03 00 284 06 53	1st	Exp	164	★★★

Peñiscola	964+				
Hostería del Mar Carretera de Benicarló Peñiscola 12598	48 06 00 48 13 63	1st	Mod	86	★★★
Marina Av. José Antonio, 42 Peñiscola 12598	48 08 90 48 08 90	4th	Inexp	19	★

CATALONIA AND THE LEVANT

HOTELS	Phone # FAX #	Class	Price	Rooms	Stars
Costa Blanca					
Alicante	96+				
Palas C. Cervantes, 5 Alicante 03002	520 93 10	2nd	Mod	42	★
Residencia Palas Pl. Ayuntamiento, 6 Alicante 03002	520 66 90	2nd	Mod	53	★
Altea	96+				
Altaya Calle Generalísimo, 115 Altea 03590	584 08 00	3rd	Inexp	24	★
Benidorm	96+				
Bilbaíno Av. Virgen del Sufragio, 1 Benidorm 03500	585 08 04 585 08 05	3rd	Inexp	38	★★
Cimbel Av. de Europa, 1 Benidorm 03500	585 21 00 586 06 61	1st	Mod	140	
Calpe	96+				
Roca Esmaralda Ponent, 1 Calpe 03710	583 61 01 583 60 04	1st	Mod	212	★★
Venta La Chata Carretera Valencia, km 150 Calpe 03710	583 03 08	3rd	Inexp	17	★★★
Denia	96+				
Rosa Pda. Marines, 98 Denia 03700	578 15 73 578 15 73	2nd	Mod	39	★
Guardamar del Segura	96+				
Guardamar Av. Puerto Rico, 11 Guardamar del Segura 03140	572 96 50 572 95 30	3rd	Mod	52	★

CATALONIA AND THE LEVANT

HOTELS	Phone # FAX #	Class	Price	Rooms	Stars
Jávea	**96+**				
Parador de Jávia Playa del Arenal, 2 Jávea 03730	579 02 00 579 03 08	1st	Exp	65	★★
La Manga del Mar Menor	**968+**				
Sol Galua Hacienda Dos Mares and Grand Vía La Manga del Mar Menor 30370	56 32 00 56 32 54	2nd	Exp	177	★
Moraira	**96+**				
Moradix Moncayo, 1 Moraira 03724	574 40 56 574 45 25	3rd	Inexp	30	★
Swill Moraira Carretera de Calpe Moraira 03724	574 71 04 574 70 74	1st	Exp	25	★★★
Playa de San Juan	**96+**				
Almirante Pocardy Av. de Niza, 38 Playa de San Juan 03540	565 01 12 565 71 69	2nd	Mod	68	★
Sidi San Juan Playa San Juan Playa de San Juan 03540	516 13 00 516 33 46	Deluxe	Exp	176	★★★
Santa Pola 96+					
Polamar Playa de Levant, 6 Santa Pola 03130	541 32 00 541 31 83	2nd	Mod	76	★★

Costa Brava

Cadaqués	**972+**				
Playa Sol Platja Pianch, 3 Cadaqués 17488	25 81 00 25 80 54	2nd	Exp	49	★
S'Aguarda Carretera de Port-Llegat, 28 Cadaqués 17488	25 80 82 25 87 56	2nd	Mod	27	★★

CATALONIA AND THE LEVANT

HOTELS	Phone # FAX #	Class	Price	Rooms	Stars
Cambrils					
Moníca Galcerán Marquet, 3 Cambrils 43850	36 01 18 79 36 78	2nd	Mod	56	★★
L'Escala	972+				
Nieves-Mar P. Martim, 8 L'Escala 17130	77 03 00 10 36 05	2nd	Mod	80	★
Lloret de Mar	972+				
Excelsior P. Mossen J. Verdaguer, 16 Lloret de Mar 17310	36 41 37 37 16 54	2nd	Mod	45	★
Marsol P. Mossens J. Verdaguer, 7 Lloret de Mar 17310	36 57 50	2nd	Mod	87	★
Rigat Park Platja de Fanals Lloret de Mar 17310	36 52 00 37 04 11	1st	Exp	104	★★
Roger de Flor C. Turó de l'Estelat Lloret de Mar 17310	36 48 00 37 16 37	1st	Ext	93	★★★
Palafrugel	972+				
Aigua Blava Platja de Fornells Palafruget 17255	62 20 58 62 21 12	1st	Exp	85	★★★
Casamar C. Nero, 3 Llafranc Palafruget 17211	30 01 04 61 06 51	3rd	Inexp	20	★★
Castell de Peratallada Pl. del Castell Pealafrugel 17210	63 40 21 63 40 11	NR	Exp	5	★★★
Garbí Costa Daurada, 20 Calella Palafrugel 17210	61 40 40 61 58 03	2nd	Mod	30	★

CATALONIA AND THE LEVANT

HOTELS	Phone # FAX #	Class	Price	Rooms	Stars
Hostalillo C. Bellavista, 22 Tamariu Palafrugel 17211	61 02 50 61 02 17	2nd	Mod	70	★
Parador de Aiguablava Aiguablava Palafrugel 17255	62 21 62 62 21 66	1st	Exp	87	★★
Sant Roc Pl. Atlantic, 2 Barri Sant Roc Palafrugel 17210	61 42 50 61 40 68	3rd	Mod	42	★

Sant Feliú de Guíxols   972+

HOTELS	Phone # FAX #	Class	Price	Rooms	Stars
De la Gavina Pl. de la Rosaleda S'Agaró Sant Feliú de Guíxols 17220	32 11 00 32 15 73	Deluxe	VExp	74	★★★★
Murla Park P. dels Guíxols, 22 Sant Feliú de Guíxols 17220	32 04 50 32 00 78	1st	Exp	89	★★
Rex I Rambla del Portalet, 16 Sant Feliú de Guíxols 17220	82 18 09	R3rd	Inexp	25	★

Tossa de Mar   972+

HOTELS	Phone # FAX #	Class	Price	Rooms	Stars
Hotel Diana Pl. de España, 6 Tossa de Mar 17320	34 18 86 34 11 03	R2nd	Inexp	21	★★★
Mar Menuda Platja de Mar Menuda Tossa de Mar 17320	34 10 00 34 00 87	2nd	Mod	50	★★★
Sant March C. Nou, 9 Tossa de Mar 17320	34 00 78	R3rd	Inexp	30	★

Costa Dorada

Cambrils de Mar   977+

HOTELS	Phone # FAX #	Class	Price	Rooms	Stars
Mónica C. Galcerán Marquet, 3 Cambrils de Mar 43850	36 01 16 79 36 78	2nd	Mod	56	★★

CATALONIA AND THE LEVANT

HOTELS	Phone # FAX #	Class	Price	Rooms	Stars
Salou	**977+**				
Carabela Roc C. Pau Casals, 108 Salou 43840	37 01 66 37 07 62	2nd	Mod	96	★
Planas Pl. Bonet, 3 Salou 43840	38 01 08	2nd	Inexp	100	★★
Sant Carles de la Rápita	**977+**				
Juanito Platja Platja Miami Sant Carles de la Rápita 43540	74 04 62	4th	Inexp	35	★★
Llansola C. San Isidro, 98 Sant Carles de la Rápita 43540	74 04 03	3rd	Mod	18	
Miami Park Av. Constitución, 33 Sant Carles de la Rápita 43540	74 03 51	2nd	Mod	80	
Plaça Vella C. Arsenal, 31 Sant Carles de la Rápita 43540	77 24 53 74 43 97	3rd	Mod	21	
Sitges	**93+**				
Romantic y la Renaixenca C. Sant Isidre, 33 Sitges 08870	894 83 75 894 81 67	4th	Mod	55	★★★
Subur Maritim P. Martim, 72 Sitges 08870	894 15 50 894 04 27	2nd	Exp	46	★
Terramar P. Maritim, 80 Sitges 08870	894 00 50 894 56 04	1st	Exp	209	★★
Vilanova i La Geltrú	**93+**				
Sovli 70 P. Ribes Roges, 1 Vilanova i La Geltrú 08800	815 12 45 815 70 02	3rd	Mod	30	★

CATALONIA AND THE LEVANT

HOTELS	Phone # FAX #	Class	Price	Rooms	Stars
Poblet	**977+**				
Masia del Cadet **Les Masies** **Poblet 43448**	87 08 69 87 03 26	NR	Inexp	12	★★
Tarragona	**977+**				
España **Rambla Nova, 49** **Tarragona 43003**	23 27 07	4th	Inexp	40	★★
Imperial Tarraco **P. Palmeres** **Tarragona 43003**	23 30 40 21 65 66	1st	Mod	170	★★
Lauria **Rambla Nova, 20** **Tarragona 43004**	23 67 12 23 67 00	2nd	Mod	72	★
Valencia	**96+**				
Albergue Juvenil Colegio "La Paz" **Av. del Puerto, 69** **Valencia 46002**	361 74 59	YH	Inexp		
Bristol **C. Abadia San Martín, 3** **Valencia 46002**	352 11 76	R2nd	Inexp	40	★
Continental **C. Correos, 8** **Valencia 46002**	351 09 26 351 09 26	R2nd	Mod	43	
Excelsior **C. Barcelonina, 5** **Valencia 46002**	351 46 12	2nd	Mod	67	★
Inglés **C. Marqués de** **Dos Aguas, 5** **Valencia 46002**	351 64 26 394 02 51	2nd	Mod	62	★
Moratín **C. Moratín, 15** **Valencia 46002**	352 12 20	Hs3rd	Inexp	12	
Reina Victoria **C. Barcas, 4** **Valencia 46002**	352 04 87 352 04 87	1st	Exp	97	★★

SPECIAL RESTAURANTS

(By Region)

NOTE: Because restaurant prices are not fixed, we use the following price categories:

Very Expensive (VExp)	**$40+**
Expensive (Exp)	**$30+**
Moderate (Mod)	**$15-30**
Inexpensive (Inexp)	**$15 or less**

(dinner for one with house wine)

Closing days are indicated by the obvious abbreviations of M, T, etc., with Su for Sunday and Th for Thursday. In some cases an establishment closes only for lunch or only for dinner, which we indicate by M/l *(closed Monday for lunch)*, or T/d *(closed Tuesday for dinner)*, etc.

Note, most resort restaurants close for one month or for the season in winter, while other restaurants generally close for one month in summer. Check the listing in the text for specifics.

MADRID AND NEW CASTILE				
RESTAURANTS	**Phone #**	**Price**	**Stars**	**Closed**
Aranjuez	***91+***			
Casa José **Abastos, 32** **Aranjuez 28300**	**891 14 88**	**Exp**	★★★	**Su/d, M**
Rana Verde **C. Reina, 1** **Aranjuez 28300**	**891 13 25**	**Mod**	★	
Madrid	***91+***	**(Many restaurants close in August)**		
Amparo, el **Puigcerdá, 8** **28001**	**431 64 58** **575 54 91**	**VExp**	★★★★	**Su**
Armstrongs **Jovellanos, 5** **28004**	**522 42 30**	**Mod**	★	
Bidasao **Claudio Coello, 24** **28004**	**431 20 81**	**Exp**	★★★	**S, Su**

MADRID AND NEW CASTILE

RESTAURANTS	Phone #	Price	Stars	Closed
Bola, La C. de la Bola, 5 28013	547 69 30	Mod	★★	Su, S/l
Botín C. Cuchilleros, 17 28005	266 42 17	Mod	★★	
Brasserie de Lista José Ortega y Gasset, 6 28006	435 28 18 576 28 17	Mod	★★	Su, S/l
Cafe de Oriente Pl. de Oriente, 2 28013	241 39 74	Exp	★★	Su, S/l
Casa Paco Puerta Cerrada, 11 28005	366 31 66	Mod	★	Su
Casa Gallega Pl. San Miguel, 8 28005	547 30 55	Mod	★★★	
Cenador del Prado, El C. del Prado, 4 28014	429 15 61	Exp	★★★★	Su, S/l
Chateaubriand, Le C. Virgen de los Peligros, 1 28004	532 33 41	Mod	★	Su
Ciao Madrid Argensola, 7 28004	308 25 19	Mod	★	Su, S/l
Foster's Hollywood Velázquez, 80 28005	435 61 28	Inexp		
Gabrieles, Los Echegaray, 17 28004		Inexp		
Gure-Etxea Pl. De La Paja, 12 28005	365 61 49	Exp	★★★	Su
Hylogui C. Ventura de la Vega, 3 28004	429 73 57	Mod	★★	Su/d

MADRID AND NEW CASTILE

RESTAURANTS	Phone #	Price	Stars	Closed
Ingenio, El Leganitos, 10 28013	541 91 33	Mod	★	Su
Laurques C. Ventura de la Vega, 16 28004	429 61 74	Inexp	★	M, Su/l
Mentidero de la Vila, El Santo Tomé, 6 28004	308 12 85 318 87 92	Exp	★★	Su, S/l
Paelleria Valenciana Caballero de Gracia, 12 28005	531 17 85	Inexp	★★	Su, S
Pescador, El José Ortega y Gasset, 75 28006	402 19 90	Exp	★★★	Su
Principe de Viana Manuel de Falla, 5 28036	457 15 49 457 52 83	Exp		Su, S/l
Puebla Ventura de la Vega, 12 28006	429 67 13	Inexp	★	Su
Saint James C. Juan Bravo, 12 28006	575 00 69	Exp	★★	Su
Trainera, La Lagasca, 60 28001	576 05 75 575 47 17	Exp	★★★	Su
Zalacaín Álvarez de Baena, 4 28006	561 48 40	VExp	★★★★★	Su, S/l
Toledo	*925+*			
Asador Adolfo Calle La Granada, 6	22 73 21	Exp	★★★	Su/d
Botica, La Plaza de Zocodover, 13	22 55 57	Mod	★	Su/l
Cardinal Paseo Recaredo, 24	22 49 00	Mod	★	

MADRID AND NEW CASTILE

RESTAURANTS	Phone #	Price	Stars	Closed
Casa Aurelio Calle Sinagoga, 1	22 20 97	Mod	★	W
Emperador, El Carretera del Valle, 1	22 46 91	Inexp	★	M
Hierbabuena C. Cristo de la Luz, 9	22 34 63	Mod	★	Su
Mesón Aurelio Calle Sinagoga, 6	22 13 92	Mod	★	M
Nido, El Pl. de la Magdalena, 5		Inexp		

OLD CASTILE AND LEON

RESTAURANTS	Phone #	Price	Stars	Closed
Ávila	**918+**			
Molina de La Losa, El Bajada de La Losa, 12	21 11 01	Mod	★★★	M
Rastro, El Pl. del Rastro, 1	21 31 43	Mod	★	
Burgos	**947+**			
Autoservicio Bonfin C. Cadena	20 61 93	Inexp		All eves.
Casa Ojeda C. Vitoria, 5	20 90 52	Mod	★★	Su/d
Fernán Gonzáles C. Calera, 19	20 94 42	Expd	★★★	
Gaona Virgen de la Paloma, 41	20 61 91	Mod	★	M
Mesón del Cid Pl. Santa María, 8	20 90 52	Mod	★★★	Su/d
Rincón de España C. Nuño Rasura, 11	20 59 55	Mod	★	T
La Rioja Region	**941+**			
Marixa Sancho Abarca, 8 Laguardia	10 01 65	Mod	★★	

RESTAURANTS	Phone #	Price	Stars	Closed
OLD CASTILE AND LEON				
Terete Lucrecia Arana, 17 Haro	31 00 23	Mod	★★★	M,Su/d
León	*987+*			
Nuevo Racimo de Oro Pl. San Martin, 8	21 47 67	Mod	★★	W. or Su/d
Adonias C. Santa Nonia, 16	20 67 68	Mod	★★	Su
Casa Pozo Pl. de San Marcelo, 15	22 30 39	Mod	★★	Su/d
Salamanca	*923+*			
Bardo, El C. Compañia, 8	21 90 89	Inexp		M
Chez Victor Espoz y Mina, 26	21 31 23	Exp	★★★★	M, Su/d
Posada, La C. Aire, 1	21 72 51	Mod	★	
Rio de la Plata Pl. del Peso, 1	21 90 05	Mod	★★	M
Sablon, Le Espoz y Mina, 20	26 29 52	Mod	★★	T
Segovia	*911+*			
Mesón de Cándito Pl. Azoguejo, 5	42 59 11	Exp	★★	
José María C. Cronista Lecea, 11	43 44 84	Exp	★★	
Mesón del Duque C. Cervantes, 12	43 05 37	Exp	★★	
La Oficina C. Cronista Lecea, 10	43 16 43	Mod	★	M
La Taurina Pl. Mayor, 8	43 05 77	Mod	★	
Valladolid	*983+*			
Figon de Recoletos, El Acera de Recoletos, 3	39 60 43	Mod	★★★	Su/d
Mesón La Fragua Paseo de Zorrilla, 10	33 87 85	Exp	★★★★	M, Su/d

OLD CASTILE AND LEON

RESTAURANTS	Phone #	Price	Stars	Closed
Mesón Panero Marina Escobar, 1	30 70 19	Exp	★★★	Su

ANDALUSIA

RESTAURANTS	Phone #	Price	Stars	Closed
Baeza	**953+**			
Juanito Paseo Arca del Agua	74 00 04	Mod	★	Su, M/d
Sali Passaje Cardenal Benavides, 15	74 13 65	Inexp		W/d
Cádiz	**956+**			
Anteojo, El C. Alameda de Apodaca, 22	22 13 20	Mod	★	M
Faro, El C. San Félix, 15	21 25 01	Mod	★	
Sardinero, El Pl. San Juan de Dios	28 25 05	Inexp	★	M
Córdoba	**957+**			
Blasón, El José Zorrilla, 11	48 06 25	Exp	★★	
Caballo Rojo, El Cardenal Herrero, 28	47 53 75	Exp	★★	
Churrasco, El Romero, 16	29 08 19	Exp	★	
Mesón Bandolero Torrijos, 6	41 51 76	Exp	★★	
Mesón el Burfaero Calleja La Hoguera, 5	47 27 19	Inexp	★★	
Triunfo, El Cardinal González, 29	47 55 00	Inexp	★	
Costa De La Luz				
El Puerto de Santa María	**956+**			

ANDALUSIA				
RESTAURANTS	**Phone #**	**Price**	**Stars**	**Closed**
El Patio Rufina Vergara, 1	54 05 06	Mod	★	
Sanlúcar de Bar- rameda	**956+**			
Bigote Bajo de Guia	36 26 96	Mod	★	
Mirador Doñana Bajo de Guia	36 42 05	Mod	★	
Costa Del Sol				
Estepona	**952+**			
Benamara 11 k east along N-340	288 37 67	Inexp	★	lunches
Marbella	**952+**			
La Hacienda 9 k east along N-340	283 12 67	Exp	★★★	M, T
La Fonda Pl. Santo Cristo, 10	277 25 12	Exp	★★★★	Su, + lunch
Nerja	**95+**			
Casa Luque Pl. Cavana, 2	252 10 04	Exp	★★	M
Portofino Puerta del Mar, 4	252 01 60	Mod	★	Lunches
Granada	*958+*			
Alcaicería Placeta de la Alcaicería	22 43 41	Mod	★	
Cunin Pecsaderia, 9	25 07 77	Exp	★★	M
Mesón Andaluz Elvira, 17	25 86 61	Inexp	★	T
Ruta del Veleta Carretera de Sierra Nevada, 50	48 61 34	Exp	★★★	Su/d
Sevilla Oficios, 12	22 88 62	Exp	★★	Su/d
Málaga	*952+*			
Antonio Martín Paseo Marítimo, 4	222 21 13	Exp		Su/d

ANDALUSIA

RESTAURANTS	Phone #	Price	Stars	Closed
Café de Paris C. Vélez Málaga, 8	222 50 43	Exp	★★	Su
La Cancela C. Denís Belgrano, 3	222 31 25	Inexp		W

Ronda   952+

Don Miguel Pl. de España, 3	287 10 90	Mod	★★	Su
Pedro Romero Virgen de la Paz, 18	287 11 10	Mod	★	

Seville   95+

Albahaca, La Pl. Santa Cruz, 12	422 07 14	Exp	★★	Su
Alcázares, Los C. Miguel de Manara, 10	421 31 03	Mod	★	Su
Alquería, La (Hacienda Bena-zuza) Sanlucar la Mayor	570 33 44	Exp	★★★	
Asador Ox's C. Betis, 61	427 95 85	Exp	★★	Su
Egaña Oriza San Fernando, 41	422 72 11	Exp	★★★★	Su, S/l
Florencia Av. Eduardo Dato, 49	453 35 00	Exp	★	
Hostería del Laurel Pl. Venerables, 5	422 02 95	Mod		
Isla, La C. Arfe, 25	421 26 31	Exp	★★	M
Modesto C. Cano y Cueto, 5	441 68 11	Mod	★	W
Pelo Roteta Farmacéutico Murillo Herrera, 10	427 84 17	Exp	★★★	Su
Pizzeria San Marco C. Betis, 66	428 03 10	Inexp	★	M
Rio Grande C. Betis, 61	427 39 56	Exp		
San Marco C. Cuna, 6	421 24 40	Exp	★★★	Su

ANDALUSIA

RESTAURANTS	Phone #	Price	Stars	Closed
Úbeda	*953+*			
Cusco Parque de Vandevira, 8	75 34 13	Mod		M/d

ESTREMADURA

RESTAURANTS	Phone #	Price	Stars	Closed
Cáceres	*927+*			
Atrio Av. de España, 30	24 29 28	Exp	★★★	Su/d
Figón de Eustaquio, El Pl. San Juan, 12	24 81 94	Mod	★★	
Guadalupe	*927+*			
Hospederia del Real Monasterio Pl. Juan Carlos I	36 70 00	Mod	★★	
Cerezo Gregorio López, 12	36 73 79	Inexp	★★	
Mérida	*924+*			
Briz C. Féliz Valverde Lillo, 5	31 93 07	Inexp	★★	
Casa Benito C. Santa Eulalia, 13	31 55 02	Inexp	★	
Nicholás Félix Valverde Lillo, 13	31 96 10	Mod	★★	Su/d
Trujillo	*927+*			
Hostal Pizarro Pl. Mayor, 13	32 02 55	Mod	★★	
Mocón la Cadena Pl. Mayor, 8	32 14 63	Inexp	★	
Mesón la Troya Pl. Mayor, 10	32 13 64	Inexp	★★★	

GALICIA, ASTURIAS, AND CANTABRIA

RESTAURANTS	Phone #	Price	Stars	Closed
Basque Coast				
Donastia	**943+**			
Akelarre Passeo del Padre Orcolaga, 56	21 20 52 21 92 68	Exp	★★★★	M, Su/d
Alotza Kalea Fermin Calbeton, 7	42 07 82	Mod	★★	W
Arzak Kalea Alto de Miracruz, 21	27 84 65 27 27 53	VExp	★★★★★	M, Su/d
Panier Fleuri Paseo de Salamanca, 1	42 42 05 42 42 05	Exp	★★★★★	W, Su/d
Hondarribia	**943+**			
Ramón Roteta Irun	64 16 93	Exp	★★★	Th, Su/d
Laredo	**942+**			
Ramona Alameda José Antonio, 4	60 71 89	Mod	★	
Risco Alto de Laredo	60 50 30	Mod	★★	W
Santander	**942+**			
Bodiga del Riojano Rio de la Pila, 5	21 67 50	Mod	★★	
Molino, El Puente Arce	57 50 55	Exp	★★★	M, Su/d
Zarauz	**943+**			
Karlos Arguiñana Mendilauta, 13 Zarauz 20800	13 00 00 13 34 50	Exp	★★★★	W, Su/d
Costa del Rias				
Muros	**981+**			
Muradana Av. Marina Español, 107 Muros 15250	82 68 85	Inexp	★	
O Grove	**986+**			
Posada del Mar, La C. Castelao 202	73 01 06	Mod	★	Su/d

GALICIA, ASTURIAS, AND CANTABRIA

RESTAURANTS	Phone #	Price	Stars	Closed
Pontevedra	**986+**			
Casa Solla Carretera de La Toya	85 60 29	Exp	★★★	Su/d, Th/d
Doña Antonia Soportales de la Herreria, 9	84 72 74	Exp	★★★★	Su
Vilagarcia de Arousa	**986+**			
Chocolate Av. Cambados, 151	50 11 99 50 67 62	Exp	★★★	Su/d
Costa Verde				
Comillas	**942+**			
Capricho de Gaudí, El Barrio de Sobrellano	72 03 65	Exp	★	M
Gijon	**98+**			
Casa Victor C. Carmen, 11	534 83 10	Mod	★	Su/d
Luarca	**98+**			
Leonés Paseo Alfonso X el Sabio, 1	564 09 95	Exp	★★	
Ribadeo	**982+**			
O Xardin C. Reinante, 20	10 02 22	Mod	★	M
Oviedo	**985+**			
Cabo Peñar Melquiades Alvarez, 24	522 03 20	Inexp	★	
Casa Fermín C. San Francisco, 8	21 64 52	Exp	★★★	Su/d
Raitan, El Pl. Trascorrales, 6	21 42 18	Mod	★	Su/d
Trascorrales Pl. de Trascorrales, 19	22 24 41	Exp	★★	Su
Santiago de Compostela	**981+**			
Alameda Puerta Fajera, 15	58 66 57	Mod	★	
Anexo Vilas Av. Villagarcia, 21	59 86 37	Exp	★★	M

GALICIA, ASTURIAS, AND CANTABRIA

RESTAURANTS	Phone #	Price	Stars	Closed
Don Gaiferos C. Nueva, 23	58 38 94	Exp	★	Su
Nova Gallihea C. Franco, 56	58 27 99	Mod	★	
O'Sotano C. Franco, 8	56 50 24	Inexp	★	
Reyes Católicos Pl. Obradioros, 1	58 22 00	Mod	★★	
San Clemente Pl. San Clemente, 6	58 08 82	Mod	★	Su/d
Toñi Vincente Av. Rosalia de Castro, 24	59 41 00 59 35 54	Exp	★★★★	Su

ARAGÓN AND NAVARRE

RESTAURANTS	Phone #	Price	Stars	Closed
Estella	*948+*			
Navarra C. Gustavo de Maeztu, 16	55 10 69	Exp	★	M, Su/d
Olite	*948+*			
Casa Zanito Mayor, 16	74 00 02	Mod	★	
Tubal Pl. de Navarra, 2 Tafalla	70 08 52	Mod	★★★	M, Su/d
Pamplona	*948+*			
Europa Espoz y Mina, 11	22 18 00 22 92 35	Exp	★★★	Su
Hartza C. Juan de Labrit, 19	22 45 68	Exp	★★	M, Su/d
Iruna, Casa Pl. del Castillo, 44	22 20 64	Inexp	★	
Josetxo Pl. Principe de Viana, 1	22 20 97	Exp	★★★	Su
Otano C. San Nicolas, 5	22 70 36	Mod	★	Su/d

ARAGÓN AND NAVARRE

RESTAURANTS	Phone #	Price	Stars	Closed
Zaragoza	**976+**			
Asador de Aranda, El Arquitecto Magdalena, 6	22 64 17	Mod	★★★	Su
Mar, La Pl. Aragñon, 12	21 22 64	Exp	★★	Su
Matilda, La Casta Álvarez, 10	44 10 08	Exp	★★	Su
Tres Hermanos C. San Pablo, 45	44 10 85	Inexp		T

CATALONIA AND THE LEVANT

RESTAURANTS	Phone #	Price	Stars	Closed
Barcelona	**93+**			
Agut C. Gignas, 16	315 17 09	Inexp	★★	M, Su/d
Agut d'Avignon C. Trinitat, 3	302 60 34	Exp	★	
Botafumeiro C. Mayor de Gràcia, 81	218 42 30 415 58 48	VExp	★★★	
Brasserie Flo C. Jonqueres, 10	319 31 02	Mod	★★	
Burger King Rambla de Canaletes, 135	302 54 29	Inexp		
Can Gaig Pas. de Maragall, 402	429 10 17	VExp	★★★★	M
Can Majó Almirall Aixada, 23	221 54 55	Exp	★★	Su/d
Caracoles, La P. Escudellers, 14	302 31 85	Mod	★	
Cangrejo Loco, El Moll del Gregal, 29-30	221 17 48	Mod	★	
Corts Catalanes, Les Gran Via de les Corts Catalanes, 630	301 03 76	Inexp		
Dama, La Avinguda Diagonal, 423	202 06 86 200 72 99	Exp	★★★	

CATALONIA AND THE LEVANT

RESTAURANTS	Phone #	Price	Stars	Closed
Eldorado Petit C. Dolors Monserda, 51	204 51 53 280 57 02	VExp	★★★★	Su
Egipte C. Jerusalem, 12	317 74 80	Inexp	★	Su
Font del Gat P. Santa Madrona	424 02 24	Mod		M
Jaume de Provença Provença, 88	430 00 29	VExp	★★★	M, Su/d
Kentucky Fried Chicken C. Ferrán, 1-3	412 51 54	Inexp		
Neichel Av. de Pedralbes, 16bis	203 84 08	VExp	★★★★★	Su, S/l
Pitarra C. d'Avinyò, 56	301 16 47	Inexp		Su
Raim D' or Can Maxim C. Bonsucces, 8	302 02 34	Inexp	★	Su
Senyor Parellada Carrer Argentería, 37	315 50 94	Mod	★★	Su
Siete Portas Passeig Isabel II, 14	319 30 33	Mod	★★	
Tick-tack-toe Moll del Grega, 20-21	221 00 66	Mod	★	W, Su/d
Via Veneto C. Ganduxer, 10	200 72 44	VExp	★★★	Su, S/l
Costa Blanca				
Alicante	96+			
Delfin Expanada de España, 12	521 49 11	Exp	★★	
Quo Vadis Pl. Santisima Faz, 3	521 66 60	Mod	★	Th
Altea	96+			
Monte Molar Caretera Valencia	584 15 81	Exp	★★★	W
Moraira	96+			
Girasol, El Moraira	574 43 73	Exp	★★★★	M

CATALONIA AND THE LEVANT

RESTAURANTS	Phone #	Price	Stars	Closed
Costa Brava				
Cadaqués	**972+**			
Galiota, La C. Narciso Monturiol, 9	25 81 87	Exp	★★	
Sant Feliú de Guíxols	**972+**			
Can Toni C. Sant Martiria, 29	32 10 26	Exp	★★★★	M
Eldorado Petit, El Rambla Vidal, 23	32 18 18 32 14 69	Exp	★★★	W
Tossa de Mar	**972+**			
Es Molí Tarull, 5	34 14 14	Exp	★★★	M
Costa Dorada				
Cambrils de Mar	**977+**			
Joan Gatell/Casa Gatell P. Miramar, 26	36 00 57	Exp	★★★	M, Su/d
Poblet	**977+**			
Masia del Cadet Les Masies	87 03 33	Inexp	★	M
Tarragona	**977+**			
Galería, La Rambla Nova, 16	23 61 43	Mod	★	Su, W/d
Puda, La Muelle Pescadores, 25	21 15 11	Mod	★★	
Valencia	**96+**			
Oscar Torrijos Dr. Sumsi, 4	373 29 49	Exp	★★★	Su
Plat II, El C. Ciscar, 3	395 15 11	Mod	★★	
Rio Sil C. Mosén Femades, 10	352 97 64	Exp	★	
Romeral, El Gran Vía Marquês del Turia, 62	395 15 17	Inexp	★	M
Timonel, El C. Felix Pizcueta, 13	352 63 00	Mod	★	M

INDEX

C

F

S

Favorite People, Places & Experiences

ADDRESS:	NOTES:

Name

Address

Telephone

Name

Address

Telephone

Name

Address

Telephone

Name

Address

Telephone

Name

Address

Telephone

Name

Address

Telephone

Favorite People, Places & Experiences

ADDRESS:	NOTES:

Name

Address

Telephone

Name

Address

Telephone

Name

Address

Telephone

Name

Address

Telephone

Name

Address

Telephone

Name

Address

Telephone

Favorite People, Places & Experiences

ADDRESS:	NOTES:

Name

Address

Telephone

Name

Address

Telephone

Name

Address

Telephone

Name

Address

Telephone

Name

Address

Telephone

Name

Address

Telephone

Favorite People, Places & Experiences

ADDRESS:	NOTES:

Name

Address

Telephone

Name

Address

Telephone

Name

Address

Telephone

Name

Address

Telephone

Name

Address

Telephone

Name

Address

Telephone

Favorite People, Places & Experiences

ADDRESS:	NOTES:

Name

Address

Telephone

Name

Address

Telephone

Name

Address

Telephone

Name

Address

Telephone

Name

Address

Telephone

Name

Address

Telephone

Favorite People, Places & Experiences

ADDRESS:	NOTES:

Name

Address

Telephone

Name

Address

Telephone

Name

Address

Telephone

Name

Address

Telephone

Name

Address

Telephone

Name

Address

Telephone

Favorite People, Places & Experiences

ADDRESS:	NOTES:

Name

Address

Telephone

Name

Address

Telephone

Name

Address

Telephone

Name

Address

Telephone

Name

Address

Telephone

Name

Address

Telephone

Favorite People, Places & Experiences

ADDRESS:	NOTES:

Name

Address

Telephone

Name

Address

Telephone

Name

Address

Telephone

Name

Address

Telephone

Name

Address

Telephone

Name

Address

Telephone

Favorite People, Places & Experiences

ADDRESS:	NOTES:

Name

Address

Telephone

Name

Address

Telephone

Name

Address

Telephone

Name

Address

Telephone

Name

Address

Telephone

Name

Address

Telephone

Favorite People, Places & Experiences

ADDRESS:	NOTES:

Name

Address

Telephone

Name

Address

Telephone

Name

Address

Telephone

Name

Address

Telephone

Name

Address

Telephone

Name

Address

Telephone

Favorite People, Places & Experiences

ADDRESS:	NOTES:

Name

Address

Telephone

Name

Address

Telephone

Name

Address

Telephone

Name

Address

Telephone

Name

Address

Telephone

Name

Address

Telephone

Favorite People, Places & Experiences

ADDRESS: **NOTES:**

Name

Address

Telephone

Name

Address

Telephone

Name

Address

Telephone

Name

Address

Telephone

Name

Address

Telephone

Name

Address

Telephone

Favorite People, Places & Experiences

ADDRESS: **NOTES:**

Name

Address

Telephone

Name

Address

Telephone

Name

Address

Telephone

Name

Address

Telephone

Name

Address

Telephone

Name

Address

Telephone

Favorite People, Places & Experiences

ADDRESS:	NOTES:

Name

Address

Telephone

Name

Address

Telephone

Name

Address

Telephone

Name

Address

Telephone

Name

Address

Telephone

Name

Address

Telephone